Personal Finance

Personal Finance

Lawrence J. Gitman
The University of Tulsa

The Dryden Press
Hinsdale, Illinois

Design by Harry Voigt

Cover photograph by Leon Lewandowski

Copy editing by Judith Lynn Bleicher

Cartoon research by Jo-Anne Naples

In Memory of My Stepfather—Stanley M. Krohn, Jr.

Preface

The field of personal finance is crowded with texts. They vary in organization, topical coverage, method of presentation, and teachability. Given the large number and variety of texts already published, you might ask, "Why would anyone write yet another one?"

My answer is simple. None of the existing texts has incorporated the necessary degree of *teachability*. While many present the topical material, they fail to make the learning process enjoyable and exciting. Teachers and students at universities, junior colleges, and community colleges have referred to texts in this field as dry and unexciting. Their reactions have motivated me to write a text with the major objective of presenting the key concepts, tools, and techniques of contemporary personal finance in such a way that they can be easily read and comprehended.

Before I began writing the book, the publisher surveyed many faculty members to obtain objective information about the good and bad points of existing texts. Taking into account these responses, as well as student feedback and my own experiences in teaching personal finance courses, we developed the plan for a text that would incorporate the desired approach, coverage, and special features that would benefit both students and teachers. The distinguishing features of this text are its organization, topical coverage, readability, special features, pedagogical features, and supplementary materials.

Organization

The book is organized in a logical but novel fashion. It approaches the personal financial management process in a manner similar to that of a business firm managing its finances. The personal balance sheet is used as a pivotal point around which the chapters are arranged. As an organizational structure, it provides for the logical development of the entire process, beginning with various tools and techniques of planning and ending with the ultimate disposition of the estate. Within this logical order, each chapter is a complete entity. Thus professors wishing to cover the text in any other order will find that the chapters can be rearranged without losing continuity.

The book is divided into six parts. Part 1 is devoted to personal financial statements, planning, and taxes. It includes a discussion of the Tax Reform Act of 1976 and the Tax Reduction and Simplification Act of 1977. Part 2 is concerned with the management of financial assets. It covers cash and savings instruments, fundamentals of stock and bond investments, transactions in security markets, investment companies, commodities, and options. Part 3 discusses the management of nonfinancial assets, including real estate (for both housing and investment), automobiles, furniture, and appliances. Part 4 describes the liability management process, including the various types of open account borrowing and consumer loans. Part 5 considers primarily life insurance, health care plans and insurance, and property and liability insurance. Part 6 is devoted to retirement and estate planning.

Topical Coverage

Each chapter presents key concepts, tools, and techniques; and each illustrates their use in personal financial management activities. Real-world situations and newsworthy developments provide additional insight and added perspectives as boxed items separate from the textual material. These items are particularly useful in stimulating class discussion of the concepts themselves.

Readability

The text is unusually readable. Words and sentence structure have been chosen with reading level in mind. Standard reading level studies of the material were made, using both the Dale-Chall and the Flesch formulas, in order to assure that the material would be easily comprehended. Straightforward subheadings, cartoons, boxed items, and other visuals were integrated into each chapter in order to further enhance readability.

A number of special features, some of them mentioned earlier, enhance the teachability and contemporary approach of the book:

1. The balance sheet model around which the text is organized provides a structure for assessing the effects of personal finance decisions on the individual's net worth.
2. All recent consumer legislation and tax law reforms are discussed (including the Tax Reform Act of 1976 and the Tax Reduction and Simplification Act of 1977).
3. The chapter on financial planning and budgeting includes a detailed illustration of the entire budgeting process.
4. The personal tax chapter not only describes the fundamentals of taxation but also discusses the process of preparing a tax return—and is illustrated with a filled-out 1977 Form 1040.
5. Coverage is given of both the traditional investment media and commodity and options transactions.
6. The chapter on real estate discusses not only personal housing decisions but also the purchase of real estate for investment purposes.
7. The estate planning discussion provides, in addition to the various legal and tax considerations, coverage of the basic techniques for maximizing the size of an estate and minimizing estate taxes.
8. Each chapter contains at least two boxed items presenting some controversy, opinion, or new development related to the personal financial management process.
9. Cartoons related to the topical material highlight relevant points.

Each part of the book begins with an overview of its chapters and topics, and each chapter begins with a discussion of its key learning objectives. Besides the boxed items and cartoons already mentioned, the book contains a generous number of tables and figures that enhance as well as simplify the text. At the end of each chapter the key terms are listed, along with twelve or more review questions that can be used by students to test their grasp of the material. Case problems highlighting the important analytical topics and concepts are also included as end-of-chapter materials.

The last item in the chapter is a listing of selected references to other texts as well as to recent articles from personal finance publications, such as *Money, Changing Times,* and *Consumers Digest.* Following the final chapter is a comprehensive glossary containing not only brief definitions of the most important terms but also the number of the chapter in which each term is explained.

Supplementary Materials

For those desiring more material, there is a workbook, the *Workbook for Personal Finance.* Each chapter in the workbook includes:

—key terms used in the text
—concepts that highlight the principles of the chapter
—questions intended to spark thought and develop an understanding of sound personal financial management practices
—financial decisions that the individual family will have to make at various points in time
—sources of further information on specific topics
—a section to test understanding, which allows the student to quickly assess the knowledge gained from the text
—activities and forms, which provide materials for students who wish to work with their own financial situations.

For the professor a comprehensive *Instructor's Manual* has been prepared. It begins with a discussion of the book's rationale and a suggested course outline, and it describes general approaches for effective use of the text. The manual includes for each chapter:

—teaching aids, which provide specific suggestions, guides, and supplementary sources of material that can be used when covering the chapter
—answers to all end-of-chapter review questions
—solutions to all end-of-chapter case problems
—true-false questions for use in quizzes and examinations
—multiple choice questions for use in quizzes and examinations.

Acknowledgments

Numerous persons have made significant contributions to this text. Without their expertise, classroom experience, guidance, general advice, and reassurance, the book could not have been written. And only through feedback from the students who have been exposed to various drafts of the manuscript have I been able to maintain my conviction that a truly *teachable* personal finance text could be developed. I am most appreciative of the hundreds of academicians and practitioners who have created the body of personal finance knowledge that is contained in this book. I particularly wish to thank the two persons who most significantly helped develop the text—Gary W. Eldred, of the University of South Carolina, for his contribution to the insurance and retirement planning chapters, and Stephan R. Leimberg, Chairman of the Department of Estate Planning at the American College, for his contribution to the estate planning chapter.

The Dryden Press, which shares my objective of providing a truly teachable text, relied on the experience and advice of a number of excellent reviewers: Joel J. Dauten, Arizona State University; Henry Hatcher, City College of San Francisco; Darrell D. Hilliker, Suffolk Community College, Eastern Campus; Carole J. Makela, Colorado State University; Arnold M. Rieger, The College of Staten Island; and R. R. Zilkowski, William Rainey Harper College. Special thanks go to three persons who not only reviewed various portions of the manuscript but who also participated in the final review process: Maurice L. Crawford, San Diego State University; John L. Grimm, Youngstown State University; and Grant J. Wells, Ball State University.

Because of the wide variety of topics covered in the book, I called upon the expertise of a number of Tulsa-based experts. I am grateful to them for their insights and awareness of recent developments in the "real world." I would particularly like to thank: Harold W. Grimmer and Rodger P. Erker, McGraw-Breckinridge Realtors; James A. Buchan, Northwest Mutual Life Insurance Company; W. Wayne Learned, Sooner Federal Savings and Loan; Fred J. Morgan, Tulsa Teachers Credit Union; Charles W. Wiseley, Paine Webber Jackson and Curtis, Inc.; Roger P. Bond, First Continental Mortgage Company; Robert L. Moore, Jr., Liberty Mortgage Company; Robert H. Reins, Mercantile Bank and Trust Company; Tommy L. Holland, The University of Tulsa College of Law; and Alvin E. Thiessen, Farmers Insurance Group.

A number of my colleagues at The University of Tulsa have also provided expertise, as well as encouragement and support: Louis E. Boone, Benton E. Gup, Edward A. Moses, and Larry E. Wofford. A special word of thanks to Xymena S. Kulsrud for providing materials as well as insights gained from many years of teaching personal finance. For updating and critiquing my tax discussions, I want to thank my colleague and tax expert, Patrick A. Hennessee.

I would also like to express my appreciation to Carole J. Makela, Head of Consumer Sciences and Housing at Colorado State University, for her preparation of the workbook and for her assistance in preparing the Instructor's Manual. I also greatly appreciate the research assistance of Kersi P. Damri and the superhuman efforts of Margaret F. Ferguson, who converted my handwritten manuscript into typescript. The editorial staff of The Dryden Press has been most cooperative, and I would like to thank Garret L. White, publisher; Ray A. Ashton, managing editor; Judith L. Bleicher, copy editor; and Jo-Anne Naples, cartoon researcher and copy editor. Special thanks go to my developmental editor, Paul R. Jones, without whose vision and constant encouragement the book would likely not have developed into the truly teachable text that it is.

Finally, my wife, Robin, and son, Zachary, have played important parts in providing needed support and understanding during the writing of the book. I am forever grateful to them and hope that the text will provide answers to the many questions that arose during the hundreds of hours I was away from them.

Lawrence J. Gitman
Tulsa, Oklahoma
January 1978

Contents

Part 4 Managing Your Liabilities   361

Part 1

Financial Statements, Planning, and Taxes

Personal Balance Sheet	
Assets	Liabilities and Net Worth
Financial Assets	Liabilities
Nonfinancial Assets	Net Worth

This part of the text sets the stage for the discussion of various aspects of personal financial management. Chapter 1 describes the goals and operating environment of personal financial management. Attention is also given to the determinants of personal income as they relate to age, education, career, and lifetime earnings. Chapter 2 discusses preparing and interpreting personal financial statements, including the income statement and balance sheet. In Chapter 3, the procedures for establishing financial goals and preparing budgets are described. And Chapter 4 examines the key principles of personal taxation at the federal, state, and local government levels.

1
The Importance of Personal Financial Management

It is the aim of this chapter to provide you with:

1. An understanding of the fundamental concepts and the importance of personal financial management.

2. A knowledge of the types of goals to consider when managing your personal finances and the respective significance of those goals.

3. Insight into the effect of inflation on consumer prices and consumption.

4. An understanding of the role of the consumer and the impact of the economy on the personal finance environment.

5. A knowledge of the various determinants of personal income.

6. A brief outline of the text and its principle of organization.

Throughout your life you will be bombarded with opportunities and alternatives. You will have to make decisions concerning your education, career, family status, life-style, and finances. The decisions you make will be greatly affected by your personal financial situation. At the same time, the outcomes of your decisions will have an impact on your personal finances. Insight into the principles and practices of contemporary personal financial management will allow you to make better decisions.

Life is a process that becomes more and more complicated with age. When you were a child, life was simple; you were given a lot of attention, you were fed and cared for, and you spent most of your time playing. You

3

had few responsibilities—financial or otherwise. As you grew older you began to care for yourself, and you assumed certain responsibilities with respect to hygiene, education, and work. Currently, you may or may not feel that your responsibilities are very significant. Your parents may be footing the bill for college, and they may continue to provide support as long as you remain in college and pass your courses. Or you may be working your way through school because you do not receive enough parental support, scholarships, or grants to pay for your education.

Regardless of your current life structure, you can expect life to continue to become more complicated as you grow older. The number of your dependents is likely to increase, your income is going to increase, you may purchase a home, and you will probably assume many other new responsibilities. Although these responsibilities may add pleasure and satisfaction to your life, at the same time they are likely to make it a bit more complicated. One of the key factors complicating your life will be the state of your finances; as a matter of fact, most of life's problems can somehow be related to or eliminated by proper handling of finances.

The Goals of Personal Financial Management

Personal financial management allows individuals or families to achieve their personal financial goals more easily. Although most people do not have the same goals, similar financial principles are required in order to facilitate goal achievement. By following the procedures for effective financial management, individuals can get the most for their money in terms of both satisfaction and material goods. The three sections below contain a general discussion of personal goals as they relate to quality of life, consumption, and wealth accumulation. The following section considers the role of money in personal financial management.

Quality of Life

Your quality of life is closely tied to the level or standard of living you maintain. The presence or absence of certain material items such as a home, cars, and jewelry are commonly associated with quality of life. Large, expensive, or "fancy" items are viewed as evidence of higher standards of living. The ability to spend money for entertainment, health, education, variety in life, art, music, and travel also contributes to the quality of life. Although many other factors—geographical location, public facilities, local costs of living, pollution, traffic, and population density—also affect the quality of life, it is primarily wealth that is viewed as a determinant of an individual's quality of life. Of course, many so-called wealthy people live quite plain lives, choosing to save or invest their money rather than spend it on luxuries and frills. It is important to

Quality of Life Is Important to All

Source: Saturday Review, 31 July 1971, p. 18. Reprinted by permission of Sidney Harris.

recognize that their quality of life is not necessarily any less than that of the person who is a flamboyant consumer.

Perceptions of what is a desirable quality of life vary among socioeconomic strata. While people in the lower socioeconomic strata might consider the ownership of a large, expensive car part of a high-quality life, those in the upper socioeconomic strata might consider membership in a country club and an annual trip abroad requisites for a high-quality life.

By planning certain future purchases and financial activities, you can set goals which are consistent with your desired quality of life, even though you may not be able to describe in precise detail the quality of life you wish to attain. In general, most people attempt to increase their wealth in order to obtain a comfortable and secure standard of living and those items commensurate with the quality of life they desire; few seriously aim at becoming millionaires. By carefully planning your finances using the principles outlined in this text you should be able to provide yourself the best quality life given your current financial position, your income potential, your future career opportunities, and your level of motivation.

Consumption

As indicated in the preceding section, the level of consumption often has a direct effect on the quality of life. Past consumption, although no longer under your control, is important since it may have set limits on current and future consumption opportunities. Given a certain level of income, you can consume currently, or save, or invest a portion of the income for future consumption. The determination of your consumption requirements—both current and future—is an important input to your personal financial management process.

Current Your current consumption is based on the necessities of life and your marginal propensity to consume. A minimum level of consumption is that which obtains only the *necessities of life*: food, clothing, and shelter. Although the quantity and types of food, clothing, and shelter purchased may differ among individuals depending on their wealth, these items in some amount are essential for survival in today's society.

Marginal propensity to consume refers to the percentage of each dollar of income that is spent for consumption. People exhibiting high marginal propensities to consume may do so because their income is low and they must spend a large portion of it for necessities. Conversely, individuals earning large amounts quite often have low marginal propensities to consume, since the cost of necessities represents only a small proportion of their income. Still, it is not unusual to find two people with significantly different incomes and the same marginal propensity to consume due to differences in standards of living. The person making more money may believe it is essential to buy either better quality and/or more items and thus may spend the same percentage of each dollar of income during the current period as the person making far less.

Future Future consumption is based on anticipated living requirements, expected increases in the cost of living, and the desired standard of living. By considering these factors simultaneously, you can better plan your future consumption requirements, thereby allowing any residual earnings to be placed in some savings or investment media, if that is your goal.

Over the past thirty or more years, we have experienced extended periods of inflation. Figure 1-1 illustrates the past inflationary behavior and its effects on consumer prices (i.e., the cost of living). The *Consumer Price Index (CPI)*, which is plotted in this figure, shows the relative cost of

Figure 1-1 **Consumer Price Index (CPI), 1906–1976**
(1967 = 100)

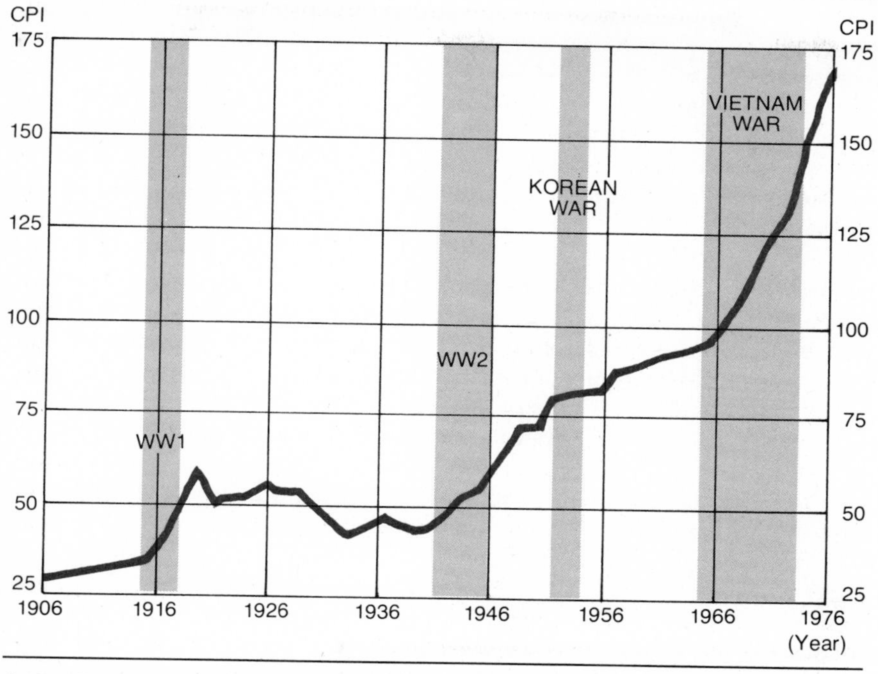

Source: Reprinted with permission from *Changing Times* Magazine, © 1977 Kiplinger Washington Editors, Inc., "Why Inflation Is So Hard to Stop," Table, page 35 (April 1977).

a bundle of goods and services over the past seventy years. For instance, the bundle of goods the consumer paid $100 for in 1967 cost approximately $170 in 1976. By April of 1977 the cost of this same bundle of goods had risen to $179.60. Most consumers expect this inflationary behavior of the market to continue into the future. And future inflation will mean an increase in the *cost of living*; in other words, the cost of any given bundle of goods and services will rise. Therefore, although your marginal propensity to consume and your income may remain the same in the future, inflation can cause a decline in your standard of living. For this reason, it is most important to establish future consumption goals and to direct current plans and activities so as to achieve those goals. Current and future consumption goals will affect the quality of life.

Wealth Accumulation

A person's *wealth* at any point in time represents the total value of all items such as bank accounts, stocks, bonds, autos, and homes he or she owns. People accumulate wealth by saving, investing, or purchasing *tangible property*, which represents items that last for long periods of time. The accumulation of wealth quite often results from savings and investment, which represent forms of nonconsumption that act as a storehouse for future consumption. Most individuals have certain wealth accumulation goals that can be stated in terms of achieving specified levels of savings, investment, or tangible property. In general, the goal of most people is to accumulate as much wealth as possible while maintaining the level of current consumption necessary to live the desired quality of life.

Savings Savings represent money that has been set aside in some interest-earning form. A large number of savings institutions exist; they are described in detail later in the text. Many people establish savings goals by planning to place a specified amount from each paycheck into their savings accounts. Quite often these savings goals are set in order to accumulate a specified amount needed to purchase tangible property

Inflation: A Way of Life?

Inflation means a rise in the general level of prices. Nobody wants inflation, but it has become all too familiar in the world today. A point is reached when inflation tends to become self-perpetuating. When inflation occurs, each dollar we have buys fewer goods and services. In the years between 1955 and 1975, the ability of our dollar to purchase goods and services declined about 50 percent.

The burden of inflation tends to fall more heavily on those who live on incomes that remain the same or rise more slowly than prices. Prices push up wages, and wages push up prices. This is known as the *wage-price spiral*, and it is a vicious circle. Increases in the productivity of labor tend to dampen the inflationary impact of rising costs. If the cost of wages in a factory increases by 10 percent and productivity simultaneously increases by 8 percent, then a difference of only 2 percent is passed on to the consumer in the form of increased prices. However, when costs rise rapidly, it is often difficult for productivity to keep pace with them.

The 1973 war in the Middle East is a good example of a situation in which costs of an important raw material and fuel rose at a rate far above any increases in productivity. The war resulted in severe oil shortages, which in turn heightened the price of not only oil but almost all commodities, since most are dependent on this form of energy for their production. As a result of this and additional oil cost increases over the past few years, the present economy has been compared to a pussy cat in need of vitamin dosages from Washington. But it now seems that the economy is more like a bloated lion, still bloated with inflation but showing signs of slowly stirring and beginning to roar. The questions in many people's minds are: When? For how long? How loud?

such as a car or a boat, to pay for education, to finance a trip. Regardless of the motive, the establishment of savings goals as part of the overall wealth accumulation scheme is an important aspect of personal financial management.

Investment The purchase of stocks, bonds, and other types of *securities* that are expected to provide the purchaser with interest, dividends, or increased value is called *investment.* Although investments are viewed as more "risky" than savings, investors expect to receive larger returns from investments than from savings. Investment, just as savings, represents a form of nonconsumption, since income that is channeled into this form cannot be used for consumption in the current period. Of course, the proceeds from selling an investment can be used for consumption. The important point is that the current value of investments represents another form of accumulated wealth, which should contribute toward achieving maximum wealth accumulation. The wise investment of funds aids in the fulfillment of wealth accumulation goals.

Tangible Property Tangible property refers to long-lived physical items, for example, real estate, automobiles, jewelry. These items, accumulated by past consumption, maintain some portion of their value over long periods of time. Some of the items, such as automobiles and boats, may depreciate in value, while other items, such as a home and jewelry, may increase in value. Some items of tangible property represent necessity items, while others may be acquired solely to enhance the quality of life. By intelligently purchasing items of tangible property, you can enhance your wealth. Because of our inflationary economy, many items of tangible property are likely to be worth more in the future than was originally paid for them; and, during the intervening years, these items provide a needed or desired service. Quite often—especially for those in the upper economic classes—tangible property is purchased solely for the expected appreciation in value. Purchases of real estate and classic automobiles fall into this category. Regardless of the motive for purchase, carefully planned tangible property purchases will make maximum contributions to your accumulated wealth.

The Role of Money

Money is the common denominator by which all financial transactions are gauged. It is the medium of exchange used as a measure of value in our economy. Although most people would probably agree that those items or services that have the best value are not necessarily the most expensive, it is generally assumed that cost and value are closely related. Without the standard unit of exchange provided by the dollar, it would be quite difficult to set specific personal financial goals and to measure progress with respect to these goals. Money as we know it today is therefore the key consideration in establishing financial goals. In order to better understand the role of money in personal financial management, it is worthwhile to look at the relationship between money and utility and money and goals.

Money and Utility *Utility* refers to the amount of satisfaction a person receives from purchasing certain types or quantities of goods and services. Quite often the utility or satisfaction provided, rather than cost, acts as the overriding factor in the choice between two items of differing price. A special feature may provide additional utility in one item, causing it to be the preferred item. This added utility may result from the actual usefulness of the special feature or may result from the status, or "snob appeal," it is expected to provide. Regardless, different people receive different levels of satisfaction from similar items, and this satisfaction is not necessarily related to the cost of the item.

Consideration of the utility of certain actions is very important in the personal financial management process. When alternative qualities of life, consumption patterns, and forms of wealth accumulation are evaluated, not only their cost but, more importantly, their utility should be considered. Your financial goals must be established in light of your own utility disposition, not that of a consultant or professional financial planner, for the utility of any given item may vary with the goals and desires of individuals. Personal financial management aims to maximize utility or satisfaction in both the short and long run. This is often, but not always, consistent with the maximization of wealth, for utility and wealth are not perfectly correlated.

Money and Goals As indicated in the preceding section, the goal of personal financial management should be to maximize overall utility over your lifetime. Since usable measures of utility have yet to be developed, personal financial management goals must be stated in terms of money—the prevailing unit of exchange. By assigning monetary values to the consumption (current and future) of certain items believed to provide desired levels of satisfaction, and by assigning monetary values to levels of saving, investment, and tangible property providing desired levels of satisfaction, financial goals consistent with quality-of-life goals can be established.

The Personal Finance Environment

The environment in which personal finance goals are established and decisions are made contains three different groups, each attempting to fulfill certain goals. Although the goals of each of these groups are not

"I felt more inner peace when we were Presbyterians."

Many People Are Ruled by the Dollar

Source: Changing Times, September 1974, p. 2. Reprinted with permission from *Changing Times* Magazine, © Kiplinger Washington Editors, Inc., 1974.

necessarily inconsistent, they do impose certain constraints on each other. The three key groups are government, business, and consumers. Each is discussed separately below, and a final section considers the effects of the interactions of these groups on the economy.

Government

In attempting to provide for and protect us, government at all levels—federal, state, and local—places a large number of constraints on business and consumers, as indicated in Figure 1-2. The two chief areas of governmental control are taxation and regulation.

Taxation The federal government levies taxes on income; state governments tax sales and income; and local governments levy taxes primarily on real estate and personal property. The largest tax bites for consumers

Figure 1-2 **Personal Finance Environment**

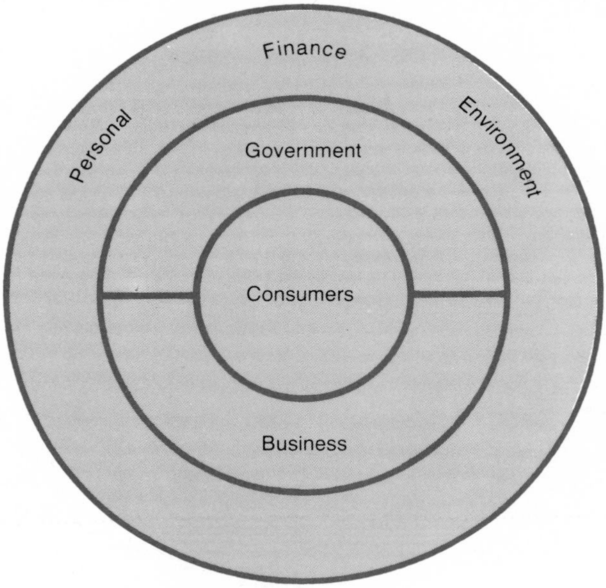

result from federal income taxes, which may take as much as 70 percent of earnings. These taxes are levied on a progressive basis so that the greater the taxable income, the higher the rate at which taxes are paid. A great deal of attention must be devoted to considering the effects of taxes on financial management activities. Due to the constraints of the tax structure on personal financial decisions and the potential magnitude of taxes, decisions must be evaluated on an "after-tax" basis.

Regulation Federal, state, and local governments place a large number of regulations on consumer- and citizen-related activities. Most of these regulations are aimed at protecting the consumer from fraudulent and undesirable actions by sellers and lenders. These government regulations require certain types of businesses to have licenses, to maintain certain hygienic standards, to adequately disclose financial charges, to warrant their goods and services. Other laws protect sellers from adverse activities by consumers, for example, shoplifting and nonpayment for services rendered. Certainly, any decisions relating to achieving personal financial goals should take into consideration both those legal requirements that protect consumers and those that constrain their activities.

Business

Businesses are a key ingredient of our free enterprise system. Their presence creates a competitive environment in which consumers may select from an array of goods and services. There are, of course, certain industries, such as public utilities, in which the degree of competition or choice provided the consumer is limited by the government for economic reasons. As indicated in the preceding section, all businesses are in some way directly or indirectly limited by the laws of some governmental body. Consumers need to understand the role and effects of business on their financial plans since the activities of business largely affect the cost and availability of goods and services in our economy. An understanding of various business activities should permit consumers to make better purchases and help them determine which business firms to deal with.

Consumers

The consumer is the party around which the personal finance environment is centered. The consumer must operate within the financial environment resulting from the actions of government and business. Of course, through their elected officials and by their purchase actions,

Keeping Up with the Joneses

Whatever the consequences, "keeping up with the Joneses" at the expense of other economic and political objectives is the lifelong ambition of most Americans. Despite the fact that many American families do not earn high wages, it is acknowledged that the United States has the highest standard of living in the world. Electrical gadgets, automobiles, and homes are all within the reach of most Americans.

However, according to Dr. Philip Crane, an Illinois Congressman, taxes take the biggest chunk of the household budget. If they continue to grow at their current pace, private sector industries may starve for want of funds. At present, 80 percent of the investment capital available is being filtered to the government bureaucracy, which Rep. Crane cites as the chief cause of inflation and unemployment. Furthermore, it is the private sector, which has made the U.S. economy the envy and despair of rivals everywhere, that provides most of this capital. Rep. Crane warns that, in the words of President Ford, "a government big enough to give us everything we want is a government big enough to take from us everything we have." Most consumers are hopeful that the Carter administration will fulfill its campaign goal of significantly cutting the cost of government.

Source: Adapted with permission from "Your Money and Your Life," *Consumers Digest,* May/June 1977, pp. 19–20.

consumers can affect government and business, respectively. But lobbies and consumer groups are necessary for any real impact; the individual consumer is unwise to expect to change government or business independently. As a consumer, you are best off accepting the existing financial atmosphere and planning your transactions within it. Consumers and their wants are central to the personal finance environment. The government provides services financed by tax receipts and places certain regulations on business and consumers in order to protect the interests of both parties. Business employs consumers to produce, sell, and provide the services needed to enhance the quality of their lives in our free enterprise system. It is thus the interaction of government, business, and consumers that determines the environment in which personal financial decisions must be made.

Economic Conditions

Our economy is a result of the interaction of government, business, and consumers as well as the economic situation in other nations. Although the goal of the government is to regulate the economy and provide economic stability and high levels of employment, swings in economic activity do occur. There are some political and economic factors that just do not yield to governmental regulation. A typical economic cycle contains four stages: expansion, recession, depression, and recovery. Each of these stages as it relates to employment is depicted in Figure 1-3.

Figure 1-3 **The Economic Cycle**

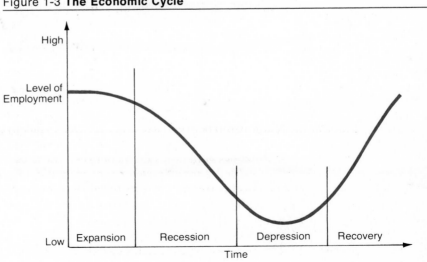

Over the past three decades, the government has been reasonably successful in keeping the economy out of a depression, although we have experienced periods of rapid expansion or inflation followed by periods of deep recession. The effect of inflation on consumers is clearly seen in the rapid rise in prices exhibited in the Consumer Price Index (CPI) in Figure 1-1.

Although you as a consumer cannot directly affect the level of economic activity, understanding the implications of certain economic conditions is important to your financial decisions. In many cases, current economic conditions warrant delaying purchases until conditions change; in other cases, for instance when inflation is anticipated, making purchases that had been planned for the future may be financially wise. Since our economy has been characterized by inflationary tendencies in recent years, it is generally best not to delay purchases: most items can be expected to become more expensive in the future.

The key factor ultimately controlling the quality of your life as reflected in your consumption and wealth is the amount of income you can expect to earn. In the absence of any inheritances or existing wealth, your income will depend on your age, your education, and your career. Although there are obvious exceptions, such as the shoeshine boy who develops a small business into a huge shoe polish manufacturing operation, generally, in our society, the closer you are to middle age, the more educated you are, and the more professional or managerially oriented your job, the greater your income will be. Each of these determinants of income—age, education, career—is discussed separately in the following sections. A final section discussing your lifetime earnings is also included.

Determinants of Personal Income

Age and Income

Although age is a variable over which you have no real control, it is interesting to look at the relationship between age and income. Typically, people with low incomes fall into the very young and very old age groups, while the period of highest earnings generally occurs between the ages of thirty-five and fifty-five. (See Table 1-1 for a breakdown of annual income for various age groupings.) This distribution results because those below age thirty-five are just developing their trade or moving up in their jobs, while those above fifty-five are likely to be working only part-time or to be completely retired. When setting financial goals and making financial plans, consideration should be given to expected changes in income as they relate to your age. Of course, someone without proper education,

Table 1-1 **Distribution of Income on the Basis of Age**
(March 31, 1976, Data)

Annual Wage or Salary Income	Age of Head of Household (Percent Earning Income within Ranges)				
	14 to 34	35 to 44	45 to 54	55 and Over	Total
$5,999 and Below	19.6%	11.7%	13.2%	40.3%	24.7%
$6,000 to 7,999	9.7	6.5	6.4	10.9	9.0
$8,000 to 9,999	11.2	7.0	6.5	8.4	8.7
$10,000 to 11,999	11.2	8.1	7.3	7.0	8.5
$12,000 to 14,999	15.5	14.2	11.4	8.6	12.0
$15,000 to 24,999	26.5	35.7	33.2	16.2	25.5
$25,000 to 49,999	6.0	15.0	19.8	7.6	10.5
$50,000 and Over	0.3	1.8	2.2	1.0	1.1
Total	100.0%	100.0%	100.0%	100.0%	100.0%
Average Income	$11,474	$17,091	$18,233	$11,452	$13,779

Source: Adapted from data in U.S. Bureau of the Census, "Money Income in 1975 of Families and Persons in the United States," *Current Population Reports*, Series P-60, no. 104 (Washington, D.C.: U.S. Government Printing Office, 1977), Table 11, p. 37.

career choice, and motivation cannot fairly anticipate the types of age-income distribution depicted in Table 1-1. As a matter of fact, for less-motivated individuals, annual income may remain relatively constant over their working life except for inflationary wage increases. This situation should be avoided by those who wish to use the tools of personal financial management to improve the quality of their lives.

Education and Income

Level of formal education is a controllable factor believed to affect an individual's potential income. It is obviously not true that all people with equivalent formal educations earn similar incomes. Formal education is a tool which properly applied can help carve out an income. The breakdown of income on the basis of formal education in Table 1-2 shows that, on the average, heads of households having more formal education earn higher annual incomes than those with less formal education. Although this is not a cause-and-effect relationship, it suggests that in order to enhance your earning opportunities you should obtain a good formal education.

Career and Income

Your choice of a field of education is closely related to your choice of level of education and is likely to determine the type of career you

"What else do you do besides graduate?"

A College Degree Does Not Insure Success

Source: Changing Times, August 1971, p. 29. Reprinted with permission from *Changing Times* Magazine, © Kiplinger Washington Editors, Inc., 1971.

choose. Of course, formal education is not a prerequisite for many types of careers, such as sales, service, and certain types of clerical work. But generally, the more responsibilities for decision making associated with a given career, the greater the annual income that career is expected to provide. The breakdown of the average income of a head of household in various occupations presented in Table 1-3 demonstrates that the highest earnings occur among professional and managerial workers, whose formal education is likely to include a college degree. Table 1-4 provides a breakdown by occupation of the average annual income for various professional careers and clearly indicates that those in professions requiring greater formal education typically earn higher annual incomes. Only when your educational and career goals have been set can your personal financial goals be established with a view to your expected lifetime earnings. Thus educational and career decisions are vital to effective personal financial management.

Table 1-2 **Distribution of Income
on the Basis of Formal Education**
(March 31, 1976 Data)

| Annual Wage or Salary Income | Years of School Completed (Percent Earning Income within Ranges) | | | | | | | Average Years School Completed |
| | Elementary | | High School | | College | | | |
	Fewer than 8 Years	8 Years	1 to 3 Years	4 Years	1 to 3 Years	4 Years	5 or More Years	
$5,999 and Below	53.8%	40.9%	31.9%	17.9%	14.1%	8.9%	5.9%	10.1
$6,000 to 7,999	11.7	12.4	11.7	8.8	6.6	3.9	3.8	11.7
$8,000 to 9,999	8.7	8.7	9.4	10.1	8.2	5.9	4.3	12.3
$10,000 to 11,999	6.4	8.3	9.1	9.3	9.2	7.6	5.4	12.4
$12,000 to 14,999	7.3	10.2	11.9	13.0	13.7	11.2	9.7	12.5
$15,000 to 24,999	9.8	15.6	20.7	30.6	33.6	35.2	33.5	12.8
$25,000 to 49,999	2.2	3.8	5.0	9.7	13.5	23.9	30.8	14.3
$50,000 and Over	0.1	0.1	.3	0.6	1.1	3.4	6.6	16.6
Total	100.0%	100.0%	100.0%	100.0%	100.0%	100.0%	100.0%	12.1
Average Income	$7,571	$9,432	$10,987	$14,184	$16,007	$20,433	$24,134	—

Source: Adapted from data in U.S. Bureau of the Census, "Money Income in 1975 of Families and Persons in the United States," *Current Population Reports*, Series P-60, no. 104 (Washington, D.C.: U.S. Government Printing Office, 1977), Table 12, p. 39.

Your Lifetime Earnings

Over your lifetime you can expect to earn a great deal of income. If you begin to establish realistic financial goals and apply the principles of personal financial management, you should be able to use this income in a fashion that will allow you to achieve the desired quality of life. Although your current weekly income may seem quite small, the average male is expected to earn about $460,000 over his lifetime. Of course, estimated lifetime income increases with education. Figure 1-4 illustrates the significant relationship between educational level and estimated lifetime earnings. Individuals with college degrees can expect to earn over $760,000 during their lives, while those who have fewer than eight years of formal education can only hope to earn about $280,000 in their lifetimes. Comparison of the nearly $500,000 of lifetime earnings of persons having completed only four years of high school with the $760,000 of those who completed four years of college (as shown in Figure 1-4) suggests that the approximate lifetime value of a college degree is $260,000 (that is, $760,000 minus $500,000). This fact tends to suggest that on the average a college education is financially justifiable.

Although many people tend to concern themselves with only their day-to-day financial affairs, all of the data suggest that by using a long-run

Table 1-3 **Distribution of Income of Males on the Basis of Occupation, 1976**

Annual Wage or Salary Income	Percent Earning Income within Range									
	Professional and Managerial Workers	Clerical and Kindred Workers	Sales Workers	Craftsmen and Kindred Workers	Operatives, Including Transportation Workers	Service Workers	Farm Laborers and Foremen	Laborers Except Farm	Farmers and Farm Managers	Total
$6,999 and Below	6.9%	13.0%	12.1%	8.7%	16.4%	34.4%	48.8%	21.6%	35.1%	14.1%
$7,000 to 9,999	7.7	19.4	9.2	10.8	15.4	17.2	20.6	17.2	17.4	12.4
$10,000 to 14,999	17.8	32.9	21.3	27.6	30.3	21.4	17.8	30.9	16.9	24.3
$15,000 to 24,999	37.5	27.2	35.5	42.3	31.4	21.9	9.2	25.3	17.1	33.4
$25,000 and Over	30.1	7.5	21.9	10.6	6.5	5.1	3.6	5.0	13.5	15.8
Total	100.0%	100.0%	100.0%	100.0%	100.0%	100.0%	100.0%	100.0%	100.0%	100.0%
Average Income	$21,834	$13,327	$18,822	$16,082	$13,713	$11,247	$8,610	$12,347	$13,052	$13,779

Source: Adapted from data in U.S. Bureau of the Census, "Money Income in 1975 of Families and Persons in the United States," Current Population Reports, Series P-60, no. 104 (Washington, D.C.: U.S. Government Printing Office, 1977), Table 13, p. 44.

Table 1-4 **Professional Occupations and Annual Income**

Occupation	Estimated Average Annual Income
Doctors	$49,500
Dentists	38,000
Lawyers	37,200
Engineers	22,900
Natural Scientists	
Geologists	16,000
Physicists	17,800
Chemists	17,500
Biologists	18,500
Social Scientists	
Economists	24,700
Psychologists	32,000
Statisticians	21,000
Teachers	
Elementary School	11,235
High School	11,825
College	16,705
Accountants	19,600
Social Workers	13,500

Source: Estimates from various portions of U.S. Bureau of Labor Statistics, *Occupational Outlook Handbook, 1976–1977 Edition*, Bulletin 1875 (Washington, D.C.: U.S. Government Printing Office, 1976).

time horizon, people can direct their current actions toward activities that will enhance the quality of their lives on a long-term basis.

An Overview of the Text

The material presented here is divided into six parts, each of which is devoted to the explanation of an important aspect of personal financial management. (See Figure 1-5 for a model of this division.) Each part is introduced with a brief description of its contents. Part titles are generally indicative of the subject matter under consideration.

Part 1: Financial Statements, Planning, and Taxes
Part 2: Managing Your Financial Assets
Part 3: Managing Your Nonfinancial Assets
Part 4: Managing Your Liabilities
Part 5: Protecting Yourself and Your Assets
Part 6: Retirement and Estate Planning

The organizational scheme of the text is based on a simple *balance sheet.* A key financial statement, the balance sheet is discussed in greater depth in Chapter 2. In essence, it presents *assets*—what is owned—and

Do You Like Hard Work?
Consider a Career in Business Management

Perhaps the most varied of all professions is business management. While some managers work for mammoth multinational corporations, others spend their time in activities such as running retail chains in the Midwest or organizing small firms in the South. The Bureau of Labor Statistics predicts a 22 percent increase in management jobs by 1986, with a 46 percent increase just for bank officers and financial managers. For those who enjoy the challenge and competition, a business career can be intellectually stimulating.

Starting on the road to a management career usually means working in one of three broad specialties: manufacturing, marketing, or finance. A profile of Bob Odear, a marketing executive, illustrates how the business management profession ranks today.

On most days, 40-year-old Bob Odear, who helped prove that women would buy higher-priced panty hose in supermarkets, arrives in his office at the Hanes Corp. in Winston-Salem at 7:30 in the morning. Without eating lunch, he stays at his desk until 6:30 p.m. Sometimes he works at home for two or three hours more.

Those are the easy days. The hard part is travelling: Odear puts in at least one week a month on the road. Recently he spent Monday in Albuquerque, Tuesday in San Francisco, Wednesday in Boise, Thursday in Cincinnati and Friday in Dayton. "After a while you don't know what city it is, and it really doesn't matter," Odear says.

Odear joined Hanes in 1971 as marketing director of L'eggs, just after the new panty hose were introduced in their now famous plastic eggshells. "The competition called our whole approach Hanes' folly," Odear says.

L'eggs are now sold in supermarkets everywhere, and sales have quadrupled. Odear has also unearthed a market for new L'eggs products—queen-size, all-sheer and support panty hose and knee-hi stockings that now account for 86% of all L'eggs sales. Last year he was named vice president in charge of new ventures for all Hanes supermarket products. He earns over $60,000, plus a car.

Odear spends most of his time ruling on staff recommendations. "I try to pick out weaknesses in proposals and then ask the right questions. Then I sit down with my people—the operations, research and marketing managers—and find out what's on their minds. No discipline has a lock on the truth. You'd be surprised how often a good marketing idea comes from a production person, or vice versa."

Odear graduated Phi Beta Kappa from the University of Kentucky and then got an M.B.A. at Harvard, class of '62. Before going to Hanes, he helped sell Lincolns and Mercurys for Ford and Winstons and Camels for R. J. Reynolds—proof that a good marketing man can sell almost anything.

Source: Excerpted from "The Heady Business of Building Profits," MONEY Magazine, March 1977, by special permission; © 1977, Time Inc.

Figure 1-4 **Lifetime Earnings and Educational Level**
(Males, 1972 to Death; Thousands of Dollars)

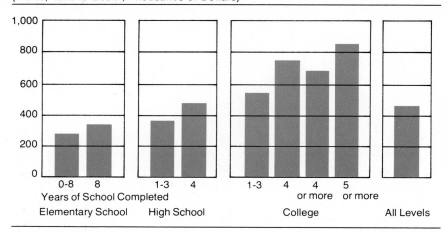

Source: U.S. Bureau of Labor Statistics, *Occupational Outlook Handbook, 1976–1977 Edition,*
Bulletin 1875 (Washington, D.C.: U.S. Government Printing Office, 1976), Chart 10, p. 19.

liabilities and *net worth*—debts and personal wealth, respectively. Since
the balance sheet reflects an individual's financial picture at any point in
time, the logical breakdown and investigation of this statement provides
the best structure for presenting the key principles of personal financial
management. It is the purpose of this text to help you understand these
principles and so prepare you to achieve the quality of life you desire.

Figure 1-5 **An Overview of the Major Parts of the Text**

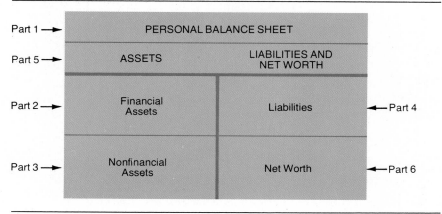

Summary

The goals of personal financial management are related to quality of life, consumption, and wealth accumulation. To some extent, economic strata determine marginal propensity to consume. The enhancement of wealth, or ownership, is one of the most important goals of the personal financial management process. Inflation can have a powerful impact on consumer prices and therefore on an individual's ability to consume. The Consumer Price Index (CPI) is a commonly cited indicator of the impact of inflation on consumer prices. Although money plays an important role in the personal finance process, the consumer must also consider the utility, or satisfaction, of certain financial activities.

The environment in which personal finance decisions are made results from the interaction of government, business, and consumers. Government affects personal finance decisions most directly through taxes and regulations. Business provides the marketplace in which these decisions must be made. As a result of the interaction of government, business, and consumers, the economy passes through various economic cycles, which include four basic stages: expansion, recession, depression, and recovery. An understanding of the economy can aid in making financial decisions.

Personal income is another important factor controlling the quality of life and wealth. Factors such as age, education, and career can have significant effects on income. In general, the closer to middle-age and the more educated people are, and the more professional their career, the higher their personal income will be.

Key Terms

assets	net worth
balance sheet	quality of life
Consumer Price Index (CPI)	recession
consumption	recovery
cost of living	tangible property
depression	securities
expansion	standard of living
inflation	utility
liabilities	wealth
marginal propensity to consume	

Review Questions

1. What is the standard of living? What are the factors that affect one's quality of life?

2. How are consumption patterns related to one's quality of life?

3. What is the marginal propensity to consume? Is it possible for two people with very different incomes to have the same marginal propensity to consume?

4. Define *inflation* and explain its effect on the consumer. How does it relate to the cost of living and the Consumer Price Index (CPI)?

5. What are the various forms in which wealth can be accumulated? Discuss.

6. Explain the role of money and utility in achieving the goal of personal financial management.

7. "It is the interaction of government, business, and consumers that determines the environment in which personal financial decisions must be made." Discuss.

8. Why should personal financial decisions be evaluated on an "after-tax" basis?

9. What are the stages of an economic cycle? Explain their significance for one's personal finances.

10. "All people having equivalent formal educations earn similar incomes." Do you agree or disagree with this statement? Explain your position.

11. Why do employers consider it so important for candidates they interview for positions in their firms to have a college education?

12. Can education be assigned a monetary value? If so, what are your future expectations for your own education?

Case Problems

1-1 Consumption: A Social Issue?

The U.S. Census Bureau indicates that there are 26 million poor people in the U.S. today. The following are income and expense data on two hypothetical families.

	Family X	Family Y
Income		
Salary	$15,500	$ 9,000
Subsidies		
Food Stamps	0	2,600
Housing Subsidy	0	2,000
Medical Benefits	0	900
Clothes Received through Charity	0	1,000
Total Income	$15,500	$15,500

Expenses

Income Taxes	$ 3,900	$ 1,300
Living Expenses (includes		
groceries, medical, vacation, etc.)	11,690	11,690
Total Expenses	$15,590	$12,990

Questions

1. How much is the current consumption for each family?

2. How much are each family's savings or withdrawals from savings? (Savings = income − expenses.)

3. Which family do you think is the poorest? Explain.

4. Discuss what you consider to be the overriding social issue relating to government subsidies for "poor people."

1-2 Accountant or Management Trainee?

Roger Kaufman will soon receive his bachelor's degree in accounting and finance from a large midwestern university. Because Roger has maintained a very high grade point average during his educational career, he has been swamped with job offers. He is, however, considering making a decision between the following two job offers:

1. One of the Big Eight accounting firms has offered him employment as their audit staff assistant at an annual salary of $14,400. His job will be to audit the books of large corporations which have this CPA firm as their accountant. During the first two years of his tenure with the firm, he will be stationed in various cities where the corporation's offices are located. Thus he will be away from his home, his family, and his young bride. Further, every summer the company will send him to its training school in Virginia. If he qualifies as a CPA after joining the firm, he is assured of a very bright future. He could be made a manager within five years and a partner three to five years after that. This would increase his earnings fourfold.

2. The second opportunity is the position of a management trainee in the Managerial Planning and Finance Division of a large petroleum company. Besides a monthly salary of $1,400, other benefits offered him include a two-week vacation every year and liberal retirement, health, and insurance benefits. This division is headed by the Vice-President, Managerial Planning and Finance, and includes a number of managerial positions. However, in terms of seniority, there will be at least twenty-five people above Roger, if he joins the company. He will not reach the manager level for ten to fifteen years. The job will not require any traveling at all.

The atmosphere and location of both firms are unusually good.

Questions

1. What are the advantages and disadvantages that Roger must consider in evaluating the two job offers?

2. Having considered the pros and cons of both jobs, which would you recommend he accept? Why?

3. List in order of importance, and discuss, five factors you feel must be present in order for you to consider a job opportunity acceptable.

Selected References

"Big Fight Over How to Protect the Consumer." *U.S. News & World Report,* 26 January 1976, pp. 40–41.

Blodgett, Richard. *All About Money.* New York: Quadrangle/The New York Times, 1973.

Cosgrave, Gerald P. *Career Planning: Search for a Future.* Toronto: University of Toronto Faculty of Education, 1973.

"Does It Pay to Go to College?" *U.S. News & World Report,* 24 January 1977, pp. 59–60.

Guzzardi, Walter, Jr. "The Uncertain Passage from College to Job." *Fortune,* January 1976, pp. 126–129 ff.

Haldane, Bernhard. *Career Satisfaction and Success: A Guide to Job Freedom.* New York: American Management Association, 1974.

"How Americans Pursue Happiness." *U.S. News & World Report,* 23 May 1977, pp. 60–76.

"How Life Will Change for Americans in Years Ahead." *U.S. News & World Report,* 12 January 1976, pp. 54–56.

"Jobs to Help You Pay for College." *Changing Times,* May 1977, pp. 17–20.

Karnasky, Denis S. *A Primer on the Consumer Price Index.* St. Louis: Federal Reserve Bank of St. Louis, July 1974.

Porter, Sylvia Field. *Sylvia Porter's Money Book: How to Earn It, Spend It, Save It, Invest It, Borrow It and Use It to Better Your Life.* Garden City, N.Y.: Doubleday, 1975.

Reddin, W. J. *The Money Book.* New York: Scribner's, 1972.

Rose, Sanford. "We've Learned How to Lick Inflation." *Fortune,* September 1976, pp. 100–105 ff.

Seixas, Suzanne. "How to Handle a Job Interview." *Money,* October 1976, pp. 55–66.

Solomon, Ezra. *The Anxious Economy.* San Francisco: W. H. Freeman, 1975.

"The Way Living Costs Vary in 40 Areas." *U.S. News & World Report,* 9 May 1977, p. 93.

"What Recruiters Watch for in College Graduates." *Nation's Business,* March 1976, pp. 34–36.

"Where the Jobs Will Open Up Over the Next Decade." *U.S. News & World Report,* 27 December 1976 and 3 January 1977, pp. 82–83.

"Why Inflation Is So Hard to Stop." *Changing Times,* April 1977, pp. 33–36.

"You Don't Need College for These Jobs." *Changing Times,* September 1976, pp. 22–24.

2
Your Financial Statements

It is the purpose of this chapter to explain:

A Preview of
Chapter 2

1. Procedures for monitoring and evaluating your financial progress.

2. Methods for preparing a personal balance sheet or statement of financial position.

3. The various types of personal assets and liabilities.

4. The meaning, importance, and methods for calculating net worth.

5. Techniques for preparing and interpreting the income statement.

6. The various types of personal income and expenses.

7. The calculation and interpretation of the contribution to savings or investment.

In order to effectively manage your personal finances, it is important to have procedures available for measuring how well you are doing. Although you are accountable only to yourself, while businesses must report to the government, to lenders, and to owners, the basic financial reporting techniques of business can be adapted to the personal financial management process. An understanding of how to prepare and evaluate personal financial statements should help you in periodically assessing your progress toward achievement of whatever financial goals you have set.

Imagine you were left aboard a drifting ship. Not knowing where you were within the vast expanse of the ocean, you would first need to determine your location; and, with the assistance of certain navigational aids—the most important of which would be the compass—you would plot your course to safety. Note that without a compass you would have been unable to accurately determine your location, and you could not have periodically checked your progress toward the desired destination. Financial statements are like compasses; people use them to gauge their financial position at various points in their lives in order to judge their progress toward their financial goals.

In order to periodically assess your financial condition, you will require some measures of both *financial position* and *financial performance*. Your financial position can be thought of as your wealth at a certain point in time, while your financial performance describes your income and expenses over a specified period of time. An understanding of how to prepare and interpret personal financial statements is one of the cornerstones of personal financial management. Without some standards by which to measure your financial condition, it would be most difficult to establish financial goals and to evaluate your progress toward those goals.

The Balance Sheet

The *balance sheet*, or *statement of financial position*, describes a family's—or individual's—wealth at a certain point in time. This statement is most commonly used as a barometer of long-run progress toward achievement of financial goals. The balance sheet derives its name from the fact that "it must balance," which means that everything must be accounted for. The statement contains three basic account classifications: *assets*, *liabilities*, and *net worth*.

Assets

Assets are items owned by the family. These are normally tangible items, although in certain instances they may be intangible. An item is classified as an asset regardless of whether it has been purchased for cash or whether its purchase was financed with borrowing. In other words, even if an asset has not been fully paid for, it is considered owned by the family. An item that is leased by the family, of course, is not shown as an asset since it is actually owned by someone other than the family. Table 2-1 lists some of the assets commonly held by a family. As in Table 2-1, assets are usually grouped into two broad categories: *financial* and *nonfinancial*. Financial assets are various forms of liquid funds, while nonfinancial assets include physical assets that are normally acquired not to earn a return but rather for the service they provide. It is important that all assets be shown on the balance sheet at their current *fair market value*, which may differ considerably from their original purchase price.

Table 2-1 **Assets Commonly Held by a Family**

Financial Assets	Nonfinancial Assets
Cash	**Real Estate**
On Hand	Home and Property
In Checking Accounts	Investment Property
Savings Deposits	**Automobiles**
At Banks	**Boats, Motors, Trailers**
At Credit Unions	**Recreational Equipment**
At Savings and Loans	**Personal Property**
At Other Institutions	Furniture
Investments	Clothing
Corporate Bonds	Jewelry
Government Bonds	Other
Corporate Stocks	**Business Ownership**
Cash Value of Life Insurance	
Other	
Money Loaned Out	

Fair market value is the price that the asset can reasonably be expected to sell for at the date of the statement.

Financial Assets Financial assets are normally *liquid*, which means they can be readily converted into cash. They include cash, savings deposits, investments, and money loaned out. Cash may be held either in the form of cash on hand or as a *demand deposit*—a checking account in banking jargon. Savings, or *time deposits*, as they are referred to by bankers, may be held in a savings account at a bank, a credit union, or a savings and loan. Investments include primarily corporate bonds, government and municipal bonds, and corporate stocks, along with the cash value of life insurance. Loans made by the family to outsiders are referred to as money loaned out. Only loans that are expected to be repaid should be included in this category. More detailed descriptions, along with discussions of certain strategies for acquiring various financial assets, are included in subsequent chapters of this text.

Nonfinancial Assets Nonfinancial assets are normally not as liquid as financial assets since they are usually purchased for the required or recreational services they provide. Typically, real estate, representing the family's home and property, appears as one of the key nonfinancial assets on the personal balance sheet. Any automobiles, boats, motors, trailers, and any other recreational equipment should be shown as nonfinancial assets on the balance sheet. All these items, including furniture, clothing, and jewelry, must be shown at their fair market value. If the family has any business ownership interests in nonincorporated businesses, the value of these interests should be included as a nonfinancial asset. Such interests normally are associated with small businesses. Of course, assets other than those included in Table 2-1 may exist and should be included in the family's balance sheet.

For more mature families, the balance sheet may show real estate investments in various types of income-generating property. It is important to recognize that real estate that is being leased to the family, as well as any other leased assets, should *not* be shown as an asset on the family's balance sheet. A family that is leasing the services of an asset does not own the asset and, therefore, must not represent it as such on their balance sheet.

Three points to remember are:

1. All assets should be entered on the balance sheet at their fair market value.

2. Only owned—not leased—items should be included on the family's balance sheet.

3. Although an asset is not fully paid for, it should still be included on the balance sheet.

The best way to determine your assets is to ask the question, "What do I own?" All items eliciting positive responses should be included.

Liabilities

Liabilities represent the debts of the family. These debts could result from department store charges, bank card charges, installment loans, or mortgages on real estate. Regardless of the source of a liability, these items are owed by the family and must be repaid in the future. Some liabilities are *due* in the very near future, while others are long-term and must be paid off over a period of years. Short-term liabilities are normally incurred for convenience while long-term liabilities are incurred to purchase nonfinancial assets, which are expected to provide service for an extended period of time. Table 2-2 presents a listing of common types of liabilities that may appear on a family's balance sheet. The level and status of an individual's liabilities are factors that potential lenders give careful consideration. Very high levels of debt and the presence of overdue debts are both viewed with a great deal of disfavor by potential lenders.

Bills outstanding include all items that must be completely paid for in the near future. These bills normally represent short-term obligations resulting from charges for the purchase of clothes, other less expensive items, consumable goods, and services. Items such as bank card charges, charge account balances, utility bills, rent, insurance premiums, taxes, medical bills, repair service bills, and any other bills are classified as bills outstanding. *All outstanding charges—even if you have not received the*

Loans Help Improve the Quality of Life

Source: Changing Times, December 1975, p. 8. Reprinted by permission of Edwin Lepper, from *Changing Times:* the Kiplinger Magazine.

bill—must be shown as bills outstanding. In other words, a charge incurred prior to the balance sheet statement date that remains unpaid should be included as a liability, regardless of whether a bill for the charge has been received.

Installment loan balances include all debts (other than mortgages on real estate) for which a series of installment payments are required over a specified period of time—usually six months to four years. Installment

Table 2-2 **Liabilities Commonly Owed by a Family**

Bills Outstanding	**Mortgage Loans**
Bank Card Charges	Home
Charge Account Balances	Investment Property
Utility Bills	Other
Rent	
Insurance Premiums	**Other Loans**
Taxes	Bank
Medical Bills	Educational
Repair Service Bills	Stocks and Bonds
Other Bills	Other
Installment Loan Balances	
Automobile	
Appliances and Furniture	
Other	

loans are generally used to finance such purchases as automobiles, appliances, furniture, and boats. *Mortgage loans* are associated with real estate purchases and normally have lives of ten years or more. Mortgage loans normally result from the purchase of a home; sometimes, however, people invest in real estate in order to earn income from renting it out or to profit from increasing market values. Mortgage loans may result from other types of real estate purchases, for example, the purchase of an apartment or office building. They are normally paid on an installment basis, and only the outstanding loan balance should be shown on the balance sheet. In Chapter 12, which explains the various types of borrowing arrangements available, mortgage loans are described in greater detail.

Other types of loans must be shown on the balance sheet as well. These may be bank loans requiring single payments, educational loans, loans used to purchase stocks or bonds, or other specialized loans. With these loans, as with the mortgage loans, *only the outstanding loan balance should be shown as a liability*, since at a given point in time it—not the initial loan balance—is the amount owed. More detailed discussions of the various types of loans and the loan negotiation process are included in subsequent chapters.

Net Worth

A family's *net worth* is the amount of actual wealth, or *equity*, it has in the assets it owns. Net worth can be viewed as the amount that would remain after the family sold all of its assets for their estimated value and paid all liabilities and debts. The accounting relationship between assets, liabilities, and net worth is called the *balance sheet equation*:

$$\text{Assets} - \text{Liabilities} = \text{Net Worth} \tag{2.1}$$

Once the market value of assets and the level of liabilities have been established, net worth is easily calculated by subtracting liabilities from assets. If a family's net worth is less than zero, the family is viewed as *technically bankrupt.* This form of bankruptcy does not mean that the family will be thrown in the poorhouse, but it does reflect the absence of adequate financial planning. In the long-run financial planning process, the level of net worth is quite important. Once a family has established a goal of accumulating a certain level or type of wealth over a specific period of years, progress toward that goal is best analyzed by monitoring net worth. Net worth represents wealth at a given point in time. It should be obvious that increasing wealth positions are preferred to decreasing wealth positions, and high wealth or net worth positions are generally preferred to low net worth positions. The importance of net worth will be emphasized more in Chapter 3, which is devoted to the topic of financial planning.

Balance Sheet Format

The balance sheet begins with the *date* at which the various asset, liability, and net worth figures recorded on it are measured. All assets are listed on the left side of the statement, and all liabilities are listed on the right. The net worth entry is shown on the right side of the statement just below the liabilities. The subheadings included in Tables 2-1 and 2-2 may be used to break the statement into various categories. Often the totals of these categories will be shown as subtotals in the statement. Regardless of how the various assets and liabilities are categorized, the statement should *balance:* According to the balance sheet equation, total assets should equal the total of liabilities and net worth. The general format of a balance sheet is depicted in Table 2-3.

Table 2-3 **General Format of the Balance Sheet**

Date	
Assets	Liabilities and Net Worth
Total Assets	Total Liabilities
	Net Worth
Total =	Total

A Sample Balance Sheet—Art and Betty Johnston

The relationship between assets, liabilities, and net worth, and the general format of the balance sheet are best illustrated with an example. To this end, we will examine the balance sheet of Art and Betty Johnston, a young family described briefly in the following color section. Art and Betty's balance sheet for the year ended 31 December 1978 appears in Table 2-4. This statement is best evaluated by looking at Art and Betty's assets, liabilities, and net worth separately.

Table 2-4 **Balance Sheet for Art and Betty Johnston**
(Year Ended 31 December 1978)

Assets		Liabilities and Net Worth	
Financial Assets		**Liabilities**	
Cash		Bills Outstanding	
On Hand	$ 40	Bank Card Charges	$ 40
In Checking Accounts	220	Charge Account Balances	90
Savings Deposits		Utility Bills	60
At Banks	650	Taxes	80
At Savings and Loans	1,800	Repair Bill	30
Investments		Installment Loan Balances	
Corporate Bonds	1,000	Auto Loan (Credit Union)	1,500
Government Bonds	350	Furniture Loan (American	
Corporate Stocks	840	Furniture)	300
Cash Value of Life Insurance	100	Mortgage Loan	
Total Financial Assets	$ 5,000	(First Savings and Loan)	32,200
		Personal Loan from	
		Parents	1,700
		(2) Total Liabilities	$36,000
Nonfinancial Assets			
Real Estate		**Net Worth** [(1) − (2)]	$14,000
Home and Property	$35,000		
Automobiles			
1976 Cutlass Sedan	2,500		
1974 Volkswagen Bug	800		
Recreational Equipment	400		
Personal Property			
Furniture	2,000		
Clothing	800		
Jewelry	1,000		
Stamp Collection	2,500		
Total Nonfinancial Assets	$45,000	**Total Liabilities**	
(1) Total Assets	$50,000	**and Net Worth**	$50,000

The Art and Betty Johnston Family

Art and Betty Johnston were married one and one-half years ago and currently have no children. Art, who is twenty-three years old, has just completed his first year as a sales representative for a large soap manufacturer. He is quite satisfied with his job and expects to continue his career in the sales and marketing area. Art's boss recently assured him that the company is most pleased with his performance and that they have "big plans" for him. Betty, who is twenty-one, still has one more year of college remaining before she receives her degree in special education. She currently works part time in the library at the university and expects to take a job in the public schools once she receives her degree. The Johnstons live in their own home, which they purchased in December 1977. Art and Betty love to travel; snow skiing is one of their favorite pastimes. They plan to have children in a few years, but wish to devote their current efforts toward developing some degree of financial stability.

Art and Betty's Assets Given their ages, Art and Betty's asset position looks quite good. The dominant asset is their home, which they purchased one year ago. Another item that strengthens their asset position is a stamp collection, which was a wedding gift from Betty's grandparents. In investments, Art and Betty have a total of $2,290 spread among government bonds, corporate bonds, corporate stock, and the cash value of their life insurance. The Johnstons' cash of $260 and savings deposits of $2,450 are liquid assets, which should allow them to meet their bill payments and cover many small unexpected costs. But the real strengh of Art and Betty's financial position cannot be evaluated without examining their debts, or liabilities, since they may be highly indebted as a result of borrowing to purchase certain of their assets, especially their home.

Art and Betty's Liabilities Looking at the Johnstons' liabilities, we can see that the primary liability is the $32,200 mortgage on their home. As might be expected, since they purchased their home only one year ago, the amount of the mortgage on it is still quite large relative to its estimated market value of $35,000. The Johnstons' *equity*, or actual ownership interest in the home, is approximately $2,800 ($35,000 market value minus the $32,200 outstanding mortgage loan). The Johnstons' bills outstanding, which total $300, do not seem too great. It is likely that these bills must be paid, at least partially, within the next month, since monthly billing cycles are most common. Other debts shown on the balance sheet include: a $1,500 balance on an installment loan used to purchase one of their cars, a $300 balance on an installment loan used to purchase furniture, and a $1,700 balance on a personal loan made by their parents to finance the down payment on their house. Contrasting the Johnstons' total liabilities of $36,000 to their total assets of $50,000 provides a more realistic view of their present wealth position.

Art and Betty's Net Worth The Johnstons' balance sheet in Table 2-4 shows their net worth as $14,000, the amount necessary to cause the balance sheet to balance. Considering Art and Betty's ages (twenty-three and twenty-one, respectively), they seem to be doing quite well. Their above average net worth can be explained by the fact that they received a $10,000 inheritance eighteen months ago. The $14,000 net worth figure is the amount Art and Betty would have if they sold their assets for the $50,000 at which they are valued on the balance sheet and from these proceeds repaid their debts of $36,000. Of course, Art and Betty are not expected to take such action, but by calculating their net worth at specified points in time, they can measure the results of their financial plans and decisions on their wealth position. As might be expected, increasing wealth positions are preferred.

The Income Statement

While the balance sheet describes a family's financial position at a certain point in time, the income statement describes the various financial activities that have occurred over a certain period of time—normally one year—and allows the comparison of actual financial outcomes to budget goals. (This will become clearer in Chapter 3, which is devoted to financial planning and budgeting.) The statement also evaluates savings or investments made during the period, which can, of course, be positive or negative.

The income statement consists of three major parts: *income, expenses,* and *contribution to savings or investment*. The name of the statement may be a bit misleading, for it shows not just income but also expenses, which are deducted from income to determine the contribution to savings or investment. A description of each of these three component parts follows.

Income

Items shown as income on the income statement include earnings received as wages, salaries, bonuses, and commissions; earnings on investments and savings; and proceeds from the sale of assets. Only income that has actually been received should be shown as income. This approach forces an honest representation of the way things were during the year—not the way they are or were expected to be. It is always possible that there could be a default on the payment of income earned. Common sources of income, which would be shown on the income statement, are listed in Table 2-5.

Table 2-5 **Sources of Income**

Wages and Salaries
Bonuses and Commissions
Dividends Received
Interest Received
   From Security Investments
   From Loans to Others
Gains and Losses on the Sale of Securities
Proceeds from Sale of Assets
Other Items
   Rent Received
   Tax Refunds
   Pension or Annuity Income
   Miscellaneous Income

A few items in Table 2-5 require clarification. Interest can be received either on bonds held as an investment or from loans made to others. Any gains or losses on the sale of securities are shown as positive or negative income, respectively. These entries represent the amount by which the sale price of the security differs from its initial purchase price. If the sale price is greater than the initial purchase price, the difference is shown as a gain; if the sale price is less than the initial purchase price, the difference is shown as negative income, or a loss. The tax implications of these transactions are discussed in Chapter 4, which is devoted to personal taxes. Proceeds from the sale of assets, such as furniture or a car, are shown as income. Other items of income include rent received from leased assets, any tax refunds received, any pension or annuity income received, and other miscellaneous types of income for the period. Total income is determined, of course, by adding all sources of income received during the period being evaluated.

Expenses

Items shown as expenses on the income statement represent money used for any of numerous possible outlays. Due to the large number of possible expense items, it is perhaps easiest to categorize expenses by the types of benefits they provide, as in Table 2-6. The listing of expenses given there is certainly not all-inclusive, but it should provide some feel for possible types and categories of personal expenditures. Other schemes for categorization are possible; for example, categories could be based on distinctions between goods and services or necessities and luxuries. The financial planning and budgeting process, which is described in detail in Chapter 3, relies quite heavily on the categorization of expenses in order to provide meaning to personal financial forecasts.

Just as only the amount of income received is shown as income, only the amount of expenses actually paid out is shown on the income statement. If an item—particularly an asset—is acquired through borrowing, only the net or actual dollars of money paid out (i.e., purchase price

Personal Income Growth (1975–1976): How Did Your State Do?

The table and associated figure presented below show the 1976 levels and rates of growth (1975 to 1976) for personal income on a state-by-state basis. Since consumer prices rose by only about 5 percent in 1976, it appears that during this period the average consumer was favorably affected by the 9.1 percent growth in personal income. How did your state do? See if you can explain its behavior relative to that of the other states.

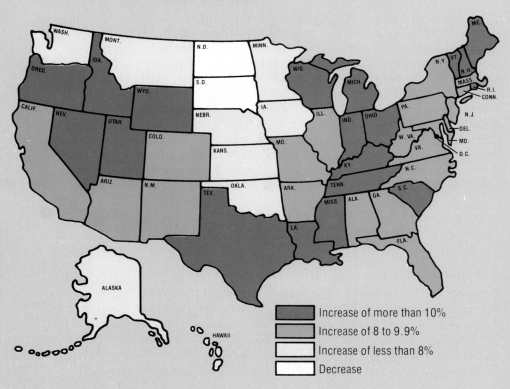

Increase of more than 10%
Increase of 8 to 9.9%
Increase of less than 8%
Decrease

minus the amount borrowed) is included as an expense. Any items purchased on credit or for which a portion of the purchase was financed with borrowing are not shown as expenses on the income statement; the financed portion of these outlays is not viewed as an expense until it is actually paid off. Any credit purchases of this type are instead shown as an asset and corresponding liability on the balance sheet. Payments against these loans are shown on the income statement in the year they are actually made. In other words, the income statement is presented on a *cash basis,* which means that only cash income and cash expenses are shown. Included in the cash expenses are actual payments against loans

State	Personal Income Per Capita 1976	Change 1975–76		State	Personal Income Per Capita 1976	Change 1975–76	
Alabama	$ 5,105	Up	9.8%	Montana	$5,600	Up	3.1%
Alaska	$10,178	Up	6.7%	Nebraska	$6,240	Up	2.2%
Arizona	$ 5,817	Up	9.4%	Nevada	$7,337	Up	10.0%
Arkansas	$ 5,073	Up	9.9%	New Hampshire	$5,973	Up	11.1%
California	$ 7,164	Up	8.6%	New Jersey	$7,269	Up	8.2%
Colorado	$ 6,503	Up	8.4%	New Mexico	$5,213	Up	9.3%
Connecticut	$ 7,373	Up	5.9%	New York	$7,100	Up	8.2%
Delaware	$ 7,290	Up	8.1%	North Carolina	$5,409	Up	9.9%
D.C.	$ 8,648	Up	11.6%	North Dakota	$5,400	Down	6.6%
Florida	$ 6,108	Up	8.3%	Ohio	$6,432	Up	10.3%
Georgia	$ 5,571	Up	9.8%	Oklahoma	$5,657	Up	7.6%
Hawaii	$ 6,969	Up	4.7%	Oregon	$6,331	Up	10.1%
Idaho	$ 5,726	Up	10.6%	Pennsylvania	$6,466	Up	8.8%
Illinois	$ 7,432	Up	9.4%	Rhode Island	$6,498	Up	10.4%
Indiana	$ 6,257	Up	10.6%	South Carolina	$5,126	Up	11.1%
Iowa	$ 6,439	Up	6.0%	South Dakota	$4,796	Down	2.6%
Kansas	$ 6,495	Up	7.4%	Tennessee	$5,432	Up	10.7%
Kentucky	$ 5,423	Up	11.0%	Texas	$6,243	Up	10.8%
Louisiana	$ 5,386	Up	10.0%	Utah	$5,482	Up	11.0%
Maine	$ 5,385	Up	12.5%	Vermont	$5,480	Up	10.4%
Maryland	$ 7,036	Up	8.9%	Virginia	$6,276	Up	8.5%
Massachusetts	$ 6,585	Up	8.6%	Washington	$6,772	Up	7.8%
Michigan	$ 6,994	Up	13.4%	West Virginia	$5,394	Up	9.1%
Minnesota	$ 6,153	Up	5.8%	Wisconsin	$6,293	Up	10.9%
Mississippi	$ 4,575	Up	12.2%	Wyoming	$6,723	Up	10.6%
Missouri	$ 6,005	Up	9.4%	**U.S. Average**	**$6,441**	**Up**	**9.1%**

Source: Data from U.S. Department of Commerce. Figure reprinted from *U.S. News & World Report,* 23 May 1977. Copyright 1977 U.S. News & World Report, Inc.

Table 2-6 **Expense Category Breakdown**

Housing	**Taxes**
Mortgage Payment	Property
Rent	Income
Repairs and Additions	**Appliances, Furniture, or Other Assets**
Household Services	Purchases
Utilities	Installment Payments
Gas and Electric	Repairs and Maintenance
Garbage Service	Home Accessories
Telephone	**Health and Hygiene**
Water	Laundry and Dry Cleaning
Cable TV	Cosmetics
Food	Barber and Hairdresser
Groceries	**Recreation, Entertainment, and Vacation**
Dining Out	Admissions
Automobile	Alcoholic Beverages
Purchase or Loan Payment	Hobby Supplies
Gas and Oil	Film and Developing
License Fees	Cigarettes and Tobacco
Repairs	Sports Equipment
Lease	Records and Tapes
Medical	Vacation and Travel
Doctor Bills	**Other Items**
Dental Bills	Postage and Stationery
Hospital Bills	Personal Allowance
Drugs and Medicine	Books and Magazines
Child Care	Tuition
Clothing and Shoes	Legal Fees
Insurance	Dues and Club Memberships
Life	Gifts
Health	Church and Charity
Auto	Pets
Homeowner's	Miscellaneous Unclassified Expenses

obtained during the period—not the amount of the loans incurred. Total expenses for the period are determined by adding together all uses of cash, or expenses, listed on the income statement.

Contribution to Savings or Investment

The third component of the income statement presents the net result of the period's activities. The contribution to savings or investment for the period is obtained by subtracting the period's total expenses from its total income. Although the income statement seems to indicate that dollars for savings or investment result from "what is left over" after all expenses are paid, the amount to be contributed to savings and/or investments must be determined by personal financial goals. The income statement is only an after-the-fact report of what actually was contributed during a particular period.

"All I'll have left this year after taxes will be you."

Tax Expenditures Are Necessary But Unpleasant

Source: Reprinted by permission from *My Shell Was Recalled!* (New York: Dow Jones Books, 1974), p. 109.

The contribution to savings or investment item on the income statement does allow you to determine how you did during the period. Its value can be negative, zero, or positive. A negative value indicates that the period's expenses have exceeded its income, thereby resulting in a *deficit* that must be covered by either reducing savings or investments or by borrowing. When businesses have expenses in excess of income, they are said to be *operating in the red,* since in business red ink is used to show deficits. A zero contribution to savings or investment indicates that the period's expenses are exactly equal to the income from the period. A positive contribution to savings or investment indicates that the period's expenses were less than the income for the period, and therefore a *surplus* resulted, which could be used to increase savings or investment or to reduce outstanding debts. Surpluses are obviously preferable to deficits.

When a deficit exists, a family or individual can meet this deficit by drawing down savings or investments or by borrowing. The effect of borrowing would not be felt until subsequent periods when the loan would have to be repaid. When a surplus exists, the amount of the surplus can be put into savings or an investment medium, or used to repay outstanding debts. The effect of repaying outstanding debts would be to reduce future expenses.

Balance Sheet Effect of Surplus When a positive contribution to savings or investment results (and the value of all other assets has not declined), the effect is to *increase* net worth. This increase results because an asset—savings or investment—increases without a corresponding increase in any liability. In order for the balance sheet equation (Equation 2.1, presented earlier) to balance, an increase in assets without any increase in liabilities must result in an increase in net worth. If the surplus is used to reduce a liability, an increase in net worth is still the result. By way of illustration, assume that Balance Sheet A in Table 2-7 represents a family's balance sheet on 31 December 1977. If the family income statement for 1978 showed a contribution to savings or investment (i.e., surplus) of $1,500 and these funds were used to increase an asset, Balance Sheet B in Table 2-7 would represent the family's financial position on 31 December 1978. If the $1,500 surplus were used instead to repay a debt, Balance Sheet C in Table 2-7 would reflect the family's

Table 2-7 **Impact of a Positive Contribution to Savings or Investment (a Surplus) on the Balance Sheet**

Balance Sheet A
31 December 1977

Assets		**Liabilities and Net Worth**	
		Total Liabilities	$22,000
Total Assets	$30,000	Net Worth	8,000
Total	$30,000	*Total*	$30,000

Balance Sheet B
31 December 1978 ($1,500 Surplus Added to Assets)

Assets		**Liabilities and Net Worth**	
		Total Liabilities	$22,000
Total Assets	$31,500	Net Worth	9,500
Total	$31,500	*Total*	$31,500

Balance Sheet C
31 December 1978 ($1,500 Surplus Used to Repay Liabilities)

Assets		**Liabilities and Net Worth**	
		Total Liabilities	$20,500
Total Assets	$30,000	Net Worth	9,500
Total	$30,000	*Total*	$30,000

financial position on 31 December 1978. Regardless which use is made of the surplus, the family's net worth increases by the amount of the surplus (i.e., $1,500) from its level of $8,000 at the end of 1977 to $9,500 at the end of 1978.

Balance Sheet Effect of Deficit While *surpluses add* to net worth, *deficits reduce* net worth. Again, in order for the balance sheet equation (Equation 2.1) to balance, this has to be the case. If the deficit is financed by reducing savings or investments without a corresponding change in liabilities, a reduction in net worth results. If it is financed by borrowing without changing assets, the net worth is still reduced, as the example in Table 2-8 indicates. Balance Sheet X in Table 2-8 represents a family's

Table 2-8 **Impact of a Negative Contribution to Savings or Investment (a Deficit) on the Balance Sheet**

Balance Sheet X
31 December 1977

Assets		Liabilities and Net Worth	
		Total Liabilities	$22,000
Total Assets	$30,000	Net Worth	8,000
Total	$30,000	Total	$30,000

Balance Sheet Y
31 December 1978 ($1,500 Deficit Financed by a Reduction in Assets)

Assets		Liabilities and Net Worth	
		Total Liabilities	$22,000
Total Assets	$28,500	Net Worth	6,500
Total	$28,500	Total	$28,500

Balance Sheet Z
31 December 1978 ($1,500 Deficit Financed by Borrowing)

Assets		Liabilities and Net Worth	
		Total Liabilities	$23,500
Total Assets	$30,000	Net Worth	6,500
Total	$30,000	Total	$30,000

financial position on 31 December 1977. Assume that the family's income statement shows a negative contribution to savings or investment (deficit) of $1,500 for 1978. Balance Sheets Y and Z show the two alternatives for meeting the deficit. In Balance Sheet Y, the $1,500 deficit is financed by reducing assets, while in Balance Sheet Z the deficit is financed by borrowing. Regardless of the fashion in which the deficit is financed, the family's net worth decreased by $1,500, from $8,000 at the end of 1977 to $6,500 at the end of 1978.

In summary, surpluses, regardless of how they are used, result in increases in net worth; and deficits, regardless of how they are financed, result in decreases in net worth. Since increases in net worth are associated with growing financial strength, while decreases in net worth indicate declining financial strength, surpluses are preferred. The importance of increasing net worth will be discussed in greater detail in Chapter 3.

Income Statement Format

The format of the income statement is outlined in Table 2-9. It is headed with the dates defining the period covered by the statement—typically, one year, although quarterly or even monthly statements are sometimes prepared. The first set of entries includes all income items and a total income figure. Following the income entries, the expenses are listed and totaled. Although it is not essential, the readability of the statement is greatly enhanced by including the various expense category headings. These headings permit a better understanding of general areas of expenditure and simplify the budget control process, which is described in Chapter 3. The final entry representing the contribution to savings or investment is shown as the result obtained by subtracting the total expenses from the total income. This entry constitutes the "bottom line" of the statement and is basically a summary of the results of the financial activities during the designated period.

Table 2-9 **General Format of the Income Statement**

	Dates
Income	
Item 1	
Item 2	
.	
.	
.	
(1) *Total Income*	
Less: Expenses	
Item 1	
Item 2	
.	
.	
.	
(2) *Total Expenses*	
Contribution to Savings or Investment	[(1) − (2)]

A Sample Income Statement—Art and Betty Johnston

Art and Betty Johnston's income statement for the year ended 31 December 1978 (Table 2-10) serves to illustrate the relationship between total income, total expenses, and the contribution to savings or investment, along with the general format of the income statement. This statement, which was prepared using the background material presented earlier, along with the Johnstons' balance sheet (Table 2-4), is best evaluated by separate analyses of their income, expenses, and contribution to savings or investment.

Income Art's wages clearly represent the family's chief source of income, to which the $980 of income earned by Betty in her part-time job is a supplement. Other sources of income include $42 of dividends received on the common stock they own and $148 of interest received on their savings deposits and bond investments. Art and Betty's total income for the year ended 31 December 1978 amounts to $12,370. The amount of income becomes much more meaningful when viewed in light of the expenses made during the year.

Expenses Art and Betty's major expenses as shown in Table 2-10 can be attributed to their home mortgage loan, food, and income taxes. Other expenses during the year included gas and electricity, auto loan payments, gas and oil for the cars, clothing and shoes, insurance, furniture loan payments, health and hygiene, recreation, tuition, and books. The total of all expenditures shown on the income statement is $11,920. Note that although the expense categories on Art and Betty's income statement are quite similar to those given in Table 2-6, they are not identical. As indicated earlier, these categories should be set up in a manner most suitable to the individual's—or family's—data requirements. Keep in mind, too, that the expense items shown represent actual cash outlays made by the Johnstons during the year ended 31 December 1978.

Contribution to Savings or Investment The Johnstons' contribution to savings or investment of $450 for the year is found by subtracting the total expenses of $11,920 from the total income of $12,370. Since the $450 is greater than zero, their contribution to savings or investment is, of course, positive. This surplus of $450 could be used to increase savings, to invest in stocks or bonds, or to repay outstanding debts. The correct strategy depends on Art and Betty's financial goals. (Strategies with respect to savings, investment, and debt repayment are discussed in subsequent chapters.) If the contribution to savings or investment had been negative, this would have indicated that the Johnstons had to withdraw savings, liquidate investments, or borrow an amount equal to the deficit in order to meet their financial commitments during the year

Table 2-10 **Income Statement for Art and Betty Johnston**
(Year Ended 31 December 1978)

Income	
Wages and Salaries	
Art Johnston	$11,200
Betty Johnston	980
Dividends Received	42
Interest Received	148
(1) *Total Income*	$12,370
Less: Expenses	
Housing	
Mortgage Payment	$ 3,084
Repairs and Additions	250
Utilities	
Gas and Electric	480
Telephone	120
Water	45
Food	1,500
Automobile	
Loan Payments	846
Gas and Oil	320
Repairs	80
Medical Payments and Drugs	180
Clothing and Shoes	300
Insurance	
Life	190
Property and Casualty	315
Auto	240
Taxes	
Income (includes social security)	1,590
Property (included in mortgage payment)	0
Furniture Loan Payment	300
Health and Hygiene	320
Recreation, Entertainment, and Vacation	780
Other Items	
Tuition and Books (Betty)	680
Gifts	100
Loan Payment (parents)	200
(2) *Total Expenses*	$11,920
Contribution to Savings or Investment [(1) − (2)]	$ 450

ended 31 December 1978. With their *surplus* of $450, the Johnstons have made a positive contribution to their net worth; had this figure been negative, a decrease in net worth would be expected (assuming all other

asset values remain unchanged from the previous period). In short, the Johnstons have done all right in the year ended 31 December 1978.

Your financial statements—the balance sheet and income statement— should provide the information needed to examine your financial position. With a thorough understanding of your financial status, you should be able to better direct your financial plans and activities toward achievement of your personal financial goals.

Preparing and Interpreting Financial Statements

Preparation of Financial Statements

Financial statements should be prepared at least once each year and are typically prepared in conjunction with the preparation of budgets. In order to simplify the financial statement preparation process, a *ledger*, or financial record book, should be set up. The ledger should contain a separate section for assets, liabilities, sources of income, and expense items. Separate accounts can then be established for each item within each section. Whenever a change (i.e., an addition or subtraction) in any of these accounts occurs, the appropriate entry should be made in the ledger. The objective of this system is to provide up-to-date data for use in financial planning as well as for preparing financial statements. Without current data, the likelihood of omitting any of these items from the planning process or the financial statements is much greater. Of course, if your finances are not very complicated, you may be able to maintain accurate records using some other, less sophisticated arrangement. Regardless of the arrangement used, it is of key importance that some type of records providing accurate information for use in preparing the balance sheet and the income statement be maintained.

Interpreting Financial Statements

Each time you prepare your financial statements you should analyze them in order to assess how well you are doing compared to past periods and in light of your financial goals. A few items to consider with respect to each statement are given below.

Balance Sheet When evaluating your balance sheet, you should be most concerned with the net worth figure, since it indicates your worth at a given point in time. By comparing your current net worth to that of past years, you can get an idea of how well you are doing. An increasing net worth position is most desirable. You may also want to evaluate the levels

One College Student's Finances

Upon completion of high school in 1974, Olivia Barrett enrolled in a small college in Oklahoma. Although Olivia's original intent was to study law or economics, she became interested in business administration after taking a course titled Introduction to Business. This spring Olivia will graduate with a bachelor's degree in business administration, with a major in finance. She is pleased with her choice of a career in business and hopes someday to start her own business. Olivia believes that her financial position and performance for the year ended 31 December 1978 are rather typical of a college senior. Note that in order to bring her balance sheet into balance she has shown a net worth of *negative* $1,175.

Olivia Barrett
Balance Sheet
(Year Ended 31 December 1978)

Assets		Liabilities and Net Worth	
Cash and Checking Accounts	$ 50	Loans	$3,500
Personal Effects	400	Net Worth	− 1,175
Income Tax Refund Due	300		
1974 Mustang	1,575	*Total Liabilities and*	
Total Assets	$2,325	*Net Worth*	$2,325

Olivia Barrett
Income Statement
(Year Ended 31 December 1978)

Income		
Scholarship	$ 900	
Summer Job (after taxes)	1,950	
Student Loan	1,100	
Gifts: From Parents	400	
From Uncle	1,200	
Total Income		$5,550
Less Expenses		
Tuition, Room, and Board	$3,845	
Recreation	525	
Miscellaneous	815	
Gifts	110	
Clothing	300	
Books and Periodicals	105	
Total Expenses		5,700
Increase in Borrowing		($150)

Olivia has accepted a position with a local savings and loan and looks forward to the day when her liabilities can be reduced and she can show a positive net worth value on her balance sheet.

of various assets and liabilities in order to determine whether or not the mix of these items is consistent with your stated financial goals.

Income Statement When evaluating your income statement, primary concern should be placed on the *bottom line*, which shows the amount of the contribution to savings or investment resulting from the period's activities. This figure indicates how well you have done during the period. As indicated earlier, positive values are preferable, since they represent positive contributions to net worth. Analysis of the individual income and expense items in light of both previous period performances and budgeted performances should provide insight into how well you are doing with respect to achievement of your stated financial goals.

Summary

Your financial statements—the balance sheet and income statement— allow you to measure your financial position and financial performance. The balance sheet, or statement of financial position, consists of three major accounts: assets, liabilities, and net worth. It describes your financial condition at a specified point in time. The balance sheet must balance, which means that the total assets must equal the sum of all liabilities and net worth. Assets include items such as cash, savings, investments, cars, and home and are listed on the left-hand side of the statement. Liabilities (which include unpaid bills, installment and other kinds of loans, and mortgages) and net worth are shown on the right-hand side of the balance sheet. All assets are shown on the statement at their current market value, while liabilities entered on the statement represent the amounts currently owed on all outstanding debts.

The income statement describes the various financial activities that have taken place over a specified period of time, normally one year. The statement has three component parts: income, expenses, and contribution to savings or investment. The contribution to savings or investment is found by subtracting the total expenses from the total income of the period. The contribution may be positive, zero, or negative. A positive contribution, or surplus, can be used to increase savings or investment or to repay an outstanding loan. A negative contribution, or deficit, can be financed by reducing savings or investment or by borrowing. Since surpluses tend to increase net worth and deficits tend to decrease net worth, surpluses are preferred. Income, which includes wages and salaries, dividends, and interest is shown at the top of the statement, followed by expenses, which include items related to housing, utilities, food, automobiles, and medical services. The contribution to savings or investment, which is the difference between total income and total expenses, is shown as the bottom line of the statement.

Both the balance sheet and income statement should be prepared periodically, typically at the end of each year. These statements can be used to evaluate past performance and as an aid in preparing financial plans and budgets.

Key Terms

assets
balance sheet
balance sheet equation
bottom line (of income statement)
cash basis
contribution to savings or investment
deficit
demand deposit
equity
expenses
fair market value
financial assets
financial performance

financial statements
income
income statement
ledger
liabilities
liquidity of assets
net worth
nonfinancial assets
operating in the red
statement of financial position
surplus
technically bankrupt
time deposit

Review Questions

1. For each item in the left column, match the appropriate item given in the right column.

(a) Balance sheet
(b) Time deposit
(c) Liquid assets
(d) Surplus/deficit
(e) Income statement
(f) Liabilities
(g) Demand deposit
(h) Expenses greater than income
(i) Income
(j) Assets

(1) Money owed
(2) Checking account
(3) Earnings
(4) Financial position
(5) Items owned
(6) Savings account
(7) Financial assets
(8) Financial performance
(9) Contribution to savings or investment
(10) Deficit

2. Distinguish between financial and nonfinancial assets. Classify the following under the appropriate heading.

(a) Furs
(b) Promissory notes
(c) Gold bars
(d) Priceless paintings
(e) Pickup trucks

3. Chris Jones is preparing his balance sheet as of 31 March 1977. He is having difficulty classifying two items and asks your help:

(a) He rents a house for $250 a month.

(b) On 21 March 1977, he bought a diamond ring for his wife and charged it using his VISA card. The ring cost $400, but he has not yet received the bill.

4. Susan Findley plans to study law at Yale University. The cost of law school is estimated at between $20,000 and $25,000. She has about $5,000 in a savings account and no other assets. She wishes to get a bank loan. Explain to Susan (a) the various types of loans that exist and (b) what kind of loan she can get.

5. State the balance sheet equation, and explain when a family may be viewed as technically bankrupt.

6. Deborah Lee bought a new house with a fair market value of $35,000. She has an outstanding mortgage loan of $33,700. How much is her equity in the house?

7. What is an income statement? Why is it important for good personal financial management? What are its three components?

8. Name some of the major sources of income a person may have.

9. William George bought a car for $4,700. Since he did not like its color, he sold it six months later for $3,500. How much was his gain or loss on the transaction?

10. "An income statement should be prepared on a cash basis." Explain what *cash basis* means. How and where are credit purchases shown when statements are prepared on a cash basis?

11. Can contributions to savings or investment be negative? What does this indicate? How does it affect net worth?

12. Describe some of the items you would consider when evaluating your balance sheet.

13. Explain why primary emphasis in the evaluation of an income statement is placed on its "bottom line." Discuss how you might go about analyzing your own income statement.

2-1 The Balance Sheet: A Banker's Friend

Case Problems

Richard and Elizabeth Walker are required by their banker to submit their balance sheet dated 30 June 1977 in support of an application for a $2,000 home improvement loan. They have come to you for help in preparing it. Their assets and liabilities are as follows:

Cash on hand		$ 70
Balance in checking account		180
Balance in savings account with Mid-America Savings		650
Bills outstanding		
Telephone	$ 20	
Electricity	70	
Charge account balance	190	
BankAmericard/VISA	180	
Master Charge	220	
Taxes	400	
Insurance	220	1,300
Home and property		34,000
Home mortgage loan		18,000
Automobiles		
1977 Chevy Nova	$3,000	
1975 Ford Pickup	4,800	7,800
Installment loan balances		
Auto loan	4,500	
Furniture loan	500	5,000
Personal property		
Furniture	1,050	
Wearing apparel	900	1,950
Investments		
U.S. Government Savings Bonds	500	
Stock of WIMCO Corporation	3,000	3,500

Questions

1. From the above data, prepare Richard and Elizabeth Walker's balance sheet, dated 30 June 1977.

2. Evaluate the balance sheet based on the following factors:

(a) Liquidity
(b) Equity in their dominant asset
(c) Net worth

3. If you were the banker, how would you feel about giving them the loan if the balance sheet data were all you had on which to base your decision? Explain.

2-2 How Did We Do in 1977?

Chuck and Judy Schwartz have been worried about their finances for more than a year. Chuck is a petroleum engineer for Phillips Petroleum Company. Judy attends the state university, where she is majoring in finance. She also tends to the housekeeping chores and maintains detailed records of all items of income and expense. Judy wishes to find out how well she managed their finances in the last year. In order to evaluate their financial performance, Judy has amassed the following data for the year ended 31 December 1977.

Chuck's salary	$20,000
Reimbursement for travel expenses	1,950
Interest on	
Savings account	110
Bonds of Alpha Corporation	70
Groceries	3,500
Rent	3,600
Utilities	720
Cash and auto expenses	650
Judy's tuition	1,400
Books, magazines, and periodicals	280
Clothing and other miscellaneous expenses	2,700
Cost of photographic equipment purchased with	
charge card	2,200
Amount paid to date	1,600
Chuck's travel expenses	1,950
Purchase of a new car (cost)	6,000
Outstanding loan balance	4,200
Purchase of bonds of Alpha Corporation	5,500

Questions

1. Using the information given above, prepare an income statement for the Schwartz family for the year ended 31 December 1977.

2. Based on your findings in Question 1, assess the Schwartzes' performance, commenting on the following:

(a) Their total income
(b) Their total expenses
(c) Their contribution to savings or investment
(d) The resulting increase or decrease in net worth

Bailard, Thomas E.; Biehl, David L.; and Kaiser, Ronald W. *Personal Money Management*. Chicago: Science Research Associates, 1977.

Cohen, Jerome B. *Personal Finance: Principles and Case Problems*. 5th ed. Homewood, Ill.: Richard D. Irwin, 1975.

"Guidelines for an Annual Audit." *Business Week*, 2 February 1974, pp. 68–71.

How to Read a Financial Report. New York: Merrill Lynch, Pierce, Fenner & Smith, 1973.

"How to Tell Profits from Puffery in an Annual Report." *Changing Times,* January 1977, pp. 25–28.

Janeway, Eliot. *You and Your Money: A Survival Guide to the Controlled Economy.* New York: David McKay, 1972.

Kristol, Irving. "The High Cost of Equality." *Fortune,* November 1975, pp. 199–200.

Lang, Larry R., and Gillespie, Thomas H. *Strategy for Personal Finance.* New York: McGraw-Hill, 1977.

Persons, Robert H., Jr. *The Practical Money Manager.* New York: Scribner's, 1974.

Rolo, Charles J. "Family Finance, 1776: A Bicentennial Backward Look." *Money,* July 1976, pp. 39–40.

"Which Family Records Should You Hang On To?" *Changing Times,* December 1974, pp. 37–40.

"Who Are Industry's Highest Paid Executives?" *U.S. News & World Report,* 6 June 1977, pp. 75–77.

Wolf, Harold A. *Personal Finance.* Boston: Allyn & Bacon, 1975.

3
Financial Planning and Budgeting

It is the objective of this chapter to explain and illustrate:

A Preview of Chapter 3

1. Methods for preparing and interpreting financial plans and budgets that are consistent with your financial goals.

2. The importance and interrelationship between short-run and long-run financial goals.

3. The manner in which schedules of future income and expense are estimated and prepared.

4. Procedures for constructing and balancing your budget.

5. Methods for summarizing your budget and evaluating any monthly budget surpluses and deficits.

6. One approach for maintaining budget records and controlling expenditures.

The periodic assessment of your financial position using the balance sheet and income statement is only the first step in managing your personal finances. In order to reach your financial potential and maintain your desired quality of life, you need to initiate a positive personal financial management program. This will require you to prepare plans and budgets that can act as navigational aids in plotting the course toward achievement of both your short-run and long-run financial goals. Although conscientious planning of your finances may force you to make certain short-run sacrifices, it should allow you to achieve your long-run goals and so provide you with higher levels of overall satisfaction.

Most individuals have certain *life goals* which they wish to achieve. Although these goals may not be entirely financial, the ability to achieve most of them depends on realizing a certain level of financial success. The absence of goals—financial and otherwise—results in a depressing and unexciting life with little direction and few prospects for the future.

Money is not necessarily the key to happiness, but its presence in amounts adequate for the fulfillment of financial goals allows people to devote more of their energy to the achievement of life goals and personal happiness. Since most people are not favored with unlimited funds throughout their lifetimes, their management of personal finances becomes a job of planning how to spend, save, and invest income in order to achieve as many lifetime goals as possible. Although without financial planning it may be possible to achieve certain financial goals, the presence of financial plans should improve goal achievement possibilities.

Establishing Financial Goals	The establishment of financial goals is the first step in the overall financial planning process. These goals, once set, provide direction for the financial planning process. In other words, it is not possible to prepare plans for attaining goals that are not yet formulated. Nor is it possible to enter the financial planning process without a knowledge of current financial position. Methods for evaluating the current financial position by preparing personal financial statements were described in the preceding chapter. After the current financial position is evaluated, both long-run and short-run financial goals must be established. Once they have been defined, budgets consistent with them can be prepared each year. Normally, *long-run financial goals* are set first and then a series of *short-run financial goals* are established in line with the long-run goals. Long-run goals are set for the years between the present and retirement, while short-run goals are normally set for one or two years ahead. These goals must be established with reference to the entire family unit—not on the basis of only one person's priorities.

Long-Run Financial Goals

Since it is quite difficult to be precise about future developments and desires, long-run financial goals are normally established in a somewhat general manner. They should indicate the wants and desires of the family unit over the next thirty to forty years. Of course, it is not easy for many

"I know you want to be affluent, but we
just can't afford it."

Financial Goals Should Be Realistic

Source: Changing Times, March 1974, p. 34. Reprinted with permission from *Changing Times* Magazine, © Kiplinger Washington Editors, Inc., 1974.

people to predict what they will want thirty or so years from now, but if they at least give some thought to the problem, they should be able to establish tentative long-run financial goals.

It should be obvious that, as the size and age of the members of the family unit change, so will many of the family's long-run goals. Long-run goals must be flexible enough to allow for changes as well as strong enough to shape short-run financial decisions. For example, an individual might set a goal of retiring at age fifty-five with a net worth of $200,000. This same individual might later decide to purchase a condominium in Florida at age fifty and retire at age sixty-two with a net worth of $225,000. But, although the long-run goal is changed, the short-run goals will remain fairly consistent: either long-run goal requires substantial regular contributions to savings and investments for the accumulation of the desired net worth.

Many families have found that the best procedure for establishing a set of mutually agreeable long-run goals is a meeting of the entire family at which the suggestions of each family member can be taken into consideration. Goals are most effective when set in reference to certain *goal dates* over a period of thirty to forty years. Goal dates are points in the future when certain financial activities are expected to be concluded; they may serve as checkpoints in the progress toward some financial goals or as deadlines for the achievement of others. For example, one goal may be the purchase of a boat in 1982 (the goal date), and another goal may be a net worth of $200,000 in 2005, with goal dates 1985 and 1995 set as checkpoints for the attainment of net worth of $75,000 and $140,000, respectively.

Goal dates are often set at intervals of two to five years for the first ten to twelve years and at five-year intervals thereafter. Of course, setting long-term goals and goal dates for periods extending twenty to twenty-five years into the future should be the prerogative of the parents, since it is likely that children will be on their own at that time and retirement will be the parents' key concern.

As time passes and long-term goals become short-term goals, adjustments in the financial plans can be made. The possibility also exists that as the actual financial outcomes are realized, the goals themselves may have to be changed. In other words, the family may recognize that goals were set either too high or too low. If the goals appear to be too high in light of the financial outcomes, they must be revised and made more realistic, while if they are clearly too low, they should be reevaluated and set at a level that forces the family to make financially responsible decisions rather than squandering surplus funds.

Short-Run Financial Goals

Short-run financial goals for each year should be consistent with the achievement of the long-run goals. These short-run goals thus become the key input into the *budget*—a tool used to plan for short-term income and expenditures. The immediate goals of individual family members, the family's expected income for the year, and the family's long-term financial goals must all be taken into account when these short-term goals are defined. In addition, the family must consider both its financial position, as reflected by the current balance sheet, and its spending in the year immediately preceding, as reflected in the income statement for that period. Short-term planning should also include the establishment of an emergency fund containing three to six months of income. This special savings account serves as a safety valve that can be used in case of financial emergencies—for example, a temporary loss of income.

The family's effectiveness in reaching its short-term goals significantly affects its ability to achieve long-term goals. If many short-term goals are not attained, the likelihood of achieving long-term goals is greatly reduced. In setting short-term goals, current desires must not be allowed to override the requirements for achieving long-term goals. Given the general disposition of people to prefer current satisfactions over satisfactions in the distant future, this may be the greatest challenge involved in setting short-term goals. Short-run sacrifices may be necessary to provide for a comfortable future, and realizing this fact ten or twenty years too late may make important financial and life goals unattainable. For example, college seniors who wish to become medical doctors may have to forego jobs paying around $12,000 a year in order to attend medical school at a cost of $6,000 per year for three or more years. Of course, upon completion of their medical education, they can expect to earn more than $40,000 per year practicing medicine.

Examples of Goals—Art and Betty Johnston

In Chapter 2 you were introduced to Art and Betty Johnston, whose financial data were used to develop financial statements dated 31 December 1978. Throughout this chapter the Johnstons' financial data will continue to be used to illustrate various aspects of financial planning and budgeting. The Johnstons' long-range and short-range financial goals, which they set on 31 December 1978, are described below.

Long-Range Financial Goals of the Johnstons Since Art and Betty Johnston are twenty-three and twenty-one years old, respectively, they have set their most distant long-range financial goal thirty-five years from now—a point in time at which Art would like to retire. Table 3-1 presents a summary of Art and Betty's long-range financial goals. They arbitrarily set their goal dates at the years 1981, 1985, 1990, 1995, 2000, 2005, and 2013. With the passage of time, they will probably adjust both the goals and goal dates. Although most of their goals do not have dollar amounts attached, Art and Betty can use them to provide direction to their short-range financial plans. In the planning process, the Johnstons made rough estimates of the costs of achieving their various long-range goals and then set the short-range goals necessary to attain them. For instance, in order to have $10,000 saved by 1990 for the purchase of a new home, it might be necessary for them to save approximately $900 per year over the 1979–1990 period (i.e., $10,000 saved over eleven years, or $10,000/11).

Short-Range Financial Goals of the Johnstons In the final week of December 1978, Art and Betty Johnston set their short-run financial goals for the coming year. They considered three factors: (1) their current financial condition as reflected in their balance sheet dated 31 December 1978 (Table 2-4); (2) their income statement dated 31 December 1978 (Table 2-10), from which they were able to evaluate their past spending in order to estimate their spending requirements for 1979; and (3) their long-run financial goals (Table 3-1), with which the short-run goals had to

Table 3-1 **Art and Betty Johnston's Long-Range Financial Goals**
(1 January 1981 to 31 December 2013)

1981
Pay off all loans other than mortgage
Save money for new home
Begin to build an investment portfolio
Start family (Betty stops teaching)
Buy new car (replace Volkswagen, trade every three years)

1985
Build investment portfolio
Have second child
Save money for new home
Buy station wagon (replace Cutlass, trade every three years)

1990
Betty resumes teaching
Buy new home
Purchase new furniture

1995
Buy sailboat
Purchase summer home
Accumulate net worth of $55,000

2000
Send children to college
Buy third car for children
Accumulate net worth of $85,000
Travel to Europe
Remodel home

2005
Children finish education
Buy larger sailboat
Travel to Australia
Accumulate net worth of $135,000

2013
Sell home and buy condominium
Retire from jobs
Accumulate net worth of $210,000

be consistent. Art and Betty's short-run financial goals for the coming year along with their expected costs of achievement are given in Table 3-2.

In order to simplify the process of eliminating expenditures in the event that sufficient funds are not available, the Johnstons assigned priorities to their short-range goals. The first four items seem to be

Table 3-2 **Art and Betty Johnston's Short-Range Financial Goals**
(Year Ended 31 December 1979)

Priority	
1	Betty finish school ($500)
2	Purchase new tires for Cutlass ($240)
3	Purchase career clothes for Betty ($350)
4	Buy three new suits for Art ($250)
5	Accumulate net worth of $15,500
6	Take two-week vacation to Canada ($600)
7	Buy workshop equipment ($300)
8	Take ski trip to Colorado ($300)
9	Purchase electric garage door opener ($180)

necessities, and the fifth appears to be associated with their long-run net worth goal. The remaining items are extras, or luxuries, that the Johnstons would like to acquire during the year but probably can do without. Once they have prepared their budget, the Johnstons will be able to determine which of their short-run goals they can afford to achieve during the coming year.

The Budgeting Process

Once you have established your short-term goals, you should prepare a budget for the coming year that is consistent with them. The *budget* is a short-term financial planning device designed to allow you to achieve your short-term financial goals. As such, it makes a positive contribution toward the achievement of your long-run financial goals. Your budget contains estimates of income and expenses, including savings and investments, for the coming year. It is usually divided into monthly intervals, although in some cases other time intervals may be more convenient.

The budget preparation process has three stages: estimating income, estimating expenses, and finalizing the budget. When estimating income and expenses, you should take into account any anticipated changes in the cost of living and their impact on your budget components. If your income is fixed—not expected to change over the budgetary period—increases in various items of expenditure will probably cause the purchasing power of your income to deteriorate. Because we do live in an inflationary economy, it is imperative that the effects of changing price levels on both income and expenditure be reflected in your budget.

What You'll Earn and Pay in 2000 A.D.

Twenty-five years from now, a senior airline pilot will be paid $292,500 a year.

That is the good news—for him.

Here is the bad.

If he lives in Dutchess County, N.Y., his new kitchen cabinet will be installed by a carpenter who makes $128,200.

Or, if home, sweet home is in San Francisco, his leaky faucet will be fixed by a plumber who makes $137,200.

Those are the projections of Manplan Consultants, a Chicago-headquartered management consulting firm. They are based on past wage trends, plus the effect of inflation.

Here is how the firm says other annual salaries will escalate:

1975	2000
$15,000	$67,500
$20,000	$90,000
$25,000	$112,500
$30,000	$135,000
$35,000	$157,500
$40,000	$180,000
$45,000	$202,500
$50,000	$225,000

"These projections are on the conservative side," says George S. Swope, Manplan Consultants partner who directed the study.

"By the year 2000, based on the same trends, the minimum wage should be at least $19,800."

Then there are taxes.

For each $1,000 in federal taxes you pay now, Mr. Swope says, figure on Washington taking $8,600 then.

And, of course, a shrunken dollar. In the year 2000, today's $1 bill will be worth 30 cents.

Source: Reprinted by permission from "What You'll Earn and Pay in 2000 A.D.," *Nation's Business,* November 1975, pp. 6, 8. Copyright 1975 by Nation's Business, Chamber of Commerce of the United States.

Estimating Income

Once the short-run financial goals have been established, the first step in the budget preparation process is that of estimating income for the coming year. Since bills are most commonly rendered and paid monthly, it is best to estimate income as well as expenses using monthly time intervals. The forecast of income takes into consideration all income expected for the year, for example: take-home salaries of husband and wife, any bonuses or commissions expected, interest income, dividend income, rental income, annuity income. Any items expected to be received for which repayment is required are not considered income. For example, a loan is treated not as a source of income, but rather as a liability for which scheduled repayments are required.

Estimating Expenses

The second stage of the budgeting process is the most difficult. It involves estimating (on a monthly basis) the expenditures for the coming year using the actual expenditures from previous years (as found on income statements for those past periods) along with the stated short-run financial goals. Families without past expenditure data must use a "needs approach" to develop spending forecasts. By first projecting their needs based on necessities and then attaching dollar values to these needs, estimates of expenditures can be made. Discussions of estimated expenditures with friends and relatives should help in developing realistic values for expenses included in the budget.

Initially, achievement of all short-run goals should be built into the expense estimates. To do this effectively, the cost of achieving the goal as well as the timing of the expenditure should be estimated. Any current or short-run contributions toward achievement of long-run goals should also be quantified and appropriately scheduled in the budget. Scheduled additions to savings and/or investments are often included as expenditures, since they are required by the family's goals. If the inclusion of all of these items does not allow the budget to balance, certain of them may, in the final analysis, have to be removed from the budget.

It is best to estimate expenses based on current price levels and then to increase these estimates by a percentage that reflects the anticipated rate of inflation. For example, if the monthly food bill is estimated at $100, and 8 percent inflation is expected in food prices, the estimated monthly food expenditure would be budgeted at $108—$100 plus ($100 × 8 percent). In order to avoid omitting important entries, reference to a list of common expense categories like that in Table 2-6 is useful when preparing the budget. An expense category for *fun money* that contains an allocation for each family member should be included. This money, which family members use however they wish without reporting how they spend it, gives each family member some degree of financial independence and thus helps provide for a healthy family budget relationship.

Finalizing the Budget

Once income and expense estimates have been made, the budget can be finalized. This involves comparing the projected income and the projected expenses on both an annual and a month-to-month basis. A balanced budget results when the total income for the year equals or exceeds the total expenses for the year.

Monthly Budget Deficits Yet even though the budget for the year may balance, expenses in certain months may exceed income, causing a monthly *budget deficit,* or income in some months may exceed expenses, causing a monthly *budget surplus.* Two remedies exist: (1) It may be possible to transfer expenditures from months in which budget deficits occur to months in which budget surpluses exist or, conversely, to transfer income from months with surpluses to months with deficits. (2) Savings, investments, or borrowing may be used to cover temporary

The Urban Family Budget: Recent Statistics

The Bureau of Labor Statistics has developed several sets of budgets which describe a specified manner of living for various types of families. These budgets were first developed in 1967 (the base year) and are updated for later years by adjusting for price level and income tax changes that have occurred over the intervening years.

The table included below shows three budgets for one such family. This budget-type family consists of a thirty-eight year old husband, employed full time; a wife who manages the house; a boy of thirteen; and a girl of eight. At this middle stage in the life cycle, after about fifteen years of married life, the family is well established, has average inventories of clothing, home furnishings, major durables, and other equipment. The three levels of budgets are described as lower, intermediate, and higher. For the intermediate budget, the U.S. urban average cost was $15,318 in the autumn of 1975. The cost for the lower budget was $9,588, or 37.4 percent less than the intermediate. The higher budget amounted to $22,294, or 45.5 percent above the intermediate budget. These budgets include all normal consumption expenditure for the family.

A corresponding budget based on your family size and style would be a good starting point for setting your target budget. A wide variation from these expenses should make you study your spending habits a bit more carefully.

deficits. Since the budget for the year is balanced, the need for funds to cover these shortages is only temporary. Once a month having a budget surplus is reached, funds used to cover deficits can be returned to savings and investments, or loans can be repaid. Either of the preceding remedies for a monthly budget deficit in a balanced annual budget is possible, but the second is probably more practical.

Unbalanced Annual Budget Situations in which the budget for the year is not in balance are more difficult to cope with. Three approaches exist: One is to *liquidate enough savings and/or investments, or to borrow enough*, to meet the total budget deficit for the year. This action is *not recommended* because it violates the objective of budgeting. The purpose of the budgeting process is to set expenditures at a level that provides for a reasonable standard of living while making positive contributions toward the achievement of long-run goals. Drawing down savings or investments in order to make the budget balance tends to reduce net worth. People who take this approach are not living within their means.

A second approach is to *cut lower priority expense items* out of the budget in order to bring the total budget into balance. This approach is

Annual Budget Costs for an Urban Family of Four Persons for the Year 1975

Item	Lower Budget		Intermediate Budget		Higher Budget	
	Dollars	Percent	Dollars	Percent	Dollars	Percent
Consumption						
Food	$ 2,952	30.8	$ 3,827	25.0	$ 4,819	21.6
Housing	1,857	19.4	3,532	23.1	5,353	24.1
Transportation	702	7.3	1,279	8.3	1,658	7.4
Clothing, Personal Care	1,019	10.6	1,434	9.4	2,083	9.4
Medical Care	818	8.5	822	5.3	857	3.8
Other[1]	447	4.7	831	5.4	1,371	6.1
Total Consumption	7,795	81.3	11,725	76.5	16,141	72.4
Other Items[2]	436	4.6	701	4.6	1,182	5.3
Social Security	576	6.0	834	5.4	841	3.8
Personal Income Taxes[3]	781	8.1	2,058	13.5	4,130	18.5
Total Cost	9,588	100.0	15,318	100.0	22,294	100.0

[1]Includes reading materials, recreation, tobacco, education, and miscellaneous.
[2]Includes gifts, contributions, life insurance, and occupational expenses.
[3]Federal and state taxes.
Source: U.S. Bureau of Labor Statistics, *Autumn 1975 Urban Family Budget and Comparative Indexes for Selected Urban Areas* (Washington, D.C.: U.S. Government Printing Office, 1976).

"You'll have to make up your mind. Do you
prefer a balanced diet or a balanced budget?"

Balanced Budgets Often Require Sacrifices

Source: George Dole in *Changing Times*, June 1976, p. 18. Reprinted by permission of the cartoonist.

preferred over the first approach, for it forces the budget to balance without using some external source of funds. Low-priority expenses are those items associated with the short-run financial goals believed to be least important. Some people using this technique to bring their budgets into balance divide their expenses into two groups—inflexible and flexible. *Inflexible expenses* are those that must be made on the basis of either contracts or necessity. Items such as mortgage payments, loan payments, and utility bills are examples of inflexible expenses. *Flexible expenses* are for noncontractual items that are not necessities, such as recreation, entertainment, and certain clothing purchases. These flexible expenses can be cut from the budget in order to bring it into balance.

A third approach is to *increase income* by assuming a second, part-time job or by finding an alternative job that pays more. This is probably the most difficult approach for it is likely to result in a significant change in leisure activities and life-style. Persons with no savings or investments to liquidate and unable to meet expenses for necessity items may find that taking a second job or changing jobs provides the only feasible course of action for balancing their budgets.

Budget Summary Once all monthly deficits have been considered and the total annual budget has been balanced, the budget is finalized. The income for the year equals or exceeds the year's expenses, and tentative plans have been made for covering expected monthly deficits. At this point, the preparation of a *budget summary*—which shows for each month the estimated income and estimated expenses, the amount of any surplus or deficit, and the cumulative surplus or deficit at the end of each month— provides an overview of the financial situation in the year to come. By analyzing the cumulative surplus or deficit, the timing and amount of shortage or excess funds can be evaluated and the practicality of the method chosen for covering monthly deficits can be determined. The use of the budget summary statement can greatly simplify the problems in preparing and interpreting budgets. The entire budget finalization process, including the budget summary statement, is illustrated in a later section of this chapter.

The Budget Format

As shown in Table 3-3, the finalized budget is normally broken into three basic sections: income, expenses, and the difference between them (income minus expenses), which may be either a surplus or a deficit.

Table 3-3 **The Budget Format**

	Jan.	Feb.	. . . . . .	Dec.	Annual Total
Income					
Item 1					
Item 2					
.					
.					
.					
(1) *Total Income*			. . . . . .		
Expenses (Includes Scheduled Contributions to Savings and Investment)					
Item 1					
Item 2					
.					
.					
(2) *Total Expenses*			. . . . . .		
Surplus (or Deficit) [(1) − (2)]					

Within the first two sections, the individual items of income and expense are shown separately. Usually, the budget shows monthly figures as well as an annual total for each income and expense item. In many situations there are so many budget entries that it is better to break the budget into separate schedules, one for estimated income, one for estimated expenses (including savings and investments), and a budget summary that can replace the single budget statement. The income and expense schedules can be prepared separately, and the budget summary can be used to bring these components together to determine the amount of any surpluses or deficits.

Sample Budget—Art and Betty Johnston

Using their short-run financial goals (Table 3-2) and their past financial statements (see Tables 2-4 and 2-10), Art and Betty Johnston prepared their budget for the 1979 calendar year. The Johnstons' budget was developed using separate schedules of estimated income and expense along with a budget summary, as described above.

Schedule of Estimated Income Art and Betty Johnston's schedule of estimated income for the year ended 31 December 1979 shown in Table 3-4 provides an item by item breakdown for each month of the coming year. The Johnstons' total annual income, which is derived primarily from Art's wages, is expected to be $13,243. Using the amount of take-home pay rather than the entire salary to draw up this schedule, as the Johnstons did, eliminates any need to show taxes or social security payments in the expense portion of the budget. Note the lapse in Betty's income during the months of June, July, and August; this is due to the fact that she will quit her library job just before she graduates from college in June but will not take a teaching job until September.

Schedule of Estimated Expenses The Johnstons' schedule of estimated expenses for the year ended 31 December 1979 is presented in Table 3-5 on page 72. Most of the expense items the Johnstons listed were categorized and included in Table 2-6. Note that Art and Betty have built $40 per month into their budget as fun money. The fun money is to be divided equally between them, and they will not report to each other on the disposition of their share of it.

Another significant aspect of their schedule of estimated expenses is the $200 included under new savings and/or investments. In light of the scheduled debt repayment, Art and Betty estimate that putting that amount aside will enable them to easily exceed their net worth goal of $15,500. (It should be recalled from Chapter 2 that the reduction of liabilities, which occurs when debts are repaid, will increase net worth as long as there is no corresponding reduction in assets.) By paying on the scheduled home mortgage, auto loan, furniture loan, and parents' loan, the Johnstons are reducing their liabilities by over $4,000, which should easily allow them to increase their net worth from its 31 December 1978 level of $14,000 to the desired level of $15,500 at 31 December 1979.

Table 3-4 **Schedule of Estimated Income for Art and Betty Johnston**
(Year Ended 31 December 1979)

Source	Jan.	Feb.	Mar.	Apr.	May	June	July	Aug.	Sept.	Oct.	Nov.	Dec.	Total
Art's Take-Home Salary	$825	$825	$825	$825	$825	$825	$825	$825	$825	$825	$825	$825	$9,900
Betty's Take-Home Salary	95	95	95	95	95	0	0	0	535	535	535	535	2,615
Art's Bonus												500	500
Interest			45			45			45			45	180
Dividends			12			12			12			12	48
Total Income	$920	$920	$977	$920	$920	$882	$825	$825	$1,417	$1,360	$1,360	$1,917	$13,243

It should also be noted that the Johnstons built in additional costs in order to adequately reflect the effect of inflation on certain of the budgeted items. They did this by adjusting actual 1978 expenditures upward by the percentages which they believed accurately reflected the rate of price increase expected for certain budget items.

Aside from the above, the schedule of estimated expenses shown in Table 3-5 is self-explanatory. Of course, it represents only the Johnstons' first estimate of their expenses. This first trial aims at the achievement of all of the Johnstons' short-run goals listed in Table 3-2.

Finalizing the Johnstons' Budget Reviewing Art and Betty Johnston's initial schedule of expenses, we can see that the initial estimate results in total expenses of $14,219. This figure is greater than that for their total estimated income of $13,243 (Table 3-4). Clearly, the budget is not balanced: a budget deficit of approximately $1,000 exists. In order to bring the budget into balance, Art and Betty cut certain low-priority goals from their budget, rescheduled some of their loan payments, and reduced their fun money allocation. The specific individual adjustments are listed below:

The Family Budget in the Year 2001

In 1976 a Chicago firm, Manplan Consultants, made projections about the future costs of a variety of consumer purchases, using a 6 percent rate of inflation. Their projection of selected living costs in the year 2001 are given below. For comparison the actual 1976 costs of these items are also shown. It is interesting to note the significant differences between the 1976 costs and the costs for associated items in the year 2001. Can you imagine paying $1.50 for the Sunday newspaper or $3.22 for a Big Mac? How will you be able to pay these high costs? If your 1976 earnings were $12,000, you would need $51,500 of annual earnings in order to maintain your current standard of living. Hard to believe, isn't it?

1. Eliminated purchase of workshop equipment costing $300.
2. Eliminated ski trip to Colorado costing $300.
3. Eliminated purchase of electric garage door opener costing $180.
4. Rescheduled $200 of repayment on loan from parents.
5. Reduced allocation of fun money by $120 for the year ($10 per month).

The total expense reduction of $1,100 lowered the total scheduled expenses for the year to $13,119, which falls within the total income estimate of $13,243. These changes are noted on the adjusted schedule of expenses by the deletion of the initial values and the writing in of the adjusted amounts (see Table 3-6). The expense totals after these adjustments have been made are given in the final line of the schedule. Once these adjustments are made and estimated annual expenses no longer exceed estimated annual income, the budget is balanced.

The Johnstons' final step in the budgeting process was to analyze monthly surpluses and deficits in order to estimate whether or not savings, investments, or borrowing should be used to meet any monthly

	1976	2001
Car (Lower Price)	$ 4,000.00	$ 17,160.00
College Tuition (Private)	3,800.00	16,302.00
College Tuition (State)	1,000.00	4,290.00
House (Average Size)	40,000.00	171,600.00
Apartment (Low Price Suburban—Monthly)	175.00	751.00
Newspaper, Sunday	.35	1.50
Soap (Bar)	.30	1.29
Toothpaste	.60	2.57
Ground Beef (1 Pound)	1.09	4.67
Hot Dogs (Package)	.99	4.25
Bread (Small Loaf)	.50	2.15
Sirloin Steak (1 Pound)	1.79	7.68
Coffee (1 Pound)	2.00	8.58
Bologna (1 Pound)	.99	4.25
Lettuce (Head)	.59	2.53
Paper Towels (Roll)	.30	1.29
Bus Fare (Local)	.50	2.15
Big Mac	.75	3.22

Source: Data copyright © 1976 Manplan Consultants, Chicago, Illinois. Reprinted by permission.

Table 3-5 Art and Betty Johnstons' Initial Schedule of Estimated Expenses
(Year Ended 31 December 1979)

Item	Jan.	Feb.	Mar.	Apr.	May	June	July	Aug.	Sept.	Oct.	Nov.	Dec.	Total
Home Mortgage	$257	$257	$257	$257	$257	$257	$257	$257	$257	$257	$257	$257	$3,084
Electric Garage Door Opener		60	60	60									180
Gas and Electric	50	50	50	30	30	40	40	50	50	40	40	50	520
Water	5	5	5	5	5	10	10	15	5	5	5	5	80
Groceries	140	140	140	140	140	140	140	140	140	140	140	140	1,620
Dining Out	25	25	25	25	25	25	25	25	25	25	25	25	300
Workshop Equipment									150	150			300
Clothing	30	30	80	30	30	30	30	30	230	40	40	40	640
Betty's Tuition		500											500
Auto Loan	75	75	75	75	75	75	75	75	75	75	75	75	900
Furniture Loan	25	25	25	25	25	25	25	25	25	25	25	25	300
Parents' Loan									100	100	100	100	400
New Tires for Cutlass	80	80	80										240
Gasoline and Oil	40	40	40	40	40	40	40	40	40	40	40	40	480
Auto License		50											50
Income Taxes (assumed equal to withholding)													0
Property Taxes												350	350
Telephone	15	15	15	15	15	15	15	15	15	15	15	15	180
Homeowner's Insurance						158						157	315
Auto Insurance		120						120					240
Health Insurance (paid by Art's employer)													0
Life Insurance											190		190
Medical and Dental	25	25	25	25	25	25	25	25	25	25	25	25	300
Laundry, Cosmetics, Hair Care	30	30	30	30	30	30	30	30	30	30	30	30	360
Gifts				10	20			20				100	150
Recreation and Entertainment	50	50	50	50	50	50	50	50	50	50	50	50	600
Vacation								600				300	900
Charitable Contributions	30					10			20				60
Miscellaneous	25	25	25	25	25	25	25	25	25	25	25	25	300
Fun Money	40	40	40	40	40	40	40	40	40	40	40	40	480
Savings and Investments (to achieve $15,500 of net worth)												200	200
Total Expenses	$942	$1,642	$1,022	$882	$832	$995	$827	$1,522	$1,302	$1,082	$1,122	$2,049	$14,219

Table 3-6 Art and Betty Johnston's Adjusted Schedule of Estimated Expenses
(Year Ended 31 December 1979)

Item	Jan.	Feb.	Mar.	Apr.	May	June	July	Aug.	Sept.	Oct.	Nov.	Dec.	Total
Home Mortgage	$257	$257	$257	$257	$257	$257	$257	$257	$257	$257	$257	$257	$3,084
Electric Garage Door Opener													0
Gas and Electric	50	50	50	30	30	40	40	50	50	40	40	50	520
Water	5	5	5	5	5	10	10	15	5	5	5	5	80
Groceries	140	140	140	140	140	140	140	80	140	140	140	140	1,620
Dining Out	25	25	25	25	25	25	25	25	25	25	25	25	300
Workshop Equipment													0
Clothing	30	30	80	30	30	30	30	30	230	40	40	40	640
Betty's Tuition		500											500
Auto Loan	75	75	75	75	75	75	75	75	75	75	75	75	900
Furniture Loan	25	25	25	25	25	25	25	25	25	25	25	25	300
Parents' Loan											100	100	200
New Tires for Cutlass	80	80	80										240
Gasoline and Oil	40	40	40	40	40	40	40	40	40	40	40	40	480
Auto License		50											50
Income Taxes (assumed equal to withholding)													0
Property Taxes												350	350
Telephone	15	15	15	15	15	15	15	15	15	15	15	15	180
Homeowner's Insurance						158						157	315
Auto Insurance		120						120					240
Health Insurance (paid by Art's employer)													0
Life Insurance											190		190
Medical and Dental	25	25	25	25	25	25	25	25	25	25	25	25	300
Laundry, Cosmetics, Hair Care	30	30	30	30	30	30	30	30	30	30	30	30	360
Gifts				10	20	10		20				90	150
Recreation and Entertainment	50	50	50	50	50	50	50	50	50	50	50	50	600
Vacation								600					600
Charitable Contributions	30								20			10	60
Miscellaneous	25	25	25	25	25	25	25	25	25	25	25	25	300
Fun Money	30	30	30	30	30	30	30	30	30	30	30	30	360
Savings and Investments (to achieve $15,500 of net worth)												200	200
Total Expenses (adjusted)	$932	$1,572	$952	$812	$822	$985	$817	$1,512	$1,042	$822	$1,112	$1,739	$13,119

deficits. To do this, Art and Betty prepared the budget summary that appears in Table 3-7. The first two columns list the estimated income and expense totals for each month from Tables 3-4 and 3-6, respectively. Column 3 shows the surplus or deficit for each month. The total surplus of $124 for the year should add to the Johnstons' savings or investments or allow them to repay a portion of one of their outstanding loans. Column 4 presents a running total of the surpluses or deficits shown in column 3.

Table 3-7 **Budget Summary for Art and Betty Johnston**
(Year Ended 31 December 1979)

Month	Estimated Income (1)	Estimated Expenses (2)	Surplus (Deficit) [(1) − (2)] (3)	Cumulative Surplus (Deficit) (4)
Jan.	$ 920	$ 932	$ (12)	$ (12)
Feb.	920	1,572	(652)	(664)
Mar.	977	952	25	(639)
Apr.	920	812	108	(531)
May	920	822	98	(433)
June	882	985	(103)	(536)
July	825	817	8	(528)
Aug.	825	1,512	(687)	(1,215)
Sept.	1,417	1,042	375	(840)
Oct.	1,360	822	538	(302)
Nov.	1,360	1,112	248	(54)
Dec.	1,917	1,739	178	124
Total	$13,243	$13,119	$124	$ 124

Note that although monthly deficits occur only in January, February, June, and August, the magnitude and timing of these deficits result in a cumulative deficit for the months January through November. In order to cover these deficits, Art and Betty were able to arrange an interest-free loan from their parents. Had they been required to use their savings to finance these temporary deficits, they would have had to forego some of the interest on savings included as part of their estimated income. If the Johnstons had been completely unable to obtain funds to cover these temporary deficits, they would have had to reschedule their planned expenses or income.

Budget Records and Control

Accurate records and control procedures must be maintained to assure that the budget has some effect on the financial planning process. A good financial plan and budget are not enough; records are needed in order to maintain control over income and spending, for preparing financial statements, and for planning future spending. It is not necessary for the family to account for every penny of income and expenditure during a given period. Since most families are not interested in devoting great amounts of time to maintaining detailed records, record-keeping and control procedures used should not be so technical as to become burdensome.

A sophisticated budget record and control system includes: (1) setting up the record book, (2) recording actual expenditures, (3) closing accounts periodically, (4) controlling budget expenditures, and (5) closing the books and preparing year-end financial statements. A detailed description of each of these phases is presented below. The system described here is relatively sophisticated, but from it you should be able to develop your own more practical budget record and control procedures.

Setting Up the Record Book

In order to maintain accurate records for controlling the budget and planning future expenditures, a *budget record book* should be kept. A loose-leaf binder with separate pages for each income and expense account serves this purpose quite well. Each account should be numbered, and an index of accounts should appear at the front of the binder. The account title and number should head each page of the record book. Grouping similar categories of accounts and tabbing these sections facilitates reference to individual accounts. Duplication and confusion can be avoided by giving only one person the responsibility for recording all income and expenditures in the record book.

Recording Actual Expenditures

At the beginning of each budget period (month, quarter), the amount budgeted for each expense item should be recorded in the record book. As income is received and money is expended, entries should be made in the appropriate accounts. The amount expended for a given item should be deducted from that item's account balance in order to maintain a running balance of the amount yet available for expenditure in the current period. When the balances in each account are kept up-to-date in this way, the probability that accounts will be overspent is reduced. Instead of making these entries each day, many people prefer to maintain all expenditures on a *master expense sheet* from which the entries are posted to the record book at specified intervals of time, such as every three days. Still, these expenditures must be entered frequently enough to assure that accounts are not overspent.

Closing Accounts Periodically

At the end of each period, all accounts should be closed; that is, the end-of-period balance should be determined. Then the amount budgeted for the next period should be added to this end-of-period balance in order to determine the balance on hand at the beginning of the new period. In theory, the balance of each account should be zero at the end of each budget period, but this normally occurs only for those accounts from which a single payment equal to the budgeted amount is required—mortgages, loans, or insurance, for example. Other accounts may end up with either positive balances, indicating the budget was underspent, or negative balances, indicating the budget was overspent.

Controlling Budget Expenditures

When accounts are closed at the end of each period, surpluses and deficits should be subjected to some analysis. The presence of a surplus need not cause concern; but a deficit, which indicates that the account is operating in the red, requires attention. An account deficit that occurs in only one period is not as problematical as a deficit that recurs in a series of periods. One way of dealing with a deficit is to cut back expenditures in future periods for the account affected. If recurring deficits indicate an account may have been underbudgeted, the budget may need to be adjusted to a level sufficient to cover the outlays. Budget adjustments of this type are usually accomplished by reducing the amount budgeted for other accounts that may be either overbudgeted or nonessential. In all cases, however, accounts must balance so that the annual budget will balance. Only in exceptional situations should budget adjustments be financed by drawing down savings or investments or by borrowing.

Envelope System Another method of monthly budget control, the *envelope system*, is often used for expenditures for which the budgeted amount is spent on a number of individual purchases. Examples of these types of accounts are groceries, clothing, or gas and oil. Under this system, at the start of each period an amount of money equal to the budgeted amount for each of the accounts is placed into separate envelopes labeled with the account name. All expenditures made on these accounts are paid using the money enclosed within the appropriate envelope. When the funds within the envelope are exhausted, the period's spending for that budget item is concluded. With this system, the balance of any of these accounts can be checked merely by finding out how much money remains in the envelope. The envelope system has been found to be quite effective in controlling expenditures in selected accounts.

Total Monthly Budget Control Control is important not only in individual accounts, but also in the total budget for the period. By examining end-of-period balances for the total of all accounts, it is possible to determine whether a net budget surplus or deficit exists. Based on this finding, appropriate action can be taken to assure a balanced budget for the year. The existence of total period surpluses is advantageous, since the surplus funds can be used for savings, investments, or debt repayment. Total period deficits, however, signal the need for corrective action, which normally consists of adjusting spending in subsequent months in order to end the year with a balanced budget.

Budget Records and Control—An Illustration

Two techniques used by Art and Betty Johnston during 1978 in the budget record and control process—monitoring an account and summarizing total budget activity—are described separately below.

Monitoring an Account Table 3-8 presents the Johnstons' grocery expense record for January through March of 1979. In January, $140 was budgeted and only $132 was actually spent; the month ended with an $8 surplus. In February, $140 was again budgeted, but $159 was spent. Although the Johnstons' spending during February was $19 over their budget ($159 − $140), the month ended with only an $11 deficit since the $8 surplus from January was in the account. During March, $140 was budgeted and $127 was actually spent; but, since the month began with an $11 deficit, the month-end balance was $2 ($13 surplus for March minus $11 deficit carried over from February). All in all, Art and Betty appear to have made reasonable budget estimates and maintained good control over their grocery expenses. Had there been surpluses in all months or deficits in all months, some type of budget adjustment would have been necessary.

Summarizing Total Budget Activity In addition to monitoring individual accounts, the Johnstons maintained an *actual budget summary* of accounts showing the balance at the beginning of the month, the budgeted amount, the actual expenditures made, and the end-of-month balance for each account, along with the total expenditures for all accounts. Their summary statement for January through March of 1979 appears in Table 3-9. The format of the statement makes it easy to analyze the behavior of individual accounts as well as the total budget and to make adjustments in amounts budgeted for future months, if necessary. The summary statement is also useful in preparing future budgets, since it facilitates evaluation of actual expenditures. For exam-

Table 3-8 Art and Betty Johnston's Grocery Expense Record
(January through March 1979)

Date	Item	Amount Budgeted	Amount Expended	Account Balance
1/1/79	**January Budget**	$140		$140
1/3/79	Groceries		$ 52	88
1/9/79	Milk and Eggs		4	84
1/11/79	Girl Scout Cookies		5	79
1/15/79	Groceries		60	19
1/26/79	Pop and Snacks		11	8
1/31/79	January Totals	$140	$132	$ 8
2/1/79	**February Budget**	$140		$148
2/2/79	Groceries		$ 65	83
2/10/79	Snacks		15	68
2/15/79	Groceries		55	13
2/23/79	Dinner Party		24	−11
2/29/79	February Totals	$140	$159	$−11
3/1/79	**March Budget**	$140		$129
3/10/79	Groceries		$ 60	69
3/12/79	Sirloin		9	60
3/16/79	Groceries		50	10
3/26/79	Snacks and Pop		8	2
3/30/79	March Totals	$140	$127	$ 2

ple, an analysis of individual items makes it quite clear that the end-of-month $111 deficit in March—which contrasts strikingly with the January and February surpluses of $8 and $55, respectively—is attributable primarily to the high medical and dental bills incurred during that month.

Closing the Books and Preparing Year-End Financial Statements

The final steps in the budget control process are *closing the books* for the year by calculating the end-of-year account balances and then, using this data, preparing the balance sheet and income statement (refer back to Tables 2-4 and 2-10). At the year end, actual expenses in each account can be determined by totalling the monthly expense values given in the actual budget summary for the account. Only after you have prepared your year-end financial statements can you determine whether you have achieved your stated budget goals. Your net worth as indicated on your year-end statements can then be compared to your net worth objective in order to assess the overall effectiveness of your budgeting process.

Table 3-9 Art and Betty Johnston's Actual Budget Summary
(January through March 1979)

Item	January Beginning Balance (1)	January Expenditures (2)	January Ending Balance [(1) − (2)] (3)	February Budget (4)	February Beginning Balance [(3) + (4)] (5)	February Expenditures (6)	February Ending Balance [(5) − (6)] (7)	March Budget (8)	March Beginning Balance [(7) + (8)] (9)	March Expenditures (10)	March Ending Balance [(9) − (10)] (11)
Home Mortgage	$257	$257	$ 0	$ 257	$ 257	$ 257	$ 0	$257	$ 257	$ 257	$ 0
Gas and Electric	50	55	−5	50	45	50	−5	50	45	40	5
Water	5	5	0	5	5	4	1	5	6	4	2
Groceries (Table 3-8)	140	132	8	140	148	159	−11	140	129	127	2
Dining Out	25	0	25	25	50	40	10	25	35	70	−35
Clothing	30	80	−50	30	−20	15	−35	80	45	25	20
Betty's Tuition	0	0	0	500	500	500	0	0	0	0	0
Auto Loan	75	75	0	75	75	75	0	75	75	75	0
Furniture Loan	25	25	0	25	25	25	0	25	25	25	0
Parents' Loan	0	0	0	0	0	0	0	0	0	0	0
New Tires for Cutlass	80	70	10	80	90	70	20	80	100	70	30
Gasoline and Oil	40	25	15	40	55	25	30	40	70	30	40
Auto License	0	0	0	50	50	45	5	0	5	0	5
Property Taxes	0	0	0	0	0	0	0	0	0	0	0
Telephone	15	25	−10	15	5	10	−5	15	10	25	−15
Homeowner's Insurance	0	0	0	0	0	0	0	0	0	0	0
Auto Insurance	0	0	0	120	120	120	0	0	0	0	0
Life Insurance	0	0	0	0	0	0	0	0	0	0	0
Medical and Dental	25	0	25	25	50	0	50	25	75	180	−105
Laundry, Cosmetics, Hair Care	30	15	15	30	45	40	5	30	35	45	−10
Gifts	0	0	0	0	0	0	0	0	0	0	0
Recreation and Entertainment	50	90	−40	50	10	20	−10	50	40	60	−20
Vacation	0	0	0	0	0	0	0	0	0	0	0
Charitable Contributions	30	30	0	0	0	0	0	0	0	0	0
Miscellaneous	25	10	15	25	40	40	0	25	25	55	−30
Fun Money	30	30	0	30	30	30	0	30	30	30	0
Savings and Investments	0	0	0	0	0	0	0	0	0	0	0
Totals	$932	$924	$ 8	$1,572	$1,580	$1,525	$ 55	$952	$1,007	$1,118	$−111

Source Key:
Columns (1), (4), and (8)—Initial Budgeted Amounts from Table 3-6
Columns (2), (6), and (10)—Actual Expenditures during Month

Summary

Personal financial planning provides a logical framework within which to make financial decisions consistent with your long-run financial goals. A good financial plan should provide funds for both long-run and short-run goals. Long-run financial goals should be established for your productive lifetime. They do not necessarily have to be stated in dollar amounts, but they should be specified in general terms. Each year your short-run financial goals should be set in a fashion consistent with the achievement of the long-run goals. These short-run goals are stated in dollar terms so that they can be evaluated in light of your projected income.

After establishing short-run goals, the budget should be prepared in a fashion consistent with as many of these goals as possible. The first step in the budget preparation process is estimating the income to be received during each month of the coming year. Estimating monthly expenditures

The Average Grocery Shopper: 20 Bucks' Worth

The table below gives a breakdown of $20 spent on various grocery items by the average shopper in 1975. Analysis of the breakdown should provide you with useful data for evaluating your own grocery shopping expenditures.

Average Shopper's Expenditure of a $20 Bill in Supermarkets and Grocery Stores: 1975

Product	Amount	Product	Amount
Perishables	$9.97	Dry groceries (continued)	
Baked goods, snacks	1.21	Dried foods	$ .24
Dairy products	1.22	Soft drinks	.49
Frozen foods	1.00	Sugar	.29
Fresh meat and provisions	3.80	All other	1.37
Fresh fish	.14	Other groceries	2.42
Fresh poultry	.48	Paper goods	.49
Produce	2.12	Soaps, detergents	.36
Dry groceries	5.71	Other household supplies	.44
Beer	.86	Pet foods	.30
Wine and liquor	.13	Tobacco products	.70
Baby foods (excluding cereals, formulas)	.07	Groceries	.13
Cereals and rice	.33	General merchandise	1.00
Candy and chewing gum	.21	Health and beauty aids	.72
Canned foods	1.19	Prescriptions	.08
Coffee and tea	.53	Housewares	.21
		All other general merchandise	.89

Source: Supermarketing Magazine, Gralla Publications, September 1976. Reprinted by permission.

using past spending data along with the short-run financial goals is the next step. And finalizing the budget by bringing it into balance is the last step. In order to balance the annual budget, it may be necessary to eliminate certain low-priority goals. Furthermore, you may have to use savings, investments, or borrowing; reduce expenditures; or increase income. A budget summary that shows monthly and cumulative surpluses and deficits can simplify the balancing procedure.

When the budget is placed into operation, it is imperative that appropriate records and controls be used to assure the success of the budgeting process. A record book containing accounts for all items of income and expenditure during each budget period provides the type of information necessary for budget control. At the end of every budget period all accounts in the record book are closed and any surplus or deficit balances are carried forward to the following month. For budget control purposes, an actual budget summary, which shows actual budget expenditures for each period, is often maintained. This facilitates any adjustments that may be necessary by making it easy to evaluate spending. At the end of each year all budget accounts are closed and the financial statements—balance sheet and income statement—are prepared and analyzed.

Key Terms

actual budget summary
balanced budget
budget
budget deficit
budget summary
budget surplus
closing the books
envelope system
flexible expenses
fun money

goal dates
inflexible expenses
life goals
long-run financial goals
master expense sheet
record book
schedule of estimated expenses
schedule of estimated income
short-run financial goals
take-home salary

Review Questions

1. What is a budget? Name the three basic steps in the budget preparation process.

2. Distinguish between short-run and long-run financial goals. Be sure to mention: (1) flexibility, (2) goal dates, and (3) the key input to the budget.

3. What is a budget deficit, and how does it differ from a budget surplus?

4. The Smith family have prepared their budget for the year 1978. They have divided it into twelve monthly budgets. In spite of the fact that only one monthly budget balances, they have managed to balance the budget for the year. What remedies are available to the Smith family for meeting the monthly budget deficits?

5. Below is a portion of the Cook family's budget record for April 1978. Fill in the blanks in columns 6 and 7.

Item No. (1)	Item (2)	Amount Budgeted (3)	Amount Expended (4)	Beginning Balance (5)	Monthly Surplus or (Deficit) (6)	Cumu- lative Surplus or (Deficit) (7)
1	Rent	$250	$250	$20	$_____	$_____
2	Groceries	220	195	−15	_____	_____
3	Telephone	15	28	−5	_____	_____
4	Utilities	60	55	15	_____	_____
5	Recreation and Entertainment	20	25	−50	_____	_____

6. Using examples, describe the envelope system for controlling expenditures in selected accounts.

7. Why is it important to analyze actual budget surpluses or deficits at the end of each month?

8. How can accurate records and control procedures be utilized to assure effectiveness in the financial planning process?

9. Discuss the procedures and importance of closing the books, which is the final step in the budget control process.

10. (a) Dave and Betty Williamson are preparing their budget for the year 1978. Their only source of income is Dave's salary, which amounts to $1,500 a month before taxes. Betty wants to show this sum of money as their income, whereas Dave argues that his net salary of $1,250 is the correct value to show.

(b) Betty wants to make a provision for fun money, an idea which Dave cannot understand. He says, "Why do we need fun money when everything is provided for in the budget?"

Help the Williamsons reconcile their differences, giving reasons to support your answers.

11. Do you think it is possible for a person to purchase more items if he or she maintains a budget? Explain.

12. Prepare a record of your income and expenditure for the next thirty days and then draw up your personal budget for the following month.

Use the budget to control and regulate the following month's expenditures. Discuss the impact of the budget on your spending behavior. Also comment on any differences between your expected and actual spending patterns.

3-1 A Budget for the Bakers

Evelyn and Harold Baker are a young couple living in a small community in upstate New York. They have a seven year old daughter, Gloria, who goes to the neighborhood public school. Harold is a foreman in the shipping and packaging department of Excel Industries, earning $12,000 a year after taxes. Overwhelmed by the current rise in prices due to inflation, Harold plans to set up a budget. He hopes it will help Evelyn and him control their expenses and live within their means.

The Baker family's expenditures for 1978 were as follows:

Gas and Electricity	$ 720	Home Mortgage	$3,600
Water	60	Life Insurance	350
Groceries	3,000	Laundry	120
Telephone	300	Recreation and Entertainment	252
Dentist	220	Miscellaneous	240

All expenses are expected to remain constant in 1979, with the following exceptions:

a. Gas and electricity rates will rise by 5 percent.

b. Grocery prices are expected to rise by 2 percent.

c. Telephone charges are expected to increase by $5 per month.

d. The entire family goes for dental checkups twice a year, in March and October.

e. Harold pays life insurance premiums in February and August. He has bought an additional life insurance policy of $10,000, and this is expected to increase his total premiums by $450 per year to a total of $800 per year.

All other expenditures are paid for in equal monthly amounts.

Questions

1. Using the data presented above, prepare the Bakers' monthly budget for the calendar year 1979.

2. Interpret the resulting budget and advise the Bakers on their finances as reflected in the budget.

3. Would you recommend that they continue to prepare budgets? Explain.

3-2 Europe or a Balanced Budget?

John and Irene Sullivan are a young married couple in their late twenties. John is a computer analyst for American Airlines and makes $16,000 a year after taxes. Irene works as a stenographer for Xerox Corporation. Her net take-home pay is $10,000 per annum. She is pregnant and expects her first child in late October. However, in May, the Sullivans plan to spend their vacation in Europe. Since they wish to assess their approximate finances for 1978, they have drawn up their budget as shown below.

Income

John's Take-Home Salary		$16,000
Irene's Take-Home Salary		10,000
Total Income		$26,000

Expenses

Necessities		$12,000
Trip to Europe		8,000
Fun Money		1,800
Addition to House (nursery for child)		2,500
New Car for Irene	$5,000	
Less: Sale Proceeds from Old Car	3,500	1,500
Savings		3,000
Total Expenses		$28,800

In addition, John and Irene have $4,000 in a savings account with Central Savings & Loan Association and $500 in a checking account with the Bank of Commerce. They also have investments in Arco, Inc., the fair market value of which is $18,000. Irene has a Triumph sports car, which she wishes to trade for a Toyota Hatchback before the child's arrival. They are very excited about going to Europe, especially since American Airlines has promised them free air tickets. At the same time, they are worried since their budget will not balance. As a last resort, they come to you for help.

Questions

1. Provide the Sullivans with the requested advice.

2. Suggest any alternatives that they might pursue in order to fulfill their stated goals.

3. What recommendation might you offer the Sullivans with respect to their use of personal financial planning in order to avoid situations such as the one that currently confronts them? Explain.

Selected References

Auerbach, Sylvia. *Your Money: How to Make It Stretch.* Garden City, N.Y.: Doubleday, 1974.

"Building Future Income with Savings." *Changing Times,* November 1975, p. 41.

Burnes, Scott. *Squeeze It Till the Eagle Grins: How to Spend, Save, and Enjoy with Your Money.* Garden City, N.Y.: Doubleday, 1972.

"Can a Budget Really Help You Manage Your Money?" *Better Homes and Gardens,* June 1976, pp. 4–8.

Donaldson, Elvin F., and Pfahl, John K. *Personal Finance.* New York: Ronald Press, 1971.

"Educational Expenses." *Consumers' Research,* April 1977, p. 41.

"Family Spending: How Patterns Are Changing." *U.S. News & World Report,* 6 December 1976, p. 92.

"How Does Your Spending Compare?" *Changing Times,* October 1976, pp. 6–11.

Main, Jeremy. "Bringing Your Budget Back to Earth." *Money,* May 1974, pp. 26–30.

"Make a New Budget for Times Like These." *Changing Times,* May 1975, pp. 6–11.

Mittra, Sid. *Personal Finance: Lifetime Management by Objectives.* New York: Harper & Row, 1977.

"One Family's Budgeting Plan—It's Easy and It Works!" *Changing Times,* July 1977, pp. 43–47.

Reaching Your Financial Goals. Chicago: Money Management Institute, Household Finance Corporation, 1971.

"Setting Up Housekeeping—How to Cut the Costs." *Changing Times,* August 1976, pp. 44–47.

"Spending and Saving: Readers Tell How They Do It." *Changing Times,* November 1976, pp. 21–23.

Troelstrup, Arch W. *The Consumer in American Society: Personal and Family Finance.* New York: McGraw-Hill, 1974.

Watkins, Arthur Martin. *Dollars and Sense: A Guide to Mastering Your Money.* New York: Quadrangle/The New York Times, 1973.

"When Your Budget Signals Danger." *Changing Times,* February 1977, pp. 33–35.

4

Personal Taxes

A Preview of
Chapter 4

This chapter will examine and illustrate:

1. The economics and terminology of federal income taxation.

2. The basic calculation procedures used to determine your federal taxes.

3. The legal requirements and procedures established by the federal government to control the filing of tax returns.

4. A federal income tax return.

5. Some of the most common techniques for reducing your tax payments.

6. Taxes levied by governmental units other than the federal government.

The payment of taxes is an important, necessary, and unpopular expenditure that can significantly affect your personal finances. Taxes must be considered not only in the financial planning and budgeting process, but also in making decisions on all aspects of personal finance. Since you are legally required to pay taxes, it is in your best interest as a potential taxpayer to gain a thorough understanding of them. Knowledge of tax laws can help you take advantage of opportunities to reduce your taxes and thereby increase the amount of after-tax dollars available for achieving your financial goals.

In order to pay the costs of governments—federal, state, and local—a variety of taxes are levied on both consumers and business. The proceeds received by the government as a result of taxation are used to pay governmental operating costs as well as to provide for our national defense, our highways, parks, and police, and social and educational services that are often taken for granted. Many people argue that government wastes our money. Because the government collects and spends billions of dollars each year, it should not be surprising to find that its operation, which requires hundreds of thousands of people, may not be perfectly efficient.

Regardless of our feelings concerning taxes and their use by government, taxes are a very real expenditure that most working people must make. Of the types of taxes that currently exist, the largest and most important one to the consumer is the personal income tax. Although the primary user of income taxation is the federal government, personal income taxes are also levied by state and local governments. Taxpayers are typically divided into two groups: corporations and all others. Corporations have their own tax rates, while individuals and other noncorporate taxpayers are taxed at a different set of rates. This chapter is concerned only with taxes on the individual.

Principles of Federal Income Taxation

The federal income tax law for corporations and all others was systematically outlined in the *Internal Revenue Code* of 1939. In 1954 this code was revised to further clarify and more precisely state the provisions of the 1939 law. Since 1954 there have been a number of amendments to the code that have attempted to simplify it and eliminate infrequently used provisions, as well as to repeal and modify other provisions. The sections of the code and its amendments deal with the tax effects of practically all business and personal transactions. The *Tax Reform Act of 1976* was one of the most extensive tax reform measures ever passed. The most recent modification of our federal income tax laws was the *Tax Reduction and Simplification Act of 1977.* The enforcement of federal tax laws is placed in the hands of the Internal Revenue Service (IRS), which is part of the U.S. Treasury Department. The IRS is responsible for making sure that people pay their taxes as required by the various tax codes. Performance of this function, although greatly simplified as a result of widespread computer usage, requires the work of thousands of IRS employees.

The Economics of Taxation

Income taxes provide the major source of revenue for the federal government. Income taxation is used not only to raise revenue but also to encourage economic activity. This encouragement has been in the form of preferential tax treatment that allows investors the opportunity for tax-free returns and tax-sheltered income. Although the Tax Reform Act of 1976 deleted certain preferential tax treatments, there are still many tax provisions which encourage economic activity. Personal income taxes are scaled on a progressive rate. This means that the higher your taxable income is, the higher the percentage of it that is taken in taxes. The economic rationale for the progressive income tax is that the taxes you pay should be based not only on your income, but also on your ability to pay. Clearly, the better understanding you have of the income tax system and its laws, the easier it is to reduce your tax liability.

Your Take-Home Pay

Income taxes are usually collected on a "pay-as-you-go" basis: Your employer withholds (deducts) a portion of your income every pay period and sends it to the Internal Revenue Service. After the close of your taxable year, you calculate the taxes you owe and file your income tax return. At the time of filing, you receive full credit for the amount of taxes withheld from your income over the year. Depending on whether the taxes withheld are greater than or less than the actual taxes you incurred, you will either receive a refund from or owe money to the Internal Revenue Service. Withholdings commonly include: the federal withholding tax, the Federal Insurance Contributions Act tax (social security, or FICA, as it is commonly called), state and local taxes, and other items. Your take-home pay, or *net earnings*, can be determined by subtracting the amount withheld from the amount of your *gross earnings*.

Federal Withholding Taxes The amount of federal withholding taxes deducted from your gross earnings each pay period depends on both the level of your earnings and the number of withholding exemptions you have claimed. *Exemptions* are deductions in the amount withheld from your income; they are based on the number of people your income supports. If you believe your actual taxes owed (*tax liability*) will be lower than suggested by the withholding tables, you may under certain conditions claim additional exemptions in order to allow your employer to withhold less. You can also elect to have your employer withhold amounts greater than prescribed by the withholding tables. It is important to recognize that federal withholding taxes on earnings are levied only on the incomes of employees.

FICA The combined old age, survivor's, disability, and hospital insurance tax under the Federal Insurance Contributions Act (FICA) is levied on both employer and employee. This "social security" tax applied to the first $16,500 of an employee's wages in 1977. The employer withholds the FICA tax from the employee's gross earnings (up to $16,500) and then matches the withheld amount. The total FICA tax, which includes the employee's and the employer's contribution, is submitted to the Internal Revenue Service at specified times by the employer.

Both the employee and the employer thus make social security and hospital insurance (FICA) contributions on the basis of the employee's wages. The current rates as well as the scheduled increases in these rates are given in Table 4-1. In 1977, with a tax rate of 5.85 percent and a wage base limitation of $16,500, the maximum amount of taxes an employee had to pay was $965.25 (5.85% × $16,500). Of course, this amount also represented the maximum amount an employer would have to contribute for an employee. Assume that in 1978 you earned $14,000. Your FICA contribution would be $847 (6.05% × $14,000), and your employer would also contribute $847. Note that, although Table 4-1 presents future FICA

Table 4-1 **FICA Contribution Rates**
(Percentages of Gross Income)

Years	Social Security	Hospital Insurance	Total FICA Contribution
1974–1977	4.95%	0.9%	5.85%
1978–1980	4.95	1.1	6.05
1981–1985	4.95	1.35	6.30
1986–2010	4.95	1.5	6.45
2011–	5.95	1.5	7.45

contribution rates, it is likely that the maximum amount of gross earnings to which these rates apply will be raised. Individuals who work for more than one employer during the year and who thereby pay FICA taxes over the taxable limits can receive credit for the overpayment on their income tax returns.

State and Local Income Taxes State and local income taxes—unlike federal income taxes—differ from state to state. These taxes, if levied, are generally tied to the individual's level of earnings. While state and local income taxes that have been withheld (or paid) are deductible on the federal return, federal taxes may or may not be deductible on the state or local return, depending on state and local laws. It is not unusual, especially in large cities, to have local income taxes amount to as much as 1 percent of income. And in some states, the state income tax amounts to as much as 15 percent of taxable income. Further discussion of state and local taxes is included in the final part of this chapter.

Other Items Employers may withhold money in addition to that mentioned above for their employees. For example, they may withhold voluntary contributions to a retirement fund or payment for life and health insurance coverage in excess of standard benefits. These additional deductions, of course, lower take-home pay.

Determining the Amount of Taxable Income

Although various sections of the Internal Revenue Code (IRC) define the key components of taxable income, the actual amount of taxable income is often difficult to determine. The hundreds of sections in the Code describing numerous conditions and exceptions surrounding the tax treatment and/or deductibility of certain items attest to the complexity of our tax system. The questions an individual must ask to determine what is taxable income are: Is it income? Whose income is it? Is an expenditure deductible? How much is deductible? Table 4-2 illustrates the procedure for computing taxable income. The items listed in the right-hand column are general classifications which are described in detail in the Internal Revenue Code. A discussion of the key items shown in the left-hand column of Table 4-2 follows.

Table 4-2 **Computation of Individual Taxable Income**

Gross Income	Wages, Salaries
	Dividends Received
	Interest Received
	Gains on Sales or Exchanges
	Annuities, Pensions
	Net Business Profits
	Farm Income
	Commissions, Bonuses, Tips
	Rents and Royalties
	Prizes
	Alimony
	Net Lottery and Gambling Winnings
minus	
Deductions from Gross Income	Trade or Business Expenses
	Travel Expenses
	Transportation Costs
	Outside Salesperson's Expenses
	Employee's Reimbursed Expenses
	Depreciation Allowable
	Losses from Sales or Exchanges
	Net Operating Loss Deduction
	Self-Employed Retirement Plan Payments

Individual Retirement Account Payments
Moving Expenses
Interest Forfeited on Premature Withdrawals
  from Time Savings Accounts
Alimony Paid
Long-Term Capital Gain Deduction
Expenses Incurred from Producing
  Rents and Royalties

equals

Adjusted Gross Income

minus

Excess Itemized Deductions (Itemized Nonbusiness Expenses minus Zero Bracket Amount)[a]

Charitable Contributions
Taxes Paid (Nonbusiness)
Interest Paid (Nonbusiness)
Nonbusiness Casualty and Theft Losses
Medical and Dental Expenses
Certain Investor's Expenses
Certain Employee Expenses, Such as
  Union Dues

equals

Tax Table Income

minus

Exemptions

Taxpayer
Spouse
Dependents
Blind
Aged (65 or Over)

equals

Taxable Income

---

[a] *Zero bracket amount* is explained later in this chapter.

Gross Income All income (before any deductions) that is subject to federal taxes is considered gross income. Certain types of income that are classified as *tax exempt* are excluded from gross income and are not listed on the tax return. A partial list of types of tax exempt income (income not considered income for tax purposes) is included in Table 4-3. In addition

Table 4-3 **Partial Listing of Tax-Exempt Income**

Accident and health insurance premiums paid by employers
Allowances received by dependents of people in the armed forces
Child support payments
Compromise settlement of will contest
Disability payments (limited in some cases)
Gifts
Inheritances
Loans (principal) repaid, but interest is taxable
Scholarships and fellowships (limited as to amount and time)
Social security and disability benefits
Veterans' disability pensions

to the items included in Table 4-3, which are examples of completely excluded income, there are some forms of income, such as dividend income, that may be partially excluded. For example, the first $100 of dividend income received from a domestic corporation is excluded from taxable income.

Deductions from Gross Income The acceptability of certain deductions from gross income is dependent on legislative decisions. Each tax amendment has had some effect on the allowability of deductions from gross income. In order for deductions from gross income to be allowable, they must be ordinary and necessary. *Ordinary* means that the item is common and expected in the general industry or type of activity in which the taxpayer is engaged. *Necessary* means that the item is appropriate and helpful in furthering the taxpayer's business or income-producing activity. As can be seen in Table 4-2, most deductions from gross income are various types of trade and business expenses. The Internal Revenue Service, of course, considers not only the reasonableness of a deduction but also the reasonableness of the amount deducted. After these allowable deductions are subtracted from gross income, the *adjusted gross income* remains.

Adjusted Gross Income Adjusted gross income is an important calculation in computing an individual's federal income tax. Certain itemized deductions are limited by adjusted gross income, which becomes "tax table income" for taxpayers who are eligible to use the tax tables and who do not itemize deductions.

Itemized Nonbusiness Expenses (Deductions from Adjusted Gross Income) Deducting itemized nonbusiness expenses allows taxpayers to reduce their adjusted gross incomes by the amount of their allowable personal expenditures in excess of the zero bracket amount (which will be explained later in the chapter). The Internal Revenue Code describes the types of itemized nonbusiness expenses, including personal, living, and family expenses, that can be deducted from adjusted gross income. Some of the more common itemized nonbusiness expenses are listed in Table 4-2. To encourage *gifts and contributions* to charitable organizations, a deduction is allowed for the amount of such contributions up to a maximum of 50 percent of adjusted gross income. The contribution must be made to qualified recipients as outlined in a list published by the Internal Revenue Service. The Internal Revenue Code also allows the taxpayer to deduct certain *taxes* from adjusted gross income, including state, local, and foreign income taxes; state, local, and foreign real property taxes; state and local personal property taxes; and state and local general sales and gasoline taxes.

Another deduction is permitted for all interest paid or incurred on borrowing during the taxable year, although the Internal Revenue Service has not established what is a "reasonable" amount of interest. The Tax Reform Act of 1976 requires taxpayers to deduct *prepaid interest* over the period of the loan, if the interest represents the cost of using borrowed funds during each taxable year in the period. Any personal casualty losses, such as theft, are deductible (see Chapter 15); they are limited to the amount of each loss in excess of $100.

A deduction of the amount by which expenses exceed 3 percent of adjusted gross income is allowed for medical expenses paid during the taxable year (including dental expenses). The expenses allowed are those incurred in the diagnosis, cure, mitigation, and treatment of disease and injury, and in the prevention of disease. Specifically, they include costs related to doctors, hospitals, corrective devices such as eyeglasses, transportation, medicine and drugs (exceeding an amount equal to 1 percent of adjusted gross income), and schooling for the physically or mentally handicapped. Of course, any portion of these expenses for which the taxpayer has been reimbursed by an insurance company cannot be counted as a deductible expense. The cost of medical insurance is an exception to the limitations on medical expenses. A deduction of one-half of medical insurance premiums (paid by the taxpayer) up to a maximum of $150 is allowed. The balance of medical insurance premiums paid is deductible as part of medical expenses.

Zero Bracket Amount Instead of itemizing personal deductions (nonbusiness expenses), a taxpayer can use the *zero bracket amount,* which is a type of blanket deduction. The zero bracket amount is so named because a zero tax rate applies to this amount of the taxpayer's income. The amount varies depending on the filing method used. Table 4-4 summarizes the zero bracket amount for various filing alternatives. For unmarried individuals (including unmarried heads of households) the zero bracket amount is $2,200; for married taxpayers filing a joint return it is $3,200; and for married taxpayers filing a separate return it is $1,600.

Each individual taxpayer "elects" either to itemize deductions or to use the zero bracket amount (which prior to the Tax Reduction and Simplification Act of 1977 was referred to as the standard deduction). The decision is not irrevocable, however, and taxpayers who find they have chosen the wrong option and paid too much may recompute their tax using the other method and claim a refund for the difference. For example, suppose you computed and paid your taxes, which amounted to $2,450, using the standard deduction. A few months later you find that, had you itemized your deductions, your taxes would have been only

Loopholes: They Could Help You Pay No Taxes

What is a tax loophole? Perhaps it can best be described as someone else's tax deduction. In these days of rising prices and heavy tax burdens, the judgment handed down by Judge Learned Hand in *Commissioner* v. *Newman* [159 F.2d 848 (CCA-2, 1947)] comes to mind:

Over and over again courts have said that there is nothing sinister in so arranging one's affairs as to keep taxes as low as possible. Everybody does so, rich or poor, and all do right, for nobody owes any public duty to pay more than the law demands: taxes are enforced exactions, not voluntary contributions. To demand more in the name of morals is mere cant.

The Winner family—Pam, Jack, and two young children—pays no income taxes. Although the family's income is $19,000, Jack supports his mother, Ruth, and can claim her as a dependent. Jack invested in a real estate partnership in 1975 in order to receive the benefits of certain tax write-offs that were available, while still expecting to make a profit on the sale of the real estate, which was planned for 1980. The computation of the Winners' taxes for 1976 is given on the following page.

$1,950. Using the appropriate forms, you can file an *amended return* showing a $500 refund ($2,450 − $1,950). In order to avoid having to file an amended return as a result of using the wrong deduction technique, it is best to estimate your deductions using both itemized and standard deductions and then choose the alternative that results in the lower taxes. Amended returns should be filed in order to correct *any* error in the original tax return, whether the correction results in a tax refund or an additional tax payment.

Tax Table Income For those taxpayers who itemize deductions and are eligible to use the tax tables, *tax table income* is adjusted gross income less *excess itemized deductions*. Excess itemized deductions are simply the

Salary and Wages Earned		$18,850
Interest Earned: Dividends	$ 350	
Less: Exclusion	(200)	150
Gross Income		$19,000
Less Employees' Business Expenses		(1,500)
Adjusted Gross Income		$17,500
Itemized Deductions		
Casualty Loss"	$1,000	
Real Estate Investment Write-off	2,000	
Property Taxes	1,500	
Interest (Home Mortgage, Car Loan)	2,800	
Contribution to Charities	350	
Tax Preparation Charges	100	
Medical Insurance	150	
Total Itemized Deductions	$7,900	
Less Zero Bracket Amount	(3,200)	
Excess Itemized Deductions		(4,700)
Tax Table Income		$12,800
Tax		$ 792
Credit for Contribution to Candidates Running for Public Office	$ 50	
Credit for Child Care	800	(850)
Tax Payable		None

"During 1976, the Winners suffered a casualty loss due to a fire in their home. Eleven hundred dollars of the loss was not recovered from the insurance company. All but $100 of that amount is deductible.

Like the Winners, you should attempt to minimize your taxes while operating within the confines of the existing tax laws. Learn about tax loopholes.

Table 4-4 **Zero Bracket Amount for Various Filing Alternatives**

Filing Status	Zero Bracket Amount
Single Persons and Heads of Households	$2,200
Married Persons Filing Joint Returns and Surviving Spouses	3,200
Married Persons Filing Separate Returns	1,600
Dependent Children with Unearned Income[a]	Limited to earned income

[a]Where children are under nineteen or students and qualify as income tax dependents of their parents, they must file a return if they have gross income of $750 or more *and* if the gross income includes any amount of unearned income. In addition, their zero bracket amount is determined only on the basis of their earned income.

taxpayer's itemized deductions in excess of the zero bracket amount. Some taxpayer's must make certain adjustments prior to computing tax table income. Generally, this added computation involves:

1. married taxpayers filing separate returns and itemizing deductions,

2. taxpayers who are claimed as dependents of other taxpayers, and

3. certain taxpayers with foreign income.

Married taxpayers with nine or fewer exemptions and $40,000 or less of tax table income and unmarried taxpayers with three or fewer exemptions and $20,000 or less of tax table income are generally eligible to use the tax tables. (Complications exist that may preclude an individual from using the tax tables.) The tax tables incorporate the zero bracket amount, personal exemptions, and the general tax credit in order to simplify the computation process for the taxpayer.

Exemptions Deductions from tax table income based on the number of persons supported by the taxpayer's income are called *exemptions*. The ordinary exemption allowed a taxpayer, spouse, and any *dependents*—which includes children or other relatives earning less than $750 and for whom the taxpayer pays at least 50 percent of support—is $750 per person. Children who are younger than nineteen or are full-time students can earn more than $750 during the year and still be claimed as exemptions by their parents. Students receiving more than half of their support from their parents and earning more than $750 (regardless of age) can be claimed as exemptions by their parents *and* on their own tax returns (by themselves). This double exemption is permitted for a married student as long as a joint return is not filed with the spouse. An additional exemption of $750 each is allowed for taxpayers and their spouses who are sixty-five years of age or older or who are blind. For example, a woman filing a joint return with her blind spouse and having three dependent children would have six exemptions—one for herself, one for her spouse, one for her spouse's blindness, and three for their children.

"That's the way it goes: your peak earning years—our peak *taking* years."

Earnings and Taxes Are Closely Related

Source: My Shell Was Recalled! (New York: Dow Jones, 1974), p. 142. Reprinted by permission of Sidney Harris.

She would therefore receive a $4,500 ($750 × 6) deduction in addition to those itemized or standard deductions from her adjusted gross income.

Tax Credits Once taxable income has been determined, the tax *liability,* or amount of taxes owed, must be calculated. This is done either with the help of a table or by applying certain specified formulas. Because our federal income taxes are *progressive taxes,* the higher our taxable income, the higher is the rate of taxation. Taxpayers are allowed to make certain deductions known as *tax credits* from their tax liability. In reducing the tax liability, these tax credits can result in a refund. The Tax Reform Act of 1976 permits an individual taxpayer to claim the greater of the following two credits: $35 per exemption or 2 percent of taxable income up to $9,000 not exceeding $180. The Tax Reduction and Simplification Act of 1977 incorporated these credits into the tax tables. Therefore, tax table users automatically get the larger of the two credits simply by using the tables. Another credit introduced with the Tax Reform Act of 1976 is 20 percent of child or dependent care expenses paid for the purpose of being gainfully employed. Numerous other credits are available for the purchase of property and equipment used in a trade or business, political contributions, the federal tax on gasoline purchased for off-highway usage, and old age, to mention a few. Note that tax credits, because they are deducted directly from tax liability, directly lower taxes.

Cash versus Accrual Basis The most common method used by taxpayers to account for income and expense items is the *cash basis*. In this system, all items of income and expense are recognized for tax purposes in the period in which the actual cash receipt or payment takes place. Under the *accrual basis*, items of income and expense are recognized when the obligation to receive or pay them is incurred. For example, suppose that your employer always pays you your wages two weeks after you have completed the work. If you calculate taxable income on the cash basis, the wages you earn in the last two weeks of December cannot be claimed as income for the calendar year since you will not receive payment until January. But if you make your calculations on an accrual basis, the wages for the last two weeks in December can be claimed as income for the calendar year, even though you do not actually receive these wages in December. The same is true for items of expenditure. The relative ease of maintaining records of cash income and expenditure during the tax year using the cash basis makes it the more popular system.

Capital Gains and Losses

Capital gains and losses are items of income or expense that may be eligible for special tax treatment. Because these gains and losses may be taxed differently from normal personal income, it is important to understand how they are taxed. Since capital gains and losses receive more favorable tax treatment than items of normal income, they are an important consideration in the personal tax planning process. To make the best use of capital gains and losses, it is necessary to understand the difference between capital and noncapital assets and between short-term and long-term gains, as well as how the sale of a home is taxed. Each of these topics is discussed briefly below.

Capital and Noncapital Assets A *capital asset* is property owned and used by the taxpayer for personal purposes, pleasure, or investment—for example, a home, an automobile, household furnishings, and stocks or bonds. Items such as interest in a business and various business inventories, copyrights, and other business assets are considered *noncapital assets* for purposes of determining the taxpayer's personal income taxes. A *capital gain or loss* therefore can occur when the sale or exchange of a capital asset takes place. A *capital gain* results when a capital asset is sold for more than its original cost. The amount of the capital gain can be found by subtracting the cost from the sale price. If the sale price is less than the cost of the capital asset, a *capital loss* results.

Short-Term and Long-Term Gains A capital gain or loss can be either short-term or long-term, depending on the length of time the capital asset is owned. Ordinarily, a gain from the sale or exchange of property is included in income in its entirety and taxed at ordinary income tax rates. But if the gain on the transaction is a *long-term capital gain*—that is, a gain arising from the sale or exchange of a capital asset which has been held by the taxpayer for longer than the holding period required by IRS standards—it is subject to a lower tax.

The rate at which long-term capital gains are taxed is approximately equal to one-half the normal tax rate, since only 50 percent of the gain is shown as taxable income. A *short-term capital gain*—a gain on the sale of a capital asset that is not held for the required holding period—receives no favored income tax treatment. A short-term capital gain is treated as ordinary income and taxed at the ordinary tax rates. In 1977, the holding period for long-term gains and losses was *nine months*; after 1977 the holding period is *one year*.

The IRS allows certain capital losses—whether they are long-term or short-term—to be deducted from ordinary income. These deductible losses must result from the sale of some *income-producing capital asset*, such as stocks and bonds, at less than their initial cost. A capital loss on the sale of a non-income-producing asset such as a home or automobile does not provide any tax relief for the taxpayer except in certain situations where offsetting capital gains exist. Due to the rather technical nature of these computations, further detail is not included here.

Selling Your Home If you sell your home and purchase a new home within eighteen months, any gain made on the sale of the old home will not be taxable unless the amount paid for the new home is less than that for which the old home was sold. If a new home is not purchased within eighteen months of the sale of the old home, taxes must be paid on any gains from that sale. If the purchase price of the new home is greater than the sale price of the old home, no taxes will be levied. If the cost of the new home is less than the sale price of the old home, the amount by which the price of the old residence exceeds that of the new residence is subject to capital gains tax treatment. For example, assume you sell your first home, which you purchased three years ago for $25,000, for $33,000. In this case you would have an $8,000 ($33,000 − $25,000) capital gain. Within eighteen months of the sale of your old home, you purchase a new home for $30,000. In this case you have to claim a $3,000 long-term capital gain ($33,000 − $30,000) on which taxes will be due. Had the new home instead cost $40,000, no taxes would be due in the current year since the $40,000 purchase price exceeded the $33,000 for which the old home was sold. If you decide at some point in the future to retire into a rental unit, you will have to pay a capital gain on the amount by which the proceeds on the sale of your house exceed the purchase price of the first home you bought. If you are sixty-five or over when you sell your last home, no tax of any kind will be due on the sale.

Methods of Filing

There are a number of methods to choose from in filing your tax returns. Your choice will depend on your marital status as well as the amount of income you earn. The two basic types of returns are joint returns and individual returns.

Joint Returns A husband and wife may file a joint return if they are married as of the last day of the year. In the joint return both the gross income and the deductions of the husband and wife are totaled. While there are two taxpayers on a joint return, there is only one adjusted gross income amount and only one taxable income. A couple generally benefits by filing a joint return rather than separate returns, but in some instances separate returns can be more advantageous. For example, if one spouse has substantial medical expenses and a moderate income while the other has no medical expenses and a low income, filing separately may provide a tax savings.

Individual Returns The taxpayer may also file an individual return, either as a single individual or as a *head-of-household*. When married persons file separately from their spouses, they file as if they are single individuals. Of course, the total exemptions claimed by married individuals filing separately cannot exceed the total exemptions they are eligible for as a married couple. A head-of-household is a single individual who maintains a household that is the principal residence of a dependent. One example of a head-of-household would be a single person who pays more than half the cost of keeping up his or her parents' home. Single persons, married persons filing separately, and heads-of-households all have their taxable incomes taxed under *differing tax rates.* These rates are, of course, different from the rates levied on joint returns.

Filing Requirements

The IRS requirements with respect to filing are based on achievement of specified levels of income. Individuals earning more than the specified minimums must file income tax returns. The income levels at which individuals had to file income tax returns in 1977 are given in Table 4-5 for certain of the more common situations. Of course, persons with no tax liability but for whom income has been withheld must also file income tax returns in order to receive a tax refund of the amount withheld.

Table 4-5 **Income Tax Filing Requirements (1977)**

Filing Status	Minimum Income
Single Individual	$2,950
Single Individual, 65 or Older	3,700
Married Couple, Joint Return	4,700
Married Couple, Joint Return, One Spouse 65 or Older	5,450
Married Couple, Joint Return, Both 65 or Older	6,200
Surviving Spouse	3,950

Estimated Taxes Because the federal withholding taxes are taken only from income earned on a regular basis and paid in the form of wages, the Internal Revenue Service requires certain people to make estimated tax payments on income earned from other sources. This requirement allows the principle of "pay as you go" to be applied not only to wages subject to withholding but also to other sources of income. The payment of estimated taxes is most commonly required of investors, consultants, lawyers, business owners, and various other professionals who are likely to receive income in a form that is not subject to withholding. The IRS requires taxpayers expecting to have $100 or more of total estimated taxes to file a declaration of estimated taxes (Form 1040 ES) in the following cases:

1. If they can reasonably expect to receive more than $500 of gross income from sources other than wages subject to withholding.

2. If they can reasonably expect that their gross income will exceed:

a. $20,000 in the case of a single individual (or a married individual treated as single), a head-of-household, a surviving spouse, or a married individual entitled to file a joint declaration of estimated tax, whose spouse does not receive wages;

b. $10,000 in the case of a married individual entitled to file a joint declaration of estimated tax, where both spouses receive wages;

c. $5,000 in the case of a married individual not entitled to file a joint declaration of estimated tax with his or her spouse.

The declaration of estimated taxes is normally filed with the tax return. The amount of estimated taxes must then be paid in four quarterly installments. Failure to estimate and pay these taxes can result in a penalty charge levied by the IRS, although no penalties are levied unless the error in payment exceeds 20 percent.

Year-End Tax Payments At the end of the tax year, those taxpayers required to file must determine the amount of their tax liability—the amount of taxes that they owe as a result of the past year's activities. The tax year covers the period 1 January through 31 December. Taxpayers are asked to file their returns as soon after the end of the tax year as possible. They must file their returns by 15 April of the year immediately following the tax year (or by the first business day after that date if it falls on a weekend or federal holiday). Depending on whether the taxes withheld plus any estimated tax payments is greater than or less than the taxpayer's tax liability, the taxpayer will either receive a refund or will have to pay additional taxes. For example, assume that you had $2,000 withheld and paid estimated taxes of $1,200 during the year. After filling out the appropriate tax forms, your tax liability amounts to $2,800. In this case you have overpaid your taxes by $400 ($2,000 + $1,200 − $2,800) and will therefore receive a $400 refund from the IRS. If, on the other hand, your tax liability had amounted to $4,000, you would have a balance due the IRS of $800 ($4,000 − $2,000 − $1,200).

Time Extensions It is possible to receive an extension of time for filing your federal tax return. An automatic two-month extension, which makes the due date 15 June, can be applied for simply by submitting the appropriate form (Form 4868). In filing for an extension, the taxpayer must estimate the taxes due and remit that amount with the application for extension. Beyond the two-month automatic extension, other extensions can be requested, but they are not automatic; the IRS must be convinced that granting them is justified.

IRS Audits of Returns Since the taxpayers themselves provide the key information and fill out the necessary forms in paying their taxes, the IRS cannot be certain that taxes have been correctly calculated. In order to validate tax returns insofar as possible, the IRS more or less randomly selects some returns for audit. IRS audits attempt to confirm the validity of these returns by carefully analyzing the data reported in them. In the course of an audit, the IRS may deem it necessary to arrange a meeting with the taxpayer being audited. At this meeting the taxpayer is asked to explain and document certain deductions taken. Even when documentation is provided, the IRS agent can still question the legitimacy of deductions. If the taxpayer and the IRS agent cannot settle the disputed items on an informal basis, certain formal appeal arrangements exist. IRS district personnel then hear the taxpayer's case and make a recommendation. If this recommendation is still not acceptable to the taxpayer, the case can be taken to the Appellate Division of the IRS. Finally, if satisfaction is not obtained from the hearing before the Appellate Division, the case can be brought before the U.S. Tax Court.

Because some day you might be audited by the IRS, it is important to maintain satisfactory tax records. Although the IRS does not specify any type of record-keeping system, it is a good idea to keep track of the source or use of all cash receipts and cash payments. Notations with respect to the purpose of expenditures are important, as well as proof that you actually made the expenditures for which you claimed deductions. Typically, audits question both the amounts and the legitimacy of deductions, as well as whether all income received is properly reported. Since the IRS can take as many as three years from the date of your filing to audit your return and, in some cases, an unlimited period of time, records and receipts used in preparing your returns are best kept on hand several years. Severe financial penalties as well as prison sentences can result from violating tax laws. In sum, at the same time you take advantage of all legitimate deductions in order to minimize your tax liability, you must be sure, too, that you properly report all items of income and expenditure as required by the Internal Revenue Code.

Tax Preparation Services and Advisors

Many people prepare their own tax returns each year. Typically these "do-it-yourselfers" have fairly simple returns which can be prepared without a great deal of difficulty. Of course, some taxpayers with quite complicated financial circumstances may also invest their time in preparing their own returns. The Tax Reduction and Simplification Act of 1977 was aimed at simplifying the process of filing a tax return. It is estimated that 95 percent of all taxpayers will be able to take advantage of the simplified system. If so, more taxpayers should be able to file their own returns without expert help. And actually, there are numerous IRS informational publications to aid persons who do prepare their own returns. Nonetheless, because our tax laws and tax forms are complex, many taxpayers prefer to rely on either the IRS or private preparation services and advisors for assistance in preparing their tax returns.

The IRS The Internal Revenue Service not only makes available various publications for use in preparing tax returns, it also provides direct assistance to taxpayers. The IRS will actually compute taxes for those whose adjusted gross income from wages, salary and tips, dividends, interest, and pensions and annuities is $40,000 or less if they do not itemize deductions. Persons who use this IRS service are required to fill in certain data, sign the return, and send it to the IRS on or before 15 April of the year immediately following the tax year. The IRS figures your tax to "give you the smallest tax." You are then sent a refund, if your withholding exceeds your tax liability, or a bill, if your tax liability is greater than the amount of withholding. If you do not wish or qualify for this total tax preparation service, you can still obtain IRS assistance in preparing your return. The IRS provides a toll-free service through which taxpayers can have questions answered.

What Are the Odds of Getting Audited?

Year in and year out, the IRS is interested in ascertaining whether the returns filed by individuals are true and accurate. This is done both manually and with the help of the computer. Completeness and accuracy of tax forms is checked manually, but it is left to the computer to provide mathematical verifications of "disallowable" items. Statistics show that errors existed in four million returns out of the 81 million that underwent screening in 1975. Believe it or not, half of these resulted in refunds to taxpayers averaging $93 each.

The computer is programmed to screen excessive or improper items on your return. If it comes across one, then you will be notified of it in writing by your IRS regional service center. This does not necessarily mean the whole return will be examined, but it could lead to an audit. The table given below indicates the percentage of various kinds of returns that were selected for audit in 1975. Note that the odds of being picked for audit are for each given year, and not once in a lifetime.

A sophisticated program called the Discriminant Function System (DIF) chooses returns for audit by assigning weights to various items of income and deductions. All returns are scored, and those with the highest scores are chosen for audit. Of all returns audited in 1975, 68.8 percent were thus chosen. The DIF weighting system is a closely guarded secret, even exempt from the Freedom of Information Act. Of the DIF audits conducted in 1975, 23 percent resulted in no change in the taxpayer's liability; 6.6 percent resulted in refunds to taxpayers totaling $302.8 million; and 70.4 percent resulted in $5.3 billion in additional taxes and penalties assessed.

No one knows how many times the IRS incorrectly levies taxes. Taxpayers

Private Tax Preparation Services Many taxpayers prefer to use private tax preparation services because (1) they are concerned about accuracy and minimizing their tax liability as much as possible, and (2) they believe the complexity of the tax forms makes preparation too difficult and too time consuming. Taxpayers who do not wish to prepare their returns and have relatively common types of income and expenditure might consider using a *national tax service*. The most well-known national tax service is H & R Block. There are also a number of *local tax preparation services*. Caution is recommended in selecting a tax preparation service, since differing levels of competency exist. National services are generally preferable to local services because they usually have better trained staff and exhibit greater concern for their reputation.

1975 IRS Audit Statistics

Type of Return	Total Filed	Total Audited	Percent
Individual, Nonbusiness			
Under $10,000 Adjusted Gross Income, Standard Deductions	30,279,027	220,909	0.7%
Under $10,000 Adjusted Gross Income, Itemized Deductions	12,937,460	561,393	4.3
$10,000 to $50,000 A.G.I.	27,765,747	689,459	2.5
$50,000 and Over A.G.I.	471,803	59,230	12.6
Individual, Business			
Under $10,000 A.G.I.	4,724,378	135,389	2.9
$10,000 to $30,000 A.G.I.	4,293,098	97,544	2.3
$30,000 and Over A.G.I.	800,249	74,634	9.3
Individual Total	81,271,762	1,838,568	2.3

Source: Annual Report, Commissioner of Internal Revenue.

normally receive four notices of taxes allegedly due before any forcible collection is made. The individual can take recourse by seeking the services of a tax counsellor, but most audits require only the taxpayer—not the IRS—to furnish evidence of the items in question. Accuracy, maintaining up-to-date records, and verifying claims lessen your chances of an IRS tax audit and make it easier for you to respond to an audit, should one be conducted.

Source: Adapted from Robert S. Rosefsky, "What Causes Your Taxes to Be Audited," *Flightime*, March 1977, p. 10. Reprinted with permission from Flightime Magazine carried aboard Continental Airlines, © 1977 East/West Network, Inc.

Taxpayers whose finances are more complex generally employ a certified public accountant (CPA) or an attorney with tax training. Both types of professionals not only know the various tax loopholes but are able to provide the taxpayer with advice on how to defer income, qualify for deductions, and generally minimize tax liability. This type of advice helps the taxpayer understand how to maximize net worth over the long run. Tax attorneys generally devote most of their attention to counseling taxpayers in the area of tax planning, while CPAs tend to be more concerned with the actual preparation of returns. The services provided by CPAs and tax attorneys can be expensive and thus are usually best used only by those taxpayers whose financial situation is relatively complicated.

When selecting a tax advisor, it is a good idea to examine credentials as well as fee schedules. Friends and relatives whose financial circumstances are similar to yours may be able to recommend a tax service. The person you choose to prepare your returns will provide you with various guidelines and forms to be used in gathering and organizing the information needed for this task. You should follow these guidelines closely and provide all information requested in order to make sure your tax returns are completely and accurately prepared; the accuracy of the tax return

IRS Toll-Free Tax Assistance

To Call IRS Toll Free for Answers to Your Federal Tax Questions, Use Only the Number Listed Below for Your Area

Caution: *"Toll-free" is a telephone call for which you pay only local charges and no long-distance charge is involved. Therefore, please use a local city number* **only** *if it is not a long-distance call for you. Otherwise, use the general toll-free number provided.*

To help us provide courteous responses and accurate information, IRS occasionally monitors telephone calls. No record is maintained of the taxpayer's name, address or social security number.

If you find it necessary to write rather than call us, please address your letter to your IRS District Director for a prompt reply.

Tax Advice to Taxpayers.—We are happy to answer questions to help you prepare your return. But you should know that you are responsible for the accuracy of your return and for the payment of the correct tax. If we do make an error, you are still responsible for the payment of the correct tax, and we are generally required by law to charge interest.

Source: U.S. Department of Treasury, Internal Revenue Service, *1976 Federal Income Tax Forms* (Washington, D.C.: U.S. Government Printing Office, 1976), p. 30.

can be no better than the accuracy of the information provided. If you have maintained the type of budget records described in Chapter 3, the information required should be readily available.

Before signing the completed return, it is a good idea to check it, since you must accept primary responsibility for its accuracy. In 1977, the IRS began requiring persons who prepare tax returns for pay to sign each return as preparer, enter their social security number and address, and furnish a copy of the return to each taxpayer. This requirement should encourage those who operate tax services to act responsibly in preparing tax returns.

Now that we have looked at the general principles of federal income taxation we can begin to examine the key aspects of calculating taxable income: (1) tax rates applicable to the various types of personal income, (2) basic tax forms and schedules, (3) a sample tax return, and (4) techniques available for reducing tax payments.

Calculating Taxable Income

Tax Rates

Tax rates levied on personal income vary with amount of taxable income and filing status. Table 4-6 presents a portion of the 1977 Tax Table applicable to persons with a taxable income of $40,000 or less. After calculating their tax table income, taxpayers can use this table to determine their tax liability. For example, a married person filing jointly who has two exemptions and a tax table income of $17,190 would have a $2,199 tax liability, as indicated in Table 4-6, for tax table income between $17,150 and $17,200.

Table 4-7 presents the tax schedules used when taxable income exceeds the tax table limits. Three separate schedules—X, Y, and Z—are included in this schedule. The schedules vary according to filing status. For example, married taxpayers filing a joint return use Schedule Y. Take the case of married taxpayers who wish to file a joint return and have $75,000 of taxable income. Their tax liability is calculated from Schedule Y as follows:

$$\$24,420 + 0.55 \, (\$75,000 - \$67,200) = \$24,420 + \$4,290 = \$28,710.$$

Note that the maximum tax rate on personal income is 70 percent, which is levied on taxable income above $102,200 for individuals and $203,200 on joint returns.

The *average tax rate* is determined by dividing tax liability by taxable income. The married couple who filed jointly with a tax table income of

Table 4-6 Portion of 1977 Tax Table for Incomes Less than $40,000

1977 Tax Table B—MARRIED FILING JOINTLY (Box 2) and QUALIFYING WIDOW(ER)S (Box 5)
(Continued)

(If your income or exemptions are not covered, use Schedule TC (Form 1040), Part I to figure your tax)

If line 34, Form 1040 is— Over	But not over	And the total number of exemptions claimed on line 7 is— Your tax is—							
		2	3	4	5	6	7	8	9
11,600	11,650	1,037	910	751	573	397	235	78	0
11,650	11,700	1,046	918	760	583	406	243	86	0
11,700	11,750	1,054	927	770	592	415	252	94	0
11,750	11,800	1,063	935	779	602	424	260	102	0
11,800	11,850	1,071	944	789	611	434	269	110	0
11,850	11,900	1,080	952	798	621	443	277	118	0
11,900	11,950	1,088	961	808	630	453	286	126	0
11,950	12,000	1,097	969	817	640	462	294	134	0
12,000	12,050	1,105	978	827	649	472	303	142	0
12,050	12,100	1,114	986	836	659	481	311	150	0
12,100	12,150	1,122	995	846	668	491	320	158	3
12,150	12,200	1,131	1,003	855	678	500	328	166	11
12,200	12,250	1,139	1,012	865	687	510	337	174	19
12,250	12,300	1,148	1,020	874	697	519	345	183	27
12,300	12,350	1,156	1,029	884	706	529	354	191	35
12,350	12,400	1,165	1,037	893	716	538	362	200	43
12,400	12,450	1,173	1,046	903	725	548	371	208	51
12,450	12,500	1,182	1,054	912	735	557	380	217	59
12,500	12,550	1,190	1,063	922	744	567	389	225	67
12,550	12,600	1,199	1,071	931	754	576	399	234	75
12,600	12,650	1,207	1,080	941	763	586	408	242	83
12,650	12,700	1,216	1,088	950	773	595	418	251	91
12,700	12,750	1,225	1,097	960	782	605	427	259	99
12,750	12,800	1,235	1,105	969	792	614	437	268	107
12,800	12,850	1,245	1,114	979	801	624	446	276	115
12,850	12,900	1,255	1,122	988	811	633	456	285	123
12,900	12,950	1,265	1,131	998	820	643	465	293	131
12,950	13,000	1,275	1,139	1,007	830	652	475	302	139
13,000	13,050	1,285	1,148	1,017	839	662	484	310	148
13,050	13,100	1,295	1,156	1,026	849	671	494	319	156
13,100	13,150	1,305	1,165	1,036	858	681	503	327	165
13,150	13,200	1,315	1,173	1,045	868	690	513	336	173
13,200	13,250	1,325	1,182	1,054	877	700	522	345	182
13,250	13,300	1,335	1,190	1,063	887	709	532	354	190
13,300	13,350	1,345	1,199	1,071	896	719	541	364	199
13,350	13,400	1,355	1,207	1,080	906	728	551	373	207
13,400	13,450	1,365	1,216	1,088	915	738	560	383	216
13,450	13,500	1,375	1,225	1,097	925	747	570	392	224
13,500	13,550	1,385	1,235	1,105	934	757	579	402	233
13,550	13,600	1,395	1,245	1,114	944	766	589	411	241
13,600	13,650	1,405	1,255	1,122	953	776	598	421	250
13,650	13,700	1,415	1,265	1,131	963	785	608	430	258
13,700	13,750	1,426	1,275	1,139	972	795	617	440	267
13,750	13,800	1,437	1,285	1,148	982	804	627	449	275

If line 34, Form 1040 is— Over	But not over	And the total number of exemptions claimed on line 7 is— Your tax is—							
		2	3	4	5	6	7	8	9
15,200	15,250	1,756	1,591	1,426	1,266	1,080	902	725	547
15,250	15,300	1,767	1,602	1,437	1,277	1,089	912	734	557
15,300	15,350	1,778	1,613	1,448	1,288	1,099	921	744	566
15,350	15,400	1,789	1,624	1,459	1,299	1,108	931	753	576
15,400	15,450	1,800	1,635	1,470	1,310	1,118	940	763	585
15,450	15,500	1,811	1,646	1,481	1,321	1,127	950	772	595
15,500	15,550	1,822	1,657	1,492	1,332	1,137	959	782	604
15,550	15,600	1,833	1,668	1,503	1,343	1,146	969	791	614
15,600	15,650	1,844	1,679	1,514	1,354	1,156	978	801	623
15,650	15,700	1,855	1,690	1,525	1,365	1,165	988	810	633
15,700	15,750	1,866	1,701	1,536	1,375	1,176	997	820	642
15,750	15,800	1,877	1,712	1,547	1,385	1,187	1,007	829	652
15,800	15,850	1,888	1,723	1,558	1,395	1,198	1,016	839	661
15,850	15,900	1,899	1,734	1,569	1,405	1,209	1,026	848	671
15,900	15,950	1,910	1,745	1,580	1,415	1,220	1,035	858	680
15,950	16,000	1,921	1,756	1,591	1,426	1,231	1,045	867	690
16,000	16,050	1,932	1,767	1,602	1,437	1,242	1,054	877	699
16,050	16,100	1,943	1,778	1,613	1,448	1,253	1,064	886	709
16,100	16,150	1,954	1,789	1,624	1,459	1,264	1,073	896	718
16,150	16,200	1,965	1,800	1,635	1,470	1,275	1,083	905	728
16,200	16,250	1,976	1,811	1,646	1,481	1,286	1,092	915	737
16,250	16,300	1,987	1,822	1,657	1,492	1,297	1,102	924	747
16,300	16,350	1,998	1,833	1,668	1,503	1,308	1,111	934	756
16,350	16,400	2,009	1,844	1,679	1,514	1,319	1,121	943	766
16,400	16,450	2,020	1,855	1,690	1,525	1,330	1,130	953	775
16,450	16,500	2,031	1,866	1,701	1,536	1,341	1,141	962	785
16,500	16,550	2,042	1,877	1,712	1,547	1,352	1,152	972	794
16,550	16,600	2,053	1,888	1,723	1,558	1,363	1,163	981	804
16,600	16,650	2,064	1,899	1,734	1,569	1,374	1,174	991	813
16,650	16,700	2,075	1,910	1,745	1,580	1,385	1,185	1,000	823
16,700	16,750	2,086	1,921	1,756	1,591	1,396	1,196	1,010	832
16,750	16,800	2,099	1,932	1,767	1,602	1,407	1,207	1,019	842
16,800	16,850	2,111	1,943	1,778	1,613	1,418	1,218	1,029	851
16,850	16,900	2,124	1,954	1,789	1,624	1,429	1,229	1,038	861
16,900	16,950	2,136	1,965	1,800	1,635	1,440	1,240	1,048	870
16,950	17,000	2,149	1,976	1,811	1,646	1,451	1,251	1,057	880
17,000	17,050	2,161	1,987	1,822	1,657	1,462	1,262	1,067	889
17,050	17,100	2,174	1,998	1,833	1,668	1,473	1,273	1,076	899
17,100	17,150	2,186	2,009	1,844	1,679	1,484	1,284	1,086	908
17,150	17,200	2,199	2,020	1,855	1,690	1,495	1,295	1,095	918
17,200	17,250	2,211	2,031	1,866	1,701	1,506	1,306	1,106	927
17,250	17,300	2,224	2,042	1,877	1,712	1,517	1,317	1,117	937
17,300	17,350	2,236	2,053	1,888	1,723	1,528	1,328	1,128	946
17,350	17,400	2,249	2,064	1,899	1,734	1,539	1,339	1,139	956

Source: U.S. Department of Treasury, Internal Revenue Service, *1977 Federal Income Tax Forms* (Washington, D.C.: U.S. Government Printing Office, 1977), p. 34.

$17,190 had an average tax rate of 12.8 percent ($2,199 ÷ $17,190). For the couple with the taxable income of $75,000, the average tax rate was 38.3 percent ($28,710 ÷ $75,000). A comparison of these average tax rates makes the progressive nature of the federal tax structure apparent: tax schedules are set up in such a way that the more you earn, the larger the percentage you pay to the government in the form of taxes. As indicated earlier, since only one-half of long-term capital gains is claimed as

Table 4-7 1977 Tax Schedules for Individuals Who Cannot Use the Tax Tables

1977 Tax Rate Schedules

If you cannot use one of the Tax Tables, figure your tax on the amount on Schedule TC, Part I, line 3, by using the appropriate Tax Rate Schedule on this page. Enter tax on Schedule TC, Part I, line 4.
Note: Your zero bracket amount has been built into these Tax Rate Schedules.

SCHEDULE X—Single Taxpayers Not Qualifying for Rates in Schedule Y or Z

Use this schedule if you checked **Box 1** on Form 1040—

If the amount on Schedule TC, Part I, line 3, is: / Enter on Schedule TC, Part I, line 4:

Not over $2,200............ —0—

Over—	But not over—		of the amount over—
$2,200	$2,700	14%	$2,200
$2,700	$3,200	$70+15%	$2,700
$3,200	$3,700	$145+16%	$3,200
$3,700	$4,200	$225+17%	$3,700
$4,200	$6,200	$310+19%	$4,200
$6,200	$8,200	$690+21%	$6,200
$8,200	$10,200	$1,110+24%	$8,200
$10,200	$12,200	$1,590+25%	$10,200
$12,200	$14,200	$2,090+27%	$12,200
$14,200	$16,200	$2,630+29%	$14,200
$16,200	$18,200	$3,210+31%	$16,200
$18,200	$20,200	$3,830+34%	$18,200
$20,200	$22,200	$4,510+36%	$20,200
$22,200	$24,200	$5,230+38%	$22,200
$24,200	$28,200	$5,990+40%	$24,200
$28,200	$34,200	$7,590+45%	$28,200
$34,200	$40,200	$10,290+50%	$34,200
$40,200	$46,200	$13,290+55%	$40,200
$46,200	$52,200	$16,590+60%	$46,200
$52,200	$62,200	$20,190+62%	$52,200
$62,200	$72,200	$26,390+64%	$62,200
$72,200	$82,200	$32,790+66%	$72,200
$82,200	$92,200	$39,390+68%	$82,200
$92,200	$102,200	$46,190+69%	$92,200
$102,200	....	$53,090+70%	$102,200

SCHEDULE Y—Married Taxpayers and Qualifying Widows and Widowers
If you are a married person living apart from your spouse, see page 7 of the instructions to see if you can be considered to be "unmarried" for purposes of using Schedule X or Z.

Married Filing Joint Returns and Qualifying Widows and Widowers

Use this schedule if you checked **Box 2 or Box 5** on Form 1040—

If the amount on Schedule TC, Part I, line 3, is: / Enter on Schedule TC, Part I, line 4:

Not over $3,200............ —0—

Over—	But not over—		of the amount over—
$3,200	$4,200	14%	$3,200
$4,200	$5,200	$140+15%	$4,200
$5,200	$6,200	$290+16%	$5,200
$6,200	$7,200	$450+17%	$6,200
$7,200	$11,200	$620+19%	$7,200
$11,200	$15,200	$1,380+22%	$11,200
$15,200	$19,200	$2,260+25%	$15,200
$19,200	$23,200	$3,260+28%	$19,200
$23,200	$27,200	$4,380+32%	$23,200
$27,200	$31,200	$5,660+36%	$27,200
$31,200	$35,200	$7,100+39%	$31,200
$35,200	$39,200	$8,660+42%	$35,200
$39,200	$43,200	$10,340+45%	$39,200
$43,200	$47,200	$12,140+48%	$43,200
$47,200	$55,200	$14,060+50%	$47,200
$55,200	$67,200	$18,060+53%	$55,200
$67,200	$79,200	$24,420+55%	$67,200
$79,200	$91,200	$31,020+58%	$79,200
$91,200	$103,200	$37,980+60%	$91,200
$103,200	$123,200	$45,180+62%	$103,200
$123,200	$143,200	$57,580+64%	$123,200
$143,200	$163,200	$70,380+66%	$143,200
$163,200	$183,200	$83,580+68%	$163,200
$183,200	$203,200	$97,180+69%	$183,200
$203,200	....	$110,980+70%	$203,200

Married Filing Separate Returns

Use this schedule if you checked **Box 3** on Form 1040—

If the amount on Schedule TC, Part I, line 3, is: / Enter on Schedule TC, Part I, line 4:

Not over $1,600............ —0—

Over—	But not over—		of the amount over—
$1,600	$2,100	14%	$1,600
$2,100	$2,600	$70+15%	$2,100
$2,600	$3,100	$145+16%	$2,600
$3,100	$3,600	$225+17%	$3,100
$3,600	$5,600	$310+19%	$3,600
$5,600	$7,600	$690+22%	$5,600
$7,600	$9,600	$1,130+25%	$7,600
$9,600	$11,600	$1,630+28%	$9,600
$11,600	$13,600	$2,190+32%	$11,600
$13,600	$15,600	$2,830+36%	$13,600
$15,600	$17,600	$3,550+39%	$15,600
$17,600	$19,600	$4,330+42%	$17,600
$19,600	$21,600	$5,170+45%	$19,600
$21,600	$23,600	$6,070+48%	$21,600
$23,600	$27,600	$7,030+50%	$23,600
$27,600	$33,600	$9,030+53%	$27,600
$33,600	$39,600	$12,210+55%	$33,600
$39,600	$45,600	$15,510+58%	$39,600
$45,600	$51,600	$18,990+60%	$45,600
$51,600	$61,600	$22,590+62%	$51,600
$61,600	$71,600	$28,790+64%	$61,600
$71,600	$81,600	$35,190+66%	$71,600
$81,600	$91,600	$41,790+68%	$81,600
$91,600	$101,600	$48,590+69%	$91,600
$101,600	....	$55,490+70%	$101,600

SCHEDULE Z—Unmarried or legally separated taxpayers Who Qualify as Heads of Household

Use this schedule if you checked **Box 4** on Form 1040—

If the amount on Schedule TC, Part I, line 3, is: / Enter on Schedule TC, Part I, line 4:

Not over $2,200............ —0—

Over—	But not over—		of the amount over—
$2,200	$3,200	14%	$2,200
$3,200	$4,200	$140+16%	$3,200
$4,200	$6,200	$300+18%	$4,200
$6,200	$8,200	$660+19%	$6,200
$8,200	$10,200	$1,040+22%	$8,200
$10,200	$12,200	$1,480+23%	$10,200
$12,200	$14,200	$1,940+25%	$12,200
$14,200	$16,200	$2,440+27%	$14,200
$16,200	$18,200	$2,980+28%	$16,200
$18,200	$20,200	$3,540+31%	$18,200
$20,200	$22,200	$4,160+32%	$20,200
$22,200	$24,200	$4,800+35%	$22,200
$24,200	$26,200	$5,500+36%	$24,200
$26,200	$28,200	$6,220+38%	$26,200
$28,200	$30,200	$6,980+41%	$28,200
$30,200	$34,200	$7,800+42%	$30,200
$34,200	$38,200	$9,480+45%	$34,200
$38,200	$40,200	$11,280+48%	$38,200
$40,200	$42,200	$12,240+51%	$40,200
$42,200	$46,200	$13,260+52%	$42,200
$46,200	$52,200	$15,340+55%	$46,200
$52,200	$54,200	$18,640+56%	$52,200
$54,200	$66,200	$19,760+58%	$54,200
$66,200	$72,200	$26,720+59%	$66,200
$72,200	$78,200	$30,260+61%	$72,200
$78,200	$82,200	$33,920+62%	$78,200
$82,200	$90,200	$36,400+63%	$82,200
$90,200	$102,200	$41,440+64%	$90,200
$102,200	$122,200	$49,120+66%	$102,200
$122,200	$142,200	$62,320+67%	$122,200
$142,200	$162,200	$75,720+68%	$142,200
$162,200	$182,200	$89,320+69%	$162,200
$182,200	....	$103,120+70%	$182,200

Source: U.S. Department of Treasury, Internal Revenue Service, *1977 Federal Income Tax Forms* (Washington, D.C.: U.S. Government Printing Office, 1977), p.43.

income, the tax rate on these gains is equal to only one-half of the taxpayer's average tax rate. For this reason, long-term capital gains are the most advantageous form of income from the standpoint of taxation.

Tax Forms and Schedules

The Internal Revenue Service requires taxpayers to file their tax returns using certain specified tax forms. These forms and a variety of instruction booklets on filling them out are made available to taxpayers free of charge. Tax forms can be obtained at the post office, at banks, at a local IRS office, or by writing or calling the IRS. All persons who filed tax returns in the previous year are automatically sent a booklet containing tax forms and instructions for preparation of returns for the current year. Inside the booklet is a form that can be used to obtain additional tax forms. Form 1040 is the main form used for filing personal taxes. Numerous others exist for filing various tax-related returns and information.

Form 1040 All individuals use Form 1040 along with its accompanying schedules for filing their tax returns. Schedules which accompany Form 1040 are named and briefly described in Table 4-8. The use of these

Table 4-8 **Description of Schedules Accompanying Form 1040**

Schedule	Description
A	For itemized deductions
B	For gross dividends and interest in excess of $400 each
C	For profit (or loss) from a personally owned business
D	For income (or loss) from the sale or exchange of capital assets
E	For income from pensions, annuities, rents, royalties, partnerships, estates, trusts, etc.
F	For income from farming
G	For use in income averaging
R & RP	For credit for the elderly
SE	For reporting net earnings from self-employment

schedules, which provide detailed guidelines for calculating certain entries on the first two pages of Form 1040, varies among taxpayers, depending on the relevance of these entries to the individual financial situation. Pages 1 and 2 of this form summarize all items of income and deduction and note the taxable income (see Table 4-9 later in the chapter).

Other Tax Forms In addition to Form 1040, other tax forms may be necessary: (1) to provide detailed information needed to report other sources of income, (2) to support certain deductions, and (3) to qualify for certain credits. Reference to certain of these forms can be found in Form 1040 (see, for example, lines 23, 24, 30, and 49 on Form 1040 presented in Table 4-9). Space does not permit further description and discussion of these forms in this chapter.

Richard and Evelyn Grant Family

Richard and Evelyn Grant are both thirty-three years old. They have been married for eleven years and have three children—Tom (nine years old), Dick (seven years old), and Jane (three years old). Richard is a staff accountant for a major oil company, which is headquartered in the Grants' hometown of Anywhere, Oklahoma. Evelyn Grant, who has one and a half years of college education, works part time as a salesclerk in a major department store. During 1977 Richard's salary totaled $20,115, while Evelyn earned $4,261. Richard's employer withheld taxes of $3,700, while Evelyn's employer withheld only $328 of her income for tax purposes. The Grants were paid $1,500 in dividends on securities held jointly and $1,250 in interest during the year. Richard kept the books of his brother's auto sales business and netted $3,000 from this activity during the year. Since no taxes were withheld from this outside income, Richard made estimated tax payments totaling $500 during the year. His detailed records indicate that during the year he and Evelyn had a total of $3,691 of nonbusiness expenses. Richard had also incurred $480 of travel expenses (not reimbursed) attending certain accounting seminars at the suggestion of his employer.

A Sample Tax Return—Richard and Evelyn Grant

An examination of the 1977 tax return data for the Grant family (see color section) elicits the basic calculations required in preparing Form 1040. Although the supporting schedules and forms are not included here, the necessary totals obtained from these schedules and forms are given.

Richard Grant has kept detailed records of his income and expenditures, which he uses not only for tax purposes but also as an important input to his budgeting process. Using this information, Richard hoped to prepare his 1977 tax return in a fashion that would allow him to reduce his tax liability as much as possible. He knew that filing a joint return was best in his particular case. The Grants' completed Form 1040 (pages 1 and 2) is shown in Table 4-9. The key entries on this form are described separately below.

Gross Income The Grants' gross income during 1977 is calculated on lines 8 through 21 of Form 1040. Richard and Evelyn's total wages and salaries (line 8) amount to $24,376 ($20,115 plus $4,261). To this total is added $1,250 (line 9) of interest and $1,300 (line 10c) of dividends. Although the Grants actually received $1,500 (line 10a) of dividends, $200 (line 10b)—$100 for Richard and $100 for Evelyn—are excluded. Note that the dividend exclusion is $100 for each spouse only if: (1) the securities are held in joint names or (2) the ownership of the securities is

Table 4-9 Form 1040 for Grant Family

Form **1040** U.S. Individual Income Tax Return	Department of the Treasury—Internal Revenue Service	**1977**

For the year January 1–December 31, 1977, or other taxable year beginning _____ , 1977 ending _____ , 19 ____

Use IRS label. Otherwise, print or type.	First name and initial (if joint return, give first names and initials of both) **RICHARD D. and EVELYN F.**	Last name **GRANT**	Your social security number **444 32 2222**
	Present home address (Number and street, including apartment number, or rural route) **105 SOUTH STREET**	For Privacy Act Notice, see page 3 of Instructions.	Spouse's social security no. **445 33 5555**
	City, town or post office, State and ZIP code **ANYWHERE, OKLAHOMA 74193**	Occupation Yours ▶ **ACCOUNTANT** Spouse's ▶ **SALESWOMAN**	

Presidential Election Campaign Fund ▶
Do you want $1 to go to this fund? . . . . ☒ Yes ☐ No
If joint return, does your spouse want $1 to go to this fund? . ☒ Yes ☐ No
Note: Checking "Yes" will not increase your tax or reduce your refund.

Filing Status
Check Only One Box

1 ☐ Single
2 ☒ Married filing joint return (even if only one had income)
3 ☐ Married filing separately. If spouse is also filing, give spouse's social security number in the space above and enter full name here ▶
4 ☐ Unmarried Head of Household. Enter qualifying name ▶ .... See page 7 of Instructions.
5 ☐ Qualifying widow(er) with dependent child (Year spouse died ▶ 19 ___). See page 7 of Instructions.

Exemptions

Always check the "Yourself" box. Check other boxes if they apply.

6a ☒ Yourself   ☐ 65 or over   ☐ Blind — Enter number of boxes checked on 6a and b ▶ **2**
b ☒ Spouse   ☐ 65 or over   ☐ Blind
c First names of your dependent children who lived with you ▶ **Tom, Dick, Jane** — Enter number of children listed ▶ **3**

d Other dependents:

(1) Name	(2) Relationship	(3) Number of months lived in your home.	(4) Did dependent have income of $750 or more?	(5) Did you provide more than one-half of dependent's support?

Enter number of other dependents ▶

7 Total number of exemptions claimed . . . . Add numbers entered in boxes above ▶ **5**

Income

8	Wages, salaries, tips, and other employee compensation. (Attach Forms W-2. If unavailable, see page 5 of Instructions.)	8	**24,376**	00
9	Interest income. (If over $400, attach Schedule B.)	9	**1,250**	00
10a	Dividends (If over $400, attach Schedule B) **1500** 00 , 10b less exclusion **200** 00 , Balance ▶	10c	**1,300**	00
	(See pages 9 and 17 of Instructions)			
	(If you have no other income, skip lines 11 through 20 and go to line 21.)			
11	State and local income tax refunds (does not apply if refund is for year you took standard deduction) . . .	11	0	
12	Alimony received	12	0	
13	Business income or (loss) (attach Schedule C)	13	**3,000**	00
14	Capital gain or (loss) (attach Schedule D)	14	0	
15	50% of capital gain distributions not reported on Schedule D	15	0	
16	Net gain or (loss) from Supplemental Schedule of Gains and Losses (attach Form 4797) . .	16	0	
17	Fully taxable pensions and annuities not reported on Schedule E	17	0	
18	Pensions, annuities, rents, royalties, partnerships, estates or trusts, etc. (attach Schedule E) . .	18	0	
19	Farm income or (loss) (attach Schedule F)	19	0	
20	Other (state nature and source—see page 9 of Instructions) ▶	20	0	
21	Total income. Add lines 8, 9, and 10c through 20 . . . . ▶	21	**29,926**	00

Adjustments to Income *(If none, skip lines 22 through 27 and enter zero on line 28.)*

22	Moving expense (attach Form 3903)	22	0			
23	Employee business expenses (attach Form 2106)	23	**480**	00		
24	Payments to an individual retirement arrangement (from attached Form 5329, Part III)	24	0			
25	Payments to a Keogh (H.R. 10) retirement plan	25	0			
26	Forfeited interest penalty for premature withdrawal	26	0			
27	Alimony paid (see page 11 of Instructions)	27	0			
28	Total adjustments. Add lines 22 through 27 . . . . ▶				28	**480**	00
29	Subtract line 28 from line 21				29	**29,446**	00
30	Disability income exclusion (sick pay) (attach Form 2440)				30	0	
31	Adjusted gross income. Subtract line 30 from line 29. Enter here and on line 32. If you want IRS to figure your tax for you, see page 4 of the Instructions . . . . ▶				31	**29,446**	00

235–057–2

split so that each spouse receives more than $100 in dividends. The first of these requirements was met by the Grants. Also included in the Grants' gross income is the $3,000 (line 13) Richard received for keeping his brother's books. The Grants' total gross income (line 21) is therefore $29,926.

Form 1040 (1977)

Page 2

Tax Computation	32 Amount from line 31		32	29,446 00
	33 If you itemize deductions, enter excess itemized deductions from Schedule A, line 41		33	491 00
	If you do NOT itemize deductions, enter zero.			
	Caution: *If you have unearned income and can be claimed as a dependent on your parent's return, check here* ▶ ☐ *and see page 11 of the Instructions. Also see page 11 of the Instructions if:*			
	● You are married filing a separate return and your spouse itemizes deductions, OR			
	● You file Form 4563, OR			
	● You are a dual-status alien.			
	34 Tax Table Income. Subtract line 33 from line 32		34	28,955 00
	Note: See Instructions for line 35 on page 11. Then find your tax on the amount on line 34 in the Tax Tables. Enter the tax on line 35. However, if line 34 is more than $20,000 ($40,000 if you checked box 2 or 5) or you have more exemptions than those covered in the Tax Tables for your filing status, use Part I of Schedule TC (Form 1040) to figure your tax. You must also use Schedule TC if you file Schedule G (Form 1040), Income Averaging.			
	35 Tax. Check if from ☒ Tax Tables or ☐ Schedule TC		35	4,848 00
	36 Additional taxes. (See page 12 of Instructions.) Check if from ☐ Form 4970, ☐ Form 4972, ☐ Form 5544, ☐ Form 5405, or ☐ Section 72(m)(5) penalty tax		36	
	37 **Total.** Add lines 35 and 36 . . . . ▶		37	4,848 00
Credits	38 Credit for contributions to candidates for public office	38	0	
	39 Credit for the elderly (attach Schedules R&RP)	39	0	
	40 Credit for child and dependent care expenses (attach Form 2441) .	40	0	
	41 Investment credit (attach Form 3468)	41	0	
	42 Foreign tax credit (attach Form 1116)	42	0	
	43 Work Incentive (WIN) Credit (attach Form 4874)	43	0	
	44 New jobs credit (attach Form 5884)	44	0	
	45 See page 12 of Instructions	45	0	
	46 **Total credits.** Add lines 38 through 45		46	0
Other Taxes	47 **Balance.** Subtract line 46 from line 37 and enter difference (but not less than zero) . . . . ▶		47	4,848 00
	48 Self-employment tax (attach Schedule SE)		48	0
	49 Minimum tax. Check here ▶ ☐ and attach Form 4625		49	0
	50 Tax from recomputing prior-year investment credit (attach Form 4255)		50	0
	51 Social security tax on tip income not reported to employer (attach Form 4137)		51	0
	52 Uncollected employee social security tax on tips (from Form W–2)		52	0
	53 Tax on an individual retirement arrangement (attach Form 5329)		53	0
	54 **Total tax.** Add lines 47 through 53 . . . . ▶		54	4,848 00
Payments	55 Total Federal income tax withheld (attach Forms W–2, W–2G, and W–2P to front)	55	4,028 00	
	56 1977 estimated tax payments (include amount allowed as credit from 1976 return)	56	500 00	
	57 Earned income credit. If line 31 is under $8,000, see page 2 of Instructions. If eligible, enter child's name ▶............	57	0	
	58 Amount paid with Form 4868	58	0	
	59 Excess FICA and RRTA tax withheld (two or more employers) . . .	59	0	
	60 Credit for Federal tax on special fuels, etc. (attach Form 4136) . .	60	0	
	61 Credit from a Regulated Investment Company (attach Form 2439)	61	0	
	61a See page 13 of Instructions	61a	0	
	62 **Total.** Add lines 55 through 61a . . . . ▶		62	4,528 00
Refund or Due	63 If line 62 is larger than line 54, enter amount **OVERPAID** . . . . ▶		63	0
	64 Amount of line 63 to be **REFUNDED TO YOU** . . . . ▶		64	0
	65 Amount of line 63 to be credited on 1978 estimated tax . . . . ▶	65	0	
	66 If line 54 is larger than line 62, enter **BALANCE DUE.** Attach check or money order for full amount payable to "Internal Revenue Service." Write social security number on check or money order . . . ▶ (Check ▶ ☐ if Form 2210 (2210F) is attached. See page 14 of Instructions.)		66	320 00

Under penalties of perjury, I declare that I have examined this return, including accompanying schedules and statements, and to the best of my knowledge and belief, it is true, correct, and complete. Declaration of preparer (other than taxpayer) is based on all information of which preparer has any knowledge.

Please Sign Here

Richard D. Grant   3/12/78
Your signature   Date

Evelyn F. Grant   3/12/78
Spouse's signature (if filing jointly, BOTH must sign even if only one had income)

Paid preparer's signature and identifying number (see instructions)

Paid preparer's address (or employer's name, address, and identifying number)

☆ U.S. GOVERNMENT PRINTING OFFICE : 1977—O—235-057

235–057–1

Deductions from Gross Income The only deduction the Grants had from their gross income was the $480 of expense Richard incurred while attending accounting seminars. This deduction is shown on line 23.

Adjusted Gross Income After subtracting the $480 deduction from the gross income and allowing for any other exclusions, the Grants' adjusted gross income of $29,446 is shown on line 31.

Itemized or Zero Bracket Amount In order to determine whether to take the itemized or zero bracket amount, the Grants had to compare the total itemized expenses of $3,691 to the zero bracket amount of $3,200. Since the itemized nonbusiness expenses amounted to $3,691, which is greater than the maximum $3,200 zero bracket amount, the excess itemized deduction of $491 ($3,691 − $3,200) was entered on line 33. Subtracting this amount from the adjusted gross income resulted in tax table income of $28,955 (line 34).

Exemptions For each exemption claimed, the Grants received an exemption of $750. Since the Grants claimed five exemptions (line 7), they received a total exemption of $3,750 (5 × $750). The exemption deductions are built into the tax tables. Thus, in order to receive credit for them, the Grants had to select the proper column (column 5) of the tax table to find their tax.

Taxes The amount of taxes owed by the Grants was calculated using their tax table income ($28,955). Since this amount was less than $40,000, they used the tax tables, a portion of which was shown in Table 4-6. The resulting tax was $4,848 (line 35).

Tax Credits A tax credit equal to $35 per exemption or 2 percent of taxable income (but no more than $180) was available to the Grants in 1977. They qualified for the maximum $180 credit, which was deducted from their tax liability. (This credit is incorporated into the tax tables; therefore it did not have to be calculated.) The credit has already been reflected in the $4,848 tax calculated above.

Tax Payment or Refund Because the total amount of tax withheld of $4,028 (line 55)—$3,700 from Richard's salary and $328 from Evelyn's wages—plus the total estimated tax payments of $500 (line 56) amounted to only $4,528 (line 62), the Grants will have a tax balance due the IRS. By subtracting the total taxes withheld (line 62) from the total tax liability (line 54), the amount due the IRS is found to be $320. The Grants must therefore remit $320 along with the signed Form 1040 (and supporting schedules and forms) to the nearest IRS District Office by 17 April 1978 (since 15 April 1978 is a Saturday). Had the total taxes withheld (line 62) exceeded the Grants' tax liability (line 54), they would have received a refund for the difference from the IRS. Refund checks are typically received one to two months after the tax return is filed.

Reducing Tax Payments

Many taxpayers—especially those with moderate to high incomes—use various techniques to minimize their tax liability. *Tax avoidance,* or minimizing tax payments, should not be confused with tax evasion. In avoiding taxes, the taxpayer accurately reports all items of income and expenditure but attempts to use legitimate deductions and computational procedures to minimize the taxes. *Tax evasion,* which is against the law, involves a failure to accurately report income, expenditure, and tax liabilities as well as to pay taxes. Persons found guilty of tax evasion are subject to severe financial penalties and prison terms. A few of the more common, legitimate methods of tax reduction are described briefly below.

Bless Us, O Lord, and These, Thy Loopholes

Ever since last year, when the Rev. Kirby Hensley defeated the IRS in court, the tax men have had reason to worry. Thanks to his self-created church, Hensley got back $13,000 when he won a dispute over his 1969 federal income taxes. With a bit of determination and effort—to say nothing of prayer—other middle-income taxpayers can wind up owing little or no tax if they set themselves up, like Hensley, as church pastors.

The initial move is to be ordained and get a church charter—a relatively easy gambit. Hensley's Universal Life Church in Modesto, Calif., will do the honors by mail for a $2 ordination charge and a monthly $2 chartering fee. Then, to qualify for the tax break, aspiring holy men—or women—must take a vow of poverty, conduct almost any kind of religious services, turn over their income to their church, and meet the IRS's paperwork requirements. In return, the church can grant them a modest, tax-free living allowance (IRS might pass $8,000) and provide a "parsonage," including upkeep costs (in all, perhaps another $4,000).

Tax Haven. IRS would unquestionably look the arrangement over carefully and might well take sudden ministers to court, with all the legal fees that implies. But the technical tax haven exists because of the difficulty of distinguishing between one man's honest religion and another's faith in the rewards of tax dodging. If the IRS was hoping that no one would notice the loophole, it was bound to be disappointed. Last week in a *National Enquirer* (circ. 3,805,112) article Hensley claimed that he has ordained 3.5 million people since 1962. "If Congress takes these tax breaks away from everyone—all the churches—that's fine with me," says the illiterate minister and building contractor. "Until then, I think everyone should be allowed to share the wealth."

Source: Time, 10 February 1975, pp. 74–75. Reprinted by permission from TIME, The Weekly Newsmagazine; Copyright Time Inc. 1975.

Income Averaging Persons whose income shows extreme fluctuations can reduce their tax liability in peak income years by *income averaging*— spreading their income evenly over a period of five years. Schedule G (Form 1040) provides a step-by-step method for determining whether income should be averaged. Generally speaking, income averaging is advantageous if the balance after subtracting $3,000 from the current year's taxable income is greater than 30 percent of the total taxable income for the immediately preceding four years. For example, assume your current year's taxable income is $13,000 and your taxable income in the preceding four years was $5,000, $5,000, $8,000, and $10,000 (total $28,000). Subtracting $3,000 from current taxable income leaves $10,000. Since $10,000 is more than 30 percent of the $28,000 of total taxable income from the preceding four years, income averaging should be considered. Because of the progressive nature of our tax structure, the averaging of increasing streams of taxable income allows the taxpayer to reduce the average tax rate applied. Taxpayers are free to average income in any year they find such action will reduce their taxes.

Income Splitting Another method of reducing income tax liability is a technique known as *income splitting*, whereby the taxpayer shifts a portion of his or her income to related individuals in lower tax brackets. This can be done by creating a trust or custodial account (see Chapter 17) or by making outright gifts of income-producing property to family members. For example, parents with $25,000 of taxable income and $18,000 of corporate bonds that pay $1,000 in annual interest might give the bonds to their two-year-old child. The $1,000 annual interest would then belong to the child, who would probably have to pay little or no tax on this income. Thus the parents' taxable income would be reduced by $1,000. Income splitting is quite often done in order to reduce taxes while at the same time building savings for covering certain future outlays, such as the expense of a child's college education. According to what is known as the "fruit-of-the-tree" doctrine, individuals cannot give away income (fruit) alone; they must give away or place in trust the income-producing property (fruit-bearing tree) as well. Further tax implications of gifts to dependents are discussed in Chapter 17.

Bunching Deductions Sometimes taxes can be reduced by *bunching deductions*, a technique which can be used effectively by persons with middle incomes (approximately $12,000 to $20,000). This involves planning to make few tax-deductible expenditures in one year and many in the following year. The standard deduction can then be used in the low-expenditure year, while deductions can be itemized in the high-expenditure year. In the low-expenditure year, the zero bracket amount will be greater than the actual expenditures made; in the high-expenditure year, the actual expenditures, which are itemized, will be considerably greater than the zero bracket amount. Taxpayers wishing to bunch deductions must, of course, take into account the fact that taxable income is computed on a cash basis. The net effect of bunching deductions is to reduce taxes by maximizing total deductions over a period of years.

Other Techniques Planning for capital gains instead of ordinary income, investing in tax shelters, buying tax-exempt securities, and claiming business expenses are other techniques used to reduce taxes. Wealthy individuals may have an opportunity to receive future capital gains income instead of ordinary income. By receiving long-term capital gains, they can lower the taxes they must pay, since only one-half of these gains must be claimed for tax purposes. They therefore are effectively taxed at only one-half of the normal tax rate. Another opportunity available to the wealthy is *tax shelters*—investments that capitalize on certain tax write-offs. Certain types of real estate and oil investments offer these tax shelters, or write-offs, which effectively reduce the amount of taxable income.

Investment in *tax-exempt securities*, which are bonds that pay interest that is not taxed as income, also provide an opportunity for reducing taxable income. Further discussion of tax-exempt securities, which are issued by city and local governments, is presented as part of the discussion of bonds in Chapter 6. Some people reduce taxes by claiming certain types of travel, meals, and entertainment as a business—rather than personal—expense. Thus these otherwise nondeductible expenditures may be deducted from taxable income. Although the IRS takes a close look at such deductions, persons in higher tax brackets are often able to reduce their taxes with them. Still other methods of tax reduction that take advantage of certain loopholes in the tax laws do exist, but discussion here must be limited to the above. Most important, however, is that before attempting to take advantage of these opportunities for tax reduction, you make certain you are operating within the law. Penalties for tax evasion can be quite severe.

Although federal income taxes are typically the largest taxes which confront an individual, there are other types of personal taxes. Additional federal taxes may be levied on income as well as on specific types of transactions. At the state and local level, income, property ownership, sales transactions, and licenses may be taxed. Because most persons earning income, owning property, or merely making purchase transactions have to pay many of these other types of taxes, it is important that their implications for the individual's financial condition be understood.

Other Sources of Personal Taxation

"That's nothing. . . . Listen to him explain
this other deduction!"

The IRS May Disallow Certain Deductions
Source: Reprinted by permission from *My Shell Was Recalled!* (New York: Dow Jones Books, 1974),
p. 68.

For example, a person saving to purchase a new automobile costing
$7,000 should realize that the state and local sales taxes as well as the cost
of license plates and registration may add $500 to the total cost. Brief
descriptions of these additional forms of personal taxation are given
below.

Additional Types of Federal Taxation

Social security taxes, excise taxes, and estate and gift taxes are some of
the federal taxes not based solely on income. Probably the most pronounced of these are the social security taxes, which are paid by most
individuals and their employers.

Social Security Taxes Most common of the social security taxes is the
FICA (Federal Insurance Contributions Act), which in 1977 was levied
on the first $16,500 of personal income. Not only does the employee pay
this tax, but the employer is required by law to match it. A detailed
discussion of this tax was presented at the beginning of this chapter,
where the FICA contribution rates were included in Table 4-1. Another
social security tax is the *federal unemployment tax,* which must be paid
by an employer on the basis of each employee's income. Although only
employers have to pay this tax, you may benefit from it in the form of

unemployment compensation should you lose your job. Unemployment benefits, although largely funded through this tax, are typically administered by state governments. Self-employed individuals must pay a *self-employment tax,* which is calculated on their income above $400. The tax is intended to pay for the same benefits that are provided to employed persons through the FICA tax.

Excise Taxes Taxes levied by the federal government on the purchase of certain luxury items and services such as jewelry, automobiles, gasoline, telephone service, tobacco products, and liquor are called *excise taxes.* These taxes are added on to the purchase price of products and services considered luxuries by the federal government.

Estate and Gift Taxes The federal government and state governments both tax estates and gifts. *Estate taxes* are levied on the value of the estate left at the death of its owner. These taxes therefore reduce the amount of the inheritance passed on to the heirs. *Gift taxes* are levied on a gift; they must be paid by the giver and are based on the value of the gift given. A detailed discussion of these federal taxes is included in the final part of Chapter 17, which is concerned with estate planning.

Other Federal Taxes Duties on imports, entrance fees to federal facilities such as parks and museums, and taxes on special types of transactions are still other types of federal taxation. Note that none of the federal taxes described in the preceding sections can be claimed as deductions for federal income tax purposes.

State Taxes

In order to finance their operating costs, state governments levy a variety of taxes. Probably the largest source of state revenue is taxes levied on sales transactions. Other sources are income taxes, property taxes, and licensing fees.

State Sales Tax Most consumer purchases are taxed. Although these sales taxes vary from state to state, they typically range from 3 to 6 percent. Most states exempt certain items that are viewed as necessities of life from this tax—for example, groceries, medical services, and rent. Sales taxes are levied by the merchant at the point of sale. The merchant is then responsible for remitting these taxes to the appropriate state authorities. Most states allow the merchant to retain a small portion of the taxes as payment for performing the collection function.

Taxpayers who itemize their nonbusiness expenses can deduct sales taxes from their income. The IRS provides tables for computing this deduction. Because sales taxes are tied to purchases, there is really no practical way to avoid them. When making or budgeting for large purchases, it is a good idea to recognize that sales taxes will add to cost.

State Income Taxes Most states currently have income taxes, which range as high as 15 percent of taxable income. Although numerous states have graduated tax rates which increase with income, some have fixed rates which apply to all levels of taxable income. The calculation of these taxes is generally similar to that for the federal income tax, which makes it relatively easy for the taxpayer to file the state tax return. Like the federal government, most states operate on a "pay-as-you-go" basis by withholding a portion of income from each paycheck. A number of states allow the taxpayer to deduct federal taxes from taxable income prior to calculating their state tax liability. For federal tax purposes, persons who itemize their nonbusiness deductions can deduct all state income taxes paid.

State Property Taxes, Licensing Fees, and Other Taxes Although most states obtain their revenues from sales and income taxes, some states also tax various items of property. Since property taxes are levied primarily by local governments, a discussion of them is included in a later section of the chapter. State governments also obtain revenue from the sale of auto licenses and by licensing certain professions. In addition, many states have excise taxes on tobacco, liquor, gasoline, and other luxury items. Most also have estate and gift taxes similar to those levied by the federal government (see Chapter 17). Although many of the state taxes are deductible and so aid taxpayers in lowering their federal taxes, they nonetheless constitute an expense to be reckoned with in the financial planning process.

Local Taxes

Local governments, which include cities and counties, levy taxes in order to obtain the revenue needed to provide a variety of public services. Although the majority of local revenues come from property taxes, local governments often use income taxes, sales taxes, and licensing fees to add to their funds.

Local Property Taxes The primary source of local revenues is the taxation of real estate and other personal property, such as automobiles and boats. Since the largest source of property ownership for most people is their home, the dominant form of property taxes is the *real estate tax.* Property taxes are typically collected by the county and then distributed among other governmental bodies—the city and the school system, for example. The rate of taxation differs from community to community. The value of the property on which taxes are levied is determined by the governmental body to which the tax is paid. In general, the more expensive the home, the higher the real estate taxes, and vice versa. If deductions are itemized, these taxes can be deducted from federal income taxes. Further discussion of these taxes is included in Chapter 9, which is concerned with real estate.

Local Income Taxes Local governments—typically larger cities—sometimes levy taxes on the incomes of all those employed within their bounds. These taxes are similar to federal and state income taxes, but the rates are lower—usually 1 percent or less. Most city income taxes are withheld and therefore charged on a pay-as-you-go basis with final settlement made at the end of the year. These taxes are a deductible expenditure for federal income tax purposes.

Local Sales Taxes and Licensing Fees Some cities have sales taxes, which are collected by merchants and remitted to the state government as part of the total sales tax on certain items. The state government, whose levy makes up the major portion of the tax, then returns to the cities their portion of the collections. Licensing fees such as building permits also provide local governments with added revenue. In some states a portion of the fees collected for auto and other licenses represents a local licensing fee or property tax.

Summary

Because taxes somehow affect all individuals, an understanding of them is essential to the intelligent management of personal finances. The dominant tax in our economy today is the federal income tax. Federal income taxes provide the federal government with money required to cover its operating costs. The Internal Revenue Service (IRS), which is a branch of the U.S. Treasury Department, is responsible for the enforcement of our federal tax laws. Because the federal government—as well as certain state and local governments—operates on a pay-as-you-go basis, employers are required to withhold a portion of their employees' taxes from each period's pay. Also withheld are FICA taxes, which are used by the federal government to pay social security benefits; state and local income taxes; and certain voluntary contributions to pension or retirement plans.

To determine your taxable income, you first total your eligible income and then subtract certain deductions and exemptions from it. The IRS provides specific guidelines and tests that can be applied to determine what items can be deducted from income. Most taxpayers, when determining their tax liability, measure income and expenditures by the amount of cash received and the amount paid out, respectively, during the tax year (1 January through 31 December). When taxpayers sell personal property that has been in their possession a long time at a gain or loss, they can take advantage of the low capital gains tax. The capital gains tax applies to the sale of a home, but only under certain conditions. As long as a home sold is replaced no longer than eighteen months after its sale with a home of equal or greater value, this tax is not due.

Tax returns must be filed by 15 April of the year following the tax year. The IRS checks the accuracy of tax returns and levies severe penalties on taxpayers who attempt to avoid taxes by not reporting income, not filing a return, or intentionally filing an incorrect return. The IRS, as well as certain private tax preparation services, provides assistance in the preparation of tax returns.

Federal tax rates on personal income vary with the manner in which the taxpayer files, the number of exemptions claimed, and, most importantly, the level of income. The IRS supplies taxpayers with forms for use in filing returns. Taxes are calculated using the IRS's tax tables, and if they exceed the amount withheld, a check for the amount owed must be included with the return. If the amount withheld exceeds the tax liability, the taxpayer will receive a refund from the IRS. Taxpayers should attempt to minimize their taxes while fulfilling all of the legal requirements set out by the IRS. Although a number of tax-minimizing techniques are available, they are most often utilized by persons in high income brackets. Other types of personal taxes—on income, sales, and property—are levied by the federal government, state governments, and local governments.

Key Terms

accrual basis
adjusted gross income
amended return
audit (of returns) by IRS
average tax rate
bunching deductions
capital asset
capital gain (loss)
cash basis
deductions from gross income
dependents
estate taxes
estimated tax payments
excess itemized deductions
excise taxes
exemptions

Federal Insurance
Contributions Act (FICA)
federal unemployment tax
federal withholding taxes
filing extensions
Form 1040
gifts and contributions
gift taxes
gross earnings
gross income
head-of-household
income averaging
income splitting
income taxes
individual returns
Internal Revenue Code

Internal Revenue Service (IRS)
itemized nonbusiness expenses
joint returns
licensing fees
local taxes
long-term (short-term) capital gains
low-income allowance
net earnings
pay-as-you-go basis
prepaid interest
progressive taxes
property taxes
real estate tax
sales taxes
self-employment tax
standard deduction
state taxes
take-home pay
taxable income
tax avoidance
tax credits
tax-exempt income
tax-exempt securities
tax evasion
tax liability
tax preparation services
tax refund
tax shelters
Tax Reduction and Simplification Act of 1977
Tax Reform Act of 1976
tax table income
zero bracket amount

Review Questions

1. Discuss the following items and explain their significance with respect to personal taxes.

(a) Internal Revenue Code, 1939

(b) The Tax Reform Act of 1976

(c) The IRS

(d) Exemptions

(e) FICA

2. What does *progressive taxation* mean? What is the economic rationale underlying the progressive income tax?

3. Distinguish between gross earnings and take-home pay. What does the employer do with the difference?

4. The amount of federal withholding taxes deducted from gross earnings each pay period depends on two factors. What are these factors? Explain.

5. Larry Tolle was married on 15 January 1978. His wife Rebecca is a full-time student at the state university and earns $75 a month working in the library. How many personal exemptions will Larry and Rebecca be able to claim on their joint return? What advice would you give in the instance that Rebecca's parents pay for more than 50 percent of her support?

6. In April 1978, Kay Foland earned a salary of $1,000. Her employer, Ray Brown, deducted $220 and $60.50 as federal and state taxes, and FICA, respectively. What amount of FICA should Ray remit to the IRS on Kay's behalf to cover the month of April 1978?

7. Wendy Jones has received the following items and amounts of income during the year. Help her calculate: (a) gross income and (b) income exempt for tax purposes.

Salary	$9,500	Interest on Savings Account	$ 250
Dividend	800	Rent from Part of House Leased	900
Gift from Mother	500	Loan from Bank	2,000
Child Support from Ex-husband	2,400	Interest on Municipal Bonds	300

8. Define and differentiate between *gross income* and *adjusted gross income.*

9. Henry and Sheila Jackson are in their late seventies. Henry Jackson is blind. Is he eligible for any personal exemptions? Explain.

10. How does a tax credit differ from a deduction from income? Explain the differences resulting from a $1,000 deduction and a $1,000 tax credit for a taxpayer in the 20 percent tax bracket with $10,000 of pretax income.

11. If you itemize your deductions, certain taxes may be included as deductions. Mention three such taxes and indicate the source of these taxes.

12. Describe the two most common methods available for filing a tax return. Also discuss filing requirements.

13. Define *estimated taxes,* and explain under what conditions such tax payments are required.

14. Briefly discuss the tax preparation services available from:

    (a) the IRS

    (b) national and local services

    (c) CPAs and tax attorneys

When is each of these preferred? Discuss the relative costs.

15. Explain how the following are used in filing a tax return:

    (a) Form 1040

    (b) schedules accompanying Form 1040

    (c) tax tables and tax schedules

16. Explain how each of the following is used to reduce tax payments:

    (a) income averaging

    (b) income splitting

    (c) bunching deductions

17. Briefly explain the personal taxes other than the federal income tax which may affect personal finances.

4-1 Preparation of the Goodwins' Tax Return

Peter and Sue Goodwin are a young married couple in their early thirties. They live at 2511 E. 6th St. in Dallas, Texas. For the year 1977, Peter earned $18,000 from his job as a sales manager with Carson Corporation. During the year, his employer withheld $2,500 for income tax purposes. In addition, the Goodwins received a dividend of $400 on jointly owned stocks and $750 interest on municipal bonds. Their only child, Tom, who is ten years old, received dividends of $200 on stocks of Kraft Inc.

Given below are the amounts of money paid out by Peter during the year that are deductible for income tax purposes.

Medical and Dental Expenses	$ 200
State and Property Taxes	801
Interest Paid	1,148
Charitable Contributions	1,360
Casualty and Theft	2,030
	$5,539

Travel costs (not reimbursed) on an out-of-town business trip by Peter were:

Airline Ticket	$250
Limousine	15
Taxis	5
Lodging	60
Meals	36
	$366

Note: You should obtain a copy of Form 1040 for use in completing this case. (You may also find Table 4-6 useful.)

Questions

1. Using the preceding information, prepare a joint tax return for Peter and Sue Goodwin for the year ended 31 December 1977. Prepare their

return in a manner that will result in the legally smallest tax liability—either itemize their deductions or take the zero bracket amount.

2. How much have you saved the Goodwins as a result of your treatment of their deductions?

4-2 John Cavander: Bartender or Tax Expert?

John Cavander, who is single, is a bartender at the Twin Towers Supper Club in Atlanta. During the year, his gross income was $12,700, made up of tips and wages. He has decided to prepare his own tax return since he cannot afford the services of a tax expert. After preparing his return, he has come to you for advice. The following is his worksheet:

Gross Income: Wages	$ 8,000
Tips	4,700
Adjusted Gross Income	$12,700
Less: Itemized Deductions	(900)
	$11,800
Less: Zero Bracket Amount	(2,200)
	$ 9,600
Less: Personal Exemption	(750)
Tax Table Income	$ 8,850

John believes that if people's net income falls below $10,000, the federal government considers them "poor" and allows them to take both an itemized deduction and a zero bracket amount.

Questions

1. Calculate John Cavander's taxable income.

2. Explain to him the difference between itemized deductions and the zero bracket amount.

3. How would the IRS feel about the return he prepared?

Selected References	

Battersby, Mark E. "Correcting Your Tax Mistakes before the IRS Does." *Consumers' Research*, March 1976, pp. 31–32.

Brittain, John A. *The Payroll Law for Social Security.* Washington: Brookings Institution, 1972.

"The Coming of Tax Reform: Read the Fine Print." *Forbes*, 11 August 1977, pp. 21–23.

"Despite New Law, You Can Still Find Tax Shelters." *U.S. News & World Report*, 22 November 1976, pp. 83–85.

Edgerton, Terry. "A New Way to Shelter Stock Gains." *Money*, March 1977, pp. 77–78.

How to Prepare Your Personal Income Tax Return. Englewood Cliffs, N.J.: Prentice-Hall, annual.

"If the IRS Calls You in for an Audit—." *U.S. News & World Report*, 11 April 1977, pp. 96–98.

"If You Decide to Take on the U.S. Tax Collector—." *U.S. News & World Report*, 11 July 1977, pp. 72–74.

Josephus, Stuart R. *Tax Planning Techniques for Individuals.* New York: American Institute of CPA's, 1971.

"Need Help with Your Tax Return?" *Changing Times*, February 1977, pp. 7–10.

"Practical Answers to Your Tax Problems." *Changing Times*, January 1977, pp. 31–32.

Ross, Irwin. "The Tax Practitioner's Act of 1976." *Fortune*, April 1977, pp. 103–108 ff.

Seixas, Suzanne. "25 Taxing Questions That Sometimes Stump the IRS." *Money*, January 1977, pp. 66–72.

Sider, Don. "How to Survive a Tax Audit." *Money*, February 1976, pp. 37–40.

"The Tax Reform Act of 1976—Law and Explanation." Chicago: Commerce Clearing House, 1977.

"Tips on How to Cut Your Income Tax." *U.S. News & World Report*, 28 February 1977, pp. 47–50.

"We *Still* Need Better Income Tax Laws." *Changing Times*, May 1977, pp. 25–28.

"When IRS Gets Your Tax Return." *U.S. News & World Report*, 28 March 1977, pp. 78–80.

Part 2

Managing Your
Financial Assets

Personal Balance Sheet	
Assets	Liabilities and Net Worth
Financial Assets	Liabilities
Nonfinancial Assets	Net Worth

Financial assets may include cash, savings instruments, investment company shares, commodities, and options. The subject of this part is their characteristics, the types of transactions involving them, returns they may be expected to yield, and their appropriate utilization for the attainment of financial goals. Chapter 5 discusses the various types of cash and savings instruments in which funds may be placed: checking accounts, savings accounts, and others. Chapter 6 presents the characteristics and fundamentals of making stock and bond investments. In Chapter 7, the topics are the mechanisms and procedures available for making transactions in the securities markets, sources of investment information, and various types of investment strategies. And Chapter 8 is concerned with the different types and characteristics of investment companies and investment programs, including mutual funds, commodity trading, and trading in options.

5
Cash and Savings Instruments

In order to provide an understanding of the purposes of cash and savings balances and the methods for maintaining them, this chapter examines the following:

A Preview of Chapter 5

1. The considerations involved in selecting institutions and instruments to hold cash balances.

2. The reasons for maintaining cash balances and the basic forms in which they can be held.

3. The procedures for opening, maintaining, and periodically reconciling a checking account.

4. Various types of checks and bank conveniences for meeting special payment or withdrawal requirements.

5. The different types of savings accounts and the techniques used to calculate interest paid on them.

6. The similarities and differences in services offered by the most popular savings institutions in our economy.

7. Alternative savings instruments—in particular, U.S. Savings Bonds and certificates of deposit.

Cash and savings balances are two of the most important financial assets you have. They are the primary resources available to you for meeting both planned and unexpected expenditures. For any given period of time in your adult life, you will need to find answers to questions such as:

131

"How much cash do I need?" "How much cash should be placed in savings?" "Where should I keep my cash balances?" The effective management and control of cash and savings will make it easier for you to attain your financial goals.

There are a number of ways to hold cash. At the most basic level, cash can be carried by an individual in a pocket, billfold, or purse. Some people may keep their cash under a mattress, in a cigar box, or in a dresser drawer. But these spots, though directly under the individual's control, are far less secure than any of the vast array of financial institutions that have been established to safeguard cash: banks, savings and loans, and credit unions, to mention a few. On the other hand, there is still some minimal level of pocket money necessary for smooth functioning in today's economy. Parking meters, admissions to theaters and sports events, bus and taxi fares, and various other items often require ready cash. People who retain cash in excess of such requirements subject themselves needlessly to the risk of loss due to theft or some calamity such as fire.

Cash may be used for either of two basic purposes: *consumption* or *savings*. Cash held for consumption is used to acquire and pay for those items needed in the current period, while savings represent a storehouse of consumption that may be maintained for any of a number of possible reasons. Whether it is held for consumption or savings, excess cash—above and beyond the amount needed for pocket money—should be placed in a financial institution that will safeguard it and, in many cases, provide some type of return on it. Although there are sometimes charges for the services extended by these institutions, the benefits provided generally outweigh the costs.

Cash Balances

Any form of funds that already is or can readily be converted into cash with a minimum of expense and administrative effort is a cash balance. As such, a cash balance is a *liquid balance*. The basic types of cash balances are pocket money, demand deposits, and savings deposits.

Pocket Money

As indicated in the introduction to this chapter, the term *pocket money* is used to refer to all currency and coin physically under the control of an individual or family. This includes cash on the person or in the home and excludes cash held by a second party (such as a commercial bank or savings and loan) on behalf of the individual or family. Although people have been known to hoard cash due to their lack of confidence in financial institutions, the only valid justification for maintaining a cash balance in the form of pocket money is its convenience in making small planned and/or unexpected expenditures. Pocket money should be kept to a minimum, since the risk of its loss, theft, or destruction always exists.

Demand Deposits

Checking accounts held at commercial banks are demand deposits. The law currently permits only commercial banks to hold checking accounts. The term *demand deposit* indicates the fact that the withdrawal of these funds must be permitted whenever demanded by the account holder: the bank, when presented with a valid check, must immediately pay the amount indicated. Money held in checking accounts is therefore liquid and can easily be used to pay bills and make purchases. Checking accounts are important in our economy; statistics of the *Federal Reserve System,* which is the official organization governing our nation's banking system, indicate that over 30 billion checks are written each year and that demand deposits are the largest component of the money supply.

Because checks are generally accepted in payment of bills and taxes and in the purchase of goods and services, demand deposit balances are a common and important type of cash balance. One of the primary advantages of demand deposits is that in almost all banks they (and any other deposit accounts in the bank) are insured for up to a total of $40,000 per account holder by the Federal Deposit Insurance Corporation, which is an agency of the Federal Reserve System. Another advantage is that the use of checks to pay bills provides a convenient type of record-keeping system for use as proof of payment and in calculating income taxes at the end of the year. In short, the widespread use of demand deposits can be attributed to the safety and relative convenience of checks in paying bills and other obligations. And demand deposits may become even more numerous if the law is changed to permit banks to pay interest on them—which may occur in the near future.

Savings Deposits

The third type of cash balance, savings deposits, may be kept in commercial banks, savings and loan associations, credit unions, and other institutions. Interest is paid on them. Commercial bank savings deposits are referred to as *time deposits* since they are expected to remain untapped for a longer period of time than do demand deposits. Since interest income is received on savings deposits but not on demand deposits, savings accounts are preferable to demand deposits when the depositor's purpose is to accumulate money for a future expenditure or to hold money to cover unexpected expenditures.

While financial institutions generally retain the right to require a savings account holder to wait a certain number of days before receiving payment of a withdrawal, most are willing to pay withdrawals immediately. The institutions that hold savings deposits insure them up to a specified maximum amount per account holder through various insuring agencies. Of course, in addition to withdrawal policies and insurance, the rate and method of calculating interest paid on savings accounts are important considerations in choosing the financial institutions in which savings are to be placed.

Why Maintain Cash Balances?

The individual reasons for holding cash balances largely affect the form in which they are maintained. The three basic motives are: (1) convenience, (2) planned expenditures, and (3) unexpected expenditures.

Convenience Cash is a readily acceptable form of payment in our country; its availability makes the purchase-sale transaction quite simple. For this reason, most people maintain some type of cash balance. In fact, since all people must make economic transactions in order to survive, convenience is probably the primary motive for maintaining some form of cash balance.

Planned Expenditures Every consumer must make certain planned expenditures. These may be large or small and may or may not be covered by 100 percent cash. Especially in the case of more expensive items, a portion of the purchase price is usually paid for with borrowed funds—a topic discussed at greater length in Part 4. Cash needed for current expenditures, for example, clothing and food, may be drawn from current income, while cash for major purchases of such items as appliances may be obtained from savings. Planning the availability of cash goes hand-in-hand with planning the expenditure of cash. The financial planning and budgeting process discussed in Chapter 3 presented procedures that can be used to provide the cash needed to make planned expenditures.

Unexpected Expenditures The third basic motive for maintaining cash balances is a precautionary one. Many people set aside cash in order to provide a cushion for meeting unexpected expenditures, such as automobile repairs, medical bills, and household repairs, or for taking advantage of unexpected opportunities, such as a sale or bargain price on a planned purchase. The presence of excess balances allows people to make these unexpected expenditures without lowering their standard of living. Maintenance of cash balances for this purpose thus allows individuals to achieve their financial goals without risking damaging financial setbacks.

Most adults in the U.S. have at least one checking account at a commercial bank; many people open their first checking account upon graduation from high school. Checking account balances represent an important component of our money supply, and they streamline the purchase-sale process. The following six sections describe methods for opening a checking account, checking account procedures, monthly statements, the negotiable order of withdrawal (NOW)—another type of checking account—special types of checks, and other related conveniences.

Checking Accounts

Opening a Checking Account

Choosing a Bank Factors that may influence your choice of the bank where you will maintain a checking account are: convenience, cost, and services provided. Many people choose a bank solely on the basis of convenience factors such as business hours, location, number of drive-in windows, and number of branches. In some states (for example, California and Ohio) branches of a bank can be spread throughout a community, while in other states (for example, Illinois and Oklahoma) branch banks are prohibited. Ease of access is obviously an important consideration: most people prefer to bank near their home or place of employment.

In some areas checking accounts are free, which means that a service charge is not levied. Some banks even provide personalized checks to customers at no cost. At the other extreme are banks that charge a basic monthly fee—eight to ten cents per check written—in addition to their charge for printing checks. The cost of banking services should be estimated based on the average number of checks to be written per month.

Services provided differ from bank to bank. Depending on their size, banks may rent safe deposit boxes, pay utility bills for their depositors out of their accounts, make loans, provide financial counseling, and offer various types of bank cards and check-cashing services. Although proximity to home or work is generally the basis for bank choice, consideration of all these convenience, cost, and service factors is advised.

Signature Card Once you have selected a bank, the checking account must be opened. To do this you generally fill in your name, address, phone number, and signature—and sometimes your place of employment and occupation—on a *signature card*. The signature on this card will be compared to the signature on checks drawn on your account in order to check their validity. A sample signature card filled out by James C. and Mary Morrison is shown in Figure 5-1.

Figure 5-1 **Signature Card for the Morrison's Account**

MERCANTILE BANK AND TRUST COMPANY, Tulsa, Oklahoma
PERSONAL CHECKING ACCOUNT AGREEMENT
AUTHORIZED SIGNATURES   Acct. No. 1-234-567-8

1. *James C. Morrison*   3. _____

2. *Mary Morrison*   4. _____

TWO COMPLETE CARDS REQUIRED........ PLEASE SIGN IN INK

Acct. Name _____ James C. and Mary Morrison _____ Date Opened April 10, 1978

Phone _____ 987-654-3210

☐ INDIVIDUAL   ☒ JOINT, PAYABLE TO EITHER OR SURVIVOR
                                      ☐ JOINT, BOTH SIGNATURES REQUIRED

DEPOSITOR(S) AGREE TO THE TERMS OF THE DEPOSITORY AGREEMENT
ON THE REVERSE SIDE HEREOF

NA. 13-C-3

Source: Courtesy of Mercantile Bank and Trust Company, Tulsa, Oklahoma.

After the signature card has been filled out, a number is assigned to your account. The signature card is filed according to this account number. The account number appears on the card and is also printed in a special ink on the checks and deposit slips you receive. (Your checks and deposit slips will have other numbers along with your account number. These are called "routing symbols," and they play an important part in the check-clearing process.) In order to activate your new account, a deposit must be made. The bank may require a minimum deposit to open a new account.

Joint or Single Account Two people who wish to open a checking account may decide to have a joint account. In this case, both individuals must sign the signature card. Either of them can then sign checks written on the account. The Morrisons' signature card shown in Figure 5-1 indicates that their account is jointly held. One advantage of the joint account over two single accounts is that it lowers the cost of any service charges the bank may make. More important, however, is the fact that if one of the partners dies, the title to the account passes to the surviving partner. In the case of a married couple, this means that if one spouse dies, the surviving spouse, after fulfilling a certain legal time requirement, can draw checks on the account. If the deceased partner had a single account, the surviving partner could not take possession of it until the estate of the deceased partner had been probated, which often takes years.

Accounts jointly held do have disadvantages: It is difficult to keep accurate balances when each partner is writing checks against the account, and it is possible for one partner to drain the account and take off with the money. To overcome the difficulty in keeping records of balances, partners in a joint account can share a single checkbook or use two checkbooks, dividing the account balance between them. Careful selection of partners or—in cases where partners lack confidence in each other—requiring both signatures on checks drawn on the account makes it unlikely that one partner will abscond with the entire amount in the account.

One Reason for Opening a Swiss Bank Account

Opening a Swiss bank account is a good hedge against inflation, one expert says.

"Inflation has become a way of life for our federal government," says James Kelder, author of "How to Open a Swiss Bank Account" (Thomas Y. Crowell Co., New York, $9.95).

"That means the dollar has become a soft currency. It will continue to lose value compared to a hard currency like the Swiss franc."

Here is Mr. Kelder's case for putting your savings in hard (meaning shrink-resistant) money such as Switzerland's.

In late 1970, the dollar was worth 4.31 Swiss francs. So a $1,000 deposit in a Swiss bank would have given you a balance of 4,310 Swiss francs.

Since then, the dollar has diminished in value.

On Sept. 1, 1976, the dollar was worth only 2.47 Swiss francs. So the 4,310 francs in the Swiss bank was worth $1,744.93.

In addition, the account would have earned at least 3.5 percent interest, compounded annually. That would have added another 438.1 francs, or $177.36.

The total: $1,922.29.

The same $1,000 deposited in an American bank would still be worth $1,000 plus interest.

Swiss bankers welcome small accounts as well as large ones.

"Many of Switzerland's most respected banks will open an account for $100 or less," Mr. Kelder says.

Of course, there are drawbacks, such as these:

• Swiss banks pay interest on only the first 50,000 francs in a non-Swiss account.

• Nonresidents are allowed only one interest-earning account.

• The Swiss government collects a 30 percent withholding tax on all interest income. Americans, however, can get five sixths of the tax refunded.

And then, there is no Federal Deposit Insurance Corp. insurance of Swiss accounts.

Source: Reprinted by permission from "One Reason for Opening a Swiss Bank Account," *Nation's Business,* November 1976, p. 8. Copyright 1976 by Nation's Business, Chamber of Commerce of the U.S.

"Henry! Have you been writing checks
on my joint account?"

Joint Checking Account Partners Must Cooperate

Source: Changing Times, June 1970, p. 46. Reprinted with permission from *Changing Times* Magazine, © Kiplinger Washington Editors, Inc., 1970.

Checking Account Procedures

Writing Checks When you write a check, you fill in on the appropriate lines the name of the person to whom it is made out, the amount, and the date. The amount of the check is both printed in numerals and written in script in order to assure accuracy; if these amounts do not agree, the written amount is considered legally correct. It is important to sign the check the same way you signed the signature card; otherwise, it may not be accepted by your bank. It is also a good idea to write somewhere on the check the name of the item or service for which the check is payment. For example, in the personal check written by Mary Morrison shown in

Figure 5-2, Mary has noted that the $25.17 made out to Gulf Oil Company is payment due on her Gulf credit card (see lower left-hand corner). This information can be used for both budgeting and tax purposes at some future date.

Whenever a check is written or a deposit made, a corresponding entry must be made in the *checkbook ledger*, which is provided with the checkbook for maintaining accurate records of all transactions in the account. By subtracting the amount of each check written and adding the amount of each deposit made to the previous balance, the account balance can be kept up-to-date. (See the portion of the Morrisons' checkbook ledger shown in Figure 5-2.) Good records of transactions and an accurate balance figure help avoid overdrawing the account.

The Check-Clearing Process Clearing a check involves a series of bookkeeping entries on the part of the banks involved. Today's computer sophistication has greatly simplified and speeded up this process. One of the keys to the clearing process is the use of *Magnetic Ink Character Recognition (MICR)*. Checks and deposit slips are encoded with numbers referring to the routing of the check, a bank identification number, and the account number, all of which are read by a machine. The machine, which is linked to a computer, both sorts the checks and transmits the appropriate information to the account records. The MICR encoding and routing symbols appear in the lower left portion of a check. See them, for example, on the Morrisons' check in Figure 5-2 (1039 0106). The routing symbols are also shown on the right-hand side of both checks and deposit slips. In the case of the Morrisons' check and deposit slip in Figure 5-2, these symbols are given as

$$\frac{86-106}{1039}$$

In order to further simplify the routing of checks and deposits, the account number is MICR-encoded at the bottom of each check and deposit slip. The Morrisons' account number (1 234 567 8), encoded in MICR symbols, appears on their check and deposit slip in Figure 5-2.

Once the information has been transmitted, a series of bookkeeping entries takes place. First, the amount of the check is deducted from the balance. If there are service charges, they are accumulated and deducted at the end of the month. Second, the amount of the check is transferred to the account in which it is deposited. The check may be deposited within the same bank, or it may be deposited in a different bank. Regardless, the funds are transferred via certain bookkeeping entries to the appropriate recipient.

Even with MICR, it often takes three or four days for a check to clear.

Figure 5-2 **Basic Checking Account Transactions**

James C. Morrison
Mary Morrison
1765 SHERIDAN DRIVE
TULSA, OKLA. 74145
SAMPLE VOID   180

86-106
1039

July 22 19 78

PAY TO THE ORDER OF _Gulf Oil Company_ $25.17

Twenty-five & 17/100 ———————— DOLLARS

M Mercantile Bank
and Trust Company Tulsa, Okla.

MEMO _Gulf Credit Card_   Mary Morrison

⊕ 1:1039 0106: 1 234 567 8

DELUXE CHECK PRINTERS—DC

CHECK NO.	DATE	CHECKS ISSUED TO OR DESCRIPTION OF DEPOSIT	(−) AMOUNT OF CHECK	√ T	(−) CHECK FEE (IF ANY)	(+) AMOUNT OF DEPOSIT	BALANCE
		PLEASE BE SURE TO **DEDUCT** ANY PER CHECK CHARGES OR SERVICE CHARGES THAT MAY APPLY TO YOUR ACCOUNT					$276 40
178	7/8	Safeway	53 86				222 54
179	7/11	Cash	35 00				187 54
180	7/22	Gulf Oil Company	25 17				162 37
181	7/23	First Tool Service	6 00				156 37
—	7/24	Deposit				436 15	592 52
182	7/26	First Mortgage Co.	297 60				294 92

CHECKING ACCOUNT DEPOSIT TICKET

James C. Morrison
Mary Morrison
1765 SHERIDAN DRIVE
TULSA, OKLA. 74145
SAMPLE VOID

DATE _July 24_ 19 78

_____

M Mercantile Bank
and Trust Company Tulsa, Okla.

CASH	CURRENCY	32	00
	COIN		
CHECKS	105 763	350	00
	288	54	15
TOTAL FROM OTHER SIDE			
TOTAL		436	15
LESS CASH RECEIVED			
NET DEPOSIT		436	15

86-106
1039

USE OTHER SIDE FOR ADDITIONAL LISTING

BE SURE EACH ITEM IS PROPERLY ENDORSED

1 234 567 8

DELUXE DCD-3 CHECKS AND OTHER ITEMS ARE RECEIVED FOR DEPOSIT SUBJECT TO THE TERMS AND CONDITIONS OF THIS BANK'S COLLECTION AGREEMENT

Source: Courtesy of Mercantile Bank and Trust Company, Tulsa, Oklahoma.

Typically, when the bank that is drawn on is in the same city as the bank that receives the deposit, the check will clear within one day. Checks drawn on banks geographically distant from those in which the depositor's checking account is held often take as long as a week to clear. Care should therefore be taken in writing checks against recent deposits to an account, since the funds deposited may not be available. When this occurs, the check "bounces" due to insufficient funds. On the other hand, people sometimes knowingly write checks against nonexistent balances, recognizing that the delay in the check-clearing process makes it possible for them to deposit funds to cover the check a few days later. This strategy of "playing the float" is a form of fraud and is against the law.

Making Deposits Deposit slips are normally included within your checkbook and are also readily obtained from your bank. Filling out a deposit slip on which the components of your deposit are itemized is the first step in making a deposit. Normally, separate entries for currency, coin, and checks are included. Each check to be deposited is listed separately on the slip. (See the sample deposit slip prepared by the Morrisons in Figure 5-2.) The second step is endorsing all of the checks to be deposited. To protect against possible loss of these endorsed checks, it is common practice to precede your endorsement with the words "For deposit only" or "Pay to the order of XYZ Bank." Your endorsement should duplicate your name as spelled by the remitter on the front of the check. If the way your name is written on the check differs from the way you signed the signature card, you should sign your correct signature below your endorsement. In order to further assure that the deposit is properly entered into your account, it is a good idea to write your account number below your endorsement(s).

Your deposit can be submitted to your bank in a number of possible ways: at the bank during normal banking hours; at a remote banking facility, such as a drive-in window; in the bank's *night depository*, a protected type of mail slot on the exterior of the bank, in the special envelopes banks usually provide for after-hours deposits; and by mail, in the self-addressed, stamped deposit envelopes most banks provide for this purpose. Some employers offer employees the opportunity to have their payroll checks deposited directly to their accounts. In any case, you should obtain a receipt for your deposit and enter the amount of the deposit into your checkbook ledger.

The use of night depositories and banking by mail is not advised if cash is to be deposited since the opportunity for an unaccountable loss exists; the loss of checks can normally be proven. Of course, when checks are deposited, a delay in the availability of the funds may result due to the time required for the check to clear. This delay is increased when deposits are mailed, since it may take an additional two to three days for them to reach the bank. Similarly, receipts from the bank verifying the deposits will require a few more days to arrive through the mail. It is thus advisable to consider any time factors involved in the required availability of funds when selecting a method for making a deposit.

Overdrafts When a check is written for an amount greater than the current account balance, the result is an overdraft. Poor bookkeeping on the part of the account holder or a delay in the bank's receipt of a deposit can be the cause. Of course, if the overdraft is proven to have been intentional, the bank could initiate legal proceedings against the account holder. The action taken by a bank on an overdraft depends on the amount involved and the strength of the relationship between the bank and the account holder. In many cases, the bank stamps the overdrawn check with the words "insufficient funds" and returns it to the person to whom it was written. The account holder is notified of this action, and a penalty fee of three to five dollars is deducted from the checking account. (See, for example, the notice of insufficient funds received by the Morrisons shown in Figure 5-3.) When the bank uses this procedure, the

Figure 5-3 **A Notice of Insufficient Funds**

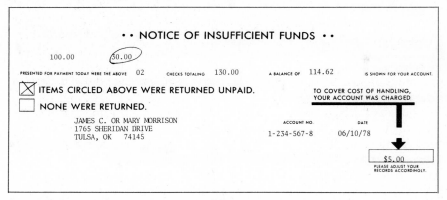

Source: Courtesy of Mercantile Bank and Trust Company, Tulsa, Oklahoma.

person to whom the check was written recognizes that the check has bounced. Many vendors require an individual whose check bounces to pay a service charge of three to ten dollars in addition to the original amount for which the check was written. They also usually refuse to accept checks drawn on that account thereafter.

In instances where a strong banking relationship has been established between the account holder and the bank, the account holder is a major customer of the bank, or arrangements have been made for overdraft privileges, the bank will go ahead and pay a check that overdraws the account. Account holders with overdraft privileges are usually not notified of overdrafts; the bank merely provides them with a temporary loan to cover the amount overdrawn. These types of arrangements are given various names, such as "checking plus" or "personal line of credit." In cases where overdraft privileges are not prearranged but the bank pays the check, the account holder is usually notified by the bank and charged a penalty fee for the inconvenience. Of course, the check does not bounce, and the remitter's credit-worthiness is not damaged. It is best to make sure that all checks you write are covered by the balance in your account, thereby avoiding the possible embarrassment associated with overdrafts.

Stopping Payment Occasionally it is necessary to *stop payment* on a check which has been issued. This may be due to any of a number of possible reasons, for example: (1) checks or a checkbook are lost or stolen, (2) a service or merchandise paid for by check is found to be faulty, or (3) a check is issued as part of a contract which is not carried out. Payment on a check is stopped by notifying the bank. Normally, the account holder must fill out a form describing the check by number and date, amount, and the name of the person to whom it was written. Sometimes stop payment orders can be initiated over the telephone, in which case a written follow-up is normally required.

Once a stop payment order has been issued, the tellers in the bank are told not to pay on the given check. At the same time, the stop payment information is placed in the computer in order to reject the check if it is presented by another bank in the check-clearing process. Most banks require account holders who wish to stop payment on a check to sign a statement relieving the bank of any liability if, by error, payment is made on the check in question. A fee ranging from two to five dollars is also usually charged for stopping payment on a check. Note, too, that payment can be stopped only on regular checks drawn on a demand deposit account; certified and cashier's checks cannot be stopped.

Monthly Statements

Once each month your bank will send you your bank statement, which will contain canceled checks and deposit slips along with an itemized statement of transactions within your account. (See the Morrisons' August 1978 bank statement shown in Figure 5-4.) In some parts of the country, banks do not return the deposit slips with the statement. Bank statements are most often rendered toward the end of each month, although in large banks they may be sent out on a staggered basis so that

The Slowest Cash Drawer in the West

Some customers, as well as all banks, have strong reasons for welcoming changes in check-cashing practices. Novelist E. M. Nathanson (*The Dirty Dozen*) recently found himself in the middle of one kind of minor crisis that couldn't happen in an age of electronic banking. His report:

The check arrived at my post office box in South Laguna, Calif. on a Saturday—a bad beginning, for there is nothing that can be done with a check on Saturday except admire it. Drawn on the Chase Manhattan Bank account of my literary agent in New York, it was for several thousands of dollars more than I'd seen in a long while. I lusted after that check, as did a long list of creditors. I spent the next day paying bills and sent some out in the mail.

Monday morning I was at the American State Bank in Newport Beach a few minutes after nine. This admirable institution is not your average prison-like fortress. You enter a magnificently designed and handsomely furnished rotunda. Graceful gestures from charming female tellers invite you to superbly comfortable chairs around an immense low circular desk. When I presented my check for deposit, however, my Thurberish reverie was shattered. "It will take two weeks to clear," said the teller.

"But I must have it cleared immediately," I protested. "The check is good . . . The money is there . . . This is an old and respected firm in American letters. There are checks out against it . . . coming in . . . maybe today . . ." If the bank didn't act quickly, there would be nothing to stop those checks from bouncing— not even an overdraft checking account, which I had shunned because I wanted no further access to easy and expensive debt.

The check and I were conveyed to Gerald R. Martin, assistant vice president and cashier. "A minimum of ten working days is the ordinary procedure," he confirmed. The check had two strikes against it: it was large and it was "out of state," a somewhat derogatory appellation implying that California and New York are not part of the same political union and federal banking system.

"Can't it be cleared by wire?" I urged. "Or telephone?" Surely, two bankers talking to each other—one at Chase Manhattan, one at American State—could work out a fast transfer. Martin was dubious. In his 27 years of banking experience nothing like that had ever worked. "Why don't you just put it in for collection?" he asked calmly.

"I can't wait two weeks!"

Catching my gist, he suggested a plan: "We can airmail the check to Chase Manhattan and instruct them to transfer the money to our bank's own account at First National City Bank and wire us the confirmation. We ought to have it by Thursday at the latest." That afternoon, Martin airmailed my check to Chase Manhattan.

In the next few days, I asked executives of Wells Fargo, Laguna Federal, United California Bank and Bank of America how long it might take to clear a check like mine through their institutions. The longest estimate was three weeks; the shortest, four or five days. There was no way to clear a check by telephone, all agreed.

I called Martin on Wednesday. "Nothing," he said. Thursday and Friday: "Nothing." On Friday I telephoned Chase Manhattan and was told they had sent the wire two days earlier. Martin searched his bank and telephoned Western Union, but no such wire was found. He then phoned First National City Bank: no record of such a deposit, he was told. He telephoned Chase Manhattan. A man there said the money had been transferred and the wire of confirmation had been sent even though Citibank claimed never to have heard of American State Bank. "I can't believe it," Martin said to me. "We're correspondent banks. They send us a statement every month."

Twilight zone. With a sigh, Martin capitulated. "We'll let you have some of your money," he said. "Lord knows exactly where it is, but I know it's there, you know it's there and they know it's there. We're not worried."

Only then did Martin reveal to me that I was not alone in this type of misadventure. He had a store of horror tales: people evicted from apartments, stranded at airports and hotels, losing large sums in business deals, all because the procedures to transfer funds rapidly are inadequate. Apparently, it seldom occurs to banks—or to their customers—that for a few dollars' interest a bank can easily extend enough short-term credit to cover incoming checks until deposits clear. As a relatively new customer, I didn't even consider asking for a loan.

The following Monday, Chase Manhattan's telegram finally arrived. Investigation uncovered its unfortunate history. It had arrived in Santa Ana on Wednesday and was relayed the same day to the Western Union agency closest to the bank, in Costa Mesa. The next day it was placed in an envelope and mailed—mailed!—to American State Bank.

Three Saturdays after I received the check from my New York agent came this from my Newport Beach bank:

Mr. Nathanson—

A note to tell you we got our money today! Chase Manhattan never sent the money to First National City Bank. They mailed us a cashier's check.

Words for this transaction fail me.

Maybe you could make some money on a short story about "Banks."

(signed) Martin

Source: "The Slowest Cash Drawer in the West," reprinted from the February 1976 issue of MONEY Magazine by special permission; © 1976, Time Inc.

Figure 5-4 **The Morrisons' August 1978 Statement**

STATEMENT OF CHECKING ACCOUNT

POST OFFICE BOX 45448
TULSA, OKLAHOMA 74145
PHONE 918/628-1200

MAIN BANK: 42nd at SO. DARLINGTON
DRIVE-IN: 42nd at SO. FULTON
MEMBER F.D.I.C.

Mercantile Bank
and Trust Company

JAMES C. OR MARY MORRISON
1765 SHERIDAN DRIVE
TULSA, OK 74145

1-234-567-8

ON	YOUR BALANCE WAS	NO.	WE SUBTRACTED CHECKS TOTALING	LESS ACTIVITY CHARGE	NO.	WE ADDED DEPOSITS OF	MAKING YOUR PRESENT BALANCE
JULY 31 78	15.10	19	602.95	2.85	4	681.75	91.05

DATE	CHECKS			DEPOSITS	BALANCE
AUG 2 78					15.10
AUG 3 78				225.00	240.10
AUG 3 78	25.17				214.93
AUG 4 78	14.75	15.50		200.00	384.68
AUG 7 78	50.00				334.68
AUG 9 78				6.75	341.43
AUG 10 78	10.00	16.80			314.63
AUG 11 78	21.37				293.26
AUG 18 78	4.18	8.00			281.08
AUG 19 78	7.27	30.00	45.80		198.01
AUG 23 78	3.50	12.44	24.83		157.24
AUG 23 78	25.00				132.24
AUG 25 78	132.00				.24
AUG 30 78	149.07			250.00	101.17
AUG 30 78	7.27	2.85			91.05

SEE REVERSE SIDE

Source: Courtesy of Mercantile Bank and Trust Company, Tulsa, Oklahoma.

some people receive them earlier in the month. You can use the monthly statement to verify the accuracy of your account records and to reconcile differences between the statement balance and the balance shown in your checkbook ledger. The monthly statement is also an important source of information for your tax records.

Account Reconciliation It is advisable to reconcile your bank account as soon as possible after receipt of your monthly statement. The reconciliation process can uncover errors in recording checks or deposits, in addition or subtraction, and occasionally in the bank's processing of the checks. It also helps you avoid overdrafts by periodically forcing you to verify your account balance. Any differences in your account balance as reflected in your checkbook ledger and the bank statement can be attributed to three basic factors, assuming neither you nor the bank has made any errors: (1) Certain checks which you have written and deducted from your checkbook balance have not yet been received by your bank and therefore remain outstanding. (2) Certain deposits you have made and added to your checkbook balance have not yet been credited to your account by the bank. (3) Certain service (activity) charges levied on your account by the bank have not yet been deducted from your checkbook balance.

The following steps facilitate the reconciliation of your account:

1. Upon receipt of your bank statement, arrange all canceled checks in ascending order based on their sequence numbers or issuance dates.

2. Compare each check to the entry recorded for it in your checkbook ledger to make sure no recording errors exist. Place a mark in your checkbook ledger alongside each entry compared.

3. List the checks outstanding—those deducted in your checkbook but not returned with your bank statement (those not checked off in step 2). Total their amount.

4. Compare the deposit slips returned with the statement to deposits shown in your checkbook. Total the amount of outstanding deposits—those shown in your checkbook ledger but not yet received by the bank—as indicated on your statement and by the deposit slips returned with it.

5. Deduct the amount of any service charges levied by the bank from your checkbook ledger balance.

6. Subtract the total amount of checks outstanding (from step 3) from your bank statement balance, and add to this balance the amount of outstanding deposits (from step 4). The resulting value should be the same as your checkbook balance. If it is not, you should check all addition and subtraction in your checkbook ledger. You have probably made an error.

Often the reverse side of your bank statement will provide a form for reconciling your account along with a step-by-step description of how to use it. Although a number of different approaches to reconciliation exist, the one described above is the most straightforward.

The reconciliation of the Morrisons' account for August 1978 appears in Table 5-1. The month end account balance reflected in their bank statement (Figure 5-4) was $91.05. Their checkbook ledger balance was $310.47. The bank statement showed $2.85 in service charges for the month. After going through the canceled checks, the Morrisons found checks outstanding for a total of $476.59. An evaluation of the deposits received by the bank revealed that a total amount of $693.16 was still in transit at the statement date. Since the actual checkbook balance after adjustment for service charges was equal to the calculated checkbook balance, the Morrisons' checking account appeared to be in good order. If the account had not reconciled correctly, the accuracy of entries and calculations in the checkbook ledger would have had to be checked.

Table 5-1 Reconciliation of the Morrisons' Checking Account (August 1978)

Checkbook Balance	$310.47
Less: Service Charges	(2.85)
New Checkbook Balance	$307.62
Bank Statement Balance	$ 91.05
Less: Outstanding Checks	(476.59)
Plus: Deposits in Transit	693.16
Checkbook Balance	$307.62

Tax Records The canceled checks returned with your monthly bank statement are an excellent source of tax information. They can be reviewed along with deposit slips in order to evaluate past expenditures and income. Although you may maintain accurate records of these items as part of your budgeting process, the canceled checks provide proof of payment, which you might need if the Internal Revenue Service should decide to audit your tax return. Thus it is advisable to indicate on the front of your checks at the time of writing them the name of the item(s) or service(s) which they are used to purchase. It is also important to retain your bank statements, including canceled checks, for a period of five years, since an audit can still be conducted several years after a return is submitted.

The NOW Account

Although the commercial bank is the only institution currently permitted to maintain checking accounts, or demand deposits, certain savings institutions have lobbied heavily for this privilege, though so far with little success. The establishment of *negotiable order of withdrawal* (NOW) accounts in several states is, however, the first step in this direction. The NOW account is similar to a checking account except that it often requires advance notice of withdrawal. Federal law currently prohibits payment of interest on such accounts in most parts of the country, but where interest payments are permitted—for example, in Massachusetts and New Hampshire—they are paid at the same rates as on savings accounts. Thus, the NOW account in those two states may be viewed either as an interest-paying checking account or as a savings account against which checks can be issued. There are no service charges on the negotiable orders of withdrawal made on NOW accounts. Although the fate of the NOW account is still uncertain, it does represent an attractive alternative to the demand deposit account. Since the number of these accounts is currently quite limited, they are not discussed further in this text.

Special Types of Checks

Because there is no way to be absolutely sure that checks are good, it is often necessary to somehow verify them for a seller. This is quite common in the case of large purchases or when the buyer's bank or the buyer is not in the area where the purchase is made. The most common instruments used to guarantee payment in such situations are certified checks, cashier's checks, and traveler's checks.

Certified Check To certify a check, you make it out to whomever is to be paid and take it to your commercial bank. The bank will immediately deduct the amount of the check from your account and then stamp the check to indicate its certification. There is normally a small charge for this service. In effect, the bank has guaranteed that the check is good. And since the bank has become the guarantor, it normally will not return the canceled check to you, but rather will keep the check for its own records.

Cashier's Check Anyone can buy a cashier's check from a commercial bank. These checks are most often used by people who do not have checking accounts. They can be purchased for fifty cents to a dollar and are sometimes issued at no charge to bank customers. In exchange for an appropriate amount of money—the amount of the check plus a service charge—the bank issues a check drawn on itself.

Traveler's Checks A number of the larger financial institutions—such as First National City Bank, American Express Company, and Bank of America—issue traveler's checks, which can be purchased at any commercial bank in denominations ranging from $10 to $1,000. A fee of 1 percent is charged on their purchase. If properly endorsed, traveler's checks are accepted by most businesses in the U.S. and can be exchanged for local currencies in most parts of the world. Since these checks are not valid unless properly countersigned by the purchaser and since they are insured against loss or theft by the issuing agency, they provide a safe, convenient, and popular form of money with which to travel.

Special Bank Conveniences

Not only do banks provide the services described above, but they also offer a number of other conveniences: safe deposit boxes, drive-in and walk-up windows, automated tellers, and electronic funds transfer systems.

Safe Deposit Boxes A safe deposit box is a drawer in a bank's vault that can be rented. The annual rental fee depends on the box size; small boxes can be rented for $5 to $10 per year, while large boxes cost hundreds of dollars per year. When you rent a box, you receive a key to it. The bank retains another key. The box can be opened only when both keys are used. This arrangement protects items in the box from theft and makes it a valuable storage place for jewelry, contracts, stock certificates, titles, and other special documents.

Drive-in and Walk-up Windows Both drive-in and walk-up windows handle the basic deposit-withdrawal and check-cashing transactions. Other, more complex transactions, such as the purchase of traveler's or certified checks, are not normally handled at a drive-in or walk-up facility. For the convenience of their customers, banks usually keep their drive-in and walk-up windows open before and after regular banking hours.

Automated Teller Recent advances in computer technology have resulted in the development and use of automated tellers by many of the nation's banks. A type of remote computer terminal at which bank customers can make deposits, withdrawals, and other types of basic transactions, the automated teller is a completely mechanical device and can operate twenty-four hours per day, seven days a week. Banks are beginning to locate these terminals in shopping centers, office buildings, and other places suited to enhance and protect their competitive position. These types of facilities will become more numerous over the next few years.

Electronic Funds Transfer System (EFTS) Another recent development which uses today's computer technology, the electronic funds transfer system (EFTS), attempts to eliminate the need for cash or checks. Each person has a credit card which can be used to make all transactions. Stores have point of sale (POS) terminals similar to cash registers. By inserting the customer's card into the terminal and punching in certain data relating to a specific transaction, the amount of the transaction is transferred via computer from the customer's account to the vendor's account. Although EFTS has been used on a very limited basis, it is expected to become much more common in the next five to ten years. Ultimately, people will need no cash or checks; instead, they will have one credit card with which all transactions can be made. A series of computers will make the necessary bookkeeping entries at the time of the transactions, thereby allowing up-to-date information on all accounts. The bounced check will be a thing of the past.

EFTS: Is It the Answer?

The U.S. banking system is menaced by its own success. In spite of computers handling dull and laborious jobs, clerical costs keep on rising. Statistics show that a medium-sized bank in a large city handles, on an average, 12,500 checks each business day. A very large bank with many branches may process 2 million a day. The entire U.S. banking system handles approximately 130 million a day or about 30 billion checks per year.

As so often in the past, that electronic genius, the computer, has come to the rescue—this time in the form of the electronic funds transfer system, EFTS. In place of pieces of paper (checks and deposit slips), EFTS uses electronic messages. The required information is fed directly into the computer, which then processes the transactions in the accounts of those who pay and those who are paid.

Under this system, the banking institutions will install point of sale (POS) terminals at retail stores. Customers who wish to deposit or withdraw money through these terminals will be able to do so by using an encoded plastic card. In effect, the POS terminal is a branch banking office. It is a convenience for the customers, since they can pay their bills and utility charges all in a day's shopping spree. Many retailers, however, are not interested in EFTS if it is limited to only one financial institution. They wish to be assured of a wide range of choices among different banking institutions and a cost savings greater than the cost of installation and operation of these sophisticated systems.

Certainly, if robberies became obsolete due to the use of EFTS, its social benefit in terms of money and human lives would be inestimable. But what would be the consequences if an error crept into the system? Think about it!

Source: Adapted with permission from "Retailers and EFT: Both Chicken and Egg Have to Come First," *Management Controls,* January-February 1977, pp. 10–13, © Peat, Marwick, Mitchell & Co.

Maintaining Savings Accounts

As indicated earlier in this chapter, savings deposits are an important method of holding cash balances, not only because they earn interest and thus provide some return on available funds, but also because they permit the accumulation of money for planned future expenditures and cover necessary but unexpected expenditures. This part of the chapter describes three important aspects of savings accounts: calculating interest on savings, savings institutions, and insured savings.

Determining Interest on Savings

Interest received on savings is a form of income paid to the saver by the institution in which the savings are placed. Savings institutions will let you know the true or *effective rate of interest* paid on your savings, which differs from the stated or *nominal rate of interest.* The effective rate of interest is the annual rate of interest; it reflects the actual rate at which deposits earn interest. The nominal rate of interest represents the rate that can be applied to deposits without consideration for the time period and/or methods utilized to determine the amount of interest. An understanding of the effects of the compounding period on the effective rate of interest and the methods used to calculate interest on savings provides a rational basis for selecting savings media.

Compounding Period The effective rate of interest you receive on your savings is dependent on the period over which interest is compounded. *Compounding* interest involves paying interest not only on the initial deposit but also on any interest accumulated from period to period. It is the standard method for paying interest on savings accounts. The period of time over which interest is compounded affects the effective rate of interest. For a given nominal rate, the more frequently interest is compounded, the higher the effective rate of interest. Table 5-2 presents

Table 5-2 Interest Earned for Various Compounding Periods Using a 5 Percent Nominal Rate of Interest
($1,000 Initial Deposit)

Year	Compounding Period			
	Annually	Quarterly	Weekly	Continuously
1	$1,050.00	$1,050.94	$1,051.25	$1,051.27
2	1,102.50	1,104.47	1,105.13	1,105.17
3	1,157.63	1,160.74	1,161.76	1,161.83
4	1,215.51	1,219.86	1,221.30	1,221.40
5	1,276.28	1,282.00	1,283.90	1,284.02
Effective Rate	5.000%	5.094%	5.125%	5.127%

the amount that results at the end of five years when $1,000 is compounded at a 5 percent nominal rate of interest annually, quarterly, weekly, and continuously; it clearly demonstrates that the more often interest is compounded, the higher the effective rate of interest. Thus, when interest is compounded continuously, which means every microsecond, the highest effective rate of interest is obtained.

Methods Used to Calculate Interest The actual point in time that a deposit is made affects the amount of interest earned on it. Some savings institutions pay interest for the entire month on all deposits received before the tenth of the month and remaining in the institution through the end of the month. Others pay interest quarterly and require deposits to remain in the account through the quarter in order to receive any interest. There are several basic techniques used by savings institutions to determine what balances are eligible to receive interest for a given compounding period. The four most common are: *FIFO, low balance, LIFO,* and *actual balance.*

FIFO The first-in-first-out (FIFO) technique deducts any withdrawals during the interest period from the earliest amount on deposit for the period. This approach penalizes the saver by removing the longest-lived deposits when withdrawals occur. The result is that the interest paid over the period is lower than under any of the other techniques.

Low Balance Under the low balance arrangement, interest is paid on the lowest balance remaining on deposit throughout the entire interest period. Interest is not paid on deposits made during the period, and withdrawals during the period tend to substantially reduce the interest earned and penalize the saver.

LIFO The last-in-first-out (LIFO) system deducts withdrawals during the period from the most recent deposit made during the period. This provides much better returns than the FIFO or low balance approach, since the interest lost through withdrawals is that on the shortest-lived deposits and is therefore minimized.

Actual Balance Interest is paid on a *daily* basis in the actual balance system, so that each dollar on deposit receives the appropriate amount of interest for each day. For example, a deposit made on the tenth of the month and withdrawn on the twenty-first of the month would earn interest for the ten full days it was on deposit. Deposits do not have to be made by a certain date and remain through the end of the period in order to receive interest; instead, the interest is paid on the actual balance maintained on a day-to-day basis. This approach, which many financial institutions have adopted, maximizes the interest return.

"Could I ask how *often* it's compounded?"

Compounding Frequency Affects the True Rate of Interest
Source: Reprinted by permission of Sidney Harris.

The differences in interest earned under each of these techniques can be demonstrated using the account transactions shown in Table 5-3 for a given quarter (thirteen-week period). Assuming interest is paid on this account at an annual rate of 5 percent and that a deposit must be received on or before the tenth of the first month of the quarter to receive interest for the quarter (except, of course, in the case of the actual balance technique), the total interest earned during the quarter under each of the four techniques described above would be as given in Table 5-4.

Under all but the actual balance plan, the only deposit eligible to receive interest for the quarter is the week 1 deposit of $4,000. Under the FIFO technique, the withdrawal at the beginning of week 5 of $2,000 is deducted from the $4,000 deposit, therefore resulting in only $2,000 on which the quarterly interest is paid. The interest amounts to $25. Under the low balance technique, the lowest balance remaining on deposit

Table 5-3 **Account Transactions during Quarter**

Beginning of Week	Transaction	Amount	Account Balance
Initial Balance	—	—	$ 0
1	Deposit	$4,000	4,000
3	Deposit	3,000	7,000
5	Withdrawal	2,000	5,000
8	Deposit	1,000	6,000
End of Quarter	—	—	6,000

Table 5-4 **Interest Earned under Alternative Computation Techniques for Account Transactions Given in Table 5-3**
(Annual Rate of Interest: 5 Percent)

Technique	Interest Earned during Quarter
FIFO	$25.00
Low Balance	50.00
LIFO	50.00
Actual Balance	70.19

throughout the period, which is $4,000, earns interest for the quarter. The interest earned in this case amounts to $50. Under the LIFO technique the $2,000 withdrawal at the beginning of the fifth week is deducted from the deposit of $3,000 at the beginning of the third week. Since the initial deposit, which is the only deposit eligible to receive interest (i.e., on deposit before tenth of month beginning quarter), is not affected by this withdrawal, the interest is earned on the entire $4,000. The interest earned in this case totals $50.

Using the actual balance technique, interest is paid on a daily basis, without consideration for the dates of deposits and withdrawals. The account balances shown in Table 5-3 are: $4,000 for weeks 1 and 2; $7,000 for weeks 3 and 4; $5,000 for weeks 5, 6, and 7; and $6,000 for weeks 8, 9, 10, 11, 12, and 13. Calculating the interest on these balances using the 5 percent annual rate results in interest for the period of $70.19.

Clearly, from the standpoint of the account holder, the actual balance technique is most desirable, and finding a savings institution which pays interest on the actual balance should not present any great problem. Note, however, that this technique may be referred to as the "payment of daily interest," which should not be confused with "daily compounding of interest." *Payment of daily interest* refers to the fact that interest is paid on the actual balance, while *daily compounding of interest* indicates how the actual rate of interest is paid.

Savings Institutions

A number of types of savings institutions offering a variety of savings plans and services are present in our economy. Limitations of space preclude description of all aspects of these institutions, but some of the important characteristics and services they provide are outlined here. The most common savings institutions are commercial banks, mutual savings banks, savings and loan associations, and credit unions.

Commercial Banks In addition to checking accounts, commercial banks offer their customers a number of types of savings accounts. Most prevalent among these is the *passbook account,* which is a regular savings account on which the annual interest paid is approximately 5 percent. Although legally commercial banks can make depositors wait thirty to sixty days to receive a requested withdrawal, they rarely, if ever, require any waiting period. The passbook account holder may or may not be given a passbook in which all transactions are recorded. Instead of a passbook, some banks issue separate deposit receipts and then at the end of the quarter send each depositor a statement on which all account transactions for the period are itemized. Passbook accounts at commercial banks are quite popular due to the convenience of maintaining both checking and savings accounts at one financial institution.

Commercial banks also offer *special savings accounts.* These accounts, the names of which may vary from bank to bank, offer a slightly higher rate of interest (1/4 to 1/2 percent) than the passbook account but in exchange require the account holder to maintain a specified minimum balance of $200 to $500 for a specified period of time such as a quarter of a year. If the account holder does not maintain the balance as required, the interest is paid on the account as if it were a passbook account.

A third type of savings account offered by the commercial bank is the *club account.* These accounts are established for special purposes, such as saving money for Christmas shopping. Banks set up these types of accounts in order to attract additional deposits from customers. The club account acts as a budgeting device for the customer by requiring specified weekly or monthly deposits, which are aimed at achieving some type of savings goal, for example, $500 for Christmas shopping or a vacation. To assist club members in making sure that scheduled deposits are made, the bank often issues them some type of coupon book. The book contains a series of coupons—one for each required deposit—showing the date and amount of each individual deposit. The rate of interest paid on club accounts is generally below the rate paid on passbook accounts since the bank must perform additional clerical chores to establish and maintain them.

Mutual Savings Banks Mutual savings banks are a special type of savings institution found primarily in the New England area of the United States.

They accept deposits on which interest is paid at a rate slightly above that paid on a similar account in a commercial bank. Depositors in a mutual savings bank are actually the bank's owners; the word *mutual* as used in finance indicates a type of cooperative ownership. The mutual savings bank accepts deposits and, after deducting the expenses of doing business from its earnings, distributes the profits to the owners in the form of dividend payments, which are technically equivalent to interest payments. Although these payments are dividends, they are classified as interest for income tax purposes. This treatment also applies to dividends received from the other types of "mutual" savings institutions to be discussed below. Normally, instead of distributing all profits, only enough to provide depositors with a stated return of, say, 5.25 percent is distributed. Any remaining profits are reinvested in order to provide greater protection for depositors. Like commercial banks, mutual savings banks offer an assortment of savings accounts, but the rate of interest paid by the latter is consistently 1/4 to 3/4 percent above the rate paid by the former.

Savings and Loan Associations Savings and loan associations are considerably more prevalent than the mutual savings bank. The most common type of savings and loan is a mutual association in which the depositors actually own the institution and the returns they receive are called dividends rather than interest. The other type is owned by a group which may or may not include some depositors. Depositors in this case receive interest instead of dividends on their deposits. Regardless of their organizational structure, savings and loans are important since they channel the savings of individuals into mortgage loans for purchasing and improving homes. This role of the savings and loan is discussed in detail in Chapters 9 and 12.

The savings opportunities provided by the savings and loan association do not differ significantly from those provided by commercial banks or mutual savings banks. A variety of passbook, special savings accounts, and club-type accounts is available. The dividends or interest paid on deposits are on a par with the rates paid by mutual savings banks—1/4 to 3/4 percent above that of commercial bank savings accounts. The existence of numerous branch offices in large cities, along with the attractive rates of dividends or interest paid, account for the popularity of savings and loan associations.

Credit Unions The credit union, which is a type of mutual association, draws together the savings of its members. These savings are lent out to members (at quite favorable rates) or invested in certain types of securities. Membership in a credit union is normally limited to a group of people having some common bond, such as the same employer, the same church, or the same community. A person who qualifies for membership in a credit union may join by making a minimum deposit, which may be five dollars or less and which buys a share in the credit union. In many of the smaller credit unions, members participate on a volunteer, part-time basis in the management and operation of the institution. Larger credit unions use paid full-time employees. Because the credit union is run to benefit the members, the rate of interest paid on savings is normally $1/2$ to $1^1/_2$ percent above the rates paid by other savings institutions. As a mutual association in which the savers own shares, the credit union pays dividends, not interest on savings.

Unlike commercial banks, mutual savings banks, and savings and loan associations, most credit unions offer only one type of savings account to their members. This passbook-type account pays dividends at a rate that is not known by the savers until the end of the savings period, since the dividends paid in each period depend on the credit union's earnings for that period. Of course, the credit union does estimate expected dividends. Since credit unions permit members not only to receive a favorable return on their savings but also to borrow money at advantageous rates (no more than 1 percent per month on the unpaid balance), they are quite popular. Most of them also provide free life insurance up to a maximum amount for each dollar deposited at no direct cost to the member. Of course, since they use a portion of their income to pay insurance fees, their dividends might be higher if no insurance premium were provided. A number of credit unions have experimented with share draft plans, which are similar to the NOW accounts discussed above. Although these plans have met a great deal of resistance, members of credit unions may be able to write checks against their deposits in the future.

Insured Savings

Savings deposits are almost always insured, regardless of the type of institution in which they are held. The insuring agency provides protection against failure of the institution for up to some maximum amount of a depositor's total accounts. Table 5-5 shows the insuring agencies, insurance limits, and approximate percent of institutions of each type insured by the agencies listed. It can be seen from Table 5-5 that in the case of commercial banks, mutual savings banks, and savings and loan associations the insurance plan is supported by the federal government. In the case of credit unions the plan is privately supported through their national organization. In almost all cases, those institutions not insured by one of these federal or national plans receive insurance through a state-chartered or independent insuring agency.

The presence of insured deposits at almost all savings institutions makes it possible for consumers to feel confident that their savings deposits are protected. They must keep in mind, however, that regardless

Table 5-5 **Insured Savings Institutions**

Savings Institution	Insuring Agency	Amount of Insurance	Approximate Percent Insured [a]
Commercial Bank	Federal Deposit Insurance Corporation (FDIC)	$40,000/depositor	99
Mutual Savings Bank	Federal Deposit Insurance Corporation (FDIC)	$40,000/depositor	67
Savings and Loan Association	Federal Savings and Loan Insurance Corporation (FSLIC)	$40,000/depositor	90
Credit Union	National Credit Union Administration (NCUA)	$40,000/depositor	70

[a] These figures represent the approximate percent of all such institutions that are insured by the corresponding insuring agency listed here. The institutions not included in these percentages are, for the most part, insured by a state-chartered or independent insuring agency. Details can be learned by inquiry.

Source: The "approximate percent insured" values have been estimated using data found in the fact books or annual reports of the associations of these different types of savings institutions.

of how many accounts they have in an insured institution, the insurance limit applies to the total of their deposits in that institution and its branches. For instance, an individual with three accounts in one commercial bank totaling $55,000—a checking account balance of $5,000 and two savings accounts, one with a $30,000 balance at the home office and another with a $20,000 balance at a branch office—is covered by only $40,000 of insurance. Of course, if one of the savings deposits were transferred to another bank or savings institution, it would be insured for up to $40,000 and the total amount in all accounts would then be protected. Thus not only the existence of insurance on deposits but also the maximum amount insured per depositor must be taken into account in establishing savings and checking accounts.

Certificates of deposit, U.S. Savings Bonds, and life insurance and pension plans are alternatives to savings accounts. But although these savings instruments provide more attractive returns, they tend to reduce the liquidity of the savings. In other words, there is generally a penalty for withdrawing funds thus held prior to a specified date. These forms of savings are normally maintained for some planned expenditure or solely as investments.

Other Savings Instruments

Certificates of Deposit

Savings certificates, or *certificates of deposit* (CDs), are issued by certain savings institutions in exchange for deposits. Most commonly, they are issued in denominations of $500, $1,000, and multiples thereof, with maturities ranging from ninety days to one or more years. The rate of interest paid on money held with a CD is higher than the rate paid on savings accounts. Interest on a CD account may be paid periodically over its life or at maturity. CD purchasers in effect agree to leave their funds with the savings institution for a specified period of time in exchange for a favorable rate of interest. If they wish to get their money back prior to maturity, they normally receive only the passbook savings rate minus some penalty charge—less than the earnings from a savings account. CDs therefore should not be purchased unless they can be held to maturity. Certificates of deposit are generally available at commercial banks, mutual savings banks, and savings and loan associations. A wide variety of maturities and interest rates are therefore available. The CD should be strongly considered as a savings medium for funds expected to be idle for a known period of time.

Also available are negotiable CDs, large CDs issued by commercial banks at quite favorable rates with ninety-day or longer maturities. Negotiable CDs are normally issued in denominations of $100,000 or more. Unlike CDs of smaller denominations, these large CDs may be sold by the holder to a third party. This feature allows purchasers to get their money back prior to maturity without paying a penalty. Although these large CDs are purchased primarily by business firms, they are sometimes also obtained through commercial banks or stock brokerage firms, which break them into several parts. For large amounts of savings ($10,000 or more), this arrangement might provide the most attractive returns. Your banker or stockbroker can make you aware of these types of opportunities.

U.S. Savings Bonds

A safe and popular savings instrument available to everyone is the U.S. Savings Bond. These bonds are issued in various denominations and maturities by the U.S. Treasury in order to assist in financing the federal government. Because both the payment of interest and the repayment of the principal are guaranteed by the government, U.S. Savings Bonds are a very safe investment. They can be purchased and redeemed at banks at no charge. Savings bonds are not negotiable; they are issued to a person or persons and are registered in the name(s) of the holder(s). The fact that the bonds are registered protects purchasers against their loss or destruction. They can be redeemed prior to their stated maturities without any direct penalty to the purchaser, and the interest received on them is exempt from all state and local income and personal property taxes. There are two series of U.S. Savings Bonds available currently: Series E and Series H.

Series E The Series E Bonds are purchased for 75 percent of their face value and accumulate to their face value over a five-year period. (For instance, a $100 Series E Bond can be purchased for $75 and redeemed five years later for $100.) They can be purchased in denominations ranging from $25 to $10,000. Individuals cannot purchase more than $10,000 of Series E Bonds each year.

Interest earned on Series E Bonds is not paid periodically; instead, it takes the form of the difference between the initial purchase price and the face value at maturity. The nominal rate of interest received over the life of a Series E Bond is currently 6 percent compounded semiannually, which is equivalent to an effective rate of 6.09 percent. As an incentive to hold a bond to maturity, the rate of interest accumulated each six months increases from an initial level of 3.73 percent for the first six months up to 12.93 percent for the last six-month period. The redemption values and rates of interest associated with a $100 Series E Bond are given in Table 5-6.

Table 5-6 Redemption Values and Rates of Interest over the Life of a $100 Series E Bond

Time since Purchase (Years)[a]	Redemption Value	Rate of Interest Earned during Period	Effective Rate of Interest from Purchase to End of Period
0 to 1/2	$ 75.00	3.73%	3.73%
1/2 to 1	76.40	5.34	4.54
1 to 1 1/2	78.44	5.00	4.69
1 1/2 to 2	80.40	4.98	4.76
2 to 2 1/2	82.40	5.24	4.86
2 1/2 to 3	84.56	5.39	4.95
3 to 3 1/2	86.84	5.53	5.03
3 1/2 to 4	89.24	5.92	5.14
4 to 4 1/2	91.88	6.09	5.25
4 1/2 to 5	94.68	12.93	6.09
5	100.80		

[a]Although the groupings of years appear to overlap, the intent is that each upper limit encompass the number of years less than or equal to it. Thus, for example, in the category 1 to 1 1/2 the purchase was made more than 1 year ago but less than or exactly 1 1/2 years ago. This applies also to Table 5-7.

Although it may be redeemed any time after sixty days from its purchase, a Series E Bond must be held to maturity to earn the 6+ percent return over the five-year holding period. It can be held as long as ten years beyond maturity, during which time it will continue to receive a 6.09 percent return. The interest it earns does not have to be reported to the IRS as taxable income until the bond is redeemed.

Series H Series H Bonds may be purchased at face value in denominations of $500, $1,000, $5,000, or $10,000. No more than $10,000 of these bonds can be purchased by one individual in a single year. Rather than accumulating to some future value like Series E Bonds, Series H Bonds pay interest semiannually. Although the effective interest return over their ten-year maturity is 6.09 percent (6 percent compounded semiannually), the interest rate for each semiannual period increases from 4.2 percent for the first 6 months to 5.8 percent for the next 4½ years and 6.51 percent for the next 5 years. Table 5-7 presents the effective rates of interest from purchase to the end of each semiannual period on a Series H Bond.

Table 5-7 **Effective Rates of Interest for Various Holding Periods for a Series H Bond**

Time since Purchase (Years)	Effective Rate of Interest from Purchase to End of Period	Time since Purchase (Years)	Effective Rate of Interest from Purchase to End of Period
0 to ½	4.20%	5 to 5½	5.69%
½ to 1	4.99	5½ to 6	5.75
1 to 1½	5.25	6 to 6½	5.80
1½ to 2	5.38	6½ to 7	5.84
2 to 2½	5.46	7 to 7½	5.87
2½ to 3	5.51	7½ to 8	5.91
3 to 3½	5.55	8 to 8½	5.93
3½ to 4	5.58	8½ to 9	5.96
4 to 4½	5.60	9 to 9½	5.98
4½ to 5	5.62	9½ to 10	6.09

Although a Series H Bond can be redeemed for its face value any time after six months from its purchase, the longer the bond is held, the larger the effective yield received on it. Series H Bonds can be obtained in exchange for outstanding Series E Bonds at their current redemption value, providing the E Bonds have a current redemption value of $500 or more. If an exchange is made, any deferred interest on the E Bonds can continue to be deferred until the H Bond is redeemed.

In sum, savings bonds provide very safe and reasonably good returns—if they are held to maturity. Series E and Series H Bonds can be redeemed after sixty days and six months, respectively, from their purchase without penalty.

In addition, there are various plans for those who wish to set aside savings regularly that allow Series E Bonds to be purchased on a payroll deduction basis.

Life Insurance and Pension Plans

In certain types of life insurance and pension plans, a portion of the payments is allowed to accumulate as savings. Although funds are channeled into these media primarily to provide insurance and retirement income, they can coincidentally generate some savings. Since these plans require periodic payments, the funds thus accumulated are sometimes called "forced" savings. Further discussions of the savings aspects of life insurance and pension plans are presented in Chapters 13 and 16.

Summary

Cash balances are maintained for one of three reasons: convenience, planned expenditures, or unexpected expenditures. Individuals maintain these balances in the form of pocket money, demand deposits, or savings deposits. Checking accounts (demand deposits) are held only by commercial banks and may be opened by anyone willing to make the minimum deposit required. Interest is not paid on checking accounts. The bank at which a checking account is maintained is normally selected on the basis of convenience, cost, and services provided.

The procedures involved in opening and operating a checking account are quite simple. Maintaining accurate records of account transactions minimizes the chances of overdrafts. Each month a bank statement showing all transactions and fees for the month is sent to the account holder. Since the statement shows the actual account balance, it must be reconciled with the checkbook ledger. The reconciliation process uncovers any errors in either the checkbook ledger or the bank records. Aside from the standard check written on a checking account, certified checks, cashier's checks, and traveler's checks are available to meet special checking needs.

Banks also offer special conveniences such as safe deposit boxes, drive-in and walk-up windows, automated tellers, and electronic funds transfer systems in order to simplify and streamline banking procedures. Another type of checking account—the negotiable order of withdrawal (NOW)—has been experimented with by a number of financial institutions, but has not yet met with much success.

Savings accounts are used to accumulate money for planned future expenditures. In the process of selecting savings institutions, special attention must be given to the effective rate of interest. The effective, or true, rate of interest is largely dependent on the length of the period over which the nominal, or stated, rate of interest is compounded. The method used to calculate interest also affects the returns received from savings. Passbook accounts, special savings accounts, and club accounts are offered by commercial banks. Other common financial institutions, including mutual savings banks, savings and loan associations, and credit unions, offer a variety of savings plans. Nearly all of these institutions insure accounts through federal or national agencies for up to $40,000 per depositor.

Other types of savings opportunities include certificates of deposit, U.S. Savings Bonds, and savings plans connected with certain types of life insurance and pension programs. U.S. Savings Bonds, which are available in two series—Series E and Series H—provide a convenient and safe savings mechanism that appeals to many people.

Key Terms

account reconciliation
automated teller
cashier's check
certificate of deposit (CD)
certified check
check
checkbook ledger
club account
commercial bank
compounding (of interest)
credit union
demand deposit
electronic funds transfer system (EFTS)
effective rate of interest
Federal Deposit Insurance Corporation (FDIC)
Federal Reserve System
financial institution

liquid balance
Magnetic Ink Character Recognition (MICR)
mutual savings bank
negotiable order of withdrawal (NOW) account
night depository
nominal rate of interest
overdraft
passbook account
pocket money
safe deposit box
savings and loan association
signature card
special savings account
stop payment
time deposit
traveler's check
U.S. Savings Bond

Review Questions

1. Define (a) consumption and (b) savings. Explain their relationship. Explain the importance of effectively managing both.

2. List and discuss the three basic motives for holding cash.

3. Distinguish between liquid cash and pocket money.

4. What is a joint checking account? Mention its advantages and disadvantages.

5. Is it possible for a check to bounce due to insufficient funds when the ledger shows a balance adequate to cover it?

6. "The strategy of playing the 'float' is a form of fraud and is against the law." Explain what is meant by "playing the float" and cite an instance.

7. Describe three different ways in which you can deposit a check in your bank account. Given an option of selecting either a bank with free banking facilities at a rather inconvenient location or a nearby bank that charges ten cents per check, which would you prefer, and why?

8. What precautions can be taken to avoid bouncing checks?

9. What are the different types of instruments offered by the banking system to the business community as a safeguard against bad checks?

10. Describe the procedure for stopping payment on a check.

11. "The electronic funds transfer system (EFTS) eliminates the need for cash or checks." In light of this statement, describe this system, and discuss its effect on people who try to play the "float."

12. Define and distinguish between the effective rate of interest and the nominal rate of interest. A savings and loan association that pays 5.50 percent interest (compounded daily) on its savings accounts actually pays an effective rate of 5.73 percent. Explain why.

13. Briefly describe the different techniques used to determine the savings balances that are eligible to earn interest. Which approach would you prefer your savings institution to adopt?

14. What does the sign, "Member FDIC," which is often displayed in a bank, mean to a depositor?

15. Distinguish between a passbook account, a special savings account, and a club account.

16. What are savings institutions? Mention the most common types, and describe the working of any two.

5-1 Reconciling the Pattersons' Checking Account

Case Problems

Nick and Rosalyn Patterson opened their first checking account at The Barclays Bank on 15 September 1978. They have just received their bank statement for the period 6 September 1978 through 5 October 1978. The statement and ledger are shown below:

BANK STATEMENT

THE BARCLAYS BANK
800-231-4567

NICK & ROSALYN PATTERSON
2128 E. 51ST ST.
DETROIT, MICHIGAN

STATEMENT PERIOD SEPT. 6 to OCT. 5, 1978

	Opening Balance	Total Deposits for Period		Total Charges for the Period	Ending Balance
	— 0 —	$569.25		$373.86	$195.39

Date	Withdrawals (Debits)			Deposits (Credits)	Balance
SEP. 15				$360.00	$360.00
SEP. 23				97.00	457.00
SEP. 25	$ 45.20			9.25	421.05
SEP. 30				103.00	524.05
SEP. 30	3.00 BC				521.05
OCT. 4	65.90	49.76	45.00		360.39
OCT. 5	165.00				195.39

RT = Returned Checks   DM = Debit Memo   BC = Bank Charges
FC = Finance Charges   CM = Credit Memo

Checkbook Ledger Sheet

Check #	Date 1978	Details	Check Amount	Deposit Amount	Account Balance
—	Sept. 15	Deposit cash—gift from wedding		$360.00	$360.00
—	'' 23	Nick's wages from library		97.00	457.00
101	'' 23	Kroger's—groceries	$ 45.20		411.80
102	'' 27	Michigan Bell Telephone bill	28.40		383.40
—	'' 30	Nick's wages for library work		103.00	486.40
103	Oct. 1	Univ. book store—college books	65.90		420.50
104	'' 1	K-Mart—sewing material	16.75		403.75
105	'' 1	G. Heller—apartment rent	165.00		238.75
106	'' 2	Blue Cross—health insurance	17.25		221.50
107	'' 3	Kroger's—groceries	49.76		171.74
108	'' 4	Cash, gas, entertainment, laundry	45.00		126.74
—	'' 5	Rosalyn's salary—Universal Corp.		350.00	476.74

Questions

1. From the information above, prepare a bank reconciliation for the Pattersons as of 5 October 1978.

2. Comment upon the procedures used as well as your findings.

5-2 Maximizing Interest

Jane and Andy Williams wish to open a savings account and are currently in the process of selecting a savings institution. Having taken a course in personal finance, Andy knows that he should inquire with respect to: (1) the effective rate of interest and (2) the methods adopted for determining the balance on which the interest is paid.

Questions

1. Discuss the four basic techniques used to determine what balance is eligible to receive interest for the period.

2. Use the following account transaction data to determine the balances on which Jane and Andy will be eligible to receive interest for the second quarter of 1978 under each of the four techniques. (Assume that deposits must be received on or before the 15th of the first month of the quarter in order to receive interest for the quarter. There are thirteen weeks in a quarter.)

Account Transactions for Quarter Ended 30 June 1978

Beginning of Week	Transaction	Amount	Account Balance
Initial Balance	—	—	$1,000.00
2	Deposit	$2,000.00	3,000.00
5	Deposit	1,000.00	4,000.00
7	Withdrawal	2,500.00	1,500.00
9	Withdrawal	1,000.00	500.00
11	Deposit	4,000.00	4,500.00
End of Quarter	—	—	4,500.00

3. Assuming the effective rate of interest is 6 percent and using the balance data given, calculate the amount of interest earned under each of the four techniques for the quarter ended 30 June 1978.

4. Based upon your analysis in question 3, which of the four techniques would allow Jane and Andy to maximize their interest earnings? Explain.

"Are Those Bank Services in a Package a Good Buy?" *Changing Times,* March 1976, p. 14.

"The Battle Over NOW Accounts Goes National." *Business Week,* 22 March 1976, pp. 153–154.

Edgerton, Terry. "A New Tax Shelter for Your Savings." *Money,* August 1976, pp. 48–54.

"Electronic Banking: A Retreat from the Cashless Society." *Business Week,* 18 April 1977, pp. 80–90.

Flannery, Mark J., and Jaffer, Dwight M. *The Economic Implications of an Electronic Monetary Transfer System.* Lexington, Mass.: Lexington Books, 1973.

"Get Ready for Cashless, Checkless, Living." *Changing Times,* October 1975, pp. 6–10.

Selected References

Gup, Benton E. *Financial Intermediaries: An Introduction.* Boston: Houghton Mifflin, 1976.

"Inkless Fingerprints Help Fight Bad Checks." *Business Week,* 28 February 1977, pp. 33 ff.

"The Ins and Outs of Safe-Deposit Boxes." *Money,* April 1977, p. 112.

"A Look at Some Ways People Are Saving Money." *U.S. News & World Report,* 22 March 1976, pp. 77–78.

Money-Market Investments: The Risk and the Return. New York: Morgan Guaranty Trust Company of New York, 1970.

"Once-Meek Credit Unions Take On the Banking Industry." *U.S. News & World Report,* 21 February 1977, pp. 85–86.

"Picking the Best Checking Account." *Consumer Reports,* January 1975, pp. 34–38.

Rose, Sanford. "Checkless Banking Is Bound to Come." *Fortune,* June 1977, pp. 118–121 ff.

"Take Another Look at U.S. Savings Bonds." *Changing Times,* March 1975, pp. 25–27.

"Things a Credit Union Can Do for You." *Changing Times,* January 1976, pp. 35–38.

"Those Buck-Passing Bank Machines." *Money,* February 1976, pp. 46–48.

Weberman, Ben. "Cash Like a Flash." *Forbes,* 1 April 1977, pp. 42–45.

Your Savings and Investment Dollar. Chicago: Money Management Institute, Household Finance Corporation, 1973.

6
Fundamentals of Stock and Bond Investments

In order to indicate how investments in stocks and bonds may fit in with personal financial goals, this chapter examines the following:

A Preview of
Chapter 6

1. The fundamental characteristics of stocks and bonds.

2. The risks and potential returns in the form of either income or expected growth in value offered by the most common types of stocks and bonds.

3. The basic facts about common stock investments, especially those concerning issuers, voting rights, dividends, and measures of return.

4. The methods used to classify common stock with respect to its behavior under various economic conditions, the techniques used to value common stock, and common stock investment considerations.

5. The rights, types, and investment considerations related to preferred stock, and the basic differences between preferred and common stock.

6. The most important aspects of bond purchases, particularly those concerning issuers, prices, bond characteristics, and investment considerations, as well as the risk-return behavior of bonds as compared to stocks.

The purchase of stocks and bonds may provide you with an opportunity to earn a higher return than you could earn with any of the various savings instruments. But while the earnings from stocks and bonds may be higher, the risk of achieving lower than expected returns from these

169

financial assets is also greater. If you are willing to take some risk, you can select from a nearly unlimited number and variety of investment opportunities the one with the risk-return characteristics most suitable for you.

Investment differs from saving in that the process of investing is one in which the future benefits are not known with certainty. Savings, which were discussed in the preceding chapter, are funds placed in some institution or instrument providing returns at a specified rate over a known period of time. Although the motives for saving and investing are quite similar—to earn a return on funds—the savings process is a more conservative strategy aimed at fulfilling necessary short-run goals. Investing, although it can be done in a "conservative" manner, is intended to earn returns consistent with long-run goals such as providing for retirement income.

The term *investment* as used here refers to money placed in some medium that is expected to provide a positive return over a certain period of time. Investments may be made in a variety of items—stocks, bonds, real estate—each with their own risk-return characteristics. Although the savings arrangements described in Chapter 5 could be classified as a form of investment, only those arrangements not based on deposits that are described throughout the next three chapters will be referred to here as investments.

Characteristics of Stock and Bond Investments

Stocks are shares of ownership in a corporate form of business, while _bonds_ are certificates indicating that a corporation has borrowed a certain amount of money which it has agreed to repay in the future. Stocks and bonds are the most common types of *securities,* which are obligations of issuers that provide purchasers with an expected or stated return on the amount invested.

Basic Types of Securities

Stocks and bonds, the two basic types of securities, have a number of key characteristics. Both are issued by *corporations,* which are business firms that have been chartered by the state and given legal status. The corporation can sue and be sued, can make and enter into contracts, and has all of the legal rights of an individual. Unlike *sole proprietorship* and *partnership* forms of business, which have their income taxed as personal income, corporations are subject to a special tax rate that may or may not be more favorable than the personal tax rates, depending on the amount of taxable income earned. One other difference between corporations and sole proprietorships and partnerships is that owners of corporations have *limited liability*, which means that they can lose no more than they invest. The owners of sole proprietorships and partnerships have *unlimited liability*, which means their potential losses can go beyond their investment in the firm. This feature has contributed greatly to the dominance of the corporate form of business in the United States.

Common Stock Common stock is the most basic form of corporate ownership. It is a form of *equity capital*, which means that each share purchased represents an investment in the equity, or ownership, of the firm. The purchaser of common stock normally receives the right to one vote in all corporate elections for each share that is owned. Common stockholders do not receive any type of guarantee or assurance that they will receive favorable returns on their investments. They are last in line to recover any portion of their investment should the firm fail; in most cases, they do not receive much of their investment if a business is liquidated (that is, all assets are sold and proceeds are used to satisfy debts). The amount paid in *dividends*, or earnings distributed to the stockholders, is normally determined quarterly by the board of directors of the corporation, who are elected by the stockholders. Dividend income is one of two possible motives for purchasing shares of common stock. The other is price appreciation. Many people buy stock in the expectation that its price will increase, thereby allowing them to sell it at a profit.

As indicated in Chapter 4, income received in the form of dividends is taxed as normal income, while income earned as the result of selling a security for more than its original purchase price may be taxed as a *capital gain*. The length of time a security must be held before the profit on its sale can be taxed as a capital gain was recently changed. Prior to 1977, the required period of ownership was six months; in 1977 it became nine months; and for subsequent years it has been set at twelve months.

If this time requirement is met, capital gains are taxed at a rate equal to one-half the normal tax rate and no more than 35 percent. If the security is not held long enough before it is sold, the profit is taxed at normal rates. Assume, for example, that you just sold 100 shares of the RZX Company common stock for $60 per share. Also assume that the stock was originally purchased two years ago for $50 per share and that during the current year you received $1.25 per share in cash dividends from the stock. For tax purposes you would have a long-term capital gain of $1,000 ([$60/share − $50/share] × 100 shares) and $125 ($1.25/share × 100 shares) of dividend income. Ignoring the dividend exemption (see Chapter 4), your taxable income from this transaction would be $625 ($500 capital gains + $125 cash dividends) since only one-half of the capital gain is taxed, while all of the dividend income is eligible for taxes.

Preferred Stock Preferred stock is a special type of ownership, or equity, capital. Purchasers of preferred stock expect to receive a stated dividend periodically. The amount of this dividend is stated when the stock is first issued. The board of directors of the issuing corporation can elect not to pay this dividend in any period. This action is not viewed favorably by the common stockholders since the claims of the preferred stockholders must be satisfied before dividends can be paid to the common stockholders.

Most preferred stock is *cumulative,* which means that all dividends *passed* (not paid in a period) accumulate and must be paid prior to giving the common stockholders any dividends. Preferred stockholders not only receive preference with respect to dividends, but they also have preference over the common stockholders in the case of liquidation of the firm. Because they have these privileges, however, preferred stockholders normally do *not* receive any voting privileges. Although preferred stock is traded in the marketplace, most purchasers buy it for the fixed dividend return rather than for any anticipated appreciation in its market price. Since its dividend return is fixed, preferred stock is not nearly as popular an investment as is common stock. In addition, because it takes precedence over common stock in the above-mentioned cases, many corporations avoid using preferred stock financing on the ground that it is not in the best interest of the "true" owners of the firm, the common stockholders.

Bonds Bonds represent a form of *debt capital,* which means that funds raised through the sale of bonds are borrowed funds. Bond purchasers do not normally receive any voice in the management of the firm. They expect to receive interest payments at specified times and to be paid back the face value or bond *principal* at maturity. Corporate and government bonds normally have face values of $1,000 and maturities of ten to thirty years. Interest on corporate or government bonds is usually paid semiannually and is expected to be higher than that paid on savings instruments. Failure to pay interest by the corporation or government will result in *default,* which may then force the corporation or government into bankruptcy. A corporation must pay all interest due bondholders prior to distributing dividends to preferred and common stockholders.

Risks in Security Investments

In selecting securities for investment, it is advisable to consider the possible risks or uncertainties associated with the various investment opportunities. The basic types of risk, which are discussed below, are business risk, financial risk, market risk, purchasing power risk, and interest rate risk.

Business Risk It is possible that the business firm that has issued the security will fail. Failure of a firm may be due to economic or industry conditions and/or management actions. It is not unusual for stockholders to receive nothing when a business fails. Bondholders, on the other hand, are likely to receive some—but not necessarily all—of the amount owed them due to their preferential situation. Although failure of the firm is the most severe outcome, in general *business risk* is the degree of uncertainty associated with the firm's earnings and consequent ability to pay interest and dividends.

Financial Risk Financial risk is related to the mix of debt and equity financing used by the firm. The greater the proportion of debt to equity the firm has, the larger its financial risk. High proportions of debt indicate that the firm must meet large interest payments; if the firm is unable to meet contractual interest payments, it could be forced into bankruptcy.

Market Risk Market risk results from the behavior of investors in the securities markets. Changes in their behavior as reflected in the market price of any one security may or may not be related to fundamental changes in the issuing firm's performance. Changes in political, economic, and social conditions or changes in investor tastes and preferences may cause the market price of a security to rise or fall. Although it is quite difficult to estimate this type of risk, the potential investor can evaluate past price movements in order to get a feel for the degree of market risk for a given security.

Purchasing Power Risk Possible changes in price levels within our economy also result in risk. In periods of rising prices, the purchasing power of the dollar declines. This means that a smaller quantity of some commodity can be purchased with a given number of dollars than could have been purchased in the past. In periods of declining price levels the purchasing power of the dollar increases. An awareness of purchasing power risk and changes in purchasing power allows investors to select investments that are best for the given price levels and thus protect themselves against changes in purchasing power. In general, investments whose values move with price changes are most profitable during periods of price rise and those that provide fixed returns are preferable for periods of price decline.

Interest Rate Risk It is primarily *fixed income securities*—securities including bonds and preferred stocks that offer purchasers a fixed periodic return—that are affected by interest rate risk. As interest rates change, the prices of these securities fluctuate, decreasing with increasing interest rates and increasing with decreasing interest rates. The prices

"If I learned one thing, it's that there's a
high risk in high-risk investments."

High Risk Investments Should Be Avoided
Source: Reprinted by permission of Sidney Harris.

of fixed income securities drop when interest rates increase in order to provide purchasers of the security with the same rate of return as would be available on similar securities. Increases in price due to declining interest rates result from the fact that the return on a fixed income security is adjusted downward to a competitive level by upward adjustments in its market price. The changes in the interest rates that cause these adjustments are a result of fluctuations in the supply of and/or demand for money. These fluctuations are caused by various economic actions of the government or the interactions of business firms, consumers, and financial institutions.

Returns from Security Investments

The returns from security investments are available as income or growth (i.e., appreciation in value). While some securities provide either income or growth, most offer both of these types of return. Of course, the mix of these two types of return differs from security to security.

Income Income in the form of dividends on stock and interest from bonds is often the primary motive for investment in securities. People who invest to obtain income look for securities that provide regular and predictable patterns of income distribution. Preferred stocks and bonds, which are expected to pay known amounts at specified periods of time (semiannually or quarterly, for example), are usually good income investments. Common stock pays the least certain dividends, if any, and is thus the least reliable type of security for providing income.

Growth The other type of return available from security investments is growth, which is reflected in an increase in the market value of the security. Generally, securities that provide greater growth potential through capital appreciation have lower levels of income, since the firm achieves its growth by reinvesting its earnings instead of paying dividends to the owners. Stocks—more specifically, common stocks—are usually acquired for their growth potential. And, as indicated above, the appreciation in stock price may receive the favorable capital gains tax treatment if the stock has been held for the required period of time. Although preferred stock and bond prices do fluctuate, these securities are normally purchased not for growth but rather for the dependable income they provide.

Risk-Return Tradeoff

The risks associated with a given security investment are inversely related to the returns. This means that the higher the risk, the greater the expected return from the security. Investors are compensated for taking higher levels of risk by the expectation of higher returns. Since most people are believed to be risk averse—to dislike taking risks—they must be given some incentive to take risks. If the same return a high risk security offered could be received from a security with lower risk, investors would naturally opt for the latter. Or, looking at it in another way, investors would choose the highest return available for a given level of risk. The inverse relationship between risk and return is depicted in Figure 6-1.

Although the inverse nature of the relationship depicted is not

Figure 6-1 **Risk-Return Relationship**

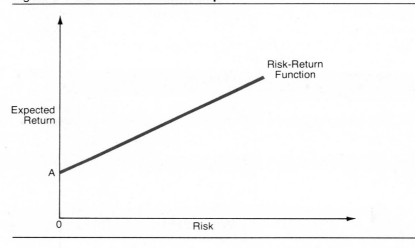

immediately apparent in Figure 6-1, it is inherent in the fact that increasing risk is a negative factor, while increasing return is a positive factor. Table 6-1 generalizes the risk-return tradeoff for better quality bonds, preferred stocks, and common stocks. Note in Figure 6-1 (point A) that it is possible to receive a positive return for zero risk; this is sometimes referred to as the riskless rate of interest, which is often measured by the return on a government security.

Table 6-1 **Generalized Risk-Return Ratings for Better Quality Securities**

Security	Risk	Return	
		Income	Growth
Corporate Bonds	Least	Very Steady	Usually None
Preferred Stock	Average	Steady	Variable
Common Stock	Most	Variable	Most

Source: Adapted with permission from *How to Invest* (New York: Merrill Lynch, Pierce, Fenner & Smith, 1971), p. 21.

Common stock investments are very popular due to the diversity of issuers and the almost endless combinations of risk-return tradeoffs available. Although, in general, common stocks are more risky than preferred stocks or bonds, they do provide opportunities to earn very large returns through appreciation in value. The return potential on preferred stocks and bonds is much more limited. Another aspect of the appeal of common stock investments over bond investments is the fact that common stock prices can range anywhere from less than one dollar per share up to hundreds of dollars per share. Bonds, however, normally sell at $500 or more per bond. The lower prices of common (and preferred) stocks thus make them quite attractive to the small investor. The important aspects of common stock investments are discussed in the following sections.

Issuers of Common Stock

Common stock can be issued by any corporation in any line of business whose charter authorizes the issuance of shares. A certificate for 100 shares of stock in The Williams Companies is shown in Figure 6-2. Although all corporations have stockholders, not all have publicly traded shares. Corporations whose shares are not publicly traded are often referred to as *closed corporations*, while corporations whose shares are traded publicly are called *open corporations*. Of course, the stock of some public corporations is not traded on the major security exchanges and is therefore difficult for investors to obtain. Aside from the initial sale of common stock when a corporation is formed, subsequent sales of additional common stock may be made through public offerings, rights offerings, or with warrants. Rights offerings and warrants have some special characteristics that common stock investors should know about.

Rights Offerings When a firm makes a new issue of common stock, it is required (in many states) to allow the current stockholders to purchase new shares in proportion to their existing share ownership. This right of the existing stockholders to be given an opportunity to maintain their proportional ownership is known as a *preemptive right*. For instance, if a stockholder currently owns 10 percent of the firm's stock and the firm plans to issue 5,000 additional shares, that stockholder will be given an opportunity to purchase 500 shares, or 10 percent of the new shares issued. In order to efficiently carry out the rights offering, the firm issues rights—negotiable instruments allowing the holder to purchase a certain number of shares of the new issue at a specified price—to each shareholder. These rights normally must be exercised within a few months. Because the *exercise price* at which the new shares can be purchased is usually below the prevailing market price, rights have value and may be sold in the marketplace.

Warrants Another technique used to sell shares of common stock, a warrant, provides for the purchase of shares at a certain price over some specified period of time. The purchase price of shares specified by warrants is usually higher than the market price at the time of issue. This means that it is not desirable to exercise warrants when issued; they become valuable only after the market price of the stock rises above the exercise price. For instance, a warrant may allow the holder to purchase three shares of common stock at $30 per share. If the current market price of the stock is $25 per share, the holder will not want to exercise the

What's Your Investment Identity Quotient?

The most important ingredient in successful investing is a knowledge of the amount of risk you can afford to take. To judge that risk, ask yourself four basic questions:

1. Am I able to pay for the basic necessities of my life?
2. Do I have sufficient insurance to protect my family?
3. Do I have enough ready cash to cover contingencies?
4. Will a slight fall in the price of securities ruin my daily routine?

At 28, Philip John Neimark lost interest in his job and quit. He vowed he would make his first million by the time he was thirty. In fact, he made his first million in the very risky commodities market by the time he was twenty-nine. According to Neimark, any person with a little capital, a good informed judgment, and a risk-taking ability can become a millionaire. His advice is to "explore any broad field where expertise counts." To determine an individual's risk-taking ability, Neimark has developed the Investment Identity Quotient (I.I.Q.). The I.I.Q. dynamically combines two factors important in determining an individual's capacity for "risk": amount of available capital and stage of life.

The first factor is a comparison of cash on hand to what is needed to pay bills over the next twelve months and is rated on a scale of zero to two. Assuming a fairly stable income and a modest standard of living, it is determined as follows:

0   In debt, or cash on hand less than half of one year's expenses.
1   Cash on hand substantially more than half of one year's expenses.
2   Cash on hand several times (or more) one year's expenses.

The second factor is age, which is rated on a scale of zero to three. This is as important as the individual's monetary situation.

warrant. But when the market price of the shares exceeds $30, rising to $40 per share, for example, the exercise of the warrant becomes very profitable. Warrants therefore do have value and are traded in the security markets. They are most commonly issued by corporations in order to make preferred stocks and bonds more attractive investments or as part of a merger or acquisition. When warrants are exercised, a corporation issues new shares of common stock.

Voting Rights

The holders of common stock normally receive voting rights, which means that for each share of stock held, they receive one vote. In certain

---

0   Ages 65 and over.
1   Ages 54 through 64.
2   Ages 29 through 53.
3   Ages 28 and under.

An individual's I.I.Q. is the sum of the ratings of these two factors. Neimark interprets I.I.Q.s in the following way:

0   You are virtually incapable of any real financial gain. You will have to go outside your economic structure in some way in order to raise your I.I.Q. to the next level.
1   Minimum level of I.I.Q. You have the means to raise yourself to a higher level, from which you can then attain wealth.
2   Average financial position. Your I.I.Q. will either move up to 3 or down to 1 within the next ten years.
3   Good position. You have the leverage to make yourself rich, and soon. Survey your possibilities and act quickly.
4   You are wealthy—whether it's in dollars or possibilities. Make that wealth real, and totally secure.
5   Ideal I.I.Q.

Thus a zero I.I.Q. implies old age, no money to spare, no time to learn from mistakes, and hence no capacity to bear risks. An I.I.Q. of 3, however, indicates some money to spare—perhaps $5,000—youth, and consequently time to take risks and learn from mistakes. What's your I.I.Q.?

Source: Adapted with permission from "Your Guide to Safe and Profitable Investments at Any Age." *Consumer's Digest Magazine,* May/June 1977, pp. 1, 32–36.

Figure 6-2 **Sample Stock Certificate for 100 Shares of The Williams Companies**

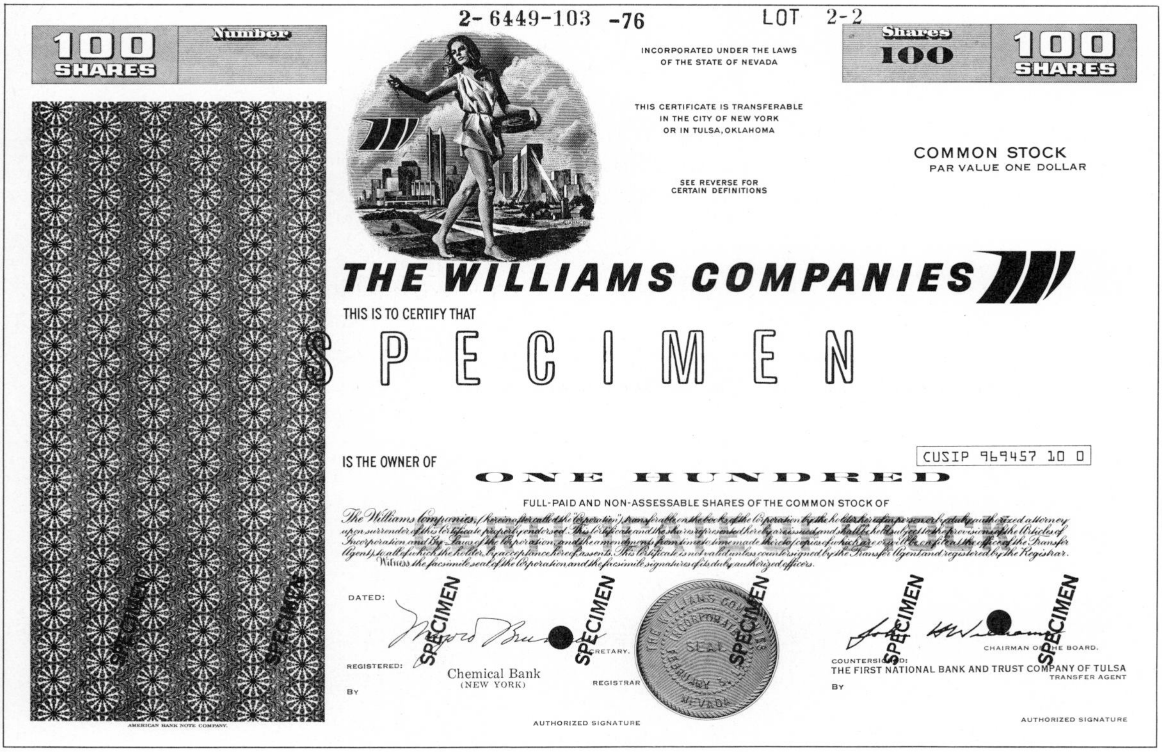

Source: Courtesy of The Williams Companies, Tulsa, Oklahoma.

instances common stock may be designated as nonvoting stock at the time of its issue, but this is the exception, not the rule. Although two basic voting systems exist, the small stockholders need not concern themselves with them, since regardless of the system, the chance that they will be able to affect the corporate control with their votes is quite slim. Corporations have annual stockholders' meetings at which new directors are elected and any special issues are voted on. Since most small stockholders are unable to attend these meetings, they assign their votes by *proxy* to another person in order to vote their stock. A proxy is merely a written statement assigning voting rights to another person. In Figure 6-3, a proxy for The Williams Companies common stock is shown. Normally the existing directors are able to gain proxy voting rights for the majority of shares and thus perpetuate their terms in office. Occasionally, if a large group of discontent stockholders exists, a *proxy battle* may occur between the directors and the discontent group of stockholders.

Figure 6-3 **A Proxy for The Williams Companies' Common Stock**

THE WILLIAMS COMPANIES

PROXY
For Common Stock

PROXY
For Common Stock

The undersigned stockholder of The Williams Companies hereby appoints JOHN H. WILLIAMS and JOSEPH H. WILLIAMS, jointly and severally with full power of substitution, as proxies to represent and vote all of the shares of Common Stock the undersigned is entitled to vote at the Annual Meeting of Stockholders of The Williams Companies to be held on the 2nd day of May, 1977, at 11:00 a.m., local time, at One Kennedy Building, 321 South Boston Avenue, Tulsa, Oklahoma, and at any and all adjournments thereof, as directed on the following matters:

WITH   WITHOUT
(X)   ( )

Authority to vote for the election of the four persons named as nomineees for director of the Company, each to hold office for a term of three years and until a successor has been elected or qualified.

FOR   AGAINST   ABSTAIN
(X)   ( )   ( )

Ratification of the appointment of Arthur Young & Company as auditors for 1977.

and, in the discretion of one or more of said proxies acting, upon any other business as may properly come before the meeting and at any and all adjournments thereof.

(Continued, and to be signed, on the reverse side.)

(Continued from other side.)

The shares represented by this proxy will be voted as directed. UNLESS OTHERWISE DIRECTED, THIS PROXY WILL BE VOTED FOR THE ELECTION OF FOUR DIRECTORS AND FOR THE RATIFICATION OF THE APPOINTMENT OF ARTHUR YOUNG & COMPANY AS AUDITORS, ALL AS SET FORTH IN THE PROXY STATEMENT.

A. Small Stockholder
Any Street
Any Town, U.S.A.

The undersigned hereby acknowledges receipt of the Proxy Statement dated March 18, 1977.

Dated this ___*15th*___ day of ___*APRIL*___ 1977.

A. Small Stockholder

Please sign exactly as name appears hereon, date and return promptly.

THIS PROXY IS SOLICITED ON BEHALF OF THE MANAGEMENT OF THE COMPANY

Source: Courtesy of The Williams Companies, Tulsa, Oklahoma.

Types of Dividends

Corporations can pay dividends to the common stockholder in cash and/or additional stock. *Cash dividends* are most common. Since firms can pay dividends from earnings accumulated from previous periods, stockholders may receive dividends even in periods during which the firm shows a loss. Cash dividends are normally distributed on a quarterly basis in an amount determined by the firm's directors.

Occasionally, the directors may declare a *stock dividend* as a supplement to or in place of cash dividends. Stock dividends are new shares of stock issued to existing stockholders. Although they often satisfy the needs of investors, stock dividends have no value, since in an accounting sense, they represent the receipt of something already owned by the stockholder. Usually after a stock dividend has been paid, the per share stock price drops by just enough to cause the value of the old share plus the stock dividend to just equal the original share price. When a firm declares a 10 percent stock dividend, each shareholder receives $1/10$ of a share of stock for each share owned. In other words, a stockholder with 100 shares of stock in a firm which declared a 10 percent stock dividend would receive ten new shares of stock. Since all stockholders receive 10 percent increases in their ownership, their proportion of ownership in the firm remains unchanged by stock dividends.

Of course, the shareholder who has received a stock dividend may sell the new shares in order to get a cash dividend. (It is important to recognize that stock dividends are not taxed until they are sold, whereas cash dividends—excluding the dividend exemption—are taxed in the year they are received.) But the value of that shareholder's holdings in the firm is reduced by the amount of the proceeds from such a sale. Stock dividends therefore do not represent real dollar income but rather a type of "psychic income," which may satisfy the stockholder's need to receive something from the firm.

Stock Splits

Stock splits are often initiated by a firm's directors in order to affect the trading activity of the stock in the marketplace. *Stock splits* are a type of trade: old shares for given amount of new shares. In the normal stock split the stockholder receives more than one share of the new stock for each old share. For instance, in a 2 for 1 stock split, a person owning 200 old shares would receive 400 new shares of stock. Of course, the market price of the new shares is expected to decline in proportion to the increase in the number of shares: in a 2 for 1 split, for example, the market price per share would be reduced by half. If the before-split market price was $50 per share, the after-split market price would be $25 per share. The person owning 200 shares at $50 per share prior to the 2 for 1 split would hold 400 shares at $25 per share after the split.

Occasionally, in order to stimulate trading activity in a stock selling at a low price, firms announce *reverse stock splits*, which means that each existing share is exchanged for less than one new share. A 1 for 2 stock split, for instance, means that one new share is issued in exchange for two old shares of stock. The effect of reverse stock splits is to increase the market price of the stock in proportion to the stock split. For instance, if a stock currently selling for $5 was split 1 for 2, the new price would be $10 per share. Regardless of how stocks are split, stock splits have no value in and of themselves; they are merely intended to enhance the trading activity of the stock. If this effect is obtained, it may then tend to drive up the stock price. Generally speaking, investors prefer regular stock splits and look unfavorably on reverse splits.

Common Stock Measurements

There are a number of terms commonly used to describe certain attributes of common stock—par value, book value, earnings per share, and price-earnings ratio. Some pertain to the value of stock, while others refer to its performance.

Par Value A stated value that used to be placed on stock certificates, par value was not intended to represent the value of a stock, but rather the minimum price at which the stock could sell without causing the shareholder to assume any liability for the firm's actions. Par value is no longer important; it does not reflect value. Many stocks issued today are, in fact, no-par stocks, which should attest to the virtual insignificance of par value. Occasionally, stocks do sell for less than their par value, although in most instances they sell above par.

Book Value The value of a firm as determined by accounting represents the book value of common stock. The firm's liabilities and preferred stock value are subtracted from the value of its assets. Thus, if a firm's assets were sold for amounts just equal to its book (accounting) value and all debts (and preferred stock) were paid off, what would remain would be the book value of common stock. For example, assume the RZX Company has total assets of $12 million, liabilities of $8 million, and preferred stock valued at $1 million. The book value of the firm's common stock is $3 million ($12 million − $8 million − $1 million). If book value is divided by the number of shares outstanding, the result is the book value per share. If the RZX Company has 100,000 shares of common stock outstanding, its book value per share is $30 ($3,000,000 ÷ 100,000 shares). Although some stocks have market prices below their book values, this does not necessarily mean they are poor investments; they may be excellent investments.

Earnings per Share (EPS) The claim on earnings for each share owned during the current period is what is known as earnings per share (EPS). EPS is calculated by dividing all earnings that remain after the claims of preferred stockholders (if any) are satisfied by the number of shares of common stock outstanding. For example, assume the above-mentioned RZX Company had earnings of $250,000 available for its common stockholders as a result of the current year's operations. Since the firm has 100,000 shares of common stock outstanding, its annual earnings per share would be $2.50 ($250,000 ÷ 100,000 shares). The value of earnings per share is considered quite important by most stockholders since it represents the amount that the firm has earned on behalf of each outstanding share of common stock. Note, however, that the firm's directors may choose not to pay dividends in this amount, or in any amount.

Price/Earnings Ratio (P/E) When the prevailing market price per share is divided by the annual earnings per share, the result is the price/earnings ratio (P/E), which is viewed as an indicator of investor confidence and expectations with respect to a given security. The higher the P/E, the more confidence investors are presumed to have in a given security, and vice versa. In the case of the RZX Company, whose shares are currently selling for $60, its price/earnings ratio is 24 ($60/share ÷ $2.50/share). This means that the RZX Company stock is selling for 24 times earnings. P/E ratios are quite important to many investors since they provide some feel for the general expectations or "growth" of the firm.

Classifications of Common Stock

Common stock is often classified on the basis of its performance under various conditions as blue-chip, growth, income, speculative, cyclical, or defensive stock.

Blue-Chip Stocks Those stocks known to provide a stable and safe return are *blue-chip stocks.* They are issued by the most stable and strongest companies, such as IBM and General Electric, and provide uninterrupted streams of dividends and good long-term growth prospects. Their proven records of earnings and dividends make them attractive investments when stable and reasonably predictable returns are desired. Due to the high levels of investor confidence and the higher than average predictability associated with blue-chips, they normally sell at high P/E ratios.

Growth Stocks Stocks whose earnings have increased at an above average level over the recent past are *growth stocks.* These stocks normally do not pay out more than about 25 percent of earnings since the firm's rapid growth potential requires that its earnings be retained and reinvested. The very high growth expectations for these stocks usually cause them to sell at quite high P/E ratios. Because these stocks are expected to achieve high levels of price appreciation, they appeal to investors desirous of capital gains income rather than dividend income. A listing of growth stocks would include companies such as McDonald's, Pizza Hut, and Texas Instruments.

Income or Speculative Stocks Stocks which have appeal primarily on the basis of the dividends they pay out are known as *income stocks*. They have fairly stable streams of earnings, a large portion of which are distributed in the form of dividends. Investors buy these stocks for the income they provide and do not concern themselves with their P/E ratios or their potential for price appreciation.

Speculative stocks, on the other hand, are purchased in the hope that their price per share will increase. Rather than basing their investment decisions on a proven record of earnings, those who purchase speculative stocks gamble that some new information, discovery, or production technique will favorably affect the growth of the firm and inflate the price of the stock. For example, companies whose stock is considered speculative may have recently discovered a new drug or located a valuable resource such as oil. The value of speculative stocks and their P/E ratios tends to fluctuate a great deal as additional information with respect to the firm's future is received. Investors in speculative stocks should be prepared to experience losses as well as gains.

Cyclical or Defensive Stocks Stocks whose price movements tend to follow the business cycle are called *cyclical stocks*. This means that when the economy is in an expansionary stage (recovery or inflation), the prices of cyclical stocks increase; and when the economy is in a contractionary stage (recession or depression), they decline. Most cyclical stocks are found in basic industries—automobiles, steel, and lumber, for example—which are quite sensitive to changes in economic activity. Investors who purchase cyclical stocks try to do so just prior to their expansionary phase and to sell the stocks before the contraction occurs. The prices and returns from *defensive stocks*, unlike those of cyclical stocks, are expected to remain stable during periods of contraction in business activity. For this reason, they are often called countercyclical. The stocks of certain public utilities are one example of defensive stocks. Basically income stocks, their earnings and dividends in effect hold up the market price during periods of economic decline. This characteristic makes them quite popular investments for investors desiring a safe but certain return.

Common Stock Value

The value of common stock as viewed by current and potential investors may be based on a number of considerations. Probably most important of

A Dividend Scoreboard

All but one of these 50 stocks, once among the favorites of professional portfolio managers seeking capital gains rather than income, are now paying dividends. Growth seekers used to ignore dividends or avoid companies paying them, but dividends now are helping restore confidence in growth stocks. Their yields, as a percentage of recent prices for the stock, are often three or four times what they were five years ago. In the same period, their price/earnings ratios, a key indicator of value to investors, have sunk to enticingly low levels. We rank the stocks here in descending order of dividend yields at the end of the first quarter of 1977.

Source: Reprinted from "A Dividend Scoreboard," MONEY Magazine, August 1977, by special permission; © 1977, Time Inc.

	Dividend Yield		Price/Earnings Ratio	
	1977	1972	1977	1972
1. Schlitz	4.5%	1.1%	9.6	32.1
2. Avon	4.4	1.1	15.5	55.3
3. Coca-Cola	4.1	1.2	15.6	42.5
4. Simplicity	4.0	0.6	12.9	44.2
5. Chesebrough-Pond's	3.7	1.4	13.0	34.1
6. American Home Products	3.7	1.7	16.6	32.9
7. IBM	3.6	1.4	17.1	35.4
8. Warner-Lambert	3.6	1.5	13.4	28.6
9. Dr Pepper	3.6	0.9	14.6	56.7
10. Bristol-Myers	3.5	1.9	12.5	24.5
11. Pfizer	3.5	1.6	11.9	27.7
12. Emery Air Freight	3.5	1.0	16.0	49.8
13. Lubrizol	3.5	0.9	12.0	34.6
14. 3M Co.	3.4	1.2	16.4	35.7
15. Eli Lilly	3.4	1.0	14.5	37.8
16. Anheuser-Busch	3.2	0.9	15.0	36.5
17. Procter & Gamble	3.2	1.6	15.1	28.5
18. Upjohn	3.1	1.6	13.0	33.1
19. J.C. Penney	3.1	1.3	11.6	28.0
20. Emerson Electric	3.0	1.4	14.8	33.0
21. Sears	2.9	1.5	14.2	28.2
22. Carnation	2.9	1.1	12.3	26.4
23. Corning Glass	2.9	1.4	12.4	31.1
24. Eastman Kodak	2.9	1.1	18.7	37.7
25. Black & Decker	2.8	1.0	15.2	44.9

	Dividend Yield		Price/Earnings Ratio	
	1977	1972	1977	1972
26. American Express	2.8%	0.9%	12.2	32.5
27. Dow Chemical	2.7	2.0	11.2	22.2
28. Merck	2.7	1.4	16.2	39.1
29. Schering-Plough	2.6	0.8	12.8	39.6
30. Philip Morris	2.4	1.3	11.7	21.0
31. Xerox	2.4	0.6	11.0	46.8
32. Int'l Flavors	2.3	0.6	17.7	58.5
33. Abbott Laboratories	2.2	1.5	13.2	25.6
34. AMP	1.9	0.7	16.0	36.7
35. Motorola	1.8	0.6	14.2	29.3
36. Halliburton	1.8	1.0	10.4	27.8
37. Perkin-Elmer	1.8	0.6	15.5	44.4
38. Longs Drug	1.7	0.6	17.2	46.2
39. Johnson & Johnson	1.6	0.4	18.0	55.2
40. Texas Instruments	1.6	0.5	18.8	37.1
41. American Hospital	1.5	0.6	15.3	47.8
42. Polaroid	1.5	0.3	13.6	94.8
43. Schlumberger	1.4	0.7	16.0	35.8
44. Masco	1.3	0.3	11.9	39.2
45. Burroughs	1.2	0.3	14.6	40.9
46. K mart	0.9	0.4	16.1	41.3
47. Baxter Travenol	0.7	0.3	16.9	59.6
48. Disney	0.4	0.1	16.1	63.5
49. McDonald's	0.2	0.0	15.4	60.6
50. Digital Equipment	0.0	0.0	18.1	59.3

these is the relationship of supply to demand for the stock. The greater the number of shares offered for sale (supply) with respect to the number of shares sought for purchase (demand), the lower the price, and vice versa. There are three basic theories of stock value—fundamental, technical, and random walk—which are described separately below.

Fundamental Theories The fundamental theories of security analysis are based on the belief that the true value of a security such as common stock is determined by its expected stream of future earnings. The higher the expected future earnings, the higher the value of the stock; and the lower the level of expected future earnings, the lower the value of the stock. The fundamental value of a security can be estimated by an analysis of the potential sales and earnings of a company using economic

A Profile of the Typical Stockholder

A survey of stockholders conducted by the New York Stock Exchange in 1975 revealed some interesting data, which are shown below. According to the survey findings, the typical stockholder was a professional or technical person, had a median income of $19,000, was age fifty-three, and had attended college for four or more years. Although females had a slight edge, the stockholders were almost equally divided between males and females.

Survey Highlights

Item	1970	1975
Number of individual shareowners (in thousands)	30,850	25,270
Median household income	$13,500	$19,000
Number of adult female shareowners (in thousands)	14,290	11,750
Number of adult male shareowners (in thousands)	14,340	11,630
Median age of shareowners	48	53

and industry-based factors. One of the most common fundamental approaches involves estimating the average annual earnings per share expected in the future and then multiplying this value by the expected price/earnings ratio. For example, assume that a stock that normally sells for 22 times earnings is expected to earn (annually) $3.20 per share in the future. Using this method, the fundamental value of the stock would therefore be $70.40 per share (22 × $3.20). Once the fundamental, or true, value of the stock has been determined, purchase or sale decisions can be made. If the true value is above the current market price, the stock is a good buy, since it is "underpriced"; but if the fundamental value is below the current market price, the stock is "overpriced" and should therefore be sold.

Selected Characteristics of Stockholders

Annual Income	1970		1975	
	Number (in Thousands)	Percent	Number (in Thousands)	Percent
Under $5,000	2,389	8.44	780	3.34
$5,000–$9,999	5,779	20.42	2,636	11.27
$10,000–$14,999	8,346	29.49	4,552	19.46
$15,000–$24,999	7,670	27.10	8,778	37.53
$25,000 and Over	4,114	14.55	6,642	28.40
Total	28,298	100.00	23,338	100.00
Age				
Under 34	6,721	22.04	4,156	16.82
35–44	5,801	19.02	3,976	16.09
45–54	7,556	24.78	5,675	22.97
55 and Over	10,414	34.16	10,889	44.12
Total	30,492	100.00	24,696	100.00
Education				
3 Years High School or Less	3,566	12.68	1,621	6.93
4 Years High School	8,697	30.92	6,580	28.13
1–3 Years College	5,867	20.86	5,301	22.67
4 Years College or More	9,999	35.54	9,886	42.27
Total	28,129	100.00	23,388	100.00

Source: Adapted with permission from "Shareowners in Public Corporations," *The New York Stock Exchange 1976 Fact Book* (New York: New York Stock Exchange, 1976), pp. 48–50.

Technical Theories The belief that security prices are solely the result of the forces of supply and demand characterizes the technical theories of stock value. Technical analysis does not rely on earnings data but rather is concerned with forecasting changes in supply and demand and the resulting stock price movements. The basic premise underlying technical theories is that past patterns of market movement will occur again in the future and can therefore be used to make predictions. The advocates of technical analysis are often called *chartists*, since they normally keep charts plotting daily stock price and market index movements in order to find patterns and trends. They have developed numerous terms such as "head and shoulders" and "ascending triangle" to describe patterns that are believed to signal certain price movements. Investors who believe in the technical theories base their purchase and sale decisions on the signals generated by their charts. Although the technical analysts rely strictly on predictions of supply and demand, ignoring true value, they have been able to perform reasonably well over the recent past.

Random Walk Theory Some would suggest that stock price movements are strictly random events, that there are really no patterns in stock price movements. Known as the random walk theory, this hypothesis actually rejects both fundamental and technical theories on the basis that price changes are really random numbers. Random walk theorists suggest that securities can be selected intelligently by using certain statistically based approaches. Although this theory does find some acceptance, the difficulty of applying it has led investors to devote most of their attention to fundamental and technical theories of stock price movement.

Common Stock Investment Considerations

Common stock has both advantages and disadvantages. Its advantages are twofold: First, its potential returns in the form of both dividend income and price appreciation may be quite good. Although common stock performance in certain years has been poor, the record of the average share of common stock over extended periods of years has been favorable. The returns on some common stocks are considered virtually unlimited since there are no constraints on dividend payments or stock price. Second, at least part of the income from stock investments—that due to its appreciation in price—may be taxed as long-term capital gains at half (or less) of the normal tax rates.

Risk, the problem of timing purchases and sales, and the uncertainty of yield are disadvantages associated with common stock. Although potential common stock returns may be high, the risk or uncertainty associated with the actual receipt of an expected return may also be great. In general, the higher the expected return, the greater the risk involved in actually receiving the return. Even though careful selection of stocks may somewhat reduce risk, the risk-return tradeoff cannot be completely eliminated. In other words, high returns on common stock are in no way guaranteed; they may or may not occur depending on numerous economic, industry, and company factors, all of which are beyond the investor's control.

The timing of purchases and sales is closely related to risk. Many investors purchase a stock, hold it for a period of time during which the price drops, and then sell it below the original purchase price, at a loss. The proper strategy, of course, is to buy stocks low and sell high, but the problem of predicting price movements makes it difficult to implement. The investor must always be abreast of the stock market and stock price movements. In general, because of the risk associated with common stock price movements and the fact that common stock dividends do not have to be paid, common stock is probably not the best investment if a steady income is desired. However, there are many stocks which provide generous, dependable incomes plus moderate growth.

Preferred stock is an income-oriented type of security commonly purchased by large institutional investors and most often issued by public utilities. It is sometimes issued as part of a merger transaction between firms. Preferred stock is a form of ownership, but its fixed return characteristic often causes it to be viewed as a type of debt. Although preferred stocks are traded in the securities markets, their investment appeal can be attributed to the income they provide to their holders in the form of dividends.

Preferred Stock Investments

Rights of Preferred Stockholders

As indicated at the beginning of this chapter, preferred stockholders are given preference over common stockholders with respect to income and assets. The company must pay the stated dividend to preferred stockholders prior to distributing any dividends to common stockholders. The same type of preferential treatment is given preferred stockholders in situations in which the firm is being liquidated. In the process of liquidation, the claims of preferred stockholders must be fully satisfied prior to those of common stockholders. Preferred stockholders, however, are given only a fixed dollar dividend, while common stockholders, who take a great deal more risk, may receive anywhere from zero to a very high dividend payment. Preferred stockholders also are normally not given voting rights. Even though they are owners, their preferential treatment over common stockholders costs them a voice in management. It is usually *only* when their dividends are "passed" (not paid) for a certain number of consecutive quarters that preferred stockholders are given the right to elect a specified number of directors.

Types of Preferred Stock

A number of types of preferred stock are available for investment consideration. While the various types are not widely divergent, certain key features of preferred stock do affect investment planning.

Cumulative or Noncumulative Most preferred stock is cumulative, which means that any dividends passed by the directors in past periods must be paid prior to distributing any dividends to common stockholders. For example, assume a firm has outstanding a $4 preferred stock, which means that $4 per year or $1 per quarter is the stated dividend, on which the last two dividends have been passed. Before any dividends can be paid to the common stockholder, the preferred stockholder must be paid the $2 of past dividends plus the current dividend of $1. Had the preferred stock been noncumulative, only the current $1 dividend would have had to be paid prior to distributing any earnings to the common stockholders.

Participating or Nonparticipating Most preferred stocks are nonparticipating, which means that the preferred stockholder receives only the stated amount of dividends. Occasionally a participating preferred stock issue is made. These issues allow the preferred stockholder to share in the distribution of dividends once the common stockholder has received a specified dividend. An example might be a preferred stock in which the preferred stockholders participate equally with the common stockholders on a per share dividend basis once the common stockholders have received a specified per share dividend. Participating preferred stock is issued only in instances where a firm is unable to obtain needed financing using more conventional types of securities.

Conversion Feature It is not unusual to find preferred stocks that are convertible, which means that the holder has the opportunity to exchange the preferred stock for shares of common stock. Convertible preferred stock can be exchanged for a specified number of shares of common stock during a specified period of time. For example, a share of preferred stock may be convertible into two shares of common stock anytime after April 1, 1986. The holder of a share of convertible preferred stock may elect to convert the stock or may continue to hold the convertible preferred instead.

The decision whether or not to convert depends on many factors, including the market price of the common stock and the length of time remaining until the conversion option expires. Convertible preferred stock has appeal since it provides fixed dividend income while offering price appreciation opportunities quite similar to those obtained with the common stock into which it is convertible. By including this conversion feature in new preferred stock issues, many firms have been able to make preferred stock an attractive investment.

Call Feature Preferred stock may be callable, which means that the issuing company can repurchase the stock at a specified price during a certain period of time. All convertible preferred stock has this feature, and quite often nonconvertible issues will be callable. The "call price" is normally stated in advance or is somehow tied to the prevailing market price of the preferred stock. The call feature allows the issuer to retire the preferred stock. In the case of convertible preferred stock, the issuer can force the preferred stockholders into converting the preferred, by calling it when the call price is lower than the prevailing market price.

Preferred Stock Investment Considerations

Preferred stock may be an attractive investment for those interested in receiving a fixed income while still being an owner of the firm. Although the fixed income of preferred stock along with its possible appreciation in value does have appeal, preferred stock is not especially popular among small investors. Because of its fixed dividend return, fluctuations in the market price of preferred stocks are primarily attributable to changes in interest rates and/or dividend rates of other fixed income securities.

As pointed out earlier, preferred stock is commonly held by certain financial institutions in order to "round out" their investment portfolio. When investments in preferred stock are being considered, those that are convertible should be given high priority, for they provide not only a guaranteed return but also some of the benefits of common stock price movements. Of course, the purchase of any security depends largely on the needs of the investor. For example, a retired person who wishes to receive regular income but does not have enough to buy a $1,000 bond may find preferred stock the perfect investment. The lack of popularity of preferred stock investments is probably due to the fact that other more attractive investment instruments exist.

Bond Investments

Bonds, which are the negotiable debt instruments of corporations or governments, are far more popular investments than preferred stocks for establishing a fixed income. The purchaser of a bond receives periodic interest over the life of the bond and the face value of the bond—the amount that was originally lent to the issuer—at maturity. Bond interest is generally paid semiannually, and bond maturities range from five to

Figure 6-4 **Sample Bond ($1,000 Face Value) for The Williams Companies**

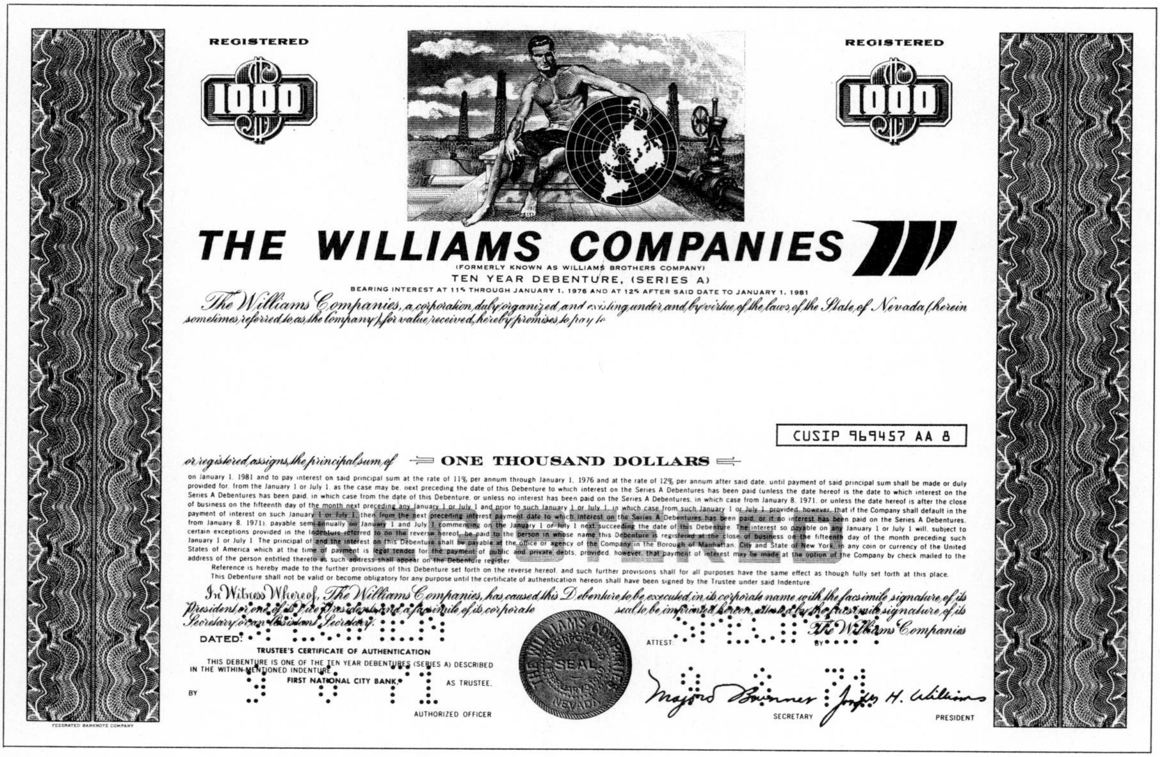
REGISTERED

1000

REGISTERED

1000

THE WILLIAMS COMPANIES

(FORMERLY KNOWN AS WILLIAMS BROTHERS COMPANY)

TEN YEAR DEBENTURE, (SERIES A)

BEARING INTEREST AT 11% THROUGH JANUARY 1, 1976 AND AT 12% AFTER SAID DATE TO JANUARY 1, 1981

The Williams Companies, a corporation duly organized and existing under and by virtue of the laws of the State of Nevada (herein sometimes referred to as the Company) for value received, hereby promises to pay to

CUSIP 969457 AA 8

or registered assigns, the principal sum of ONE THOUSAND DOLLARS

on January 1, 1981 and to pay interest on said principal sum at the rate of 11% per annum through January 1, 1976 and at the rate of 12% per annum after said date, until payment of said principal sum shall be made or duly provided for, from the January 1 or July 1, as the case may be, next preceding the date of this Debenture to which interest on the Series A Debentures has been paid (unless the date hereof is the date to which interest on the Series A Debentures has been paid, in which case from the date of this Debenture, or unless no interest has been paid on the Series A Debentures, in which case from January 8, 1971, or unless the date hereof is after the close of business on the fifteenth day of the month next preceding any January 1 or July 1 and prior to such January 1 or July 1, in which case from such January 1 or July 1, provided, however, that if the Company shall default in the payment of interest on such January 1 or July 1, then from the next preceding interest payment date to which interest on the Series A Debentures has been paid, or if no interest has been paid on the Series A Debentures, from January 8, 1971), payable semi-annually on January 1 and July 1 commencing on the January 1 or July 1 next succeeding the date of this Debenture. The interest so payable on any January 1 or July 1 will, subject to certain exceptions provided in the Indenture referred to on the reverse hereof, be paid to the person in whose name this Debenture is registered at the close of business on the fifteenth day of the month preceding such January 1 or July 1. The principal of and the interest on this Debenture shall be payable at the office or agency of the Company in the Borough of Manhattan, City and State of New York, in any coin or currency of the United States of America which at the time of payment is legal tender for the payment of public and private debts, provided, however, that payment of interest may be made at the option of the Company by check mailed to the address of the person entitled thereto as such address shall appear on the Debenture register.

Reference is hereby made to the further provisions of this Debenture set forth on the reverse hereof, and such further provisions shall for all purposes have the same effect as though fully set forth at this place.

This Debenture shall not be valid or become obligatory for any purpose until the certificate of authentication hereon shall have been signed by the Trustee under said Indenture.

In Witness Whereof, The Williams Companies, has caused this Debenture to be executed in its corporate name with the facsimile signature of its President or one of its Vice Presidents and a facsimile of its corporate seal to be imprinted hereon, attested by the facsimile signature of its Secretary or an Assistant Secretary.

DATED:

TRUSTEE'S CERTIFICATE OF AUTHENTICATION

THIS DEBENTURE IS ONE OF THE TEN YEAR DEBENTURES (SERIES A) DESCRIBED IN THE WITHIN-MENTIONED INDENTURE.

FIRST NATIONAL CITY BANK, AS TRUSTEE,

BY

AUTHORIZED OFFICER

ATTEST:

The Williams Companies

BY

SECRETARY

PRESIDENT

FEDERATED BANKNOTE COMPANY

Source: Courtesy of The Williams Companies, Tulsa, Oklahoma.

thirty years. Because the denominations of bonds are commonly in the $1,000 range, generally only large institutions and wealthy individuals actively deal in bond investments. A sample bond issued by The Williams Companies is shown in Figure 6-4. Although certain risks relating to both interest rates and purchasing power are associated with bond investments, there is such a wide variety of bonds available that investors willing to devote sufficient time can find bonds which conform to their investment needs.

Issuers of Bonds

The issuers of bonds available for investment consideration include corporations, municipalities, and the federal government. Their special roles and the characteristics of the bonds they issue are described separately below.

Corporate Bonds Corporations sell bonds in order to raise funds needed for expansion and growth. Most corporate bonds have maturities of twenty to thirty years and are listed and traded on an organized security exchange or in the over-the-counter market. Although the most common denomination of these bonds is $1,000, their prices in the marketplace are quoted as a percentage of the $1,000 face value. For example, a $1,000 bond selling at 87¹/₈ has a market value of $871.25 (0.87125 × $1,000). The stated interest return on corporate bonds at time of issue varies depending on the quality of the bond, which is determined by the financial condition of the issuer.

Municipal Bonds State and local governments often issue bonds to finance certain projects. These *municipal bonds* are quite popular among persons in high tax brackets, even at lower interest rates than those on corporate bonds, since the interest received on them is exempt from federal and in many cases state taxes. Table 6-2 indicates the difference in yields between taxable interest bonds and tax-free municipal bonds for taxpayers in high tax brackets. According to the table, for instance, a tax-exempt municipal bond that pays interest at a rate of 6 percent is equivalent to a bond that receives no exemption and pays interest at a

Table 6-2 **Converting Tax-Exempt Yields to Equivalent Taxable Yields for Persons in High Tax Brackets**[a]
(Taxable Income in Thousands)

Joint Return	$20 to $24	$24 to $28	$28 to $32	$32 to $36	$36 to $40	$40 to $44	$44 to $52	$52 to $64	$64 to $78	$78 to $88	$88 to $100	$100 to $120	$120 to $140
Tax-Exempt Yield	32	38	39	42	45	% Tax Bracket 48	50	53	55	58	60	62	64
4.00	5.88	6.25	6.68	6.90	7.27	7.69	8.00	8.51	8.89	9.52	10.00	10.53	11.11
4.50	6.62	7.03	7.38	7.76	8.18	8.65	9.00	9.57	10.00	10.71	11.25	11.84	12.50
5.00	7.35	7.81	8.20	8.62	9.09	9.62	10.00	10.64	11.11	11.90	12.50	13.16	13.89
5.50	8.09	8.59	9.02	9.48	10.00	10.58	11.00	11.70	12.22	13.10	13.75	14.47	15.28
6.00	8.82	9.37	9.84	10.34	10.91	11.54	12.00	12.77	13.33	14.29	15.00	15.79	18.67
6.50	9.56	10.16	10.68	11.21	11.82	12.50	13.00	13.83	14.44	15.48	16.25	17.11	18.06
7.00	10.29	10.94	11.48	12.07	12.73	13.46	14.00	14.89	15.56	16.67	17.50	18.42	19.44
7.50	11.03	11.72	12.30	12.93	13.64	14.42	15.00	15.96	16.67	17.88	18.75	19.74	20.83
8.00	11.76	12.50	13.11	13.79	14.55	15.38	16.00	17.02	17.78	19.05	20.00	21.05	22.22
8.50	12.50	13.28	13.93	14.66	15.45	16.35	17.00	18.09	18.89	20.24	21.25	22.37	23.61
9.00	13.24	14.06	14.75	15.52	16.36	17.31	18.00	19.15	20.00	21.43	22.50	23.68	25.00

[a]To see what a taxable-interest bond would have to yield to equal your take-home yield in a tax-free municipal bond, find your taxable income bracket. Then find the yield in the left-hand column of a tax-free bond you might buy and read across until you find what percentage interest you would have to receive from a taxable security to equal that yield.

Source: Reprinted with permission from *Investments for a Changing Economy* (New York: Merrill Lynch, Pierce, Fenner & Smith, May 1977), p. 15.

"What if EVERYONE puts his money in
tax-free municipal bonds?"

Municipal Bond Interest Bypasses the IRS
Source: Reprinted by permission of Sidney Harris.

rate of 10.91 percent for an individual paying taxes at a 45 percent rate
($6\% \div [1 - .45]$). In general, the higher the tax bracket, the more
attractive municipal bonds become; they are especially attractive to
wealthy individuals desiring fixed income from their investments.

Because there is such a diversity of municipal bonds available, investors must be careful to assess the quality of the bond in order to
make sure that the issuer will not default and the bond can be sold prior
to maturity, if necessary. Although it may not seem that the issuer of
municipals would default on either interest or principal payments, it does
occasionally occur, especially on issues of small communities.

Federal Government Bonds The federal government also sells bonds
in order to finance its activities. These bonds make up part of the so-
called *national debt*. Ranging in maturity from three months to twenty-
eight or more years, these bonds come in many forms, including treasury
bills, treasury notes and treasury bonds, and savings bonds, which were
discussed in Chapter 5. The interest returns on these government issues are lower than returns on corporate issues since the risk of default

is viewed as nonexistent. Because of their riskless nature and fixed returns, investment in government bonds appeals to more conservative investors who wish to receive a reasonable, but certain, return.

Treasury Bills are issued in 91 to 360 day maturities with interest returns that reflect the existing financial conditions. They are readily marketable and can be purchased in denominations of $10,000 or more through a broker or bank or directly from the Federal Reserve. They are sold below their face value (at a discount) and can be redeemed for face value at maturity. The size of the discount from face value and the time required to attain maturity determine the interest return received.

Treasury Notes normally have one to five year maturities and sell with interest rates slightly above that on treasury bills. They are also quite marketable and may be purchased in denominations of $1,000 or more. They have a stated rate of interest that is paid semiannually to all holders.

Treasury Bonds are issued with initial maturities of five to twenty-eight years and generally have interest rates above treasury bills and notes due to their higher purchasing power and interest rate risks. Treasury bonds are also very marketable and can be purchased in $1,000 denominations. As in the case of treasury notes, the stated rate of interest on treasury bonds is paid semiannually.

Characteristics of Bonds

Bonds differ according to the specifications and conditions under which they are issued. The following discussion considers some of the characteristics of bonds, particularly of corporate bonds, since they are probably most appealing due to the diversity of risk-return possibilities they offer.

Legal Aspects When corporations issue bonds, an *indenture*, which is a legal contract clearly stating all obligations of the issuer, is drawn up. Within the indenture, the dates and amounts of interest and principal payments are stated along with other provisions designed to protect the quality of the bond. In order to make sure that the indenture is not violated by the issuer, a *trustee*, which is generally a large commercial bank, is appointed to enforce the indenture. Though hired by the issuer, the trustee protects the interests of the bondholders. Quite often in order to aid in the bond preparation and sale process, the issuer may use an *investment banking* firm, which is paid for its advisory and selling assistance.

Unsecured or Secured Bonds can be issued on the creditworthiness of the company or with specific assets held as collateral. Unsecured bonds are called *debentures,* while secured bonds are referred to as *mortgage bonds, collateral trust bonds,* or *equipment trust obligations.* Mortgage bonds, which are the most common type of secured bond, have real property (land, buildings, equipment) pledged against them; collateral trust bonds have stocks and bonds owned by the issuer pledged against them; and equipment trust obligations are secured by certain types of equipment.

In the instance of default, the holders of debentures have a general claim on the firm's assets. When a firm defaults on secured bonds, the specific assets held as collateral are liquidated and the proceeds are used to satisfy the bondholders' claims. If, after liquidating the collateral, the claims of secured bondholders have not been satisfied, they become general creditors for the remainder of their claims. In order to protect debenture holders from having assets pledged against subsequent bond issues, a clause can be included in the indenture requiring that the debenture holders share equally in the liquidation of any pledged assets. Secured bonds are generally viewed as a safer investment than debentures since specific assets stand behind them and can be used to satisfy the bondholders' claims. Of course, since only firms having strong financial positions can sell debentures, they are still generally very safe investments.

Senior or Subordinated The claims of certain bondholders are sometimes subordinated to the claims of other bondholders or lenders. The claims of *subordinated debentures* are not especially strong; normally they are viewed as nearly equivalent to those of a stockholder. The bonds to which the debentures are subordinated are often referred to as *senior debt* since the claims of these lenders are superior to those holding subordinated bonds. Purchasers of subordinated debentures are normally given higher interest returns and an opportunity to convert their bonds into common stock as compensation for the higher degree of risk they assume.

Conversion Feature Like preferred stocks, some corporate bonds are convertible into a specified number of shares of common stock. The conversion feature is outlined in the indenture at the time of issuance. The price per share at which conversion can be made is set above the market price at the time of issuance, but the expectation is that when the stock price exceeds the conversion price, bondholders will convert to common stock. Sometimes conversion is limited to only a certain period of years while the bond is outstanding. Most convertibles are debentures, and most subordinated debentures are convertibles. The conversion feature enhances the marketability of these issues since it provides purchasers with an opportunity for investment appreciation: they share in the growth of the firm in a fashion similar to that of the common stock-holder. Because they offer this advantage, convertible bonds typically have a lower interest rate than do similar nonconvertible bonds.

For a better understanding of the alternatives a convertible bond offers its purchaser, consider a $1,000 bond that is convertible into twenty-five shares of common stock. This means that the conversion price is $40 per share of common stock ($1,000 ÷ 25). If at the time of issue the common stock had a market price of $30, conversion would not be attractive since the bond would be worth only $750 (25 × $30) once converted. If the stock price rises above the $40 conversion price, the price of the bond will probably rise also. For instance, if the market price of the stock rises to $50, conversion would be attractive; but, since the bond price will rise to $1,250 (i.e., 25 × $50), many people may not convert the bond. They still have the benefit of the fixed interest payment of the bond along with the price movement of the stock. Convertible bonds, because they offer fixed income as well as prospects for price appreciation similar to common stocks, are attractive to people who are not necessarily interested in receiving maximum current income from their investments.

Call Feature The call feature, which allows the issuer to repurchase the bond at a prespecified price, is often included as part of a bond issue. Call features do not normally come into effect until the bond has been outstanding for five or more years. The call feature is always included as part of a convertible bond because it allows the issuer to "force" bondholders to convert the bonds into common stock once the common stock price exceeds the conversion price. In other cases the use of the call feature permits a firm that no longer needs debt financing to retire debts prior to their maturity.

Bond Ratings

Potential bond investors can obtain unbiased evaluations of the quality of various bonds through bond ratings. The two chief bond ratings are provided by Moody's Investors Service, Inc., and Standard & Poor's Corporation. These companies assign ratings to bonds on the basis of quality and degree of risk. As Table 6-3 illustrates, Moody's and Standard & Poor's ratings are quite similar. It can be seen that as one moves down the classification schemes, the bonds become lower quality invest-ments. Investors should consult either of these bond ratings in order to make sure that the bonds they purchase are consistent with the level of risk they are willing to take. These ratings can be obtained at banks, brokerage firms, or libraries. Although they are not infallible, bond ratings do provide free and useful insights for investors.

Table 6-3 **Moody's and Standard & Poor's Bond Ratings**

Moody's	Interpretation	Standard & Poor's	Interpretation
Aaa	Prime Quality	AAA	Bank Investment
Aa	High Grade	AA	Quality
A	Upper Medium Grade	A	
Baa	Medium Grade	BBB	
		BB	
Ba	Lower Medium Grade or Speculative	B	Speculative
B	Speculative	CCC	
		CC	
Caa	From Very Speculative	C	
Ca	to near or in Default		
C		DDD	In Default (Rating
		DD	Indicates the Relative
		D	Salvage Value)

Source: Reprinted by permission of Moody's Investors Service, Inc; reprinted by permission from Standard & Poor's N.Y.S.E. Stock Reports.

Bond Prices

The price of a bond depends on a number of factors, including its interest rate, the number of years to maturity, and the prevailing returns on similar bonds. The most common type of corporate bond is the *registered bond,* on which interest checks are automatically mailed to the bondholder. The other type of bond is the *coupon bond,* which provides interest coupons that are detached and redeemed at specified dates. The popularity of registered bonds is attributed to the fact that there is too much risk involved in handling coupon, or "bearer," bonds, since coupons can be easily lost or stolen. In order to understand why the market price of these bonds may differ from their face values, it is necessary to understand discounts and premiums, yields to maturity, and interest rate effects.

Discounts and Premiums Once a bond is issued, it is not unusual for its market price to deviate from its face value. When a bond is selling below its face value, it is said to be selling at a *discount*; when it is selling above its face value, it is selling at a *premium.* Bond discounts and premiums result from the fact that other bonds of similar risk (with similar ratings) are selling for higher or lower rates of interest, respectively, than the *coupon* (or stated) rate on the bond. Changes in the interest returns on similar-risk bonds are brought about by changes in the supply and demand for money. These supply and demand changes normally result from changes in economic activity. In order for the bond to be attractive to investors, it must provide a return that is competitive with similar-risk bonds; since the rate of interest paid to bondholders is fixed, the price must be adjusted in order to allow investors to receive a competitive return on the bond.

For example, a bond with a face value of $1,000 and a 7 percent coupon rate would be expected to sell for $1,000 as long as similar-risk bonds are selling at 7 percent returns. If the *market rate* of interest on the similar-risk securities increases, the price of the bond will drop in order to allow the investor to receive a competitive return. The amount of the discount will depend on the prevailing interest rates and the time to maturity of the bond. The closer the market rate to the coupon rate and the closer to maturity the bond, the smaller the amount of the discount.

In effect, the discount allows the coupon rate of the bond to become competitive, since, as the price drops, the coupon rate represents a higher percentage return. Of course, when the market interest rates fall below the coupon rate on the bond, the reverse process will result, and the price of the bond will rise above its face value. Table 6-4 presents the bond prices associated with varying market rates of interest for the bond with the 7 percent interest rate described above. The bond is assumed to have just been issued with a twenty year maturity.

Table 6-4 **Bond Prices for Varying Market Interest Rates**
(7 Percent Stated Interest Rate, 20 Year Maturity, $1,000 Bond)

Market Rate of Interest	Bond Price	Discount, Premium, or Face Value
4%	$1,407	Premium
5	1,249	Premium
6	1,115	Premium
7	1,000	Face Value
8	902	Discount
9	817	Discount
10	745	Discount

Yield to Maturity The annual rate of return that a bondholder purchasing the bond today and holding it until it matures would receive is the bond's *yield to maturity*. The yield to maturity reflects two types of return: the actual interest income and the payment of face value at maturity. If a bond is purchased for its face value, its yield to maturity equals the stated rate of interest. But if it is purchased at a discount, its yield to maturity is greater than the stated rate because in addition to receiving the stated rate, the face value, which is greater than the initial investment, is received at maturity. Of course, if a premium is paid for the bond, the opposite is true; the yield to maturity is less than the coupon rate.

Equation 6.1 provides the formula for calculating an approximate yield-to-maturity for a $1,000 bond:

$$\text{Approximate yield-to-maturity} = \frac{I + \dfrac{\$1,000 - N}{n}}{\dfrac{N + \$1,000}{2}} \qquad (6.1)$$

where:

I = annual interest payment in dollars
N = the amount paid to purchase the bond
n = the number of years remaining to maturity of the bond

Assume, for example, that you are contemplating the purchase of a $1,000, 8 percent coupon bond, with fifteen years remaining to maturity, at a discount for $910. If $I = \$80$ (0.08 [$1,000]), $N = \$910$, and $n = 15$

Tax Exempt Municipals May Be the Answer

Paul David of San Juan, California, a successful fifty-five year old attorney, earned a taxable income of $40,000 annually from his partnership in a law firm. Over the years, he had built up a nest egg of $125,000, which he deposited in various savings institutions. The $125,000 earned interest at a rate of 6 percent, providing him additional income of $7,500 a year. Because he was in a high income tax bracket, the federal taxes took $2,622 of his $7,500 each year. In addition, the State of California took another $769 in taxes. This left David with $4,109 after taxes from the interest on his savings.

David resented paying such high taxes, so he visited his broker, Jay Reynolds, to ask his advice on some tax-free investment deals. His broker recommended the new Aa-rated bonds of the Los Angeles Department of Water and Power due in 2015. These were available with 6¾ percent interest coupons at a price of par ($1,000) or a yield of 6.75 percent.

Making a few quick calculations, Reynolds said, "One hundred twenty-five bonds, besides being tax-free, will earn you $8,437.50 a year in interest. Since neither the government nor the State of California will deduct any taxes, you will earn an extra $4,328.50 over and above your $125,000."

In response to his question about the amount of commission Reynolds would expect to be paid, David was told, "Since these bonds are sold over-the-counter, our firm makes money on the spread and does not directly charge you any commission on the transaction." The next day the deal was closed. The moral to this story is that you should BECOME AN INFORMED INVESTOR!

Source: Reprinted with permission from "Bonds to Save Taxes," *The Bond Book* (New York: Merrill Lynch, Pierce, Fenner & Smith, July 1975), p. 8.

years, the approximate yield-to-maturity for this bond will be 9.01 percent:

$$\text{Approximate yield-to-maturity} = \frac{\$80 + \dfrac{\$1,000 - \$910}{15}}{\dfrac{\$910 + \$1,000}{2}} = \frac{\$86}{\$955} = \underline{9.01\%}$$

This is above the 8 percent stated rate since the bond is purchased at a discount from its face value. Equation 6.1 is valid for any $1,000 bond regardless if it sells at a discount or a premium.

Interest Rate Effects As indicated above, interest rate fluctuations in the marketplace directly affect the prices at which bonds sell. If market rates of interest increase, the prices of bonds are discounted in order to provide a competitive yield-to-maturity; if market rates of interest decline, bond prices are increased in order to adjust the yield-to-maturity to a level that is competitive with the prevailing rate of interest. If you purchase a bond with the intention of holding it to maturity, changes in the market rates of interest will not affect the actual return you receive; in other words, you will get the yield to maturity expected as long as you hold the bond to maturity. If you must sell a bond prior to maturity, however, the effects of changing interest rates upon the price at which you sell may be significant.

Bond Investment Considerations

Bonds are attractive investments for those who wish to receive periodic and predictable patterns of income from their investments. High-grade (bank investment quality) bond investments provide nearly certain income along with the return of the investment at maturity. Although investment in high-grade bonds is viewed as quite conservative, its appeal lies in the fact that it provides a safe return exceeding that available from various savings instruments.

The primary danger of corporate bond investments lies in the potential effects of interest rate movements on the bond price. Over the past ten years the general trend in interest rates has been upward, which has tended to lower bond prices on outstanding bonds having lower stated interest rates. Bonds therefore do not protect investors from the inflationary pressures of our economy. It is important for the bond investor to assess the potential effects of interest rate movements and inflation on bond prices when evaluating various investment alternatives.

Summary

The basic types of securities are common stock, preferred stock, and bonds. The basic risks that must be considered when selecting security investments include business risk, financial risk, market risk, purchasing power risk, and interest rate risk. An inverse relationship exists between these risks and the expected security returns, which may be received in the form of periodic income or growth in the market price of the securities.

Common stock is a popular investment due to the diversity of risk-return combinations available. Only the shares of the larger corporations are actively traded. Common stock may be purchased in the marketplace, through public offerings or rights offerings, or by exercising warrants. Common stockholders vote in corporate elections and may pass their votes to others by signing a proxy statement. Dividends on common stock may be paid in cash or in stock. Sometimes stock splits are initiated in order to stimulate trading activity in the firm's shares. Par value and book value are historical accounting-based measures of stock value. The earnings per share and the price/earnings ratio are often used to assess the returns on common stock. On the basis of performance, common stock is often classified as blue-chip, growth, income or speculative, and cyclical or defensive. The three basic theories of common stock value are: (1) the fundamental theory; (2) the technical, or chartist, theory; and (3) the random walk theory. Common stock investment offers opportunities for both income and profit through price appreciation. Disadvantages are related to the risk associated with its returns, the difficulty of timing purchases and sales, and the relatively low dividend returns.

Preferred stock, which is a form of ownership that is given preference over common stock in the distribution of dividends and—in case the firm is liquidated—assets, is occasionally issued by corporations. Preferred stockholders do not normally receive voting privileges. Most preferred stock pays dividends on a nonparticipating and cumulative basis. Preferred stock can be convertible and/or callable. Its appeal lies in the fixed income it provides, while its chief disadvantage is that there are many more attractive investments available today.

Bonds may be issued by corporations, municipalities (in which case they are tax-exempt), and the federal government. Since corporate issues have the broadest appeal, they are given primary attention. An indenture is the legal document describing a corporate bond issue; it is enforced by the trustee. Bonds may be unsecured debentures or they may be secured by a variety of corporate assets. Bonds may also be senior to the claim of another security or subordinated to another security's claim. Like preferred stocks, bonds may be convertible or callable. Bond ratings are published by a number of companies. The market price of a bond depends on the relationship between the stated rate of interest, the market rate of interest, and the number of years to maturity. Depending on the relationship of these factors, bonds may sell at a premium (above), at a discount (below), or at their face value. Bond investments provide fixed and relatively safe returns, but upward interest rate movements and inflation do affect them adversely.

Key Terms

blue-chip stock	market risk
bond	mortgage bonds
bond discount	municipals
bond premium	noncumulative preferred
business risk	nonparticipating preferred
call feature	open corporation
capital gain	participating preferred
chartists	partnership
closed corporation	par value
collateral trust bond	preemptive right
common stock	preferred stock
conversion feature	price/earnings ratio (P/E)
corporation	principal
coupon bond	proxy
cumulative preferred	purchasing power risk
cyclical stock	random walk theory
debt capital	registered bonds
default	reverse stock split
defensive stock	rights offering
earnings per share (EPS)	securities
equipment trust obligations	senior debt
equity capital	sole proprietorship
exercise price	speculative stock
financial risk	stock dividend
fundamental theory of value	stock split
growth stock	subordinated debenture
income stock	technical theory of value
indenture	treasury bills, notes, and bonds
interest rate risk	trustee
investment	unlimited liability
investment banking	warrants
limited liability	yield-to-maturity
market rate of interest	

Review Questions

1. Name and describe the key characteristics of the two basic types of securities.

2. What is meant by the risk-return tradeoff? On what axes is it plotted? What is the riskless rate of return?

3. What are rights? How do they differ from warrants?

4. Explain the terms *proxy* and *proxy battle* as they relate to the voting rights of common stockholders.

5. How does a stock split differ from a stock dividend?

6. What are the basic classifications of common stock? Explain the difference between income and growth stock.

7. What is preferred stock? What claims do preferred stockholders have when a firm is liquidated?

8. Distinguish between a cumulative and a noncumulative preferred stock.

9. What is participating and nonparticipating preferred stock? Under what circumstances would you expect participating preferred stock to be issued?

10. Discuss the call feature as part of a preferred stock issue.

11. "The issuers of bonds available for investment consideration include corporations, municipalities, and the federal government." Briefly discuss the characteristics of the bonds issued by each of them.

12. What is a bond indenture? What role does a trustee play with respect to a bond indenture?

13. What are the basic types of unsecured bonds? What can happen to the subordinated debt holder in the instance of bankruptcy?

14. Explain the system of bond ratings used by Moody's and Standard & Poor's.

15. What is the importance of calculating bond yields?

16. What effects do current market interest rates have on the price of outstanding bonds?

17. What are bond discounts and bond premiums?

Case Problems

6-1 An Investment Plan for the Stewarts

Lee and Althea Stewart are the working parents of two school-age children. Lee earns $15,000 a year as a high school English teacher; Althea brings home another $12,000 from her job as an executive assistant. The Stewarts live rather modestly in a suburban housing development. Their monthly expenditures, including mortgage and car payments, amount to $900. During ten years of marriage, they have saved

$8,000. Their only other protection comes from a $25,000 life insurance policy.

Lee Stewart is anxious to invest some of the family savings in the stock market. He is not deterred by the contrary advice of a stockbroker, who has told him to wait until those savings have increased to at least $10,000. He argues that the time has come to begin planning for his children's education.

Questions

1. Would you recommend that the Stewarts make security investments, or would you agree with the stockbroker?

2. Prepare an investment plan for the Stewarts, taking into consideration:

(a) The risks involved in security investments

(b) The relative returns expected from different types of securities

(c) The risk-return tradeoff from the investments chosen

6-2 Neil Hudson's Choice of Investment Media

Neil Hudson is a twenty-six year old management trainee at the Monsanto Chemical Company. He is a bachelor, with no plans for matrimony. His annual salary is $18,000, and his monthly expenditures come to approximately $900. He has managed to save at the rate of $3,500 a year. His company pays the premium on his $15,000 life insurance policy. Since Neil's entire education was financed by scholarships, he was able to save $3,000 from the summer and part-time jobs he had while a student. Altogether he has a nest egg of $6,500, of which he wishes to invest at least $4,500. The remaining $2,000 will be kept in a savings account with Best Federal Savings & Loan Association at 5¼ percent interest. This amount is to be used only in case of an emergency. Although Neil can afford to take more risks than someone with family obligations, he does not wish to be a speculator. He wants to increase his net worth over the long run.

Questions

1. What are the options open to Neil?

2. What chances does he have of raising his net worth if he invests $4,500 in:

(a) Growth stocks?

(b) Blue-chip stocks?

(c) Speculative stocks?

(d) Corporate bonds?

(e) Municipal bonds?

3. Discuss the factors you would consider when analyzing these alternative media.

4. What recommendation would you give Neil with respect to the available investment alternatives? Explain.

Selected References

"Convertible Bonds: Stocks and Bonds in One Bundle." *Changing Times*, April 1975, pp. 36–38.

D'Ambrosio, Charles A. *Principles of Modern Investments*. Chicago, Ill.: Science Research Associates, 1976.

Dines, James. *How the Average Investor Can Use Technical Analysis for Stock Profits*. New York: Dines Chart, 1974.

Dreyfus, Patricia A. "A Better Break for the Small Investor." *Money*, March 1976, pp. 41–43.

———. "The Ripening Optimism about Growth Stocks." *Money*, August 1977, pp. 34–37.

Ehrbar, A. F. "The Trouble with Stocks." *Fortune*, August 1977, pp. 89–93.

Engel, Louis. *How to Buy Stocks,* 5th ed. New York: Bantam Books, 1972.

"High Risks—and Rewards—in High-Yield Bonds." *Dun's Review*, June 1977, pp. 121–124.

"Investing in Tax-Exempts." *Business Week*, 25 July 1977, pp. 127–134.

"Municipal Bonds: High Yields, High Risk." *Business Week*, 29 December 1975, p. 114.

Perham, John C. "What the Proxy Statements Don't Tell." *Dun's Review*, January 1976, pp. 36–40.

"Picking Stocks That Will Beat the Averages." *Changing Times*, March 1976, pp. 7–10.

Rolo, Charles J. "Judging What a Stock Is Worth." *Money*, May 1977, pp. 45–47.

Sherwood, Hugh C. *How to Invest in Bonds*. New York: McGraw-Hill, 1974.

Stevenson, Richard A., and Jennings, Edward H. *Fundamentals of Investments*. St. Paul, Minn.: West Publishing, 1976.

"Undervalued Stocks? Where?" *Dun's Review*, March 1976, pp. 71–74.

Vaughn, Donald E. *Survey of Investments*. 2d ed. Hinsdale, Ill.: Dryden Press, 1974.

"What Experts See for Stocks in Years Ahead." *U.S. News & World Report*, 23 February 1976, pp. 56–58.

Wycoff, Peter. *Language of Wall Street*. New York: Hopkinson and Blake, 1973.

skip

7

Making Transactions in Securities Markets

In order to clarify and illustrate the procedures involved in analyzing, selecting, and making security transactions, this chapter will discuss the following:

A Preview of Chapter 7

1. The types, organization, regulation, and operating procedures of the key securities markets and stock exchanges.

2. The various kinds of transactions and the procedures for making transactions with the aid of a stockbroker.

3. The requirements, procedures, and potential payoffs and losses involved in using borrowed funds to make security purchases.

4. The sources of information that can be used to evaluate the quality as well as the past performance of potential investments.

5. The common approaches used to evaluate investment information and develop strategies for timing investment transactions.

An individual may have an excellent understanding of the physical characteristics of boats but still be unable to operate them and navigate across a body of water. In the same sense, a thorough knowledge of stocks and bonds is not enough to permit you to carry out your investment goals. In order to operate an investment program, you need to understand the institutions, mechanisms, and procedures involved in making security transactions. To navigate through the vast array of stocks and bonds, you must know how to gather and interpret relevant information and be familiar with the strategies available for making purchase and sale decisions.

The preceding chapter presented the fundamentals of stock and bond investing, including the basic characteristics of the most common types of security investments and the differences in their risk-return characteristics. We now turn our attention to the nature of the various markets and the process of making securities transactions.

Securities Markets

The phrase *securities markets* describes the marketplace in which stocks and bonds are traded. The *capital market* is the marketplace in which long-term securities (those with lives or maturities greater than one year) are traded, while the *money market* is the marketplace for short-term securities. Since most individuals cannot deal in the money market due to the large denominations required, this chapter will consider only the capital market, in which all stock and bond transactions take place. Both types of markets provide a vital mechanism for bringing together the purchasers and sellers of securities for the purpose of making transactions. Without the development of securities markets, it would have been difficult for business firms to grow into the large corporations of today.

Types of Markets

The securities markets can be divided into two basic parts: the primary market and the secondary market. The *primary market* is the market in which new securities are sold to the public. The *secondary market* is the market in which old securities are sold. A security is traded in the primary market only when it has just been issued by a corporation. Subsequent transactions in which it is sold by one investor to another take place in the secondary market. Trading in the secondary market, where various types of "stock exchanges" exist, is more prevalent, especially among small investors who may not be able to conveniently make purchases in the primary securities market.

Primary Markets When a corporation sells a new security issue, a number of financial institutions participate in the transaction. The corporation will probably use an *investment banking* firm, which specializes in *underwriting* (selling) new security issues. The investment banker will give the corporation advice with respect to pricing and other aspects of the issue and will sell the new securities or arrange for a *selling group* to do so. The selling group is normally made up of a large number of stock brokerage firms, each of which accept the responsibility for selling a certain portion of the new issue. Occasionally on very large issues of securities, the originating investment banker will bring in other underwriting firms as partners and form an *underwriting syndicate* as an attempt to spread the risk associated with selling the new securities. In such cases, each underwriter forms a selling group responsible for selling its portion of the new issue. Figure 7-1 depicts this selling process for a new security issue.

Figure 7-1 **Organization of New Security Selling Process**

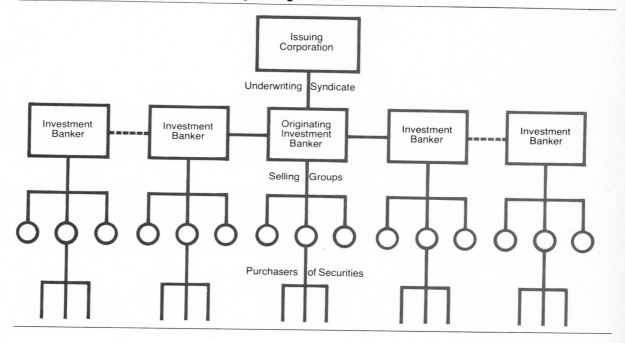

In the course of selling a new security, both the underwriting firm and the selling firms are compensated by receiving discounts from the anticipated sales prices. In other words, the underwriting and selling firms buy the securities at a price below that at which they will sell them. The discount is the difference between the price they pay and the sale price. A potential purchaser of a new issue must be provided a *prospectus,* which is a document describing the firm and the issuer. Certain agencies of the federal government have the responsibility of making sure that all information included within a prospectus is an accurate representation of the facts. Sometimes investors have trouble purchasing new security issues because all shares allocated to the stockbrokers have been sold— often prior to the official sale date. Of course, if new shares are sold using *rights* or *warrants,* which were discussed in Chapter 6, the ability to purchase new shares may be considerably more limited, since only the holders of these instruments can purchase the shares.

Secondary Markets The secondary markets for securities exist in order to permit the buyers and sellers of securities to make transactions. Included among the secondary markets are the various *security exchanges,* in which the buyers and sellers of securities are brought together. Both organized and over-the-counter securities exchanges exist. The organized exchanges typically handle transactions in the securities of larger, better-known companies, and the over-the-counter exchanges handle transactions in the securities of smaller, less well-known firms. The *over-the-counter market* is basically a mass telecommunications network linking buyers and sellers, while the *organized exchanges* are well-structured institutions where the market forces of supply and demand are brought together. Since most transactions of small investors are made in the secondary market, primary emphasis will be given to it throughout this chapter.

Organized Security Exchanges

The forces of supply and demand for various securities are brought together in the organized security exchanges. In these exchanges, the floor is laid out according to the different types of securities, and *members* of the exchange can trade only *listed* securities on the floor of the exchange. Members of an exchange are said to own a "seat" on the exchange. This privilege is obtained by meeting certain financial specifications and requirements. Only the securities of companies that have met certain "listing requirements" are traded on the exchange, and those companies must comply with regulations established to assure that they do not make financial or legal misrepresentations to their stockholders. Not only must the firms comply with the rules of the specific exchange but they must also fulfill certain requirements established by the Securities and Exchange Commission (SEC), which is a regulatory agency of the federal government. A few of the larger exchanges are described below.

New York Stock Exchange The New York Stock Exchange (NYSE) is the largest and most prestigious organized security exchange. It handles the major portion of the dollar volume of securities transactions and accounts for approximately 65 percent of the total annual share volume. Membership on the NYSE is limited to 1,366 seats. The cost of a seat has ranged from $17,000 to $500,000; most recently seats have sold for $100,000 or more. Most are owned by stock brokerage firms. The largest of these firms—Merrill Lynch, Pierce, Fenner & Smith—owns seven seats.

The listing requirements on the NYSE are the most stringent of all organized exchanges. In order to be listed on the NYSE, a firm must have at least 1,800 stockholders each owning 100 shares or more. It must also have a minimum of one million shares of stock outstanding, of which 800,000 are publicly held; it must have demonstrated earning power of $2.5 million before taxes at the time of listing; and, finally, it must pay a listing fee. The ten companies listed on the NYSE with the largest number of common stockholders in 1976 are shown in Table 7-1. Firms

Table 7-1 Ten NYSE Companies Having the Largest Number of Common Stockholders, 1976

Company	Number of Stockholders
American Telephone & Telegraph	2,934,000
General Motors	1,311,000
Exxon	707,000
International Business Machines	589,000
General Electric	530,000
General Telephone & Electronics	500,000
Gulf Oil	372,000
Texaco	362,000
Ford Motor	352,000
Consolidated Edison	303,000

Source: Reprinted with permission from *The New York Stock Exchange 1976 Fact Book* (New York: New York Stock Exchange, 1976), p. 37.

failing to continue to meet listing requirements can be *delisted.* Over 1,200 firms accounting for over 1,700 different stocks and over 1,300 different bonds are currently listed on the NYSE.

American Stock Exchange The American Stock Exchange (AMEX) is the second largest exchange. Its organization and procedures are quite similar to those of the NYSE. Membership costs and listing requirements on AMEX are not quite as stringent as for the NYSE. There are approximately 500 seats on AMEX and over 1,000 listed stocks and 150 listed bonds. AMEX is believed to handle approximately 25 percent of all share volume. It and the NYSE are the dominant organized security exchanges: in combination they handle about 90 percent of all shares traded.

Regional Stock Exchanges A number of regional stock exchanges such as the Midwest Stock Exchange, the Pacific Coast Stock Exchange, and the Boston Stock Exchange, also exist. In all, there are eleven regional exchanges that deal primarily in the trading of securities with local and regional appeal. Most of these regional exchanges are modeled after the NYSE, but their membership and listing requirements are considerably more lenient. It is not unusual for these regional exchanges to list securities also listed on the NYSE or AMEX in order to enhance their trading activity. The total activity on the regional stock exchanges accounts for only about 7 percent of the annual volume on organized exchanges.

Over-the-Counter Market

The over-the-counter market (OTC) is not a specific institution like the organized stock exchanges, but rather an intangible relationship between the buyers and sellers of securities. The market is linked together by a mass telecommunications network. Unlike the organized security exchanges, many of the trades in the OTC market are negotiated directly between buyer and seller. Most government and corporate bonds as well as a numerical majority of stocks are traded in the OTC market, which has no listing requirements: all nonlisted securities are traded there. Traders known as *broker-dealers* make markets in certain securities by offering to either buy or sell them at stated prices.

The *bid* and the *ask* price represent, respectively, the highest price offered at which a security may be purchased and the lowest price at which it is offered for sale. The OTC market is linked through the National Association of Security Dealers Automated Quotation System (NASDAQ), which provides up-to-date bid and ask prices on thousands of securities and allows buyers and sellers to locate each other in order to consummate transactions. Buyers and sellers of the less active OTC securities, which are not traded on the NASDAQ system, must find each other through references or through known *market makers*, who specialize in making markets in certain securities.

Regulation of Securities Markets

The Securities and Exchange Commission (SEC), an agency of the federal government, was established to enforce the Securities Exchange Acts of 1933 and 1934. These acts were aimed at regulating not only the operation of security exchanges and the securities markets, but also the disclosure of information on both new and outstanding listed securities. In addition to the regulations of the SEC, there are laws in most states on the sale of securities within their borders. These "blue sky" laws protect investors by preventing firms from attempting to sell nothing but "blue sky." The exchanges themselves also perform a self-regulatory function through their governing bodies.

The OTC market is regulated by the National Association of Securities Dealers (NASD), which is made up of all brokers and dealers in OTC securities. NASD is a self-regulatory organization that polices the activities of brokers and dealers in order to make sure the association's standards are upheld. The SEC supervises the activities of NASD, thus providing investors further protection from fraudulent activities.

General Market Conditions: Bull or Bear

The market is said to be bullish or bearish depending on whether the prices of stocks are generally rising or falling, respectively. Changing market conditions generally stem from changing investor attitudes, changes in economic activity, and certain governmental actions generally aimed at stimulating or slowing down the economy. *Bull markets* are favorable markets normally associated with investor optimism, economic recovery, and governmental stimulus, while *bear markets* are unfavorable markets normally associated with investor pessimism, economic slow-downs, and government control. It is not unusual to find individual securities that are bullish in a bear market or bearish in a bull market. Market conditions—bull or bear—are difficult to predict and usually can only be identified once they exist.

To take advantage of the full spectrum of market opportunities, you must not only be aware of the mechanism available for accessing the securities markets, but you must also understand the various types of orders that may be placed and the services available to help you make transactions.

Making Security Transactions

Stockbrokers

Stockbrokers, sometimes called "account executives," purchase and sell securities for their customers. They must be licensed by the exchanges on which they place orders and abide by the strict ethical guidelines of the exchanges and the SEC. These stockbrokers work for brokerage firms, which own "seats" on the organized security exchanges. Thus the members of the security exchange actually execute orders transmitted to them by the brokers in the various sales offices. For example, the largest stockbrokerage firm, Merrill Lynch, Pierce, Fenner & Smith, has brokerage firms located in most major cities in the U.S. Orders from these offices are transmitted to the main office of Merrill Lynch and then to the floor of the stock exchange (NYSE, AMEX, or other), where they are executed. Confirmation that the orders have been executed is transmitted back to the broker placing the order and then to the customer. This

Figure 7-2 **How Stocks Are Bought and Sold on the New York Stock Exchange**

How Stocks Are Bought and Sold on the New York Stock Exchange

1. An account executive receives a round-lot market order from an investor by telephone.

2. The order goes to the wire room of the local office, where it is sent by teletype to the New York headquarters . . .

3. . . . and simultaneously to the floor of the New York Stock Exchange . . .

4. . . . where it is given to the firm's floor broker . . .

5. . . . who executes it, bargaining for the best possible price, at the appropriate trading post.

6. Confirmation is teletyped to the local office . . .

7. . . . where it is received . . .

8. . . . and relayed to the account executive so that he can notify the customer of the price he paid—or received—for the stock. It takes only two or three minutes to buy or sell a popular stock.

Source: Reprinted with permission from *How to Invest* (New York: Merrill Lynch, Pierce, Fenner & Smith, 1971).

process, which can be carried out in a matter of minutes with the use of sophisticated telecommunications networks, is illustrated in Figure 7-2.

Orders for the over-the-counter (OTC) securities must be executed through *market makers* in the given security. The NASDAQ system, along with available information on who makes markets in certain securities, allows the broker to execute orders in OTC securities. Normally, OTC transactions can be executed rapidly since most market makers maintain inventories of the securities in which they deal in order to provide a continuous market. Although the procedure for executing orders on organized exchanges differs from that in the OTC market, you as an investor place orders with your broker, regardless of the market in which the security is traded.

How to Choose Your Broker

What would you tell someone who asked you how to select a broker?

Financial Marketing Services Corp. asked that question in a survey of stockholders. The survey was financed by Paine, Webber, Jackson & Curtis, a New York–based brokerage firm.

Here are the answers and the percentage of replies for each. Some of those polled offered more than one suggestion. Thus, the total exceeds 100 percent.

	Percent
Pick a large, well-known firm	28
Ask someone who is successful as an investor to recommend a broker	23
Interview several brokers	21
Select an experienced broker	19
Find a broker with a reputation for integrity	16
Pick someone you feel comfortable with	11
Check on services available	6
Compare commission rates	4
Ask a banker or lawyer to suggest a name	3

At the same time, many of these investors place little reliance on a broker's advice.

Asked if customers know as much about picking stocks as their brokers do, 48 percent said this is generally not true. Forty-seven percent said it is generally true.

Source: Reprinted by permission from "How to Choose Your Broker," *Nation's Business,* September 1976, p. 10. Copyright 1976 by Nation's Business, Chamber of Commerce of the United States.

Selecting a Stockbroker You should select a stockbroker who understands your investment goals and can effectively assist you in pursuing these goals. If you choose a broker whose own disposition toward investing is quite similar to yours, you should be able to avoid conflict and establish a solid working relationship. It is probably best to ask friends or business associates to recommend stockbrokers. It is not important—and often not even advisable—to know your stockbroker personally. A strict business relationship eliminates the possibility that social concerns will interfere with achievement of your investment goals. This does not mean, of course, that your broker's sole interest should be commissions. Responsible brokers make a concerted effort to establish a long-term broker-client relationship with their clients; they do not "churn accounts"—attempt to cause their clients to make many transactions in order to get numerous commissions.

Brokerage Services In addition to facilitating purchase and sale transactions for a commission, stockbrokers offer their clients a variety of other services. The stockbrokerage firm, or "house," normally provides a wide variety of free information ranging from stock and bond guides that summarize the activity of securities to research reports on specific securities or industries. Quite often the house will have a research staff that will periodically issue analyses of economic, market, industry, or company behavior and relate these behaviors to recommendations it makes to buy or sell certain securities. It is the job of your stockbroker to provide you with the type of information that is most relevant to your investment goals. As a client of a large brokerage firm, you can expect to periodically receive monthly bulletins discussing market activity and possibly including a recommended investment list. Also, you will receive a statement describing all of your transactions for the month, commission charges, interest charges, dividends received, and your account balance.

Most brokerage offices have electronic equipment of some sort that provides up-to-the-minute stock price quotations and world news. Stock price information can be obtained from either the quotation board (a large screen that electronically displays all NYSE and AMEX security transactions within a few minutes after they take place) or by keying into the telequote system, which relies on a computer terminal to provide a capsule description of almost all securities and their prices. World news, which can significantly affect the stock market, is obtained from a news wire service subscribed to by the brokerage office. Most offices also have a reference library for use by the firm's clients.

Brokerage firms will also hold your certificates in their safe for you in order to protect against their loss. The stocks kept thus by the firm are said to be held in "street name" since the broker can liquidate them for you without having to obtain your signature. You are protected against

"Are you interested in a growth stock,
high dividends, a share in America's future,
or do you just want to make a buck?"

Stockbrokers Should Know Their Clients' Investment Goals

Source: Reprinted by permission of Sidney Harris.

the loss of the securities that are held by your broker by the Securities Investor Protection Corporation (SIPC), an agency of the federal government that insures each customer's account against the financial failure of the brokerage firm. SIPC insurance covers each customer's account for up to $50,000 of securities held by the brokerage firm and up to $20,000 in cash balances held by the firm. Note, however, that the SIPC insurance does not guarantee that the dollar value of the securities will be recovered; it only guarantees that the securities themselves will be returned. Some brokerage firms insure customer accounts for amounts in excess of the required $50,000 of SIPC insurance. For example, Merrill Lynch, Pierce, Fenner & Smith insures its customers for an additional $450,000, thereby providing total coverage of up to $500,000 per account. Certainly, in light of the diversity and quality of services available among stockbrokerage houses, careful consideration should be given not only to your selection of a stockbroker but also to your choice of a firm.

Odd or Round Lot Transactions Security transactions can be made in either odd or round lots. An *odd lot* consists of less than 100 shares of a security, while a *round lot* represents a 100-share unit or multiple thereof. Since all transactions made on the floor of the major stock exchanges (New York and American) are made in round lots, the purchase or sale of odd lots requires the assistance of a special type of broker, the odd lot broker, on the floor of the exchange. The additional fee charged for the odd lot broker's services in making these types of transactions encourages round-lot transactions. Small investors, who are generally in the early stages of their investing programs and do not account for the majority of security transactions, are primarily responsible for odd lot transactions.

Brokerage Fees For executing purchase and sale transactions on behalf of their clients, brokerage firms receive commissions. Brokerage commissions are currently said to be negotiated, which means that the fees are not fixed. In practice, brokerage firms establish fee schedules that are applied to small transactions; these fees are not really negotiated. The small investor may nonetheless find that the fee schedule differs from brokerage firm to brokerage firm. On the larger, "institutional" trades, the negotiation of commissions actually does take place.

The suggested fee schedule currently used by one large brokerage firm is given in Table 7-2. Although this schedule does not specifically levy a

Table 7-2 **Suggested Brokerage Fee Schedule**
(June 1977)

Value of Transaction	Fees for an Odd Lot or 100 Shares
Under $1,000	$10.50 + 2.0% of the value of the transaction
$1,000 – $2,500	$15.50 + 1.5% of the value of the transaction
$2,500 – $5,000	$23.00 + 1.2% of the value of the transaction
Above $5,000	$83.00

premium on odd lot transactions, the fixed-cost fee component does tend to raise the per share cost of odd lot transactions. Using the fee schedule in Table 7-2 to calculate brokerage fees on a purchase of eighty shares of stock XYZ at $20 per share, the total value of the transaction would be $1,600 (80 shares × $20/share) and the brokerage fee would therefore be:

$$\$15.50 + 1.5\%(\$1,600) = \$15.50 + \$24.00 = \$39.50$$

A common rule-of-thumb is that brokerage fees are approximately 2 percent of the value of the transaction.

Aside from the brokerage fees, there are also certain transfer taxes charged by the state in which the transaction takes place, which is usually New York, since both the NYSE and AMEX are located there. These transfer taxes are levied only on the seller. In addition, a relatively insignificant federal registration fee of approximately one cent per $500 is levied by the SEC on the seller in the transfer of listed securities.

The brokerage commissions on bond transactions differ from those on stock transactions. They usually range from $2.50 to $5.00 per bond for $1,000 corporate bonds and are thus decidedly lower than the commissions on stock transactions. The magnitude of brokerage commissions is an important consideration in making security transactions since they tend to raise the overall cost of purchasing securities and lower the overall proceeds from the sale of securities.

Types of Orders

Investors can place several different kinds of orders to make security purchase or sale transactions. The type of order chosen normally depends on the investor's goals and expectations with respect to the given transaction. The three basic types of orders are the *market order*, the *limit order*, and the *stop-loss order*.

Market Order An order to buy or sell stock at the best price available at the time the order is placed is a market order. The process by which these orders are transacted was described above and depicted in Figure 7-2. These orders are executed through an auction process which attempts to allow *buy orders* to be filled at the lowest price and *sell orders* to be filled at the highest price, thereby providing the best possible deal to both purchasers and sellers of a security. Because of the speed with which market orders are transacted, the purchaser or seller of a security can be sure that the price at which the order is transacted will be very close to the market price at the time the order is placed.

Limit Order An order to either buy at a specified price or lower or sell at or above a specified price is a limit order. When a limit order is placed, the broker transmits the order to a specialist dealing in the given security on the floor of the exchange. The specialist makes a notation in his or her "book" indicating the limit order and limit price. The order is executed as soon as the specified market price or better exists and all other such orders with precedence have been satisfied. The order can be placed to remain in effect until a certain date or until canceled. Also, specialists may periodically clear their books, thereby eliminating all unexecuted limit orders.

Assume, by way of example, that you place a limit order to buy 100 shares of a stock currently selling at 20¹/₂ (security market terminology for

Discount Brokers Can Save You Money

The difference is big enough so that, as small investors regain an interest in a recovering stock market, they might also want to consider making their transactions through discount commission brokers—bare-bones operations that dispense with fancy offices, research analysts, and sales personnel and simply execute the orders of their customers.

To see what the savings might be on a typical transaction, we [Consumer Reports] queried some big brokerage houses and some discount brokers about the costs of buying one round lot (100 shares) of a $30 stock. [A $30 stock was chosen since it represents about the average price of a share traded on the New York Stock Exchange in the spring of 1976.] The commissions for buying 100 shares of that stock ranged from a high of about $59 at Merrill Lynch, Pierce, Fenner & Smith, Bache Halsey Stuart, and Dean Witter & Co., three of the largest brokerage houses, to a low of $23 at Burke, Christensen & Lewis Securities, Inc., a Chicago discounter. . . .

The table below compares the commission rates charged for four typical stock trades by three of the country's largest brokerage houses and by eight discount brokers. New York State transfer tax and SEC fee are not included. Commission prices, rounded to the nearest dollar, are as of mid-August.

To do business with a discount broker, you phone your order into a trading desk, which buys or sells the stocks you want and later confirms the trade by mail. Most brokers have toll-free 800 numbers or accept collect calls. By "settlement day" (five business days after the transaction), you must either send the firm a check for the securities you bought or deliver the stock certificates of the securities you sold.

It's not unusual for a discounter to ask a new customer to put down all or some of the cash required for the first buy order, or to furnish the stock certificates before the first sell order. Some firms, interested in serving only active customers who trade frequently, require new customers to pay a certain amount of commissions in advance. . . .

Most discounters (like some big brokerage firms) have a minimum fee per transaction, which tends to discourage orders under $1000 or so. The minimums range from $15 to $30, with most between $20 and $25.

Source: Excerpted from "What You Should Know about Discount Stock Brokers," *Consumer Reports,* October 1976, pp. 588–591. Copyright 1976 by Consumers Union of the United States, Inc., Mt. Vernon, NY 10550. Reprinted by permission from Consumer Reports, October 1976.

What It Costs to Trade Stocks

	$30 Stock		$50 Stock	
	Commission on 50 Shares	Commission on 100 Shares	Commission on 50 Shares	Commission on 100 Shares
Big Brokers				
Merrill Lynch, Pierce, Fenner & Smith (Regular)[a]	$38	$59	$52	$80
Merrill Lynch, Pierce, Fenner & Smith (Sharebuilder)	26	47	42	68
Bache Halsey Stuart	40	58	53	80
Dean Witter & Co.	38	59	54	82
Discounters				
Source Securities, New York City[a]	25	35	33	35
Quick & Reilly, New York City[b]	30	35	30	43
StockCross, Boston[c]	29	34	29	34
Kulak, Voss & Co., Springfield, Va.	25	40	35	54
Daley, Coolidge & Co., Cleveland	26	43	37	57
Burke, Christensen & Lewis Securities, Chicago[d]	23	23	23	23
Letterman Transaction Services, Newport Beach, Calif.	24	36	40	60
Charles Schwab & Co., San Francisco	24	40	40	60

a For a person who generates $250 or less in commissions per year; lower rates for people who trade more.

b For market orders; limit orders cost slightly more.

c Orders must be accompanied by 20 per cent collateral in cash or securities. Limit orders cost $10 more.

d For orders executed on Midwest Stock Exchange, or third market; orders executed on New York Stock Exchange will probably cost more.

$20.50) at a limit price of $20. Once the specialist has cleared all similar orders received before yours and once the market price of the stock has fallen to $20 or less, the order is executed. It is possible, of course, that your order might expire before the stock drops to $20. Although a limit order can be quite effective, it can also keep you from making a transaction. If, for instance, you wish to buy at $20 or less and the stock price moves from its current $20.50 price to $32 while you are waiting, your limit order has caused you to forego an opportunity to make a profit of $11.50 ($32 − $20.50) per share, or $1,150. Had you placed a market order, this profit would have been yours. Limit orders for the sale of a stock are similarly disadvantageous when the stock price closely approaches but does not attain the minimum sale limit before dropping substantially. Generally speaking, limit orders are most effective when the price of a stock is known to fluctuate greatly, since there is then a better chance the order will be executed.

Stop-Loss Order An order to sell a stock when the market price reaches or drops below a specified level is a stop-loss or *stop order.* Used to protect the investor against rapid declines in stock prices and limit loss, the stop order is placed on the specialist's book and activated when the stop price is reached. At that point in time the stop order becomes a market order to sell. This means that the stock is offered for sale at the prevailing market price, which is likely to drop below the price at which the order was initiated by the stop. For example, imagine that you own 100 shares of OEF, which is currently selling for $25. Because of the high uncertainty associated with the price movements of the stock, you decide to place a stop order at $21. If the stock price drops to $21, the specialist will sell all your OEF stock at the best price then available. If the market price increases, nothing will be lost by placing the order. It may be advisable to raise the level of the stop and thus lock in a higher level of profit when the price does increase.

Short Sale Transactions

Most security transactions are "long transactions" made in anticipation of increasing security prices in order to profit by buying low and selling high. The *short sale* transaction is made in anticipation of a decline in the security price. Although not as common as long transactions, the short sale is often used by the more sophisticated investor to profit during a period of declining prices.

When investors sell a security short, their broker borrows the security and then sells it on their behalf. The borrowed shares must, of course, be replaced in the future. If the investors can repurchase the shares at a lower price and then return them to the owner, their profit is the difference between the proceeds of the initial sale and the repurchase price. If they repurchase the shares at a price higher than the price at which the security was sold, they sustain a loss. Because the shares sold are borrowed shares, there are numerous rules and regulations governing the short sale process. One, for example, permits stocks to be sold short only when the last change in the market price of the stock has been upward.

The short sale process can be illustrated using a simple example, which ignores brokerage fees. Assume that Art Johnston wishes to sell 100 shares of ABC at $52.50 per share. After Art meets the necessary requirements, his broker borrows the shares and sells them, obtaining proceeds of $5,250 (100 shares × $52.50/share). If the stock price goes down, as Art expects, he will repurchase the shares at the lower price. Say the price drops to $40 per share and Art repurchases the 100 shares. Art will make a profit since he has been able to replace the shares for $4,000 (100 shares × $40/share), which is below the $5,250 in proceeds obtained from the sale of them. Art's profit will be $1,250 ($5,250 − $4,000). If on the other hand the stock price rises to, say, $60 per share, Art will sustain a loss of $750 ([$60.00/share] [100 shares] − [$52.50/share] [100 shares]). Art, or anyone who sells short, is betting on a price decline. In the preceding example, Art, of course, would have to pay brokerage fees, which would result in decreased profits or increased losses. Because of the high risk involved in short sales, you should ask your broker to familiarize you with all their possibilities and pitfalls before committing yourself to them.

Borrowing to Purchase Securities

It is possible to borrow a portion of the amount necessary to purchase securities. *Buying on margin,* as this is called, is a common practice that allows investors to use other people's money (borrowed money) in an attempt to heighten their overall return.

Making Margin Purchases The *margin requirements,* which specify the proportion of each dollar used to purchase a security that the investor must provide, are set by the Federal Reserve System (Fed). Most recently, the margin requirement has been around 50 percent, which means that at least 50 percent of each dollar invested must be the investor's; the remaining 50 percent or less may be borrowed. For example, you could purchase $5,000 worth of stock by putting up only $2,500 of your own money and borrowing the remaining $2,500 if the margin requirement is 50 percent. It is believed that the Fed can depress or stimulate, respectively, stock market activity by raising or lowering the margin requirement.

In order to make margin purchases, approval of your broker is required. You must also have minimum equity of $2,000 in cash or securities on deposit with your broker and agree to let the shares you purchase be loaned out to short sellers. Once the necessary requirements are met, the brokerage firm will loan you the needed funds and retain the securities you purchase as collateral. Brokerage houses usually charge interest on those funds at a rate ½ to 1 percent above the prime rate of interest (i.e., the rate of interest charged on loans to the highest quality business borrower). It is not unusual for brokerage houses to establish their own in-house margin requirements, which are more restrictive than those of the Federal Reserve System. It is also possible to obtain loans for purchasing securities from your commercial bank, but the Fed's margin requirements still apply, even though they may be a bit more difficult to enforce. Along with the above-mentioned requirements, stock exchanges and brokerage houses insist that margin purchasers put up additional money as collateral when the stock price falls to a level at which their equity represents less than 25 percent or so of the current market value. This is called a *maintenance margin* requirement and is illustrated below.

Assume that the margin requirement is currently 50 percent but your brokerage firm has an in-house margin requirement of 60 percent. In addition, the maintenance margin requirement is 25 percent and your brokerage firm charges 7 percent interest on margin loans. If you wish to purchase a round lot (100 shares) of LMN, which is currently selling for $50 per share, you can either make the purchase entirely with your own money or you can borrow a portion of the purchase price. The cost of the transaction is $5,000 ($50/share × 100 shares). If you borrow, you will have to put up only $3,000 of your own money (60 percent × $5,000); you can borrow the $2,000 balance ($5,000 purchase price − $3,000 of your money). Table 7-3 compares the rates of return you will receive when margin is used and when it is not in two cases: (1) a $10 per share increase in the stock price and (2) a $10 per share decrease in the stock price. It is assumed the stock was held for one year, and all brokerage commissions are ignored.

As indicated in Table 7-3, the use of margin allows you to increase the return on your investment when the stock price increases. The return on your investment when the stock price increases from $50/share to $60/share is 20 percent without margin and 28.67 percent with the use of margin. But when the stock price declines from $50/share to $40/share, the return on your investment is negative 20 percent without margin and negative 38 percent with margin; the use of margin magnifies the loss on your investment. If the stock price drops below $26.67/share, the total market value of your stock will be less than $2,667 ($26.67 × 100 shares). If you have used margin to borrow $2,000, your investment or equity will be less than $667 ($2,667 market value − $2,000 borrowing). Your investment will thus be less than 25 percent ($667 ÷ $2,667) of the current market value of your stock. Since you will be in violation of the maintenance margin requirement, your broker will probably require you to increase your investment. Clearly, the risks inherent in buying on

Table 7-3 **The Impact of Margin on Investment Returns**

	Without Margin		With Margin	
Dollars invested				
Your investment	$5,000		$3,000	
Borrowing	0		2,000	
Total purchase (100 shares @ $50)	$5,000		$5,000	
Sell stock for $60/share one year later				
Gross proceeds (100 shares @ $60)	$6,000		$6,000	
Less: Interest @ 7% of borrowing	0		140	
Net proceeds	$6,000		$5,860	
Less: Total investment	5,000		5,000	
Net profit (loss)	$1,000		$ 860	
Return on your investment	$\dfrac{\$1,000}{\$5,000} = 20\%$		$\dfrac{\$\ 860}{\$3,000} = 28.67\%$	
Sell stock for $40/share one year later				
Gross proceeds (100 shares @ $40)	$4,000		$4,000	
Less: Interest @ 7% of borrowing	0		140	
Net proceeds	$4,000		$3,860	
Less: Total investment	5,000		5,000	
Net profit (loss)	($1,000)		($1,140)	
Return on your investment	$\dfrac{(\$1,000)}{\$5,000} = (20\%)$		$\dfrac{(\$1,140)}{\$3,000} = (38\%)$	

margin make it vital for you to thoroughly acquaint yourself with the cost-benefit tradeoffs involved before using margin purchases in your investment program.

Information with respect to companies of interest, specific industries, securities markets, and the economy in general can provide an important input into the investment decision process. There are literally thousands of sources of investment information, including raw data on performance, various indexes of market and economic performance, and advisory information about security purchase and sale decisions. Naturally, individuals have personal preferences for certain types of analyses, but as a beginning investor you should probably concentrate on the more common sources of information, which are described here: stockholders' reports, financial news, brokerage firms, subscription services, and investment advisors.

Sources of Investment Information

Stockholders' Reports

Operating data on individual business firms can be obtained from their stockholders', or annual, reports. These reports provide a wealth of information, including balance sheets and income statements for the most recent period of operation as well as summarized statements for several prior years. The balance sheets and income statements for these business firms are quite similar in form to the personal financial statements examined and illustrated in Chapter 2. Many stockholders' reports describe the firm's business activities, development, and plans for future operation and discuss the firm's future outlook. Financial ratios describing past and future performance may also be included, among many other relevant statistics. A sample page from The Williams Companies' 1976 Stockholder's Report is shown in Figure 7-3. A great deal of insight into the company's past, current, and future operations can be obtained by studying the information in the stockholder's report. These reports are sent to all stockholders and can be obtained by anyone directly from the company, through a brokerage firm, or at a large library. They are a free and useful source of investment information.

Financial News

The most common source of financial news, which describes the behavior of the economy, the market, an industry, or a particular company, is the local newspaper. In most cities with a population of 250,000 or more, newspapers devote at least two pages to the presentation of financial items, and of course big city newspapers such as the *New York Times* and the *Los Angeles Times* provide investors with an abundance of financial information.

Other, more specific sources of financial news include the *Wall Street Journal* and *Barron's Weekly*. These financial newspapers operate on a subscription basis and are devoted in their entirety to articles on the behavior of the economy, markets, industries, and specific companies. The most comprehensive and up-to-date coverage of financial news is provided daily by the *Wall Street Journal. Barron's Weekly* concentrates on the week's activities as they relate to the financial markets and individual security prices. Other sources of investment information are business publications such as *Forbes, Fortune*, the *Commercial and Financial Chronicle, Business Week, U.S. News & World Report*, and the *New York Stock Exchange Magazine*. In addition, the government publishes magazines containing financially related items that can be found in most libraries or may be subscribed to, possibly free of charge. The *Federal Reserve Bulletin* and the newsletters of the Federal Reserve Banks are such free sources of information.

Figure 7-3 **A Page from a Stockholder's Report**
(The Williams Companies, 1976)

Stock Information

At the close of business in 1976, more than 23,000 investors held NYSE-listed securities of The Williams Companies having a market value of about $900 million, 70 percent of which was represented by common stock. WMB is the company's symbol on both the New York and Pacific Stock Exchanges. During 1976, a daily average of 41,000 shares of The Williams Companies' common stock was traded.

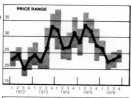

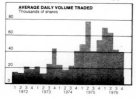

Common Stock

As of year-end 1976, The Williams Companies had 24,762,496 shares of its common stock outstanding. In January 1976, the Board declared a quarterly dividend of 25 cents per share, an increase from the previous quarterly rate of 15 cents per share. After adjustment for a two-for-one split declared in January 1975, the high and low quarterly sales prices for the company's common stock on the New York Stock Exchange for the last two years are as follows:

Quarter		1st	2nd	3rd	4th
1975	High	$32⅝	$37⅜	$35½	$32⅜
	Low	24	29¾	28	22½
1976	High	$29	$24⅞	$25⅝	$26⅛
	Low	24⅛	20	20½	22¼

After adjustment for the 1975 stock split, dividends per share on The Williams Companies' common stock for the last two years are as follows:

Quarter	1st	2nd	3rd	4th	Total
1975	$.15	$.15	$.15	$.15	$ .60
1976	$.25	$.25	$.25	$.25	$1.00

Preferred Stock

Also traded on the New York and Pacific Stock Exchanges is The Williams Companies' convertible preferred stock. As of December 31, 1976, the company had outstanding 115,255 shares of convertible preferred stock. The high and low quarterly sales prices for such stock on the NYSE for the last two years are as follows:

Quarter		1st	2nd	3rd	4th
1975	High	$58½	$67	$60	$58⅛
	Low	46	57	51	43
1976	High	$50½	$43⅛	$44½	$44⅞
	Low	45	38	40½	40

Dividends on The Williams Companies' convertible preferred stock have been 20 cents per share per quarter for each of the last two years. Each share of preferred is convertible into 1.8 shares of common stock.

Warrants

Williams' outstanding warrants expired on January 2, 1976.

Source: Courtesy of The Williams Companies, Tulsa, Oklahoma.

Economic Data Summaries and analyses of economic events can be found in all the sources of financial information mentioned above. Economic data include news items related to the actions of government and their effects on the economy, political and international events as they pertain to the economy, and statistics related to price levels, interest rates, the federal budget, and taxes.

Market Data Most commonly presented in the form of indexes, or averages, market data describe the general behavior of the securities markets. Indexes are based on the price movements of a select group of securities over a long period of time. Most frequently cited are those calculated by Dow Jones, Standard & Poor's, the New York Stock Exchange, and the American Stock Exchange.

Dow Jones Averages The "Dow" consists of four basic averages: (1) an industrial average based on 30 stocks; (2) a transportation average based on 20 stocks; (3) a utility average based on 15 stocks; and (4) a composite index based on 65 industrial, transportation, and utility stocks. Most often cited is the industrial average, which is shown in Figure 7-4 along with the name of the stocks included in it.

Standard & Poor's Averages Standard & Poor's averages are quite similar to the Dow Jones averages except that they consist of a larger number of stocks. There are four: (1) an industrial average based on 425 stocks; (2) a utility average of 50 stocks; (3) a railroad average of 25 railroad stocks; and (4) a composite index for all 500 stocks used to determine the first three averages. The Standard & Poor's averages, like the Dow

What's Read Most in Annual Reports

Fancy, four-color bar charts showing how the company has done over the years?

Reports on company acquisitions?

Not many stockholders find them of key interest in annual reports.

That's what Winthrop C. Neilson, principal, Georgeson & Co., says. The New York investor relations firm asked small investors a number of questions about annual reports and the information the reports contain.

One question: What sections of the annual report interest you most? The replies:

Earnings per share	31%
Stockholder letter	19%
Statistics	15%
Future prospects	12%
Financial highlights	9%

Ranking lowest in reader interest were acquisitions and company history, one percent each. Photos and proxy statements were of most interest to two percent.

Replies to other questions in the survey—and stockholders' replies:

Jones averages, are quoted in the *Wall Street Journal* as well as many other sources of investment information.

New York Stock Exchange Index The New York Stock Exchange publishes a number of indexes consisting of all common stocks, all industrial stocks, all transportation stocks, all finance stocks, and all utility stocks listed on the exchange. These indexes are also cited in the *Wall Street Journal* and other financial news sources.

American Stock Exchange Index Similar to the New York Stock Exchange Index, the American Stock Exchange Index includes indexes of stocks listed on the AMEX and is cited in basically the same places as the other indexes discussed.

Industry Data The *Wall Street Journal, Barron's,* local newspapers, and various financial news magazines contain industry data. Standard & Poor's *Industry Surveys* provide descriptions and statistics for various industries. *Business Week* and other magazines include indexes of industry performance and price levels. Other industry-related data can be obtained from industry trade associations, one example of which is the American Petroleum Institute for oil companies.

	Yes	No	Some
Do you know the dividends on your stocks?	74%	19%	7%
Do you know the earnings per share?	43%	49%	8%
Do you know the names of the companies' top officers?	21%	59%	20%

Fifteen percent of stockholders say they don't read annual reports. Twenty-five percent spend less than five minutes reading them; 26 percent spend six to 15 minutes; 20 percent, 15 to 30 minutes; 14 percent, more than half an hour.

The value of the annual report as an image-builder wasn't examined.

"The study was made several years ago," says Mr. Neilson. "But informal surveys we have made since then show virtually identical results."

Source: Reprinted by permission from "Selling Know-How Abroad," *Nation's Business,* February 1976, pp. 6, 8. Copyright 1976 by Nation's Business, Chamber of Commerce of the United States.

Figure 7-4 **The Dow Jones Industrial Average (DJIA)**
(Friday, 27 May 1977)

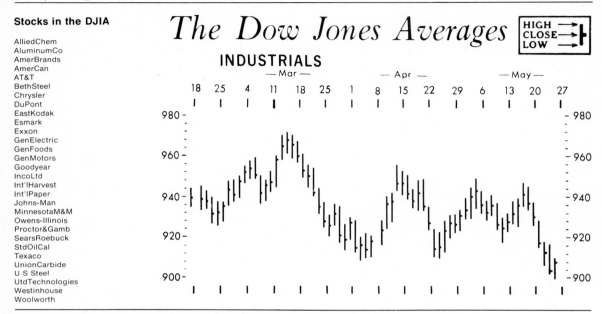

Stocks in the DJIA

AlliedChem
AluminumCo
AmerBrands
AmerCan
AT&T
BethSteel
Chrysler
DuPont
EastKodak
Esmark
Exxon
GenElectric
GenFoods
GenMotors
Goodyear
IncoLtd
Int'lHarvest
Int'lPaper
Johns-Man
MinnesotaM&M
Owens-Illinois
Proctor&Gamb
SearsRoebuck
StdOilCal
Texaco
UnionCarbide
U S Steel
UtdTechnologies
Westinhouse
Woolworth

Company Data Articles about the performance and new developments of companies are included in local newspapers, the *Wall Street Journal, Barron's,* and most news magazines. The prices of the securities of all listed companies and the most active over-the-counter stocks are quoted daily in the *Wall Street Journal* and weekly in *Barron's.* Many daily newspapers contain stock price quotations, though in the smaller ones the listing may be selective; in some cases only stocks of "local interest" are included.

The quotations in the *Wall Street Journal* give not only the most recent price of each stock but also a great deal of additional information. Figure 7-5 contains a portion of the 27 May 1977 NYSE stock price quotations from the *Wall Street Journal.* The Williams Companies' (Williams) quotation is highlighted in the table and will be used for illustrative purposes. A glance at the quotation shows that the stock prices are quoted in eighths of a dollar, with the fractions reduced to their lowest common denominator ($^2/_8$, $^4/_8$, and $^6/_8$ are expressed as $^1/_4$, $^1/_2$, and $^3/_4$, respectively). Since the quotation presented was published in the 27 May 1977 *Wall Street Journal,* the actual transactions reported are those of 26 May 1977. There is a one-day lag in reporting. A closer look at the

Figure 7-5 **NYSE Stock Price Quotations**
(27 May 1977)

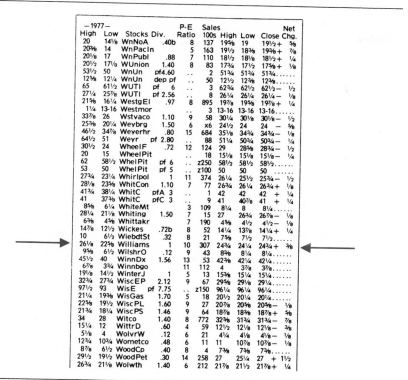

—1977— High	Low	Stocks	Div.	P-E Ratio	Sales 100s	High	Low	Close	Net Chg.
20	14 1/8	WnNoA	.40b	8	137	19 5/8	19	19 1/2	+ 5/8
20 3/8	14	WnPacIn		5	163	19 1/2	18 3/8	19 3/8	+ 7/8
20 1/8	17	WnPubl	.88	7	110	18 1/2	18 1/8	18 1/2	+ 1/4
20 1/2	17 1/8	WUnion	1.40	8	83	17 3/4	17 1/2	17 5/8	+ 1/8
53 1/2	50	WnUn	pf4.60	..	2	51 3/4	51 3/4	51 3/4	......
12 5/8	12 1/4	WnUn	dep pf	..	50	12 1/2	12 3/8	12 3/8	......
65	61 1/2	WUTI	pf 6	..	3	62 3/4	62 1/2	62 1/2	− 1/2
27 1/4	25 7/8	WUTI	pf 2.56	..	8	26 1/4	26 1/4	26 1/4	− 1/8
21 5/8	16 1/4	WestgEl	.97	8	895	19 7/8	19 5/8	19 7/8	+ 1/4
1 1/4	13-16	Westmor		..	3	13-16	13-16	13-16	......
33 7/8	26	Wstvaco	1.10	9	58	30 1/4	30 1/8	30 1/8	− 1/2
25 3/8	20 1/4	Weybrg	1.50	6	x6	24 1/2	24	24	− 5/8
46 1/2	34 7/8	Weyerhr	.80	15	684	35 1/8	34 3/4	34 3/4	− 1/8
64 1/2	51	Weyr	pf 2.80	..	88	51 1/4	50 3/4	50 3/4	− 1/4
30 1/2	24	WheelF	.72	12	124	29	28 5/8	28 3/4	− 1/2
20	15	WheelPit		..	18	15 1/8	15 1/8	15 1/8	− 1/4
62	58 1/2	WhelPit	pf 6	..	z250	58 1/2	58 1/2	58 1/2	......
53	50	WhelPit	pf 5	..	z100	50	50	50	......
27 3/4	23 1/4	Whirlpol	1	11	374	26 1/4	25 1/2	25 3/4	− 1/2
28 1/8	23 5/8	WhitCon	1.10	7	77	26 3/4	26 1/4	26 3/4	+ 1/8
41 3/4	38 1/4	WhitC	pfA 3	..	1	42	42	42	+ 1/4
41	37 3/8	WhitC	pfC 3	..	9	41	40 7/8	41	+ 1/4
8 5/8	6 1/4	WhiteMt		3	109	8 1/4	8	8 1/4	......
28 1/4	21 1/8	Whiting	1.50	7	15	27	26 3/4	26 7/8	− 1/8
6 3/8	4 5/8	Whittakr		7	190	4 5/8	4 1/2	4 1/2	− 1/8
14 7/8	12 1/2	Wickes	.72b	8	52	14 1/4	13 7/8	14 1/4	+ 1/4
10	6 1/2	WiebdtSt	.32	8	21	7 5/8	7 1/2	7 1/2	......
26 1/8	22 5/8	Williams	1	10	307	24 3/4	24 1/4	24 3/4	+ 3/8
9 5/8	6 1/2	WilshrO	.12	9	43	8 3/8	8 1/4	8 1/4	......
45 1/2	40	WinnDx	1.56	13	53	42 3/8	42 1/4	42 1/4	......
6 7/8	3 3/4	Winnbgo		11	112	4	3 7/8	3 7/8	......
19 1/8	14 1/2	WinterJ	1	5	13	15 3/8	15 1/4	15 1/4	......
32 3/4	27 3/4	WiscEP	2.12	9	67	29 5/8	29 1/8	29 1/4	......
97 1/2	93	WisE	pf 7.75	..	z150	96 1/4	96 1/4	96 1/4	......
21 1/4	19 3/8	WisGas	1.70	5	18	20 1/2	20 1/4	20 1/4	......
22 5/8	19 1/2	WiscPL	1.60	9	27	20 7/8	20 5/8	20 5/8	− 1/8
21 3/4	18 1/4	WiscPS	1.46	9	64	18 7/8	18 3/8	18 7/8	+ 5/8
34	28	Witco	1.40	8	772	32 3/8	31 3/4	31 3/4	− 7/8
15 1/4	12	WittrD	.60	4	59	12 1/2	12 1/8	12 1/8	− 3/8
5 1/8	4	WolvrW	.12	6	21	4 1/4	4 1/8	4 1/8	− 1/8
12 3/4	10 3/4	Wometco	.48	6	11	11	10 7/8	10 7/8	− 1/8
8 7/8	6 1/2	WoodCp	.40	8	4	7 3/8	7 3/8	7 3/8	......
29 1/2	19 1/2	WoodPet	.30	14	258	27	25 1/4	27	+ 1 1/2
26 3/4	21 1/8	Wolwth	1.40	6	212	21 7/8	21 1/2	21 7/8	+ 1/4

Source: Wall Street Journal, 27 May 1977, p. 23. © Dow Jones & Company, Inc. 1977. All rights reserved.

quotation reveals that the first two columns, labeled High and Low, contain the highest and lowest price at which the stock sold during the year to date. The figure immediately following the abbreviated company name (the ticker symbol used for quotations) is the cash dividend expected to be paid on each share during the year. The next entry is the price/earnings (P/E) ratio, the current market price divided by the per share earnings for the most recent one-year period. Since it is believed to reflect investor expectations concerning the firm's future activities, the P/E ratio is commonly referred to by investors in the process of evaluating potential investments.

The daily volume follows the P/E ratio; 30,700 shares of The Williams Companies were traded 26 May 1977. The next entries, in the High, Low, and Close columns, contain the highest, lowest, and last (closing) price, respectively, at which the stock sold on 26 May. The final column shows the net change between the current day's closing price and the closing price on the preceding day. The Williams Companies closed up $^3/_8$ on 26 May 1977, which means that it must have closed at 24$^3/_8$ ($^3/_8$ point lower) on 25 May 1977. Not all price quotations are as easy to read as this one, since often a number of other notations and footnotes are included. In the *Wall Street Journal*, a key explaining notations follows the stock price quotations.

Brokerage Firms

Brokerage firms provide their clients with investment information prepared by their own research staffs or, in the case of new issues, with *prospectuses*, which are documents prepared by a firm describing aspects of its issue. The cover of the seventy-seven page prospectus describing a 1976 bond issue of The Williams Companies is shown in Figure 7-6.

Reports on certain industries or securities prepared by the house's *back-office research* staff may be issued on a scheduled basis and often contain lists of securities within certain industries classified as to the type of investment return they provide and the type of market behavior they are expected to have. Often the brokerage house will issue lists of securities classified as either "buy" or "sell," depending on the research staff's analysis of their anticipated market behavior. Occasionally brokerage houses issue extensive analyses of specific securities along with recommendations as to the type of investment returns expected and whether or not to buy or sell. Recognizing that brokerage houses receive their income from commissions which are generated through the purchase-sale process, you should be certain that you—not your broker or the house research staff—are making the final decision on how your money is to be invested.

Subscription Services

There are a number of subscription services that provide information and recommendations with respect to various industries and specific securities. These services normally cost from fifty to a few hundred dollars per year and should be subscribed to only by the more active investor. You will normally be able to review these materials at the office of your brokerage firm, and your broker may provide you with relevant portions of these reports. Probably the best-known financial services are those provided by Standard & Poor's Corporation, Moody's Investors Service, and the Value Line Investment Survey. Each of these companies offers an array of subscription services. Both Standard & Poor's and Moody's publish yearly manuals that contain historical facts and financial data on thousands of corporations. These manuals are broken down into industry

Figure 7-6 Cover of a Prospectus for a Bond Issue

PROSPECTUS

$150,000,000

The Williams Companies

9.40% Sinking Fund Debentures due March 15, 1996

Application has been made to list the Debentures on the New York Stock Exchange and Pacific Stock Exchange.

Interest payable on March 15 and September 15 in each year.

THESE SECURITIES HAVE NOT BEEN APPROVED OR DISAPPROVED BY THE SECURITIES AND EXCHANGE COMMISSION NOR HAS THE COMMISSION PASSED UPON THE ACCURACY OR ADEQUACY OF THIS PROSPECTUS. ANY REPRESENTATION TO THE CONTRARY IS A CRIMINAL OFFENSE.

	Price to Public (1)	Underwriting Discounts (2)	Proceeds to Company (3)
Per Debenture	100.00%	1.125%	98.875%
Total	$150,000,000	$1,687,500	$148,312,500

(1) Plus accrued interest from March 15, 1976 to date of delivery (from September 15, 1976 in the case of Debentures to be issued on or after September 15, 1976 as described under "Delayed Delivery Contracts").

(2) The Company has agreed to indemnify the Underwriters against certain liabilities, including liabilities under the Securities Act of 1933. See "Underwriting."

(3) Before deducting expenses estimated at $362,500.

Debentures in limited amounts are offered by the Company, through the several Underwriters, for delayed delivery not later than October 1, 1976, to certain institutional purchasers, all as more fully described under "Delayed Delivery Contracts." The Underwriters have agreed to purchase from the Company all Debentures not contracted to be sold for delayed delivery, and such Debentures are offered by the Underwriters subject to prior sale, withdrawal, cancellation or modification of the offer, without notice, to delivery to and acceptance by the Underwriters, and to certain further conditions. It is expected that delivery of such Debentures will be made at the office of Lehman Brothers Incorporated, New York, N.Y., on or about April 1, 1976, against payment in New York funds.

LEHMAN BROTHERS
INCORPORATED

REYNOLDS SECURITIES INC.

The date of this Prospectus is March 24, 1976.

Source: Courtesy of The Williams Companies, Tulsa, Oklahoma.

groups. On a monthly basis, Standard & Poor's also publishes a *Stock Guide* and a *Bond Guide,* both of which summarize the financial condition of a few thousand issues.

Separate reports on specific companies are another valuable type of subscription service. Recommended lists of securities broken down into groups on the basis of investment objectives constitute still another type of service. In addition to these common subscription services, there are numerous *investment letters*, which periodically advise subscribers on the purchase and sale of securities. Investors may also obtain, through subscription chart books, graphs showing stock prices and volume over a period of time. Although the annual cost of investment subscription services is tax deductible, these services should be purchased only by the more active investor. Indeed, you can look at copies of many of these materials without charge at your brokerage house or public library.

Investment Advisors

Investors who have been quite successful often establish themselves as professional investors and investment advisors. In this latter role, they attempt to develop investment plans consistent with the financial objectives of their clients. Professional investment advisors may operate their own individual business or they may be associated with large firms that employ research staffs and quite often publish various subscription materials. Many of the better-known investment advisors limit their business to a select group of wealthy individuals who have similar investment objectives, while others accept clients with diverse objectives. Generally, professional advisors do not accept clients with assets of less than $50,000, and the more elite advisors are likely to require considerably larger holdings. Annual fees for advisory services, which may involve the complete management of the client's money, are likely to range from 0.25 percent to 2 percent of the money managed.

A recent trend is for the large commercial banks, such as First National City Bank of New York, and other independent advisory services to provide investment advice to those with assets of $5,000 to $10,000 for fees in the 1 to 2 percent range. In any case, there is no guarantee that investment advisors will perform better than their clients could independently, although in all likelihood they will. Of course care should be taken in the selection of advisors to assure that their investment planning is based on their clients' financial objectives and not their own.

Investment Strategies

Without a plan for attaining your investment goals, your investment activities may be more of a hobby than an integral part of your overall financial plans. It is therefore of utmost importance that you carefully formulate strategies for selecting securities that fit your investment goals.

It is also essential to time your investment activities in order to take advantage of changes in the security market. This portion of the chapter describes some of the key aspects of investment strategy.

Investment Goals

Although it is difficult to list all of the possible investment goals the individual has to choose from, it is nonetheless important to establish such goals and develop financial plans consistent with them. "To earn a 5 percent after-tax return by investing in a portfolio evenly split between blue-chip and speculative stocks," is one way of expressing an investment goal. It is generally advisable not only to specify the level of return and type of securities (as above), but also to specify the *form* in which the *total return* is expected to be received. This makes it easier to select securities that are consistent with established goals. The two basic forms of investment return are *dividend (or interest) yield* and *capital gains*.

Dividend Yield The dividend yield on a common stock represents the percent return provided by the dividends paid. It is calculated by dividing the per share dividend by the prevailing market price. Dividends provide a form of current income, which often appeals to investors whose goal is to receive retirement or supplementary income from their investments. Take, for example, the stock of the XYZ Company, which is currently selling for $60 a share and paid cash dividends of $2.40 per share during the past year. Its dividend yield would be 4 percent ($2.40 ÷ $60). The yield, or *yield-to-maturity*, is more difficult to determine for a bond. Fortunately, bond yields are published in various sources, including the *Wall Street Journal*. The important point to remember is that if periodic income is one of your investment goals, you should select securities that offer high dividend or interest yields.

Capital Gains As was indicated in Chapter 4, capital gains result from selling a security for a profit. Many people purchase securities, especially common stock, for this kind of long-run profit rather than to provide income in the form of interest or dividends. For an example of a capital gain, assume that the XYZ Company stock mentioned above was purchased for $56.60 and held for one and one-half years, at the end of which it was sold for $60.00. Excluding brokerage costs and personal taxes, this would produce a $3.40 capital gain ($60.00 − $56.60). Expressed as a percentage of the original purchase price, this gain would represent a 6 percent ($3.40 ÷ $56.60) return, which, when combined with the 4 percent dividend yield calculated earlier, would result in a 10 percent total return on the investment. Some *speculative* traders purchase stocks with the intention of gaining on the day-to-day fluctuations in price. These *day traders* are gamblers, and their strategies are risky in the extreme.

It is advisable to evaluate the total return on a security in light of your investment goals. Since it is often difficult to select securities that provide only dividends or only capital gains, you will be wise to recognize and measure the contribution each security might make to your overall investment return. Careful selection of securities on this basis should result in a mix of dividend yield and capital gains appropriate to your goals.

Security Analysis

Various kinds of analyses—of the economy, of the securities markets, of the industry of concern, and of the firm on which the security is issued—help in the evaluation of the quality and general desirability of a security investment. Most such analyses are done by the research departments of large brokerage firms.

Economic Analysis The first step in security analysis is assessing the present and future behavior of the economy. By studying certain economic indicators, expectations with respect to the nature of the economy can be formulated. One important factor that must be considered is the actions of the government in regard to spending, taxes, and interest rates. Although it is impossible to predict actual economic outcomes, the study of various statistics and economic forecasts can aid in the judicious selection of securities. For instance, during a recessionary period bonds may be more attractive, while in an expansionary period stocks generally have greater appeal. In fact, specific bonds or stocks chosen for investment will depend on anticipated economic activity.

Market Analysis The second step in analyzing a security is an examination of the securities markets—both their current state and movements anticipated in them. The results of the economic analysis should provide meaningful input to the market analysis. If a recession is predicted, a bear, or downward, market would be expected; while if inflation is anticipated, a bull, or upward market would be the forecast. The analysis of market behavior is vital to those who are interested in capital gains and do not necessarily wish to hold securities for a long period of time. Forecasts of security market behaviors based on the relevant stock averages such as the Dow Jones Industrial Average can be obtained either from a broker or through various subscription services. Expectations about the behavior of the securities markets can significantly affect an investor's choice of stock or bond investments.

Industry Analysis The goal of industry analysis, which is the next stage in security analysis, is to determine the general behavior of a particular industry under various economic conditions. This is accomplished by studying the past behavior of the industry and drawing some conclusions about its future behavior, as well as by examining whether the demand for its products and services enhances its potential success. These findings should be related to the results of the economic analysis in order to determine whether or not the performance of the given industry over the near future will be favorable. Also, the behavior of the securities of companies within the industry during periods of economic activity similar to that which is forecast should be examined to determine the future attractiveness of the industry's securities. Often security analysts will analyze a number of industries in order to determine the best industry to invest in under the economic circumstances they expect to evolve. These industry analyses are generally available from your stockbroker.

Company Analysis Once an industry has been determined to have investment potential, the analyst will look at the securities of companies within the industry to determine the "best" investments. Two of the variables investors and security analysts concern themselves with are *earnings per share (EPS)* and the *price/earnings ratio (P/E)*.

Earnings per Share (EPS) As indicated in Chapter 6, the amount earned by the firm for each share of common stock outstanding is the earnings per share. Investors concern themselves with both the reported and the projected EPS value. Historic, actual, and sometimes projected values for EPS for stocks of major interest are periodically reported in the *Wall Street Journal* and other financial publications. Individuals interested in investing in the common stock of a certain company should evaluate the levels and expected trend of its EPS; in general, the higher the EPS, the more attractive the securities are as investment opportunities.

Price/Earnings Ratio (P/E) Another popular tool in security analysis, the price/earnings ratio is calculated by dividing the current market price per share by the most recent annual earnings per share (see Chapter 6). Like *EPS*, the P/E ratio is cited in numerous places, including, of course, the *Wall Street Journal*. It is generally believed that the higher the P/E, the more confidence investors have in the future of the firm, and vice versa. This relationship stems from the fact that the higher the P/E ratio, the more investors are paying for expected future benefits and the less they are paying for current earnings. P/E ratios generally fall in the range from 10 to 50, although during periods of economic expansion, the stocks of growth firms like IBM have been known to sell for more than fifty times earnings.

The analysis of P/E ratios as part of the stock selection process is more or less standard, since a true reading of a firm's stock cannot really be obtained by looking at its price or earnings separately. The P/E ratio offers some insight into stock price behavior because it considers both price and earnings movements simultaneously. For example, when the stock price increases from $40 to $60 per share, while annual earnings per share increase from $2.50 to $4.00, the P/E ratio decreases from 16 ($40 ÷ $2.50) to 15 ($60 ÷ $4). In this case, although the earnings per share have increased from $2.50 to $4.00, the per share price has not increased correspondingly, and so the P/E ratio has declined. Basically, the P/E ratio of a stock reflects the general sentiment of those in the marketplace toward it as an investment.

In short, the formal process of security analysis attempts to link expected economic behavior to market activity and then to the behavior of individual industries and the securities of the firms within them. The type of analysis performed by the small investor is limited primarily to company analysis. This normally involves a study of price, earnings, and the relationship between them as indicated in the price/earnings ratio. A basic investments text or materials available from your stockbroker will provide you with a more detailed discussion of the various aspects of security analysis.

Security Selection

Although numerous techniques of analysis exist for selecting security investments, small investors normally make their investment decisions without resorting to very sophisticated analytical procedures. Stockholders' reports, prospectuses for new issues, research studies provided by brokers, and other informational inputs can help you become familiar with proposed security investments and analyze the basic financial data on earnings, dividends, and price behavior. Once you feel comfortable with a proposed investment and find other sources (broker, research studies, friends) who agree with your selection, you should make the investment. Of course, no matter how much formal analysis you use in the selection process, there is no guarantee that you will "pick a winner."

Security Portfolios

Sophisticated investors devote their attention to constructing diversified *portfolios* of securities. These portfolios consist of stocks and bonds selected not only for the returns expected but also for their combined risk-return behaviors. According to the *theory of diversification*, by combining securities with dissimilar risk-return characteristics a portfolio

When to Sell: The Hemline Theory and More

. . . How do you know when to sell a stock? One often-heard answer: when stocks in general start going down. Investors who believe that the direction of the market is of paramount importance do not worry much about timing the sale of individual issues. Instead, they concentrate on finding a formula that alerts them when the overall market is about to suffer a sinking spell.

The formula may feed on data from the front page, the financial page or even the fashion page. What matters to true believers is whether it works. The fashion page? Don't laugh. The axiom that when hemlines fall, the market will fall has a leg up on some other theories. Skirt watchers can point out that the introduction of the midiskirt coincided with the bear market of 1970 and that the disappearance of the knee when the midiskirt caught on heralded the stock debacle of 1973.

For some unconventional analysts, politics provides the formula. Election watchers note that there have been bear markets the year after eleven of the 16 presidential elections since 1913 (see "An Election-Year Stock Market Strategy," *Money*, August [1976]).

A public health specialist has even developed a theory that mental illness is bearish. M. Harvey Brenner of the Johns Hopkins School of Hygiene and Public Health observes "a significant relationship" between bad economic news and rising admissions to mental hospitals. He finds that people in higher socioeconomic groups (like businessmen) crack up the soonest when recessions loom.

According to a theory based on more orthodox financial data, General Motors stock sounds the knell of record-breaking markets. In its simplest form, the theory holds that a bull market is finished unless GM climbs to an all-time high within four months after the stock market hits a new high. In October 1965, for example, the Dow Jones industrial average closed at 960.82, then a record, and GM sold at a record $113.75. The Dow went on climbing, but not GM. Thus the GM theory flashed a sell signal in February 1966, shortly before the market tailed off.

The stock market hasn't reached new high ground since 1973—and doesn't seem about to—but the GM theory could prove useful soon again. In September [1976] the Dow came within striking distance of its record high closing of 1051.7. If that level is surpassed, GM will have to take off dramatically to avoid giving yet another sell signal. In mid-November it was selling for $44 less than its best price.

Investors looking for broader-based—and more frequent—clues to market action often turn to "Fed watching." Here the rule is to unload your stocks whenever the Federal Reserve Board appears to be tightening credit. Signals include increases in bank reserve requirements—the proportion of total loans outstanding that have to be backed by a bank's deposits; in the "discount rate" the Fed charges member banks when they borrow money to meet reserve requirements; or in margin requirements—the down payment investors must make on purchases of securities. When a pattern of credit tightening emerges, the sell signal is loud and clear. For example, from January through July of 1973 the Fed raised the discount rate six times. People who got the message early could have taken their profits out of the market near its peak.

Source: "When to Bail Out of Your Stocks," excerpted from the December 1976 issue of MONEY Magazine by special permission; © 1976, Time Inc.

of securities with an acceptable and relatively certain return can be constructed. This type of portfolio selection, however, is quite complex mathematically, and is generally practiced only by the large financial institutions. Nonetheless, small investors can and should combine securities with different earnings behaviors to reduce the risk in their investments. For example, investing in the stock of a meat packer and the stock of a flour mill may provide a relatively stable level of earnings, since when meat sales increase flour sales decrease, and vice versa.

Timing Investment Decisions

There are a number of basic techniques for timing investment decisions which can assist investors in profiting as much as possible on their investments and minimizing losses. Three of the more common ones are dollar cost averaging, formula timing, and the use of charts.

Dollar Cost Averaging To use the dollar cost averaging approach, investors purchase a fixed dollar amount of a security at specified points in time. This tends to keep the cost of the security at a reasonable level. For example, suppose you operated on a strategy of investing $300 per quarter (every three months) in the stock of XYZ Company, as indicated in Table 7-4. Although the per share price of your stock ranged from $10 to $25, the average cost per share at the end of the year was $15.58 ($1,200 ÷ 77 shares). Your strategy allowed you to purchase more shares when the price was low and thus average out the purchase of the smaller number of shares when the price was high. Had you invested the total $1,200 in quarter 1, you would have been able to purchase only forty-eight, instead of seventy-seven, shares. Dollar cost averaging is best used as part of a long-run investment strategy by individuals who are willing to make a fixed-dollar investment at certain points in time.

Table 7-4 Dollar-Cost Averaging Investment

Quarter	Amount Invested (1)	Price per Share (2)	Number of Shares [(1) ÷ (2)] (3)
1	$ 300	$25	12
2	300	15	20
3	300	10	30
4	300	20	15
Total	$1,200		77

"Sell!"

Timing of Investment Decisions Is Sometimes Easy
Source: Reprinted by permission of Sidney Harris.

Formula Timing By establishing certain indicators for buying or selling, formula timing plans attempt to force an investor to buy low and sell high. They often rely on price-earnings ratios (P/E) as signals. When the P/E of a given security drops to a certain point, that is a signal to buy; while when it rises to a predetermined level, that is a signal to sell. For example, the rule might be to buy XYZ when its P/E ratio is less than 8 and to sell it if its P/E ratio is greater than 18. The use of formula plans is intended to introduce some degree of rationality into investment activities. The basic principle is to substitute these decision rules for human judgment, since people have a tendency to wait too long, thereby losing some of the potential profit, when it comes to purchasing or selling a security. Formula plans may also be based on variables other than the price/earnings ratio, such as price, earnings, economic indicators, or proportions of securities held. Care should be taken in making formula plans to be sure that the formulas established are consistent with the investor's goals.

Chartist Approach Discussed in the preceding chapter, the chartist approach is a type of formula plan founded on charting trends in security prices and stock market averages. Chartists prespecify, on the basis of given chart formations, when purchase or sale actions are to be taken. The chartist theories and formations are quite well developed, and there are numerous books on charting available to the interested investor. Although there is a great deal of disagreement among investment analysts about the effectiveness of the use of charts, many chartists have become quite wealthy as a result of their approach. Like all strategies for timing investment decisions, the use of charts does not guarantee success, but it does force investors to develop logical strategies for fulfilling their investment goals.

Special Security Purchase Arrangements

A number of special arrangements exist whereby investors can purchase stocks. The more common of these include: stock purchase options and plans, Monthly Investment Plans (MIP), and investment clubs.

Stock Purchase Options and Plans As part of their compensation, key employees of a corporation are often given an opportunity to purchase a given number of shares of the corporation's stocks at a price specified when the option is granted. At issue, stock purchase options have no value. The firm's purpose in issuing them is to motivate these employees to work hard and move the firm forward so that the market price of the stock and therefore the value of their option will rise. A few years after the issue, the employees may be able to exercise their options and purchase the stock at a price below its market value. They can then either sell it for an immediate profit or hold it to achieve further gains from the future price appreciation. The gain on the sale, if the stock is held the required length of time, would be a long-term capital gain, which would be taxed at a lower rate than normal income. (See Chapter 4 for a discussion of this tax treatment.) These options, if offered to you, may provide a very attractive source of income.

Stock purchase plans allow all employees to buy into the firm. These plans often include some kind of arrangement for the employer to make matching contributions toward the purchase of shares by the employees. The price at which shares are purchased is normally based on some type of average. Employees are often required to hold the stock purchased for a specified period of time before selling it. Like stock purchase options, purchase plans serve as a form of employee compensation, as well as to stimulate employee interest in the firm's success.

Monthly Investment Plans (MIP) A form of dollar cost averaging and a type of forced savings, the monthly investment plan is an arrangement that benefits long-term investors. For each plan, a monthly or quarterly investment of $40 to $1,000 must be made in the same NYSE security on a regular basis. Since a fixed dollar amount is invested periodically, fractional shares are issued as needed. For example, if you invest $100 per month in XYZ and during a given month pay $16 per share, you would receive 6.25 shares of XYZ ($100 ÷ $16/share) for that month. Certain rules and regulations for participating in these plans are established by the various brokerage firms. Brokerage commissions are charged on transactions, and the broker has the option of discontinuing the plan if the participant skips a payment. If your investment goal is long-run price appreciation, you may wish to look into the MIPs and other similar arrangements available at brokerage firms and large commercial banks, since these types of plans may assist you in achieving this goal.

Investment Clubs Investment clubs are often formed by a group of people in order to pool their knowledge in the hope of making better investment decisions and to further educate members on how to make investments. Club members are required to make scheduled contributions into the club's treasury. The resultant pool of funds is then invested in securities that are mutually agreed on by the club's members. A legal partnership agreement binds and protects the members of the club. The clubs generally attempt to make investments of good quality aimed at providing favorable returns over the long run; they normally do not speculate in high-risk securities. Generally, various members of the club are responsible for analyzing certain possible stock or bond investments and presenting their findings to the membership. Through this process, the club selects what it believes to be the best investments given the overall investment goals of its membership. These clubs provide an excellent opportunity for the inexperienced investor to learn more about the investment world and how to make intelligent investment decisions. The National Association of Investment Clubs offers various publications and regional and national meetings through which club members can learn new investment techniques and strategies. Your broker can assist you in forming or becoming a member of an investment club. For the beginning investor, club membership is an excellent idea.

Summary

Investment transactions take place in the capital market rather than the money market. New issues of securities are traded in the primary market, while the resale of securities takes place in the secondary market. Investment banking firms often underwrite new security issues. A prospectus is normally prepared and distributed to interested parties when a new security issue is made. Securities are listed and traded on an organized exchange or are traded in the over-the-counter market. The securities markets are regulated by the Securities and Exchange Commission, as well as various state securities commissions. The conditions of the securities markets are described as "bear" or "bull" depending on whether the security prices in general are falling or rising. Stock and bond transactions can be made through stockbrokers, who are paid a commission to purchase and sell securities for their customers. Aside from executing purchase and sell orders, stockbrokers perform numerous other services for their clients. Although the standard unit in which securities are traded is 100 shares, security transactions can be made in smaller quantities. The basic types of security orders include the market order, the limit order, and the stop-loss order. Some investors sell short in the hope of gaining from an expected decrease in the security's prices. Customers who meet certain legal and brokerage firm requirements may borrow money in order to finance a portion of their security purchases.

Information for use in making investment decisions can be obtained from a wide range of sources, including stockholders' reports, the financial news, and business magazines. Additional investment information can be obtained from stock indexes and averages, from brokerage firms, through any of a number of subscription services, or from an investment advisor. Before formulating an investment strategy, investment goals, which are an integral part of an individual's overall personal financial plan, should be established. The dividend yield and capital gains from a security are used to compute its total return. The formal security analysis process includes an analysis of the economy, the market, the industry, and the company. Sophisticated security analyses are normally performed by the back-office research staff of brokerage firms. Earnings per share and price/earnings ratios are the variables most commonly considered when analyzing securities.

Selection of securities should be based on inputs from the various sources of investment information, the findings of security analyses, and the individual's investment goals. More sophisticated investors attempt to create portfolios of securities using the theory of diversification. The common techniques for timing investment decisions include dollar cost averaging, formula timing, and the chartist approach. A number of special security purchase arrangements such as stock purchase options, stock purchase plans, Monthly Investment Plans, and investment clubs are available to those who qualify and are interested.

American Stock Exchange (AMEX)
ask price
bear market
bid price
broker-dealers
bull market
buy orders
capital gain
chartist approach
delisting (securities)
diversification (theory of)
dividend yield
dollar cost averaging
earnings per share (EPS)
exchange members
formula timing
investment banking
investment clubs
limit order
listed securities
maintenance margin
margin purchases
margin requirement
market maker
market order
money market
Monthly Investment Plan (MIP)
National Association of Securities Dealers (NASD)
New York Stock Exchange (NYSE)
odd lot

over-the-counter market
portfolio (securities)
price/earnings ratio (P/E)
primary market
prospectus
purchase plans
regional stock exchanges
rights
round lot
secondary market
Securities and Exchange Commission (SEC)
Securities Investor Protection Corporation (SIPC)
security analysis
security exchanges
secondary market
selling group
sell orders
short sale
speculative (day) traders
stock averages (indexes)
stockbroker
stockholder's report
stock options
stop-loss order
total return
underwriting
underwriting syndicate
warrants

1. Explain what is meant by the *securities market*. Briefly describe the various markets.

2. How does a primary market differ from a secondary market?

3. What are organized security exchanges? What is the difference between the New York Stock Exchange and the American Stock Exchange? Are stocks of all companies traded on the floor of the American Stock Exchange listed? Explain.

4. Explain the difference between a bear market and a bull market.

5. Who is a stockbroker? How does the selection of a broker play an important role in the purchase of securities?

6. "Stockbrokers, besides facilitating purchase and sale transactions, offer a variety of additional services to their clients." What are these services? Explain.

7. Explain how you can buy and sell odd lots of listed stocks.

8. Name and describe three basic types of orders. Assume George Sanford places an order for 100 shares of Kodak with a broker who is a member of the NYSE. Explain how the order will be processed.

9. What is a short sale? Explain the logic behind short sales.

10. What are margin requirements? Helen Emerson wants to buy 200 shares of PEPSICO, which is currently selling in the market for $25 a share. Rather than liquidate all her savings, she decides to borrow through her broker. The brokerage firm has an in-house margin requirement of 60 percent and charges 7 percent interest on margin loans. What would be the interest cost of the transaction to Helen if she sells the stocks at the end of one year?

11. What are the various sources from which a person can obtain investment information? What kinds of information are available?

12. Define and discuss the use of dividend yield, capital gains, and total return as measures of investment return.

13. Briefly define *earnings per share (EPS)* and *price/earnings ratios (P/E)*, and discuss their role in analyzing potential stock investments.

14. Outline several techniques used in timing investment decisions.

15. What is a Monthly Investment Plan? Explain how it works.

16. Does a small investor find any advantages in belonging to an investment club? Explain.

Case Problems

7-1 How Much Must I Pay in Broker's Fees?

Barbara Moses would like to distribute $14,000 among investments in the stocks of various corporations. She has consulted her broker, Paine Webber & Co., regarding the current market conditions and placed orders for the shares itemized below.

Item	Number of Shares	Company Name	Purchase Price per Share
1	100	Amarex	$ 15
2	200	SKF	25
3	50	Phillips	50
4	20	CITGO	100
5	300	Union Carbide	10

Questions

1. From the suggested brokerage fee schedule given in Table 7-2, compute the total brokerage fees Barbara would have to pay on these transactions.

2. Calculate the broker's commissions using the rule of thumb rate—2 percent of the value of the transaction, and compare the resulting commissions to those found in question 1.

3. Differentiate between odd and round lot transactions. Classify each of Barbara's transactions as odd or round lot.

7-2 Investment Advice for the Gordons

A middle-aged couple, Allen and Lena Gordon, recently inherited $20,000 from one of their relatives. Allen earns a comfortable living as a sales manager for Smith and Johnson, Inc. Since they do not have any children and do not need the money, they have decided to use it to enter the securities market. However, they are neither familiar with the manner in which transactions take place, nor do they know how to select a broker. They have come to you for guidance.

Questions

1. Evaluate the various securities markets, and then recommend the best one for the Gordons.

2. What characteristics should they look for in a stockbroker? Take into consideration brokerage services and brokerage fees.

3. Based on your analysis, decide whether they should buy odd lots or round lots.

4. Evaluate the types of orders that can be placed, and recommend some investments for the Gordons.

7-3 Which Stock Should We Buy?

Rebecca and Albert Reynolds have been married for two years. Rebecca earns $17,000 a year as a floor manager for a large department store. Albert is a third-year law student who makes about $200 a month working at a part-time job for a local law firm. They currently have in their savings account about $2,000, which they want to invest in stocks. They do not plan to make any large expenses, but rather their goal is to increase their net worth. Given below are data on the stocks from which the Reynolds would like to make their final selection.

Year	Name of Company	Average Price per Share	Earnings per Share	Average Dividend per Share	Dividend Yield	P/E
1975	Playboy	$ 6	$0.12	$0.08		
	Texaco	30	3.06	1.70		
	McDonald's	42	2.17	0.05		
	IBM	268	13.35	10.00		
	CITGO	60	5.12	2.70		
1976	Playboy	8	0.22	0.10		
	Texaco	29	3.20	1.80		
	McDonald's	45	2.72	0.06		
	IBM	275	15.94	10.00		
	CITGO	59	7.98	2.80		
1977	Playboy	7	0.80	0.12		
	Texaco	27	3.75	2.00		
	McDonald's	40	3.40	0.10		
	IBM	260	17.50	10.00		
	CITGO	61	9.00	3.00		

Source: *Wall Street Journal*, 27 May 1977, pp. 23–24.

Questions

1. Calculate the dividend yield and the price/earnings ratio for each stock each year.

2. On the basis of the above data, evaluate the potential risk of each of the securities shown.

3. Evaluate the potential returns of each security.

4. In light of their investment goals and your analysis of the risks and returns of the stocks, make a stock purchase recommendation to the Reynolds.

Selected References

Branch, Ben. *Fundamentals of Investing.* Santa Barbara, Calif.: Wiley-Hamilton, 1976.

"Buying Stocks on Margin." *Changing Times*, July 1975, pp. 13–14.

Christy, George A., and Clendenin, John C. *Introduction to Investments.* New York: McGraw-Hill, 1975.

Dreyfus, Patricia A. "Tying Your Investments to the Indexes." *Money*, May 1976, pp. 87–94.

Edgerton, Jerry. "Amateur Investors Who Outperform the Pros." *Money*, February 1977, pp. 42–45.

Farrell, Maurice L. *Dow Jones Investor's Handbook.* Princeton, N.J.: Dow Jones Books, 1975.

"Five Ways to Invest, from Low Risk to High." *Business Week*, 29 December 1975, pp. 56–66.

"How to Invest for Income." *Changing Times*, July 1977, pp. 6–10.

"How to Invest Safely." *U.S. News & World Report*, 14 June 1976, pp. 74–75.

"Investment Pools: A Way to Diversify and Cut Risks." *Changing Times*, June 1976, pp. 6–11.

Jessup, Paul F. *Competing for Stock Market Profits.* New York: Wiley, 1974.

Neal, Charles V. *How to Keep What You Have: Or, What Your Broker Never Told You.* Garden City, N.Y.: Doubleday, 1972.

"The Right Way to Read the Stock Market Averages." *Changing Times*, April 1977, pp. 39–41.

Rolo, Charles J. "Predicting How the Market Will Move." *Money*, June 1977, pp. 61–68.

Rukeser, Louis. *How to Make Money in Wall Street.* Garden City, N.Y.: Doubleday, 1974.

Snyder, Linda. "Wall Street's Discount Houses Are Selling Hard." *Fortune*, March 1977, pp. 117–118 ff.

Sprecher, Ronald C. *Introduction to Investment Management.* Boston: Houghton Mifflin, 1975.

"Those Investment Advisory Services—What You Get for Your Money." *Changing Times*, August 1977, pp. 24–28.

"Where Should You Invest Your Money Now?" *Changing Times*, May 1977, pp. 6–10.

8

Investment Companies, Commodities, and Options

A Preview of Chapter 8

In order to provide an understanding of the fundamental characteristics of investment companies, commodities, and options, this chapter examines the following:

1. The types, characteristics, and methods of making transactions in investment company shares, commodities, and options.

2. The different kinds of investment companies, the cost of investment company transactions, and the classifications of investment companies on the basis of the securities they buy.

3. The motives and available arrangements for purchasing mutual fund shares.

4. The special features of mutual funds and the sources and procedures available for analyzing and selecting mutual funds.

5. The operation of the commodities markets and the rationale and methods for making futures transactions in commodities.

6. The two most common types of options, puts and calls; the operation of the options market; and the procedures for making options transactions.

Sometime during your lifetime you are likely to find that security investments offer the returns you require to fulfill your financial goals. In order to fully understand the investment opportunities available to you, you will need to complement your understanding of the basics of stock and bond investments with a knowledge of the functions, characteristics, and risk-return behavior of investment companies, commodities, and options. Each of these latter media offers risk-return opportunities that you may not be able to obtain from stock and bond investments.

The investor who is interested in receiving the benefit of professional portfolio management but does not have sufficient funds to purchase a diversified portfolio of securities may find the purchase of investment company shares quite attractive. An *investment company* is a company that owns a diversified portfolio of securities which are professionally chosen on the basis of certain specified criteria. The best-known type of investment of this nature is the *mutual fund*. The investor willing to accept higher risk may find *commodity investments* quite attractive. These investments are actually contracts to purchase a commodity, such as sugar, at a specified price at some future date. Because small movements in commodity prices significantly affect the value of these investments, they are quite risky. Another alternative would be to purchase *options*, which are rights to purchase or sell a security at a specified price over a stated period of time. The purchase of options is a speculative tool which allows the investor to take calculated risks based on future security price movements. The costs, risk-return characteristics, institutional structure, and methods for making transactions in investment company shares, commodities, and options are the subject of this chapter.

An *investment company* can be viewed as a financial institution that gathers funds from numerous investors. It uses these funds to purchase securities issued by a variety of corporations. The investors actually receive shares of stock in the company in exchange for their money. Since the sole function of the investment company is to invest in the securities of other companies, the company shareholder is in effect indirectly investing in a wide variety of securities. The main appeal of the investment company for the investor is based on the fact that one share of its stock gives the holder a claim on a diversified portfolio of securities, while in the market, the amount of money paid for that share might not permit the purchase of more than one share of a single stock. The professional portfolio managers employed by the company to lend their expertise to the selection of good security investments are another advantage of the investment company. The basic investment company structure is depicted in Figure 8-1.

Investment Company Fundamentals

Types of Investment Companies

There are two basic types of investment companies: in *closed-end companies* the number of ownership shares is limited, while in *open-end companies* it is not. In both, the managers of the company exercise the voting rights of shares held, and investment activities are regulated either directly or indirectly by various governmental agencies such as the Securities and Exchange Commission.

Figure 8-1 **Basic Investment Company Structure**

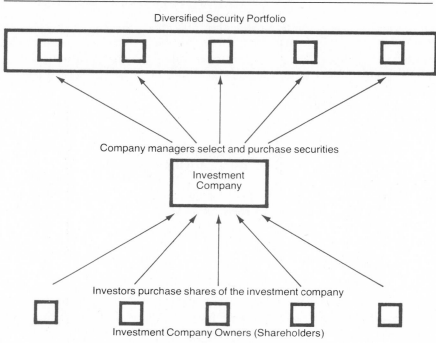

Diversified Security Portfolio

Company managers select and purchase securities

Investment
Company

Investors purchase shares of the investment company

Investment Company Owners (Shareholders)

Closed-End Companies Only a small portion of investment company activity is accounted for by closed-end companies. They issue a fixed number of shares, which may be listed and traded on an organized security exchange, and therefore have only a fixed amount of funds to invest in various securities. Once issued, their shares can be purchased or sold only in the security markets. Shares are traded in the same fashion as for any corporate stock; brokerage commissions must be paid on purchase and sale transactions. Note that closed-end investment company share prices are affected not only by the value of the securities that underlie them but also by the general behavior of the securities markets. Some of the better-known closed-end investment companies are Lehman Corporation, Madison Fund, and Niagara Share Corporation.

Open-End Companies (Mutual Funds) The dominant type of investment company is the open-end, or mutual, fund. These funds issue as many shares as are demanded and thus, unlike the closed-end companies, do not have a fixed amount to invest. A few of the better-known mutual funds are Guardian Mutual Fund, Putnam Equities Fund, and Windsor Fund. The open-end company will sell or buy back its own shares at a

"Get me some crumbs of whatever
the mutual funds are gobbling up."

Professional Management Is One Benefit of Mutual Fund Investment
Source: Reprinted by permission of Sidney Harris.

price that is based on the current value of the securities the fund owns.
The price at which it sells or buys back its own shares is referred to as the
net asset value (NAV) per share. This value is calculated at least once a
day and represents the worth of a share in the fund; it is found by dividing
the market value of all securities held in the fund less any liabilities of the
fund by the number of fund shares outstanding. For example, assume
that at the end of a day the value of all assets held by the fund is
$10,500,000 and there are 400,000 shares outstanding. If the fund's
liabilities resulting from paying management are $500,000, the net asset
value per share will be $25 ([$10,500,000 − $500,000] ÷ 400,000 shares).
Figure 8-2 is an excerpt of the mutual fund quotations reported for
Thursday, 26 May 1977, in the Friday, 27 May 1977, *Wall Street Journal.*
An explanation of the values reported is given at the top of the figure. The
quotation for Putnam Equities Fund, which is highlighted, indicates that
a share of this fund will cost $10.35 (with the maximum commission

Figure 8-2 **Mutual Fund Quotations**
(27 May 1977)

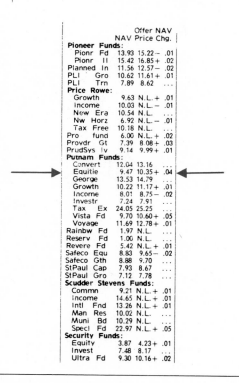

included), while it can be sold for its net asset value (NAV) of $9.47, which is four cents higher than the NAV for the previous day.

Mutual Fund Cost Considerations

Unlike the cost of closed-end investment company share purchases and sales, which are treated in the same fashion as any common stock transaction, the cost of mutual fund (open-end investment company) transactions varies. Mutual fund shares are therefore classified as *load* or *no-load*, depending on whether or not transaction charges, or "loads," are assessed. In addition to such charges, administrative and management costs and taxes may mean reduced returns for mutual fund investors.

Load Funds Load funds normally charge a purchase fee equal to from 7 to 8.5 percent of the purchase amount. The 8.5 percent maximum sales commission was established in 1975 as a result of actions taken by the National Association of Securities Dealers (NASD), which is a self-regulatory organization of brokers and dealers. This commission charge, or load, is normally levied only on the purchase; a commission is not charged on the sale of shares back to the investment company. The amount of the load is deducted from the money put up for the purchase of shares. For example, if you wished to purchase $1,000 worth of the XYZ Fund and the loading fee were 7 percent, you would end up buying only $930 worth ($1,000 − 7%[$1,000]) of the fund. The other $70 would be divided between whoever sold you the shares and the fund. Recalling that on stock transactions, purchase and selling commissions were about 2 percent each, it should be clear that the cost of load funds is high, even in light of the fact that the loading is charged only on the purchase, not on the sale, of the shares. Because in certain instances the load could be excessive, the SEC has the power to oversee the level of the loads and has provided a mechanism whereby any prepaid load is refunded if the shares are sold within a specified period of time after purchase.

No-Load Funds Well-managed no-load funds have a great deal of appeal. They are mutual funds that do not use formal sales channels requiring payment of sales commissions and therefore do not charge any load. Shares of no-load funds are sold through advertisements in newspapers and other financial media. For this reason, however, it is more difficult to become acquainted with these no-load funds. Occasionally, a no-load fund will have a 1 to 2 percent *back-end load*, a fee for redeeming mutual fund shares.

Management and Administrative Costs Mutual funds employ professional managers who are responsible for making all decisions with respect to the purchase and sale of the securities owned by the fund. The fee these managers are paid for their services is normally set as a percentage of the total assets of the fund and usually ranges between 0.25 and 0.5 percent of the dollar amount of total assets. The larger the fund, of course, the lower the rate. These fees as well as the administrative costs of operating the fund are deducted from the value of the fund assets when calculating the net asset value per share.

Earnings and Taxes

Two important aspects of investment companies are the sources of their earnings and their tax consequences. The *earnings* of investment companies may be received in three basic forms: (1) interest income from corporate and government bonds, (2) dividends from stock, and (3) gains from selling securities for more than their initial purchase price. Each of these forms of earnings is taxable income. Of course, management fees and administrative costs are deducted from all earnings prior to their taxation. To avoid double-taxation, most investment companies choose to be taxed as *regulated investment companies.* This means that by meeting certain conditions and distributing almost all earnings to the shareholders, they can avoid having earnings taxed as company income. Of course, the earnings received by the investment company shareholders will be taxed according to the breakdown provided them by the fund.

Classification of Investment Companies

Investment objectives and types of securities purchased serve as a means of classifying investment companies. Objectives are usually clearly stated, and the company managers are responsible for making purchase and sale decisions consistent with them. In fact, fund managers are typically hired on the basis of their expertise in the types of activities required by fund objectives. A number of the common classifications of investment companies are briefly described below.

Bond and Preferred Stock Funds Funds that purchase diversified portfolios of either bonds or preferred stocks attempt to provide safe, predictable returns to their investors. These types of funds are currently not especially popular investments.

Diversified Common Stock Funds The most popular types of funds, diversified common stock funds, account for more than 50 percent of all investment company assets. Their investments in diversified portfolios of common stock provide a wide range of income-growth combinations. Some invest only in blue-chip stocks, while others are known to invest in more speculative types. (See Table 8-1 for a list of stocks popular among mutual funds.) Since there is a broad range of common stock funds, investors should identify the objectives and performance of any funds they are interested in prior to investment. Table 8-2 provides a breakdown of securities owned by the Putnam Equities Fund, a diversified common stock fund with a primary objective of growth. (The cover of the prospectus for this fund is shown later in the chapter in Figure 8-3.)

Table 8-1 **Stocks Mutuals Like Best: The Fifty Favorites**
(as of March 31, 1976)

	Value of Holdings (Millions)	Funds Holding Stock	Total Shares Held	Change from Three Months Earlier
IBM	$2,016	392	7,695,700	Up 1.3%
Exxon	854	222	9,098,700	Down 2.5%
AT&T	669	174	11,836,600	Up 6.0%
Eastman Kodak	599	191	5,039,900	Up 0.04%
Digital Equipment	511	107	2,912,500	Up 11.0%
General Motors	508	149	7,244,700	Up 16.5%
Philip Morris	448	103	8,019,300	Up 3.2%
Dow Chemical	447	120	4,156,600	Up 1.9%
Union Carbide	385	130	5,336,300	Up 2.5%
Burroughs	375	116	3,649,600	Up 0.3%
McDonald's	374	102	5,840,900	Down 0.9%
Ford	356	82	6,246,700	Up 11.4%
Monsanto	337	98	3,827,500	Down 3.0%
U.S. Steel	308	109	5,815,200	Up 0.8%
R. J. Reynolds	257	72	4,132,500	Up 0.9%
Texaco	253	96	9,444,100	Down 5.5%
Texas Instruments	253	78	2,020,500	Up 3.8%
Du Pont	252	74	1,727,900	Up 2.4%
General Electric	252	116	4,790,600	Down 5.3%
Xerox	233	140	4,190,300	Up 4.4%
Schering-Plough	229	83	4,026,400	Down 4.3%
Standard Oil of California	225	83	6,630,500	Down 11.4%
Minnesota Mining & Manufacturing	224	98	3,491,200	Down 0.4%
Atlantic Richfield	220	106	2,498,500	Down 6.1%
Merck	215	99	2,887,800	Down 3.8%
International Paper	214	88	3,028,700	Down 7.8%
Schlumberger	212	91	2,707,900	Down 5.8%
Kresge	209	101	5,774,800	Down 0.8%
Northwest Airlines	209	69	7,358,100	Up 1.9%
Bristol-Myers	207	68	2,807,800	Down 10.8%
Warner-Lambert	203	60	5,691,100	Down 4.6%
Phillips Petroleum	202	77	3,612,100	Up 5.1%
Continental Oil	201	77	5,914,600	Down 0.4%
Citicorp	201	81	5,709,600	Down 13.6%
Mobil Oil	198	112	3,413,800	Down 7.5%
Georgia-Pacific	198	44	3,671,100	Down 5.9%
Weyerhaeuser	197	53	4,056,300	Down 10.9%
Sears, Roebuck	194	98	2,526,000	Up 2.4%
Kerr-McGee	189	73	2,654,400	Down 13.9%
Travelers	181	64	5,705,300	Down 2.4%
CBS	180	62	3,414,700	Down 1.6%
Deere	179	59	2,812,100	Down 9.2%

Table 8-1 **continued**

	Value of Holdings (Millions)	Funds Holding Stock	Total Shares Held	Change from Three Months Earlier
Standard Oil (Indiana)	177	85	3,743,800	Down 12.9%
St. Regis Paper	175	38	3,933,400	Up 13.8%
Avon	173	75	4,090,500	Down 4.4%
General Telephone & Electronics	173	99	6,603,400	Down 4.6%
Sperry Rand	172	62	3,508,500	Down 4.9%
Tenneco	168	62	5,941,200	Up 9.6%
Johnson & Johnson	167	71	1,860,600	Up 1.4%
Union Camp	166	40	2,844,500	Up 5.6%

Source: Reprinted by permission of Vickers Associates, Inc., Huntington, NY 11743. Table appeared in *U.S. News & World Report,* 19 July 1976.

Balanced Funds Bonds, preferred stocks, and common stocks of a variety of industries or companies are combined in the portfolios of balanced funds. These funds are believed to account for as much as 25 percent of all mutual fund assets. They attract investors who wish to receive a reasonably good—but safe—return on their investments. While the money invested in a balanced fund is usually fairly secure, capital growth is not as great as that expected from investment in a diversified common stock fund. The balanced fund generally appeals to persons who do not wish to build their own portfolios and would like to diversify across various security types.

Mutual Fund Funds A relatively new development, these funds invest in a portfolio of mutual funds, thereby spreading risk over a quite large group of securities. One disadvantage of this type of fund is that it must pay loading fees of 7 to 8.5 percent on the shares of load funds it acquires for its portfolio. The mutual fund itself, however, is permitted to charge only 1 to 3 percent loadings on the sale of its shares. Due to its probable overdiversification and the large amount of fees it must pay to set up a portfolio, this type of fund is not an especially attractive investment.

Dual Funds A special kind of closed-end investment company, the dual fund purchases securities with both income and growth attributes. The shares of this fund are designated as either income or growth shares. Purchasers of income shares receive the income from the securities owned by the fund, while purchasers of growth shares receive the capital gains from the fund. A minimum level of annual income is often guaranteed with the income shares. These funds are established with limited lives of around fifteen years. When they are liquidated, the

Table 8-2 Securities Owned by a Mutual Fund

PUTNAM EQUITIES FUND, INC.

SECURITIES OWNED — December 31, 1975

Number of Shares		Cost (††)	Market Value (†††)	Number of Shares		Cost (††)	Market Value (†††)
	COMMON STOCKS — 87.0%(*)				Electronics — 5.4%		
	Consumer Products — 18.0%			26,500	Fairchild Camera & Instrument Corp.	$ 1,185,278	$ 993,750
115,000	Franklin Mint Corporation	$ 1,551,684	$ 2,903,750	42,000†	National Semiconductor Corporation	1,877,498	1,722,000
58,000	Polaroid Corporation	2,043,906	1,798,000			3,062,776	2,715,750
55,200†	Tandy Corporation	1,466,160	2,870,400				
30,000†	Tandycrafts, Inc.	223,452	401,250		Aerospace — 4.6%		
47,100	Woolworth (F.W.) Company	1,003,044	1,036,200	61,000†	General Dynamics Corporation	1,595,466	2,295,125
		6,288,246	9,009,600			1,595,466	2,295,125
	Restaurant Chains — 13.9%				Drugs and Medical — 2.0%		
30,000	Denny's, Inc.	540,000	615,000	47,800	Hospital Corp. of America	1,175,571	979,900
35,000†	McDonald's Corporation	1,475,006	2,043,125			1,175,571	979,900
92,000†	Pizza Hut, Inc.	1,602,993	1,909,000				
160,000	Sambo's Restaurants, Inc.	1,851,903	2,400,000		Natural Resources — 1.0%		
		5,469,902	6,967,125	21,300	Boise Cascade Corporation	511,632	503,213
	Office Equipment — 11.9%					511,632	503,213
64,000†	Data General Corporation	1,702,151	2,392,000		Miscellaneous — 1.3%		
16,000†	Digital Equipment Corp.	1,953,145	2,190,000	49,000†	Combustion Equipment	1,650,124	655,375
6,000	International Business Machines Corporation	1,342,661	1,345,500			1,650,124	655,375
		4,997,957	5,927,500		TOTAL COMMON STOCKS	37,039,969	43,485,000
	Services — 11.0%			Par Value			
39,500	Lawson Products, Inc.	815,750	711,000				
60,000	Servicemaster Industries Inc.	1,503,125	1,650,000		Commercial Paper — 13.0%		
110,000	UAL, Inc.	2,227,077	3,121,250	$ 650,000	Farm Credit Bank 1/7/76 — 5.1% (††††)	648,895	648,895
		4,545,952	5,482,250	1,615,000	Ford Motor Credit Corp. 1/5/76 — 1/26/76 5.5% (††††)	1,611,855	1,611,855
	Energy and Related — 10.1%			1,887,000	General Electric Credit Corp. 1/6/76 — 1/14/76 5.4% (††††)	1,874,671	1,874,671
32,800	Houston Natural Gas Corporation	810,111	1,599,000	1,554,000	GMAC Corp. 1/8/76 — 1/20/76 5.4% (††††)	1,545,282	1,545,282
15,000	Hughes Tool Co.	693,872	643,125	821,000	Sears, Roebuck Acceptance 1/9/76 — 1/28/76 5.4% (††††)	814,255	814,255
12,400	National Mine Service Co.	494,325	350,300		TOTAL COMMERCIAL PAPER	6,494,958	6,494,958
87,000†	Vetco Offshore Industries, Inc.	2,044,566	2,457,750		TOTAL SECURITIES	$43,534,927	$49,979,958
		4,042,874	5,050,175				
	Insurance — 7.8%						
43,000	American International Group, Inc.	1,830,087	2,150,000				
61,100	Colonial Penn Group, Inc.	1,869,382	1,748,987				
		3,699,469	3,898,987				

(*) Percentages indicated are based on market value of total investments.

† Non-income producing security.

†† The aggregate identified cost of securities for federal income tax purposes was substantially the same.

††† Market value is based on stock exchange or over-the-counter quotations, computed at the last reported sale price on December 31, 1975, or, if no sale was reported, at bid price at the close of business on that day.

†††† The rate of interest shown is based on cost and is an average for each issuer.

Source: Putnam Equities Fund, Inc., prospectus dated 30 April 1976, Boston, Massachusetts, p. 21. Reprinted by permission.

holders of income shares receive their original investment, and the excess proceeds are distributed among the growth shares. The success of this type of fund depends on how well its manager selects securities with both income and growth attributes.

Specialty Funds Most often, specialty funds are funds that invest in relatively high-quality companies within a specific industry. Some spe-

Those Bouncing New Tax-Exempt Funds

Now Wall Street has a new breed of wonder child: mutual funds that invest in tax-free municipal bonds. . . . Like other mutual funds, the new investment vehicles consist of professionally managed, diversified portfolios. They make it possible for relatively small investors to take advantage of the fact that interest on municipal bonds isn't subject to federal income tax. Traditionally, municipals have appealed most to the well-to-do. . . .

But it's not just the very prosperous who can profit from tax-exempt investments. If you're a single taxpayer whose net income after exemptions and deductions is $12,000 to $14,000 a year, you're in the 29% federal income tax bracket; typically that would mean a gross income in the $14,000 to $16,000 range. In the 29% bracket a tax-exempt yield of 6% is the equivalent of a taxable yield of 8.45%, which is higher than the current yields on high-grade corporate bonds. For a couple with a net income between $24,000 and $28,000 a year filing a joint return, a 6% tax-exempt yield equals a taxable yield of 9.38%. . . .

Sponsors of the new managed funds believe they have clear-cut advantages. . . . Small investors benefit because the minimum initial investment can be as little as $100; it usually runs between $1,000 and $2,500. Additional shares may be then purchased in increments of anywhere from $25 to $100. Large and small investors alike should benefit—at least in theory—from flexibility in the fund's portfolios. Donald Spiro, president of Oppenheimer Management Corp., which recently offered a muni-fund to the public, points out that "if there's a change in rates, fully managed portfolios can take advantage of it." When interest rates go up, the funds can maintain the market value of their shares by selling longer-term issues and reinvesting in short-term municipal bonds.

Some muni-funds will offer a variety of special services to shareholders, including automatic reinvestment of dividends and automatic transfer of money into the fund from a checking account or paycheck. The Federated Tax-Free Income Fund can be used like a checking account that pays tax-free interest, though the checks you write must be for at least $500. Companies that sponsor other types of funds besides a muni-fund will allow investors to transfer from one fund to another at no charge.

Source: "Those Bouncing New Tax-Exempt Funds," excerpted from the January 1977 issue of MONEY Magazine by special permission; © 1977, Time Inc.

cialty funds invest in firms in similar situations. For example, the Small Business Investment Company (SBIC) is a closed-end investment company that invests solely in small business firms. The objectives of specialty funds may be growth, income, or some combination of both.

Money Market Funds As a result of the prevailing high interest rates being paid on money market instruments in 1973–1975, money market funds were established to invest in short-term debt instruments such as certificates of deposit and treasury bills. The appeal of these funds is closely tied to the prevailing interest rates: in periods of high interest rates, they are often lucrative; but in periods of low interest rates, their value is limited. One attractive feature of these funds is that they allow small investors to make money market investments indirectly that would require minimum purchases of $10,000 if made directly. Another is the high liquidity of money market funds.

Performance (Go-Go) Funds Performance as measured by total return earned on the shareholder's investment is the emphasis of performance, or "go-go," funds. The managers of these funds are quite aggressive; they buy and sell securities, often holding them only for short periods of time. Their investment strategies are speculative in the sense that they attempt to trade securities in order to earn on small share price movements. Investment in go-go funds should be made only by those willing to take the risks commensurate with the higher than average returns expected from them. Of course, it is probably best to let the professional fund managers make these investments for you rather than engage in such speculative ventures on your own.

Although the most common types of investment companies are described in the preceding sections, there are numerous others whose objectives with respect to income and growth differ from those of the aforementioned. Table 8-3 categorizes the investment companies discussed above according to types of securities held and primary objectives. Many of the possible motives and considerations for making investments in these companies are discussed in the next part of the chapter.

Since most investment company transactions are made in mutual fund shares, this part of the chapter is devoted to certain essential aspects of mutual fund transactions, in particular, motives for purchase, methods of purchase, special features, and considerations and techniques involved in buying mutual fund shares.

Making Mutual Fund Investments

Table 8-3 **Classifications and Characteristics of Investment Companies**

Classification of Investment Company	Types of Securities in Portfolio	Primary Objective—Growth (G) or Income (I)
Balanced Funds	Bonds, Preferred Stock and Common Stock	G-I Combination
Bond Funds	Bonds—Corporate or Government	I
Diversified Common Stock Funds	Common Stock	Variety of G-I Combinations
Dual Funds	Stock and Bonds	G or I
Money Market Funds	Money Market Instruments	I
Municipal Bond Funds	Bonds—State and Local Government	I (Tax Exempt)
Mutual Fund Funds	Mutual Funds	G
Performance (Go-Go) Funds	Speculative Common Stock	G
Preferred Stock Funds	Preferred Stock	I
Specialty Funds	Common Stock in a Specific Industry	G-I

Motives for Purchasing Mutual Funds

The most common motives for purchasing mutual fund shares include diversification, professional management, financial return, and convenience.

Diversification The primary motive for investing in mutual funds is the *ability to diversify* and diminish risk by indirectly investing in a number of different types of securities and/or companies. A person with only $100 to invest might at most be able to diversify into only four securities, while the same $100 invested in mutual fund shares might provide a claim on a diversified portfolio of fifty securities. In order to better understand the degree of diversification achieved by mutual funds, refer to the historic portfolio diversification for mutual funds in Table 8-4.

Professional Management The second major appeal of the mutual fund is its professional management. Of course, management is paid a fee from the fund's earnings, but the contribution of a full-time expert manager should be well worth its cost. Purchase and sale decisions made by professionals should provide better results than those that the average investor could achieve. Fund managers who do not perform are expected to be fired.

Table 8-4 **Portfolio Diversification of Mutual Funds**
(Percent of Total Common Stock by Industries, 1965, 1970, 1975)

	1965	1970	1975
Agricultural Equipment	0.43%	0.14%	0.41%
Aircraft Manufacturing and Aerospace	2.80	0.90	1.71
Air Transport	3.87	1.47	1.91
Auto and Accessories (Excluding Tires)	4.61	3.15	2.42
Building Materials and Equipment	1.27	4.31	2.41
Chemicals	6.46	5.46	8.15
Containers	1.22	0.44	0.46
Drugs and Cosmetics	4.09	5.96	8.04
Electrical Equipment and Electronics (Excluding TV and Radio)	6.14	6.45	4.46
Foods and Beverages	2.54	4.59	3.89
Financial (Including Banks and Insurance)	10.46	9.12	7.21
Machinery	1.51	1.42	1.72
Metals and Mining	3.79	3.60	3.12
Motion Pictures	0.12	0.26	0.36
Office Equipment	4.98	7.53	7.87
Oil	12.12	10.41	14.20
Paper	1.58	1.69	3.03
Public Utilities (Including Telephone and Natural Gas)	10.52	10.52	5.48
Railroad	3.57	1.43	1.55
Railroad Equipment	0.26	0.30	0.30
Retail Trade	2.53	5.27	3.46
Rubber (Including Tires)	1.19	1.75	1.13
Steel	2.28	0.24	2.07
TV and Radio	1.58	0.64	1.54
Textiles	1.15	0.48	0.46
Tobacco	1.42	2.05	2.41
Miscellaneous[a]	7.51	10.42	10.23
Totals	100.00%	100.00%	100.00%

Note: Composite industry investments drawn as of the end of calendar year 1975 from the portfolios of forty of the largest investment companies, whose total net assets represented 53.3 percent of total net assets of all Institute member companies.
[a] Includes diversified industrial companies not readily assignable to specific industry categories.

Source: 1976 Mutual Fund Fact Book (Washington, D.C.: Investment Company Institute, 1976), p. 23. Reprinted by permission.

Financial Return As indicated above, professional management is expected to result in returns exceeding those that the small investor could generate. Still, the relatively high purchase fee coupled with the management fee have a tendency to reduce the returns actually earned on mutual fund investments. Mutual fund investments must therefore earn higher returns than other investments. And while they are generally expected to earn a safer, more predictable return than self-made portfolios, there is no guarantee—only the expectation—that this will actually be the case.

Convenience Finally, the fact that mutual fund shares can be purchased through a variety of sources also adds to their appeal. Then, too, prospectuses of mutual funds, which clearly state their investment objectives, greatly simplify the selection. This convenience coupled with the above-mentioned diversification, professional management, and expected financial returns make the mutual fund appealing to the small investor, who otherwise would be unable to reap similar benefits.

Methods of Purchasing Mutual Funds

Mutual fund shares can be purchased using one of three possible methods: the regular account purchase, voluntary savings accumulation plans, and contractual savings accumulation plans.

Regular Account Purchase Persons who buy mutual fund shares on a transaction-by-transaction basis rather than under some type of prearranged purchase program make regular account purchases which are one-time purchase transactions. To make this kind of purchase, the investor expends a specified amount of money; the loading, or purchase, fee is then levied against this amount. Although the percentage amount of this fee declines with the size of the transaction, it is expected to be in the range of 7 to 8.5 percent for most transactions made by the small investor. For example, if you wish to make a regular account purchase of $5,000 of mutual fund shares and the loading fee is 8 percent, the cost of the transaction is $400 (0.08[$5,000]). Any dividends or capital gains earned on this investment are distributed to the shareholders at prespecified points in time or reinvested, depending on what arrangements have been made. Reinvestment plans are discussed in a later section.

Voluntary Savings Accumulation Plans In voluntary savings accumulation plans an investor opens an account by making an initial purchase of mutual fund shares ranging from $25 to $500, depending on the fund's requirements. The investor is then expected to make regular minimum purchases of the fund's shares ranging from $25 to $100; larger purchases can, of course, be made at any time. This type of plan is similar to the Monthly Investment Plans (MIPs) for security purchases described in Chapter 7. Since additional purchases of the fund's shares are made each period, the voluntary savings accumulation plan is a type of dollar-cost averaging plan. The load on purchases of shares under this plan is calculated in the same fashion as is done on regular account purchases. Since these plans have no stated life, they may be liquidated at any time without penalty. Failure to make a planned purchase does not result in any penalty, but it may cause the company to put you on a regular account purchase arrangement. The advantage of the voluntary accumulation plan over the regular account purchase arrangement is that it allows you to make smaller purchases than the minimums required under the regular account arrangement. The forced savings aspect of these plans also has appeal for some investors.

Contractual Savings Accumulation Plans There is a built-in penalty for not abiding by a contractual savings accumulation plan. This type of plan differs from the voluntary plan in that the purchaser agrees to make regular contributions over a specified period of time. The time period over which contributions are made is frequently ten years. The total commissions on all purchases to be made over the life of the plan are paid in the first few years. This arrangement is referred to as a "front-end load," and because in effect it requires commissions to be paid in advance, it provides investors with an incentive to abide by the plan. Investors who drop out of this kind of plan sacrifice the prepaid loads on subsequent purchases and find that the number of shares they possess is less than what they could have obtained through a regular account purchase. The Securities and Exchange Commission (SEC) requires contractual accumulation plans to give a full refund of prepaid loads to persons who cancel within forty-five days of their enrollment and to give persons who cancel within eighteen months of enrollment a refund of 85 percent of the total prepaid sales commissions paid.

Contractual savings accumulation plans are offered only by load funds, since no-load funds have no mechanism to provide an incentive to continue investing. Because of the high sales commissions in the early years of these plans, sales representatives have strongly promoted them. At the same time, the SEC as well as state regulatory agencies have imposed restrictions on them, since the high front-end loadings tend to severely penalize persons wishing to cancel. The SEC has attempted to force investment companies to spread the loadings over more years; and certain states, such as California, Illinois, Ohio, and Wisconsin, have gone so far as to prohibit entirely the sale of contractual savings accumulation plans. As a result of the growing governmental regulation of these plans, their popularity has declined dramatically over the last five years.

Special Features of Mutual Funds

Mutual funds have a variety of features which can prove valuable to investors, including automatic reinvestment plans, systematic withdrawal plans, insurance against loss, and retirement plans.

Automatic Reinvestment Plans Plans are often available whereby the share owners can elect to have dividends, interest, and capital gains realized on their holdings automatically reinvested in additional shares. Fractional shares are issued, if needed in order to permit the reinvestment of the total amount of earnings. The advantage of these plans, which are often required under the savings accumulation plans discussed above, lies in the fact that no loading is charged on this purchase transaction. Note, however, that the net amount earned from dividends and interest is reduced by the management fee prior to reinvestment. For tax purposes, of course, it makes no difference whether or not dividends, interest, and capital gains realized are automatically reinvested. For investors who wish to increase their investments in fund shares, these plans provide an excellent vehicle that can save loading fees.

Systematic Withdrawal Plans Quite often a mutual fund will provide some kind of systematic withdrawal plan which pays out specified amounts each period to the shareholders. To participate in these plans, the shareholders are usually required to have a minimum investment (i.e., net asset value) in the fund of $5,000 to $10,000. The size of the withdrawal must normally be $50 or more per month. Depending on how well the fund has done and the specified amount of the withdrawals, the check may or may not actually represent the return of part of the owner's initial investment. In other words, in some cases the dividends, interest, and capital gains after management fees may be greater than the withdrawal, resulting in an automatic accumulation of additional shares in the plan. On the other hand, if the fund has not performed well, the withdrawals could eventually completely deplete the original investment of funds.

Under systematic withdrawal plans, the most common arrangement is to specify the withdrawal as a *fixed dollar amount* per period as indicated above. Another type of arrangement specifies a *fixed number of shares* which are to be liquidated each period so that the shareholder may receive the proceeds. Since the net asset value of the shares is likely to fluctuate each period, this plan provides a varying amount of dollar income depending on the prevailing net asset value. In still another type of arrangement, only a *fixed percentage of the net asset growth* is paid to the shareholder. Under this plan, since the percentage is less than 100, some reinvestment is always provided for. In periods where asset values have not grown, no withdrawal takes place. Finally, there is one kind of plan that provides for withdrawal of *all earnings* in the form of dividends, interest, and capital gains (less management fees). Under this plan the initial investment remains untouched since only earnings on it are paid out. None of these withdrawal plans is permanent; all may be altered or discontinued at any time at the option of the shareholder. They are most useful to those who desire fixed periodic income from their investment. Investors interested in one of these plans should check to be sure that it is available from the mutual fund in which they intend to invest.

Insurance against Loss A number of mutual funds currently make available insurance policies covering losses realized on the mutual fund investment. These insurance policies require that the investment be held for at least ten years and that all dividends, interest, and capital gains earned on the shares be reinvested in additional shares. The premiums on these policies are forfeited and the coverage canceled if the shares are sold prior to the minimum holding period specified in the policy. The insurance covers the loss experienced when mutual fund shares are sold for less than was originally paid for them. For example, assume you paid $12,000 for mutual fund shares which you purchased ten years ago, and today you sell these shares for $10,000. If you had a ten-year policy insuring against losses, the insurance company would pay you $2,000 ($12,000 − $10,000). The availability of mutual fund insurance is often used to stimulate the purchase of shares in a given fund. On an economic basis, the insurance is not worth its cost; the chance that you would experience a loss on shares held for ten or so years on which all earnings have been reinvested is small.

Retirement Plans As a result of certain government legislation, self-employed individuals are permitted to divert a portion of their pretax income into certain approved mutual fund investments. The eligibility of mutual funds as acceptable investments under this arrangement enhances their investment appeal to self-employed persons. A more detailed discussion of the use of mutual funds as part of retirement planning is included in Chapter 16.

Buying Mutual Fund Shares

In order to buy mutual fund shares that are appropriate to your investment goals, it is advisable to know not only how to make the transaction but also how to obtain and evaluate information with respect to the quality of specific funds. This section considers the various sources of mutual fund information, methods for measuring mutual fund performance, and the process of making the transaction.

Sources of Information Information with respect to the objectives, characteristics, management, and past performance of a mutual fund can be obtained from the fund's prospectus, which is available from a sales representative. Both the National Association of Securities Dealers (NASD) and the SEC require that mutual fund prospectuses and advertising be accurate representations of the facts. Thus prospectuses and other sales information should provide reliable information. The cover of the prospectus for the Putnam Equities Fund is shown in Figure 8-3. It

Figure 8-3 **Cover of a Prospectus for a Mutual Fund**

PUTNAM EQUITIES FUND, INC.

A Mutual Fund Seeking Capital Appreciation

Putnam Equities Fund, Inc. (the "Fund") is a mutual fund. Its address is 265 Franklin Street, Boston, Massachusetts 02110, and its telephone number is (617) 423-4960.

The Fund's investment objective is to seek capital appreciation by investing its assets primarily in common stocks. Portfolio investments are selected entirely on the basis of their possibilities for capital appreciation and current income is only an incidental consideration (dividends, if any, are expected to be small). Shares of the Fund should be regarded as speculative and are designed for investors who understand and are willing to accept the risk of loss involved in seeking capital appreciation. There is no assurance that the Fund's objective will be achieved, and there is no protection against loss of value of a shareholder's investment. The value of the shares of the Fund will fluctuate with changes in the market value of its investments. **The Fund may purchase securities for short-term trading. This speculative activity may involve greater risks and costs and is more fully described on page 2 of this Prospectus.**

The Fund's investment adviser is The Putnam Management Company, Inc. (the "Adviser"), which has been advising mutual funds since 1937, and today manages nine publicly owned investment companies known as The Putnam Group with net assets in excess of $1.88 billion at April 21, 1976. Affiliates of the Adviser advise a number of institutional accounts which, in the aggregate, are substantial in size. The management fee payable by the Fund to the Adviser is at the annual rate of 50/100 of 1% of the first $100,000,000 of average net asset value, and 40/100 of 1% of the average net asset value in excess of $100,000,000, and is subject to certain adjustments — see "Investment Adviser", page 6.

Shares of the Fund may be purchased from securities dealers at the public offering price which fluctuates with changes in the market value of the Fund's portfolio securities and is the net asset value per share, plus a sales charge of a maximum of 8.5% of the offering price or 9.3% of the net amount invested (reduced on sales of $10,000 or more — see page 10). A shareholder's initial investment and each subsequent investment must be at least $500, except under certain Plans. (See "How to Buy Shares", page 10.) Shares may be redeemed at their net asset value. (See "How May Shares Be Repurchased or Redeemed?", page 12.)

The investor is advised to retain this Prospectus for future reference.

THESE SECURITIES HAVE NOT BEEN APPROVED OR DISAPPROVED BY THE SECURITIES AND EXCHANGE COMMISSION NOR HAS THE COMMISSION PASSED UPON THE ACCURACY OR ADEQUACY OF THIS PROSPECTUS. ANY REPRESENTATION TO THE CONTRARY IS A CRIMINAL OFFENSE.

TABLE OF CONTENTS

Prospectus dated April 30, 1976

Source: Putnam Equities Fund, Inc., Prospectus dated 30 April 1976, Boston, Massachusetts, p. 1. Reprinted by permission.

contains a brief statement of the fund's objective and the table of contents for the prospectus. The securities owned by this fund on 31 December 1975 were shown earlier, in Table 8-2.

Other sources of information are similar to those for stock and bond investments given in Chapter 7. Publications such as the *Wall Street Journal, Barron's,* and *Forbes* provide useful data and articles concerned with mutual funds. Probably one of the best general sources of informa-

Learning More about a Mutual Fund

You, too, can invest more wisely.

So says one expert.

Take mutual funds.

Their prospectuses are a gold mine of information, states Yale Hirsch, author of the yearly "Mutual Funds Almanac."

But most mutual fund investors never read these documents, he adds. Why?

"Because they are forbidding documents filled with highly technical jargon. The fund industry knows it and wants to make them easier to read. But Washington and the legal profession are slow to change ways."

Every prospectus, Mr. Hirsch says, will tell you things like these:

The fund's basic investment policy in detail.

Not all growth—or income—funds are alike. Some growth funds, for example, invest in big, established firms like IBM or Xerox. Others look for new companies, here or overseas, or turnaround situations.

The prospectus spells out, too, if the fund sells short, uses leverage or tries to outguess market trends.

Investment restrictions.

Those are no-nos for the fund's portfolio manager. Like not buying or selling real estate, commodity contracts, or puts and calls.

Portfolio turnover.

How long the fund holds on to the stock it buys. A 100 percent rate means a complete turnover in one year's time. Does it intend to be a long-term investor or a short-term trader?

Fund management.

The prospectus identifies directors or trustees, and members of the fund's advisory board—if it has one. Also their occupation for the last five years, which may reveal inexperience when it exists.

Litigation.

Is anyone suing the fund? If so, the prospectus says so and explains why in detail.

Statement of investments.

This shows, among other things, what the fund paid for the stocks it owns. Check to see if it has picked winners or lots of lemons.

That's much more, Mr. Hirsch says, than you may know about a stock.

Only a mutual fund always has a prospectus available. That's because its shares are always being sold.

Not so with stocks, except new issues.

Source: Reprinted by permission from "Learning More about Your Mutual Funds," *Nation's Business,* July 1975, pp. 6–7. Copyright 1975 by Nation's Business, Chamber of Commerce of the United States.

tion on mutual funds is *Fundscope,* a monthly publication devoted entirely to discussion and analysis of mutual funds. It is, of course, not advisable to rely solely on the information provided by a salesperson since, although it may be accurate, it may not include comparisons of the fund to other funds having similar objectives.

Measuring Fund Performance The performance of mutual funds is usually measured with reference to the investment of a certain amount at a specified point in time. Comparisons are made of the net asset values of shares that result after a period of years from $10,000 investments. Statistics based on the assumption that all dividends, interest, and capital gains were reinvested in additional shares are presented as either the dollar amount of net asset value achieved or the annual compound rate of growth in net asset value realized. For example, a $10,000 investment in the QRS Growth Fund ten years ago with all dividends and capital gains reinvested might have a net asset value of $25,650. This would represent an annual rate of return of approximately 11 percent. These types of performance statistics are a good means for comparing the different funds.

Again, small investors should not rely solely on the statistics provided in a prospectus or by a mutual fund sales representative since the data from these two sources are intended to show only the positive aspects of the fund under consideration. One excellent source of comparative performance statistics is published annually each August in *Forbes.* An excerpt from the 1976 Forbes Fund Ratings is shown in Figure 8-4. Other sources of comparative statistics which are sold on a subscription basis are *Johnson's Investment Company Charts* and Weisenberger's *Investment Companies, Mutual Funds, and Other Types.* These sources not only compare the performance of the funds' management, but they also relate fund performance generally to the behavior of the securities markets to permit the investor to assess the relative advantages of investing in mutual fund shares versus investing in individual securities. These sources can normally be obtained at your stockbrokerage firm.

Note that performance statistics report only what has happened in the past. Although past performance does act as a barometer for the future, it is important to be sure that major changes in fund management are not expected since management is of key importance to a fund's success. Also, if you consider investing in a new fund that has no past performance statistics, you must rely almost completely on knowledge of the expertise of the managers in order to develop expectations about future performance. The quality of fund managers is the key factor affecting the relative performance of mutual fund shares.

Making the Transaction Transactions in mutual fund shares can be made either through a broker who is authorized to sell shares or through

Figure 8-4 Excerpt from 1976 Forbes Fund Ratings

Performance Ratings — In UP Markets	In DOWN Markets		Latest 12 Months Gain	10-Year Average Annual Growth Rate	Latest 12 Months Dividend Return	Total Assets 6/30/76 in Millions	% Change 1976 vs. 1975	Maximum Sales Charge	Annual Expenses Per $100
C	D	**Standard & Poor's 500 Stock Average**	9.5%	1.0%	3.7%				
		FORBES Stock Fund Average	7.6%	0.3%	2.7%				
		Stock Funds (Load)							
C	D	Plitrend Fund	11.7%	0.9%	-2.9%	$ 9.7	2.1	8.50%	$1.36
A	F	Polaris Fund (started 8/68)	5.1	—	none	37.5	-7.2	8.50	0.76
A	D	Progress Fund (started 8/69)	2.3	—	1.5	5.8	-3.3	8.50	1.00
D	B	Provider Growth Fund (started 2/70)	3.0	—	2.2	6.7	3.1	8.50	1.12
D	A	Provider Investors Fund (started 1/69)	15.4	—	4.7	4.4	29.4	8.50	1.12
D	A	Puritan Fund	11.8	1.4	5.5	759.0	5.2	8.50	0.52
		Putnam Funds							
A	F	Equities (started 9/67)	3.8	—	0.4	52.2	-8.6	8.50	1.08
A	D	Growth	6.5	2.8	2.3	654.0	-3.8	8.50	0.58
B	B	Investors	3.2	5.3	1.7	472.8	-6.1	8.50	0.62
A	F	Vista (started 6/68)	3.7	—	0.5	71.5	-5.1	8.50	1.03
A	C	Voyager (started 4/69)	12.1	—	none	45.8	8.3	8.50	1.41
C	A	Research Capital Fund (started 5/69)	-52.7	—	9.6	17.1	-53.9	7.25	1.09
B	F	Research Equity Fund	-1.7	-1.1	4.1	66.9	-9.6	7.25	1.27
C	C	Paul Revere Courier Fund (started 8/69)	15.1	—	2.7	3.3	13.8	8.50	1.34
C	F	Revere Fund	5.3	-4.7	2.7	6.9	-2.8	—	2.90
		SAFECO Funds							
B	D	Equity	21.4	1.8	3.2	32.4	7.3	8.50	0.63
B	F	Growth (started 2/68)	27.3	—	2.3	20.9	29.0	8.50	0.92
C	B	Income (started 10/69)	20.4	—	5.5	4.7	30.6	8.50	0.90
C	F	Salem Fund	17.3	-2.4	2.2	56.4	8.3	8.50	1.00
C	D	Schuster Fund (started 9/67)	7.0	—	1.2	15.1	33.6	8.50	1.50

Note: Forbes rates mutual funds on the basis of their performance in three rising markets and three falling markets. Funds are rated against each other rather than on an absolute scale. In up markets, the top 12.5 percent get an A+, the next 12.5 percent get an A, the next 25 percent get B, the next 25 percent get C, the lowest 25 percent get D. There is, however, some weighting toward performance in the most recent period. Also, a fund that did especially badly in a down market might rate F—failing. Funds that have not been in operation for at least ten years may not get an A+ rating.

Source: Reprinted with permission from "Forbes Fund Ratings—1976," *Forbes*, 15 August 1976, p. 69.

a fund salesperson. If your broker is not authorized to sell fund shares, he or she might be able to put you in contact with a salesperson. If you respond to an advertisement for fund shares, you will probably be called on by an authorized salesperson. In the case of no-load mutual funds, the entire transaction is carried out through the mail. In response to your request, you will be sent the relevant information for purchasing shares along with a prospectus describing fund performance. Investors should keep in mind that when salespersons are involved, they are compensated only if shares are purchased. Be sure if you make a mutual fund investment that it is consistent with your financial plans and is the best of the available alternatives. In other words, do not let the salesperson make your investment decisions; make them yourself.

Speculative Investments: Commodities and Options

Thus far in this chapter and Chapters 6 and 7, emphasis has been placed solely on investing—placing money in assets which are expected to yield some positive return over a specified period of time. Assets selected for investment may or may not be risky. Investing in high-risk assets is known as speculation. A speculator purchases assets that have quite uncertain returns and are too risky for the average investor. The speculative investments described in this part of the chapter—commodities and options—are not recommended as part of your financial plan; these types of investments should be made only with fun money that you can afford to lose without disrupting your financial plans.

Dealings in Commodities

The commodities markets provide a mechanism through which producers of certain commodities can protect themselves against future price declines on their products. Suppliers of commodities such as soybeans, frozen pork bellies, cocoa, silver, and cattle who believe that the price of their product is likely to drop prior to the time when they will have their commodity available for sale might sell a contract to deliver a specified quantity of the commodity at a specified price at some future date. The buyers of these contracts protect themselves against a price increase and guarantee themselves the future availability of a needed raw material at a known price. The various commodities are listed and traded on a number of exchanges, including the Chicago Mercantile Exchange and the New York Mercantile Exchange.

The Contract *Futures contracts* are normally written to provide for delivery of a commodity three or more months in the future. The contract represents a guarantee by the seller that he or she will deliver the commodity at a certain price on a given date. The buyer must arrange to pay for and take delivery of the commodity on this date. Thus both the seller and the buyer of a futures contract accept certain contractual obligations as the result of their transaction.

Because a wide variety of commodities are available for trading, contracts vary depending on which commodity is being traded. Table 8-5 lists some of the more common commodities along with the number of units in a contract and the unit in which the prices are quoted. For example, if a silver futures contract for delivery six months from now is quoted at 461.00, this means that to buy a contract, it is necessary to pay

Table 8-5 **Selected Commodity Contracts**

Commodity	Contract Size	Price Quotation
Cattle	40,000 pounds	cents/pound
Cocoa	30,000 pounds	cents/pound
Pork Bellies	36,000 pounds	cents/pound
Silver	5,000 troy ounces	cents/troy ounce
Soybeans	5,000 bushels	cents/bushel
Wheat	5,000 bushels	cents/bushel

461.00 cents per troy ounce. Since a silver contract consists of 5,000 troy ounces, the price of the contract would be $23,050 (461¢/troy ounce × 5,000 troy ounces). It should be clear from this example that if you plan to trade in futures contracts you must be familiar with the differing contract sizes and price quotations.

Logic of Futures Trading Because of various changes in business, weather, and international conditions, the prices of commodities fluctuate on a day-to-day basis and affect the value of futures contracts. For example, a one cent increase in the price of silver would cause the value of a futures contract in silver to increase by $50 (1¢/troy ounce × 5,000 troy ounces/contract). Because of the sensitivity of the values of futures contracts to small movements in the prices of commodities, these contracts offer high potential returns (or losses). They are thus attractive to speculators, who make commodities transactions not with any intention of ever taking delivery but rather in the hope of obtaining high profits in a short period of time. Of course, high risks are associated with these high returns. The two basic approaches used to trade in commodities differ depending on whether the price of a commodity is expected to increase or decrease.

Expected Price Increase A person who expects the price of a given commodity to rise will purchase a contract for that commodity and hold it until the price increase occurs. For example, assume today is January 1 and you purchase a silver contract (5,000 troy ounces) for delivery in May at the current price of silver, which is 461 cents per troy ounce. If the price of silver increases to 476 cents per troy ounce over the next few months and you sell the contract, you will make (ignoring any commissions) 15 cents/troy ounce (476¢ − 461¢), or a total of $750 (15¢/troy ounce × 5,000 troy ounces/contract) on the transaction. The $750 profit resulted from only a small movement in the silver price. Of course, had the price of silver instead dropped by 15 cents per troy ounce to 446 cents, you would have experienced a $750 loss.

Expected Price Decrease An individual who expects the price of a commodity to decline can attempt to capitalize on this expectation by selling a contract to deliver the commodity and, when the price of the commodity drops, purchasing a contract to cover the obligation to deliver. This strategy is quite similar to short selling, which was described in Chapter 7. For example, assume that silver futures are currently selling at 461 cents per troy ounce and you expect the price to decline. You could sell a silver contract for delivery in five months at this price. If within the five-month period the price declines to 446 and you then buy a contract to provide your promised delivery, you will have made 15 cents per troy ounce, or a total of $750 (15¢/troy ounce × 5,000 troy ounces/contract). You have in effect sold something to be delivered in the future at a higher price than you had to pay in order to acquire it. Had the price of the commodity increased instead of decreased, you would have had to purchase the commodity to be delivered at a price higher than the price at which you sold it and thus would have suffered a loss.

Since there are numerous factors that can affect the price of a commodity at a certain future date, and since small movements in commodity prices can drastically affect the value of a contract, the high risks of trading in commodity futures should be evident. In addition, certain constraints placed on the commodities markets may make it difficult to sell a futures contract as the delivery date approaches. This means that a risk of having to take delivery of the commodity itself does exist.

Making Futures Transactions Futures transactions can be made through most stockbrokerage firms. The broker can execute both buy and sell orders in futures contracts and the commission charged is less than 1 percent of the value of the contract. In order to make sure that their customers are financially able to take the risks associated with commodities trading, most brokerage firms establish a net worth minimum their clients must possess in the form of liquid assets before they can open a commodity trading account. Although these minimums vary from firm to firm, they are often in the neighborhood of $50,000. The primary source of information on commodities is the *Wall Street Journal,* which provides daily price quotations. Other information can be obtained from your stockbroker or directly from one of the commodity exchanges.

One significant aspect of commodity futures is the very low margin requirements placed on transactions. Persons with commodity trading accounts are required to put up between 5 and 20 percent of the value of the futures contract at the time of the transaction. Interest is normally not charged on the borrowed portion of the purchase price, since the money is not really paid out (or borrowed) until the actual delivery of the commodity takes place. If the price of the commodity declines over

"When you're in the commodity
market, one mistake . . ."

Commodity Futures Are High Risk Investments
Source: Reprinted by permission of Sidney Harris.

the holding period, the brokerage firm is likely to require the customer to
put up additional money as collateral on the contract. The use of low
margin on commodity transactions enhances returns received on investments but also notably increases the risks involved.

Refer back to the example from the silver market, in which an
individual purchased one silver contract and sold it after the price of
silver increased by fifteen cents per troy ounce (461¢ to 476¢) to make a
profit (ignoring any commissions) of $750 on the transaction. Had the
margin been 10 percent, the trader would have had to invest only $2,305
(10% × 461¢/troy ounce × 5,000 troy ounces of silver/contract). If the
contract had been held for three months (¼ of a year), the return on the
investment would have been 130 percent ([$750 ÷ $2,305] × 4)—a very
high return. Of course, had the price of silver declined by the same

amount, the trader would have lost 130 percent of the investment in the transaction. Although trading commodity futures can provide high potential returns, the risks of these transactions is so great that the small investor is wise to stay away from them.

Dealing in Options

Options are various types of contracts that permit an individual to either purchase or sell a specified security at a predetermined price within a certain period of time. The two most common types of options are calls and puts. A *call* is an option to purchase a specified number of shares (typically 100) of a stock at or before some future date for a specified price. Call options usually have initial lives of one month, three months, six months, or one year. The *striking price*, which is the price at which the option can be exercised, is most often set at or near the prevailing market price of the stock when the option is written. In order to purchase a call option, a specified price of normally a few hundred dollars must be paid. A *put* is an option to sell a given number of shares of a stock at or before a specified future date for a stated striking price. Like the call option, the striking price of the put is close to the market price of the underlying stock at the time of issuance. The lives and costs of puts are also quite similar to those of the call option. Although other types of options made of some combination of calls and puts exist, because calls and puts are the most common types, the discussion here is devoted solely to them.

How the Options Markets Work There are two methods of making options transactions. The first involves making a transaction through one of twenty or so call and put options dealers with the help of a stockbroker. The other and more popular mechanism is the organized options exchange. The dominant exchange on which both call and put options are traded is the *Chicago Board Options Exchange (CBOE)*. Although from its inception in April 1973 until June 1977 the CBOE dealt only in call options, it now provides an organized marketplace in which purchases and sales of both call and put options can be made in an orderly fashion. The options traded on the CBOE are standardized and are considered registered securities. Each option is for 100 shares of the underlying stock. The price at which options transactions can be made is determined by the forces of supply and demand. Options on over 100 listed securities are available on the CBOE.

A person can take one of two possible roles on the CBOE and become either an option *buyer* or an option *writer*. The buyer of options purchases and sells options that were initially written by the writer. In other words, a six-month call option for 100 shares of ABC with a striking price of $50, if exercised, would allow the buyer to purchase 100 shares of

ABC for $50 per share. The writer of the option would be responsible for providing the 100 shares of ABC. Therefore, when a person writes a call option, a contractual obligation is made to sell 100 shares of the stock to the buyer of the call at the exercise price. Writers of puts must be prepared to purchase from the buyer of the put 100 shares of the stock at the exercise price. Although probably less than half of all options are ever exercised, the option writer must be prepared to fulfill his or her contractual obligations to the option buyer. Most small investors who

Writing Call Options: A Conservative Approach?

Many investors approach the securities markets with a conservative attitude. They take it for granted that purchasing blue-chips over a span of years will provide them with capital appreciation and dividends. However, with the advent of listed options markets in 1973, a large number of investors are now viewing this activity as being aggressive in nature rather than conservative. In order to be more conservative, they are engaging in writing call options against newly acquired securities or against existing positions in their portfolios.

The advantages of writing a call option can be seen from the example of Tina Wilkerson, an investor. Tina currently owns 100 shares of Xerox stock, which is selling for $50 per share. Tina is uncertain about future movements of Xerox's stock price and wishes to protect her position in the stock. She therefore writes a six month call option against the stock at $50 per share and sells the option for $300. Tina knows that if the stock rises above $50 per share, the option will probably be exercised, but she has guaranteed herself $53 per share in this instance—the $50 per share sale price plus the $3 per share ($300 ÷ 100 shares) proceeds from the sale of the option. If the stock price drops below $50 per share, Tina knows that the option will not be exercised. But she will still have $3 per share more than she would have had if she had not written the option. If the stock price were to drop to $48 per share, she would net $51 per share ($48/share + $3/share from the option proceeds), which is more than she would have received from selling the stock. By writing the option, Tina has assured herself of receiving at least $50 per share as long as the stock price does not drop below $47 per share in the marketplace. At the same time, she has limited her gain during the period to a maximum of $53 per share.

The premium received for writing an option on a stock can be viewed as a cushion against near-term weakness in the market for the stock. It should be noted that income from premiums on options not exercised is taxed at ordinary rates, whereas a premium on an option that is exercised is added to the sale price of the delivered stock and can be taxed as a capital gain. Both the option purchaser and the option writer should act with caution. The former should commit only a small percentage of his or her assets to the purchase of options. The latter should not write "naked" call options without having any security in hand. Be sure you understand options before trying to deal in them. Whether you are writing or buying them, there are many opportunities for mistakes.

speculate in options only buy and sell options; they normally do not write them.

Logic of Option Trading The most common motive for purchasing call options is the expectation that the market price of the underlying stock will rise by more than enough to cover the cost of the option and thereby allow the purchaser of the call to profit. For example, assume that you pay $250 for a three-month call option on ABC at $60. This means that by paying $250 you are guaranteed that you can purchase 100 shares of ABC at $60 per share any time over the next three months. Ignoring any brokerage fees, the stock price must climb $2.50 per share ($250 ÷ 100 shares) to $62.50 per share in order to cover the cost of the option. If the stock price were to rise to $70 per share during the period, your net profit would be $750 ([100 shares][$70/share] − [100 shares][$60/share] − $250). Since this return would be earned on a $250 investment, it illustrates the high returns on investments that options offer. Of course, had the stock price not risen above $60 per share, you would have lost the $250 since there would have been no reason to exercise the option. Had the stock price risen to anywhere between $60 per share and $62.50 per share, you probably would have exercised the option in order to reduce your loss to an amount less than $250.

Put options are purchased in the expectation that the share price of a given security will decline over the life of the option. Purchasers of puts normally own the shares and wish to protect a gain they have realized since their initial purchase. By buying a put, they insure their gain because it enables them to sell their shares at a known price over the life of the option. Persons gain from put options when the price of the stock declines by more than the per share cost of the option. The logic underlying the purchase of a put option is exactly the opposite of that underlying the use of call options.

Making Options Transactions Your broker can easily make transactions for you in any of the options listed on the CBOE or other options exchanges. When the desired options are not listed, most brokers can locate the appropriate option dealer and negotiate the transaction. The brokerage fees on the purchase or sale of options may differ slightly depending on the exchange on which they are traded or the option dealer through which the transaction is made. As a rule of thumb, the fees are normally quite similar to those charged on transactions in listed securities.

Information and price data on options can be obtained from your stockbroker. Price quotations on the more active listed options appear daily in the *Wall Street Journal*. Trading in options is not recommended for the beginning or small investor due to the high degree of risk involved. Although high potential returns exist, the probability of achieving these returns is quite low. In many situations the exercise of the option is not attractive and the option expires, which results in a 100 percent loss on the investment in the option. Before attempting to trade in options, consult your broker, talk to an experienced investor, and read a basic text on options markets and transactions. Be sure you are aware of the risk associated with options transactions. Avoid this type of speculative investment unless you can afford the losses.

Summary

Investment companies, commodities, and options provide alternatives to stock and bond investments. Investment companies gather funds by selling shares to numerous investors and using the proceeds to purchase securities issued by a variety of corporations. These funds therefore provide small investors who do not have enough money to create their own diversified security portfolios with the benefits of diversification. The two basic types of investment companies are closed-end and open-end. The latter, often called mutual funds, issue as many shares as are demanded and stand willing to buy or sell shares at a price equal to the net asset value (NAV) per share of the portfolio. While most mutual funds are load funds—commissions are charged on the purchase of their shares—some are no-load funds.

Since investment companies are required to state their objectives, investors can use this information to select companies that provide returns consistent with their financial goals. The various types of investment companies include bond and stock funds, diversified common stock funds, balanced funds, mutual fund funds, dual funds, specialty funds, money market funds, and performance funds. The most popular type of fund is the diversified common stock fund, which invests in diversified portfolios of common stock providing a broad range of risk-return opportunities. The basic advantages of mutual fund investments include diversification, professional management, financial return, and convenience. Mutual fund shares can be purchased on regular account or through either a voluntary or contractual savings accumulation plan. Features often available as part of mutual fund purchases are automatic reinvestment plans, systematic withdrawal plans, insurance against loss, and various retirement plans. Purchases of mutual fund shares are best transacted through stockbrokers or fund salespersons.

Two of the more common types of speculative, or risky, investments are commodities and options. Commodities futures are contracts to buy or sell a commodity such as silver at a specified price at a future date. A number of markets for trading commodities exist. Because of the great deal of uncertainty associated with future commodity price movements, these investments are quite risky. Futures transactions can be made through your stockbroker, who can direct you to relevant information on the commodities markets. Options, which are contracts that permit either the purchase or sale of a specified security at a predetermined price within a certain period of time, are another type of speculative investment. The two most common types of options are calls and puts. Investors can buy and sell options traded on the options exchanges either through a stockbroker or directly through an options dealer. In options transactions there is a possibility of a 100 percent loss of the original investment. Like commodities transactions, they are too risky for the small investor.

Key Terms

automatic reinvestment plan
back-end load
balanced fund
bond or preferred stock fund
call options
Chicago Board Options Exchange (CBOE)
closed-end investment company
commodity futures
diversified common stock fund
dual fund
futures contract
front-end load
investment company
load funds

money market fund
mutual fund
mutual fund fund
net asset value (NAV) per share
no-load fund
open-end investment company
options
performance (go-go) fund
put options
regulated investment company
savings accumulation plans
specialty fund
striking price
systematic withdrawal plans
writer (of options)

Review Questions

1. Define and discuss investment companies. Distinguish between closed-end investment companies and open-end investment companies. Which are most popular?

2. What are mutual funds? Discuss what is meant by the "loading charge" on a mutual fund.

3. Distinguish between a front-end load and a back-end load as related to mutual funds.

4. Describe the manner in which the earnings of investment companies are taxed.

5. How are investment companies classified? Briefly describe any three types of mutual funds. How do the objectives of various mutual funds differ?

6. Explain the most common motives that exist for purchasing mutual fund shares?

7. What types of accumulation plans can be used to purchase mutual fund shares? Describe their differences and discuss any legal requirements that pertain to these plans.

8. What are some attractive features of mutual funds? How do automatic reinvestment plans work?

9. What types of systematic withdrawal plans are available to buyers of mutual funds?

10. What is meant by *dealing in commodities*? What is a futures contract? How do price fluctuations affect the value of futures contracts?

11. Sheikh Ahmad of Saudi Arabia purchased a futures contract on 1 January 1978 from the East-West Trading Corporation for delivery of 15,000 bushels of wheat, at a cost of $10 a bushel on 1 March 1978. On 1 January 1978 a bushel of wheat cost $10. In February the price increased to $12 a bushel. Ahmad decided to sell the contract before March. What was his profit or loss on the transaction? What would have been the effect if the price of wheat had declined to $8 a bushel?

12. How are futures transactions executed? Are clients expected to meet any financial requirements before opening a commodity trading account? Explain.

13. "The ability to use a low margin on commodity transactions enables the trader to enhance returns on investments while at the same time increasing the risks involved." Explain this statement.

14. What are options? Name and describe the most common type of options. How do options markets operate?

15. How are transactions made in options that are not listed? Do brokerage fees charged on options transactions differ from those charged on listed security transactions? Explain.

8-1 Clifford's Dilemma: Common Stock or Mutual Fund Shares?

Case Problems

For the past eight years, Clifford Swanson has been drawing an annual salary of about $19,000 working in the Management Services Division of Ace Consultants Inc. At thirty-three, he is still a bachelor, and he has accumulated about $8,000 of savings over the years. This he has kept in the Citibank Savings and Loan Association, where it earns 5¼ percent interest per year. Clifford is contemplating withdrawing $5,000 from this savings account and investing it in common stock. He believes that such an investment will probably earn him more than 5¼ percent. Bill Dover, a close friend of Clifford's who has recently taken a course in personal finance, suggests that he invest in mutual fund shares. This suggestion leaves Clifford undecided. He therefore has approached you, his broker, for advice.

Questions

1. Explain to Clifford the key motives that exist for purchasing mutual fund shares.

2. What special features of mutual funds may assist him in achieving his investment goals?

3. What type of mutual fund would you recommend that Clifford consider?

4. What recommendation would you make to Clifford with respect to his dilemma? Explain.

8-2 Jack Bought the Call Option: Was It a Good Deal?

Jack Butler, a systems analyst for Butler Baked Breads, is interested in buying 100 shares of Boeing through his stockbroker. The stock is selling at $40 a share, but as a result of new legislation removing double taxation of dividends, the price is expected to increase to $45. If Jack buys the stock at $40 per share and sells it one year later at $45 per share, his investment will have netted him $500, or a 12½ percent gain. Jack recently read an article about options in a news magazine published by a brokerage firm and as a result has decided to purchase a call option for shares of Boeing rather than buy the stock itself. He pays $400 for the option, which allows him to buy 100 shares of Boeing at $38 per share over the next ninety days.

Questions

1. How high must the stock price rise for Jack to break even on this transaction?

2. If the stock price rises to $45 per share during the period, what will be Jack's net profit?

3. What will be Jack's net profit if the stock reaches only $42?

4. Would Jack have been better off purchasing the stock (instead of the option) if he could have paid $40 a share and sold at $42 a share? Explain.

Amling, Frederick. *Investments: An Introduction to Analysis and Management.* Englewood Cliffs, N.J.: Prentice-Hall, 1974.

Ansbacher, Max C. "The Bear Facts about Puts." *Money,* August 1977, pp. 64–65.

Bellemore, Douglas H., and Ritchie, John C. *Investments: Principles/Practices/Analyses.* Cincinnati, Ohio: South-Western Publishing, 1974.

Ehrbar, A. F. "The Mythology of the Option Market." *Fortune,* October 1976, pp. 117–118 ff.

————. "Options—A Game for Bulls, Bears, and Arbitrageurs." *Fortune,* November 1976, pp. 107–108 ff.

Gastineau, Gary L. *The Stock Options Manual.* New York: McGraw-Hill, 1976.

Gould, Bruce G. *Dow Jones–Irwin Guide to Commodities Trading.* Homewood, Ill.: Dow Jones–Irwin, 1973.

Green, Timothy. *How to Buy Gold.* New York: Walker, 1975.

"How to Trade Options." *Business Week,* 7 March 1977, pp. 77–82.

Lamb, Robert. "A Wary Look at Those Tax-Exempt Mutual Funds." *Fortune,* December 1976, pp. 59–60 ff.

"Las Vegas in Chicago." *Forbes,* 1 July 1977, pp. 31–32.

Lavoie, Rachel. "Strictly for Speculators." *Money,* March 1977, pp. 68–69.

Mead, Stuart B. *Mutual Funds: Guide for the Lay Investor.* Braintree, Mass.: D. H. Mark Publications, 1971.

"Mutual Funds That Pay Tax-free Income." *Changing Times,* March 1977, pp. 6–9.

"Now—More Choices than Ever for Investors in Mutual Funds." *U.S. News & World Report,* 20 December 1976, pp. 77–78.

Sauvain, Harry C. *Investment Management.* Englewood Cliffs, N.J.: Prentice-Hall, 1973.

"Should You Invest in Gold?" *Better Homes and Gardens,* September 1975, pp. 68–69.

Smith, Keith V., and Eiteman, David K. *Essentials of Investing.* Homewood, Ill.: Richard D. Irwin, 1974.

Snyder, Linda. "The Weather and the Futures." *Fortune,* April 1977, pp. 59–60 ff.

**Selected
References**

Part 3

Managing Your
Nonfinancial Assets

Personal Balance Sheet	
Assets	Liabilities and Net Worth
Financial Assets	Liabilities
Nonfinancial Assets	Net Worth

This part of the text provides information on some basic nonfinancial assets—real estate, automobiles, furniture, and appliances—that an individual must consider in making personal financial plans. Since most of these items are necessities of life, the development of rational procedures for making good decisions with respect to their purchase, ownership, and sale is essential. Indeed, decisions regarding many of the financial assets discussed in preceding chapters, such as savings accounts, stocks, bonds, investment companies, commodities and options may be secondary to the acquisition of certain nonfinancial assets. Chapter 9 discusses housing and real estate investments. Primary emphasis is placed on choosing from alternative types of housing and the key aspects of housing purchases. Chapter 10 considers strategies related to the acquisition of automobiles, furniture, appliances, and other major nonfinancial assets.

287

9
Real Estate: Housing and Investments

To provide a basic knowledge of the considerations involved in purchasing real estate either for housing or as an investment, this chapter examines the following:

A Preview of Chapter 9

1. The alternative forms of available housing and their relative advantages and disadvantages.

2. The techniques for determining whether to rent or to buy housing.

3. The approach used to determine how much an individual can afford to spend for a home.

4. The steps involved in purchasing and selling a home.

5. The factors that must be considered when evaluating real estate investment alternatives.

6. Speculating in real estate, investing in income property, and buying limited partnership shares, real estate investment trusts, and shares in real estate investment companies.

Probably the largest single transaction you will make during your lifetime will be the acquisition of a home. Because of the major commitment of funds involved in the acquisition, repayment, and maintenance of this key nonfinancial asset, decisions on housing must be made carefully. You will need to determine what your housing requirements are, what you can afford to spend, what forms of housing are available, and how you can best go about buying a home. You may also at some time in the future wish to consider buying real estate for investment purposes. This, too, requires an in-depth understanding of the real estate market.

Because of the magnitude of the housing transaction, many people are not able to meet the financial requirements in order to purchase a home when they wish. Most, whether single or married, spend the early years of their adult lives in some type of rental unit such as an apartment or duplex. Once they have saved enough money to make the down payment necessary to buy a house, they can shop for one that fulfills their housing and budget requirements. Still, home ownership, once achieved, brings with it additional financial responsibilities: taxes, insurance, and maintenance. These, too, must be given careful consideration before the purchase of a home is finalized.

Because of the large-scale commitment associated with home ownership, it is a good idea to analyze the costs and benefits of alternate forms of housing. Since there is no universal rule with respect to which is the best, people need to know how to relate their housing needs to their present and expected income in order to make housing decisions. If the purchase of a home is the chosen strategy, there are numerous financial, nonfinancial, and borrowing problems to be resolved. Sometimes, too, real estate may be purchased as an investment. Although there are some similarities between housing and investment purchases of real estate, persons interested in real estate investments must justify them not on the basis of need but rather on strict economic grounds. This chapter discusses real estate purchases both for housing and for investment purposes. The primary emphasis is of course placed on housing decisions.

| Considering Alternative Forms of Housing | In choosing housing, it is advisable first to determine your requirements, then to analyze the alternatives—rent or buy, for example—and finally to compare the costs of these alternatives. Although renting and buying are the most common alternatives, other forms of housing such as mobile homes and condominiums do exist and might warrant consideration. |

Determining Housing Requirements

Numerous factors interact to determine an individual's housing requirements. Key among them are location, necessary physical characteristics, and, most important, the individual's ability to pay. It is advisable to clearly specify these items prior to searching for housing.

Location Housing location is closely related to convenience and transportation cost considerations. With today's rising energy costs, the proximity of the housing unit to employment, schools, public transportation, churches, shopping, and playgrounds affects the cost and convenience of a location. Of course, if reasonably priced public transportation facilities are readily accessible, these factors are less important. Other factors such as traffic, nuisances, economic level of the neighborhood, privacy, lay of the land, and scenic quality may also bear on the location decision. In order to eliminate from consideration many unacceptable alternatives, the desired geographic location should be determined before the selection of a specific residence is begun.

Physical Characteristics: Size and Other Features Housing units are available in numerous sizes, ranging from a single-room efficiency apartment to a 5,000 square foot, six-bedroom home, for example. Since size is directly related to cost, like location, it is a feature that should be defined prior to the selection process. This is probably best accomplished through a room-by-room analysis. To do this, it is necessary first to determine the number and size of each of the types of rooms needed—bedroom, bathroom, living area, office, dining area, kitchen, garage, basement—to meet near-term housing requirements. The importance of each room should be considered; for instance, if meals will rarely be eaten at home, a small kitchen should be adequate. By realistically assessing space requirements, it should be possible to specify not only the number and types of rooms needed but also the approximate number of square feet of total space.

Related considerations are room arrangement and the number of levels or stories the house should have. This may be particularly important to families with children or a parent or relative living in. Aesthetic factors, too, should be taken into account, as well as desired amenities. For instance, if the buyer wishes to have a contemporary style unit with a fireplace, this fact, should be made known to the realtor, builder, or rental agent assisting in the search. A little "window shopping" is all right, but having the desired physical characteristics of the housing unit reasonably well-defined in advance of the selection process eliminates a lot of unnecessary looking. Since the cost of housing depends primarily on size, physical characteristics, and location, it is a good idea to be sure characteristics considered essential can actually be obtained with the available financial resources.

Monthly Payment Capacity The ability to pay scheduled monthly payments as well as any maintenance costs is the single most important factor in the rental or purchase of a housing unit. If cost were not of concern, most people would live in the largest, most glamorous housing available. Unfortunately, the average person has limited financial resources from which to pay for housing. An individual's payment capacity should be known or estimated in his or her personal budget. A common rule of thumb suggests that monthly housing payments should not exceed 20 to 25 percent of gross monthly income. For example, if your gross before-tax monthly income is $1,000, you should not buy or rent property requiring payments of greater than $250 per month. In the case of a home purchase, the monthly payment as defined by this rule includes property taxes and insurance as well as the cost of the loan. Although this rule serves as a general guideline, it has been found that low-income people may spend as much as 30 percent of their monthly income for housing, while high-income earners may spend as little as 10 percent.

The Single-Family Home Buyer: A Profile

Data compiled from the Census Bureau's most recent (1973) survey of housing reveal some interesting facts on home buyers with respect to age, income, and prior housing situation. It was found that growth in home ownership occurs, in a manner of speaking, by two steps forward and one step backward—while there were 2 million households shifting from renter to owner in 1973, one million were moving in the other direction.

Table 1, which gives a percentage distribution of age of single-family home buyers, reveals that buyers under the age of thirty-five comprised nearly 50 percent of the home-buying market. From Table 2, which shows the percentage distribution of income of single-family home buyers, it is evident that the average income was $13,300—26.7 percent greater than the average income of $10,500 for *all* U.S. households in 1973. The buyers who had owned their previous residence had a higher average income than those who had rented. Newly formed households had the lowest average income. More than two of every three home purchasers in 1973 had children.

Renting

One of the two most popular methods of fulfilling housing needs is renting, which is especially common among very young adults and retired or childless families. Young adults usually rent for one (or more) of three reasons: (1) they do not have funds for the required down payment; (2) they are unsettled in terms of jobs and family status (single, engaged, or recently married); and (3) they do not want the additional responsibilities associated with home ownership. Those who do choose to

Table 1 Age of Single-Family Home Buyers
(Percentage Distribution)

Age of Head of Household	All	Previous Owner	Previous Renter	New Household
Under 25	7.0%	3.5%	13.6%	28.0%
25–34	39.0	30.1	49.4	34.9
35–44	23.8	28.6	19.2	15.1
45–54	15.3	17.9	10.4	10.8
55–64	8.3	11.5	5.5	7.3
65 and Over	5.9	8.3	1.9	3.9
Total	100.0%	100.0%	100.0%	100.0%
Median Age	36 years	40 years	32 years	30 years

Table 2 Income of Single-Family Home Buyers in 1973
(Percentage Distribution)

Income of Household	All	Previous Owner	Previous Renter	New Household
Less than $6,999	16.4%	16.1%	15.2%	22.0%
$7,000–$9,999	14.1	11.3	16.6	20.3
$10,000–$14,999	29.1	24.1	32.0	29.3
$15,000–$19,999	19.7	23.7	19.4	9.5
$20,000–$24,999	10.6	10.8	10.2	10.3
$25,000 and Over	10.1	14.0	6.6	8.6
Total	100.0%	100.0%	100.0%	100.0%
Median Income	$13,300	$14,700	$12,800	$11,300

Source: Reprinted with permission from the June 1977 issue of REALTORS® Review published by the NATIONAL ASSOCIATION OF REALTORS®. Prepared by the Department of Economics and Research.

rent should be aware of the types of units available, the significance of the rental contract, and the various advantages and disadvantages of renting.

Types of Rental Units The two basic types of rental units are apartments and houses. A variety of apartments, of various sizes and with various features, are available. Garden apartments, which are built in groups of four to six units that may be either one or two stories, are separated by landscaped green areas. Efficiency apartments are generally one-room apartments for single people. Townhouses are "up and down," or two-story apartments, usually with the bedrooms upstairs. High-rise apartments, in buildings several stories high, often have views of the city or surrounding countryside. Frequently entire houses can be rented from their owners either because they will be temporarily empty or because they are owned for rental purposes. In many parts of the country various combinations of houses with common walls are available. The most popular among these is the duplex, which is a two-unit building resembling two separate houses joined together by a common wall.

The cost and availability of rental units vary from one geographic area to another. Unfurnished units, of course, rent for less than furnished ones. The Department of Housing and Urban Development (HUD) administers various programs which provide low-rent housing opportunities for people in lower income brackets. Because such a wide variety of rental units are available, those people who wish to rent can usually find units that conform to their location, physical, and financial requirements.

Rental Contract When you rent an apartment, house, duplex, or other type of unit, you will normally be required to sign a *rental contract*, or *lease agreement*. The contract is a legal device intended to protect the *lessor* (person who owns the property) from nonpayment or some adverse action of the *lessee* (person who leases the property). Because the contract binds the lessee to various actions, it is advisable to make certain that you understand the rental contract prior to signing it. The contract specifies the *amount* of the monthly payment, the payment *date*, *penalties* for late payments, the *length* of the lease agreement, any *deposit* requirements, distribution of *expenses*, *renewal* options, and any *restrictions*, for example on pets or the use of facilities.

Most leases are for one year and require regular payments at the beginning of each month and either a deposit or the last month's payment as security against damages or some infringement of the lease agreement. Most of the deposit should be refunded to the lessee at the expiration of the lease; a portion of it is usually retained by the lessor to cover cleaning costs and any damages, regardless of how clean and unmarred the unit is left. Because the landlord has control over the deposit, a statement in writing of any damages in evidence prior to occupancy may help the lessee avoid loss of the entire amount deposited. Renters must also be sure to determine who bears expenses such as utilities and trash collection and exactly what, if any, restrictions exist with respect to usage of the property. Table 9-1 presents some questions that should be resolved before a lease agreement is signed.

Table 9-1 **Questions to Resolve before Signing a Lease**

1. What are your responsibilities, and what are those of the landlord, for any needed repairs and, in general, for keeping the property and fixtures in good condition? For example, who is responsible for painting and for making ordinary repairs like fixing faulty plumbing?

2. On what day is the rent due each month, and do you have any days of grace (permitting you to be late a number of days if necessary)?

3. What services will the landlord provide, such as heat, electric current, gas, garbage removal? Are these enumerated in the lease?

4. If you default on your obligations under the lease, are you liable for any additional charges such as landlord's legal expenses or the cost of preparing the premises for rerental?

5. Are you required to put up a deposit as security, for example, a month's rent? This is often a sore point between landlords and tenants because landlords usually do not want to pay interest on these deposits. Then too, at the end of the lease landlords often keep part and sometimes even all of the security deposit. The justification usually advanced is that the money withheld represents the cost of restoring or repairing the premises after occupancy. Take note, in the form you will be asked to sign, of what potential reasons may be listed for withholding your deposit.

Source: Adapted with permission of Macmillan Publishing Co., Inc., from *The New Adult Guide to Independent Living* by Sidney Margolius. Copyright © 1968 by Sidney Margolius.

Advantages and Disadvantages of Renting A number of *advantages* are often cited in favor of renting. One is that in order to rent, a down payment such as is required for buying is not needed. Renting permits greater mobility in that moving in and out of rental units is not as complex and costly as moving when homes must be sold and purchased. Renting also involves less work with respect to maintenance of the unit. Other advantages may be the presence of security systems, the appeal of community living, and access to certain amenities such as swimming pools and tennis courts.

The *disadvantages* of renting are primarily financial. The renter does not get any ownership as a result of monthly rent payments, which serve only to obtain use of the property. In addition, the renter does not receive any tax-deductible benefit from rent payments. Renters may also find that their rental units are not quiet, repairs are not made promptly, or landlords are uncooperative. In other words, since renters have no control over repairs, other tenants, and the general management of the apartments in which their unit is located, they are at the mercy of their landlords. Sometimes renters can form associations to effectively pressure uncooperative landlords into responding to their requests.

Owning

Home ownership remains quite popular in the U.S. today for various financial and personal reasons. As can be seen in Figure 9-1, the percentage of families owning homes has risen quite rapidly over the past thirty years. The American way of life includes home ownership as one of the basic indicators of success. Homes come in a wide variety of sizes, shapes, and prices; they can be purchased for as little as $20,000 for a one-bedroom, one-bath home to over a million dollars for a large architecturally unique estate with all imaginable amenities. When considering alternate forms of housing—especially in comparing renting and buying—special attention must be given to taxes, cost differences, and inflation. Like renting, home ownership has both advantages and disadvantages.

Figure 9-1 **Percentage of Families Owning Their Homes, 1890–1970**

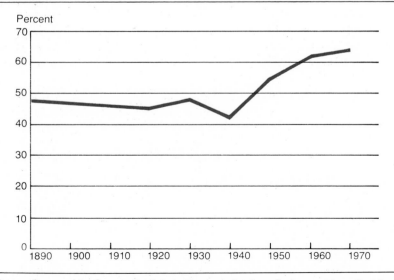

Source: Bureau of the Census. Reprinted with permission from *Savings and Loan Fact Book, 1976* (Washington, D.C.: U.S. Savings and Loan League, 1976), chart 18, p. 37.

Taxes Home ownership affects taxes in two ways. First, homeowners who itemize their deductions can deduct all of the interest paid on the loan used to finance the purchase of the home. The *tax deductibility of mortgage interest* tends to lower the actual cost of home ownership. Second, homeowners must pay *property taxes* on their homes; if homes are rented, the landlord must bear this cost (which is, of course, reflected in the monthly rent charged). Like interest, property tax payments are treated as tax-deductible expenses, which thus reduces somewhat their actual cost to the homeowner.

Comparing Rental and Purchase Costs For an example of the basic cost and tax differences between renting and purchasing, assume you are confronted with the following problem. You are trying to decide whether to rent or purchase a home. If you rent, you will have to make monthly payments of $300. If you purchase, your house will cost $35,000. You will make a $5,000 down payment using your savings, on which you are currently earning 6 percent per year. The monthly mortgage payment will be $240, of which $200 is interest and the other $40 goes toward repayment of the loan. Property taxes are expected to amount to $45 per month, and homeowner's insurance will cost $15 a month. The cost of maintaining the house is $35 per month. Table 9-2 presents a cost analysis of the rental and purchase alternatives based on the assumption that you are in the 25 percent tax bracket. Due to the fact that both interest ($200/month) and property taxes ($45/month) are tax deductible, an annual tax savings of $735 ($245/month × 12 months × .25 tax rate)

Table 9-2 Comparing Rental and Purchase Costs

Rental Cost	
Annual rent payments ($300/month × 12 months)	$3,600

Purchase Cost	
Annual mortgage payments ($240/month × 12 months)	$2,880
Plus: Annual maintenance cost ($35/month × 12 months)	420
Plus: Cost of lost interest on $5,000 down payment ($5,000 × .06)	300
Plus: Property taxes ($45/month × 12 months)	540
Plus: Homeowner's insurance ($15/month × 12 months)	180
Less: Tax benefit from tax deduction of interest and property taxes ([$200 interest/month + $45 property taxes/month] × 12 months × .25 tax rate)	−735
Less: Reduction in loan balance ($40/month × 12 months)	−480
Annual purchase cost	$3,105

results. As the cost analysis in Table 9-2 indicates, purchasing is considerably less costly than renting ($3,105/year purchase cost vs. $3,600/year rental cost). Naturally, various other considerations may enter into the rental-purchase decision.

Inflation Inflation has characterized the U.S. economic environment over the past twenty years or so. Home ownership provides protection against the loss in purchasing power that accompanies inflation. In other words, because historically housing values have appreciated faster than the rate of inflation, the purchase of a house has provided a hedge against it. While the rate of inflation has recently been 8 or 9 percent a year, housing prices in many areas have increased by 15 percent a year. The hedge that home ownership provides against inflation is manifest in Figure 9-2, which shows the median price of single-family homes relative

Figure 9-2 **Housing as a Hedge against Inflation**

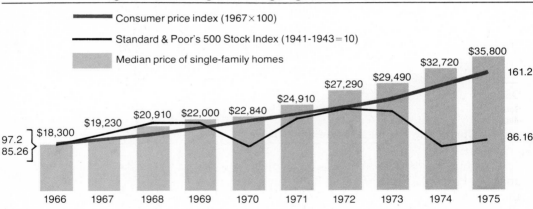

Source: "How a Small Investor Can Make Money on Rental Property," *Changing Times,* May 1976, p. 16. Reprinted with permission from *Changing Times* Magazine, © Kiplinger Washington Editors, Inc., 1976.

to the consumer price index and the Standard & Poor's stock index over the past decade. The price of single-family homes doubled between 1966 and 1975, while the consumer price index increased by 66 percent and the stock index increased by a mere 1.06 percent. The type of protection against losses in purchasing power provided by home ownership cannot be obtained through renting. Generally during inflationary periods rental costs increase, while the monthly payments of homeowners remain

"It's my wife's mother. She gave us the down payment on the house."

Down Payments Usually Come from Savings

Source: Changing Times, September 1970, p. 26. Reprinted with permission from *Changing Times* Magazine, © Kiplinger Washington Editors, Inc., 1970.

unaffected. Note, however, that this advantage of home ownership rarely allows individuals to improve the quality of their lives. Because the cost of all housing increases as a result of inflation, whatever profit they might make on the sale of their home has to be invested in the purchase of the next home if it is to be of equivalent or better size and quality. Home ownership merely permits people to maintain their standard of living.

Advantages and Disadvantages of Home Ownership A number of advantages are often cited in favor of home ownership. Feelings of independence, pride of possession, and general security are associated with owning a home. Many suggest that the quality of life of the home-owner is enhanced, since homes usually offer more space and neighborhoods where homes are owned provide more opportunities for community involvement. As indicated earlier, tax benefits available to the homeowner normally make it cheaper to own than to rent. In addition, the homeowner's monthly payments are reasonably fixed and therefore quite predictable. And since a portion of each of these payments goes toward the repayment of the loan, the homeowner's equity in the house gradually increases. Thus home ownership can be viewed as an investment, for equity is built up at the same time that the market value of the home is increased.

Home ownership does have a few disadvantages. One results from the cost and inconvenience normally associated with the sale of a home. Also, if a home is owned for only a few years, ownership may be more expensive than renting since selling costs are likely to exceed any increase in value. The inconvenience and cost of maintaining a home is another headache that a renter does not have. And a final disadvantage is that the required down payment of from 5 to 30 percent of the purchase price may reduce liquid assets (savings) to a level that is less than adequate to cover potential emergency financial needs.

Other Housing Forms

Mobile homes, cooperative apartments, condominiums, and second or summer homes are additional forms of housing readily available in most populous areas. Each of these is described separately below.

Mobile Homes Factory-produced living units, mobile homes can be transported on the highways to a desired location, where they can then be connected to utilities and used as residences. They generally provide between 200 and 600 square feet of living space and range in cost from $5,000 to $20,000, depending upon size and features; the average price is around $9,200. Although used occasionally as temporary housing, mobile homes provide permanent residences for many. As indicated, their prices are low, and seven to twelve year loans with low down payments are available. Unfortunately, however, the interest rates on these loans are high. Low maintenance costs are another attractive feature. Still, because in most parts of the country the market price of mobile homes is likely to decline over time, they are not considered good investments and do not provide any protection against inflation.

Cooperative Apartments Apartment buildings in which each tenant owns a share of the corporation that owns the apartment building are cooperative apartments. Residents lease the units they occupy from the corporation and are assessed monthly in proportion to their ownership shares, which are based on the amount of space they occupy. The assessments cover the cost of services, maintenance, taxes, and the mortgage on the entire building. These can change, depending on the actual costs of operating the building and the actions of the board of directors, which determines policies of the corporation. Members of cooperatives may find that the value of their ownership interest increases over time. Because profit is not the purpose of cooperative apartments, monthly assessments are likely to be less than the rent on similar accommodations in the more common type of apartment.

Condominiums The purchaser of a condominium receives a title to an individual unit in a group of units and a joint ownership to any areas and facilities provided for residents of all units, such as lobbies, swimming pools, lakes, and tennis courts. Since purchasers of a condominium own their own units, they arrange their own mortgages, pay their own taxes, and pay for maintenance and building services. The owners of condominium units elect a board of managers to supervise their buildings and grounds. The cost of condominiums is generally below that of home ownership since they tend to be built in a fashion that results in better use of land and lower construction costs. Although condominiums have traditionally appealed primarily to retired persons who do not want the responsibilities of maintaining and caring for their property, many younger people have now begun to buy them for similar reasons.

A Survey of Condominium Owners

There are nearly 40,000 condominium units in the Washington, D.C., metropolitan area. A recent study by the area's Council of Governments sampled owners and found these were their most frequently cited reasons for buying condominiums:
- The tax and equity benefits of owning a home.
- The reduced obligations for home maintenance in a condominium.
- Desirable locations.

Of those surveyed, 79% rated their over-all living conditions "good," and 61% scored "high" on an owner-satisfaction index. Generally, townhouse and high-rise owners were more satisfied than low-rise owners.

These were the poorest features of condominium living mentioned most often:
- The way the owners' association was set up and operated.
- Higher than expected costs, particularly the condominium fee.
- The practices and quality of the professional condominium management firms employed.

The study found no widespread abuses, such as sales misrepresentations, but did uncover frequent problems it attributed to inexperience with condominiums on the part of developers, real estate professionals and buyers. Developers were criticized for failing to give purchasers enough information soon enough.

Source: Changing Times, December 1976, p. 18. Reprinted with permission from *Changing Times* Magazine, © Kiplinger Washington Editors, Inc., 1976.

Second or Summer Homes Second or summer homes may be regular houses, beach houses, mobile homes, cooperative apartments, or condominiums. The characteristic that differentiates summer homes from other housing is that they are used as secondary or recreational residences. Sometimes they are leased during periods when they might otherwise be idle. Tax laws permit these homes to be categorized as investments only when the owner spends less than two weeks a year in them. For this reason, ownership of a second or summer home is in most instances a luxury that only the wealthy can afford.

Buying a House

At some time in your life you will probably consider buying a house. Because of the magnitude of the associated outlay and the degree of commitment which accompanies home ownership, it is important to understand all the aspects of buying a home. The factors to consider and techniques to employ in selecting, analyzing, and purchasing a home as well as the basic procedure for selling a home are discussed in the following sections.

How Much Can You Afford?

The amount you can afford to spend on a home is related to a number of basic cost considerations. Among these, the size of the mortgage loan payment is the most significant, but insurance, taxes, and maintenance and operating costs are also important.

Mortgage Payments The size of the loan you obtain to purchase a home depends on two factors: (1) the cost of the home, and (2) the size of the down payment. In order to evaluate how much you can afford to spend, you must determine how much you can put down on the home. In most cases, a minimum down payment of 5 to 30 percent of the purchase price is required. The difference between the purchase price and the down payment is the amount of the mortgage loan. Your balance sheet will provide the needed information as to the amount of savings and investments you have available for conversion into a down payment.

Assuming you do have money with which to make a down payment, you must next determine how large a mortgage loan you can handle given your income. One rule of thumb commonly used by lenders is that the *amount borrowed* to purchase a home should not be more than two times the borrower's gross annual income. Another is that monthly mortgage payments, which include loan repayment, insurance, and taxes, should not exceed 25 percent of gross (before tax) monthly income. And according to still another, the *purchase price* of a house should not exceed $2\frac{1}{2}$ times the purchaser's gross annual income. This last rule is quite similar to the first except that it assumes a 20 percent down payment.

By way of example, assume that you earn $14,000 per year and have available savings of $7,000 which can be used for a down payment on a home. Assume also that your gross monthly income is $1,167 ($14,000 per year ÷ 12 months) and that additional savings are available for meeting any additional *closing costs,* which result from various fees incurred in applying for and obtaining a mortgage loan. According to the first rule of thumb, the maximum amount that can be borrowed is $28,000 (2 × $14,000). This amount in addition to the assumed $7,000 down payment makes it possible for you to purchase a $35,000 home. Monthly mortgage payments (including insurance and taxes) can be estimated as 1 percent of the amount borrowed, in this case approximately $280 (1% × $28,000). According to the second rule, given the $1,167 per month before-tax income, the maximum monthly mortgage payment should be $291.75 (25% × $1,167). This value seems to correspond quite well with the estimated $280 monthly mortgage payment. And the purchase price of the house as prescribed by the third rule is unobjectionable since $35,000 is equal to $2\frac{1}{2}$ times gross annual income ($2\frac{1}{2}$ × $14,000). Although the rules illustrated above are not absolutes, they are practical guidelines for assessing how expensive a house you can afford.

Insurance and Taxes Aside from the loan costs, many mortgage payments include insurance and tax payments. The costs of *homeowner's insurance* vary with factors such as age of home, location, materials used in construction of the home (stone, frame, brick, etc.), and geographic area. Of course, as will be discussed in a later chapter, homeowner's insurance is actually carried only on the replacement value of the home, not on the land. Insurance costs usually amount to approximately $\frac{1}{2}$ of 1 percent of the home's market value per year. Thus the annual cost of insurance on the $35,000 home in the preceding example would be around $175 ($\frac{1}{2}$ of 1 percent × $35,000). The various types of homeowner's insurance are discussed in detail in Chapter 15.

Another component of the monthly mortgage payment may be *property taxes.* These local government taxes are levied to support schools, law enforcement, and other local services; they differ in amount from one community to another. Within a given community, individual property taxes vary with the *assessed value* of property: the more expensive the home, the higher the property taxes, and vice versa. Attention should be given property taxes in the purchase of a home for two reasons: (1) they do vary from community to community, and (2) if they are included as part of the monthly mortgage payment, differences in them can cause the mortgage payments for houses of the same price to differ.

Maintenance and Operating Expenses Aside from the monthly mortgage payments including insurance and taxes, the home buyer incurs certain maintenance and operating expenses. Maintenance costs should be anticipated even on new homes. Painting, mechanical repairs, leaks, and lawn maintenance, for example, are inescapable facts of home ownership. These costs are generally greater the older and larger the home. Indeed, a large, old home may appear to be a good buy in view of its purchase price, but because the costs of maintaining it are high, a smaller, new home might be more economical.

Another point to consider in the selection process is the cost of operating the home, specifically, the cost of utilities such as electricity, gas, water, and sewage. Because costs vary with geographic location, type of heating and air conditioning, size of home, amount of insulation, and other factors—and can be quite sizable—it is important to obtain estimates of them when evaluating houses for purchase. In many parts of the country the cost of gas is much less than that of electricity, making homes with gas rather than electric utilities far less expensive in the long run. Also, the amount of insulation should be investigated since the better insulated the home, the lower its fuel consumption and costs will probably be. Of course, if the insulation is inadequate, it may be possible to add insulation for very little additional expense.

Figure 9-3 presents a checklist that home buyers can use in uncovering and evaluating repair and remodeling problems in a house they are considering for purchase. Using estimates of these costs and those associated with home ownership mentioned above, a budget can be prepared to determine whether ownership of a given house will interfere with other financial goals. Since housing costs will be the largest single item in your budget, it is imperative that you estimate them carefully prior to committing yourself to the purchase of a home. It is sometimes also helpful to consult a loan officer at a savings and loan or some other mortgage lender, who will advise you without obligation as to how much you can afford to spend.

Old Home, New Home, or Custom Built Home

Once you have determined how much you can afford to spend for a home, you must decide whether you want an older home, a new home, or a custom built home. Your decision will be influenced by the kind of neighborhood in which you want to live, standards you have set for the physical condition of your house, and utility cost considerations.

Older Home Homes ranging in age from one to ten years are likely to be fully draped and landscaped and thereby provide cost savings over the new home. Homes ten to twenty years old may appeal to some because

Figure 9-3 Checklist for Houses

Outside House and Yard

- ☐ attractive, well-designed house
- ☐ suited to natural surroundings
- ☐ lot of the right size and shape for house and garage
- ☐ suitable use of building materials
- ☐ compatible with houses in the area
- ☐ attractive landscaping and yard
- ☐ good drainage of rain and moisture
- ☐ dry, firm soil around the house
- ☐ mature, healthy trees—placed to give shade in summer
- ☐ convenient, well-kept driveway, walks, patio, porch
- ☐ yard for children
- ☐ parking convenience—garage, carport or street
- ☐ distance between houses for privacy
- ☐ sheltered entry—well-lighted and large enough for several to enter the house together
- ☐ convenient service entrance

Outside Construction

- ☐ durable siding materials—in good condition
- ☐ solid brick and masonry—free of cracks
- ☐ solid foundation walls—six inches above ground level—eight inches thick
- ☐ weather stripped windows and doors
- ☐ noncorrosive gutters and down-spouts, connected to storm sewer or splash block to carry water away from house
- ☐ copper or aluminum flashing used over doors, windows and joints on the roof
- ☐ screens and storm windows or Thermopane glass
- ☐ storm doors

Inside Construction

- ☐ sound, smooth walls with invisible nails and taping on dry walls; without hollows or large cracks in plaster walls
- ☐ well-done carpentry work with properly fitted joints and moldings
- ☐ properly fitted, easy-to-operate windows
- ☐ level wood floors with smooth finish and no high edges, wide gaps or squeaks
- ☐ well-fitted tile floors—no cracked or damaged tiles—no visible adhesive
- ☐ good possibilities for improvements, remodeling, expanding
- ☐ properly fitted and easy-to-work doors and drawers in built-in cabinets
- ☐ dry basement floor with hard smooth surface
- ☐ adequate basement drain
- ☐ sturdy stairways with railings, adequate head room—not too steep
- ☐ leakproof roof—in good condition
- ☐ adequate insulation for warmth, coolness and soundproofing

Living Space

- ☐ convenient floor plan and paths from room to room
- ☐ convenient entry with foyer and closet
- ☐ convenient work areas (kitchen, laundry, workshop) with adequate drawers, cabinets, lighting, work space, electric power
- ☐ private areas (bedrooms and bath-rooms) located far enough from other parts of the house for privacy and quiet
- ☐ social areas (living and dining rooms, play space, yard, porch or patio) convenient, comfortable, large enough for family and guests
- ☐ rooms conveniently related to each other—entry to living room, dining room to kitchen, bedrooms to baths
- ☐ adequate storage—closets, cabinets, shelves, attic, basement, garage
- ☐ suitable wall space and room size for your furnishings
- ☐ outdoor space convenient to indoor space
- ☐ windows located to provide enough air, light and ventilation
- ☐ agreeable type, size and placement of windows
- ☐ usable attic and/or basement space
- ☐ possibilities for expansion
- ☐ attractive decorating and fixtures
- ☐ extras—fireplace, air conditioning, porches, new kitchen and baths, built-in equipment, decorating you like

Source: This information taken from the Money Management Institute booklet titled *Your Housing Dollar* (1971, p. 21), printed by the Money Management Institute of Household Finance Corporation, Chicago, Illinois.

they are in mature neighborhoods which have developed a charm of their own and have established residents. And for any of these reasons, homes that are even older may also seem attractive. Regardless of its exact age, an older home is expected to have higher maintenance costs than would a similar size and type of new home. On the other hand, the quality of construction and insulation is often better in older homes than in new homes, and they are generally conveniently located relatively close to town and near established churches and shopping. The plumbing and wiring, as well as certain structural and mechanical aspects, of an older home may not be adequate by modern standards, however; and technically qualified experts should be hired to evaluate these features before any purchase is made.

New Home If you buy a new home, you can be certain it has not been abused and that all mechanical and electrical systems are in good working order. In most localities builders construct homes on speculation that a buyer will be found. These "spec homes" vary in price, size, and other features and can be found in various stages of construction. If you can find and purchase a spec home in the final stages of construction, you will then have an opportunity to select the colors and types of carpeting, fixtures, and window dressings you wish. Like the houses themselves, the reputations of builders vary and should be checked as an indication of the quality of the home and the degree of cooperation to be expected in righting any defects after a purchase is made. In most states the builder will warrant the new home against any mechanical defects for one year. Opportunities also exist to purchase insurance against mechanical failures and material defects for up to ten years.

Custom Homes You may, if you wish, employ an established builder or architect to design and build a custom home meeting your budget and layout requirements. Though this might seem the best approach, it is actually preferable to buy an old home or new "spec" home rather than to build your first house. It is difficult to know what types of houses and what design features best suit your life-style until you have had the practical experience of living in one or more houses. And although the custom home does seem to be the ideal solution to the problem of selecting a house, only certain types of people find custom building a worthwhile experience given the headaches that almost always arise from disagreements with the builder, the numerous decisions involved, and the uncertainty as to costs incurred in the construction and decorating process. There is also a limit to the creativity that can be exercised in the construction of a custom home; a home is not a good investment if it is so unique that it will not be easily resalable.

The Purchase Transaction

Certain formal procedures are followed in the purchase of an older or spec home to assure that both the buyer and the seller are adequately protected. These procedures and the steps involved in negotiating the purchase transaction are described in the following section.

Using a Realtor A realtor—an individual licensed by state examination to provide advice and assistance in real estate transactions—can often provide you with valuable help in finding and purchasing a home in your price range. The realtor's fees are paid by the seller of the home purchased. Where two realtors are involved in the transaction, one representing the purchaser and one the seller, they usually split the commission earned on the sale. The realtor who represents you should not only understand your housing requirements but should have access to a multiple listing service in order to be able to show you a number of suitable houses. Recognizing that the commission received is greater if your realtor or realty company also represents the seller, do not allow yourself to be pushed too rapidly into a transaction where this is the case.

To list property with a realty firm, a seller must pay a commission generally in the range of 6 to 7 percent of the sale price—for example, $2,100 to $2,450 on a house sold for $35,000. In the typical fee-splitting agreement, the realtor representing the purchaser receives approximately 25 to 30 percent of the commission, $525 to $630 where the commission is $2,100. You may be able to save money by purchasing unlisted real estate since prices of listed property are often inflated to cover the commission paid the realtor. An attorney will probably be better able to help you make this type of direct transaction with a seller or builder than will a realtor. Unlisted real estate is advertised in the local newspaper as property "For Sale by Owner" and by "For Sale by Owner" signs posted in yards.

Making an Offer: Earnest Money Although most listed real estate sells within 5 percent of the asking price, you should offer to pay the asking price only after you have made an accurate survey of the market and feel that the value of the home is the value asked. The preparation of a *purchase contract* in which the offering price and all conditions of the purchase—including repairs and inspections for termites and dry rot—are clearly specified is the first step in making an offer. A real estate purchase contract, legally referred to as a "contract of sale of real estate," is illustrated in Figure 9-4. (This one is for a new loan with conventional financing.) Realtors and attorneys have standard contracts to which clauses describing any special requirements of purchase can be added.

As a second step in the negotiations, you will be expected to pay some

Figure 9-4 **Real Estate Purchase Contract**

This is a legally binding contract; if not understood seek advice from an attorney.

This form approved by the Metropolitan Tulsa Board of Realtors Permission to use is granted to Realtors only.

CONTRACT OF SALE OF REAL ESTATE

McGraw•Breckinridge
Realtors

5525 East 51st Street, Tulsa, Oklahoma 74135 - Telephone 663-1144

REALTOR®

THIS CONTRACT is entered into between .... ("Seller")
and .... ("Buyer").

Upon approval of this Contract by both Seller and Buyer, evidenced by their signatures hereto, a valid and binding contract of sale shall exist, the terms and conditions of which are as follows:

1. **SALE:** Seller agrees to sell and convey to Buyer by warranty deed and Buyer agrees to purchase the following described real estate (the "Property") located in .... County, Oklahoma: ....
....
....
together with all improvements thereon, if any, in their present condition, ordinary wear and tear excepted, and including the following personal property: ....
....

2. **PURCHASE PRICE:** The total purchase price is $.................................. payable by Buyer as follows:

$.................. on execution of this Contract, receipt of which is acknowledged by Seller, which is deposited with the Listing Broker identified below (and which shall be deposited, pursuant to the Receipt set forth below, in the Listing Broker's trust or escrow account immediately upon execution of this Contract by Seller and Buyer), as earnest money and part payment of the purchase price; and the balance of the purchase price in cash, cashier's or certified check upon delivery of the deed (the "Closing"), unless otherwise provided in paragraph 9 hereof.

3. **FINANCING CONDITIONS: A.** Buyer shall immediately apply for a conventional loan on the Property and proceed diligently to procure such loan. If, within .... days from the date of this Contract, or such longer period as Seller shall grant in writing, Buyer has not received approval of a conventional loan: (i) in an amount of not less than ....% of the purchase price (within $50.00); (ii) for a term of not less than .... years and at an interest rate of not more than ....%, plus private mortgage insurance premiums, if applicable; and (iii) with discount or points, which shall be payable by Buyer, not to exceed ....% of the loan amount; then this Contract shall be automatically null and void, in which event the abstract shall be returned to Seller and earnest money refunded to Buyer. Buyer may, however, waive this condition by notice in writing delivered to the Listing Broker on or before the expiration of the period specified for loan approval (including written extensions), in which event this Contract shall remain in effect except for this clause.

B. In connection with any such loan: (i) Buyer shall pay the tax and insurance accruals necessary to establish the escrow account; (ii) Buyer shall pay all other loan closing costs; and (iii) the loan shall not be considered approved if any conditions or restrictions unusual to such loans are imposed on Seller or any conditions or credit restrictions are imposed on Buyer by the lender.

4. **TITLE:** Seller, within .... days after approval or waiver of a conventional loan as contemplated herein, shall furnish Buyer or Buyer's lender a current Uniform Commercial Code Search certificate and abstract of title certified at least to the date of this Contract, showing a marketable title to the Property in Seller, subject only to reasonable utility easements and building restrictions of record. Buyer shall have .... days after receipt in which to have the abstract examined and furnish Seller, in care of the Listing Broker, notice in writing of any objections thereto. No matter shall be construed as a valid objection to the title under this Contract unless it is so construed under the "Real Estate Title Examination Standards" of the Oklahoma Bar Association, where applicable. In case of valid objections to the title, Seller shall have .... days or such additional time as may be agreed to in writing by Seller and Buyer to satisfy such objections. If such valid objections cannot be satisfied within the time specified in this paragraph, or Seller does not approve this Contract, the earnest money shall be returned to the Buyer, Buyer shall return the abstract to Seller, and this Contract shall be of no further force and effect.

5. **TAXES AND PRORATIONS: A.** The Seller shall pay in full: (i) all special assessments against the Property upon the date of Closing, whether or not payable in installments; (ii) all taxes, other than general ad valorem taxes for the current calendar year, which are a lien on the Property upon the date of Closing; and (iii) the cost of any item of workmanship or material furnished on or prior to the date of Closing which is or may become a lien on the Property.

B. Unless otherwise specified in paragraph 9, the following items shall be prorated between the Seller and Buyer as of the date of Closing: (i) rents, if any; and (ii) general ad valorem taxes for the current calendar year, provided that, if the amount of such taxes has not then been fixed, the proration shall be based upon the rate of levy for the previous calendar year.

6. **CONDITION OF PROPERTY: A.** On or before the date of the Closing, Seller shall furnish Buyer, at Seller's expense, a current report by a licensed exterminating company, addressed to Buyer, reflecting that buildings on the Property are free and clear of visible termite infestation and visible termite damage.

B. All fixtures and equipment relating to plumbing, heating and cooling, including ducts, electrical systems and built-in appliances will be in normal working order at Closing, ordinary wear and tear excepted. Buyer, at Buyer's expense, shall have the right to inspect such items, but shall report any such item not in normal working order in writing to Seller, in care of the Listing Broker, not later than seven (7) calendar days before Closing. Buyer shall pay the first $100.00 of repair cost. Repairs in excess of a total of $100.00 necessary to meet the foregoing standard shall be at Seller's expense. If the total estimated cost to seller of such repairs required by this paragraph exceeds $.................. Seller shall have the option to cancel and terminate this Contract within 48 hours of being advised of such estimate, unless Buyer agrees in writing to pay repair costs in excess of such sum.

C. Until Closing or transfer of possession, risk of loss to the Property, ordinary wear and tear excepted, shall be upon Seller; after Closing or transfer of possession, such risk shall be upon Buyer.

D. Unless otherwise agreed upon in writing, Buyer, by Closing or taking possession of the Property, shall be deemed to have accepted the Property in its then condition, including fixtures, equipment and appliances. No warranties, express or implied, by Seller or Seller's agents, with reference to the condition of the Property or any fixtures, equipment or appliances shall be deemed to survive the Closing.

7. **CLOSING:** Subject to the provisions of paragraphs 3 and 4 the Closing shall be held on or before ...., 19........ If valid title objections require correction, Closing shall be extended for the time permitted under Paragraph 4. At or prior to Closing Seller shall deliver to the Listing Broker a duly executed and acknowledged warranty deed conveying the Property to Buyer for delivery to Buyer upon payment of purchase price. Unless otherwise agreed in writing, possession shall be transferred ....

8. **BREACH OR FAILURE TO CLOSE:** Subject to the provisions of paragraph 3, if, after the Seller has performed Seller's obligations under this Contract, and if within five (5) days after the date specified for Closing under paragraph 7 the Buyer fails to make the payments or to perform any other obligation of the Buyer under this Contract, then all sums theretofore paid on the purchase price shall, at the option of the Seller, be retained as such or as liquidated damages for the breach of this Contract by the Buyer. The Seller and Buyer agree that such amount is a reasonable amount for liquidated damages and that it would be impractical and extremely difficult to determine actual damages. In such latter event, the Seller and Buyer agree that the undersigned Broker(s) may retain and shall be paid from such funds one-half of such retained funds, not exceeding the agreed commission for services in obtaining this Contract. If the conditions in paragraph 3 are met, or waived, the Buyer shall perform all of the obligations of Buyer hereunder, and if Seller breaches this Contract or fails to perform any of Seller's obligations hereunder, then Buyer shall be entitled either to cancel and terminate this Contract, return the abstract to Seller, and receive a refund of the earnest money or pursue any other legal remedy.

9. **SPECIAL CONDITIONS:**

10. **EFFECT:** This Contract shall be executed in triplicate and, when executed by both Seller and Buyer, shall be binding upon and inure to the benefit of Seller and Buyer, their heirs, legal representatives, successors and assigns. This Contract sets forth the complete understanding of Seller and Buyer and supersedes all previous negotiations, representations and agreements between them and their agents. This Contract can only be amended or modified by a written agreement signed by Seller and Buyer. In executing this Contract, both Seller and Buyer agree to the terms of the Receipt contained below, and Seller additionally agrees to pay the named Listing Broker the commission previously agreed upon in the Listing Agreement or other agreement of employment between them, which shall survive this Contract, for services rendered and to be rendered in this transaction.

APPROVED BY BUYER: This .... day of ...., 19........ **APPROVED BY SELLER:** This .... day of ...., 19........

....

....

Mailing Address: .... **Mailing Address:** ....

RECEIPT: The undersigned Listing Broker acknowledges receipt of the earnest money referred to in paragraph 2 and agrees to hold it in such Broker's trust or escrow account in accordance with the terms of this Contract, applicable laws, rules and regulations governing such funds. The Broker shall be entitled to accept Buyer's personal check for the earnest money and endorse it for deposit without recourse.

Dated this .... **day of** ...., **19**........

Selling Broker McGraw•Breckinridge Realtors .... **Listing Broker** ....

By: .... **By:** ....

CONVENTIONAL **Always Have Your Title Examined by an Experienced Title Attorney**

Source: Courtesy of Metropolitan Tulsa Board of Realtors, Tulsa, Oklahoma.

earnest money, usually about 5 percent of the purchase price, to assure the seller that you can get the financing needed to buy the house and are thus a good-faith buyer. The seller may decide to accept your offer and sign the purchase contract, which will then become binding on both buyer and seller. However, the seller may decide not to accept your offer and may instead make a counter-offer somewhere between the asking price and your offer. When both buyer and seller are satisfied, this bargaining process will culminate in a transaction; if one party remains dissatisfied, no transaction is made.

Financing the Purchase Once the purchase contract has been signed by both buyer and seller, the buyer must apply for a mortgage loan. This loan, which is secured against default by the house being purchased, must normally be approved within a specific number of days as stipulated in the purchase contract. Key considerations in obtaining a mortgage loan are discussed in detail in Chapter 12. Once the loan has been procured, a closing date agreeable to buyer, seller, and lender is established. At the closing the buyer pays certain costs, the buyer and seller sign the pertinent documents, the seller is paid, and the deed to the property is exchanged. The closing costs and procedures, which are sometimes quite complicated, are also described in Chapter 12.

Selling Your House

Your goal in selling your home should be to obtain the highest price possible. This objective, however, may have to be tempered by the fact that you must complete the sale within some limited period of time either because you must move to another city or because you have purchased another home and cannot support two mortgages. If at all possible, you should put your home on the market during late spring and early summer, when the real estate market is most active. Two important considerations in selling are whether or not to list your home with a realtor and the selling costs.

To List or Not to List It is generally advantageous to sell your home on your own, by advertising in the newspaper, by posting a "For Sale by Owner" sign in your yard, and by word-of-mouth. If you try this, you can expect to be bothered by realtors who "want to list your home" or "have a buyer lined up." If after a few weeks the house is unsold, it is probably advisable to list it with a real estate company. This is done by signing an exclusive contract giving the realtor the right to act as your agent in the sale of your home over a specified period of months. In its role as your agent, the real estate company will advertise your home, advise you on the appropriate price for it, show and publicize it through multiple listing services, and "qualify" prospective buyers—screen out so-called buyers who do not have the requisite funds or who merely entertain themselves by looking at houses. A listing contract with a short life, ninety days or so, will give your realtor greater incentive to sell your house quickly.

Cost of Selling If you sell your home on your own, your selling costs are usually limited to expenditures for advertising, for having a purchase contract drawn up, and for updating the title. Occasionally a seller will agree to pay a fee in order to assist the buyer in obtaining the financing needed to allow the purchase of the home. If you list your house, in addition to legal and title costs you will have to pay your realtor a commission. The 6 or 7 percent commission may seem high, but a realtor can often help you sell your house quickly at an advantageous price.

Real Estate Investments

Although real estate purchased to provide housing is a key nonfinancial asset, many people hold additional real estate for investment purposes. In this part of the chapter some of the types of real estate investments and fundamental considerations that pertain to them are discussed.

Fundamental Considerations

Before property is purchased as an investment, an expert analysis of the costs and benefits that will result should be obtained and related to similar analyses for alternative investments. This section provides only a brief description of the basic factors that affect the value of an investment in real estate, including cash flows and taxes, appreciation in value, risk and return characteristics, and the use of leverage.

Cash Flow and Taxes The *cash flow* is the annual after-tax earnings of the investor. It depends on the project in which the investment is made, but it is also affected by depreciation and taxes. Certain types of real estate investments make possible large depreciation write-offs that tend to lower taxable income. These tax deductions, which are intended to reflect the fact that certain real estate assets other than raw land deteriorate over time, provide the property owner with an allowance for this decline in value, or *depreciation*. Because of the importance of taxes to the cash flow, individual investors should call on a tax expert to evaluate proposed real estate investments in light of their income.

Appreciation in Value Certain types of real estate—especially raw land and residential lots—have experienced phenomenal growth in value over the past few years. Other types, such as apartments and duplexes, are

Real Estate May Be an Attractive Investment

Source: Changing Times, November 1968, P.27. Reprinted with permission from *Changing Times* Magazine, © Kiplinger Washington Editors, Inc., 1968.

likely to decline in value over time. The total assessment of a proposed real estate investment should include estimates of projected changes in value that may occur, as well as cash flow projections.

Risk versus Returns If you can earn 6 percent on a savings deposit, any money you invest in a real estate project will have to provide a return higher than 6 percent in order to justify your investment. In addition, the 6 percent return you receive on your savings is certain—but what about the projected returns on a real estate investment? Clearly there is an element of risk to be taken into account. The risk and return characteristics of proposed real estate investments should be viewed in light of the risks and returns associated with other financial and nonfinancial investments. The anticipated total return on the investment, as well as the predicted periodic returns, is another important consideration in the evaluation of proposed real estate investments.

Use of Leverage One appeal of investment in real estate is the high degree of leverage it permits. *Leverage* is the use of borrowing to magnify returns. Because real estate is a tangible item, investors are able to borrow as much as 80 to 90 percent of the cost of investment property. If the total return on the investment is greater than the cost of borrowing, the net profit on the investment that takes advantage of leverage is proportionately greater than that on an investment that does not involve leverage. For example, imagine that you have found a real estate investment costing

The Wild Speculation in California Homes

Last month [April 1977] Irvine Co., a big Southern California land developer, sold a new condominium in the Harbor View development in Newport Beach for $87,050. Two weeks later the buyer resold it—for $117,500. All that despite the fact that the unit is still under construction. The cycle was started by a speculator, who listed the unit for sale with a local realtor the same week that he bought it, reselling it even before the closing on his purchase.

Such incidents are now common in California, where speculators looking for windfall profits are driving an already-inflated housing market through the roof. Lenders, builders, and even municipalities are worried that the bubble might burst. In recent weeks they have started imposing restrictions—some of which might themselves be illegal—to restrict home sales to owner-occupants. The San Clemente City Council will consider a measure that would prohibit owners from selling homes until they have lived in them for at least a year. "We're studying the legality," says City Manager Gerald Weeks. "It is simply a matter of trying to keep speculators out."

Mission Viejo Co., another Orange County developer, now requires would-be buyers to sign a sworn statement that they will live in the home for at least a year. The company restricts house or condominium sales to one to a customer and cancels the deal if it finds that the home comes back on the market before it is occupied.

Irvine's lawyers have drawn up a restrictive contract that new customers will be asked to sign. If buyers try selling their homes before the year is up, "we will have the right to cancel [the purchase]," says Kenneth Agid, vice-president of Irvine Pacific Development Co., the housing arm for Irvine. But, admits Agid, "it hasn't been tested in the courts yet."

So far, at least, housing speculation is rife only in California. "There's an inadequate supply of new houses, so people are starting to bid up prices," explains Harvey Stearn, vice-president of Mission Viejo. San Diego–based real estate consultant Sanford R. Goodkin estimates that between 20% and 40% of new home purchases in the state—and in a few developments, as much as 80% of the tract—are being made by speculators. "That means you have a development where maybe 25% of the homes are either vacant or for rent," he says.

Builders worry that a collapse of the cycle could leave them with unsold

$100,000. You can either purchase it for cash or put up $10,000 of your own money and borrow the remaining $90,000 at 9 percent interest. If the project earns $11,000 per year after all expenses, including real estate property taxes and depreciation, but before the deduction of interest and taxes, the analysis of the return on your investment will be as shown in Table 9-3. In the no leverage case the investor's return will be 7.15 percent, while in the leverage case it will be 18.85 percent. Note from the above example, however, that when no borrowing is used, there is no

inventory in tracts with foreclosed homes bought by speculators. Real Estate Commissioner David H. Fox indicates that builders actually have few ways to judge demand, with speculators buying up so much of the inventory. "The builders all say there is inadequate supply because of governmental regulations, but that's greatly oversold. Actually, there are a tremendous number of tracts being built right now." Fox's office approved 82,249 lots for development in 1975–76, compared with 41,871 a year earlier.

Security Pacific National Bank, California's second largest bank, took the unusual step last month of charging an interest-rate premium of 1.25% on home loans where the purchaser will not occupy the property. Paul J. O'Brien, senior vice-president, worries that speculators cannot realize enough rental income on these luxury properties to cover mortgage and tax costs. "The speculators might be willing to take a licking for a few months," he says. "But what happens if they can't sell them? There could be quite a backlash."

No real danger. United California Bank lends only to persons who declare in writing that they intend to occupy. "The form states that they face either a $5,000 fine or up to two years in prison if they lie," says Lawrence W. Becker, president of UCB's United California Mortgage Co. division. But he adds: "We've had people look us in the eye and sign, and then go out and try to sell the house."

Despite their fears, few observers feel the boom will result in a crash—as did the overbuilt Florida market of the early 1970s. "There's a healthy demand for homes in California," explains consultant Goodkin. "Florida was overbuilt with second homes. California still needs homes." Orange County, the site of much of the speculation, is one of the fastest growing counties in the country.

Goodkin notes the recent emergence of what he calls the "single-family home syndicator" now buying up groups of homes. "Some of these investors are way overpaying for a piece of property," he says. "We are seeing some cases of speculator selling to speculator—further accelerating the inflation in housing." Shortly, Goodkin predicts "a lot of fingers will be burned, and that will alleviate the situation."

Reprinted from the 2 May 1977 issue of *Business Week* by special permission. © 1977 by McGraw-Hill, Inc.

Table 9-3 **Using Leverage in Real Estate Investments**

	No Leverage		Leverage
Owner Investment	$100,000		$ 10,000
Borrow	0		90,000
Total Investment	$100,000		$100,000
Earnings before Interest and Taxes[a]	$ 11,000		$ 11,000
Less: Interest	0	(0.09)($90,000) =	8,100
Earnings before Taxes	$ 11,000		$ 2,900
Less: Taxes (assumed 35% tax rate)	3,850		1,015
Earnings after Taxes	$ 7,150		$ 1,885
Return on Investment	$\dfrac{\$7,150}{\$100,000} = 7.15\%$		$\dfrac{\$1,885}{\$10,000} = 18.85\%$

[a]All expenses including real estate property taxes and depreciation are assumed to have been already deducted from earnings.

risk of default; but in the leverage case, minimum earnings (before interest and taxes) of $8,100 are necessary to avoid default. The risk that comes with leverage must therefore be considered along with the potential benefits. Indeed, many people have been driven into bankruptcy as the result of using too much leverage.

Speculating in Real Estate

The growth in the value of real estate in certain areas has been phenomenal over the past few decades. The increase in population, the rising affluence of Americans, and the fact that real estate is a scarce commodity have all contributed to this growth. Stories of people who bought land for $50 an acre ten years ago and have recently been offered $1,000 an acre are not unusual. The rapid growth of certain urban and recreational areas has also caused related real estate prices to skyrocket. Because many investors expect the value of selected real estate to increase, real estate is presently a quite popular investment. The key to speculation is to isolate certain areas of potential population growth and/or real estate demand and to purchase property in these areas in the hope that the expectations for their development are realized.

Raw Land Undeveloped acreage without any utilities or improvements is often purchased by land speculators either to hold for future development or merely to sell at a higher price at some later date. Speculation in raw land often occurs near an area where a new development of some type is anticipated. Both residential and commercial developments tend to increase the value of nearby property. Because of the high degree of uncertainty involved in raw land speculation, it is an activity that should be reserved for the professional real estate investor.

Residential Lots Although builders typically predominate among purchasers of residential lots, it is often possible for the individual investor to buy such lots as speculative ventures. The likelihood that these lots will appreciate is much greater than for raw acreage since the land would probably not have been subdivided had there been no positive indications of the demand for the lots. If lots are purchased when first offered for sale, there is a good chance that they will appreciate, because as homes are built on neighboring lots the value of available lots tends to increase. Of course, if you wish to invest in residential lots, you should carefully assess their quality and the demand for them in the subdivision you are considering. Opportunities to profit do exist, but risks are still high. The success of speculation in lots depends not only on location but also on the quality, size, and appeal of the houses built on them. These latter factors are obviously difficult to control.

Investing in Income Property

The purchase of income property is a relatively common type of real estate investment that provides a *tax shelter*. The real estate purchased is leased to tenants to generate income in the form of rent receipts. Because the buildings on income property can be depreciated to reduce an investor's taxable income, it is a quite popular type of investment among the wealthy. Although the primary purpose of investment in income property is to produce a cash flow, certain types of strategically located income properties also offer good opportunities for appreciation in value. There are two basic types of income property: housing units and commercial property.

Housing Units Apartment houses, duplexes, and rental houses are all housing units that provide income. This type of income property is available in a broad range of sizes, prices, and types from multifamily apartment complexes to single-family rental homes. First-time investors in real estate usually choose investments of this type. Aside from cost considerations, the major factors influencing the profitability of these investments are the occupancy rate—the percentage of available space rented over the year—and maintenance and management costs.

Commercial Property Office buildings, stores, shopping centers, and mobile home parks are examples of the variety of investments included in the category commercial property. The risks and returns on commercial

The Small Real Estate Investor Can Make Money!

To gain experience as a landlord and to keep initial risks as low as possible, it's usually wise to start with a single-family or two-family house. If your expectations go awry, you can probably sell a small house much faster than an apartment.

Sharing small houses with tenants has traditionally been a way of cutting down the owner's shelter costs. In the Park Slope section of Brooklyn, N.Y., a spruced-up neighborhood, people can buy brownstones in the mid-$40,000 range and lease out half the space for about $400 a month—enough to cover a good part of the mortgage payments and property taxes.

In Los Angeles, where prices have spiraled more rapidly than almost anywhere else in the nation, people have been acquiring property in the faded grandeur of the Hollywood Hills. Veritable mansions, some visibly in need of repairs but others well kept, have been selling for $70,000 to $220,000. Because the area is showing signs of renewed respectability, some buyers are looking for capital gains. While they wait, they're renting out the houses, or apartments in them.

With larger rental properties, everything increases—potential gains and losses and the time it takes to look after things. Walk-up apartment buildings of four to twelve units that form the core of the housing stock in inner-city areas aren't the investments they once were, advises William D. Sally, a vice president of Baird & Warner Inc., a real estate firm in Chicago. Even if the price looks temptingly low and there is no rent control, an investor will have trouble making ends meet, he says, because the buildings are likely to leak heat and to need overhauling.

According to Sally, buildings with more than 25 apartments need someone always on hand, either a superintendent who gets a free apartment or one of the owners. He adds that anyone running a property of this size will "spend long hours, seven days a week and put in a lot of hard work."

High prices haven't discouraged two Ohio investors. Frank Landgraff, a sales manager for Continental Can Co., and William Coole, a lawyer, recently purchased a pair of two-family houses in Shaker Heights, near Cleveland. The sturdy brick structures, bought for $45,000 and $57,000, have been quite profitable. What made the deals work, besides meticulous planning and calculation, was the decision to have the tenants pay the utility bills, including gas heat, on top of their rent. The owners spend one day a week handling repairs and paint jobs. "No matter how solid the house," cautions Landgraff, "there will always be something going wrong. And if you are going to make any money from the investment, you have to fix things yourself."

It's a lot easier to make money on houses bought only a few years ago than it is at current prices. In 1970 and '71, Charles Abramovitz, a New York accountant, bought a single-family house and a two-family house in Hampton Bays, Long Island. They're netting him a total of $280 a month, but he acknowledges that they wouldn't be profitable if he had paid 1976 prices and interest rates. Abramovitz, who lives in Manhattan, hires local contractors for serious repairs but does simple maintenance himself during weekends and vacations. Figuring that he stands to make a $40,000 gain if he sells both houses, he says, "I look forward someday to being an ex-landlord."

Source: "Wrenching Profits from Rental Property," excerpted from the March 1975 issue of MONEY Magazine by special permission; © 1975, Time Inc.

property are more dependent on business conditions and location than would be true for housing units. The value of commercial property—especially retail businesses—is usually enhanced by a location in high-traffic areas. Due to the need for professional management and the magnitude of the expense involved, investment in commercial types of income property is generally the domain of more sophisticated investors.

Real Estate Syndication: Limited Partnerships

Real estate syndicates are *limited partnerships* which invest in various types of real estate and are professionally managed. Managers assume the role of a general partner, which means that their liability is unlimited, while the other investors are limited partners, which means they are legally liable for only the amount of their initial investment. Most syndicate shares cost $2,000 to $5,000 each and can be purchased directly through ads in financial newspapers, through a stockbroker, or with the assistance of a commercial real estate broker.

Types of Syndicates There are both single property and blind pool syndicates. The *single property syndicate* is established to raise money to purchase a specific piece of property. For example, fifty shares at $4,000 each could be sold to buy a piece of property for $600,000. A total of $200,000 ($4,000 × 50) would come from the partners, and the remaining $400,000 would be borrowed. The *blind pool syndicate,* on the other hand, is formed by a well-known syndicator in order to raise a given amount of money to be invested at the discretion of the syndicator. The cover of the prospectus for such a limited partnership is shown in Figure 9-5. The blind pool syndicator takes a specified percentage of all income generated as a management fee. Large real estate brokerage firms commonly arrange these types of syndications.

Returns and Risks The potential returns from real estate syndications lie in the tax shield provided by depreciation and in the gains due to appreciation in property values. In effect, the tax shield allows shareholders to receive tax-free cash flows from these investments. Appreciation in value yields a capital gain, which is taxed at rates lower than those on normal personal income (see Chapter 4). The annual returns on these types of investments range between 10 and 25 percent of the amount invested; and because part of the income is used to repay the mortgage financing, the partners' equity in the property increases over time. The emphasis with respect to the type of return generated differs from syndicate to syndicate. Some emphasize tax shelters; others emphasize capital gains. Uncertainty with respect to future price appreciation, occupancy rates, changes in tax laws, and the competence of the

Figure 9-5 **Cover of a Prospectus for a Limited Partnership**

PROSPECTUS
McNEIL REAL ESTATE FUND VII, LTD.

70,000 Units of Limited Partnership Interest
$500 Per Unit
Minimum Investment - 10 Units ($5,000)
(3 Units - $1,500 for an Individual Retirement Account)

McNEIL REAL ESTATE FUND VII, LTD. is a California limited partnership ("Partnership") of which Robert A. McNeil and Pacific Investors Corporation are the General Partners. The Partnership will engage in acquiring, improving, developing, operating and holding for investment, income producing real properties.

The Partnership's objectives are to invest in properties which will (i) preserve and protect the Partnership's capital; (ii) provide capital gains through potential appreciation; (iii) provide for "tax-sheltered" cash distributions from operations; (iv) build up equity; and (v) generate tax losses in excess of current tax sheltered cash distributions during the initial years of operation which may be used to offset taxable income from other sources.

THIS OFFERING INVOLVES A HIGH DEGREE OF RISK.

Prospective investors

(1) There are tax

(2) They may not ... Partnership, because the Partnership ... and may not have identified any sp ... the event a reasonable proba ... ship during the offering, this Prospectus w ... and particularly 3. - "Unspecified ... Objectives and Policies," p. 57).

including ... the General Partners and their Affiliates, ... 800,000, (... Gross Proceeds) upon the

... interest ... ship (see "C ...

... market for the Units ... ly to ... should be purchased ... long term investment ... ed partners may ... ir investments in the event ... cy of ... any oth ... sale of Un ... significant adverse tax con ... See "Real Estate ... income Tax Consequences" p.64).

THESE SECURITIES HAVE NOT BEEN APPROVED OR DISAPPROVED BY THE SECURITIES AND EXCHANGE COMMISSION NOR HAS THE COMMISSION PASSED UPON THE ACCURACY OR ADEQUACY OF THIS PROSPECTUS. ANY REPRESENTATION TO THE CONTRARY IS A CRIMINAL OFFENSE.

NEITHER THE ATTORNEY GENERAL NOR THE BUREAU OF SECURITIES OF THE STATE OF NEW JERSEY HAS PASSED ON OR ENDORSED THE MERITS OF THIS OFFERING. ANY REPRESENTATION TO THE CONTRARY IS UNLAWFUL.

	Price to Public	Underwriting Commissions ① ②	Proceeds to Partnership ② ③
Per Unit (Minimum Investment 10 Units)	$500	$40.00	$460.00
Total Minimum..........................	$1,250,000	$100,000	$1,150,000
Total Maximum	$35,000,000	$2,800,000	$32,200,000

(Footnotes on following page)

The date of this Prospectus is May 16, 1977

Source: Courtesy of Pacific Investors Corporation.

syndicate management introduces varying degrees of risk into these types of investments. The goals of the syndicate, the expected returns, and the perceived risks should all be carefully evaluated before limited partnership shares in a real estate syndicate are purchased.

Advantages and Disadvantages The key advantages of real estate syndicate investments are professional management, convenience, potentially high returns, and low operating costs. Because the professional manager is able to keep abreast of real estate conditions and pay close attention to the investment, the likelihood of success is much greater than for small real estate investors. Syndicate investments do have some disadvantages, however. Shares are difficult to sell quickly when returns are low; there are high risks in speculating on property appreciation and occupancy rates in housing units; and possible changes in the tax laws related to depreciation such as occurred in 1976 heighten the general uncertainty as to the continued role of these investments as tax shelters.

Real Estate Investment Trusts (REITs)

The Real Estate Investment Trust (REIT) is an unincorporated business that accumulates money for investment in real estate ventures by selling shares to small investors. REITs, a special type of closed-end investment company (see Chapter 8), must abide by the Real Estate Investment Trust Act of 1960, which established requirements for forming a REIT and rules and procedures for making investments and distributing income. These trusts channel money into various types of long-term real estate investments such as apartments and office buildings. Since they are required to pay out nearly all of their earnings to the owners, they do quite a bit of borrowing to obtain financing for investments.

A number of insurance companies, mortgage banking houses, and commercial banks have formed REITs. The ownership of many is traded on the security exchanges. They are not taxed, but the income distributed to owners is taxed as personal income, which is divided into normal income and capital gain income and taxed accordingly. While REITs may earn returns in the range of 5 to 15 percent and do provide a mechanism through which the small investor can make real estate investments, they are risky. For this reason, it is advisable to invest only in the shares of the better-known REITs, which are listed on major security exchanges. The poor performance and financial collapse of many REITs during the period 1973–1975 has decreased considerably the popularity of these investments. Your stockbroker should be able to give you advice with respect to REITs and help you select REIT investments consistent with your investment goals, if you wish.

Real Estate Investment Companies

The real estate investment company is nothing more than a corporation that sells its shares and uses the proceeds to make real estate investments. It differs from the REIT in that it must pay corporate income taxes and therefore is not regulated with respect to the distribution of its income. Such companies are therefore able to retain earnings as well as borrow and thus can grow at a much faster rate than REITs. Although these companies specialize in real estate investments, they represent nothing more than another common stock investment. This perhaps explains the diversity of their performance; some have done well, while others have performed poorly. Your stockbroker should be able to provide detailed information with respect to these common stock investments.

Summary

The first step in making a housing decision is to determine housing requirements. Monthly payment capacity is the prime consideration. Housing may be rented or purchased. Rental units are available in a wide variety of types, styles, and prices. Renters are required to sign a lease which specifies various costs and restrictions related to the usage of the leased property. Since no down payment is required, renting permits a high degree of mobility; it also offers freedom from maintenance responsibilities. The disadvantage of renting lies in the fact that it does not offer the financial benefits of owning. Home ownership makes possible the deduction of interest payments and property taxes from taxable income and provides a hedge against inflation. Disadvantages of home ownership are the cost and inconvenience of selling a home and the maintenance and upkeep responsibilities associated with owning. Other less popular housing forms are mobile homes, cooperative apartments, condominiums, and second or summer homes.

Before you buy a house, you must decide how much you can afford to spend. You should have enough savings available to make a 5 to 30 percent down payment. In addition, you will need to be able to make the regular mortgage payments, which often include not only the loan repayment and interest but also the payment of property taxes and homeowner's insurance. You will have to have enough money to pay closing costs as well. Once you decide on the type of home—old, new, or custom built—you desire, you may wish to have a realtor assist you in the selection process. To make an offer on a home, you must present a purchase contract and earnest money to the seller. Once the purchase contract is accepted, you must obtain mortgage financing for the amount you need to borrow. After financing has been secured, the closing, or settlement, takes place.

Real estate has appeal as an investment due to any of several factors: tax effects provided by depreciation, a favorable cash flow, and the general expectation of appreciation in property value that it offers. The use of leverage adds risk to a real estate investment but makes higher returns possible. Speculators in real estate often purchase raw land or residential lots in expectation of future price increases. Income property—both housing units and commercial property—may appreciate in value while buildings on it can be depreciated, thereby providing some tax shelter. Other types of real estate investments that offer a variety of risk-return opportunities include: real estate syndications, or limited partnerships; Real Estate Investment Trusts (REITs); and real estate investment companies.

Key Terms

assessed value
blind pool syndicate
closing (of loan)
closing costs
condominiums
cooperative apartments
down payment
duplex
earnest money
income property
lease agreement
leverage
limited partnership

mortgage
property taxes
purchase contract
real estate investment companies
Real Estate Investment Trust (REIT)
rental contract
settlement (of loan)
single property syndicate
spec home
syndication (real estate)
tax shelters (shields)

Review Questions

1. What factors determine an individual's housing requirements?

2. What features are normally included as part of a rental contract?

3. Discuss the relative advantages and disadvantages of renting a home.

4. Why is home ownership becoming increasingly popular in the United States?

5. Does a homeowner have any advantage over a renter with respect to taxes? Explain.

6. "The purchase of a house provides a hedge against inflation." Explain.

7. List the advantages and disadvantages of home ownership.

8. What other forms of housing are available in the United States? Differentiate between a cooperative apartment and a condominium.

9. Approximately how much is the minimum down payment on a house? Cite the rules used to determine the size of mortgage loan a person can handle.

10. Distinguish between (a) old homes, (b) new homes, and (c) custom homes from the viewpoint of a prospective buyer.

11. What role does a real estate agent play in the purchase of a house?

12. What is meant by "making an offer"? What clauses are normally included in a purchase contract? What is earnest money? Explain the purchase negotiation process.

13. Explain two ways a person may go about selling a house.

14. What factors should be considered before an investment is made in real estate? Explain.

15. Distinguish briefly between: (a) a real estate syndicate, (b) a Real Estate Investment Trust, and (c) a real estate investment company.

Case Problems

9-1 The Browns' Rent or Purchase Decision

After much persuasion by Vera, his wife, and Mrs. Dean Jones, his old neighbor, Clifford Brown decided to buy a home and avoid having to make rent payments of $350 per month for an apartment. He purchased a modest three-bedroom house in the newly developing Silver Oaks Estates of North Carolina for $50,000. His down payment amounted to $8,000. Since Clifford earns approximately $18,000 a year at his job with a pharmaceutical company, he is in the 28 percent income tax bracket. He made the down payment from his available savings, on which he was earning 5$\frac{1}{2}$ percent annual interest, and borrowed the remaining $42,000 from a local savings and loan association at an interest rate of 9 percent per year. The loan has a maturity of thirty years. The monthly mortgage payment is $410, of which $300 is interest and $35 goes toward repayment of the loan principal. The remaining $75 per month ($410/month − $335/month) is used to pay annual property taxes of $660 and the annual homeowner insurance premium of $240. The monthly operating costs—such as gas, electricity, water, sewage, and maintenance—are expected to be approximately $75, which is $30 per month greater than those for the apartment the Browns had been renting.

Questions

1. Evaluate and compare the Browns' alternatives of either remaining in the apartment or purchasing the house.

2. Are there any nonquantitative factors that should be considered when making the rent-buy decision? Discuss.

3. Which alternative would you have recommended for the Browns in light of your analysis?

9-2 Financing the Sheik's California Real Estate Investment

Sheik Batumi of Kuwait wants to invest in real estate somewhere in California. After looking at various properties for about a week, he finally chooses one that his realtors have shown him. The asking price for the property is $220,000. A shrewd businessman, Sheik Batumi has arranged to purchase the property for $200,000 but does not wish to pay the full amount with his own money. He arranges instead to pay only $50,000 out of his own pocket and borrows the remaining $150,000 at 12 percent interest. The project is expected to earn $25,000 a year after all expenses, including real estate property taxes and depreciation but before deduction of interest and taxes. The Sheik will have to pay taxes of 50 percent on this investment due to his status as a foreign investor.

Questions

1. Calculate the Sheik's return on investment:
(a) Assuming he borrows $150,000 as proposed above.
(b) Assuming he pays the entire $200,000 from his own funds.

2. Using your findings above, explain why leverage is so appealing to investors. Are there any risks associated with its use? Explain.

3. Which financing alternative in question 1 would you recommend the Sheik use? Explain your answer.

Selected References

"Are There Pitfalls in Condominiums?" *Better Homes and Gardens*, April 1975, pp. 6 ff.

"Buy a House or Rent? A Fresh Look at the Options—." *Changing Times*, April 1975, pp. 13–16.

"Buying a House? Analyze the Floor Plan First." *Changing Times*, January 1977, pp. 29–30.

"Choosing an Older Home." *Consumers' Research*, March 1977, p. 2.

Davis, Joseph C. *Buying Your House: A Complete Guide to Inspection and Evaluation.* Buchanan, N.Y.: Emerson, 1975.

"Five Myths about Condominiums." *Changing Times,* December 1976, pp. 17–18.

Gray, Genevieve. *Condominiums: How to Buy, Sell, and Live in Them.* New York: Funk & Wagnalls, 1975.

Harris, Marlys. "How to Find an Affordable House." *Money,* August 1977, pp. 46–50.

"Homeowners and the Law: Your Rights and Obligations." *Better Homes and Gardens,* March 1976, pp. 16 ff.

"How a Small Investor Can Make Money on Rental Property." *Changing Times,* May 1976, pp. 15–19.

"How to Keep Down the Cost of Buying a Home." *U.S. News & World Report,* 21 March 1977, pp. 39–42.

Irwin, Robert. *How to Buy and Sell Real Estate for Financial Security.* New York: McGraw-Hill, 1975.

Levine, Mark Lee. *Real Estate Fundamentals.* St. Paul, Minn.: West Publishing, 1976.

"The New Money Target: Profitable Real Estate." *Business Week,* 1 August 1977, pp. 52–58.

Shankel, William M. *Modern Real Estate Principles.* Dallas, Tex.: Business Publications, 1977.

"Things They Must Tell You When You Lease Something." *Changing Times,* March 1977, pp. 41–42.

"Who Wins the REIT Game?" *Forbes,* 15 May 1977, pp. 132–135.

Williams, Robert L. "How to Buy a $50,000 House for $27,000." *Money,* January 1977, pp. 37–39.

Your Housing Dollar. Chicago: Money Management Institute, Household Finance Corporation, 1971.

10

Automobiles, Furniture and Appliances, and Other Assets

In order to provide a basis for the analysis, selection, and purchase of major nonfinancial assets other than a home, this chapter discusses the following:

A Preview of Chapter 10

1. The fundamental approaches available for analyzing, selecting, and purchasing major nonfinancial assets such as automobiles, furniture, appliances, and other expensive items.

2. The key motives for buying automobiles and important considerations in the analysis of automobile purchase alternatives.

3. Methods for analyzing a potential auto purchase on the basis of the prospective buyer's financial status and projected ownership costs.

4. Where to buy automobiles, auto financing considerations, maintenance of automobiles, and various aspects of auto leasing.

5. Purchase considerations, financing techniques, and maintenance factors related to the acquisition of furniture and appliances.

6. The purchase criteria for other major nonfinancial assets such as recreational vehicles, sporting goods, personal and household goods, collections, and small business ownership.

In addition to a home, automobiles, furniture, and appliances are major nonfinancial assets. They are generally purchased more frequently than is a home, and their purchase normally results in a long-term commitment of your finances. Because of their sizable effect on your financial plans, you should know how to analyze the features, reliability, purchase terms, warranties, and costs of these assets.

The automobile is probably the first major expenditure most persons make. Typically, an individual purchases an automobile every one to four years and pays anywhere from $1,000 to $10,000 for it, depending on its make, model, and age and on whether or not a trade-in is made. Because you will probably have to make an automobile purchase decision ten or more times during your life, a commonsense approach to selection and financing can help you achieve significant savings.

Furniture and appliances are other important nonfinancial assets. Although these items are probably not purchased as often as automobiles, they nonetheless represent major expenditures that require careful analysis. For example, if you buy the cheapest refrigerator on the market, you may find that it needs more frequent repairs and has a shorter usable life than a more expensive unit. This chapter discusses the key considerations in the purchase of nonfinancial assets other than housing that you are likely to acquire during your lifetime.

Automobiles

The automobile plays a major role in our society today. It is an important factor in the economy, since the auto industry provides hundreds of thousands of jobs and is a major consumer of raw materials produced by other vital industries such as steel. There is a vast array of types, styles, sizes, and colors of automobiles from which the consumer may select. In addition to domestically (U.S.) produced automobiles, a large number of "foreign," or "imported," cars are also available. Basic considerations related to the selection and purchase of an automobile are presented below.

Motives for Ownership

The most common motive for automobile ownership is to provide *transportation.* Even in some parts of the country where the ready availability of public transportation has eliminated the necessity of owning a car, the automobile still remains the most popular mode of transportation. Clearly, the amount of use that is anticipated should be a factor in determining individual automobile requirements.

Many people view the automobile not only as a mode of transportation but also as a type of *status symbol.* The bigger, more expensive, and more luxurious the car, the greater the amount of status it is believed to reflect. Although an individual's status in society is not dependent on the car he or she drives, many consumers feel that the ownership of a special type of car places them in a position of superiority over others who do not have a similarly prestigious automobile. Thus although it is not economically justifiable, the status reflected in auto ownership is an important motive

Status and Economy Are Often in Conflict
Source: Reprinted by permission of NEA.

for owning certain types of cars. Automobile advertisements, in fact, reveal the industry's reliance on status appeals in their promotional campaigns.

Another motive for owning an automobile may be to provide a *hobby*. The auto has become such a key part of American life that many people devote their free time to some sort of auto-related activity, for example, drag racing, road racing, and auto shows. People purchase cars merely for the pleasure of fixing them up or "souping them up." Numerous auto clubs exist to bring together people who share automotive hobbies and interests. Typically autos purchased for hobbies do not serve as a primary source of transportation; their purpose is to provide entertainment and, to some extent, status.

Automobiles may also be purchased as *investments*. Old, discontinued, or limited production models often appreciate in value because of their scarcity. Sometimes, too, rapid rises in the cost of new cars or, in the case of foreign and imported cars, changes in the value of the dollar in relation to other currencies result in significant increases in value. Although purchasing automobiles as an investment does offer earning opportunities, many safer investments exist. Auto investments are usually only a hobby of the wealthy.

How Much Can You Afford to Spend?

Before you shop for a car to be used as your primary mode of transportation, it is a good idea to determine how much you can afford to spend. Since your budget is set up on a monthly basis, your estimate of the amount you can afford to spend should be calculated on a per month basis.

One approach is to deduct all fixed expenses such as house payments or rent, other loan payments, and utilities from your after-tax monthly

Future Transportation for Commuters

Ten years from now, most commuters are likely to be using the same mode of transportation they're riding today, and about 85% of the time that's the private car. Many who drive have not spurned mass transit and car pooling; they never had those choices. Many people commute from homes in one suburb to jobs in another suburb, rather than following the rail and bus corridors to and from downtown.

What's likely to happen in the next ten years is an upgrading of existing systems. The next generation of rail cars and buses will be somewhat more comfortable, but most improvements will be aimed at increasing energy efficiency and economy. "You reach a point in riding comfort where the incremental increase is not worth the money," contends C. Kenneth Orski, who walks to his job as associate administrator for policy and program development at the Urban Mass Transportation Administration (UMTA).

Transportation officials have been forced to abandon greater designs and concentrate on improving what they have—for example, making a more serious effort to coordinate schedules so that commuters transferring from one bus or train or another spend less time waiting. Transit professionals also expect a proliferation of "feeder" lines, small buses and jitneys—taxicabs plying a regular route—that will pick up commuters at their doors and drop them at train and bus stations. Says Orski: "This will allow people to do away with that second car."

Subsidies will probably keep mass transit fares from rising as precipitously in the next few years as they have since the late 1960s. Transit operators, however, will have more sophisticated methods of extracting the fare from the commuter. On rail lines in San Francisco and suburban Philadelphia, travelers now buy plastic tickets that resemble credit cards from vending machines. Machines at station exits deduct fares automatically.

Whether your trips to work will get better, worse, or stay the same will depend partly on what form of transportation you use. Some likely specifics:

Driving to work will get worse, not better, for many commuters. One of the strings attached to federal mass transit aid will be that cities take steps to discourage driving. They may ban on-street parking and impose fees of $10 a day or more in municipal lots. Transportation officials are watching with interest an experiment in Singapore, where anyone who wants to drive in the central business district must pay a daily license fee. UMTA will select at least one U.S. city this year to set up an auto-free zone. It's hoped that more park-and-ride lots along bus and rail lines will lure the driver from his car outside the city limits.

The breaks that a few car poolers now get will become more widespread. They will pay reduced tolls and reduced parking fees. Car pools, along with buses, will be allowed to use express lanes and enter zones where other passenger cars are outlawed.

Taking the bus will be a more attractive alternative. In a few weeks, UMTA will announce standards for new buses—including both city buses and those that haul commuters in from the suburbs. The better buses that result will probably hit the streets by 1979. The agency is likely to require bus operators to equip at least some of the buses in their fleets with one or more features to make it easier for the elderly and handicapped, as well as others, to get on and off—wider doors, lower floors, shorter steps, ramps to take on wheelchairs, or machinery that will allow the entire bus to "kneel" at stops.

Future buses will have quieter, less smelly engines and better suspensions. Recent prototypes compared with a 1974 Ford LTD in ride smoothness, according to UMTA. Windows and destination signs will be larger, though the space per passenger probably won't be. Improved air-conditioning systems will be less prone to breakdowns.

"Articulated" buses, which bend in the middle, could carry twice as many passengers as ordinary buses, while minibuses will serve lightly populated areas and cities in off-peak hours. An increase in privately operated and community sponsored buses is likely. Housing tracts, for instance, may set up subscription bus services; more suburban firms may provide bus transportation for employees free or at low cost. "In many cases today companies provide parking lots, which are a hidden subsidy to the automobile," says Orski. "In the future they may provide a subsidy for bus or van services."

Bus riders will be the chief beneficiaries of improved traffic management— lanes for buses only, traffic lights that sense an approaching bus and stay green until it passes, signals on freeway entrance ramps that give buses the go-ahead while holding cars back. Engineers are also working on electronic systems that would keep buses evenly spaced along routes.

Going by rail will become more comfortable as railroads and subway systems continue to replace old cars with new. The latest in urban rail cars offers a quieter, less jerky ride in a more streamlined vehicle. For cities willing to pay extra, there are carpeting and seating arrangements that give everyone a little more legroom.

Cities are now reconsidering the streetcar, which could run on the old trolley rights of way or down the median strips of expressways. Streetcars without exclusive rights of way may once again run in traffic or on streets closed to cars by city fathers no longer awed by the automobile. Says Michael Ferreri, president of Simpson & Curtin, a Philadelphia transportation engineering firm, "Right now the general political feeling in the cities is 'So what if your car gets stuck.'"

Source: Excerpted from "What's Down the Line for Commuters," MONEY Magazine, March 1976, by special permission; © 1976, Time Inc.

income. (Any monthly savings deposits that are being made in order to fulfill some specific future goal should also be treated as a fixed monthly expense.) From the resulting figure, you then deduct the average amount of your variable monthly expenditures for such items as food, clothing, and entertainment. What remains is the amount that you can afford to spend each month on car ownership. Of course, you should spend only as much as is needed for the type of car that fulfills your transportation requirements—not necessarily all that is available.

Assume, for example, that your monthly after-tax income is $1,180 and your fixed expenses per month consist of: $230 for housing, $100 in installment payments, $70 in utility bills (budgeted), $50 in scheduled savings deposits, and $90 for various types of insurance. Also assume that your variable expenses for each month consist of $180 for food, $60 for clothing, and $120 for other unspecified items, including entertainment. Table 10-1 illustrates the calculation of the monthly amount available for automobile expenditures—in this case, $280.

Table 10-1 **Estimating the Monthly Amount Available for Auto Expenditures**

Monthly After-Tax Income		$1,180
Less Fixed Monthly Expenses:		
Housing	$230	
Installment Payments	100	
Utilities (Budget)	70	
Scheduled Savings Deposits	50	
Insurance	90	
Total Fixed Expenses		540
Income Available to Meet Variable Expenses		640
Less Variable Monthly Expenses:		
Food	180	
Clothing	60	
Other Unspecified Items	120	
Total Variable Expenses		360
Monthly Amount Available for Auto Expenditures		$280

Of course, the amount you spend for an automobile must be related to your financial goals and budgeted in light of your financial priorities (see Chapter 3). Once an estimate of the monthly amount you have available for auto expenditures has been made, you should evaluate the costs of owning various types of autos in order to select the most suitable one for you.

Costs of Automobile Ownership

The monthly cost of auto ownership consists not only of payment for ownership of the car but also includes the cost of insurance, licenses, gas, oil, tires, and other operating and maintenance outlays. Certain of these costs—*fixed costs*—are the same regardless of how much you drive, while others—*variable costs*—depend directly on the number of miles you drive.

Fixed Ownership Costs Installment loan payments, insurance costs, license costs, personal property taxes, and parking costs are common fixed ownership costs. If you plan to purchase a car with cash you have saved, a loan will not be needed to finance your purchase and you will have no monthly *installment payments*. However, if you must borrow to pay for your car, you will have regular payments to make on your loan. And although they are usually paid only once or twice a year, insurance costs should be calculated on a monthly basis. License costs vary from state to state and quite often depend on the year, make, and model of car. In some states the cost of licenses includes a personal property tax, while in others automobile ownership is taxed separately by the county or township. These costs may change slightly as the value of the car decreases, but they are considered fixed since they do not vary with the number of miles the car is driven. Similarly, monthly parking or garage rental fees are also a fixed cost of automobile ownership.

Variable Ownership Costs Expenditures for gas, oil, tires, and maintenance and repairs are all variable ownership costs. The greater the number of miles driven, the greater these costs will be, and vice versa. Of course, maintenance and repair costs are also affected by how the car is driven. Maintenance and repair costs per mile driven are higher when a car is abused than when it is driven in a reasonable fashion.

Total Ownership Costs The sum of estimated monthly fixed and variable auto ownership costs provides a fairly good indication of the total monthly cost of owning an auto. You can make these cost estimates with the assistance of a friend who has owned a similar type car or by using your own knowledge gained from past experience as an automobile owner. You will find that the fixed ownership costs can easily be determined by consulting the appropriate sources—bank loan officers, insurance agents, licensing agencies, and garage or parking lot attendants. Variable costs must be estimated in light of the number of miles you expect to drive each month. They will also be affected by the fuel economy and relative maintenance requirements of the auto you are considering.

Auto Ownership and Operating Costs: Recent Data

A new study offers some clues on the varying costs of owning and operating cars of different sizes.

Automobile Costs. In the typical 10-year life of a 1976-model car, it will be driven 100,000 miles, according to a Federal Highway Administration report. During that time, estimated total costs of a standard-sized car will be $17,879, or 17.9 cents a mile. For a compact car, costs will total $14,561, or 14.56 cents a mile. A subcompact, $12,638, or 12.64 cents a mile.

This table shows you the itemized costs for the three sizes of cars:

	Standard	Compact	Subcompact
Depreciation	$4,864	$3,830	$3,189
Repairs, maintenance	3,664	2,961	2,660
Replacement tires	448	387	350
Accessories added after purchase	92	86	89
Gasoline	3,193	2,281	1,652
Oil	170	170	154
Insurance	1,678	1,594	1,511
Garaging, parking, tolls, etc.	2,209	2,109	2,109
Federal, State taxes and fees	1,562	1,144	925

Note: The costs are based on operations in the Baltimore suburbs and are not national averages. All taxes—on gasoline and other things—are included in the tax total. Maryland does not have a personal-property tax, as some States do. No account is taken of finance charges or inflation.

On a daily basis. The cost per day of owning and running an automobile in its first year is $7.44 for a standard-sized car, $4.83 for a compact and $3.95 for a subcompact. In the second year, costs drop to $5.50 a day for a standard, to $4.38 for a compact and to $3.54 for a subcompact. Daily costs continue to drop as the years pass and the differences in the costs among the three sizes become narrower.

For details—. You can get the complete study, "Cost of Owning and Operating an Automobile 1976," from: Federal Highway Administration, HPA-1, 400 Seventh Street, S.W., Washington, D.C. 20590. It's free.

Source: Reprinted from *U.S. News & World Report,* 20 September 1976. Copyright 1976 U.S. News & World Report, Inc.

Assume, for example, that you are considering the purchase of a medium-size car equipped with most optional accessories. Because you cannot afford to pay the $6,500 purchase price in cash, you intend to borrow $4,500 to be repaid over three years. The remaining $2,000 down payment will be made from your savings along with proceeds from the sale of your old car. The monthly payment of your installment loan will be $147. Auto insurance will cost $240 per year, or $20 per month. The combined cost of license plates and property taxes is estimated to be $120 per year, or $10 per month. Since your job is in the heart of the city, you will have to pay $25 a month for reserved parking.

Your variable ownership costs are estimated in accordance with the fact that you expect to drive 12,000 miles per year, or 1,000 miles per month. The estimated cost of gasoline is based on the assumption that the car will average fifteen miles per gallon. With fuel costs projected at 60 cents per gallon, the cost per mile would be 4 cents (60 cents per gallon ÷ 15 miles per gallon). Since you expect to drive an average of 1,000 miles per month, the monthly cost will be $40 (1,000 miles × 4 cents per mile). The cost of oil has been estimated at $2 per month. Tires are expected to cost an average of $6 per month. Maintenance and repair costs are difficult to predict, but from past experience they are estimated at $12 per month.

Table 10-2 presents an itemized listing of all these monthly costs, both fixed and variable. Your total ownership cost per month as calculated in Table 10-2 can be estimated at $262—that is, $202 in fixed costs and $60 in variable costs. Based on an expected 12,000 miles of driving each year,

Table 10-2 **Estimating Total Monthly Auto Ownership Costs: An Example**

Ownership Cost	Monthly Amount	Cost per Mile [a]
(1) Fixed		
Installment Loan Payment	$147	$.147
Auto Insurance	20	.020
License Plates and Property Taxes	10	.010
Parking Cost	25	.025
Total Fixed	$202	$.202
(2) Variable		
Gasoline	$ 40	$.040
Oil	2	.002
Tires	6	.006
Maintenance and Repairs	12	.012
Total Variable	$ 60	$.060
Total Ownership Cost [(1) + (2)]	$262	$.262

[a] The number of miles driven per month is assumed to be 1,000.

the cost per mile will be 26.2 cents. In other words, to afford the car under consideration, you should have available $262 per month to meet the total ownership costs.

In Table 10-1 the monthly amount available for auto expenditures was estimated at $280 per month, which appears to be enough to support the ownership of the proposed car. Note, however, that although the amount of total ownership costs estimated for each month must be met, this value represents only an average cost. Therefore in some months actual cash outlays will be less than $262, while in others they are likely to be greater than $262. Even though it may not be necessary to pay out $262 each month, it is a good idea to place any unused portion of this amount in savings in order to meet expenditures that surpass the estimated monthly average.

Depreciation Cost

The amount by which the value of the automobile declines over a given period of ownership is known as *depreciation cost.* Simply stated, it represents the difference between the price at which you purchase the car and the price for which you can sell it at some future date. For example, if you purchase a new car for $6,500 and expect to keep it for three years, you will have to estimate its value three years from now in order to calculate the depreciation. By looking at the past depreciation on similar types of cars, you can roughly determine what percent of the original cost the car will be worth after three years. Assume you find that similar cars were worth 53 percent of their original purchase price at the end of three years. You can therefore expect your car to be worth about $3,450 (approximately 53 percent of $6,500) after three years. The depreciation cost over the three-year period will therefore be $3,050—about $1,017 per year, or approximately $85 per month.

Although depreciation is a cost of auto ownership, it is not incurred until the car is sold, when the proceeds will be less than the amount originally paid to purchase the car. Depreciation was not included as an ownership cost in the preceding section, since it does not result in having to spend money each month as a condition of ownership. In spite of the fact that depreciation does not affect the monthly costs of ownership, it does merit attention in the process of selecting a car to buy. Since some automobiles depreciate more rapidly than others in the same price range, it is advisable to assess carefully the depreciation expected on an auto prior to purchasing it. The impact of depreciation on your finances is felt when the car is traded in. The lower the trade-in value you realize (i.e., the greater the depreciation), the higher your monthly payments will be on your next car. As illustrated in the preceding example, this hidden cost of auto ownership can be sizable.

Additional Purchase Considerations

Other important purchase considerations are related to the automobile itself rather than the financing of its purchase. Most of these result from the wide variety of auto types, sizes, features, and warranties on the market. Although automobile manufacturers are few in number, they produce virtually hundreds of differently priced, sized, designed, and painted autos. While this vast array is one of the benefits of our free-enterprise economy, it forces consumers to do a great deal of purchase analysis in order to buy the cars best suited to their needs. A number of the more important nonfinancial purchase considerations are briefly discussed below.

New or Used? One decision you must make is whether to buy a new or used car. If you cannot afford to buy a new car, the decision is made for you. Some people always buy used cars, even though they can afford to buy a new one. Others pay more for a used car, such as a Mercedes, than it would have cost to purchase a new car of another make, such as a Chevrolet. The advantages of buying a used car are: (1) it is less expensive than a comparable new car; (2) it will not depreciate in value as quickly as a new car; and (3) because it is less expensive, the purchaser does not have to put down as much money as is required on a new car. Moreover, the purchase of used cars less than eighteen months old means a savings of 10 to 25 percent of the depreciation in value experienced when a new car is purchased.

The main disadvantage of buying a used car is the uncertainty of its mechanical condition. Although it might look good, it could still have some mechanical problems requiring maintenance and repair expenditures in the near future. Even though according to a salesperson the car has low mileage and "has been driven only to and from church by a little old lady," it is advisable to have it checked by a reputable mechanic. The twenty or so dollars spent on a thorough examination of it prior to its purchase could save hundreds of dollars.

Purchasers of used cars have another means of protecting their investment in the federal *odometer disclosure law*. The penalties for violation of this law, which requires sellers to give buyers a signed statement attesting to the fact that the mileage shown on the odometer of their used cars is correct, are quite stringent. A seller of a used car should always be asked to provide such a statement.

Prior to purchasing either new or used cars, make certain you know what you want; if you have not done this, a slick auto salesperson may cause you to purchase a car you do not need. If you wish to buy a used car, it is generally a good idea to shop for a car "for sale by owner" in order to avoid paying the added overhead charges of an auto dealer. Classified ads in local or nearby city newspapers provide an excellent source of information on used cars for sale.

Type of Car: American or Imported Some people consider only American-made autos, while others are completely indifferent to the country of origin for the cars they purchase. Generally speaking, imported cars are smaller, lighter in weight, and therefore offer better fuel economy than American cars. A few years ago people hesitated to buy imported cars because they felt both service and availability of replacement parts were uncertain. Today this concern has been eliminated in the major imports from Germany, Japan, and Sweden. Vast networks of imported car dealerships consisting of hundreds of dealers exist in the major imported auto lines, and because of the expertise of certain foreign auto manufacturers in producing smaller cars, American auto manufacturers even manufacture some of their cars abroad, for example, the Buick Opel and Mercury Capri. Nevertheless, if you consider purchasing an imported car, you should ascertain whether you will be able to receive adequate local service at a reasonable price.

Size of Car and Body Style The size and body style you wish your car to have are largely dependent on your motive for buying it. Obviously, a two-passenger compact car is not appropriate if you need the car for business. When determining size and body style, you should select from only those cars consistent with the primary use of the auto; you should not adapt your needs to fit the car. The four basic size classifications commonly used are given in Table 10-3. In most instances, there is a direct relationship between size and cost: the larger the car, the more expensive it will be.

Cars differ with respect to body styles as well as size. Again, it is important to select a car with a body style that conforms to the requirements of your usage of the auto. Most of the basic types of body styles, which are described in Table 10-4, can be obtained for each of the automobile sizes described in Table 10-3. Figure 10-1 presents a comparison of the past growth (1956–1976) and anticipated shrinkage (1976–1980) in the size of the American car. Friends and acquaintances who own cars similar in size and body to a proposed purchase may be able to offer you some insight into the pros and cons of the car you are considering.

Features: Standard and Optional Most cars have certain optional features providing a broad range of conveniences and luxuries for those willing to pay the price. It is quite unusual to find a car that does not have at least some optional features. On new cars a window sticker details each optional feature and its price, but in fact only close observation serves to determine the options on a used car. Window stickers quite often list standard features that might be considered optional on some other models, and vice versa. When shopping for a new car, make certain you are comparing comparably equipped models. The buyer should also beware of fancy-sounding adjectives used to describe some feature that is

Table 10-3 Automobile Size Classifications

Subcompacts are the smallest cars of all, seating two adults quite comfortably, but with room in back for small children only. They are especially suitable for in-town driving because of their maneuverability in traffic and in parking. Due to their less powerful engines, subcompacts do not perform as well on the highway and cannot be overloaded with optional equipment. Their small size makes them more vulnerable in an accident. Their biggest advantage is economy.

Compacts are somewhat larger and higher-priced than subcompacts and will accommodate four adults comfortably for short periods of time. They make a satisfactory all-round car for small families. Compacts are also easy to handle and are among the less expensive cars to own and operate, for they get good mileage and have lower depreciation, insurance, and repair costs.

Intermediates have lower mileage and higher upkeep expenses, but provide more space and comfort for the money. They are large enough to easily accommodate six adults and perform well in both city traffic and on the highway.

Full-size or standard cars, which include the luxury models, are the largest of all. They are the most expensive to own and operate because of their high initial cost, upkeep, depreciation, insurance rates, and lower mileage. They usually offer greater riding comfort, power, and stability than do the smaller cars, so are more suitable for extensive highway and long-distance driving. On the other hand, their bulk makes them more difficult to manage in city traffic.

Source: This information taken from the Money Management Institute booklet titled *Your Automobile Dollar,* printed by the Money Management Institute of Household Finance Corporation, Chicago, Illinois, 1975.

really not so special. For example, what is torsionmatic suspension? And do you really care?

By listing all options you desire prior to shopping for your car, you can avoid paying for features you really do not need. There are literally hundreds of options available, ranging in price from a few dollars up to $1,000 or more and including automatic transmission, a bigger engine, air conditioning, power steering, power brakes, some type of radio, a clock, power windows, power seats, rear window defroster, and special suspension. Other, appearance-related, options are two-tone or metallic paint, vinyl top, electric sun roof, whitewall tires, sport wheels, and one of many exterior trim packages. When selecting options, you should give some thought to their cost and effects, not only on performance, handling, and appearance, but also on fuel economy, reliability, repair problems, and the resale value of the car.

Table 10-4 **Automobile Body Style Classification**

Sedans (4-door and 2-door) are designed to carry several passengers, making them good family cars. They are solidly built, with central side pillars that provide extra stability in case of an accident. Two-door sedans cost slightly less and have a more streamlined appearance, but getting in and out of the back seat is more difficult. Parents of young children often prefer them because there are no rear doors to be accidentally opened.

Hardtops (4-door and 2-door) are similar in size and style to sedans, but they lack side pillars. This results in an appealing sporty look and unobstructed side vision. Because the smooth, uncluttered look of hardtops is generally more popular, they usually have higher resale value than sedans.

Station wagons are utility cars that hold more people than comparable sedans. They are particularly suitable for those who frequently carry several passengers. The large amount of space in the rear makes them ideal for hauling large items—shrubbery, camping gear, lumber, or bags of groceries. They are several hundred pounds heavier than sedans in the same make and series and are less maneuverable in traffic. With a higher price tag and lower gas mileage, station wagons are more expensive to own and operate.

Hatchbacks are designed with a hinged rear window that provides access to a large flat storage area created when the rear seat is folded down. With this feature, a subcompact or compact can become, in effect, a small station wagon. These models are valued by people who have an occasional need for cargo space but no need for the extra seating capacity or power of a standard-sized wagon.

Convertibles, once seen frequently, have declined in popularity. They have been phased out of most domestic car lines but are available in some foreign makes. The poorer insulation of convertibles results in noisier, less comfortable rides that are hotter in summer, cooler in winter. Their occupants are also more vulnerable in an accident.

Sports cars are popularly regarded as fun cars. Generally seating only two people and offering little storage space, they are perhaps the least practical of all body types. Since some of the higher-priced models offer superior engineering qualities and finely-tooled, powerful engines, they hold special appeal for automobile buffs. Even the lighter-weight, less expensive models provide status and delight along with transportation, and their sleek continental lines attract many an admiring eye.

Source: This information taken from the Money Management Institute booklet titled *Your Automobile Dollar*, printed by the Money Management Institute of Household Finance Corporation, Chicago, Illinois, 1975.

Reliability and Warranties Another factor to consider when shopping for a car—new or used—is its general *reliability*. An excellent source of this type of information is published by Consumers Union, which provides ratings of various aspects of each year's cars along with an overall rating of their quality in its annual *Buying Guide Issue of Consumer Reports*. Friends who own cars similar to the type you are interested in and mechanics at independent auto repair shops who have worked on numerous makes and models are other good sources of information on reliability. Although not every car produced by a given

Figure 10-1 **Changing Size of the American Car**

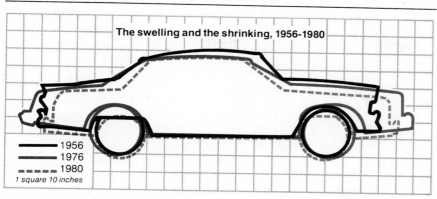

This chart shows how the standard Ford sedan grew from the 1956 Victoria to the 1976 LTD and how designers expect it to shrink—back to roughly the 1956 dimensions—by 1980. The growth was gradual; the contraction will be abrupt.

Source: Reprinted from "The Trimming of the Big American Car," MONEY Magazine, December 1975, by permission of Hans Kung.

manufacturer is equally reliable, it is possible to obtain a general idea of the quality of the makes and models you are considering and the frequency of repair they require.

On all new cars, manufacturers in effect guarantee the general reliability and quality of construction for a specified period of time in a written *warranty* stating that any defective parts and flaws in workmanship will be repaired or replaced at little or no cost to the owner. Most new car warranties cover the first twelve months of ownership or 12,000 miles, whichever comes first. A sample of the new car warranty on a 1978 Cadillac is shown in Figure 10-2.

Warranties are generally transferable, which means that if a used car is sold, the purchaser receives any warranty coverage remaining. Some auto manufacturers allow new car buyers to purchase some form of extended warranty coverage, which increases the length of time (or number of miles) the warranty remains in effect. Manufacturers also often provide warranty coverage on the internal engine parts and drive train of their cars for five years or 50,000 miles. Occasionally used car dealers warrant the drive trains of the late model cars they sell. These warranties are generally for no more than one year or 12,000 miles.

In order to have warranty work done, you are normally required to go to an authorized dealer or a repair shop designated by the dealer. The dealer will reimburse you for repairs done at an independent garage in emergency situations if the repairs are covered by the warranty. Since new car warranties are issued by the auto manufacturer, not the dealer,

Figure 10-2 **Standard New Car Warranty**

Source: Courtesy of Cadillac Motor Car Division, General Motors Corporation.

you should contact the regional manager for the given automotive line if you have trouble getting your dealer to do warranty work. It is important to read the warranty booklet included with a new car and make sure you understand the terms of the warranty. Most warranties are void if the owner has not performed routine maintenance or has somehow abused the car.

Your Old Car: Trade-In or Sell? When you buy a new or used car from a dealer and have an old car you wish to sell, the question of a trade-in arises. Most auto dealers are pleased to take trade-ins. But their interest conflicts with that of their customers: they want to get the trade-ins as cheaply as possible, while their customers want to get as much value as they can from them. The dealer typically attempts to make a profit on both the car being sold and the trade-in made. For this reason, it is best to negotiate a new car purchase without mentioning a trade-in. Once the price has been settled, you can let the dealer appraise your car to determine its trade-in, or wholesale, value. This can then be deducted from the purchase price of your new car. Estimates of wholesale value can be obtained from any of a number of used car guides or through your banker.

Although trading in your old car is convenient, it can mean a substantial loss in savings: you may be able to sell your car yourself for several hundred dollars above the wholesale price. This of course depends on the demand for the kind of car you have. The best way to sell your car is to price it reasonably, run an ad in the classified section of your local newspaper, and be honest with prospective buyers. Sometimes it helps to put For Sale signs on it and park it in a high-traffic area. Trading in your car does eliminate the inconvenience of answering phone calls and showing the car to interested buyers; and since auto dealers generally do not check out trade-ins as closely as private individuals, it may enable you to avoid having to fix up your car. It is best to evaluate the pros and cons of trading in your old car prior to shopping for a new one so that whatever the decision you can make the most of your purchase. Of course, if you sell your car before you buy another, you will have additional funds with which to make the purchase.

Other Purchase Considerations One piece of information you might note when shopping for a new car is its *EPA mileage rating*. The Environmental Protection Agency (EPA) requires manufacturers to post the number of miles per gallon their cars may be expected to get for both city and highway driving. These ratings, which are determined by the EPA through their own tests run on new cars, tend to be a little bit higher than you might get but provide an excellent instrument for comparing the fuel economy of various cars. Another factor to consider is the number of *safety features* built into the car. These features are likely to be similar in new cars since the federal government requires auto manufacturers to meet certain safety standards, but many valuable features may not be present in used cars.

Auto insurance costs, too, should be of concern. Car ratings by insurance companies are based on both their expense of repair and the horsepower with respect to weight. The higher these factors, the more expensive the insurance on them, regardless of your own driving record. It is therefore a good idea to get an estimate of insurance costs on cars you are considering for purchase. Auto insurance is discussed in greater detail in Chapter 15.

Buying an Automobile

Once you have determined how much you can afford to spend and what features you desire, you are ready to begin shopping for a car. If you plan to purchase a new car, you should go to all dealers who have cars filling your requirements. Look the cars over, ask questions, and ask the salesperson for the "best price that includes all costs." Do not even think about making an offer on a car until you have shopped around and found two or three cars that meet your specifications and are priced within your budget. One dealer selling the same brand as another may give you a better deal or more desirable car. Watch out for the sales technique known as "low-balling," in which salespeople indicate to buyers that they will sell cars for less than they actually do. This is used as an enticement to get the prospective buyer to make an offer. Be careful.

Estimating Cost A common method of estimating the dealer's cost on a new car is to deduct 20 percent from the sticker price (see Figure 10-3 for a 1978 car sticker). Most new cars can be bought for between 5 and 10 percent above dealer cost, plus preparation and delivery charges. For example, a car with a $6,500 sticker price would cost the dealer approximately $5,200 (80 percent × $6,500). Allowing for a profit margin of say 8

The Status of Imported Cars: 1977 Data

The table below illustrates the role that imported cars play in the U.S. today. With more and more attention toward energy conservation it is likely that the role of imports will continue to increase unless American auto makers are successful in producing more energy efficient autos. Let's hope that they do.

1977's Top Imports
(New-Car Sales in First Five Months)

1. Toyota	207,515
2. Datsun	167,559
3. Volkswagen	111,143
4. Honda	105,935
5. Dodge Colt	38,352
6. Subaru	29,839
7. British Leyland	29,442
8. Fiat	28,061
9. Plymouth Arrow	25,283
10. Mercedes-Benz	20,918

Source: Reprinted by permission from *Ward's Automotive Reports.*

Figure 10-3 **Window Sticker from a 1978 Cadillac**

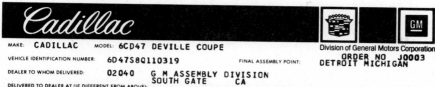

Cadillac

MAKE: **CADILLAC** MODEL: **6CD47 DEVILLE COUPE**

Division of General Motors Corporation

VEHICLE IDENTIFICATION NUMBER: **6D47S8Q110319** FINAL ASSEMBLY POINT: **DETROIT MICHIGAN** **ORDER NO J0003**

DEALER TO WHOM DELIVERED: **02040 G M ASSEMBLY DIVISION SOUTH GATE CA**

DELIVERED TO DEALER AT (IF DIFFERENT FROM ABOVE):

THE FOLLOWING ITEMS ARE STANDARD ON THIS MODEL AT **NO EXTRA CHARGE**	MANUFACTURER'S SUGGESTED RETAIL PRICE OF THIS MODEL INCLUDING DEALER PREPARATION	10444.00

Manufacturer's Suggested Retail Delivered Price for Options and Accessories installed on this Vehicle by Manufacturer

AUTO CLIMATE CONTROL	YL2 FIREMIST EXTERICR COLOR	163.00
AM/FM STEREO RADIO	CB5 VINYL ROOF - PADDED	215.00
STEEL BELTED RADIAL	YL1 LEATHER SEATING AREA	295.00
WHITE WALL TIRES	AV7 W DUAL COMFORT FRONT SEATS - 50/50	198.00
STOWAWAY SPARE TIRE	B93 D DOOR EDGE GUARDS - TWO	11.00
SOFT RAY GLASS	N37 Q TILT & TELESCOPE STEERING WHEEL	121.00
POWER DOOR LOCKS	A90 T TRUNK LID RELEASE & PULL DOWN-POWER	80.00
6 WAY DRIVER POWER	B32 F CARPETED RUBBER FLOOR MATS - FRONT	31.00
SEAT ADJUSTER	B33 R CARPETED RUBBER FLOOR MATS - REAR	15.00
HIGH ENERGY IGNITION	B36 I TRUNK MAT	12.00
DIGITAL CLOCK	C49 N REAR WINDOW DEFOGGER	94.00
FREEDOM BATTERY	K30 C CRUISE CONTROL	122.00
LAMP MONITORS	DF3 E MIRROR - RIGHT SIDE REMOTE CONTROL	34.00
CORNERING LIGHTS	D64 G MIRROR - ILLUM. VANITY - PASSENGER	50.00
AUTO TRANSMISSION	CD4 K CONTROLLED CYCLE WIPER SYSTEM	32.00
POWER STEERING	VK3 X LICENSE PLATE FRONT MOUNT PROVISION	.00
POWER WINDOWS	VJ9 AN CALIFORNIA EMISSION REQUIREMENTS	75.00
DUAL POWER BRAKES	INCLUDES TESTING, EQUIPMENT AND	
FRONT DISC BRAKES	CERTIFICATION NECESSARY FOR	
	REGISTRATION IN THE STATE OF CALIF.	
	VO1 AO HEAVY DUTY COOLING SYSTEM	47.00
	VG7 AV FRONT BUMPER REINFORCEMENT	9.00

THIS VEHICLE IS EQUIPPED WITH A GENERAL
MOTORS ENGINE PRODUCED IN A GENERAL
MOTORS PLANT OPERATED BY THE
CADILLAC MOTOR CAR DIVISION.

THIS VEHICLE HAS BEEN TESTED UNDER AND
CONFORMS TO CALIFORNIA ASSEMBLY LINE
TEST REQUIREMENTS
CALIF. STDS. (GM/MI) HC 0.41,CO 9.0,NOX 1.5.
CERTIFICATION VALUES HC 0.29,CO 3.7,NOX 1.2.

Trim	**023**	Factory Installed Options and Accessories Subtotal	1604.00
Color	**90**	Top **J** Destination Charge	456.00
		TOTAL AMOUNT does not include dealer installed options or accessories, state or local taxes or license fees, except as indicated. TOTAL AMOUNT	12504.00

This vehicle was manufactured in compliance with all applicable Federal Motor Vehicle Safety and Emission Control Standards. This label has been affixed pursuant to Federal law which prohibits its removal or alteration prior to delivery of this vehicle to the actual possession of the ultimate purchaser.

Source: Courtesy of Cadillac Motor Car Division, General Motors Corporation.

percent along with around $300 in dealer preparation and delivery charges, a potential buyer should probably offer $5,916 ($5,200 + [8 percent × $5,200] + $300). Actually it would be wise to offer a little less than this amount, perhaps $5,800, as a first try. The actual amount the buyer offers can also be determined to some extent by the time of year the transaction is negotiated. You can normally get a better deal at the end of a model year than at the start. If you are considering a used car, the wholesale price, listed in various published sources and available through your bank, is your only guide to cost. To buy a used car, you should probably offer a few hundred dollars above the wholesale price.

Making an Offer Whether you are buying a new or a used car, to make an offer you must sign a formal *auto purchase agreement* that specifies an offering price. The purchase agreement will also specify whether or not the offer includes a trade-in; when it does, the offering price will represent the amount in addition to the trade-in you are willing to pay. Because this agreement contractually binds you to purchase the car at the offering price, if accepted by the dealer, you should be certain that you want and can afford the car prior to signing such an agreement. In order to show that you are making an offer in good faith, you may be required to include a deposit of $100 or more with the agreement.

If the dealer accepts your offer, you have bought the car. Unless you offer close to the sticker price, however, the dealer will probably make a counter offer. You can accept the counter offer, reject it, or make another offer. If you reject the dealer's offer, your deposit is returned, and you can go elsewhere to make an offer. It is probably a good idea not to accept a counter offer until you have "slept on it." Hesitation is a good psychological ploy and gives you time to consider some of your other alternatives. The most important point to keep in mind is that your offer can become contractually binding; therefore, be sure that you can live with the offer you make.

Closing the Deal Once your offer has been accepted, you will need to complete the purchase transaction and accept delivery of the car. If you are not paying cash for the car, you can arrange financing through the dealer, at your bank, credit union, or a consumer finance company. The key aspects of these types of installment loans, which can be quickly negotiated if your credit is good, are discussed in Chapter 12. Prior to delivery, the dealer is responsible for cleaning up the car and installing any optional equipment. It is a good idea to make sure that all equipment you are paying for has been installed and the car is ready for use before paying the dealer.

If it is a new car, the dealer will give you sixty to ninety days to bring the car back and have any flaws you find taken care of free of charge. Because of the mass production techniques employed in the automobile industry, annoying flaws in workmanship are quite common in new cars. Used car dealers normally perform only those repairs that they have warranted on cars they sell. When you pay the dealer, you receive in addition to the car a title to it or evidence thereof, operating manuals, warranties, and other instructional materials.

Maintaining Your Automobile

Like any nonfinancial asset, the automobile must be properly maintained and repaired in order to preserve its function as well as to enhance its resale value. Maintenance and repairs should be performed by a dealership or independent garage that will stand behind its work and not do unneeded repairs. Of course, you may choose to do some of the basic maintenance yourself.

Preventive Maintenance The best way to preserve your investment, provide for the maximum effectiveness of your car's engine, and reduce the need for future repairs is to do preventive maintenance. This generally involves regularly scheduled changes and checks of various fluids and filters as well as periodic chassis lubrication and checks of battery, tires, exhaust system, and various other exterior and interior items. Scheduled preventive maintenance programs are usually prescribed by auto manufacturers, and it is a good idea to follow their guidelines.

Repairs Certain types of repairs cannot be eliminated through preventive maintenance. Replacement of brakes and exhaust systems and wheel alignments will ultimately be necessary, no matter how careful your treatment of the car, if you drive it regularly for a year or two. Engine tune-ups are another type of repair that comes with time. Although the manufacturer may specify certain scheduled tune-ups, it normally does not hurt to wait until your fuel economy begins to drop or the car starts to run poorly to make such repairs. For the most part, however, it is best to repair your car promptly to avoid damaging other components. For example, when brake pads or shoes are worn, they should be replaced; if they are not, the brake discs or drums may be damaged. In many cities and states formal safety inspections force people to keep their brake, exhaust, and suspension components in good repair.

Leasing an Automobile

An alternative to purchasing a car is *leasing*, which involves receiving the use of a car in exchange for a contractual obligation to make periodic lease payments over a specified period of time. Auto leases most commonly require monthly payments and run for two to three years. The lease payment is based on the cost of the car, the term of the lease, and the number of miles the car is expected to be driven each year. The lease payment may or may not cover the costs of maintenance. Many leases allow the lessee to purchase the car at a specified price upon termination of the lease agreement. Monthly lease payments generally amount to 3 percent of the cost of the car. For example, to lease a car costing $6,500, you would pay around $195 (3 percent × $6,500) per month.

Leasing is advantageous when the car is being used for business purposes, since the lease cost is a tax-deductible business expense. Leasing is a convenience that allows the individual to obtain use of a car without the sizable outlay often required for purchase. Most auto dealerships and certain independent auto leasing companies can arrange to lease any car desired. Since auto leasing is most often justified for business reasons, you probably will not personally lease a car during your lifetime. (Leasing an auto for personal use is more expensive than owning one because the tax benefits available to businesses that lease cars are not available to individuals who lease cars for personal use.) But if you do lease, remember that you do not own the car and it therefore should *not* be shown as an asset on your personal balance sheet.

Furniture and Appliances

Another group of nonfinancial assets that you will purchase during your lifetime consists of furniture and appliances. Although you can lease these types of assets, most people purchase them. *Furniture* includes any items used for comfort, convenience, or decoration—such as chairs, tables, sofas, paintings, and lamps—that do not by themselves perform any tasks. *Appliances,* on the other hand, do perform some type of task—for example, cleaning dishes, providing visual entertainment, or drying clothes. Ovens, dishwashers, clothes washers, televisions, and toasters are examples of appliances. Typically, appliances operate on gas or electric power and are made up of a variety of electromechanical components. The cost of both furniture and appliances can be high; therefore, it is important to carefully evaluate such items prior to purchase.

Furniture and Appliance Purchase Considerations

Because of the large variety of items that are considered furniture or appliances, the discussion in this section must be limited to only the basic factors affecting the purchase of these types of assets. The four most important considerations when buying either a piece of furniture or an appliance are purchase cost, function, operating and repair expenses, and appearance.

Purchase Cost When contemplating the purchase of furniture or appliances, you should first make certain that what you plan to spend is consistent with your financial goals and budget. Keep in mind that large pieces of furniture and appliances may have reasonably long lives and should be viewed as investments. And before you establish a maximum amount to be spent on a given item, be sure you have a reasonably accurate impression of what its price range will be. Because of the long life of these assets, it is wise to be flexible with respect to cost; you may have to live with what you buy for a number of years. Quite often an extra $50 or $100 can make the difference between a purchase that provides enduring satisfaction and one that affords constant frustration. If you do not have the funds to pay for an item you want, you may well be better off to wait until you do rather than purchase an item of inferior quality.

Function Since both furniture and appliances are purchased primarily to perform some function—for example, a chair is supposed to provide a comfortable place to sit and a clothes washer is expected to get clothes clean—they should be analyzed with respect to how well they perform. In the case of furniture, this might involve examining and testing various items in the showroom; but in the case of appliances, the average purchaser cannot easily assess differences in quality in the store. In fact, the various little features added to supplement an appliance's primary function often make it difficult to compare the products of different manufacturers. For example: Is a dishwasher with a "soak" cycle better than one without such a feature? The best way to get an indication of the quality of a given appliance is to consult some type of consumer buying guide such as the monthly magazines *Consumer Reports* (which publishes its *Annual Buying Guide* in December), *Changing Times,* and *Money.* These are valuable sources of ratings and comparative statistics on furniture, appliances, and many other consumer goods.

Operating and Repair Expenses Since most appliances require a power source such as gas or electricity, their operation involves some expense. An investigation of operating costs of various makes and models may uncover information indicating that the appliances of certain manufacturers are cheaper to operate, or that one type of power is less expensive than alternate forms. You may also find that the presence of an "optional" feature on a certain appliance increases its operating cost. Information on operating costs can be obtained from the consumer publications mentioned above and from friends who have purchased similar types of appliances. It may well be worthwhile to pay an extra $60 for a major appliance that is expected to save $30 a year in utility costs.

In addition to purchase costs and operating costs, there are also repair costs. Both the probable *frequency of repair* and the *cost of repair* for a given item should be considered prior to its purchase. In the case of furniture, the frequency of repair can be gauged by the quality of construction and types of component materials used; if the furniture is solidly built with durable materials, frequency of repair can be expected to be low. Also, the reputation of the manufacturer is usually a clue to the quality of the item, and good quality is often indicative of a relatively low frequency of repair.

Repair frequencies and their associated costs are more easily estimated for appliances than for furniture. Most consumer publications provide relevant data. One consideration in the purchase of an appliance should be the availability of factory authorized repair facilities. Generally, the better the availability of repair facilities, the lower the cost of repairs.

Appearance In our society, whether people are willing to admit it or not, it is not unusual for material possessions to be viewed as an indication of one's social stratum. Appearance is also important merely from the standpoint of visual satisfaction; the way your furniture and appliances

Appliance Service Contracts: Are They Necessary?

Nobody knows how many appliances break down the day after their warranties expire, but it's probably far fewer than many manufacturers selling service contracts would have you believe. Long before warranties expire, the barrage of letters and phone calls begins—all beseeching you to spend anywhere from $20 to $135 a year to extend the service contracts on new appliances and TVs.

Hard statistics on the economics of appliance repair bills versus service contracts are virtually nonexistent, in part because sellers are closemouthed about the topic. William Zabler, national service manager for Sears, Roebuck, claims that Sears doesn't even "keep track of the number of agreements we sell." Some government and private organizations, though, have begun gathering the statistics. Their work is hardly complete, but it tends toward the conclusion that service contracts in general are not a good buy.

Whether to purchase a service contract depends on the type of appliance and the use to which you put it. If you know you are going to subject an appliance to unusual wear, a service contract may make sense. As John Donaldson of the National Bureau of Standards puts it, "Refrigerators and freezers generally work about the same no matter who owns them, but washing machines, toasters and mixers can be worn out by a family that uses them a lot."

look strongly affects the visual environment in which you live. If you are planning to buy new furniture, you will find a large variety of decors from which to choose: contemporary, French provincial, colonial, Mediterranean, for example. Your preferences are likely to change over the course of your lifetime. Thus it is not a bad idea to purchase furniture that will fit in with various decors. The less ornate types of furniture provide greatest flexibility. Another aspect of appearance to consider is the color of the fabrics and other materials from which the furniture is constructed. It is best to coordinate and select colors that are reasonably versatile so that your furniture can be used in a variety of combinations. Of course, the cost of furniture when viewed in light of your budget may force you to be a bit less choosy in your selection.

Appliances do differ in general appearance, although decor is usually not a major consideration in purchasing them. For example, washing machines come in either top or front loading models, and refrigerators come in both side-by-side and freezer-on-top models. Most major appliances come in a number of models, colors, and designs. The choice of model—for example, top loading or front loading washing machine—can largely be left to personal preference. Major appliances that are to be in the same room should be the same color to provide a coordinated look.

You can base your decision on how the appliance performs during the first year. Repairs on color TVs usually decline after the normal 90-day warranty period. During the next few years, according to a Massachusetts Institute of Technology study, the average set requires less than one service call a year. So unless you have a lot of trouble with a set while it's under warranty, it makes little sense to spend $60 to $135 to extend your coverage for a year.

Refrigerators and freezers have a far lower repair-frequency rate than color TVs, the MIT study found. They too are repaired more during the first year of use than during the second through fifth years. Clothes dryers also require infrequent servicing, according to manufacturers. Unless you bought a lemon, spending $20 to $35 on a service contract for any of these appliances is a waste of money. Similarly, it rarely pays to take out a $40 or $50 service contract on a furnace until it is several years old and likely to need parts.

Beware! Bargains Are Not Always the Best Deal
Source: © 1977 Phil Frank. Reprinted by permission.

And some caution should be exercised, because seemingly insignificant differences in design, for example the amount of chrome hardware, may tend to cause significant differences in appearance. Of course, when you are shopping for furniture or appliances, you should give the quality with which they function, purchase costs, and expected operating and repair costs primary attention.

Shopping for Furniture and Appliances

It is a good idea to shop around for furniture and appliances. The shopping process will allow you to educate yourself with respect to the various purchase considerations mentioned in the preceding sections. Salespersons will be able to answer your questions and give you literature on items in which you are interested. In reviewing this information, you should analyze the special features of different brands; and if appliances are to be purchased, you should take particular note of safety features and warranties, as well as operating instructions. Many appliances have warranties on all parts and labor covering the first two years of ownership.

Once you have selected the basic brands and models you are interested in, you should shop for the best deal. Many furniture and appliance dealers will negotiate prices. You may be able to pay less than the amount shown on the price tag if you simply ask. You may be able to learn from friends and business associates which dealers have the best prices. It is sometimes worthwhile to consider the purchase of a floor model or second-hand item. Because furniture and appliances have fairly long lives, you may find that the savings resulting from the purchase of "used" items more than compensate for the slight wear they show. You should be sure that you know what year model you are buying—the preceding year's model or a floor model may be a bargain. And before finalizing your purchase, you should also look into who pays for delivery, whether taxes are included in the price quoted, and whether there are any installation costs. If you are able to plan the timing of your purchases, you can often take advantage of sales on furniture in January and August and on appliances in October and November.

Financing Furniture and Appliance Purchases

Because of the magnitude of the outlay in the purchase of many items of furniture or appliances, it may be necessary to borrow money in order to make the purchase. Of course, before you begin to shop, you should have some idea about whether or not you need financing. Some furniture and appliance dealers offer "90 days same as cash" or "30-60-90 day" financing arrangements, which allow you to pay for the merchandise in three monthly installments without interest. A number of the installment payment plans used to purchase these types of assets are discussed in detail in Chapter 12. If you will need financing on a purchase, you will want to analyze and compare the cost of financing plans offered by various dealers. Differences in the ultimate amount expended can be significant.

Maintaining Furniture and Appliances

To protect your investment in furniture and appliances, you should adequately maintain these items. Be sure to read and follow any cleaning instructions, owner's manuals, or operating instructions that accompany them. In the case of furniture, one important criterion for selection should be the kind of use the item will receive. When a piece of furniture is unsuitable for the use to which it is subjected, maintenance becomes difficult or impossible. For example, durability should be a prime consideration in the purchase of furniture to be used by children. If your appliances require repair, someone who is familiar with the brands you have and has easy access to replacement parts should do the work on them. Remember, the benefits of intelligent purchases can be overshadowed by poor care and maintenance.

Attention thus far in the chapter has been devoted to the more expensive nonfinancial assets (other than housing) that most people consider necessities of life. Other types of expensive nonfinancial assets can be divided into three groups on the basis of the motive for their acquisition: (1) personal and household goods, (2) recreational items, and (3) asset investments.

Other Expensive Assets: Some Basic Comments

Personal and Household Goods

Many assets—such as clothing, dishes, silverware, and small appli-ances—are necessary to allow you to function in today's society. Of course, some people are able to live with fewer such items than others: a wardrobe that contains fifteen shirts may be viewed as a necessity by some people, while others may require only seven shirts. Although a fine line exists with respect to what are necessity items and what are luxuries, the important point is that these types of items are assets for which you spend your hard-earned money. Thus you should consider carefully the costs and benefits associated with their purchase.

Items that are faddish should be avoided since their use is limited. Once in a while, though, it may give you an emotional boost to buy some article that is very much in vogue. Even if it is not really necessary, go ahead and make the purchase, but use some of the fun money you have budgeted. Try not to buy on pure emotion or impulse; ask yourself whether you really need the item and whether the same money might be better spent elsewhere or put into savings and investments. Since household and personal goods normally decline in value over time and cannot be easily sold, they are not good investments. It is advisable to plan purchases, not only of personal and household goods but of all items, to coincide with sale months. The calendar in Figure 10-4 indicates when it is best to buy various items.

Recreational Items

As a result of the shortened work week, the average individual has experienced an increase in leisure time. This free time is often devoted to some type of recreational activity that necessitates the purchase of certain assets. The required outlay may be quite small, as in the case of basketball, or quite large, as in the case of boating.

Important Considerations Before buying these items, you should be certain their purchase does not unbalance your budget or delay your progress toward your personal financial goals. Like cars, many of these assets—boats, campers, motorcycles—may depreciate rapidly in the first year or so of their lives. With this in mind, you might want to look into buying used items. Another major point to consider is that much expensive recreational equipment once acquired receives insufficient use to justify its purchase. People often purchase these types of assets based on rather limited exposure to them or to enhance their social standing rather than for serious use. If you can afford the luxury of purchasing an asset you will use on only a limited basis, that is fine. But it is wise to put off the purchase of an expensive recreational asset until you have

Figure 10-4 **A Calendar of When to Buy**

	J	F	M	A	M	J	J	A	S	O	N	D
Accessories	●							●				
Major Appliances										●	●	
Baby Needs	●				●			●		●		●
Bedding	●	●				●	●	●				
China and Glassware			●									
Drugs and Cosmetics	●											
Fabrics and Notions	●	●		●			●					
Floor Coverings	●	●				●						
Furniture	●	●				●	●	●				
Furs	●	●						●			●	
Garden Supplies			●									
Home Furnishings	●	●			●							
Hosiery		●				●						
Housewares			●		●							
Jewelry, Diamonds	●			●	●							
Lingerie and Sleepware	●			●		●						
Luggage	●				●							
Men's and Boys' Wear	●	●			●	●						
Outdoor Furniture				●								
Outerwear										●		
Resort and Cruise Wear	●											●
Silverware											●	
Sports Goods								●				
Stationery	●						●					
TV and Radios	●											
White Goods	●				●		●	●				
Women's Apparel	●				●							

Source: "Nine Commandments for Smart Shoppers," *Changing Times*, December 1973, p. 8. Reprinted with permission from *Changing Times* Magazine, © Kiplinger Washington Editors, Inc., 1973.

stabilized your finances. You should also consider any other uses for your money that might provide greater satisfaction.

Shopping Around If you are convinced that some type of major recreational expense is justified, on the basis of both expected use and your ability to afford it, then you should carefully shop for the item that best fulfills your needs. Ask someone who is an expert in the activity you are pursuing about what item is best for the type of use you will give it. You do not want to buy a high-powered ski boat if your primary objective in purchasing a boat is to be able to fish. Study patterns of depreciation in the value of the asset you are interested in and consider the possibility of buying it used. As for all major outlays, research the quality, safety, warranties, operating costs, and repair costs of alternative items. Try to get the best value per dollar. Be sure, too, that you consider insurance costs in your analysis, since separate insurance policies are required on major recreational assets. If you do not intend to make a cash purchase, study the various financing plans available. Once you acquire a major recreational asset, be sure to maintain it properly. If you find that you are not really using the asset, sell it quickly so that you can recover as much of your investment as possible.

Asset Investments

Collections Collections of certain types of assets—for example, coins, stamps, antiques, art, automobiles—can be classified as investments since the general expectation is that they will increase in value over time. Not all collections require some type of financial outlay, but those that have a monetary value will show up as nonfinancial assets on your personal balance sheet. While collections are the result of an individual's personal interests, from a strictly financial viewpoint, it is best to collect items that have a good market and are likely to appreciate in value. If the items in a collection are expensive, their value and authenticity should be confirmed by an expert prior to purchase (there are many unscrupulous dealers in collectible items). Unless you specifically budget money to be spent on a collection, outlays for this purpose should be made from fun money. One type of item commonly collected is antique furniture, which is popular due not only to its appreciation in value but also to its utility. It is both an investment and a utility item.

Small Business Ownership Another, rather different, kind of asset that you may have is an interest in some small business. Whether you own only part of such a business or the entire firm, your interest in it will be shown as an asset on your personal balance sheet. Although this asset can be classified as either a financial or a nonfinancial asset, it is considered a nonfinancial asset in this text.

If a small business is your sole source of income, any money you have invested will represent your net worth (or equity) in the business. Just as you wish to increase the net worth on your personal financial statement, you should try to increase the net worth of your small business investments. There are thousands of different types of small businesses ranging from service companies operated by one individual to small manufacturing companies that employ fifteen to twenty people. If you do consider starting or investing in some type of small business, it is a good idea to consult any of numerous books specifically devoted to the formation and management of small business. Also, the Small Business Administration (SBA), which is an agency of the federal government, provides numerous publications and advisory services. When considering small business investment, keep in mind the fact that only about two out of ten new small businesses actually survive.

Summary

Major nonfinancial assets such as automobiles, furniture, and appliances are quite important, since they are relatively expensive items that people are likely to purchase a number of times during their lives. The automobile is probably the most frequently purchased of these nonfinancial assets. The amount an individual can afford to spend monthly on auto ownership can be estimated by deducting all necessary fixed and variable monthly expenditures (other than automotive) from after-tax monthly income. The monthly auto ownership cost can be estimated based on the required finance payments, including taxes, insurance, licenses, and parking, in addition to expenditures that vary with the number of miles driven, such as gas, oil, maintenance, and repairs. By comparing the estimated total monthly cost to the amount of money available each month, it is possible to determine the feasibility of various purchase alternatives. Since depreciation in value is a cost of ownership, it, too, should be taken into account. Other purchase considerations relate to whether to buy a new or a used car, whether to buy an American or an imported car, the size and body style of the auto, the standard and optional features included, reliability and warranties, and whether to trade in or sell the old car.

To buy a car, it is a good idea to estimate the seller's cost and then offer an amount slightly above that. Once the offer is accepted, the buyer must arrange financing, and the dealer must prepare the car for delivery. At delivery the buyer receives the car and its title in exchange for payment. A car should be properly maintained to protect the investment in it. If an auto is going to be used primarily for business purposes, leasing rather than purchasing it may offer certain advantages.

Furniture and appliances represent another group of nonfinancial assets that require sizable outlays. The main considerations in purchasing these assets are cost, function, operating and repair costs, and appearance. People shopping for furniture and appliances should investigate the alternative makes and models in order to determine the type of units they desire. A number of consumer publications provide relevant information. Those who do not wish or are not able to pay cash should compare and evaluate available financing plans. Furniture and appliances should be adequately maintained in order to reduce repair costs and increase their usable lives. Other major nonfinancial assets include personal and household goods, recreational items, collections, and interests in small businesses. Careful selection and conscious avoidance of impulsive buying are important in the purchase of all these types of assets.

Key Terms

appliances
auto depreciation costs
auto purchase agreement
auto reliability
buyer's guides
EPA mileage ratings
fixed (auto) ownership costs
frequency of repair

furniture
installment payments
preventive maintenance
Small Business Administration (SBA)
total (auto) ownership costs
variable (auto) ownership costs
warranty

Review Questions

1. Describe the role of the automobile in today's society. What are the various motives for owning an automobile?

2. Why are automobile ownership costs best divided between fixed costs and variable costs? How would you differentiate between the two?

3. What is meant by *depreciation cost?* Jack Williamson purchased a new Ford Granada on 1 January 1978 for $7,000 and plans to keep it for five years. At the end of five years the car is expected to be worth 45 percent of the original purchase price. How much will that be in cash? Determine the depreciation cost per year and per month on Jack's Granada.

4. Briefly explain the nonfinancial considerations related to auto purchases.

5. Cite the advantages and disadvantages of buying a used car.

6. Describe and differentiate the characteristics of imported cars and American cars.

7. List and discuss the various classifications of automobile size and body style.

8. Explain the difference between reliability and warranty.

9. Is it preferable to trade in your car or sell it yourself? Christy has a '71 Buick that she wants to sell before going home on a summer vacation from college. In what possible ways might she sell the car?

10. Suppose you are shopping for a car. Discuss the importance, if any,

of: (a) EPA mileage ratings, (b) safety features, and (c) auto insurance costs.

11. Describe the entire process of buying an automobile, beginning with making an offer and ending with closing the deal.

12. What is auto leasing? How are lease payments determined? Why is it often preferable to lease a car for business purposes?

13. Briefly discuss the most important considerations regarding the purchase of furniture and appliances.

14. "The benefits of intelligent purchases can be overshadowed by poor care and maintenance of the assets acquired." Explain why this statement is true.

15. Aside from automobiles, furniture, and appliances, describe other nonfinancial assets that are expensive enough to require careful consideration before purchasing.

10-1 Estimating the Boardman's Monthly Auto Spending Capacity

Case Problems

Arthur and Karen Boardman live in Berkeley, a suburb of San Francisco. They have been married for ten years and have two children. Arthur earns $25,000 per year after taxes as an engineer at the San Francisco Water Works Department. For quite some time now, the Boardmans have been considering getting rid of Karen's Pinto hatchback and replacing it with a Ford station wagon. The station wagon is much better suited to the family's needs since they often go on long weekend trips in addition to their annual vacation. To discover whether they can afford a new car, the Boardmans wish to determine the amount of money they will have available each month after meeting the following expenses:

Mortgage Payment		$550	Medical	$ 40
Heat and Light		80	Entertainment	150
Water and Sewage		15	Magazines	.10
House Repairs and Maintenance		30	Insurance	100
Telephone		35	Charity and Gifts	25
Food		300	Scheduled Savings Deposits	200
Clothing: Husband	$20			
Wife	30			
Children	40	90		

Questions

1. Classify the above expenses as either fixed or variable.

2. Calculate the amount the Boardmans will have available each month for automobile expenses.

3. Might they have other sources of funds available to use in order to meet auto expenditures? Explain.

10-2 Can the Boardmans Afford the Station Wagon?

The Boardmans of Case 10-1 can buy a stripped down Ford station wagon for $6,500 from Bill White, the local Ford dealer. Before they buy the station wagon, they want to estimate the total monthly cost of maintaining it. They expect to keep the car for three years, during which they intend to drive it about 48,000 miles. With added accessories like an air conditioner and an 8-track stereo player, the car's total cost is expected to increase by $1,000. The Boardmans decide to buy the wagon with the added accessories. They make a down payment of $2,500 using some savings along with the proceeds they received from selling the Pinto hatchback. They plan to borrow the remaining $5,000 from State National Bank. The loan will be repaid in monthly installments of $164 over a period of three years.

Given below are some of the Boardmans' annual expenses expected to result from their ownership of the station wagon.

Lubricating Oil	$ 60	Repairs and Maintenance	$ 60
License Plates and Road Taxes	132	Gasoline	640
Parking Fees	240	AAA Membership	34
Tires	36	Farmer's Auto Insurance	360

Questions

1. Calculate the total ownership costs per month, dividing the expenses into their fixed and variable costs.

2. Calculate the Boardmans' ownership cost per mile using the projected annual mileage given. How large would the per mile cost be if they instead drove 20,000 miles per year?

3. If the Boardmans know that the station wagon will be worth $3,000 at the end of three years, what effect, if any, will this have on the decision to purchase? Explain.

4. Do Arthur and Karen Boardman have sufficient money available to meet the auto ownership costs? Explain. (Answer the question in light of your findings in Case 10-1. If you did not work that case, you should skip this question.)

"Are Diesel Autos Finally Going to Make It Big?" *U.S. News & World Report,* 13 June 1977, pp. 55–56.

"Buying a Used Car." *Changing Times,* January 1975, pp. 25–28.

"Buying Furniture on a Shoestring." *Consumers' Research,* January 1977, pp. 16–19.

"Commuter Vans Catch On at Corporations." *Business Week,* 28 February 1977, pp. 54–55.

Consumer Reports—Buying Guide 1977. Mount Vernon, N.Y.: Consumers Union, 1977.

Consumers' Research Magazine: Handbook of Buying Issue for Use throughout 1977. Washington, N.J.: Consumers' Research, 1976.

Edgerton, Jerry. "Japanese Cars Have Their Day in the Sun." *Money,* May 1977, pp. 50–54.

"For All the Headaches, You Can Still Start Your Own Business." *U.S. News & World Report,* 26 July 1976, pp. 43–46.

"Gems: A Good Hedge against Inflation?" *U.S. News & World Report,* 7 February 1977, p. 64.

"How Much Does Auto Upkeep Really Cost?" *Better Homes and Gardens,* August 1976, pp. 28 ff.

Klamkin, Charles. *How to Buy Major Appliances.* Chicago: Regnery, 1973.

"The Shift to Midsize Cars." *Business Week,* 14 March 1977, pp. 26–27.

"Shopping Tips: Furniture." *Changing Times,* February 1975, pp. 15–17.

"A Skeptical Look at Appliance Service Contracts." *Changing Times,* August 1976, pp. 29–31.

Tendell, Bob. *New Era Car Book and Auto Survival Guide.* New York: Holt, Rinehart and Winston, 1975.

Weathersbee, Christopher. *Intelligent Consumer: How to Buy Food, Clothes, Cars, Houses.* New York: Dutton, 1973.

Your Automobile Dollar. Chicago: Money Management Institute, Household Finance Corporation, 1975.

Your Equipment Dollar. Chicago: Money Management Institute, Household Finance Corporation, 1973.

Selected
References

Part 4

Managing Your Liabilities

Personal Balance Sheet	
Assets	Liabilities and Net Worth
Financial Assets	**Liabilities**
Nonfinancial Assets	Net Worth

The use of borrowed funds to pay for assets as well as certain goods and services has become the American way of life. Most consumer credit granted is used for financing the purchase of nonfinancial assets such as those discussed in the immediately preceding part of the text. This part of the text therefore considers the basic concepts involved in borrowing, the types of borrowing arrangements available, and methods for managing the liabilities incurred in financing asset purchases. Chapter 11 is concerned with borrowing fundamentals, open account credit, store charges, and bank credit cards. Emphasis is placed on describing why, how, where, and when these types of borrowing should be used. Chapter 12 discusses the negotiated forms of borrowing, which include notes, installment loans, and mortgages.

11

Borrowing on Open Account: Credit Cards and Bank Cards

To provide a basic understanding of the purposes, techniques, and problems of borrowing on open account, this chapter examines the following:

A Preview of Chapter 11

1. How to obtain and use open account credit—store charges and credit cards—in order to make transactions in a fashion consistent with personal financial goals.

2. Why people borrow and the benefits and dangers associated with borrowing.

3. The types of accounts available and procedures for obtaining open account credit.

4. The basic consumer legislation passed to protect the individual's rights as a borrower.

5. The major form of open account credit, the store charge; the methods used to determine finance charges; and the advantages and problems of using this type of credit.

6. The key features and considerations in the use of bank credit cards, which represent an increasingly popular source of open account credit.

The ability to plan, select, and acquire assets is not enough to insure your financial success. You must also become familiar with the opportunities and techniques available for using liabilities to finance the acquisition of assets. One important aspect of liability management is concerned with borrowing on open account, which involves using some type of store charge account or credit card in order to make transactions. Because the availability, costs, and conditions normally included as part of open account credit are likely to vary, you must learn when, in what amounts, how, and where to obtain and use this form of borrowing. A knowledge of these fundamental aspects of open account credit should enhance your ability to achieve your personal financial goals.

The economy we live in today is often called a "credit economy" because of the ready availability as well as liberal use of credit to make various types of purchases. This chapter discusses borrowing on open account, an informal method of borrowing commonly used to finance less expensive goods and services.

Fundamentals of Borrowing

Consumers, businesses, and governments all rely heavily on the use of borrowing to make transactions. Without credit, businesses could not supply the goods and services needed to satisfy consumer demand. The availability of credit to business also provides for higher levels of employment and helps raise our overall standard of living. Local, state, and federal governments use borrowing to implement various projects and programs that result not only in an increased standard of living but in additional employment opportunities as well. Borrowing therefore helps fuel our economy and enhance the overall quality of our lives. Of course, consumers in a credit economy need to know how and when to borrow, whether on an informal basis or through some type of formal negotiation.

Why Borrow?

People typically borrow money for use in paying for goods and services. There are a number of reasons for borrowing. Most commonly, borrowing is used because the total outlay is too large to be paid out of current resources. This is particularly true for people age twenty-five to forty-four, since in many cases they have not had time to accumulate the financial assets required to pay cash outright for major purchases and expenditures. As people begin to approach their mid-forties, their financial assets begin to increase and their debt obligations tend to be reduced.

Most people do not pay cash for *large outlays*, such as purchases of houses and cars, but rather borrow a portion of the purchase price. They then repay their loan on some scheduled basis. In this way, borrowing allows people to obtain the immediate use of an expensive asset even

"Humph! Trying to destroy the American way of life!"

Borrowing Is a Way of Life in the U.S. Today
Source: Bo Brown—Rothco Cartoons Inc.

though this asset may not be fully paid for until a number of years pass. Another reason people sometimes borrow is to meet a *financial emergency*—for example, to cover living expenses and make payments on other loans during a period of unemployment or to purchase plane tickets in order to visit an ill relative. As was indicated in Chapter 5, however, savings should be maintained to meet such financial emergencies and the necessity of borrowing should be avoided if at all possible.

An increasingly common motive for borrowing is *convenience.* Merchants as well as banks have made available a variety of charge cards and accounts that readily allow consumers to charge the purchase of many goods and services. Though in many cases no interest is levied, these credit card purchases represent a form of borrowing since payment is not made at the time of the transaction, and they should be shown as liabilities on the personal balance sheet. In many cases no interest is charged on these delayed payments. Borrowing is also done for *investment* purposes. As indicated in Chapters 7 and 8, investors can arrange to partially finance the purchase of certain securities with borrowed funds. Real estate investments, too, commonly involve borrowed funds.

Benefits of Borrowing

The ability to borrow, regardless of the underlying motive, provides certain benefits to borrowers, savers, merchants, and society in general.

Borrowers As indicated in the preceding section, the *borrower* benefits by being able to obtain expensive goods or services while spreading the payments for them over the future. Borrowers may also benefit from two other factors: taxes and inflation.

Taxes Because those persons who itemize their tax deductions can deduct all interest paid during the year (see Chapter 4), our tax structure provides favorable treatment for borrowers. Of course, the tax deductibility of interest does not fully eliminate the cost of borrowing. For example, assume that you paid interest of $1,000 in the current year and that you are in the 25 percent tax bracket. Table 11-1 illustrates the impact of this interest deduction on taxes, if your income after all deductions and credits other than interest is $18,000. The tax deductibility of the $1,000 in interest causes the taxes to be reduced by $250 ($4,500 − $4,250) and therefore results in only a $750 ($13,500 − $12,750) drop in income after taxes. The $1,000 interest payment actually reduced income by $750 due to the favorable tax treatment of interest. Thus although interest must be paid, our tax structure provides some relief by treating it as a tax-deductible expense.

Table 11-1 **Impact of Interest Deduction on Taxes**

	Without Interest Deduction	With Interest Deduction
Income after All Deductions and Credits but before Interest	$18,000	$18,000
Less: Interest	0	1,000
Taxable Income	$18,000	$17,000
Taxes (25 Percent)	4,500	4,250
Income after Taxes	$13,500	$12,750

Inflation Because inflation reduces the purchasing power of money, the consumer who borrows money and repays it during a period of increased inflation may benefit. The benefit results because the borrower in this situation can repay the debt in dollars "cheaper" than those initially borrowed. For example, assume that you borrowed $2,000 exactly one year ago and you must repay this amount today. Also assume that the purchasing power of a dollar, as reflected in the Consumer Price Index, is such that what cost $1.00 a year ago costs $1.15 today. In other words, the dollar today can purchase only about 87 percent ($1.00 ÷ $1.15) of what it would buy one year ago. Therefore, the $2,000 being repaid today would be worth only $1,740 (87% of $2,000) in terms of the money originally borrowed. Of course, lenders and creditors attempt to adjust the interest rates they charge to reflect the impact of expected inflation on the purchasing power of the dollar.

Savers As was pointed out in Chapter 5, certain financial institutions accept savings deposits from which they obtain funds to loan out. A major portion of the interest paid to the savings institutions on these loans is returned to the depositors. This process of *financial intermediation* benefits savers by giving them a return on their unused funds, while at the same time satisfying the needs of borrowers. Clearly, without the interest paid by borrowers, financial institutions would not be able to pay their depositors interest on savings accounts.

Merchants By offering credit to their customers, merchants can often attract and retain business that might otherwise go elsewhere. The use of credit enables them to sell expensive items such as appliances, autos, and boats that purchasers would not be able to afford were they required to pay in full at the time of purchase. Borrowing arrangements are vital to merchants in two other ways as well: they generally receive credit from their suppliers and borrow the funds needed to extend credit to their customers.

Society In the formative years of our country, borrowing from abroad enabled settlers to buy machinery and equipment needed to build production facilities. As the nation matured, institutions and mechanisms were created to gather and make available funds for borrowing by consumers, business, and government. The borrowing mechanism still remains of key importance to the growth and development of our society. Not only must consumers be able to purchase expensive goods, but business and government too must be able to obtain the financing needed to increase productive capacity, economic growth, and employment and to fulfill growing consumer demand. The ability to borrow is one of the cornerstones of the capitalistic economy in which we live.

Dangers of Borrowing

Although borrowing provides a mechanism whereby consumers, savers, vendors, and society in general can benefit, there are some dangers associated with its use.

Inflationary Effects on the Economy One problem believed to result from the excessive use of consumer credit is inflation. If consumers have too little difficulty in borrowing to purchase goods and services, the demand for these items may rapidly increase, thereby causing prices to rise. This type of *demand-pull inflation* results from too many dollars chasing too few goods and services. Although various types of governmental controls exist for regulating consumer credit, the danger of

"Charge It," "Charge It," "Charge It," . . . Look Out!

"Charge it!" Those two little words are so simple, until the time comes to pay. "I know," writes Mrs. Mary K. Mansour, an Akron, Ohio, reader of Changing Times. *"I learned the hard way about five years ago. And I still have the urge to use those magic words whenever I don't have cash."*

Let her tell how it was, in her own words.

It was easy to get credit cards then. Companies were eager to process your application and encouraged you to go use them right away. I got a gold-toned card once and even was told that I was an exceptional customer. That's when the trouble began.

We had just been married and naturally wanted the best of everything all at once. We had stable income and job security. We wanted a nice home, good clothes, a few luxuries. Did our sparse wardrobes need brightening? Ah, yes, our credit cards! How easy it was to go out and buy! With every intention of paying, we soon ran up a $500 clothing bill in one store alone.

Little by little the fever crept over me. I spent much more on items I charged than if I had to pay cash. I told myself it was all right to buy the prettier $20 handbag instead of the $10 one. It wouldn't show up on my account until next month anyhow.

As the statements rolled in, I never paid much attention to balances. I merely paid the minimum required and, as far as my creditors were concerned, I could go on charging forever. They had me hooked, although I didn't realize it until years later.

When I hit my credit limit on an account, I wouldn't charge on that account for a while, until my balance got down to where I could charge again. Our balances averaged $300 to $500 for as long as we kept charging. But I was confident that all would get paid sooner or later. And my credit cards enabled me to get all I needed for myself and my family.

By then we had two children and I had no job. I got to thinking nothing of

inflationary pressures from liberal use of credit is very real in our economy today. It is interesting to note that advertising people commonly deny that credit can have an inflationary effect. They suggest that if credit or charge account use increases the volume of sales significantly, the fixed costs per unit of producing the item are reduced, thereby resulting in no increase in cost and possibly even a decrease—a portion of which may be passed on to the customer.

Effects of Borrowing Costs Another aspect of borrowing that causes the prices of goods and services to rise is the borrowing costs themselves. Sellers must be compensated for extending credit to consumers; if consumers borrow or use credit to purchase a good or service, they pay

---

charging groceries, haircuts, plants, car repairs. Even our family doctor took credit cards.

How easy and convenient it all was. Then one day it hit us. We had $4,000 to $5,000 tied up just in charge accounts and easy payments!

We tried to figure out what we had to show for it. We couldn't account for anywhere near half of what we'd spent. The clothing was out of style, the groceries gone. In effect, we still owed our doctor. There it was, bigger than we dreamed, the bottom line telling us we were in debt and out of control.

Payments began to exceed the cash coming in. We had to juggle bills, hold off one to pay another. We got deeper in the red and could see no way out. The finance charges grew each month. There were interest charges, previous balances, service charges, late charges. We had so many bills coming in I hated to see the mailman coming. What were we to do?

A bill-consolidation loan was out of the question because, believe it or not, we had little collateral. We were too embarrassed to borrow from relatives. It was just too late.

Well, that's how it was until a year ago. We're still struggling to pay what we still owe, but we charge no more. The stress and worry about paying the bills haunted us until it actually made us sick. It was just too much to handle.

They say, "Guard your credit." You'll never know how wise that is until you've been as close to ruining it as I have. Look at those cards in your wallet. If you use them to buy things you don't really need, don't push your luck. Credit can be like a disease in a weak body. Take it from one who has been there. It's a long, rough road back from "charge it" to "cash only."

Source: "Personal Report—Hooked on Credit and Out of Control," *Changing Times,* February 1977, p. 34. Reprinted with permission from *Changing Times* Magazine, © Kiplinger Washington Editors, Inc., 1977.

interest either directly at a specified rate or indirectly in the form of an increase in the purchase price. Given the fact that consumers pay more when they use credit than when they do not, the use of credit clearly reduces the amount they can purchase. On the other hand, some would argue that the increased cost of goods and services may be offset by the fact that with credit available more goods and services are demanded, thereby possibly lowering their unit costs of production.

Overspending Probably the biggest danger in consumer credit is that it makes it easy for people to overspend, or incur more obligations for future payments than they have income available from which to pay. People who overspend eventually arrive at a point where they must choose either to be delinquent on their payments or sacrifice necessities such as food and clothing. If payment obligations are not met, the consequences are likely to be lawsuits, a damaged credit rating, or personal bankruptcy. The use of a budget as described in Chapter 3 provides a means of assessing your borrowing potential and planning for and using consumer credit while not subjecting yourself to the dangers of overspending.

Open Account Credit

Open account credit, often referred to as *charge accounts,* is a form of credit extended to a consumer in advance of any transactions. Typically a store or bank agrees to allow the consumer to buy or borrow up to a specified limit on open account. Credit is extended as long as the consumer does not exceed the established *credit limit* and payments are made in accordance with the terms specified. When a store issues open account credit it is usually applicable in that store or its branches. A Sears charge account, for example, is useful only in Sears stores; open account credit issued by banks, such as VISA/BankAmericard and Master Charge accounts, however, can be used to make purchases at a wide variety of businesses. In the remainder of this chapter attention is devoted to various characteristics and types of open account credit.

Open Account Credit Illustrated

Consumers who use open account credit can avoid paying interest charges if they pay the full amount of the unpaid account balance each time they are billed. For example, assume that in a given month an individual has charged $15.58 worth of purchases on an open account at a department store. Sometime within the next month, that individual will receive a statement from the store. The statement will show any past unpaid balances, the preceding period's payment, any new charges during the past month, and any finance charges (interest) on the unpaid

Figure 11-1 **Sample Statement Received on Open Account**

DEPARTMENT NUMBER	DATES MONTH	DAY	TRANSACTION DESCRIPTION	CHARGES	CREDITS
99	10	22	PAYMENT		25.00
65	11	04	GLOVES	4.98	
	11	04	STATE TAX	.20	
64	11	04	SKIRTLINER PT	10.00	
	11	04	STATE TAX	.40	

renberg's

TO YOUR PREVIOUS BALANCE	WE ADDED YOUR CHARGES	*WE ADDED YOUR FINANCE CHARGES	WE DEDUCTED PAYMENTS	WE DEDUCTED OTHER CREDITS	THIS IS YOUR NEW BALANCE
$ 182.00	$ 15.58	$ 2.49	$ 25.00	$	$ 175.07

Account Number	Billing Dates		Finance Charge 1½% (Annual Percentage Rate 18%) Computed On Avg. Daily Balance Of	Minimum Amount To Send
	This Month	Next Month		
	11 10 76	12 10 76	$ 165.87	$ 20.00

*To Avoid Additional Finance Charges, Pay "New Balance" Before "Billing Date" Next Month

EXPLANATION OF FINANCE CHARGES

If the "NEW BALANCE" is received by Renberg's, Inc., by the "BILLING DATE NEXT MONTH", no additional FINANCE CHARGE is imposed.

If a FINANCE CHARGE is shown on the front hereof, it is computed as follows: 1½% of the AVERAGE DAILY BALANCE as shown on the front hereof; this being an ANNUAL PERCENTAGE RATE of 18%. When the AVERAGE DAILY BALANCE for a monthly billing period is $33.33, or less, the FINANCE CHARGE for that monthly billing period, at Renberg's option, will be 50¢.

The AVERAGE DAILY BALANCE is determined by dividing the sum of the balances outstanding for each day of the monthly billing period by the number of days in the monthly billing period. The balance outstanding each day of the monthly billing period is determined by subtracting all payments and credits (excepting credits for merchandise purchased and returned within the same monthly billing period) from the previous day's balance, excluding any purchases added to the account during the monthly billing period and excluding any unpaid finance charges.

MINIMUM PAYMENT

A minimum payment of one-tenth (1/10) of the unpaid balance (adjusted to the next highest increment of $5.00) appearing on each monthly billing statement (but not less than $10.00 monthly) PLUS any amount which is past due from previous months must be received by Renberg's, Inc., by the "BILLING DATE NEXT MONTH" as shown on the front hereof.

Source: Courtesy of Renberg's Department Store, Tulsa, Oklahoma. Receivable statement invoice was designed by Mr. Sherman J. Stokes, Credit Manager, Renberg's.

balance. It is also likely to specify a minimum payment. One such statement is shown in Figure 11-1. By evaluating this statement you should be able to gain an understanding of how open account credit works.

Transactions The statement includes the itemized transactions that have occurred between the last billing date (10 October 1976) and the current billing date (10 November 1976). The first of these items is a $25 payment on the account received on 22 October. The other four items are two purchases and the state taxes on them that were charged on November 4. The total cost of these four items is $15.58, as indicated above. Had any merchandise been returned for credit, these items would also be shown on the statement as "credits," and the amounts charged for them would be deducted from the account balance.

New Balance Calculation The $182.00 previous balance shown at the bottom of the statement represents the account balance at the end of the previous billing period. The charges during the current month are added to the previous month's balance; thus $15.58 in charges during the current period is added to the $182.00 previous account balance. Also added to the previous balance are any interest charges applicable to the account—in this case, a finance charge of $2.49. (A detailed discussion of how finance charges are determined will be given in a later section of this chapter.) Finally, any payments received and other credits are subtracted from the unpaid balance to arrive at the new account balance. The $25.00 payment is the only deduction shown in Figure 11-1; apparently no other credits were received during the month. The resulting new balance on the account is $175.07.

Minimum Payment Most open accounts do not require payment of the entire new balance but do require payment of some minimum amount, usually a specified percentage of the new balance. For example, the statement in Figure 11-1 indicates that a minimum payment of $20.00 is required. At the bottom of the reverse side of the statement, the method of calculating this minimum is explained. It is figured as 10 percent of the new balance (in this case, $17.51) adjusted to the next highest increment of $5.00 (in this case $20.00). Of course, any past due charges are added to this amount. Sometimes the open account statement will have a schedule of minimum payments that will specify the minimum payment for various ranges of account balances. In our example, as long as the $20.00 minimum payment is made before the next month's billing date (12/10/77), the customer's credit privileges are not jeopardized.

Types of Charge Accounts

Charge accounts are available in a wide variety and differ primarily with respect to the type of institution issuing the credit. A brief description of each of the key types of charge accounts follows.

Thirty-Day, or Regular, Charge Accounts Commonly offered by certain types of businesses for the general convenience of their customers, the thirty-day account requires the customer to pay the full amount billed within ten to twenty days after the billing date. If payment is made within the specified period, no interest is charged. Only when payments are received after the due date is an interest penalty levied. Thirty-day accounts generally do not require the use of a charge card. These types of accounts are typically offered by electric companies, telephone companies, doctors and dentists, and repair services, for example.

Revolving Charge Accounts One very popular form of credit is the revolving charge account, which allows customers to continue to purchase goods as long as they do not exceed the credit limit established or let their account become delinquent through failure to make specified minimum payments. The line of credit, or total amount of credit customers can have at any point in time, varies with their financial assets and past credit record. These types of accounts generally require charge cards and are most common in department and clothing stores where it is likely that customers will make several purchases each month. Sometimes revolving charge accounts are referred to as *budget* or *option* charge accounts. The example discussed earlier and the statement in Figure 11-1 illustrate the technical aspects of a revolving charge account. The finance charge levied on the unpaid balance of this kind of account is usually 1½ percent per month. In addition to department and clothing stores, most large oil companies offer revolving charge accounts through their gasoline credit cards. Some of these companies, however, exclude gasoline from the revolving charge, thereby allowing only items such as tires, batteries, and accessories to be charged on a revolving basis.

Bank Credit Card Accounts An increasingly popular type of charge account is the bank credit card account, which is issued by a commercial bank and allows consumers to charge purchases at any stores accepting the appropriate credit card. This kind of account is similar to the revolving charge account except that it is not issued by a specific store. Card holders are given credit limits beyond which they are prohibited from charging. At the end of each month the bank card holder will receive a statement itemizing all charges, payments, and interest. Stores that do accept these types of cards must pay a fee in the form of a specified percentage of the sales made to people using the card. In addition to being able to make purchases on credit, holders of bank credit cards can also easily obtain *cash advances*—loans on which interest begins to accrue immediately—from designated commercial banks without having to make any formal application. The two dominant bank credit cards are VISA/BankAmericard and Master Charge. These cards are accepted by various banks and retail stores worldwide and in the U.S. by state governments, universities, medical groups, and record clubs, for example. A detailed discussion of bank credit cards is included in a later section of this chapter.

National Credit Cards National credit card accounts are similar to bank credit card accounts in that a credit card enabling the holder to charge purchases at a variety of locations is issued to qualified applicants. Typically, the businesses willing to accept these cards are travel-related—hotels, motels, airlines, and restaurants. In order to obtain one of these cards, the applicant must agree not only to pay interest on any outstanding balances but also to pay an annual fee of about $20 for the privilege of using the card. Issuers are private businesses such as American Express, Diners Club, and Carte Blanche. These national credit cards are most popular among businesspeople because of the convenience of charging travel and entertainment related to business activities. Not only the charges for such business expenses but also the fee paid to purchase the card is deductible for tax purposes. Because of the business orientation of these cards, the credit standards that must be met in order to hold them are higher than those required for bank credit cards, but the credit limit is also higher than that received on bank credit cards.

Opening a Charge Account

For the sake of convenience, people often maintain a variety of charge accounts. The ranking of items purchased using credit cards shown in Table 11-2 tends to confirm their popularity as a device for making relatively routine purchases. Although open account charges do increase the account holders' risk of overextending their budget, at the same time they serve as a useful way to keep track of expenditures. Since it is likely that you will establish charge accounts during your lifetime, you should understand the procedures used to obtain open account credit. Generally, formal credit application procedures are not required for thirty-day charges. Revolving charge accounts, bank credit card accounts, and national credit card accounts, however, all require formal application procedures as described below.

Credit Application To obtain open account credit, an application must be filled out. Applications are usually available at the store or bank with which the account is to be held. Sometimes you can have them mailed to you. Applications for national credit cards and gasoline credit cards can be found at businesses accepting these cards or obtained by request from the companies that issue the cards. The information normally requested

Table 11-2 **Ranking of Items Purchased with Credit Cards**

Rank[a]	Item
1	Clothes for Adults
2	Gasoline
3	Major Appliances
4	Children's Clothing
5	Christmas Presents
6	Gifts
7	Household Goods
8	Vacations
9	Drugs and Medicines
10	Eating Out in Restaurants for Pleasure
11	Food and Groceries
12	Toys

[a]Rankings are from the most common to the least common items purchased using credit cards.

Source: Reprinted with permission from *The General Mills American Family Report, 1974–1975: A Study of the American Family and Money* (Minneapolis: General Mills, 1975), p. 89.

on these applications is concerned with family, housing, employment and income, assets and liabilities, existing charge accounts, and credit references. It should be provided as accurately and thoroughly as possible since it will be verified in the process of the credit investigation.

Credit Investigation Once the credit application has been completed and returned to the store or bank, the applicant is subjected to a credit investigation. In the case of local department store charge accounts requested by people who have lived in the community for a few years, the entire investigation may take only a matter of minutes since the store can get a credit report from the local credit bureau over the telephone. But in situations where the local credit bureau does not have sufficient data on the applicant, the store may ask the credit bureau to investigate the applicant's credit. This may involve contacting the credit references listed on the credit application or, in the case of someone who is new to the community, corresponding with the credit bureau in the town in which the applicant previously lived. Because most local credit bureaus are connected to one another by computer, they sometimes can get credit information from other cities in a matter of minutes. Stores themselves will sometimes check with the references the applicant has provided in order to avoid having to pay a credit bureau to do so.

The local *credit bureau* is typically established and mutually owned by local merchants and banks. It collects and stores credit information from its members on people living within the community and makes this information available for a specified fee to members who request it. If the information requested can be transmitted over the phone, the cost of an inquiry is typically only a few dollars. In situations where the credit bureau must obtain, either through its own investigations or from another credit bureau, additional information in order to update the applicant's file the cost of the report may run as high as ten dollars. Local credit bureaus are linked together nationally through the Associated Credit Bureaus, Inc., which provides guidelines and mechanisms for obtaining credit information from almost any area of the United States. Note that credit bureaus merely provide credit information; they do not analyze the information and make the credit decision. That is the responsibility of the store or bank involved.

Credit Decision Using the data provided by the credit applicant along with any credit information obtained from the credit bureau, the store or bank must decide whether or not to grant credit. Quite often some type of *credit scoring scheme* is used to make the credit decision. By assigning values to factors such as income, existing debts, and credit references, an applicant's overall credit score can be developed. If it compares favorably with the established acceptable range of scores, the applicant will be given credit; if not, no credit will be extended. Sometimes borderline cases are granted credit only on a limited basis. For example, a large department store that normally limits the outstanding balance of its revolving charge accounts to $500 might give a customer who scores poorly in the credit analysis a revolving charge account with a $100 credit limit. Even when a formal credit scoring scheme is used, the credit analyst is normally empowered to offer nonstandard credit terms when such action seems appropriate. Applicants who are granted credit are notified and sent a charge card along with materials describing the credit terms and procedures to be used.

Important Consumer Credit Legislation

When you apply for consumer credit of any kind, you should be well-versed in the legal obligations of the store or bank from which you are requesting credit. There is always a possibility that your rights may be violated. Over the last decade, several important pieces of consumer legislation affecting the extension of credit have been passed. The major concerns of this legislation have been credit discrimination based on sex or marital status; disclosure of credit information; mailing, error complaints, and cash discounts on bills; disclosure of interest charges; loss of credit card; and recourse on defective merchandise charged. Each of these aspects of open account credit is discussed briefly below.

Credit Discrimination Based on Sex or Marital Status As of October 1975 the *Equal Credit Opportunity Act* made it illegal for a creditor to

© 1974 by NEA, Inc.

"All right, I'll cut out the mumbo-jumbo. The reason we can't give you bank credit is because you're only a woman."

Credit Discrimination Based on Sex or Marital Status Is Illegal
Source: Reprinted by permission of NEA.

discriminate on the basis of sex or marital status when considering a credit application. The act was passed in order to extend to women the credit rights already held by men. Specifically, the act prohibits prospective creditors from asking about an applicant's sex, marital status, and child-bearing plans. Lenders are required to view the income of women in exactly the same fashion as they do the income of men. In addition, they must consider alimony and child support as part of women's income. There are severe penalties for the violation of this law.

Disclosure of Credit Information On 25 April 1971, the *Fair Credit Reporting Act* went into effect. It includes numerous provisions, among which are the following: First, credit reports must contain accurate, relevant, and recent information about the personal and financial situation of credit applicants. Second, only bona fide users of financial information may review credit files. Third, consumers who are refused credit or who find their borrowing costs increased as the result of a credit investigation must be informed of the reasons for such actions as well as the name and address of the reporting credit agency. And perhaps most important, the credit reporting agencies must let individuals review their credit files personally and correct any inaccurate information. This legislation protects consumers with respect to the content as well as disclosure of their credit files. Of course, consumers should protect the quality of their credit rating by paying their bills promptly and meeting all other terms of open account or more formal credit agreements.

Mailing, Error Complaints, and Cash Discounts on Bills As a result of errors and abuses in credit billing and the poor handling of credit complaints that resulted primarily from the use of computer-generated bills, the *Fair Credit Billing Act* became effective in October 1975. One provision of the act requires creditors to mail bills at least fourteen days prior to the payment due date and to include all credits and refunds on the bill for the period in which they occur. Another provision requires creditors to respond within thirty days to customer inquiries concerning a billing error complaint and to resolve the complaint within ninety days of the acknowledgment. During the period the complaint is being resolved,

---

Your Credit File: Important Questions and Answers

As a result of the Fair Credit Reporting Act you have certain rights to examine as well as question your credit files. The following questions and answers may help you better understand these rights.

Q. How do I arrange to find out about my credit file?

A. Go personally to the local credit bureau (address listed in the Yellow Pages under "Credit Reporting Agencies") and ask to see your file. If an advance request is made in writing, this can be handled over the telephone.

Q. What information does the credit bureau have to give me?

A. It must disclose all information in your file, together with the sources of that information.

Q. How can I correct an error in my file?

A. If an error is noticed, ask the credit bureau to delete it. If you disagree with the findings, file a written statement to that effect. The credit bureau must at

the creditor is prohibited from collecting the bill or issuing an unfavorable credit report as a result of the disputed charge. A third provision of the act allows merchants to give cash discounts of up to 5 percent to customers who pay cash instead of using credit. Since the merchants have to pay credit card companies such as VISA/BankAmericard, Master Charge, and American Express for the privilege of accepting customers' cards, this act allows them to pass the savings on to those who choose not to use credit cards. The Fair Credit Billing Act also includes a provision concerned with the credit purchaser's recourse to the creditor; this provision is discussed in greater detail in Chapter 12.

Disclosure of Interest Charges Another major piece of consumer legislation is the *Consumer Credit Protection Act.* Commonly referred to as the *Truth in Lending Law,* it initially went into effect 1 July 1969 and was amended effective 28 October 1975. The directives for complying with the act are outlined in *Regulation Z,* which was issued by the Federal Reserve Board. Its most significant provision is the requirement that, prior to extending credit, all lenders disclose both the dollar amount of finance charges and the annual percentage rate charged. This enables credit applicants to make valid comparisons of alternate sources of credit. Such a disclosure is included on the reverse side of the statement shown earlier in Figure 11-1.

your request notify all persons who have used your file in the past two years of the changes made therein.

Q. How will I know if a credit report caused me to lose a loan?

A. If a formal credit report was involved, then you must be given the name and address of the credit bureau involved.

Q. Can just anyone get credit information on me?

A. No. It can be made available to you, to lenders, to the government, or to a court (upon a court order).

Q. What can I do if I have a complaint?

A. Call the credit bureau, and find out how much it costs to see your credit file. Get them to remove any items that are wrong or inaccurate. The law gives you a right to challenge what's said against you.

Source: Adapted with permission from *Everybody's Money,* Education Department, Credit Union National Association, Inc.

The *dollar amount* of finance charges includes all interest and fees that must be paid in order to receive the loan. The *annual percentage rate (APR)* is the true rate of interest paid over the life of the loan, and it must be calculated in the manner outlined by the law. Note that on open account credit creditors cannot specify in advance the dollar amount of interest since they do not know how much will be purchased on the account. The annual percentage rate on these accounts can be stated, however, since there are no fees charged other than interest. Remember, it is your right as a consumer to be told the dollar amount and APR on any financing you consider.

Loss of Credit Card The Consumer Credit Protection Act noted above requires each credit card to contain some form of user identification on

In Plastic We Trust

Under the Fair Credit Billing Act of 1975, merchants can give discounts of up to 5% to customers who pay in cash instead of with credit cards. In theory, both customers and merchants could benefit: cash customers wouldn't have to support their card-carrying brethren by paying the higher prices caused by widespread credit-card use; merchants would save on costly paperwork and on the fees they pay the credit-card companies (about 3% of sales for Master Charge and BankAmericard).

In practice, almost no one is benefiting because almost no one is offering discounts to cash customers. In a recent survey of dozens of companies, *Money* found only a handful offering cash discounts. A spokesman for the elegant Stanford Court Hotel in San Francisco simply murmured that cash discounts are "not appropriate. Credit cards are a service to our customers." Arthur Landen, controller of one of Chicago's largest furniture dealers, was more forthright: "If we do it across the board, we have to raise our prices by 5%." Fearing theft, many sellers, and buyers, don't like to keep a lot of cash on hand. Besides, credit cards encourage impulse buying, an urge few sellers want to dampen.

Still, it never hurts to ask. Among the firms that told us they did offer discounts, some, like the Ramada Inn in Southfield, Ind., are trying to perk up business in off-peak periods. Still others, like Dorman-Winthrop Clothiers in Los Angeles, used to charge credit-card customers extra before that practice was banned by the billing act; now Dorman-Winthrop offers discounts for cash. One restaurant, the Coach House in Chicago, has gone so far as to print two menus—one for cash customers, the other (5% higher) for users of American Express cards, the only credit card the restaurant accepts.

Source: Reprinted from "In Plastic We Trust," MONEY Magazine, September 1976, p. 42, by special permission; © 1976, Time Inc.

it—generally a picture or user signature—and limits the liability of the credit card owner in the instance the card is lost or stolen to a maximum of $50 per card. It also requires credit card issuers to send to their account holders a stamped, self-addressed envelope (used to notify the issuer if the card is lost or stolen) and an explanation of the card holder's rights at the time of issue. If the issuer fails to do this, the card holder cannot be held liable for even the first $50 of loss. In addition, companies are prohibited from sending unrequested credit cards to potential users. Credit cards can be sent only in response to a request or application for them.

Recourse on Defective Merchandise   One of the 28 October 1975 amendments to the Consumer Credit Protection Act concerned the right of credit card holders to recourse on unsatisfactory merchandise charged on their account. This amendment applies for the most part to situations in which the credit used to make a purchase is provided by someone other than the seller—through the use of a bank credit card, a national credit card, or an outright loan from some financial institution, for example. The amendment allows people who have used credit to purchase goods or services that do not perform satisfactorily to stop paying the lender if they, after "good faith" attempts, cannot satisfactorily work out their disagreement with the seller.

By placing some of the burden of guaranteeing the value of what is purchased on the lender, the amendment has caused lenders to be more concerned with the reputation of the providers of the goods or services being financed. While this amendment applies only to situations in which the amount contested exceeds $50, it does allow you to protect yourself in instances where you have financed major purchases of goods or services that prove to be defective.

Credit Card Insurance

Before the passage of the Consumer Credit Protection Act, the liability of credit card holders for charges made on lost or stolen cards was virtually unlimited. The card holder was held liable for all charges made prior to the time when the issuer received written notice that the card was lost or stolen. In order to protect themselves against the consequences of the possible loss or theft of their credit cards, many people would purchase credit card insurance. Today this is no longer necessary since the credit card holder's liability in the instance of loss or theft of the card is limited to $50. In fact, under the Consumer Credit Protection Act your liability is the lesser of two amounts: that charged on your card prior to notification of the issuer or $50. Clearly, quick notification of the issuer when a card is lost or stolen is important. In order to afford yourself maximum protection, it is a good idea to keep a list of credit card numbers along with the addresses provided by the issuers for use in situations where cards are lost or stolen and to destroy credit cards that you do not plan to use.

Credit Counselors

If you carefully plan and prepare budgets to guide you in managing your finances, it is likely you will never need to seek the advice of a credit counselor. Unfortunately, many people, through poor management of their finances, impulse buying, and general overextension of credit, find themselves in financial difficulties they are unable to resolve. People in these straits should seek professional financial counseling in order to avoid *personal bankruptcy*, which is a legal form of financial failure that provides relief to the overextended consumer.

The National Foundation for Consumer Credit sponsors nonprofit credit counseling centers in many communities. These centers are normally supported by local businesses, financial institutions, and educational, religious, and service organizations. They employ counselors who assist overextended consumers in preparing budgets for both spending and debt repayment. If necessary, the counselors will negotiate with those to whom money is owed to establish workable schedules for the repayment of outstanding debts. Quite often the counseling service will collect money from the consumer and distribute it to those owed by the consumer.

In addition to the National Foundation for Consumer Credit, various other community, social, business, and financial organizations sponsor or offer credit counseling services. A list of such services can usually be obtained from a large bank, other lending institutions, or the local Chamber of Commerce. Profit-making organizations that specialize in acting as middlemen between consumers and creditors also provide counseling services. Their counselors generally attempt to reduce the size of payments, the size of the debt outstanding, or both. Because of their high fees, however, these profit-making credit counseling services are not recommended. The best program consumers can follow is to properly budget, plan expenditures as well as debts, and maintain an emergency fund so that they will never become overextended.

Store Charges

Open account credit offered by various types of retail merchants is referred to as *store charges*. Because it is quite likely that you will use these types of charge accounts, it is a good idea to understand the following: the methods of computing finance charges, advantages and disadvantages of charge accounts, and certain precautions that should be taken in using them. Each of these items is briefly discussed below.

Methods of Computing Finance Charges

Since merchants do not know how much you will charge on your account, it is impossible for them to specify the dollar amount of interest you will be charged. But they can and must, according to the Truth in Lending Law, disclose the percent interest they charge and the method they use to compute finance charges. (See the example of such a disclosure on the reverse of the statement presented earlier in Figure 11-1.) The three basic techniques for computing finance charges are the previous balance method, the average daily balance method, and the adjusted balance method.

In the examples that follow, the transactions noted are taken from the statement presented in Figure 11-1. The monthly interest rate used is $1\frac{1}{2}$ percent, which represents an annual rate of 18 percent. (Although $1\frac{1}{2}$ percent is the most common rate, in some states usury laws governing interest rates may establish a lower interest rate ceiling on balances above a specified amount, such as $1,000.) Any credit purchases made during the current month are not subject to a finance charge if paid before the billing date specified. Finance charges are computed only on unpaid balances from previous months' purchases. In other words, if the full amount of the monthly bill is paid before the billing date of the following month, no further finance charges will result.

Previous Balance Method A commonly used method for computing finance charges, the previous balance method is the most expensive for the consumer since interest is charged on the outstanding balance at the beginning of the billing period. In Figure 11-1, $182.00 is the balance at the beginning of the period—the previous balance on which interest would be calculated. The resulting finance charge for the period using this method would be $1\frac{1}{2}$ percent of $182.00, or $2.73.

Average Daily Balance Method In the average daily balance method, the interest is applied to the average daily balance of the account over the billing period. The calculations used to compute this balance do not reflect purchases or returns of purchases made during the billing period. The interest charges and the methods of computing interest using the average daily balance were shown in Figure 11-1.

The billing period, which extended from 10 October 1976 through 10 November 1976, included 31 days. The outstanding balance for the first 11 days of the period (October 11 through October 21) was $182.00, while the outstanding balance for the remaining 20 days of the period (October 22 through November 10) was $157.00 ($182.00 − $25.00 payment). The average daily balance of $165.87 can therefore be calculated as shown in Table 11-3 by weighting the various balances according to the number of days they were in existence and then averaging them. By multiplying the average daily balance of $165.87 by the 1½ percent interest rate, the $2.49 finance charge shown on the statement in Figure 11-1 results. When the average daily balance method is used, $2.49 is the finance charge, while the previous balance method yielded a $2.73 finance charge. Thus the average daily balance method is clearly less expensive than the previous balance method and therefore preferable. It is commonly used by stores that offer revolving charge accounts.

Table 11-3 **Calculation of Average Daily Balance**

	Number of Days (1)	Balance (2)	Weighted Balance [(1) × (2)] (3)
	11	$182	$2,002
	20	157	3,140
Total	31		$5,142

$$\text{Average Daily Balance} = \frac{\$5,142}{31 \text{ days}} = \$165.87$$

Adjusted Balance Method In the adjusted balance method of calculating interest the interest charge is applied to the balance remaining at the end of the billing period (ignoring purchases or returns made during the billing period), which results in lower finance charges than under either of the other methods described. In the example, the account balance at the end of the billing period would have been $157.00 ($182.00 − $25.00 payment). When the 1½ percent interest charge is applied to this balance, the resulting finance charge is $2.36, as compared to $2.73 and $2.49 in the other two cases. A comparison of the results of using these methods is given in Table 11-4. Because the finance charge varies with the method used to determine the account balance, the wise consumer determines which method is used prior to buying on credit.

Advantages of Using Store Charges

The most significant advantage of store charges is that by charging purchases, customers can delay payment until the end of the billing period. Note, however, that because of the high cost of the finance charges levied on balances carried from period to period, there is no real advantage to delaying payment beyond the end of the billing period. The advantages to be obtained from proper use of store charges are briefly described below.

Table 11-4 **Summary of Finance Charges for Example**

Method of Determining Balance	Balance (1)	Rate (2)	Finance Charge [(1) × (2)] (3)
Previous Balance	$182.00	1.5%	$2.73
Average Daily Balance	165.87	1.5	2.49
Adjusted Balance	157.00	1.5	2.36

Interest-Free Loans   To carry charges without penalizing customers costs stores money. This is one of their business expenses, and it is reflected in the price you pay for their goods or services. Since you pay for store charges, you might as well maximize the benefits you receive from them. By delaying payment to the end of the billing period during which your purchases were made, you can receive an interest-free loan for up to thirty days. You can thus, without penalty, keep your money in some interest-earning form until the payment is due.

Record Keeping, Protection against Defects, and Credits Store charges provide detailed records of transactions in the form of monthly statements. Because there may be errors in these statements, it is advisable to save receipts and check them against the statement entries before paying. It is also easier to resolve any disagreements you might have with businesses over goods or services purchased if you have not yet paid for them. If you charge your purchases, you will have approximately thirty days to make sure that they are satisfactory. If they are not, you can refuse to pay off your account. In addition, when you purchase an item on credit and later wish to return it, you need only have the store credit your account. Some stores credit your account for returns whether the purchase was charged using the store charge or a bank charge. In this way the purchase price can be written off the books and no cash must change hands. Some stores use due bills to compensate customers who return items purchased for cash. Due bills can be used only to make purchases within the store and thus are less advantageous than the system of crediting the account, since they make another purchase necessary.

Preferred Customer Status Customers who have charge accounts normally receive preferred customer status, which provides benefits such as notification of forthcoming sales, invitations to special shopping events limited to credit card holders, and check cashing privileges. Although these benefits may be rather limited, many people find them appealing.

Convenience Some people find the use of store charges convenient since it eliminates the need to write a check each time a purchase is made. By charging all transactions during the month, the customer has only to write one check to pay each monthly bill. This convenience is a particularly important consideration for people who make a large number of transactions at a given store during the month.

Use in Emergencies A final advantage of store charges is that they provide a means for purchasing needed items when sufficient cash is unavailable. With proper budgeting and planning, the consumer should be able to avoid running short of cash, but charging a needed item because of a shortage of cash may be justifiable in some situations. A tendency to run short of cash on a regular basis, however, signals the need to reevaluate one's budget.

Disadvantages of Using Store Charges

The use of store charges has two major disadvantages: (1) there is a tendency to overspend, and (2) high interest costs add to the price of purchases.

Tendency to Overspend People who do not use budgets tend to forget that what they charge must eventually be paid for. The credit card gives them a sense of buying power that may not be supported by actual income. One of the consequences of this type of overspending is a tendency not to pay the full amount of the bill. And since consumers who overspend end up without sufficient funds to cover their bill, they make only the minimum payment and thus incur finance charges. If their overspending is not curtailed, the size of their unpaid balance carried from period to period may become so large it cannot be paid without curtailing the purchase of some necessity items. A realistic budget as well as good budget control should help avoid this type of overspending.

High Interest Costs on Unpaid Balances The rate of interest charged on unpaid balances carried from month to month is usually quite high. The 1½ percent per month commonly charged represents an 18 percent annual rate. Since most consumer loans can be obtained at annual rates between 9 percent and 15 percent, people who need to borrow money should not do so through the use of store charges. Clearly, store charges should be paid off in full each period and not used as a type of loan to finance the purchase of goods and services.

The Effective Use of Store Charges: Some Precautions

If you use charges without close coordination with your budget, you may overspend and have to carry an unpaid account balance to the following period. In order to avoid doing this, it is advisable to enter all charges (as if you had paid cash) on your budget expense record as soon as they are made (see Chapter 3). If you wait to record expenditures until you are billed for them, you will probably overspend your budget. You should charge only as much as your budget indicates you can afford.

When charging a purchase of a good or service, be sure to read the charge slip before you sign it. Make sure that the items and amounts as well as the total amount shown are correct. Once you sign the charge slip, you have in effect indicated that you have purchased and agreed to pay for whatever is shown on the slip. Most merchants will correct errors if you later discover them, but this process usually provides unneeded headaches. Also, always keep your receipts and check them against the amounts shown on your monthly statement. Make sure that the amounts charged have been correctly recorded on your statement. By checking both charge slips and monthly statements for accuracy, you may save yourself many dollars. It is not unusual for merchants to make mistakes in recording transactions, and, unless you check for errors, they may go unnoticed at your expense.

Bank Credit Cards

As indicated earlier, bank credit cards are becoming an increasingly popular form of open account credit. The two dominant bank credit cards, VISA/BankAmericard and Master Charge, should not be confused with national credit cards, such as American Express, Diners Club, and Carte Blanche. As illustrated in Figure 11-2 in the comparison of 1974 sales charged with each of the above-named cards, the bank credit cards account for far more sales than do the national cards.

Bank credit cards are usually free to those who qualify financially; applications for them can be obtained from sponsoring banks and participating merchants. Since no restrictions exist, many people have both VISA/BankAmericard and Master Charge cards. These cards can be used not only to charge goods and services but also to obtain cash advances at any of the many banks that sponsor them. Merchants who accept bank credit cards must pay a fee ranging as high as 6 percent of the dollar amount of bank credit card transactions accepted. Although this may seem costly, the opportunity to make purchases on credit is expected to appeal to consumers and add significantly to the volume of business. The remainder of the chapter briefly considers the features, use, and future prospects of bank credit cards.

Features of Bank Credit Cards

Bank credit cards are quite similar to revolving charge accounts except that they are issued by a third party—a bank—and can be used to borrow money. Because of their potential for use in thousands of businesses and

Figure 11–2 **Sales Charged Using Bank and National Credit Cards, 1974**

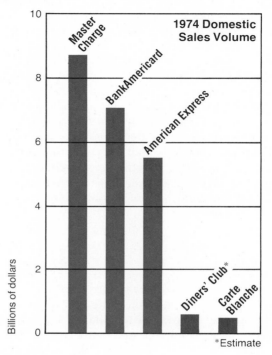

Source: "The Big Charge Cards Adjust to a Different Future." Reprinted from the 4 August 1975 issue of *Business Week* by special permission. © 1975 by McGraw-Hill, Inc.

banks, they can be of great value to consumers. Individuals who do make use of them, however, should be thoroughly familiar with their basic features.

Line of Credit The line of credit provided the recipient of a bank credit card is set by the card issuer for each card issued. It is the maximum amount the card holder can owe the issuer at any point in time. The size of the credit line is dependent on both the request of the applicant and the results of the issuer's investigation of the applicant's credit and financial status. Lines of credit offered by issuers of bank cards can reach $3,000, but for the most part they range from $300 to $1,000. Most issuers of bank credit cards do not take any action against card holders until they have extended their account balance beyond the stated maximum by 20 percent or more. For example, if your credit limit were $500, you would probably not be notified you had exceeded your credit limit until your outstanding balance had exceeded $600, which is 20 percent above the

$500 line of credit. Because in most cases account balances are only checked prior to transactions greater than $50, it is not especially difficult to exceed the credit limit established. Of course, as new and more sophisticated computer-based systems are used to monitor bank credit card accounts, credit limits will be more strictly controlled.

Merchandise Purchases Merchants who participate in a given bank credit card program can generally be recognized by the bank credit card insignia they affix to the door of their business and display in their advertisements. When you purchase goods or services with bank credit cards, the key information—account number, name, and expiration date—is imprinted from the card onto the sales slip, the amount of the purchase is filled in on the sales slip, and you are asked to sign. Be sure to check the accuracy of the purchase prices recorded before you sign the sales slip. You will be given a copy of the slip for your records. Merchants can determine whether you are the legitimate user of the card by comparing your signature with that on the card, by checking the card's number with a printed list of numbers of invalid cards, by requiring additional identification (such as a driver's license), or by verifying over the telephone that you are an account holder in good standing and that the card you present has not been lost or stolen. Merchants make these checks because bank credit card issuers hold them responsible for losses experienced as the result of accepting a lost or stolen bank credit card charge.

Cash Advances A bank credit card holder can obtain a cash advance, or loan, from any bank participating in the given credit card program. These cash advances are transacted in the same fashion as merchandise purchases except that they take place at a commercial bank. Of course, the bank, like the merchants who participate in these programs, checks to be sure the card user is legitimate and the line of credit will not be exceeded as a result of the advance. Some banks will not make cash advances for amounts less than fifty dollars.

Interest Rates on Bank Card Charges The rate of interest applied to bank card charges is usually $1\frac{1}{2}$ percent per month or an annual percentage rate of 18 percent, whether transactions involve purchases or cash advances. In some states these rates may be limited by usury laws, and in some areas the rate of interest on merchandise purchases may differ from that on cash advances. It is also not unusual for the rate of interest on cash advances above a certain amount, such as $1,000, to be lower than that on advances of smaller sums. Generally speaking, the rate of interest on bank credit cards is comparable to rates on store charges. The legal requirements with respect to disclosure of interest costs and related information are no different for bank credit cards than for other

Peeling Away Excess Credit Cards

Almost any solvent American these days can get a credit card. To qualify for a BankAmericard or Master Charge card at many banks, all you need is a decent credit rating and an income of about $7,000 a year. It doesn't take much more—$10,000 to $12,000—to qualify for one of the travel and entertainment cards—American Express, Carte Blanche or Diners Club.

The question is: How many cards do you really need to carry, and which ones? For most people, one of the bank cards may be enough. Heavy travelers may need more, but BankAmericard and Master Charge have grown so fast in the 1970s that one or both now are accepted almost anywhere credit cards can be used. Doctors, lawyers and even traffic cops in some states accept bank cards. Each of the bank cards has nearly 2 million outlets worldwide.

No travel and entertainment card comes close to that. American Express and Diners Club have about 350,000 outlets here and abroad and Carte Blanche has about 250,000. Diners Club, the oldest of all credit cards, for many years was accepted in numerous spots abroad where no other cards could be used. But both American Express and the bank cards appear to be closing this gap. Spencer Nilson, who publishes a credit-card industry newsletter, has found U.S. bank cards catching on almost everywhere in Europe.

Most establishments that once took only American Express, Carte Blanche or Diners Club cards now take bank cards too. Even the president of Carte Blanche can't name a prominent restaurant that takes his card exclusively. Still, a certain cachet clings to the travel and entertainment cards. Asked to describe the difference between Diners Club and bank cards, Diners Club president R. Newell Lusby says, "If you want to go into a suburban hardware and charge some fertilizer, you might use a bank card. But if you want to go to the finest hotels and restaurants—the Plaza-Athénée or the Tour d'Argent in Paris—you need Diners Club." He's only half right—while the Tour d'Argent does not take bank cards, a Master Charge is acceptable at the Plaza-Athénée.

Travel and entertainment cards do have a corner on some higher-priced shops such as Brooks Brothers and Van Cleef & Arpels, the jewelers. Diners Club and American Express used to stick pretty much to those types of stores. "We're not competing for the appliance store trade," says John Andersen, American Express' vice president for marketing. . . .

A bank card may not be enough, however, for people who travel very much. It is the nightmare of every business or vacation traveler to run out of money in a strange city. In such a fix, the best card to have is probably the American Express card.

American Express will cash a cardholder's check for up to $500 worth of its traveler's checks in 600 offices in 120 countries. It has installed machines in 16 U.S. airports to dispense traveler's checks up to $500 and deduct the amount from the customer's checking account. The fee for these services is the price of the traveler's checks—1% of their face value. At many U.S. hotels, cardholding guests can also cash checks up to $50, because American Express guarantees payment. It is also trying to get U.S. banks to honor its card in cash-dispensing machines.

Diners Club and Carte Blanche also have arrangements with hotels to cash checks for their members. The limit per check—$250—is higher than American Express', but far fewer hotels participate. Diners Club will advance $100 at its foreign offices and charge that amount plus a $4 fee, to the member's credit-card account—a service unavailable from American Express. . . .

Travel and entertainment cards charge a flat $20-a-year membership fee. To run up that annual charge on a bank card, at 18% interest, you'd have to have an average unpaid monthly balance of $112. By avoiding cash advances and paying promptly, bank-card members can generally escape finance charges. "I've suggested to our people to get rid of everything but bank cards in order to save membership fees," says Gerard Seagriff, travel services manager at J.C. Penney Co. Penney reimburses employees for expenses quickly, so they can avoid interest charges.

Even for prompt payers, however, bank cards may not be free too much longer. New York's Citibank has begun charging a minimum of 50¢ a month to anyone who uses his card that month. Most Minnesota banks charge $15 a year for bank cards, but the interest rate on purchases after 25 days is held to 12% by state law. Many bankers predict widespread fixed charges on bank cards within five years. . . .

With bank cards and travel and entertainment cards, you can charge almost anything. Still, you might want another card or two in your pocket. The major retail chains with their own nationwide cards—Sears, Penney and Montgomery Ward—take no outside cards. If you drive a lot and like to charge gasoline, tires and repairs, you may want a card from your favorite oil company. Sunoco and Phillips stations do take nongasoline credit cards. But acceptance is spotty at stations of some big companies—Exxon, for one.

With those major exceptions, the best combination of cards for most people seems to be Master Charge or BankAmericard (or both—they're free) and American Express. Whether you want a rug in Marrakesh, a bundle of extra cash in Monte Carlo, or a hairdo in Minneapolis, one of those cards will swing the deal.

Source: Excerpted from "Peeling Away Excess Credit Cards," MONEY Magazine, December 1976, by special permission; © 1976, Time Inc.

forms of consumer credit. In the case of purchases of merchandise and services, the specified interest rate is comparable to rates on store charges, and as with store charges, it is applied only to unpaid balances carried from previous periods. Interest on cash advances is charged on a daily basis for the actual number of days the cash advance remains unpaid.

The Statement If you use a bank credit card, you will receive monthly statements showing all transactions, payments, account balances, finance charges, credit available, and the required minimum payment. See Figure 11-3 for a sample bank credit card statement. Merchandise and cash (advance) transactions are separated in these statements due to the different methods used to calculate interest on them. Any payments received by the bank credit card issuer are applied to cash advances until they are paid off and only then applied to merchandise purchases. For example, in Figure 11-3, the entire $200 payment is used to reduce the cash (advance) balance outstanding. Note, too, that interest is applied using the adjusted balance method, which applies interest to the balance remaining at the end of the billing period.

Good-Bye BankAmericard, Hello VISA

An $8 million advertising campaign began 1 April 1977 to explain the conversion of BankAmericard to VISA. Although some 46 million persons are card holders, the name of the card differs from one country to the next. In the United Kingdom, it is the Barclay card; in Canada, the Chargex. Other names include Banco de Bilbao, Carte Bleu, Summitomo, Banc Union, and Banco Credito.

The switch to a single name, VISA, was designed to show how BankAmericard is keeping up with the life-styles of its global card holders. The move is intended to position the card not only against Master Charge, but also against such travel and entertainment cards as Diners Club, Carte Blanche, and American Express, since the VISA card will be accepted in 110 countries. Final changeover is expected to be completed by 1 October 1979.

Source: Adapted from Louis E. Boone and David L. Kurtz, *Newsletter for Contemporary Business,* March 1977, part 5. Copyright © 1977 by The Dryden Press, a Division of Holt, Rinehart and Winston, Inc. Reprinted by permission of Holt, Rinehart and Winston, Inc.

Figure 11–3 **Sample Bank Credit Card Statement**

DATE	REFERENCE NUMBER	TRANSACTION DESCRIPTION	AMOUNT
09/13/76	4640092120058221	U NEED UM TIRES	259.40
	I4644091726100494	TULSA OK	
09/28/76	4640092830008019	*** PAYMENT RECEIVED ****	200.00-
09/22/76	4640101320049319	SUNOCO DX PREMIER FREEWAY	2.00
	I4450101200203856		

RETAIN THIS PORTION FOR YOUR
RECORDS

PREVIOUS BALANCES	PAYMENTS AND CREDITS	BALANCE SUBJECT TO FINANCE CHARGE	PERIODIC RATE	FINANCE CHARGE	ANNUAL PERCENTAGE RATE	PURCHASES AND ADVANCES	NEW BALANCES
MERCHANDISE 67.25	MERCHANDISE .00	MERCHANDISE 67.25	MER 1.5%	MERCHANDISE 1.00 *	MERCH. 18%	MERCHANDISE 261.40	MERCHANDISE 329.65
CASH 278.25	CASH 200.00	CASH 78.25	CASH 1.5%	CASH 1.15 *	CASH 18%	CASH .00	CASH 79.40
TOTAL 345.50	TOTAL 200.00	TOTAL 145.50		TOTAL 2.15		TOTAL 261.40	TOTAL NEW BALANCE 409.05

* **FINANCE CHARGES** ACCRUED AFTER THE CLOSING DATE WILL APPEAR ON NEXT STATEMENT

YOUR ACCOUNT NUMBER	CREDIT AVAILABLE	CLOSING DATE	MINIMUM PAYMENT
	190.95	10/18/76	OF 21.00 BY 11/12/76

TOTAL MINIMUM PAYMENT = CURRENT MONTH'S MINIMUM PAYMENT AND AMOUNT PAST DUE FROM PREVIOUS BILLING, IF ANY. TO AVOID ADDITIONAL **FINANCE CHARGE** , PAY TOTAL NEW BALANCE BY DUE DATE.

PAYMENTS MUST BE <u>RECEIVED</u> NO LATER THAN THE "DUE DATE" TO BE CREDITED ON YOUR NEXT STATEMENT. ALL INQUIRIES MUST BE MADE WITHIN 60 DAYS.

NOTICE: SEE REVERSE SIDE FOR IMPORTANT INFORMATION

Source: Reprinted by permission.

Payments Users of bank credit cards can avoid future finance charges by paying the total new balance shown on their statement each month. For example, if the $409.05 total new balance shown in Figure 11-3 is paid by the due date of 12 November 1976, no additional finance charges will be incurred. If card holders cannot pay the total new balance, they can pay any amount as long as it is greater than the minimum payment specified on the statement. They do, however, incur additional finance charges in the following month. The minimum payment of $21 for the statement shown in Figure 11-3 represents 5 percent of the total new balance rounded to the next dollar. Had the balance been less than $200, the bank card issuer would have required a $10 payment or the total balance if it were less than $10. If card holders fail to make the minimum payment, they are in default of the bank credit card agreement they signed when they received the card, and the bank issuing the card can take whatever action is deemed necessary.

Returning Merchandise When you return merchandise purchased with your bank credit card, the merchant to whom you return it will issue a credit on your bank credit card. The credit is transacted in the same fashion as a purchase and will appear on your statement as a deduction from the statement balance. If you purchase a good or service and have problems with it, you may not have to pay the bank credit card company for the purchase if you have attempted in "good faith" and failed to resolve the problem with the merchant. This protection provided by the Consumer Credit Protection Act was described earlier. It applies only when: (1) the purchase was made within your home state or 100 miles from your current mailing address, and (2) the purchase price is greater than $50. Of course, if the problem is resolved in the merchant's favor, you will ultimately have to pay.

Effective Use of Bank Credit Cards

Bank credit cards, like store charges, can be quite helpful tools if used properly. They have the same basic advantages and disadvantages as do store charges.

Interest-Free Loans Like store charges, bank credit cards provide short-term, interest-free loans on the purchase of goods or services as long as each monthly statement is paid in full by the due date. The high rate of interest—$1^{1}/_{2}$ percent per month or 18 percent per year—on balances carried from period to period makes it inadvisable to make purchases on bank credit that cannot be paid off in full at the end of the current period. The use of the bank credit card to obtain cash advances is also inadvisable due to the high rate of interest charged on such loans. Bank credit cards should be used only to charge merchandise and services, and monthly statements should always be paid in full to avoid any finance charges. Use of the card in any other fashion signals poor personal financial management.

Consolidated Statement of Expenses Probably the most valid reason for using a bank credit card is to consolidate your records of purchases. No matter how many and varied the stores at which bank credit card transactions occur, the consumer receives only one statement that records them all. This greatly simplifies the record-keeping process. Another benefit of a consolidated statement of expenses is that only one check need be used to make the payment for the many purchases transacted. Thus not only time but also the service charges on checks can be saved.

A Word of Caution One of the real dangers of bank credit cards results from the fact that they are so easy to use. Many people have a tendency to forget they must eventually pay for the merchandise charged with their bank card. But each time they make a transaction using their bank credit card, they are incurring a liability to the issuer of the card. Bank card charges should be limited to those items budgeted. Only in financial emergencies should bank credit card holders use their credit to make nonbudgeted transactions, leave a portion of the bank card balance unpaid, or receive cash advances on account. If used properly, the convenience and widespread acceptance of bank credit cards makes them worthwhile devices for the efficient management of personal finances.

The Future of Bank Credit Cards

Due to their widespread acceptance and the rapid advances in computer technology, bank credit cards are expected to replace cash in transactions of all types. As was discussed in Chapter 5, the development and linking together of electronic funds transfer systems (EFTS) and point of sale (POS) terminals will virtually eliminate the use of currency, coin, and checks in our society. In the not too distant future, each person will have a card that can be used to make all transactions. Paychecks will be deposited directly into people's bank accounts and the banks will be authorized to make certain fixed payments from these deposits. All other transactions will be made using the credit card. They will be electronically transmitted to the appropriate bank account and result in a series of bookkeeping entries. For example, if you buy a $50 radio at Store X, your credit card will be inserted in a terminal at the store, and the account number and information regarding the purchase will be transmitted to your bank. Upon receipt of this information, the bank will deduct $50 from your account and deposit it in Store X's account. If the store's

"The rich are beginning to carry nothing but credit cards, so starting immediately, we'll have to rob from the poor and give to the destitute."

In the Future, Credit Cards Will Replace Cash

Source: Saturday Evening Post, March 1975, p. 18. Reprinted with permission from The Saturday Evening Post Company, © 1975.

account is not at the same bank as the customer's, the bank will electronically transfer the $50 to the appropriate bank.

Loans, loan payments, and payment of bills will all be transacted using the bank card. Regular statements will continue to be issued, but the system will make it virtually impossible to overdraw an account. Merchants will be certain to receive immediate and full payment for their goods and services. Although the need for pocket money to pay for inexpensive convenience items may continue for some time into the future, eventually bank cards will be used exclusively in all transactions.

Summary

People who use open account credit, whether in the form of store charges or bank credit cards, do so for several basic reasons: to finance large outlays, to cover financial emergencies, for the sake of convenience, or to finance investments. The ready availability of credit provides benefits: consumers can obtain a good or service now and pay for it later; interest payments receive favorable tax treatment; and inflation makes delayed payments advantageous. Savers, merchants, and society in general benefit from the opportunity to buy on credit. There are disadvantages to the use of open account credit, however: possible inflationary effects on the economy, the high cost of finance charges, and the consumer's tendency to overspend.

The key types of open account charges include: thirty-day, or regular, charge accounts; revolving charge accounts; bank credit card accounts; and national credit cards.

Over the past decade, certain important pieces of credit legislation, including the Equal Credit Opportunity Act, the Fair Credit Reporting Act, the Fair Credit Billing Act, and the Consumer Credit Protection Act, or Truth in Lending Law, have provided the consumer with numerous protections related to the disclosure of credit information; mailing, error complaints, and cash discounts; disclosure of interest charges; loss of credit cards; credit discrimination; and recourse on defective items purchased on credit.

Store charges are open accounts offered primarily by retail merchants, who charge interest on the unpaid account balances. The account balance on which interest is charged may be determined using the previous balance method, the average daily balance method, or the adjusted balance method. The use of store charges is appealing. They provide short-term, interest-free loans; they are convenient; they can be helpful in financial emergencies; the cost of issuing them is included in the price of merchandise; they simplify record keeping; unsatisfactory purchases and credits can be more easily handled; and the account holder receives preferred customer status. Still, these charges facilitate overspending, and the interest charges levied on unpaid balances are high.

Bank credit cards, which can be used to purchase merchandise or to obtain cash, are usually available free to those who meet certain financial requirements. The amount of the line of credit extended depends on the credit worthiness of the individual. If used correctly, bank credit cards can provide short-term, interest-free loans and also allow account holders to consolidate the records of numerous purchases in one statement. The cost of carrying unpaid balances and/or cash advances is usually 18 percent per year, which is normally too expensive to justify their use in this fashion.

In the future, the use of bank credit cards in conjunction with the computer will replace the use of both checks and cash for making most transactions.

Key Terms

adjusted balance method
American Express
annual percentage rate (APR)
average daily balance method
bank credit card
budget charge account
Carte Blanche
cash advance
Consumer Credit Protection
Act (1969, 1975)
credit bureau
credit card
credit card insurance
credit counselor
credit investigation
credit limit
credit scoring scheme
demand-pull inflation
Diners Club
Equal Credit Opportunity Act
(1975)
Fair Credit Billing Act (1975)
Fair Credit Reporting Act
(1971)

financial intermediation
interest penalty
line of credit
Master Charge
minimum payment
national credit card
National Foundation for
Consumer Credit
open account credit
option charge account
overspending
personal bankruptcy
previous balance method
regular charge account
Regulation Z
revolving charge account
store charges
thirty day charge account
Truth in Lending Law
VISA/BankAmericard
usury laws

Review Questions

1. Why do people borrow? How does the borrowing mechanism benefit savers? Are there any dangers associated with borrowing? Explain.

2. Sue Grillot works as a chemotherapist, earning $15,000 per year before deduction of interest and taxes. She is in the 20 percent tax bracket. Illustrate the impact of taxes on her borrowing costs, assuming she paid $750 in interest during 1977.

3. What is open account credit? Explain the workings of: (a) a regular charge account and (b) a revolving charge account.

4. Distinguish between bank credit cards and national credit cards. Give examples of each.

5. Briefly describe the steps involved in opening a charge account, from both the customer's and the creditor's point of view.

6. How does recent consumer credit legislation relate to: (a) credit discrimination based on sex or marital status; (b) disclosure of credit information; (c) disclosure of interest charges; (d) loss of credit card; and (e) recourse on defective merchandise purchased on credit?

7. What are the provisions of the Fair Credit Billing Act of 1975?

8. Describe the methods used for computing finance charges.

9. Explain the advantages and disadvantages of using store charges.

10. What is the line of credit? Explain.

11. How does a person make a purchase using a credit card? What are the benefits of making this type of charge? Explain.

12. How large is the rate of interest charged on a bank card? What, if any, are the legal requirements with respect to disclosure of interest rates?

13. One of the key features of bank credit cards is the monthly statement. What does this statement disclose? Why are merchandise and cash (advance) transactions separated?

14. "If used intelligently, bank credit cards can be quite useful tools." Comment on this statement.

15. "In the future, plastic money will be replaced by Electronic Funds Transfer Systems." Do you agree or disagree with this statement? Explain.

11-1 The Andersons' Department Store Statement: How Much Is Owed?

Case Problems

Sean and Amy Anderson, a couple in their late twenties, reside in Cambridge, a suburb of Boston. Sean is employed by Norton International, and Amy is a school teacher. Six months ago, they established credit at a fashionable department store, where they often make purchases. They used to pay the full amount on all their bills before the due date. Of late they have not been able to budget their expenses correctly, and when their most recent bill from the department store arrived, it showed a previous balance of $215. The store had levied a finance charge of 15 percent per annum (APR) on the unpaid amount. The Andersons' statement from the department store is on page 400. The statement covers all account activity in the thirty-one day period beginning 16 August 1978 and ending 15 September 1978.

Questions

1. Calculate the average daily balance that would be used by the department store to determine the applicable finance charges.

2. How large is the finance charge levied on the above balance?

3. Give the new balance that would be shown on the statement.

4. Using the same details as shown above, calculate the finance charges by:

Department Number	Dates Month	Dates Day	Transaction Description	Charges	Credits
100	8	30	Payment		$45.00
105	9	02	Fashion Wear	$18.26	
335	9	02	Hosiery	22.54	
271	9	02	Footwear	17.10	

To Your Previous Balance	We Added Your Charges	We Added Your Finance Charges	We Deducted Payments	We Deducted Other Credits	This Is Your New Balance
$215.00	$57.90	$?	$45.00	$0	$?

Account Number	Billing Dates This Month	Billing Dates Next Month	Average Daily Balance	Finance Charge (1¼%) Computed on Average Daily Balance	Minimum Amount to Send
070652981	9 15 78	10 15 78	$?	$?	$20.00

Note: If a finance charge is shown, it is calculated by taking 1¼ percent of the average daily balance. Purchases made during the current billing period are not included in the calculation of the average daily balance. This calculation results in an annual percentage rate of 15%.

(a) The previous balance method.

(b) The adjusted balance method.

5. Which method of computing finance charges do you prefer? Explain your answer.

11-2 Explaining Credit Card Procedures to the Carpenters

Ellwood and Angela Carpenter are a newly married couple in their mid-twenties. They reside in Columbia, Missouri. Angela is a senior at the University of Missouri and will graduate in the summer of 1978. Ellwood recently started working as a sales representative for Hoover Corporation. He supports both of them on his monthly salary of $1,050 after taxes. At present the Carpenters pay all of their expenses in cash or by writing a check. They would, however, like to use at least one of the major bank credit cards. Because neither Ellwood nor Angela is familiar with the procedure for opening a credit card account, they approach you for help.

Questions

1. Advise the Carpenters on how they should go about filling out a credit application.

2. Explain to them the procedure that the bank will probably follow in processing their application.

3. Explain how the bank arrives at a credit decision.

4. Would you offer the Carpenters any advice with respect to "the correct use of the card"? Explain.

Selected References

"Buying On Credit." *Consumers' Research*, September 1976, p. 41.

"Check Out Your Credit Rating." *Better Homes and Gardens*, May 1977, pp. 240–245.

"Cobleigh, Ira U. *What Everyone Should Know about Credit before Buying or Borrowing Again.* New York: Simon and Schuster, 1975.

"Credit Cards: Growing Concern Over Your Privacy." *U.S. News & World Report*, 23 February 1976, p. 43.

"Credit Rules That Give Women a Fair Shake." *Changing Times*, May 1977, pp. 13–15.

"Don't Be in the Dark about Credit Terms." *Better Homes and Gardens*, January 1976, pp. 45 ff.

"Don't Let the Credit Pushers Trap You!" *Changing Times*, April 1976, pp. 15–16.

Griffin, Al. *Credit Jungle.* Chicago, Ill.: Regnery, 1971.

Hendrickson, Robert A. *The Cashless Society.* New York: Dodd, Mead, 1972.

"Higher Costs Coming for Credit Card Users." *Changing Times*, December 1976, pp. 35–36.

It's Your Credit: Manage It Wisely. Chicago: Money Management Institute, Household Finance Corporation, 1970.

"Merchants of Debt." *Time*, 28 February 1977, pp. 36–40.

Meyer, Martin J. *Credit Cardsmanship: How to Survive the Credit Card Nightmare and Turn Plastic into Gold.* New Rochelle, N.Y.: Farnsworth/Hawthorn, 1971.

"New Credit Laws Give You a Better Break." *Changing Times*, November 1975, pp. 29–31.

"New Rights When You Buy on Time." *Consumer Reports*, May 1976, p. 302.

"Rating Your Credit—Another Threat to Privacy." *U.S. News & World Report*, 16 August 1976, p. 62.

"Somebody Has a File on You." *Changing Times*, August 1975, pp. 41–44.

12

Consumer Loans: Single Payment, Installment, and Mortgage

A Preview of Chapter 12

To provide a thorough understanding of consumer loans and the role they should have in financing major purchases, this chapter considers the following:

1. The fundamental aspects of single payment, installment, and mortgage loans.

2. The organization and operation of various consumer lending institutions.

3. Finance charges, annual percentage rates of interest, and other key features in single payment loan agreements.

4. Finance charges, annual percentage rates of interest, and payments required on installment loans.

5. Major components and special features of installment purchase agreements and the methods commonly used to determine interest refunds on early repayment of installment loans.

6. The types, sources, coverages, application procedures, costs and other features, and closing costs and related procedures associated with mortgage loans.

While the foregoing chapters have been devoted to financial planning and the selection and acquisition of appropriate financial and nonfinancial assets, little attention has been given the equally important problem of determining appropriate methods for financing major purchases. In the course of a lifetime, almost every individual must find answers to questions such as: "How do I obtain temporary financing?" "Where can I borrow money?" "How can I finance the purchase of a new automobile?" "What financing methods are available for purchasing a new home?" Knowledge of the sources, types, characteristics, costs, and methods for obtaining single payment, installment, and mortgage loans should provide you with the ability to resolve these and other problems related to asset financing.

The preceding chapter illustrated that although the use of open account credit is not essential to the achievement of financial goals, it does help people plan and live within their personal financial budget. More important to the long-run achievement of financial goals are single payment loans, installment loans, and mortgage loans. These long-term liabilities are most commonly used to finance the acquisition of durable assets such as appliances, furniture, automobiles, and housing that are likely to be too expensive to purchase out of current funds. Sometimes, too, they may serve to finance nondurable items, for example, education and vacations. Of course, the extent to which these types of borrowing are used must be dictated by personal financial plans and budgets. And since they provide financing to cover the cost of necessity items that cannot be purchased with current resources, proper management of these long-term liabilities is quite important.

Types and Sources of Consumer Loans

The major difference between open account credit, which was discussed in the preceding chapter, and consumer loans is the formality of the lending arrangement. While open account credit results from a rather informal arrangement, consumer loans are negotiated formal contracts that specify terms for borrowing and repaying relatively large amounts. The formality of the consumer loan is necessary since, compared to open account charges, it is long-lived and involves significant amounts of money.

Types of Consumer Loans

Consumer loans can be broken into three main categories based on type of repayment arrangement and purpose: single payment, installment, and mortgage. Each of these types of loans is briefly described below.

Single Payment Loans Single payment loans are made for a specified period of time at the end of which full payment is due. They are generally used to finance purchases that are expected to be repaid within a year and usually have maturities ranging from thirty days to one year. Sometimes single payment loans are made to finance purchases or pay bills in situations where the cash to be used for repayment is known to be forthcoming in the near future. Thus they serve as a form of *interim financing*. In other situations single payment loans are negotiated on short notice in order to meet some unexpected need.

Installment Loans Installment loans are repaid in a series of fixed, scheduled payments rather than a lump sum. These loans are typically made to finance the purchase of a good or service for which current resources are inadequate. The repayment period is usually six months or more. Table 12-1 shows the monthly payments, finance charges, and total costs of a $1,000 installment loan for a variety of annual percentage rates and maturities. Installment loans have become a way of life for most consumers; they are popular because they provide an organized mechanism that permits people to "buy now and pay later" in fixed monthly amounts that can readily be incorporated into the budget. The process of using installment loans to finance purchases is often referred to as "buying on time."

Mortgage Loans The mortgage loan, which was briefly discussed in Chapter 9, is a type of installment loan used to finance the purchase of real estate, especially homes. It is so named because the lender takes a mortgage—the legal right to the property for which the loan is made in the event the borrower defaults—in order to secure the loan. Most mortgage loans have maturities of ten to thirty years and require the borrower to make monthly payments. Without mortgage loans, most people would find it nearly impossible to purchase a home due to the magnitude of the required outlay. Although the mortgage loan is just a type of installment loan, it is given special attention in this chapter due to its overwhelming importance in the management of personal finances.

Sources of Consumer Loans

Loans can be obtained from any of a number of possible sources, including commercial banks, credit unions, consumer finance companies, life insurance companies, savings and loan associations, sales finance companies, pawnshops, remedial loan societies, and friends and relatives. The selection of a lender often depends on both the rate of interest charged and the ease with which the loan can be negotiated. Table 12-2 provides a summary of the characteristics of the major sources of non–real estate consumer loans, all of which are discussed below.

Commercial Banks Because they offer various types of consumer loans at good rates of interest, commercial banks are a popular source of

Table 12-1 **Cost and Payment Data
for a $1,000 Installment Loan**

Annual Percentage Rate	Length of Loan (Months)	Monthly Payments	Finance Charge	Total Cost
9.25	6	$171.19	$ 27.14	$1,027.14
	12	87.57	50.84	1,050.84
	24	45.80	99.20	1,099.20
	36	31.92	149.12	1,149.12
10.5	6	171.81	30.86	1,030.86
	12	88.15	57.80	1,057.80
	24	46.38	113.12	1,113.12
	36	32.50	170.00	1,170.00
12	6	172.55	35.30	1,035.30
	12	88.85	66.20	1,066.20
	24	47.07	129.68	1,129.68
	36	33.21	195.56	1,195.56
13	6	173.04	38.24	1,038.24
	12	89.32	71.84	1,071.84
	24	47.54	140.96	1,140.96
	36	33.69	212.84	1,212.84
15	6	174.03	44.18	1,044.18
	12	90.26	83.12	1,083.12
	24	48.49	163.76	1,163.76
	36	34.67	248.12	1,248.12
18	6	175.53	53.18	1,053.18
	12	91.68	100.16	1,100.16
	24	49.92	198.08	1,198.08
	36	36.15	301.40	1,301.40

Source: "Why You May Be Paying Too Much for Credit," *Changing Times*, August 1976, p. 8. Reprinted with permission from *Changing Times* Magazine, © Kiplinger Washington Editors, Inc., 1976.

consumer loans. Their rates of interest on single payment, installment, and some mortgage loans are lower than those charged by many other lenders due to the fact that they take only the best credit risks and are able to obtain relatively inexpensive funds from their depositors. Because their terms are good, the demand for their loans is generally quite high, and they can be quite selective in making consumer loans. Typically, banks lend only to customers with good credit ratings who can demonstrate an ability to make repayment in accordance with the specified terms. They also give preference to loan applicants who are account holders. The fact

Table 12-2 Major Sources of Non–Real Estate Consumer Loans

Credit Source	• Commercial Banks	• Consumer Finance Companies
Type of Loan	• single payment loans • personal installment loans • passbook loans • check-credit plans • credit card loans	• personal installment loans
Lending Policies	• seek customers with established credit ratings • often require collateral or security • prefer to deal in large loans such as auto, home improvement and modernization, with the exception of credit card and check-credit plans • determine repayment schedules according to the purpose of the loan • vary credit rates according to the type of credit, time period, customer's credit rating, and the security he can offer • may require several days to process a new credit application	• often lend to consumers without established credit ratings • often make unsecured loans • often vary rates according to the size of the loan balance • offer a variety of repayment schedules • make a higher percentage of small loans than other lenders • maximum loan size limited by law • process applications quickly, frequently the same day as the application is made
Cost	lower than some lenders because they: • take fewer credit risks • lend depositors' money, which is a relatively inexpensive source of funds • deal primarily in large loans which yield a larger dollar income without an increase in administrative costs	higher than some lenders because they: • take greater risks • must borrow and pay interest on money to lend • deal frequently in small loans which are costly to make and yield a small amount of income
Common Range of Annual Percentage Rates [a]	• 15%–18% credit card and check-credit plans • 11%–18% unsecured loans (in Canada, 11%–12%) • 8½%–12% secured loans and passbook loans	(in the United States, regulated by national and state banking laws; in Canada, there are no legal restrictions on bank rates) • 15%–36% (depending on the size of the loan and state or provincial laws; in Canada, generally from 15%–24%)
Services	• offer several different types of consumer credit plans • may offer financial counseling • handle credit transactions confidentially	• provide credit promptly • make loans to pay off accumulated debts willingly • design repayment schedules to fit the borrower's income • usually offer financial counseling • handle credit transactions confidentially

[a] Rates applicable at date of printing.

Source: This information taken from the Money Management Institute booklet titled *It's Your Credit: Manage It Wisely*, printed by the Money Management Institute of Household Finance Corporation, Chicago, Illinois, 1977.

• Credit Unions	• Life Insurance Companies
• personal installment loans	• single or partial payment loans
• lend to members only • make unsecured loans for small amounts • may require collateral or co-signer for loans over a specified amount • may require payroll deduction to pay off loan • submit all loan applications to a committee of members for approval • offer a variety of repayment schedules	• lend on cash value of life insurance policy • usually place no date or penalty on repayment • deduct amount owed from the value of policy benefit if death or other maturity occurs before repayment
lower than some lenders because they: • take fewer credit risks • lend money deposited by members, which is less expensive than borrowed money • often receive free office space and supplies from the sponsoring organization • are managed by members whose services, in most cases, are donated • enjoy federal income tax exemption	lower than some lenders because they: • take no risk • pay no collection cost • secure loans by cash value of policy
• 9%–15% (limited to 12% under federal and state credit union laws, but may be higher in some Canadian provinces)	• 5%–8% (as stated in the policy; in the United States, legal limit 8%)
• design repayment schedules to fit the borrower's income • generally provide credit life insurance without extra charge • may offer financial counseling	• permit repayment at any time • handle credit transactions confidentially

that an applicant is a good customer of the bank greatly enhances his or her chances of receiving requested financing. Although banks prefer to make loans secured by some type of collateral, it is not uncommon for them to make unsecured single payment loans to their better customers. Quite often they will lend against a passbook savings account balance or certificates of deposit. People obtain such loans in order to avoid losing interest by withdrawing deposits or cashing in certificates of deposit before the end of some specified period. The interest rate on a bank loan may be affected by the loan's size, its terms, and whether or not it is secured by some type of collateral.

Credit Unions Only members can obtain installment loans and, in some cases, single payment loans from credit unions, which were discussed in Chapter 5. Because they are nonprofit organizations with minimal operating costs, credit unions charge relatively low rates on their loans. The maximum rate of interest that federally chartered credit unions can charge their customers is 1 percent a month, or 12 percent per year. Most credit unions make loans at annual percentage rates ranging from 9 to 12 percent. They make both unsecured and secured loans depending on the amount and type of loan being requested. The maximum size of loan made by credit unions to their members is often set by certain regulatory agencies. In addition, the directors of the credit union frequently set their own in-house loan limits. Generally speaking, membership in a credit union provides the most attractive borrowing opportunities available. And an added convenience of credit union loans is that loan payments can often be deducted directly from payroll checks.

Consumer Finance Companies Sometimes called *small loan companies*, consumer finance companies make secured and unsecured, or signature, loans to qualified individuals. These companies do not accept deposits but rather obtain funds from their stockholders and through borrowing. Because they do not have the inexpensive sources of funds that banks and credit unions have, their interest rates are generally quite high, not infrequently ranging from 15 percent to 36 percent per year. The actual rates charged by consumer finance companies are regulated by interest rate ceilings set by the states in which they operate. The maximum allowable interest rate may vary with the size of the loan. State regulatory authorities also limit the maximum size and repayment period of these loans. Typically, loans made by consumer finance companies are for $2,000 or less and are secured by some type of asset. Repayment is required on an installment basis over a period of five years or less. Consumer finance companies generally make small loans to high risk borrowers. Of course, these loans are quite costly, but they may be the only alternative for people who have poor credit ratings. Some people are attracted to consumer finance companies due to the ease with which loans may be obtained from them. Because of the high rates of interest they charge, however, the individual should consider this source of borrowing only after exhausting others.

Life Insurance Companies Life insurance policy holders can often obtain loans from their insurance companies. Certain types of policies not only provide a death benefit but also have a savings function, and these can be used as collateral for loans. (A detailed discussion of life insurance is presented in Chapter 13.) Life insurance companies are required by law to make loans against the *cash value*—the amount of savings accumulated—of their customers' policies. The rate of interest on these loans is stated in the policy and by regulation cannot exceed an annual percentage rate of 8 percent. Such loans typically have no repayment date, and interest is charged on the actual amount for the period of time the loan is outstanding. A loan on a life insurance policy may never be repaid, in which case the amount of the loan outstanding plus interest is deducted from the proceeds of the policy holder or beneficiaries when the policy is retired.

When you take out a loan against the cash value of your life insurance policy, you are really borrowing your own money, and the procedure is quite simple. Forms can be obtained from your agent or by writing the company. Once completed, they are returned to the insurance company, which (normally) promptly issues you a check for the specified amount. Interest on the loan is then included as part of your premium payment. Because certain other lenders with lower rates, such as commercial banks, may be willing to lend against the cash value of life insurance, it is a good idea to investigate the alternatives prior to borrowing from your life insurance company. Generally, though, these loans are quite good. Their chief danger lies in the fact that they do not have a firm maturity date, and therefore borrowers may lack motivation to repay them. Delay in repaying these loans increases their cost to the borrower, who must continue to pay interest until the loan is retired. As indicated earlier, all borrowing must be budgeted both in amount and with respect to repayment.

Savings and Loan Associations Savings and loan associations and mutual savings banks, both of which were discussed in detail in Chapter 5, primarily make real estate mortgage loans. They accept savings deposits and loan these funds out to qualified borrowers. Although they are regulated with respect to the loans they can offer, some are now permitted to make loans on consumer durables such as televisions, refrigerators, and ranges as long as these items are part of homes being financed. Savings and loan associations are also allowed to make certain types of home improvement and mobile home loans that are secured by assets, as well as some personal loans using passbook savings as collateral.

The mortgage loans made by these institutions are always installment loans, while the others may be either installment or single payment loans. Rates of interest on mortgage loans usually range from 8 to 10 percent, while on other loans they range from 7 to 12 percent. The rate of interest in each case depends on several factors, including the type and purpose of the loan, the duration and type of repayment (installment or single payment), and the overall credit-worthiness of the borrower. Although savings and loan associations and mutual savings banks primarily offer mortgage loans, you may find in some parts of the country that you can get the type of loan you require from them at rates competitive with those of other lenders.

Sales Finance Companies Businesspeople who sell more expensive items, such as automobiles, furniture, and appliances, often provide installment financing to purchasers of their products. Because these dealers cannot afford to tie up their funds in installment contracts, they sell them to a sales finance company for cash. This procedure is often referred to as "selling paper" since merchants in effect sell their loans to a third party. When the sales finance company purchases these notes, it normally notifies the customer to make payments directly to it. Depending on whether or not the sales finance company has purchased contracts with or without *recourse*, the merchant may still be liable should purchasers default.

The largest sales finance companies are the *captive finance companies* owned by manufacturers of "big-ticket" items—automobiles and appliances. General Motors Acceptance Corporation (GMAC) and General Electric Credit (GEC) are examples of captive (sales) finance companies that purchase the installment loans made by dealers in their products. Some large commercial banks act as sales finance companies by buying paper from certain types of businesses. The cost of financing through sales finance companies is in the range of 12 to 24 percent per year. Rates are generally higher than those charged on similar loans by commercial banks and credit unions. Often when consumers let a dealer arrange financing for a purchase, they end up owing a sales finance company for a loan with unnecessarily high interest rates.

Pawnshops Loans can be obtained in exchange for some kind of collateral, or *pawn*, as it is often called, at pawnshops. The pawnshop accepts certain types of goods such as jewelry, guns, and stereos against which it lends 25 to 75 percent of their estimated market value. An individual who needs money and is unable to obtain it from other sources may turn to the pawnshop as a last resort. To pawn an item, a person need only take it to the pawnshop and have the pawnbroker appraise it and specify the amount that he or she will lend using it as collateral. The

"We have so much to live for. . . . The payments on the house, the payments on the furniture, the payments on the car . . ."

Remember: Installment Loans Must Be Repaid
Source: Boserman—Rothco Cartoons Inc.

pawnbroker is required by the Truth in Lending Law to disclose both the dollar amount and annual percentage rate of interest that will be charged on a proposed loan. If both parties agree, the pawnbroker gives the customer the specified amount of money along with a pawn ticket to be used in reclaiming the pawned merchandise and receives possession of the merchandise in return. The loan might be for anywhere from one to twelve months. It is a single payment loan that is, in effect, secured by the pawned item. If the borrower does not repay the loan as well as the interest according to the terms of the agreement, the pawnbroker will sell the pawned item and use the proceeds to satisfy the outstanding loan. If the pawnbroker nets more from this sale than is owed on the loan, this excess is supposed to be returned to the borrower. The rate of interest, which typically ranges from 20 to 40 percent per year, and many other aspects of pawnshop operations are regulated by various local and state governments.

Borrowers who use pawnshops are usually from low-income groups and often do not repay the loans they receive on pawned merchandise. Because pawnshops end up with a great deal of merchandise to sell, they operate as retail stores in which jewelry, stereos, and other items are offered for sale at attractive prices. In fact, many sell not only the used merchandise they have claimed as the result of unpaid loans but also new items they have purchased solely for resale purposes. Due to the high costs involved, the use of pawnshops as a source of loans is not advised. But as a consumer looking for a bargain on merchandise, you might find that the pawnshop offers interesting purchase opportunities.

Remedial Loan Societies In some metropolitan areas, nonprofit organizations have been set up to provide a mechanism through which the poor can get a fair deal. These remedial loan societies operate in a manner similar to a pawnshop in that they lend against physical assets, which are held as collateral. The borrower is expected to repay the amount lent along with the interest at maturity of the loan. The annual percentage rate of interest on these loans, most of which are made for a period of one year or less, is relatively low given the risks involved—12 to 18 percent per year. Like pawnbrokers, these societies sell the collateral to satisfy an unpaid loan. And similarly, if excess proceeds are obtained through the sale, the borrower will be entitled to receive these funds. Probably only about twenty of these societies exist today.

Friends and Relatives Often a close friend or relative who has excess funds will be willing to lend you money. In many cases such loans are quite attractive because little or no interest is charged. The terms will, of course, vary depending on the financial needs of the borrower, but they should be specified in a loan agreement that states the costs, conditions, and maturity date of the loan as well as the obligations of both borrower and lender. Not only does a written loan agreement reduce opportunities for disagreement and unhappiness, it also legally protects both borrower and lender should either of them die or other unexpected events occur. Still, given the potential for disagreement and conflict among friends and relatives inherent in this type of arrangement, it is advisable to borrow from friends or relatives only when the terms are considerably better than those available from one of the more traditional sources or when there are no other alternatives.

The single payment loan differs from other loans in that it is to be repaid in full on a given date. It is useful when funds for a necessary purchase are currently inadequate but expected to be available in the future. Thus it can aid in meeting emergency cash requirements, serving as a form of interim financing until more permanent financing can be arranged. This part of the chapter examines two aspects of single payment loans: (1) finance charges, annual percentage rates, and the methods of computing these rates, and (2) the important features of loan agreements.

Single Payment Loans

Finance Charges and Annual Percentage Rates

As indicated in the preceding chapter, the Consumer Credit Protection Act, or Truth in Lending Law, requires all lenders to disclose both the dollar amount of finance charges and the annual percentage rate (APR) of interest. A sample disclosure statement applicable for either a single payment or an installment loan is given in Figure 12-1. Although

Figure 12-1 **Disclosure Statement from a Loan Agreement**

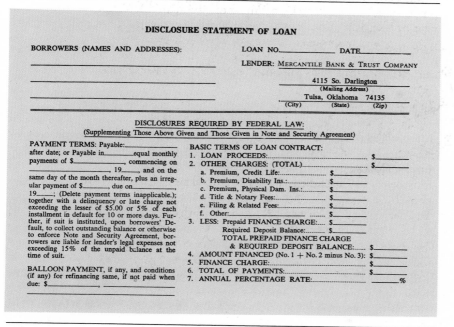

Source: Courtesy of Mercantile Bank and Trust Company, Tulsa, Oklahoma.

disclosures such as this allow you to compare the cost of various borrowing alternatives, it is still a good idea to understand the methods used to compute finance charges, since similar loans with the same *stated* interest rates may have different finance charges and APRs. The two basic methods used to calculate the finance charges on single payment loans are the *simple interest method* and the *discount method.*

Simple Interest Method Interest is charged only on the *actual loan balance outstanding* in the simple interest method. This method is commonly used on revolving open account charges, by commercial banks, and by credit unions. To see how it is applied to a single payment loan, assume that you borrow $1,000 for two years, at a 10 percent stated annual rate of interest. On a single payment loan, the actual loan balance outstanding for the two years would be $1,000 since no payments are made until the two years have elapsed. The finance charge calculated with the simple interest method, F_s, is obtained by multiplying the actual balance outstanding by the stated annual interest rate and then multiplying this product by the term of the loan (Equation 12.1).

$$F_s = Prt \qquad (12.1)$$

where:

F_s = finance charge calculated using the simple interest method
P = the principal amount of the loan
r = stated annual rate of interest
t = term of the loan stated in years

Substituting $1,000 for P, 0.10 for r, and 2 for t in Equation 12.1, F_s becomes $200 ($1,000 × 0.10 per year × 2 years).

To calculate the true, or annual, percentage rate (APR) of interest on this loan, the average annual finance charge is divided by the average loan balance outstanding, as specified in Equation 12.2.

$$\text{APR} = \frac{\text{average annual finance charge}}{\text{average loan balance outstanding}} \qquad (12.2)$$

The average annual finance charge is found by dividing the finance charge by the life of the loan. In our example, the result is $100 ($200 ÷ 2). Because the loan balance outstanding remains at $1,000 over the life of the loan, the average loan balance outstanding is $1,000. When the $100 average annual finance charge is divided by the $1,000 average loan balance outstanding, an APR of 10 percent results. Thus the APR and the stated rate of interest (also 10 percent) are equivalent. This is *always* the case when the simple interest method is used to calculate finance charges, whether loans are single payment or installment.

Discount Method The finance charges are calculated and then subtracted from the amount of the loan in the discount method. The difference between the amount of the loan and the finance charges is then lent to the borrower. In other words, finance charges are paid in advance and represent a "discount" from the stated amount of the loan. The finance charge on a single payment loan using the discount method (F_d) is calculated in the same fashion as for the simple interest loan:

$$F_d = F_s = Prt \qquad (12.3)$$

Using the above method, the finance charge, F_d, is $200.

To find the annual percentage rate (APR) on this discount loan, we can substitute the appropriate values into Equation 12.2. For this two-year loan, the average annual interest rate is $100 ($200 ÷ 2). But since on a discount loan the finance charges for the life of the loan are deducted from the stated amount of the loan, the borrower receives only $800 ($1,000 stated loan amount − $200 in finance charges). Because this is a single payment loan, the amount of the average loan balance is thus $800. When Equation 12.2 is applied to these figures, the APR for the discount loan is found to be 12.5 percent ($100 ÷ $800). Clearly, the discount method yields a higher APR on single payment loans than does the simple interest method. Table 12-3 depicts these results for the single payment loan example discussed here.

Table 12-3 **Finance Charges and APRs for a Two-Year, $1,000 Single Payment Loan with a Stated Interest Rate of 10 Percent**

Method	Finance Charges	Approximate APR
Simple Interest	$200	10.0%
Discount	200	12.5

Note that the interest computations shown in this section pertain only to single payment loans. The calculation of finance charges and APRs for installment loans is discussed later in this chapter.

Important Features of Loan Agreements

Although the finance charges on a single payment loan are an important consideration, other features of the loan agreement also deserve attention. The Truth in Lending Law made mandatory the explicit disclosure

At Last, an Understandable Consumer Loan Agreement

The Citibank of New York—one of the nation's largest banks—recently initiated a "plain English" loan agreement that can be read and understood by most customers. The agreement, which contains only one-third the words found in the form it replaced, is believed to be the first of its kind in banking. It may be an indication that the confusing legal terminology of the standard loan agreement may be on its way out. A copy of Citibank's new, understandable consumer loan note is shown on page 417.

Source: Adapted from Michel Lipman, "Reform Your Forms to Ease the 'Legalese,'" *Savings and Loan News,* June 1977, pp. 78–82. Loan note reprinted by permission of Citibank.

CITIBANK, N.A.
CONSUMER LOAN NOTE

Date _____ , 19 _____

(In this note, the words **I, me, mine** and **my** mean each and all of those who signed it. The words **you, your** and **yours** mean **Citibank, N.A.**)

Terms of Repayment

To repay my loan, I promise to pay you _____ Dollars
($ _____). I'll pay this sum at one of your branches in _____ uninterrupted _____
installments of $ _____ each. Payments will be due _____
starting from the date the loan is made.

Here's the breakdown of my payments:

1. Amount of the Loan $ _____
2. Credit Life Insurance $ _____
3. Property Insurance $ _____
4. Filing Fee for Security Interest $ _____
5. Amount Financed (1 + 2 + 3 + 4) $ _____
6. **FINANCE CHARGE** $ _____
7. Total of Payments (5+6) $ _____
   ANNUAL PERCENTAGE RATE _____ %

Prepayment of Whole Note

Even though I needn't pay more than the fixed installments, I have the right to prepay the whole outstanding amount of this note at any time. If I do, or if this loan is refinanced—that is, replaced by a new note—you will refund the unearned **FINANCE CHARGE**, figured by the rule of 78—a commonly used formula for figuring rebates on installment loans. However, you can charge a minimum **FINANCE CHARGE** of $10.

Late Charge

If I fall more than 10 days behind in paying an installment, I promise to pay a late charge of 5% of the overdue installment, but no more than $5. However, the sum total of late charges on all installments can't be more than 2% of the total of payments or $25, whichever is less.

Security

To protect you if I default on this or any other debt to you, I give you what is known as a security interest in my O Motor Vehicle and/or _____(see the Security Agreement I have given you for a full description of this property), O Stocks, O Bonds, O Savings Account (more fully described in the receipt you gave me today) **and** any account or other property of mine coming into your possession.

Insurance

I understand I must maintain property insurance on the property covered by the Security Agreement for its full insurable value, but I can buy this insurance through a person of my own choosing.

Default

I'll be in default:
1. If I don't pay an installment on time; or
2. If any other creditor tries by legal process to take any money of mine in your possession.

You can then demand immediate payment of the balance of this note, minus the part of the **FINANCE CHARGE** which hasn't been earned figured by the rule of 78. You will also have other legal rights, for instance, the right to repossess, sell and apply security to the payments under this note and any other debts I may then owe you.

Irregular Payments

You can accept late payments or partial payments, even though marked "payment in full", without losing any of your rights under this note.

Delay in Enforcement

You can delay enforcing any of your rights under this note without losing them.

Collection Costs

If I'm in default under this note and you demand full payment, I agree to pay you interest on the unpaid balance at the rate of 1% per month, after an allowance for the unearned **FINANCE CHARGE.** If you have to sue me, I also agree to pay your attorney's fees equal to 15% of the amount due, and court costs. But if I defend and the court decides I am right, I understand that you will pay my reasonable attorney's fees and the court costs.

Comakers

If I'm signing this note as a comaker, I agree to be equally responsible with the borrower. You don't have to notify me that this note hasn't been paid. You can change the terms of payment and release any security without notifying or releasing me from responsibility on this note.

Copy Received

The borrower acknowledges receipt of a completely filled-in copy of this note, including, if there is a Credit Life Insurance Charge, the Notice on the reverse.

	Signatures	Addresses
Borrower:	_____	_____
Comaker:	_____	_____
Comaker:	_____	_____
Comaker:	_____	_____

Hot Line

If something should happen and you can't pay on time, please call us immediately at (212) 559-3061.

Personal Finance Department
Citibank, N.A.

ITEM 452318 (PBR 668 REV. 7-76)

of all conditions and features of loans. Only the most important of these are discussed below.

Loan Collateral Most single payment loans are *secured* by certain specified assets. Only to the highest quality borrowers with proven credit reputations will lenders grant *unsecured* loans. For collateral, lenders accept only items that are readily marketable at a price sufficiently high to cover the principal amount of the loan—for example, an automobile, jewelry, or stocks and bonds. If a loan is obtained to purchase some physical asset, that asset may be used to secure the loan. In most cases lenders do not take physical possession of the collateral, but rather file a *lien,* a legal claim that permits them to liquidate the items that serve as collateral to satisfy their claim in the event of default. The lien is filed in the county courthouse and is a matter of public record. If borrowers maintain possession or title to *movable* property used as loan collateral, the instrument that gives the lenders title to the property in the event of default is called a *chattel mortgage.* Chattels are movable assets such as autos, TVs, and jewelry. If lenders actually take possession of loan collateral or the title to collateral, as in the case of stocks and bonds, the agreement giving them the right to sell these items in the instance of default is a *collateral note.*

Sometimes single payment loans are secured using second mortgages on real estate. A *second mortgage* is a secondary claim on the proceeds from liquidating real estate in order to satisfy unpaid claims. Because the market value of real estate is likely to be greater than the amount owed on it, second mortgages can provide an excellent source of loan collateral. For example, if you owe $20,000 on a home that currently has a net market value (i.e., after all expected sales costs) of $32,000, you have $12,000 ($32,000 − $20,000) of unused collateral value. You can use some portion of this amount to secure a loan with a second mortgage.

Sometimes, too, borrowers can secure loans by having a creditworthy friend or relative cosign for them. Of course, if they default, their cosigner is required to repay the loan, since by cosigning he or she has guaranteed it.

Maturity, or Term, of the Loan As indicated above, the maturity, or term, of a single payment loan is typically one year or less. When you request such a loan, you should be sure its term is long enough to allow you to receive the money needed for repayment but no longer than necessary since the amount of finance charges increases with time. Because the loan is to be paid in a single payment, the lender must be assured that you can repay it at the specified future date even if certain unexpected events occur in the meantime. The term of your single payment loan must therefore be reconciled with your budget as well as your ability to pay. If the money you plan to use for repayment will be received periodically over the term of the loan, an installment type of loan would probably be more suitable.

Repayment: Early or Late? The repayment of a single payment loan is expected to take place on its maturity date. Occasionally, the funds needed to repay this type of loan will be received prior to maturity. Depending on the lender, the borrower might then be able to repay the loan prior to its maturity and thereby reduce the finance charges on it. Credit unions often permit early repayment of these loans with reduced finance charges, but commercial banks and other single payment lenders either do not accept early repayments or charge a prepayment penalty on them. This penalty normally amounts to a set percentage of the interest that would have been paid over the remaining life of the loan. The Truth in Lending Law requires lenders to disclose in the loan agreement whether or not and in what amount prepayment penalties are charged on a single payment loan. It is important to examine and understand this information prior to signing a loan agreement.

Paying back a loan late should be avoided at all costs. For if you are unable to repay a single payment loan at maturity, you will be in default, and the lender could force you into bankruptcy. In instances where you cannot pay on time, it is a good idea to inform the lender in advance so that a partial payment, a loan extension, or some other arrangement can be made. If you wait until payment is already past due prior to talking with the lender, your credit rating as well as the possibility of working out an agreement with the lender will probably be reduced. Whatever you do, do not try to trick or avoid the lender; such action can severely damage your credit rating. Maintaining a favorable credit rating is vital since it can significantly affect both the cost and availability of credit to you.

Installment Loans

Installment loans, which are made to purchase certain goods and services, require the borrower to make scheduled payments over the life of the agreement. They typically require equal monthly payments over a period of six or more months. This part of the chapter discusses finance charges and APRs on installment loans, the installment purchase agreement, special features of the agreement, and early repayment considerations related to installment loans.

Finance Charges and APRs

In the preceding part of this chapter, the finance charges and annual percentage rates (APRs) of interest on single payment loans were discussed. The simple interest and discount methods of determining finance charges on single payment loans were described and illustrated. In this section the simple interest and add-on methods of computing finance charges on installment loans are the subject. For illustrative purposes, a $1,000 installment loan with a stated interest rate of 12 percent and twelve monthly installment payments will be used.

Simple Interest Method In the case of installment loans, simple interest is charged only on the outstanding balance. The required payments can be determined from financial tables, which, due to their complexity, are not discussed here. As shown in Table 12-4, the monthly payment on a $1,000, 12 percent installment loan to be repaid in twelve monthly installments is $88.85. Since the stated interest rate is 12 percent per year, monthly interest of 1 percent (12 percent ÷ 12 months) is applied to the outstanding loan balance each month. Table 12-4 illustrates how loan payments are divided into interest and principal components in calculating simple interest on an installment loan. Of the payment total of $1,066.20, $66.20 represents interest and the remaining $1,000 represents repayment of the principal. Since no finance charges other than interest have been assumed, the total finance charges are $66.20. And because interest is charged only on the outstanding balance of the loan, the annual percentage rate (APR) of interest on an installment loan calculated by the simple interest method equals the stated rate, in this case 12 percent.

Table 12-4 **Payment Analysis for a $1,000 Loan at a 12 Percent Interest Rate to Be Repaid in Twelve Monthly Installments**

Month	Outstanding Loan Balance (1)	Monthly Payment (2)	Interest [(1) × .01] (3)	Principal [(2) − (3)] (4)
1	$1,000.00	$ 88.85	$10.00	$ 78.85
2	921.15	88.85	9.21	79.64
3	841.51	88.85	8.42	80.43
4	761.08	88.85	7.61	81.24
5	679.84	88.85	6.80	82.05
6	597.79	88.85	5.98	82.87
7	514.92	88.85	5.15	83.70
8	431.22	88.85	4.31	84.54
9	346.68	88.85	3.47	85.38
10	261.30	88.85	2.61	86.24
11	175.06	88.85	1.75	87.10
12	87.96	88.85	0.89	87.96
Totals		$1,066.20	$66.20	$1,000.00

Notes: Column (1) Values for months 2 through 12 are obtained by subtracting the principal payment shown in column (4) for the preceding month from the outstanding loan balance shown in column (1) for the preceding month. Column (3) The .01 value represents the monthly interest charge of 1 percent, since the stated rate of interest is 12 percent per year.

Add-on Method Finance charges and monthly payments on installment loans are quite commonly computed on the basis of the add-on method. Equation 12.1, which was presented in the section on single payment loans, can be used for this purpose. Given the $1,000, twelve-month loan with a stated rate of interest at the 12 percent interest rate cited above, P = $1,000, r = 0.12, and t = 1; thus the computations prescribed in Equation 12.1 yield a finance charge of $120 ($1,000 × 0.12 × 1). The finance charge is added to the principal amount, and the total is divided by the number of payments to be made; this results in the amount of the monthly payment, in this case $93.33 ([$1,000 + $120] ÷ 12).

The formula given in Equation 12.4 can be applied to calculate the approximate APR on an add-on loan.

$$\text{Approximate APR} \ = \ \frac{2MF}{P(N+1)} \qquad (12.4)$$

where:

APR = annual percentage rate of interest
M = number of payments in a year
F = total finance charges
P = the principal amount of the loan
N = number of loan payments scheduled over life of loan

If M = 12, F = $120, P = $1,000, and N = 12, the approximate APR is 22.2 percent:

$$\text{Approximate APR} = \frac{2(12)(\$120)}{(\$1,000)(13)} = \frac{\$2,880}{\$13,000} = 22.2\% \qquad (12.5)$$

This rate is considerably higher than the APR of 12 percent found in the case where the simple interest method was used. The difference is due to the fact that when add-on interest is applied to an installment loan, the interest included in each payment is charged on the initial principal even though the outstanding loan balance is reduced as installment payments are made. Like the approximate APR computed above, the exact APR calculated with the add-on method is higher than the APR calculated with the simple interest method. A summary of the finance charges and approximate APRs for the above example is presented in Table 12-5.

Under the Truth in Lending Law, the exact APR must be disclosed to borrowers. Sophisticated formulas or financial tables derived from such formulas are necessary to find the exact value of the APR. You will probably never have to calculate it yourself, but as a well-informed consumer, you should understand the differences in the simple interest and add-on methods of computing finance charges. Note, too, that not

Table 12-5 **Finance Charges and APRs for a $1,000 Installment Loan at a Stated Rate of Interest of 12 Percent to Be Repaid in Twelve Equal Monthly Installments**

Method	Finance Charges	Approximate APR
Simple Interest	$ 66.20	12.0%
Add-on	120.00	22.2

only interest but also any other fees required to obtain a loan are considered part of the finance charges used in the computation of the

The Four-Year Auto Loan: An Answer to Rising Auto Prices?

NEW YORK—A growing number of new-car buyers are taking out four-year loans, instead of the once-standard three-year auto loans, to finance their wheels.

From a financial viewpoint, the four-year loan can offer a good deal. Interest rates sometimes are lower on a four-year loan. Monthly payments are smaller.

Credit executives, however, say that most people who take out four-year loans do so in order to buy more car than they otherwise would have purchased. A rational buyer (but since when have new-car buyers been purely rational?) would first pick out his car and then apply for the least-expensive loan, if he needed to borrow. Instead, most new-car credit buyers appear to decide first on the size of the monthly payment they can afford and then choose a car that they can finance within that figure.

"In retirement communities like San Diego," says Allan Gilmour, president of Ford's Ford Credit subsidiary, "a lot of retired people have used longer-term loans to buy more expensive cars." This appears to be true, he says, regardless of the buyer's income. "People who buy Pintos," he says, "will use a longer-term loan to buy more expensive Pintos. Of course, fewer people finance the Continental Mark V than a Pinto, but the ones who do will also use a longer-term loan to buy more options on the Mark V."

Price Is a Factor

Since 1973, installment loans longer than 36 months have risen to 56% from 4% of the loans that Ford Credit has purchased from dealers. At Chrysler's Chrysler Financial, James J. Madden Jr., vice president of marketing and operations services, says the percentage has risen to 60.3% from 7.6% in 1973. Overall, says Walter Kurth, new executive vice president of the National Consumer Finance Association, loans exceeding 36 months rose to 41.4% of all new-car loans in February this year from less than one-half of 1% in February 1972.

The credit executives agree that soaring prices on new cars have created the swing toward long-term loans. "Increased car prices are the basic, fundamental reason," says Mr. Madden of Chrysler. By February 1977, the average new-car price, according to the Bureau of Labor Statistics, had risen to 140.7% of the 1967 index figure of 100.

APR. In the illustrations presented in this chapter interest was assumed to represent the only finance charge on the loan.

The Installment Purchase Agreement

All of the information relative to the transaction being financed on an installment basis is included in an installment purchase agreement. This agreement specifies the obligations of both the purchaser (or borrower) and the lender. Although its form is likely to vary with the lender, it will probably contain four basic components: a sales contract, a security

---

Used-car prices have risen, too, encouraging banks and finance companies to increase the size of their car loans and to lengthen the repayment period. In 1970, the average installment purchaser financed by Chrysler borrowed $3,357 for 34.1 months; his monthly payment averaged $98. In 1976, the average installment contract was for $5,686 with monthly payments of $141 for 40.1 months.

Citibank, in New York, offers these figures for comparing the cost of a four-year and three-year auto loan:

Three-Year Loan

Total Amount Financed	$5,976
Interest Charge	$1,076
Net Amount Borrowed	$4,900
Annual Interest Rate	13.38%
Monthly Payment	$ 166

Four-Year Loan

Total Amount Financed	$6,144
Interest Charge	$1,229
Net Amount Borrowed	$4,915
Annual Interest Rate	11.40%
Monthly Payment	$ 128

The four-year borrower, using Citibank's figures, will pay about $150 more in total interest than the three-year borrower of roughly an equal amount. But the four-year borrower's lower yearly interest rate, and his smaller monthly payments, can offset this. If he merely saves the $38 difference in monthly payments for three years, he will accumulate $1,368 plus $126 in interest at 6%.

Source: Donald Moffitt, "Why Four-Year Car Loans Are Gaining Favor," *Wall Street Journal,* 6 June 1977, p. 28. Reprinted with permission of The Wall Street Journal, © Dow Jones & Company, Inc., 1977. All rights reserved.

agreement, a note, and an insurance agreement. A sample purchase agreement used for installment sales of autos or trucks by General Motors dealers and containing all four of the components mentioned is presented in Figure 12-2. The back side of the agreement (not shown) has all of the detailed provisions printed on it.

Sales Contract An important part of the purchase agreement, the sales contract is drawn up to provide adequate protection for the lender in the event that the purchaser defaults on the installment loan. The actual content and form are regulated by the state in which the contract is drawn. Sales contracts specify all key information with respect to identification of borrower, lender, and the merchandise being purchased as well as any down payment, the amount of payments, all other fees, and the finance charges and APR. Items 1–10 of Figure 12-2 represent the sales contract for the sample installment purchase agreement.

Security Agreement The security agreement (or security interest), which may be part of the sales contract, gives the installment lender control over the item being purchased. Although state laws determine whether or not the borrower retains legal title to the collateral, the lender files a lien on the collateral in order to make his or her "security interest" public. In either case, the lender retains legal control over the collateral. If default does occur, the lender can sell the collateral and use the proceeds to satisfy the unpaid loan balance and cover any costs incurred in this process. However, the lender must pay the borrower any excess funds obtained from the liquidation of the collateral. If the proceeds from liquidation are not sufficient to satisfy the loan, the borrower remains liable for the unsatisfied portion of the debt. The security agreement appears as item 12 in the installment purchase contract illustrated in Figure 12-2.

Note The formal promise on the part of the borrower to repay the lender as specified in the sales contract is contained in the note. It states the legal obligations of both the borrower and lender and outlines all details with respect to repayment, default, and disposition of collateral. The note is normally secured by the sales contract or security agreement, which provides the lender with a security interest in the assets being acquired. It is the document which, when signed by both borrower and lender, legally binds them to the terms and conditions stated therein. Although many of the detailed provisions of the note in Figure 12-2 are on the reverse side of the contract (not shown), the entire document, when signed, is considered to be the note.

Insurance Agreement Sometimes, as a condition of receiving an installment loan, the borrower is required to buy credit life insurance and

Figure 12-2 **Sample Installment Purchase Agreement**

INSTALMENT SALE CONTRACT   Dealer Number ___   Contract Number ___

Buyer (and Co-Buyer) - Name and Address (Include - County and Zip Code) | Seller - Name and Address

The seller hereby sells, and the buyer (meaning all undersigned buyers, jointly and severally) hereby purchases, subject to the terms set forth below **and upon the reverse side hereof,** the following property, delivery and acceptance of which in good order are hereby acknowledged by buyer, viz.:

New or Used	Year Model	No. Cyl.	Make Trade Name	Body Type — If Truck, Give GVW	Model No. or Series	Vehicle Identification No.

If truck—Describe bodies and major items of equipment sold—

Buyer represents that the purchase of said property is primarily for personal, family or household ☐, agricultural ☐, business (other than agricultural) ☐ use (check one).

1. CASH PRICE (including any accessories, services and taxes imposed on the cash sale) .... $_____ (1)
2. TOTAL DOWNPAYMENT—$_____ plus $_____ Trade-in _____ .... $_____ (2)
   Trade-In (Net)   Cash Downpayment   Make, Model, Year
3. UNPAID BALANCE OF CASH PRICE (Difference between Items 1 and 2).......... $_____ (3)
4. OTHER CHARGES
   *A. Cost of Required Physical Damage Insurance
       BUYER MAY CHOOSE THE PERSON THROUGH WHICH THIS INSURANCE IS TO BE OBTAINED .... $_____ (4A)
   B. Cost of Creditor Insurance for the term hereof.
       COVERAGE OF THE BUYER BY ANY SUCH INSURANCE IS NOT REQUIRED BY SELLER.
       CHECK CREDITOR   ☐ Life .... $_____ (4B)
       INSURANCE DESIRED   ☐ Disability (Accident and Health) .... $_____ (4B)
                               ☐ Other (describe) .... $_____ (4B)
       BUYER'S APPROVAL: I DESIRE TO OBTAIN THE CREDITOR INSURANCE CHECKED ABOVE FOR THE BUYER PROPOSED FOR INSURANCE.
       _____ Signature _____   _____
       (Date)   (Buyer's Signature)   (Co-Buyer's Signature)
   C. Official Fees .... $_____ (4C)
   D. Taxes Not Included in Cash Price .... $_____ (4D)
   E. License and/or Registration Fees (Itemize) .... $_____ (4E)
   F. Certificate of Title Fee .... $_____ (4F)
   G. Other (Describe) .... $_____ (4G)
5. UNPAID BALANCE—AMOUNT FINANCED (Sum of items 3 and 4) .... $_____ (5)
6. **FINANCE CHARGE** .... $_____ (6)
7. TOTAL OF PAYMENTS (Sum of items 5 and 6) .... $_____ (7)
8. DEFERRED PAYMENT PRICE (Sum of items 1, 4 and 6) .... $_____ (8)
9. **ANNUAL PERCENTAGE RATE** .... _____% (9)
10. PAYMENT SCHEDULE: The Total of Payments (Item 7) is payable at seller's office designated below or at such office of any assignee as may be hereafter designated in_____ instalments of $_____ each, commencing _____, 19____, and on the same day of each successive month thereafter, or as indicated in space below.

Any instalment which is more than twice the amount of an otherwise regularly scheduled equal instalment is a BALLOON PAYMENT. If the final instalment is larger than any of the substantially equal prior instalments, buyer may, by a new written agreement with seller, refinance such final instalment, as of the due date thereof and over a reasonable period of time, for a refinance charge computed at the Annual Percentage Rate of finance charge hereinbefore provided in Item 9.
11. DEFAULT CHARGE IN EVENT OF LATE PAYMENT If any instalment is not paid within **10** days after it is due, buyer agrees to pay a charge equal to **5%** of the unpaid instalment, if the property purchased hereunder is a truck, trailer, semi-trailer, motorcycle, agricultural machinery or off-highway equipment. Otherwise, charge shall not exceed **2%** per month of the unpaid instalment, computed on the basis of a full calendar month for any fractional month period in excess of **10** days.
12. DESCRIPTION OF SECURITY INTEREST Seller retains an interest in the property described above to secure payment and performance of buyer's obligation hereunder, including any additional indebtedness incurred as provided herein, and under any extensions or renewals hereof.
13. PREPAYMENT REBATE Upon prepayment in full buyer is entitled to a rebate of the Finance Charge (Item 6) computed in accordance with the Rule of 78. A minimum charge of $15 will be made. No rebate less than $1 will be paid.

* Covering Accidental Physical Damage to the car as outlined below (check which applies) for a term of_____months, and {including / excluding} optional coverage for Towing and Labor Costs.

Insurance Company_____
☐ Comprehensive Coverage
☐ $50 Deductible Comprehensive Coverage   {including / excluding}
☐ Fire-Theft and Combined Additional Coverage

☐ Regular $_____ Ded. Collision; or
☐ Broadened $_____ Ded. Collision; or
☐ Limited Collision (private passenger car); or
☐ Limited $_____ Ded. Collision (commercial vehicle)

Insurance shall be based upon actual value of property at time of loss, not to exceed limits of liability set forth in the policy, and shall be payable to buyer, seller or seller's assignee, as interests may appear.

NOTICE
ANY HOLDER OF THIS CONSUMER CREDIT CONTRACT IS SUBJECT TO ALL CLAIMS AND DEFENSES WHICH THE DEBTOR COULD ASSERT AGAINST THE SELLER OF GOODS OR SERVICES OBTAINED PURSUANT HERETO OR WITH THE PROCEEDS HEREOF. RECOVERY HEREUNDER BY THE DEBTOR SHALL NOT EXCEED AMOUNTS PAID BY THE DEBTOR HEREUNDER.

Executed in quintuplicate, this_____day of_____, 19____ at_____
(City)   (County)   (State)

NOTICE TO BUYER: 1. Do not sign this contract in blank. 2. You are entitled to a true copy of the contract you sign without charge. 3. Keep it to protect your legal rights.

Warning: The insurance afforded hereunder does not cover liability for injury to persons or damage to property of others.

A Buyer Signs in Ink _____   B Co-Buyer Signs in Ink _____
Seller Signs in Ink _____   By _____
                                       (Title)

Source: Courtesy of Oldsmobile Division, General Motors.

possibly credit disability insurance. These policies insure the borrower for an amount sufficient to repay the outstanding loan balance. By requiring this coverage, the seller and lender are assured that if the borrower dies or is disabled, the loan will be repaid. The seller's or lender's ability to dictate the terms of these insurance requirements is restricted by law in some states. The statement with respect to credit life insurance and credit disability insurance in the sample installment purchase agreement given in Figure 12-2 is contained in item 4B. If insurance is required as a condition of purchase, its cost must be included in the finance charges and APR disclosed by the lender. Buyers should always make sure that the cost of such insurance is reasonable since sellers or lenders often receive commissions on the sale of credit life and disability insurance. It may well be possible to purchase the required insurance at a lower cost from another source, and many state laws require that lenders permit borrowers to do so.

Special Features of Installment Purchase Agreements

The general content of installment purchase agreements was described in the preceding section. Some of the more important features of these agreements, which are normally included as clauses in the sales agreement and/or the note, are further highlighted below.

Holder in Due Course The holder in due course doctrine concerns situations in which an installment loan has been sold to a third party (perhaps a bank or a sales finance company) by the dealer from whom the installment purchase was made. In effect, it prohibits the purchaser from discontinuing payments to the lender in the event that the seller will not be responsible for defective materials. In other words, if you purchase defective merchandise from a seller who then sells your loan to a third party, you cannot stop paying the third party in order to get the seller to make good on your purchase. The amended Consumer Credit Protection Act and the Fair Credit Billing Act, which both became effective in October of 1975, and other state regulations have more or less eliminated this clause from loan agreements. In cases where the seller and the financing agency cooperate to arrange financing, the holder in due course doctrine is no longer valid. But when a purchaser independently arranges financing in order to purchase merchandise, it is likely to remain in effect, since the lender can be considered an independent third party. It is expected that future legislation will cause any holder of a consumer credit contract to be subject to all claims and defenses made by the purchaser (debtor). Such action will provide the consumer with the best protection possible on installment purchases.

Confession of Judgment Some sales contracts have confession of judgment clauses, which in effect cause purchasers (debtors) to give up their right to legally disagree or defend themselves with respect to the debt should default occur. Contracts containing this type of clause should be avoided. Recent legislation has made such clauses illegal in most states, and their complete elimination is expected in the near future.

Add-on Clause An add-on clause allows the lender to hold as security a number of items that are purchased over a period of time. The lender does not release the security interest in any of these items until the entire loan has been paid off. Borrowers should avoid installment contracts with such clauses, since they allow lenders to repossess items of merchandise already purchased and paid for if the borrower defaults on other items purchased under the agreement. If a number of items are to be purchased, it is best to have separate purchase agreements for each of them rather than one agreement with an add-on clause.

Acceleration Clause The acceleration clause allows the lender to demand immediate repayment of the entire amount of the unpaid debt if the purchaser misses a payment. Although this clause is always included in installment loans, the lender is likely to allow a late payment or levy a fixed penalty instead of accelerating the loan by exercising the acceleration clause.

Wage Assignment: Garnishment Some purchase agreements allow the lender to collect a portion of the purchaser's (borrower's) wages if the purchaser defaults on payments. By signing a purchase agreement with such a clause, the purchaser agrees to these terms and enables the lender to collect part of his or her wages without obtaining a court order. If an assignment clause is not included in the agreement, it is still possible for a lender to *garnish* a borrower's wages, which is a legal method of getting an employer to pay a portion of a borrower's wages to the lender. The borrower must, of course, be in default, and a court order must be issued to the employer in order for such action to be taken.

The Federal Garnishment Law, which was included as part of the Consumer Credit Protection Act and became effective 1 July 1970, places limitations on the portion of an employee's wages that can be garnished. It specifically limits the amount of an employee's weekly wage that can be garnished to no more than the smaller of the following: (1) 25 percent of take-home pay, or (2) the amount by which take-home pay exceeds thirty times the federal minimum hourly wage ($2.65/hour in 1978, $2.90/hour in 1979, $3.15/hour in 1980, and $3.40/hour in 1981). The law also prohibits firms from firing employees as a result of their wages being garnished to repay a single debt. Many state laws have completely prohibited garnishing or have placed more severe restrictions than the federal law on the portion of a person's wages that can be garnished.

Repossession The act of seizing collateral when the borrower defaults on an installment loan is termed *repossession*. In many states the ability of the lender to repossess collateral in the case of default is limited. But in some states collateral can be repossessed without notice and even "in effect" stolen from the borrower. Still other states require a court order to repossess loan collateral. Quite a few states have detailed procedures which must be followed by the lender when selling repossessed items in order to satisfy unpaid debts. Because there have been many abuses in the repossession of collateral—especially in automobile financing—additional federal and state regulations are expected to be forthcoming.

Balloon Clause Sometimes installment purchase agreements are set up in such a fashion that the final payment is considerably larger than all other payments. The Truth in Lending Law requires that any *balloon payment* of this sort that is included in a loan agreement must be clearly identified as such. A statement to this effect appears in the disclosure statement in Figure 12-1 and in the installment purchase agreement in Figure 12-2 (just above item 11). Because these balloon clauses have been abused by some lenders and can place borrowers in an undesirable position, a number of states prohibit their inclusion in a loan agreement. It is best not to enter into an agreement that includes such a clause, since it is difficult to know if you will be able to afford the balloon payment when it falls due. Only in situations where the borrower is expecting a known sum of money at some exact future date can the use of a balloon payment be justified.

Early Repayment: The Rule of 78 (Sum of the Digits)

In most loan agreements (and according to some state laws) the borrower is permitted to repay a loan prior to its maturity. If interest has been prepaid, the loan agreement may provide for a refund of interest when an early repayment is made. In most cases, the Rule of 78 (sometimes called Sum of the Digits) is used to determine the portion of the total finance charges the lender receives upon paying off a loan prior to its maturity. The rule is best illustrated using a simple example. Suppose you borrowed $1,000 to be repaid in twelve monthly installments. Assume that the total finance charge over the life of the loan is $80. To determine the amount the lender will receive if you repay the loan after three months, you must first add all whole numbers between 1 and 12 (1 + 2 + 3 + . . . + 10 + 11 + 12). The total is 78. If the loan is repaid after one month, the lender receives 12/78 of the total interest. If it is repaid after two months, the amount of interest paid is 23/78 of the total interest ([12

+ 11] ÷ 78), and so on. In the example, since the loan is repaid after three months, the lender receives 33/78 of the total interest ([12 + 11 + 10] ÷ 78). This amounts to $33.85 ([33 ÷ 78] × $80).

The purpose of the Rule of 78 is to allow the lender to get a fair return on loans that are repaid prior to maturity. Note that in spite of the name of this rule, the denominator in the fraction used may not always be 78. The denominator depends on the number of months in the total repayment period, while the numerator is determined by the principle illustrated above. For example, if you repay a ten month loan after two months, the lender receives 19/55 ([10 + 9] ÷ [1 + 2 + 3 + . . . + 9 + 10]) of the total finance charges. Although the use of the Rule of 78 to determine interest charges on prepayments of installment loans is most common, other rules do exist. Item 13 in the sample installment purchase agreement given in Figure 12-2 indicates that the Rule of 78 is used on prepayments under that contract.

Mortgage Loans

The *mortgage loan*, which is used to finance the purchase of real estate, was briefly described during the discussion of home purchases in Chapter 9. Because these loans are likely to represent the largest single liability on an individual's balance sheet, an understanding of the various types, features, and costs of such loans is vital to the effective management of personal finances. Mortgage loans are a special type of installment loan that is specifically used to purchase real estate. In this portion of the chapter, the types, sources, coverage, application procedures, costs and other features, and closing and related procedures are discussed.

Types of Mortgage Loans

Most people cannot afford to purchase a home for cash. The only feasible way to obtain the needed financing is through a mortgage loan. Because of the relatively large sum involved, the lender secures the loan by a mortgage on the property—a legal right to sell the property in order to repay the loan should the borrower default. Lenders normally loan no more than 70 to 95 percent of the value of the property. The borrower must therefore make a down payment of 5 to 30 percent of the value. The three basic types of mortgage loans available are the conventional loan, the FHA insured loan, and the VA guaranteed loan. Each is briefly described below.

Conventional Loan Nearly 70 percent of all mortgage loans are conventional loans. They are made by various financial institutions using their own money, which may come from deposits, borrowing, or the owners'

"... of course, if you feel that 10% and your first-born male child is too expensive, you're welcome to look elsewhere."

Shopping for Real Estate Loans Is Recommended

Source: Changing Times, March 1974, p. 22. Reprinted with permission from *Changing Times* Magazine, © Kiplinger Washington Editors, Inc., 1974.

investment. The lender bears all of the risk; there are no government loans or guarantees involved. Loans ranging to as much as 95 percent of the appraised value of the property can be obtained with maturities of twenty-five to thirty years. Note that the appraised value, which is determined by the lender, is not necessarily equal to the market value. The interest rate on conventional mortgages has most recently ranged between 8 and 10 percent.

FHA Loan An FHA loan is like a conventional loan in that it is made by a financial institution, but it is insured by the Federal Housing Administration (FHA), a branch of the U.S. Department of Housing and Urban Development (HUD). This type of insured loan is easy to obtain since lenders know that if the borrower defaults, the FHA will take over the payments and they are thus protected against loan defaults. In order to qualify for an FHA loan, the property being purchased as well as the buyer (borrower) must meet certain standards established by the FHA. These requirements vary from time to time; occasionally new FHA loan programs are established. Although FHA loans are a bit more restrictive than conventional mortgages, they have greatest appeal to those buying lower priced homes who cannot as easily qualify for the conventional loan. In 1977 the FHA would insure a loan only up to $45,000, even if the home cost more than that. Pending legislation may well raise this maximum to $60,000. These loans require minimum down payments determined by taking 3 percent of the first $25,000, plus 10 percent of the next $10,000, plus 20 percent of the next $10,000. (Of course, for homes costing more than $45,000 the purchaser must pay all the purchase costs above that amount.) Down payments on FHA loans thus vary from 3 percent to $8\frac{1}{3}$ percent of the insurable cost of the home. For example, the down payment required on a $40,000 home financed by an FHA-insured loan would be $2,750 (0.03 × $25,000 + 0.10 × $10,000 + 0.20 × $5,000), or $6\frac{7}{8}$ percent of the purchase price. The repayment period on FHA loans usually ranges from twenty-five to thirty years, and the interest rate is generally one-half percent above the conventional rate in order to cover the cost of the insurance.

VA Loan The VA loan program is available only to qualified veterans of U.S. military service. The loans are guaranteed by the Veterans Administration (VA); thus, if the borrower defaults, the VA pays the lender. Although the VA does not guarantee the entire loan, because the lender holds a mortgage against the property, the lender's risk is virtually zero under this arrangement. Besides being veterans, applicants for VA loans must meet certain VA requirements, as must the property they wish to purchase. Since lenders are not required to make VA loans, their availability to qualified veterans is in no way assured. If the VA's appraisal of the property shows it to be of a value equal to or greater than the purchase price, it is possible for the applicant to obtain the loan without down payment. Regulated by the VA, the interest rate on VA loans is generally lower than the rate charged on conventional mortgages, and the repayment period can be as long as thirty years. Before applying for a VA loan, the borrower must obtain a Certificate of Eligibility, usually from the local VA office.

Sources of Mortgage Loans

Most mortgage loans are made by savings and loan associations, which use customers' savings deposits for this purpose. The second largest source of such loans is commercial banks, which often make mortgage loans to their better customers. The third largest source is mutual savings banks (90 percent of which are located in New England); these banks use the money they receive in the form of customer deposits to make the loans. Another good source of mortgage loans is mortgage companies; these companies do not accept deposits but instead use the money of large investors to buy real estate mortgages. In some areas of the country, life insurance companies make FHA-insured and VA-guaranteed loans as well as conventional loans on expensive homes. A final source of mortgage loans is the seller of the home, who must have the money to lend and who must feel that the return from the loan will be acceptable in light of other available investments.

Mortgage Coverage

Three alternative types of mortgage coverage may be available to the borrower. The most common coverage is the *budget mortgage*, which often includes property tax and insurance payments as part of the monthly payment and can be obtained on any kind of mortgage—conventional, FHA, and VA. A *package mortgage*, which is also available for all three types of mortgage loans, allows the borrower to include the financing of major household appliances as part of the loan. Although this type of mortgage is a "good deal" for the borrower since interest rates on mortgage loans are lower than on appliance loans, it is not permitted in certain states. *Open-end mortgage* coverage, which can be obtained only in conventional loans, allows the borrower to reborrow as the loan is repaid. For example, if you had borrowed $30,000 initially and through your payments reduced the loan principal to $28,000, you could borrow an additional $2,000 against the mortgage. While the package and open-end mortgage coverages have appeal, you are most likely to use the budget mortgage for financing your home purchase.

Applying for a Mortgage Loan

Because the rate of interest, terms of the loan, and down payment are likely to differ from lender to lender, it is advisable to make sure that you have found the most advantageous loan for which you can qualify prior to making a loan application. Once you have made an application, you are informally bound to the lender. If your loan is approved, you are expected to take it; if you do not, the lender is likely to charge you a few hundred dollars for the clerical costs incurred. In some parts of the country, an application fee of $25 to $100 is charged at the time of application. You should be able to find the "best deal" by talking to your banker, a realtor, or a friend who is knowledgeable in the field of finance and by getting rate quotations from potential lenders. Although most mortgage loans are issued by savings and loans or mutual savings banks, it is advisable to look at all possibilities prior to committing yourself to a specific lender.

Costs and Other Features

There are several important factors to be considered when shopping for and negotiating a mortgage loan, including the borrowing costs and other finance charges and some additional and rather significant features of the loan agreement. These are discussed in the following sections.

Interest Rate: Fixed, Variable, or Graduated The interest on a mortgage loan is calculated using the simple interest method, which applies the stated rate of interest only to the declining loan balance. As was indicated in earlier portions of the chapter, this approach causes the stated interest rate to equal the annual percentage rate of interest. The mortgage interest rate may be fixed, variable, or graduated. *Fixed interest rates* are stated at the time the loan is negotiated and will not change over the life of the mortgage. Under this type of arrangement, the lender is required by law to state the annual percentage rate (APR) or true rate of interest charged on the loan. *Variable rate mortgages* are an increasingly common device that allows the mortgage rate to change over the life of the loan in response to economic conditions. When money is in short supply, the variable interest rate will increase, and when money is plentiful, it will drop. The *graduated rate mortgage* is another new device; it is designed to allow a young family to buy housing in anticipation of future income. These mortgages have low interest rates over the first few years and higher rates in later years. The early payments on them are therefore lower and the later payments higher. The annual percentage rate of interest over the life of the mortgage is quite similar to that on a fixed rate mortgage. Figure 12-3 presents some basic questions and their answers with respect to the graduated rate mortgage (referred to as the "Modifier" by the savings and loan association that provided this information). An understanding of these basic types of interest arrangements should assist homebuyers in selecting the best type and source of mortgage loan in light of their financial needs and situation.

Points, Down Payment, and Maturity A few other factors that affect the actual cost of a mortgage loan are points, the down payment, and the loan maturity. A *point* represents a fee equal to 1 percent of the loan amount. Points are often charged on mortgage loans for either of two reasons: (1) to raise the annual percentage rate of the loan above its stated rate or (2) to pay the lender for making the loan, as a loan origination fee. For example, if the prevailing mortgage rate is 9 percent and the maximum rate allowed by the government on FHA and VA loans is 8½ percent, the lender might charge a fee of two points, which on a $30,000 loan would be $600. The two points would allow the lender to receive a 9 percent return on this FHA loan. In theory the points on government insured or guaranteed loans must be paid by the seller. Yet it is really the buyer who pays, since the seller will adjust the sale price upward to cover the cost of the points. On conventional, FHA, and VA loans, a loan origination fee of one to two points is commonly charged. According to one rule of thumb, each point charged raises the actual interest cost by ⅛ percent. Therefore on an 8½ percent loan for which the borrower must pay two points, the actual cost would be 8¾ percent (8½ percent + [2 × ⅛ percent]).

The *down payment* also varies from loan to loan. This payment by the purchaser is most often stated as a percentage of the purchase price of the home. For instance, a 20 percent down payment on a $37,500 purchase price would mean that the purchaser must pay $7,500 (20 percent × $37,500) in cash and can borrow the remaining $30,000 ($37,500 − $7,500). Generally, the larger the down payment, the lower the number of points charged by the lender. For example, while the interest on a 90

The Variable Rate Mortgage Boom in California

In just 22 months, a half dozen or so of California's largest state-chartered stock savings-and-loan associations have loaned out nearly $5 billion in variable rate mortgages, most of it in the past 12 months.

For the two largest California S&Ls, Home Savings & Loan and Great Western Financial, 80% of all their new mortgage loans in the last 12 months have been in the form of variable rate mortgages, which now constitute 35% to 40% of their portfolios. President James F. Montgomery of Great Western Financial flatly predicted last month that 55% of GWF's portfolio this year will be VRMs. In March alone, Home S&L President Richard H. Deihl claims, "over 90% of $300 million in mortgages held in escrow were VRMs."

VRMs are mortgages that include a provision permitting the lender to adjust the interest rate in the mortgage up or down, depending on changes in the average cost of funds to the S&Ls. The maximum upward rate change in any year cannot exceed one-half of 1% or more than 2½ points over the life of the mortgage.

California's state-chartered S&Ls really first began issuing VRMs in volume in 1975, although they have been legally permitted since 1970. Federally chartered S&Ls still cannot issue or buy VRMs. However, by sometime next year Congress may pass legislation enabling federal S&Ls at least to buy VRMs in the secondary market, and perhaps to offer them. . . .

Looking ahead, the S&Ls figure the VRMs are a good hedge to put more stability into their highly cyclical earnings pattern. Right now the S&Ls are in the soaring stage: Earnings gained an average of 60% in 1976 as loan volume recovered sharply from depressed 1974 and interest spreads widened to near-record levels; and, says Jerry Gitt [a San Francisco–based S&L analyst], "Spreads should continue to widen in 1977." However, S&L managements are thinking about 1978 and beyond.

The California real estate market is playing into their hands. Prices of new homes there have spurted to above $55,000 in most markets, and prices of existing homes—the big mortgage market—in places like Orange County and San Diego have been rising even faster. Many state S&Ls are taking advantage of the trend by insisting that borrowers take VRMs on properties with mortgages of $55,000 and up.

percent loan (10 percent down payment) is 9 percent plus 2½ points, the rate on an 80 percent loan (20 percent down payment) is 9 percent plus 2 points.

The *maturity* of mortgage loans can range from ten years to thirty years. The longer the maturity, the lower the monthly payment, but also the greater the amount of interest being paid each period. Because of the outstanding appreciation in real estate values over the past few years, it is probably best to buy the most expensive home your budget permits and borrow for as long as possible. If you do buy a more expensive home, the increase in property value you will experience will be greater, thereby

---

Real estate brokers love VRMs. As one S&L executive told FORBES: "It doesn't take much selling on his [the broker's] part to convince a buyer in today's market to go for a little higher-priced house. To clinch that sale, the broker is increasingly likely to steer him to S&Ls that are actively seeking VRM business. On a more expensive house, the broker earns a larger commission."

Look at what he can promise with a VRM. If a buyer is transferred or wants to move during a tight-money period, the VRM holder has the right to transfer his mortgage at his existing contract rate, even though the interest rate on new mortgages may have risen significantly in the meantime. That is a big selling point with homeowners in California, where moving is almost a pastime.

The trend to higher-priced homes is being enfolded into the California culture. "The old rule of thumb—that no more than 25% of a family's monthly income should go for housing costs—has faded," a Great Western senior executive told a group of San Francisco analysts in March. "Most mortgage loans made in the last few years have accepted 30% to 33% of income as adequate. That's not just our bank, but pretty much a general situation in California." The working wife not only wants to work, she *has* to work.

Of course, S&Ls have not relaxed their insistence on a healthy down payment, usually 20%, which means close to $15,000 on a $70,000 house. Some families manage that by borrowing, others by taking out second mortgages, still others by both. So, for many California homebuyers, real shelter costs today are even higher than is generally recognized.

The frenzied buying in California is even beginning to worry some S&L executives. Says Home S&L's Richard Deihl: "I expect demand for homes to plateau in the next few months. If it doesn't, we're going to have to take a look at our lending policies."

Clearly, variable rate mortgages did not *create* the current frothy California housing boom—but if oversold by eager brokers, VRMs could get in trouble along with it.

Source: Reprinted by permission of *Forbes* Magazine from "VRMs Go Vroom in California," *Forbes,* 15 April 1977, pp. 110, 114.

Figure 12-3 **Questions and Answers about the Graduated Rate Mortgage (the "Modifier")**

THE ◪ODIFIER

MidAmerica Savings & Loan offers a special loan financing plan designed to enable more people to become homeowners. The following questions and answers explain this convenient payment plan.

What is the ◪ODIFIER loan?

The ◪ODIFIER loan is a financing method (conventional loan) designed to reduce monthly payments during the early years of a loan.

How does it work?

The loan terms require interest payments only, plus escrows for taxes, hazard insurance, and private mortgage insurance (if applicable) during the first five years of a loan. Thereafter, the payments will increase to fully retire the debt in the required number of years.

What's an example?

Assume the following hypothetical example:

Loan Amount	$35,000.00
Interest Rate	8.75%
Term	30 years

Principal and interest payments based on a thirty year amortization —**$275.35.**
◪ODIFIER interest only payment for the first 5 yrs.—**$255.21.**
◪ODIFIER principal and interest payments during the remaining 25 years—**$287.76.**

The ◪ODIFIER monthly payments during the first five years of the loan are $20.14 per month less than the standard thirty year loan. After five years, the ◪ODIFIER'S monthly installments would increase to an amount required to retire the debt during the remaining 25 years of the loan.

NOTE—Escrows for taxes, hazard insurance, and private mortgage insurance if required will be included in addition to the payments illustrated above. The lender cannot control changes in taxes or insurance premiums.

Who is eligible for this loan?

Any loan applicant who meets the underwriting guidelines set forth by MidAmerica Savings may qualify for this loan, based on the following conditions:
1. The loan is for 30 years.
2. The borrower occupies the property.
3. The loan meets all conditions and requirements set forth for qualification by MidAmerica Savings.

How does the ◪ODIFIER help?

The ◪ODIFIER reduces the required monthly payment during the period when the borrowers income is generally the lowest. By reducing the initial payment during the first 5 years this may enable some home buyers to purchase a home where they otherwise may have been unable to meet the financial obligation. In some cases, it may broaden the opportunity to upgrade the style or quality of home desired.

Is this plan optional?

Yes, it may be selected by the borrowers upon approval of MidAmerica Savings, as an option to a normal 30 year loan.

NOTE—The ◪ODIFIER may be discontinued by MidAmerica Savings at any time. However, should this happen, it will not affect those ◪ODIFIER loans that have already been closed.

*The above constitutes an example of ◪ODIFIER loan transaction. There is no assurance that an applicant will qualify for any loan, or that an applicant who does qualify for a loan will be able to obtain the loan amount, interest rate and/or term applied for. All loan applications are subject to review and approval by MidAmerica Federal Savings and Loan Association.

Source: Courtesy of MidAmerica Federal Savings and Loan Association, Tulsa, Oklahoma.

increasing your net worth and at the same time allowing you to maintain your standard of living if you can meet the increased cost of taxes, maintenance, and utilities. Most conventional, FHA, and VA lenders make loans with thirty-year maturities; most commercial banks make mortgage loans with maximum maturities of twenty-five years. Interest rate, fee, maturity, and down payment data on conventional loans in a variety of U.S. cities are presented in Table 12-6.

Table 12-6 **Conventional Mortgage Loan Statistics for Various Cities, 1975**[a]

	New Houses						Previously Occupied Houses					
	Contract Rate	Fees and Charges	Effective Rate	Mortgage Term (Years)	Purchase Price	Down Payment	Contract Rate	Fees and Charges	Effective Rate	Mortgage Term (Years)	Purchase Price	Down Payment
U.S. Average	8.74%	1.37%	8.96%	26.6	$43,100	23.2%	8.86%	1.18%	9.05%	24.7	$39,400	25.7%
Atlanta	8.65	2.41	9.04	29.8	53,100	19.1	8.68	2.58	9.10	28.7	52,000	18.4
Baltimore	8.58	0.63	8.67	28.7	49,900	20.6	8.90	0.03	8.90	24.4	46,800	32.9
Boston[b]	9.08	0.26	9.11	26.4	37,800	27.3	8.91	0.25	8.94	23.9	51,700	32.9
Chicago– Northwestern Indiana Consolidated Area	8.73	1.39	8.96	24.5	48,800	28.3	8.78	1.53	9.03	25.0	46,700	30.7
Cleveland	8.58	2.00	8.91	28.1	43,900	21.1	8.77	1.61	8.03	26.8	38,200	27.2
Dallas	8.49	2.71	8.93	28.8	46,900	21.3	8.72	1.31	8.93	27.3	50,000	20.5
Denver	8.70	1.30	8.91	29.7	54,700	24.9	8.94	1.25	9.14	29.1	46,400	23.0
Detroit	8.51	1.13	8.69	29.3	53,000	25.0	8.81	1.06	8.98	28.1	41,800	25.5
Houston	8.37	3.10	8.87	30.0	49,300	16.0	8.93	1.42	9.16	28.8	59,700	17.5
Los Angeles– Long Beach	8.78	1.13	8.96	29.8	54,400	22.7	8.96	1.31	9.17	29.3	51,000	22.1
Miami	8.82	3.11	9.33	27.9	42,500	18.3	8.57	3.26	9.11	26.2	56,900	25.3
Minneapolis– St. Paul[c]	8.00	0.26	8.04	27.6	54,800	28.7	7.99	0.17	8.01	27.7	46,400	27.1
New York– Northeastern New Jersey Consolidated Area	8.51	0.44	8.58	28.7	52,100	33.8	8.62	0.44	8.69	25.7	51,500	33.4
Philadelphia	8.77	1.11	8.95	25.3	50,100	31.4	8.99	0.88	9.13	23.4	45,800	33.1
St. Louis	8.71	1.03	8.87	23.8	39,600	37.9	8.90	1.07	9.08	21.9	28,100	22.2
San Francisco– Oakland	8.86	1.42	9.09	29.4	61,300	23.8	9.14	1.48	9.38	29.1	52,100	22.9
Seattle–Everett	9.09	2.24	9.45	29.0	54,200	17.4	9.12	1.99	9.45	27.7	42,000	21.8
Washington, D.C., Virginia, Maryland	8.71	0.71	8.82	29.8	44,900	15.7	8.83	0.67	8.94	27.7	65,700	27.7

[a]These are average rates and terms for conventional mortgage loans completed in early June (except where noted) as reported by the Federal Home Loan Bank Board. "Contract rate" is the interest rate stated in the loan contract. "Effective rate" reflects both ordinary interest and the initial fees and charges that boost the lender's return. It is calculated by amortizing the fees and charges over ten years.
[b]Figures for new houses are for April.
[c]Figures for new houses are for May.

Source: "Buy a House or Rent? A Fresh Look at the Options." Reprinted with permission from *The Changing Times Family Success Book,* © Kiplinger Washington Editors, Inc., 1975.

Assuming a Loan If you purchase a used home, it is sometimes advantageous to assume the loan of the seller. By so doing, you can avoid certain administrative costs, and you may be able to obtain a lower interest rate than you could on a new loan. Most mortgage agreements now contain "Due on Sale" clauses, which effectively prohibit assumptions of loans. Nonetheless, many lenders will allow you to assume such a loan if you pay one point or a stated dollar amount as an assumption fee.

Because of the potential savings in financing costs, it is advisable to investigate the possibility of assuming a mortgage loan. Note, however, that your down payment will have to equal the difference between the purchase price and the mortgage balance in order to assume a loan.

Monthly Payment At a minimum, the monthly payment required on a mortgage loan will include interest and the repayment of principal. These financing cost components (for fixed interest rate loans) are *amortized* over the life of the loan, which means they are converted into equal monthly payments. Because of the long maturities of these loans, the payments made in the early years of the mortgage are almost completely interest; only a small part of each is repayment of the principal amount borrowed. Of course, in the later years, the major share of every payment is used to reduce the principal. For a given principal amount, loan maturity, and interest rate, the monthly financing cost can be determined from a loan payment table. A portion of one of these tables showing the monthly loan amortization payments on a $30,000 mortgage, given various loan maturities and interest rates, is presented in Table 12-7. As

Table 12-7 **Monthly Loan Amortization Payments on a $30,000 Mortgage Loan for Various Maturities and Interest Rates**

Loan Maturity (in Years)	Interest Rate						
	8%	$8^1/_4$%	$8^1/_2$%	$8^3/_4$%	9%	$9^1/_4$%	$9^1/_2$%
10	$363.99	$367.96	$371.96	$375.99	$380.03	$384.10	$388.20
15	286.70	291.05	295.43	299.84	304.28	308.76	313.27
20	250.94	255.62	260.35	265.12	269.92	274.77	279.64
25	231.55	236.54	241.57	246.65	251.76	256.92	262.11
30	220.13	225.38	230.68	236.02	241.39	246.81	252.26
35	213.08	218.55	224.06	229.61	235.20	240.83	246.49

indicated in this table, for a given loan maturity, as the interest rate increases, so does the monthly payment increase; and for a given interest rate, the monthly payment decreases as the maturity increases.

Many mortgage lenders require you to include not only the amortized loan cost but also your homeowner's insurance and property tax in your monthly payments (i.e., a budget mortgage). For example, assume you borrow $30,000 at 9 percent for thirty years to purchase a home on which monthly homeowner's insurance costs are expected to be $15 and monthly property taxes are expected to be $45. Your monthly mortgage payment will be:

Loan Amortization Payment (from Table 12-7)	$241.39
Homeowner's Insurance	15.00
Property Taxes	45.00
Monthly Mortgage Payment	$301.39

The portion of your monthly payment that consists of insurance and taxes is held in escrow by the lender, who then uses it at the appropriate time to pay the insurance and property taxes on your behalf. This arrangement is disadvantageous to the borrower, who must pay this amount prematurely and thus lose interest that could be earned on it, unless the lender pays interest on the escrow account. Although some states have passed laws requiring lenders to do so, most states currently do not have legislation to this effect. It is quite likely, however, that this situation will be remedied in the near future.

Mortgage and Title Insurance Sometimes lenders require borrowers to purchase mortgage and/or title insurance. *Mortgage insurance* is an insurance policy on the life of the borrower that names the lender as the beneficiary. If the borrower dies, the mortgage is automatically paid off, thereby leaving clear title to the property for the borrower's beneficiaries. Most major insurance companies have developed mortgage insurance policies on which the insurance declines with the loan balance. This type of insurance is discussed in greater detail in Chapter 13. *Title insurance* is sometimes required by lenders as a form of protection against the possibility that the title to the property for which the loan is made will be found faulty. The cost of title insurance is usually paid by the buyer, although the seller does occasionally assume it. It ranges from $1/4$ of 1 percent to $1/2$ of 1 percent of the amount borrowed and is paid only once, normally at the closing of the loan. For example, to insure the title for the $30,000 being borrowed when the insurance rate is $1/4$ of 1 percent, the cost would be $75 (0.0025 × $30,000). Title insurance protects not only the lender but also the borrower against any flaws in the title.

Prepayment Clause Most mortgage loans have a clause concerned with the prepayment of the loan prior to its maturity date. This clause may seriously affect the borrower's ability to sell his or her home prior to the maturity of the loan. Prepayment penalties can amount to as much as 5 percent of the total loan. Since most people do not live in a home long enough to pay off the loan on it, it is best to avoid mortgage loans with these penalties. The more common type of prepayment clause is designed to keep the borrower from refinancing the house with another lender. It penalizes the borrower only for paying off the loan prior to its maturity in order to obtain new financing; when the loan is prepaid as a result of selling the house, no penalty is charged.

Closing or Settlement Costs and Procedures

Once the mortgage loan has been approved and all of the legal work with respect to the transaction has been completed, the loan closing will be scheduled. The latest date at which the closing can take place is normally specified in the purchase contract. The participants in the closing, which typically takes place at the offices of the lender, are usually the purchaser, the seller, the lender, and the realtors representing the buyer and seller. Often attorneys representing buyer and seller also attend the closing. At the closing, the deed to the property is delivered to the buyer in exchange for payment to the seller. The buyer signs a loan agreement for the amount borrowed and a mortgage agreement, which gives the lender a legal claim on the property in the event the borrower defaults. Two important aspects of the closing process are the closing costs and the execution of the deed.

Closing Costs In addition to the down payment, the purchaser must pay closing costs. These processing and title costs cover the examination of the title, the recording of legal documents in the county courthouse, the survey and appraisal of the property, the taxes on the mortgage, the acquisition of credit reports, the purchase of title insurance, and the payment of points in order to obtain the loan. In the case of FHA loans, the payment of points to adjust the interest rate is shown as a deduction from the proceeds to the seller although, as was pointed out earlier, the buyer is the one who actually pays this portion of the purchase price. It is not unusual for the processing and title costs to amount to from 1 to 4 percent of the mortgage. Also at closing certain prepayments, or escrow payments, are made, which normally include thirteen months of home-owner's insurance plus two to three months of property taxes. The insurance payment provides insurance for the first year and the amount necessary to pay for an additional month. This latter sum is placed in escrow. Some lenders let the borrower pay the first year's homeowner's insurance and require payment of only one or two month's insurance at closing. Under the Truth in Lending Law, the lender must provide "estimates" of the total amount of the closing costs—down payment, processing and title costs, and prepaid or escrow payments—at the time of the loan application. In many cases the actual closing costs will be greater than those estimated.

The Deed At the closing, the *deed*, which is a legal instrument used to transfer the title of real property from one party, known as the *grantor* (seller), to another party, known as the *grantee* (buyer), is executed and given to the buyer. The two basic types of deeds are the *quitclaim deed* and the *warranty deed.* A quitclaim deed gives the grantee whatever claim the grantor had on the property and completely relieves the grantor of further risk. In other words, the risks and consequences of flaws in the title pass to the grantee. The warranty deed is safer because the grantor warrants that the title to the property is "clean" and therefore has no flaws. The grantor in this case is liable if any flaws are subsequently discovered. In any case, because of the legal considerations involved, the title to the property should be examined by a competent attorney to make certain no flaws exist. As indicated above, the purchase of title insurance provides additional protection against any flaws that might be discovered in the future.

Summary

There are three basic types of consumer loans that are not open account forms of credit. Single payment loans are made for a specified period of time at the end of which full payment is due. They are used as interim financing and to meet emergency needs. Installment loans are repaid through a series of payments scheduled over a period of months. They are used to finance purchases of more expensive goods and services such as automobiles and appliances. Mortgage loans are a special type of installment loan; they are used to purchase real estate, especially homes, and have maturities ranging from ten to thirty years. Consumer loans can be obtained from a variety of sources including commercial banks, credit unions, consumer finance companies, life insurance companies, savings and loan associations, sales finance companies, pawnshops, remedial loan societies, and friends and relatives.

Either the simple interest method or the discount method is normally used to determine the finance charges on single payment loans. While the stated rate of interest and the annual percentage rate (APR) of interest are equal using the simple interest method, the APR that results from the discount method is higher than the stated rate of interest. Most single payment loans are secured by loan collateral on which the lender obtains a security interest by filing a lien against the property. To have this legal claim on movable property, the lender must obtain either a chattel mortgage or a collateral note. Sometimes a single payment loan can be secured if a second party signs for it. Although lenders may allow early repayment of a single payment loan, they are likely to charge a fee for such action. Late payment of these loans can result in a damaged credit rating and possibly even personal bankruptcy.

Financial tables and formulas are required to calculate finance charges and APRs for installment loans because of the periodic nature of the payments. When the simple interest method is used on these loans, the APR and stated rate of interest are equal. However, the use of the add-on method to calculate finance charges results in an APR that is considerably higher than the stated interest rate. The installment purchase agreement, which may include a sales contract, a security agreement, a note, and various insurance requirements, contains all the relevant information pertaining to the purchase and installment repayment plan. Various aspects of purchase agreements that consumers should be aware of and understand include the following: the holder in due course doctrine, confession of judgment, add-on clauses, acceleration clauses, wage assignment or garnishment, repossession, and balloon clauses. Quite often installment lenders use the Rule of 78 to determine interest refunds when loans are prepaid.

Mortgage loans are likely to be the largest liability consumers will incur during their lifetime. The common types of mortgages are conventional loans, FHA-insured loans, and VA-guaranteed loans. The down payment and annual percentage rate (APR) of interest on mortgage loans differs with the type of mortgage as well as with the mortgage lender. Mortgage loans are usually obtained from savings and loans, commercial banks, and mutual savings banks. Although the most common type of mortgage coverage is the budget mortgage, both package mortgages and open-end mortgages may be available. The actual interest rate on a mortgage loan can be fixed, variable, or graduated over the life of the loan. Points are often charged on a mortgage loan in order to raise the APR or as a loan origination fee. The portion of the monthly payment (on fixed interest rate loans) attributable to borrowing is amortized over the life of the loan. Borrowers sometimes purchase mortgage and/or title insurance. At closing, the deed changes hands and the purchaser pays the seller using his or her own money as well as the mortgage loan proceeds. Also at this time the purchaser makes any specified prepayments or escrow payments and pays any processing and title costs charged by the lender.

Key Terms

acceleration clause
add-on clause
add-on (interest) method
amortized loan
appraised value
assignment (wage)
balloon clause
budget mortgage

captive finance company
cash value (life insurance)
chattel mortgage
closing (or settlement)
collateral note
confession of judgment
consumer finance company
conventional mortgage

cosign
credit life insurance
deed
discount (interest) method
escrow payments
Federal Garnishment Law (1970)
FHA loan
fixed interest rate
garnishment
graduated rate mortgage
grantee
grantor
holder in due course (doctrine)
installment loan
installment purchase agreement
interim financing
lien
loan origination fee
mortgage companies
mortgage insurance
mortgage loan
note

open-end mortgage
package mortgage
pawnshop
points
prepayments (escrow payments)
prepayment clause
principal amount
processing and title costs
quitclaim deed
remedial loan society
repossession
Rule of 78 (Sum of the Digits)
sales contract
sales finance companies
secured (and unsecured) loans
security agreement (or security interest)
simple interest method
single payment loan
small loan company
title insurance
VA loan
variable rate mortgage
warranty deed

Review Questions

1. Briefly describe the basic types of consumer loans that are available. Discuss the sources from which these loans can be obtained.

2. Explain how you can obtain a loan against the cash value of your life insurance policy.

3. Discuss the role of savings and loan associations in providing consumer loans. Describe how these institutions are able to offer these loans.

4. What is meant by "selling paper"? Explain.

5. Explain how pawnshops operate. Are there any regulations on pawnbrokers? Which people frequent pawnshops?

6. What are single payment loans? What two methods are used to calculate finance charges on single payment loans?

7. Indicate whether the following statements are true or false and explain your response.

(a) The simple interest method is one in which interest is charged only on the average loan balance outstanding.

(b) Under the discount method, the finance charge is calculated and then added to the total amount of the loan.

(c) Most single payment loans are unsecured only for the highest quality borrowers with proven credit reputations.

(d) The instrument giving the lender title to the property in the event of default is called a lien.

8. Illustrate how single payment loans can be secured with a second mortgage.

9. Explain briefly the important features of a loan agreement that must be disclosed according to the Truth in Lending Law.

10. What are installment loans? What are they typically used for? Where can these loans be obtained?

11. A sales contract is an important part of the installment purchase agreement. Explain its role. What is the security agreement?

12. Why is a borrower often required to purchase credit life and disability insurance as a condition for receiving an installment loan? Explain.

13. Discuss each of the following special features that may be included in an installment purchase agreement.

(a) Holder in due course

(b) Confession of judgment

(c) Add-on clause

(d) Acceleration clause

(e) Wage assignment: garnishment

(f) Repossession

(g) Balloon clause

14. What is the Rule of 78? Kathy Harrington of Chicago borrowed $3,000 to be repaid in twelve monthly installments. The total finance charges over the life of the loan are $260. What is the amount that the lender will receive using the Rule of 78 if Kathy wishes to repay the loan after nine months?

15. What are mortgage loans? Briefly describe the various types of mortgage loans available.

16. Define and differentiate between budget mortgage, package mortgage, and open-end mortgage coverages.

17. For each item in the left column, match the appropriate item given in the right column.

(a) Variable rate mortgage   (1) Money paid the lender for making a loan

(b) Graduated rate mortgage

(c) Loan origination fee

(d) Down payment

(e) Mortgage insurance

(f) Closing costs

(g) Escrow payments

(h) Quitclaim deed

(2) Costs which include certain processing and title costs

(3) Buyer's contribution to the purchase price which is often stated as a percentage of the face value of the loan

(4) Prepayments which normally include three months of homeowner's insurance plus two months of property taxes

(5) A mortgage in which interest rates change over time in response to economic conditions

(6) A mortgage that allows a young family to buy housing in anticipation of future income

(7) A legal instrument which gives the grantee whatever claim the grantor had on the property, completely relieving the grantor of further risk

(8) Insurance policy on life of a mortgage borrower for which the lender is the beneficiary

12-1 Sidney's Cadillac Purchase: Choosing the Best Loan

Case Problems

Sidney Watson, a thirty year old bachelor living in Charlotte, Virginia, has been a high school teacher at Piedmont High for the past eight years. For two years he has been contemplating purchasing a Cadillac but has not been able to afford a brand new one. Recently, however, John McKenzie, a friend of Sidney's, has offered to sell his 1976 Cadillac to Sidney. John wants $7,500 for his sedan, which has been driven only 20,000 miles and is in very good condition. Sidney is eager to buy the car, but he has only about $3,000 in his savings account at the Chemical Bank. He expects to net $2,000 from the sale of his 1974 Mercury Capri, but this will still leave him short of the $7,500 figure by about $2,500. He has two alternatives for obtaining this sum:

(1) Borrow the needed $2,500 from the Charlotte Teachers' Credit Union at a fixed rate of 10 percent per annum simple interest. The loan would be repaid in a single payment at the end of two years.

(2) Obtain an installment loan requiring twenty-four monthly payments from the First National Bank of Charlotte at a 6 percent stated rate of interest. The add-on method will be used to calculate the finance charges on this loan.

Questions

1. Calculate: (a) the finance charges, (b) the APR, and (c) the size of the single payment on the loan offered by the Charlotte Teachers' Credit Union.

2. Calculate: (a) the finance charges, (b) the APR, and (c) the size of the monthly payment on the loan offered by the First National Bank of Charlotte.

3. Discuss the pros and cons of each loan and indicate which loan you would advise Sidney to accept. Explain your answer.

12-2 Evaluating a Mortgage Loan for the Newtons

Farrah and Sam Newton, both in their early thirties, have been married for five years. Sam has an accounting degree from Northwestern University and is presently employed as an assistant financial controller with Smith, Kline, and French, Inc., at an annual salary of $20,000, which leaves him with $17,000 after taxes. The Newtons have two children, ages two and four. At present they are living in a duplex but wish to buy a house in the suburbs of their rapidly developing city. They have decided that they can afford only a $45,000 house and hope to find one with the features they desire in a good neighborhood.

The taxes on such a home are expected to be $660 per year, insurance costs are expected to be $240 per year, and utility bills are estimated at $600 per year. The Newtons are considering financing their proposed home with a conventional mortgage at 9.5 percent for thirty years. The savings and loan association from which they would borrow requires a 20 percent down payment on this type of mortgage loan. Over the last five years they have been saving for the down payment on the home and now have $7,000 in their savings account at Continental Savings & Loan Association.

Questions

1. Calculate the size of the down payment the Newtons will need in order to buy the proposed home.

2. How much will their monthly mortgage payments be? (*Note:* The monthly payment required to amortize a loan of $36,000 over thirty years at 9.5 percent is $302.71.)

3. They would also like to purchase title insurance, which costs $\frac{1}{2}$ of 1 percent of the amount borrowed. How much will it cost?

4. If the seller decides to give them a 10 percent second mortgage for the difference between the $7,000 they have in savings and the required down payment, should they take it? Discuss your answer. (*Note:* The second mortgage would be repaid with monthly payments over a five-year period. The required monthly payment at the 10 percent rate for that period can be found by multiplying the amount of the second mortgage by 0.02125.)

5. What recommendation would you give the Newtons? Explain.

Selected References

"Are You over Your Head in Debt?" *Better Homes and Gardens*, June 1975, pp. 8–10.

Bailey, Fred. "There Must Be a Better Way to Finance a House!" *Better Homes and Gardens*, May 1975, pp. 6 ff.

Bernstein, Elliott. "Mortgages with Changing Monthly Payments." *Money*, September 1975, pp. 65–66.

Ficek, Edmund F.; Henderson, Thomas P.; and Johnson, Ross H. *Real Estate Principles and Practices.* Columbus, Ohio: Charles E. Merrill, 1976.

"Finding Money to Remodel the House." *Changing Times*, November 1976, pp. 6–10.

"Getting a Home Loan These Days." *Changing Times*, September 1975, pp. 6–9.

Hawver, Carl F. *Basic Principles in Family Money and Credit Management.* Washington, D.C.: National Consumer Finance Association, 1972.

Hines, Mary Alice. *Principles and Practices of Real Estate.* Homewood, Ill.: Richard D. Irwin, 1976.

"How to Shop for Credit." *Consumer Reports*, March 1975, pp. 171–178.

"If Installment Contracts Said It in Plain English . . ." *Changing Times*, July 1975, pp. 46–47.

Lavoie, Rachel. "Mortgages for Cash-Shy House Hunters." *Money*, November 1976, pp. 101–102.

Mencher, Melvin. *The Fannie Mae Guide to Buying, Financing, and Selling Your Home.* New York: Doubleday, 1973.

Meyer, Jerome I. *Wipe Out Your Debts and Make a Fresh Start.* New York: Chancellor Press, 1973.

"An Owner's Manual for Financing a Car." *Money*, December 1973, pp. 78–82.

"Pay Ahead on Your Mortgage?" *Changing Times*, July 1977, pp. 15–17.

"Should You Co-sign a Loan?" *Better Homes and Gardens*, November 1976, pp. 40–41.

Unger, Maurice A. *Real Estate: Principles and Practices.* 5th ed. Cincinnati, Ohio: South-Western Publishing, 1974.

"What If You Can't Pay Your Mortgage?" *Changing Times*, August 1975, p. 26.

"When Bill Collectors Play Rough—." *U.S. News & World Report*, 16 May 1977, p. 75.

Part 5

Protecting Yourself
and Your Assets

Personal Balance Sheet	
Assets	Liabilities and Net Worth
Financial Assets	Liabilities
Nonfinancial Assets	Net Worth

This part of the text is concerned with the various types of insurance you may purchase to protect yourself and your family against loss of income and property. Good financial planning, personal asset management, and personal liability management could prove useless if adequate protection against unexpected and damaging events is not provided for. Specifically, at the same time people implement their financial plans, they must also safeguard the assets they own against loss resulting from uncontrollable factors. The following chapters describe the types of insurance available for providing needed protection. Chapter 13 outlines the fundamental features of insurance and discusses life insurance needs, types, and purchase procedures. Chapter 14 is concerned with health insurance needs, types, sources of coverage, and planning procedures. Chapter 15 deals with basic concepts of property and liability insurance and includes specific information relevant to homeowner's, automobile, and other forms of this type of insurance.

13

Life Insurance

A Preview of
Chapter 13

By way of underlining the importance of obtaining insurance and of
clarifying not only the most significant features of life insurance but also
the appropriate steps in the selection of a life insurance policy, this
chapter examines the following:

1. The fundamental aspects of insurance policies.

2. The concepts of risk, insurance, insurable exposures, and the underwriting function as they relate to providing adequate protection for
individuals and their assets.

3. The three approaches most commonly used to determine an individual's life insurance needs.

4. The characteristics of the three basic forms of life insurance—term,
whole life, and endowment—and some aspects of other types of life
insurance.

5. The basic elements in an insurance contract, additional policy features, and certain advantages of policy ownership.

6. Life insurance company operations, life insurance costs, and the
procedures for purchasing life insurance.

Acquiring assets and incurring liabilities based upon financial plans and
budgets consistent with your overall personal financial goals is important.
Because the ability to achieve these goals depends on a continuing stream
of income, it is important to make sure that death does not disrupt this

income stream. You should therefore know how to assess life insurance needs and select and purchase the appropriate quantity and type of insurance to secure your financial goals in the event of your own death or the death of any of the members of your family.

If you or any other members of your family were to die, the achievement of your financial goals might be jeopardized. Although it may currently seem ridiculous to worry about death, it is important to recognize that it is an unpredictable event that can have detrimental effects on your family's finances, if not properly planned for. Life insurance can provide adequate financial protection for your family in the event of your premature death or that of another family member. American families purchase more life insurance than families in any other country. Presently, the total face value of life insurance in force in the United States exceeds $2.3 trillion. This means an average of about $30,000 per family, though of course many families have little or no life insurance protection while others have policies with face values ranging into hundreds of thousands of dollars.

Table 13-1 presents key statistics on life insurance in force in the U.S. Note that *ordinary insurance* is a technical term used to refer to individual insurance policies. As can be seen in the table, this class of insurance is by far the most important form of life insurance. Because life insurance does play such an important role in the financial lives of many, the basic purpose of this chapter is to show you how to determine your life insurance needs and develop and maintain a life insurance program to fulfill them. Before the specifics of life insurance are discussed, several key factors which are basic to the understanding of all types of insurance require consideration.

Fundamentals of Insurance

Each year Americans pay nearly $125 billion in insurance premiums to private life, health, and property and liability insurance companies. This amount is more than double the sum spent annually on new automobiles. If this $125 billion were divided equally among everybody in the country, it would be $600 for each individual. And yet, even though insurance is a major part of the budgets of most families, relatively few people actually understand how to get the most benefit from their coverages.

Concept of Risk

Risk is defined as uncertainty regarding economic loss. The family that wishes to protect against financial calamity must learn to deal effectively

Table 13-1 **Key Life Insurance Statistics (1976)**

Life Insurance in Force in the United States (in Millions)

Ordinary (Individual Policies)	$1,117,672
Group	1,002,647
Industrial	39,175
Credit	123,569
Total	$2,343,000

Average Amounts of Life Insurance in Force in the United States

Per Family	$30,100
Per Insured Family	35,400

Life Insurance Purchases in the United States (in Millions)

Ordinary	$212,003
Group	102,791
Industrial	6,373
Total	$321,167

Benefit Payments in the United States (in Millions)

Payments to Beneficiaries	$ 9,593
Payments to Policyholders and Annuitants	15,018
Total	$24,611

Premium Receipts of U.S. Life Insurance Companies (in Millions)

Life Insurance	$31,358
Annuity Considerations	13,962
Health Insurance	21,059
Total	$66,379

Net Rate of Investment Income of U.S. Life Insurance Companies, Including Separate Accounts (before Federal Income Taxes) 6.55%

Source: Adapted with permission from *Life Insurance Fact Book '77* (Washington, D.C.: American Council of Life Insurance, 1977), p. 7.

with risk. One way to accomplish this objective is by purchasing insurance. Other methods, though, such as risk avoidance, risk assumption, and loss prevention, are also necessary measures that most families should undertake. These are discussed in greater detail in the following paragraphs. Although life insurance is the basic subject in the remainder of this chapter, the equally important topics of health, automobile, and homeowner's insurance are treated in the following two chapters.

Risk Avoidance Perhaps the simplest way to deal with risk is to avoid the exposure to loss that creates the risk. For example, people who are afraid they might lose everything they own because of a successful lawsuit against them resulting from an automobile accident could avoid driving. Many new college graduates avoid the risk of unstable or low earnings by refusing to accept employment in jobs that pay wages on a commission only basis.

Although avoidance can be an effective way to handle some risks, it is important to recognize that such action almost always involves a cost. For instance, the people mentioned above who avoid driving may incur a considerable cost in inconvenience, and the recent graduates may forfeit an opportunity for commission earnings that would greatly surpass their guaranteed salary. Risk avoidance is an attractive way to deal with risk when the estimated cost of avoidance is less than the estimated cost of handling it in some other way. Since common sense and personal analysis play a major role in decisions of risk avoidance, general guidelines cannot be developed for establishing risk avoidance strategies.

Risk Assumption When the family or individual chooses to bear or accept risk, this is termed *risk assumption*. Risk assumption can be an effective way to handle many types of potentially small exposures to loss for which the protection of insurance would be too expensive (for example, having your personal finance text stolen). It is also a reasonable approach in situations where very large exposures which the individual cannot insure, avoid, or prevent (nuclear holocaust, for instance) are present. Unfortunately, people often assume risks because they are unaware of many of the exposures to loss that are present or because they think that their insurance offers adequate protection when in fact it does not. Therefore, one of the objectives of this and the following two chapters is to better acquaint you with the exposures to loss that you will face and to provide you with some understanding of when risk assumption is the preferred manner for handling given risks.

Loss Prevention In a broad sense, *loss prevention* can be defined as any activity that reduces the probability a loss will occur (for example, driving within the speed limit) or lessens the severity of the loss should it occur (for example, wearing a safety belt and/or shoulder strap). Loss prevention should be an important part of the risk management program of every family and individual. In fact, insurance provides a reasonable means for handling risk only when society implements effective loss prevention measures. In other words, if all individuals drove fast and recklessly, the cost of collision insurance would be too great to allow people to purchase such protection.

Insurance Defined

Insurance is a device that allows society to reduce financial risks and share losses related to uncertain events. Risk (uncertainty) can be reduced because insurers are able to combine the experiences of large numbers of people, and with the resulting data they can accurately predict the losses experienced by the population. This prediction then allows each individual who wishes to share in the insurance system to contribute a specified small amount (the insurance premium) to an insurance company in exchange for a promise that he or she will not suffer a loss up to the amount of the insurance limits. Individuals benefit because they are able to transfer their risk to the insurer. The company benefits because, if it has accurately predicted the frequency and amount of economic loss, profit or contribution to surplus will remain after all claims and expenses of operation have been paid.

Characteristics of an Insurable Exposure

Even though insurance is an ideal method for handling the uncertainties related to potential economic loss, not all risks are insurable. In order for the insurance mechanism to work well, certain criteria must be met. Several of the more important of these criteria are: (1) there must be a large group of persons with similar exposures to loss, (2) the potential loss must be fortuitous, and (3) the cost of the insurance must be relatively low. Each of these is briefly explained below.

Large Group The necessity of involving a large group of persons with similar risk exposures is due to the fact that insurers base their premium calculations on what may loosely be called "the law of averages." Unless the group is large enough to permit an accurate calculation of what average losses will be, premiums cannot be computed with sufficient accuracy to allow the insurers to make a profit. Moreover, since insurance is a loss-sharing arrangement, the premium required from each individual in a small group would have to be quite large since the company could become insolvent if only one person suffered a loss.

Fortuitous Loss A *fortuitous loss* is one that happens by chance or accident—its timing and/or the occurrence is for the most part unintentional and unexpected from the standpoint of the individual. If individual losses that were intentional or certain could be insured, insurance companies would be plagued by adverse selection—the tendency for those who anticipate a loss in the near future to seek insurance more often than others in the general population.

Low Cost The cost of an insurance premium should be relatively low with respect to the potential loss that is covered by the insurance. Thus insurance should be used only for protection against large losses that are sustained by only a very small fraction of those who buy a given coverage. A company cannot economically insure small losses because the expenses of selling and administering such policies when coupled with the claims that would be made could total nearly as much or more than the potential loss covered. Similarly, insurance cannot be offered economically for losses that occur too frequently because the premiums would soon increase beyond what most people would be willing to pay. An excellent example of the application of this latter criterion is life insurance for persons over age sixty-five. Few insurance companies will issue a new policy to people in this age category because the relatively high frequency of loss makes the premiums larger than most people believe they can afford. However, life insurance is certainly not the only type of insurance where increased frequency of loss can make the premium too high. This phenomenon has in recent years contributed to increased automobile, health, homeowner's and professional malpractice insurance premiums.

Unfortunately, too many people waste insurance dollars by insuring small losses that occur frequently when, in fact, they should focus on potentially large losses that occur infrequently and could be financially devastating. An example of this illogical decision making is those individuals who buy an automobile insurance policy with a $50 rather than a $200 deductible and yet purchase only a $10,000 bodily injury liability limit. They have expensively protected themselves against a loss of $150 ($200 less $50) while ignoring relatively inexpensive protection for tens of thousands of dollars of necessary additional liability coverage.

Underwriting

In all types of insurance, the company must decide which exposures to loss it can insure and the appropriate rates to charge. This function is called *underwriting*. Through underwriting insurers try to guard against adverse selection. In addition, underwriters design rate classification schemes so that those who buy insurance will pay a premium commensurate with their probability of experiencing a loss. The success of any insurance company is highly dependent on the quality of the work performed in its underwriting department. If the underwriting standards and/or rates are set too high, the company could lose a large amount of business. On the other hand, if standards are too loose and/or rates too low, the insurer could face large financial losses.

A basic problem facing underwriters is the choice of appropriate criteria to apply in the selection and classification of insureds. Since a perfect relationship does not exist between criteria available and loss experience, invariably some insureds believe that they are charged more than their fair share for insurance coverage. This situation is probably most apparent in underwriting for automobile insurance. Many youthful male motorists who have never had an auto accident must pay two or three times the premium that a family man age thirty-five would pay. Similarly, an auto owner who has never had a claim but lives in Manhattan is likely to pay an amount considerably in excess of what a rural driver with a poor driving record pays.

In recognition of the difficulties experienced in selecting and classifying insureds, some vocal consumer advocates have spoken for the removal of rate classifications and the application of the same rate to all insureds. This idea, however, is no solution to the problem. In fact, it would simply increase the number of complaints made about insurance because, even though a few people would receive large decreases in premiums, many more would incur rate increases. Indeed, recently in Massachusetts the rural population of the state was outraged at a proposal to eliminate place of residence from the rate classification system for automobile insurance. Of course, if such a proposal were implemented, these people would have premium increases while the motorists of Boston would receive a rate reduction.

As can be seen from the foregoing discussion, underwriting is a difficult task. It is an art, perhaps, as much as it is a science. Insurers, though, indicate that they are working to improve their underwriting capabilities in order to be able to set rates that are adequate to protect against insolvency and yet are reasonable and not excessive for the majority of policyholders.

Determining the Need for Life Insurance

As a group, Americans buy more life insurance than any other nationality (see Table 13-1). An analysis of individual insurance purchases by sex, age, income, and size of policy is shown in Table 13-2. In spite of these statistics, most families in the U.S. are actually underinsured. One reason for this is that most people do not buy life insurance until a life insurance agent convinces them they need it. And certainly most individuals and families do need some protection against the loss of income that can result from death or retirement. This section illustrates how a person's life insurance requirements can be determined. Three methods are considered: the human life value approach, the multiple earnings approach, and the needs approach. Although only the needs approach is a logical method that considers all relevant factors, the other methods are discussed because they are popularly used and you should be familiar with their shortcomings.

Table 13-2 Characteristics of Purchasers of Individual Life Insurance Policies in the U.S. (1976)

	Percent of Insurance Purchases
Sex of Insured	
Male Insureds under 15	3%
Female Insureds under 15	2
Male Adults	78
Female Adults	17
Total	100%
Age of Insured	
Under 15	4%
15–24	22
25–34	41
35–44	20
45 and over	13
Total	100%
Income of Insured	
Under $3,000	Less than 0.5%
$3,000–$4,999	1
$5,000–$7,499	7
$7,500–$9,999	11
$10,000–$24,999	54
$25,000 or More	27
Total	100%
Size of Policy	
Under $2,000	Less than 0.5%
$2,000–$4,999	2
$5,000–$9,999	5
$10,000–$24,999	27
$25,000 or More	66
Total	100%

Source: Adapted with permission from *Life Insurance Fact Book '77* (Washington, D.C.: American Council of Life Insurance, 1977), p. 14.

Human Life Value Approach

One of the oldest and best-known techniques for determining the amount of life insurance a person should have is the human life value approach. It is an attempt to convert the future earnings of an individual into a current sum. This current sum is then said to be the human life

"Maybe, like you say, they will increase in value after you're gone, but I still think you ought to have a little life insurance."

There Is No Substitute for Life Insurance!

Source: Changing Times, December 1969, p. 17. Reprinted with permission from *Changing Times* Magazine, © Kiplinger Washington Editors, Inc., 1969.

value of that person. Specifically, the human life computation considers two factors: (1) the total amount of wages that a person will earn from the present to retirement minus related income taxes and personal maintenance expenses; and (2) an appropriate interest rate at which these anticipated future net earnings can be converted into a present value amount. For example, assume that a person age twenty-five expected to net $10,000 per year after taxes and personal maintenance expenses during the next forty years and that an appropriate interest rate is 8 percent. The human life value of that person would.equal $119,246, an amount determined using special financial computations that are too rigorous for coverage in this text.

The human life value concept may be useful in certain legal proceedings or by economists concerned with studying human capital of a nation. However, it should not be employed in computing the amount of life insurance a person should buy because it fails to consider both the financial obligations and any resources external to life insurance that an individual may have.

Multiple Earnings Approach

The multiple earnings approach gains its popularity on the basis of its simplicity rather than its soundness. To calculate the amount of life insurance to purchase using this technique, you simply multiply gross annual earnings by some arbitrarily selected number. Most frequently, three, five, or in some cases, ten is used. For example, if the multiplier is five, a person who has a gross annual income of $15,000 should have $75,000 of life insurance coverage. The major shortcomings of the multiple earnings approach are the same as those cited for the human life value approach. It considers neither the financial obligations nor the resources of the individual.

Estimating Life Insurance Needs: The Multiples of Salary Chart

A family's life insurance needs typically don't require the replacement of all of after-tax income, since the family's expenses decline by approximately 25 percent when the insured person dies. Replacement of 75 percent of the breadwinner's net (after-tax) income is believed best, although 60 percent is considered adequate. The chart on page 461 can help you determine the amount of life insurance needed to replace the breadwinner's salary.

To calculate the amount of life insurance needed for either net replacement level, multiply your present gross salary by the number under that level.

If your gross income or spouse's age fall between the figures shown, take an average between the multiples for nearest salaries and ages.

Social Security benefits will be part of both levels.

If personal liquid assets (savings, predictable inheritance, retirement plan, investment, etc.) equal one year of gross salary or less, use them as part of the fund for the small-emergency reserve and final expenses. If they equal *more* than one year, subtract that extra amount from the insurance needed to replace income.

People with no personal assets who can't afford the 75% level might try for at least 60%. The average family would then face some lowering in level of living but wouldn't be financially devastated.

Needs Approach

A number of progressive life insurance companies have abandoned the human life value or multiple earnings approach and employ instead the needs approach. This method considers both the financial resources external to life insurance and the specific financial obligations that a person may have. Essentially, the needs approach involves three steps: (1) estimating the total economic resources needed; (2) determining all financial resources that would be available; and (3) subtracting the amount of resources from the amount needed in order to determine the amount of life insurance required to round out an individual's financial program.

Economic Needs In principle, the need for life insurance stems primarily from income losses resulting from death or retirement. In fact, approximately two-thirds of all payments by life insurance companies go to living policyholders rather than beneficiaries of deceased insureds.

The Multiples of Salary Chart
(for Net Income Replacement)

Your Present Gross Earnings	Present Age of Spouse							
	25 Years[a]		35 Years[a]		45 Years[a]		55 Years[b]	
	75%	60%	75%	60%	75%	60%	75%	60%
$ 7,500	4.0	3.0	5.5	4.0	7.5	5.5	6.5	4.5
9,000	4.0	3.0	5.5	4.0	7.5	5.5	6.5	4.5
15,000	4.5	3.0	6.5	4.5	8.0	6.0	7.0	5.5
23,500	6.5	4.5	8.0	5.5	8.5	6.5	7.5	5.5
30,000	7.5	5.0	8.0	6.0	8.5	6.5	7.0	5.5
40,000	7.5	5.0	8.0	6.0	8.0	6.0	7.0	5.5
65,000	7.5	5.5	7.5	6.0	7.5	6.0	6.5	5.0

[a]Assuming federal income taxes for a family of four (two children). There are four exemptions and the standard—or 15% itemized—deductions. State and local taxes are disregarded.
[b]Assuming you have only two exemptions. (Any children are now grown.)

Source: "Ideally How Much Life Insurance Do You Need?" Reprinted with permission of Citibank's *Consumer Views*, July 1976, pp. 1–2.

However, the focus in this chapter is on death protection; a discussion of retirement planning is presented in Chapter 16.

The most common financial needs that must be satisfied after the death of a family breadwinner are: (1) funds to pay off debts; (2) income to sustain the family until the children are self-sufficient; (3) income to sustain the surviving spouse for life; and (4) income to fund special financial requirements. Typically, few families even with life insurance can accumulate the resources necessary to fulfill all desired financial needs upon the death of the breadwinner. Nevertheless, it is useful to first consider all needs and then develop a hierarchy of importance for them.

Debt Liquidation Most breadwinners would prefer to leave their families relatively debt-free in the event of their death. Therefore, persons wishing to accomplish this objective must determine the average amount of their outstanding bills. Included in this amount are balances on installment loans, credit cards, department store accounts, and other

Insuring the Economic Value of the Housewife

How much life insurance will replace the services of a full-time housewife? One rule of thumb is to multiply the so-called economic value of a housewife by the number of years outside help will be needed to maintain the household. The years and amount of help depend on age of children.

There are estimates—no one knows for sure—of a housewife's economic value. One government study suggests it may now average between $6,000 and $8,000 a year, nationally, for the housewife aged 20 to 54, with spouse or children or both. Other estimates are higher, especially when there are preschool children.

The usual recommendation of $25,000 life insurance to replace the housewife's services in the home and for final expenses—based on statistics about how quickly widowers remarry—thus may or may not be adequate during a family's younger years.

Source: "Insurance for the Full Time Housewife," reprinted with permission of Citibank's *Consumer Views,* July 1976, p. 4.

similar obligations, as well as estimated funeral expenses. In addition, some heads-of-households will want to leave enough money to pay off their home mortgages and will include this amount in their debt liquidation expense estimate. The debt liquidation component of financial needs can be viewed as an estimate of the individual's average liabilities.

Family Income The amount of annual income necessary to support the family until the last child or other dependent is self-sufficient depends largely on the level of living that is deemed appropriate. If no change in living style is anticipated, then income needs will equal the breadwinner's take-home pay. Although expenses of maintaining the household may decrease somewhat because of reduced consumption, these savings may be offset if many home maintenance chores previously provided by the breadwinner now have to be purchased. Perhaps the best way to determine the amount of monthly income necessary to sustain the family is to develop a budget for all expenses that will be incurred. As discussed in Chapter 3, major items in the budget are housing costs; utilities; food; clothing; life, health, property, and liability insurance; recreation and travel; property taxes; and savings.

Surviving Spouse's Income After the children are independent, the monthly household expenses should decrease substantially. Nevertheless, the surviving spouse will still need monthly income for support for the remainder of his or her life. It is therefore necessary to estimate the amount of income needed as well as the duration of the survivor's life.

Special Financial Needs In addition to the above economic needs, some families also would like to have the resources available to meet certain special financial requirements, such as a college education fund for the children and/or surviving spouse, an emergency fund for unexpected financial burdens, or, as previously mentioned, a fund to pay off the mortgage.

Available Resources After estimating the amounts of the financial needs that a family would have upon the death of its breadwinner, a list of all resources available for meeting these needs must be prepared. For most families, money from savings and social security benefits comprise the largest non–life insurance financial resources. In addition, another very important source is any income that can be earned by the surviving spouse or children. Also, a majority of corporate employers offer some cash benefits that are payable upon the death of an employee. Many families have real estate (not including the home), jewelry, stocks, bonds, and other assets that can be liquidated in order to obtain funds to meet financial needs. After developing a complete list of available resources, some reasonable estimate of their value should be made. Although this step can be difficult because the values of some assets are not fixed, a conservative evaluation should be made of all assets.

Needs Less Resources The final step in determining the amount of life insurance required is to subtract the amount of available resources from the total amount needed to satisfy all of the financial objectives of the family. If, by chance, the amount of resources available exceeds the needs, then no life insurance for death protection should be purchased. (Of course, it still might be useful for retirement, savings, or to guarantee insurability, but these uses are considered elsewhere.) If, as in most families with children, the resources are fewer than the needs, that difference is the amount of life insurance required. Often, though, this amount will exceed the family's willingness or capacity to pay for it. In these cases, a priority ranking of needs coupled with a reassessment of available resources is necessary. For example, in the preliminary plans a college education fund might have been included while consideration was not given to income from employment of the surviving spouse or children. The family could decide, however, to have the surviving spouse seek employment and let the children work their way through college. In this manner, capacity and willingness to pay for life insurance can be adjusted to meet economic needs.

Over all, financial planning based upon the needs concept can become quite complex. However, when a family uses a competent life insurance agent who is familiar with the process, the planning stage can proceed quite smoothly. In fact, a number of major life insurance companies have computer programs set up to determine the life insurance requirements of families using the needs approach. An example of the application of this approach is given in Figure 13-1. Remember, though, that life insurance needs are not static. The amount and type of life insurance you need today will very likely differ from the amount and type suitable for you five years from now. Life insurance programs should be reviewed and adjusted at least every five years or after major changes in the family have occurred (for example, the birth of children or acquisition of a home).

Types of Life Insurance Policies

After you determine the amount of life insurance necessary to meet the financial requirements of your family, you must decide on the type of policy best suited to your family. In general, families can most efficiently satisfy their needs through the use of one of three basic types of life insurance: term, whole life, or endowment. However, because numerous other types of policies (which are mostly modifications of these three

Figure 13-1 **Sample Computer Analysis of Life Insurance Needs**

	INCOME ESTATE TO AGE 65: $		X	YEARS = $	

A detailed worksheet table showing:

- FOR (blank), AGE **34**
- ASSUMED AVERAGE MONTHLY EARNINGS FOR GOVERNMENT BENEFITS: **$700** OR DEATH BENEFITS, **$1050** OR RETIREMENT BENEFITS
- PREPARED FOR YEAR **1974**
- AGES OF: WIFE **32**, CHILD **09**, CHILD **06**

	CASH FOR YOUR FAMILY		INCOME FOR YOUR FAMILY					RETIREMENT FOR YOU	
	FINAL EXPENSE FUND	MORTGAGE CANCELLATION FUND	FOR 9 YRS. UNTIL WIFE 41 CHILD 18 CHILD 15 PER MONTH	FOR 3 YRS. UNTIL WIFE 44 CHILD 21 CHILD 18 PER MONTH	EDUCATIONAL FUND	FOR 16 YRS. UNTIL WIFE IS AGE 60 PER MONTH	LIFE INCOME FROM WIFE'S AGE 60 PER MONTH	LIFE INCOME FROM YOUR AGE 65 PER MONTH	CASH VALUE AT AGE 65
YOUR OBJECTIVES	8,000	21,000	1,000	1,000	20,000 **	600	600	800	
ASSUMED BENEFITS									
GOVERNMENT SOCIAL SECURITY	255		665	570	X		272	651	
COMPANY PENSION								300	
CASH ASSETS	7,745	21,000			20,000				
INCOME ASSETS									
OBJECTIVES UNPROVIDED BY ASSUMED BENEFITS			335	430		600	328		
TOTAL AMOUNT REQUIRED TO COMPLETE OBJECTIVES	$143,776		32,092	11,619		67,133	32,932		
UTILIZATION OF PRESENT LIFE INSURANCE	$65,000		32,092	11,619		21,289 ***		52	9,000
REMAINING AMOUNT NEEDED TO COMPLETE OBJECTIVES	$78,776					45,844	32,932		
UNFULFILLED OBJECTIVES						600	328		

$26,255 EXCESS CASH ASSETS
X $285 PER MONTH WILL BE PAID EACH CHILD FROM AGE 18 TO 22 IF IN AN ACCREDITED SCHOOL AND UNMARRIED, PROVIDED TOTAL FAMILY BENEFITS DO NOT EXCEED $665 PER MONTH.
** INTEREST COULD BE PAID ON EDUCATION FUND UNTIL EXHAUSTED.
*** THE INCOME PROVIDED WILL BE EXHAUSTED DURING YEAR 4.
BENEFITS DEPEND ON GOV'T. PROGRAM IN EFFECT WHEN BEGUN, ON ACTUAL INSURANCE, AND ON ASSETS RESULTS.

THE AMOUNTS OF THE INSURANCE ARE CALCULATED ASSUMING THAT DEATH OCCURS IN THE YEAR PREPARED. THIS IS AN ILLUSTRATION, NOT A CONTRACT.

Source: Courtesy of Mutual of New York Life Insurance Company.

types) are available, this part of the chapter also describes these hybrid forms of life insurance.

Term Insurance

Under the provisions of a *term life insurance policy,* the insurance company agrees to pay a stipulated sum if the insured dies during the policy period. The period of coverage is usually five years with premiums payable annually or semiannually. However, many other periods of coverage and payment plans are also common. Term insurance offers the most economical way to purchase life insurance on a temporary basis for protection against financial loss resulting from death. Many term policies are sold at very competitive rates through newspaper advertisements and direct mail. For example, one large company regularly runs display advertisements in the *Wall Street Journal* offering $100,000 of term insurance to males age thirty for only $197 annually. For persons age thirty-five, the corresponding premium is $217. Of course, these premiums (which are set at the time the policy is purchased) increase each year as the insured gets older, but they still will purchase a large amount of protection at a relatively low price until about age forty-five. Unfortunately, many families in the past, because of either lack of knowledge or poor advice, did not properly incorporate term insurance into their life insurance programs. But as consumers have become more sophisticated, term life insurance sales have increased dramatically. A premium schedule from a company with below average rates for level premium participating term insurance is shown in Table 13-3.

Types of Term Insurance The most common types of term insurance are straight term, renewable term, convertible term, and decreasing term. Note, though, that these term insurance features are not necessarily unique; for instance, a policy could be a straight term with both guaranteed renewable and convertible features.

Straight Term Policies written for a given number of years—for example, one, five, ten, or twenty—are called straight term policies. The annual premium on a straight term policy may increase each year or each five years. Or in many cases it will remain level throughout the policy period. Of course, a policy with a premium that increases each year will start off below the level premium amount, subsequently equal it, and then exceed it. The face amount, or coverage, of a straight term policy remains unchanged throughout the period of the policy.

Renewable Term A renewable term policy is one that may be renewed at its expiration for another term of equal length. This renewal is at the option of the insured, but the premium will increase to offset the greater chance of death at older ages. Generally, term policies may be renewed each period until the insured attains age sixty-five or seventy. Purchasers of term insurance are wise to obtain a *guaranteed renewable provision* in their policy. Otherwise, if they become uninsurable due to accident or illness during the policy period, they will lose their option to renew protection at the end of the period. This valuable feature usually is available at a modest cost.

Convertible Term A term insurance policy that allows the insureds the privilege of converting their coverage into a whole life or endowment life insurance policy (discussed in a later section) is a convertible term. The

Table 13-3 Level Premium Term Insurance Premium Schedule
(Premiums per $1,000 of Insurance; Minimum Policy Issued, $5,000—
Disability Waiver of Premium Included)

Age Nearest Birthday	5-Year Renewable Term		10-Year Term		15-Year Term		20-Year Term		Term to Age 60		Term to Age 65		Term to Age 70	
	Annual	Monthly	Annual	Monthly	Annual	Monthly	Annual	Monthly	Annual	Monthly	Annual	Monthly	Annual	Monthly
20	$ 4.44	$ .39	$ 4.37	$ .39	$ 4.47	$ .39	$ 4.53	$ .40	$ 6.51	$ .58	$ 7.42	$ .66	$ 8.54	$ .75
21	4.47	.39	4.41	.39	4.51	.40	4.59	.41	6.62	.58	7.55	.67	8.72	.77
22	4.48	.40	4.43	.39	4.56	.40	4.68	.41	6.75	.60	7.72	.68	8.91	.79
23	4.52	.40	4.47	.39	4.63	.41	4.78	.42	6.88	.61	7.88	.70	9.11	.80
24	4.57	.40	4.51	.40	4.71	.42	4.90	.43	7.01	.62	8.04	.71	9.32	.82
25	4.60	.41	4.57	.40	4.80	.42	5.03	.44	7.15	.63	8.22	.73	9.55	.84
26	4.65	.41	4.64	.41	4.92	.43	5.17	.46	7.31	.65	8.40	.74	9.78	.86
27	4.71	.42	4.70	.42	5.05	.45	5.34	.47	7.47	.66	8.61	.76	10.02	.89
28	4.79	.42	4.80	.42	5.20	.46	5.52	.49	7.65	.68	8.81	.78	10.28	.91
29	4.86	.43	4.90	.43	5.34	.47	5.73	.51	7.83	.69	9.04	.80	10.55	.93
30	4.95	.44	5.04	.45	5.52	.49	5.97	.53	8.03	.71	9.27	.82	10.84	.96
31	5.05	.45	5.19	.46	5.72	.51	6.26	.55	8.24	.73	9.53	.84	11.15	.98
32	5.19	.46	5.38	.48	5.93	.52	6.56	.58	8.46	.75	9.79	.86	11.47	1.01
33	5.35	.47	5.60	.49	6.17	.54	6.91	.61	8.69	.77	10.07	.89	11.81	1.04
34	5.55	.49	5.87	.52	6.47	.57	7.30	.64	8.93	.79	10.36	.92	12.17	1.07
35	5.79	.51	6.15	.54	6.79	.60	7.75	.68	9.19	.81	10.69	.94	12.55	1.11
36	6.06	.54	6.47	.57	7.16	.63	8.24	.73	9.49	.84	11.01	.97	12.94	1.14
37	6.40	.57	6.85	.61	7.57	.67	8.79	.78	9.80	.87	11.37	1.00	13.38	1.18
38	6.76	.60	7.28	.64	8.02	.71	9.40	.83	10.12	.89	11.76	1.04	13.81	1.22
39	7.17	.63	7.69	.68	8.54	.75	10.08	.89	10.46	.92	12.16	1.07	14.29	1.26
40	7.61	.67	8.12	.72	9.10	.80	10.83	.96	10.83	.96	12.57	1.11	14.78	1.31
41	8.09	.71	8.58	.76	9.73	.86	11.53	1.02	11.22	.99	13.03	1.15	15.32	1.35
42	8.63	.76	9.11	.80	10.44	.92	12.30	1.09	11.63	1.03	13.48	1.19	15.87	1.40
43	9.19	.81	9.71	.86	11.21	.99	13.15	1.16	12.07	1.07	14.00	1.24	16.46	1.45
44	9.82	.87	10.35	.91	12.08	1.07	14.07	1.24	12.54	1.11	14.53	1.28	17.07	1.51
45	10.52	.93	11.07	.98	13.04	1.15	15.08	1.33	13.04	1.15	15.08	1.33	17.72	1.57
46	11.30	1.00	11.88	1.05	13.94	1.23	16.19	1.43	13.58	1.20	15.67	1.38	18.42	1.63
47	12.16	1.07	12.80	1.13	14.92	1.32	17.45	1.54	14.17	1.25	16.32	1.44	19.17	1.69
48	13.11	1.16	13.81	1.22	16.00	1.41	18.68	1.65	14.79	1.31	17.00	1.50	19.94	1.76
49	14.17	1.25	14.93	1.32	17.19	1.52	20.11	1.78	15.46	1.37	17.72	1.57	20.78	1.84
50	15.34	1.35	16.20	1.43	18.49	1.63	21.66	1.91	16.20	1.43	18.49	1.63	21.66	1.91
51	16.61	1.47	17.37	1.53	19.91	1.76					19.32	1.71	22.59	2.00
52	17.92	1.58	18.65	1.65	21.59	1.91					20.20	1.78	23.58	2.08
53	19.28	1.70	20.07	1.77	23.14	2.04					21.16	1.87	24.66	2.18
54	20.80	1.84	21.61	1.91	25.00	2.21					22.19	1.96	25.81	2.28
55	22.49	1.99	23.31	2.06	27.02	2.39					23.31	2.06	27.02	2.39
56	21.28	1.88	22.65	2.00									25.88	2.29
57	22.91	2.02	24.43	2.16									26.99	2.38
58	24.70	2.18	26.37	2.33									28.17	2.49
59	26.63	2.35	28.47	2.51									29.43	2.60
60	28.76	2.54	30.76	2.72									30.76	2.72

Note: All policies shown are participating. This means that the company will pay policyholders a dividend at the end of each year. Of course, the amount of the dividend cannot be determined beforehand.

convertibility feature serves as a guarantee to the insureds that (1) they do not have to lose their insurance protection at the end of the period and

(2) upon conversion they will have lifelong protection—as long as they pay their premiums, of course. The convertible term can be useful to persons who need a large amount of death protection for a relatively low cost but who also want to continue their insurance coverage throughout their entire life. Thus, a convertible term can be purchased to provide immediately for a large amount of needed death protection, and then later when the insured has more income, the policy can be converted to whole life. The convertibility option is available with most term insurance contracts at an attractive price. It is important to recognize that many convertible term policies place some limitation upon when the conversion can take place. For example, a ten year term policy may stipulate that the conversion must be made before the end of the eighth year, or a term policy to age sixty-five may require conversion prior to age sixty-one.

Decreasing Term Because the death rate increases for each year of life, the premium for straight term policies for each successive period of coverage must increase. Table 13-4 presents mortality rates per 1,000 persons and life expectancies for various ages. Many companies offer a term policy that maintains a level premium throughout all periods of coverage, while the amount of protection decreases. These policies are called decreasing term, since the protection decreases over the life of the policy. Decreasing term can be conveniently used when the amount of coverage needed declines over time. For example, a decreasing term policy can be purchased when children are young in order to provide sufficient family income until they reach maturity. As they grow older, the amount of coverage needed decreases until the last child becomes independent and the need expires. Similarly, some families find it desirable to purchase a decreasing term policy which declines in coverage at the same rate as the balance on their home mortgage.

Advantages and Disadvantages of Term The primary strength of term insurance is that it can offer an economical way to purchase a large amount of protection against financial loss resulting from death, especially during the child-rearing years. With the guaranteed renewable and convertible options, coverage can be continued throughout the life of the insured. Of course, the costs of continued coverage will grow due to the increased chance of death. In this characteristic, then, lies the most commonly cited weakness of term insurance: the rates increase as the insured ages. And not infrequently, many people discontinue the coverage because of the increasing cost.

Criticizing term insurance on the basis of increasing cost is similar to finding fault with homeowner's insurance for not paying for a loss caused by an automobile accident. Clearly, the purpose of homeowner's insurance is not to provide automobile coverage just as the purpose of term

Table 13-4 **Mortality Rates and Life Expectancies**
(United States Total Population, 1969–1971)

Age	Deaths per 1,000	Expectation of Life (Years)	Age	Deaths per 1,000	Expectation of Life (Years)	Age	Deaths per 1,000	Expectation of Life (Years)
0	20.02	70.75	37	2.44	37.23	74	50.75	9.82
1	1.25	71.19	38	2.66	36.32	75	55.52	9.32
2	.86	70.28	39	2.90	35.42	76	60.60	8.84
3	.69	69.34	40	3.14	34.52	77	65.96	8.38
4	.57	68.39	41	3.41	33.63	78	71.53	7.93
5	.51	67.43	42	3.70	32.74	79	77.41	7.51
6	.46	66.46	43	4.04	31.86	80	83.94	7.10
7	.43	65.49	44	4.43	30.99	81	91.22	6.70
8	.39	64.52	45	4.84	30.12	82	98.92	6.32
9	.34	63.54	46	5.28	29.27	83	106.95	5.96
10	.31	62.57	47	5.74	28.42	84	115.48	5.62
11	.30	61.58	48	6.24	27.58	85	125.61	5.28
12	.35	60.60	49	6.78	26.75	86	137.48	4.97
13	.46	59.62	50	7.38	25.93	87	149.79	4.68
14	.63	58.65	51	8.04	25.12	88	161.58	4.42
15	.82	57.69	52	8.76	24.32	89	172.92	4.18
16	1.01	56.73	53	9.57	23.53	90	185.02	3.94
17	1.17	55.79	54	10.43	22.75	91	198.88	3.73
18	1.28	54.86	55	11.36	21.99	92	213.63	3.53
19	1.34	53.93	56	12.36	21.23	93	228.70	3.35
20	1.40	53.00	57	13.41	20.49	94	243.36	3.19
21	1.47	52.07	58	14.52	19.76	95	257.45	3.06
22	1.52	51.15	59	15.70	19.05	96	269.59	2.95
23	1.53	50.22	60	16.95	18.34	97	280.24	2.85
24	1.51	49.30	61	18.29	17.65	98	289.77	2.76
25	1.47	48.37	62	19.74	16.97	99	298.69	2.69
26	1.43	47.44	63	21.33	16.30	100	306.96	2.62
27	1.42	46.51	64	23.06	15.65	101	314.61	2.56
28	1.44	45.58	65	24.95	15.00	102	321.67	2.51
29	1.49	44.64	66	26.99	14.38	103	328.17	2.46
30	1.55	43.71	67	29.18	13.76	104	334.14	2.41
31	1.63	42.77	68	31.52	13.16	105	339.60	2.37
32	1.72	41.84	69	34.00	12.57	106	344.60	2.34
33	1.83	40.92	70	36.61	12.00	107	349.17	2.30
34	1.95	39.99	71	39.43	11.43	108	353.33	2.27
35	2.09	39.07	72	42.66	10.88	109	357.12	2.24
36	2.25	38.15	73	46.44	10.34			

Source: Reprinted with permission from *Life Insurance Fact Book '77* (Washington, D.C.: American Council of Life Insurance, 1977), pp. 108–109.

insurance is not to provide lifelong coverage. Rather the objective of term insurance is to provide a large amount of protection for a limited period of time. This task it accomplishes very well.

Whole Life Insurance

Few people ever outlive the need for some life insurance. Accordingly, as the name implies, *whole life insurance* is designed to offer financial protection for the entire life of an individual. However, in addition to death protection, whole life insurance has a savings element called *cash value,* which results from the manner in which premiums are paid. In fact, whole life is normally available through several different payment plans, including continuous premium, limited payment, and single premium payment. All of these payment plans provide for some amount of cash value accumulation.

Life insurance companies set aside assets which are to be used to pay the claims expected to result from the policies they issue. As time goes by, the cash value of a policy—the amount of assets allocated for each person insured—increases to reflect the greater chance of death that comes with age. If policyholders decide to cancel their contracts prior to the death of the insured, that portion of assets set aside to provide payment for the death claim which did not take place is available to them. This is called the *nonforfeiture right* of the policyholder. The logic supporting this right is based on the fact that the company collects premiums in order to pay death claims. Policyholders, by terminating their insurance contract, forfeit their right to a death benefit. Correspondingly, the company must forfeit its right to keep all of the monies paid by these policyholders for the future death benefit they will no longer be eligible to receive. This logic cannot be applied to term life insurance or various types of property and liability insurance because, upon issuing these policies, insurance companies assume that they will have to pay a claim on only a tiny fraction of the contracts sold, and consequently they collect premiums on that basis.

Types of Whole Life Policies Although a wide variety of types of whole life policies exist, only the major ones—continuous premium, limited payment, and single premium payment—are described here. A sample premium schedule for several types of participating whole life policies is shown in Table 13-5.

Continuous Premium Under a continuous premium whole life policy, individuals, upon securing coverage at a given age, pay a level premium amount each year until they die. The earlier in life the coverage is purchased, the lower the amount of the annual premium. This concept is a selling point used by life insurance agents to convince younger persons to "buy now." Their argument is that the sooner you buy, the less you pay. What they mean by this is "what you pay *annually,*" not the total payments over the life of the policy. Of course, the sooner people

Table 13-5 **Whole Life Premium Schedule**
(Premiums per $1,000 of Insurance; Minimum Policy Issued, $2,000—
Disability Waiver of Premium Included)

Age Nearest Birthday	Ordinary Life		Life Paid-Up At 65		10-Pay Life		20-Pay Life		30-Pay Life	
	Annual	Monthly	Annual	Monthly	Annual	Monthly	Annual	Monthly	Annual	Monthly
20	$13.09	$1.16	$ 14.24	$ 1.26	$37.07	$3.27	$21.93	$1.94	$17.09	$1.51
21	13.44	1.19	14.66	1.29	37.83	3.34	22.37	1.98	17.43	1.54
22	13.78	1.22	15.09	1.33	38.61	3.41	22.82	2.02	17.77	1.57
23	14.15	1.25	15.55	1.37	39.40	3.48	23.28	2.06	18.14	1.60
24	14.53	1.28	16.04	1.42	40.24	3.55	23.74	2.10	18.51	1.63
25	14.93	1.32	16.55	1.46	41.07	3.63	24.23	2.14	18.91	1.67
26	15.35	1.36	17.09	1.51	41.93	3.70	24.73	2.18	19.30	1.70
27	15.78	1.39	17.67	1.56	42.82	3.78	25.24	2.23	19.72	1.74
28	16.25	1.44	18.29	1.62	43.73	3.86	25.78	2.28	20.16	1.78
29	16.72	1.48	18.94	1.67	44.66	3.94	26.32	2.32	20.61	1.82
30	17.23	1.52	19.62	1.73	45.61	4.03	26.89	2.38	21.10	1.86
31	17.77	1.57	20.35	1.80	46.59	4.12	27.48	2.43	21.59	1.91
32	18.33	1.62	21.14	1.87	47.60	4.20	28.09	2.48	22.11	1.95
33	18.92	1.67	21.98	1.94	48.64	4.30	28.72	2.54	22.65	2.00
34	19.54	1.73	22.87	2.02	49.71	4.39	29.37	2.59	23.22	2.05
35	20.19	1.78	23.81	2.10	50.80	4.49	30.06	2.66	23.81	2.10
36	20.88	1.84	24.84	2.19	51.93	4.59	30.75	2.72	24.44	2.16
37	21.60	1.91	25.94	2.29	53.09	4.69	31.50	2.78	25.10	2.22
38	22.36	1.98	27.13	2.40	54.29	4.80	32.26	2.85	25.78	2.28
39	23.16	2.05	28.40	2.51	55.51	4.90	33.07	2.92	26.50	2.34
40	24.01	2.12	29.77	2.63	56.74	5.01	33.90	2.99	27.24	2.41
41	24.91	2.20	31.26	2.76	58.02	5.12	34.79	3.07	28.04	2.48
42	25.84	2.28	32.87	2.90	59.34	5.24	35.69	3.15	28.86	2.55
43	26.82	2.37	34.63	3.06	60.68	5.36	36.63	3.24	29.75	2.63
44	27.88	2.46	36.55	3.23	62.06	5.48	37.62	3.32	30.67	2.71
45	28.98	2.56	38.65	3.41	63.49	5.61	38.65	3.41	31.66	2.80
46	30.15	2.66	40.97	3.62	64.97	5.74	39.73	3.51	32.70	2.89
47	31.39	2.77	43.53	3.85	66.49	5.87	40.85	3.61	33.80	2.99
48	32.71	2.89	46.40	4.10	68.08	6.01	42.06	3.72	34.99	3.09
49	34.10	3.01	49.60	4.38	69.73	6.16	43.29	3.82	36.23	3.20
50	35.59	3.14	53.22	4.70	71.46	6.31	44.62	3.94	37.57	3.32
51	37.17	3.28	57.31	5.06	73.31	6.48	46.02	4.06	39.00	3.44
52	38.85	3.43	62.02	5.48	75.24	6.65	47.50	4.20	40.53	3.58
53	40.63	3.59	67.47	5.96	77.25	6.82	49.07	4.33	42.18	3.73
54	42.55	3.76	73.88	6.53	79.33	7.01	50.75	4.48	43.94	3.88
55	44.57	3.94	81.50	7.20	81.50	7.20	52.54	4.64	45.83	4.05
56	43.95	3.88	87.44	7.72	80.48	7.11	51.43	4.54	45.02	3.98
57	45.92	4.06	98.36	8.69	82.35	7.27	53.09	4.69	46.86	4.14
58	48.00	4.24	112.32	9.92	84.30	7.45	54.85	4.84	48.82	4.31
59	50.21	4.44	130.86	11.56	86.30	7.62	56.72	5.01	50.91	4.50
60	52.55	4.64	156.75	13.85	88.38	7.81	58.71	5.19	53.13	4.69

Note: All policies shown are participating.

purchase whole life, the longer they have coverage in force, but the *more* they pay in total. While good reasons (such as securing needed protection, savings, and insurability) do exist for many young persons to buy whole life, it should seldom be purchased by anyone simply because the annual premium will be less than if it is purchased at a later date. Of the variety of whole life policies available, continuous premium whole life offers the greatest death protection and the least savings per dollar of premium paid. Since the primary purpose of whole life insurance for most families is death protection rather than savings, the continuous premium policy is usually a wise choice.

Limited Payment Limited payment whole life policies are those that offer coverage for the entire life of the insured but schedule the payments to end after a limited period. For example, 20-pay life, 30-pay life, paid-up age 55, and paid-up age 65 are types of limited pay whole life policies which are frequently sold. Under the 20-pay and 30-pay life contracts, the policyholder is most often required to make twenty or thirty annual level premium payments, respectively. Under the premium schedule of paid-up at age 55, 65, or other stipulated age policies, the policyholder makes premium payments until the insured attains the stated age. Of course, for any individual, the shorter the period of time over which premiums are payable, the larger the amount of the annual premium. Upon completion of the scheduled payments, the insurance remains in force at its face value for the remainder of the life of the insured.

Some insurance companies emphasize the sale of limited pay policies to the detriment of those who purchase them. In the sales presentation, considerable attention is focused on the "large" savings element that will develop and the fact that the policyholder is relieved of having to pay premiums for the entire life of the insured. However, this logic is often misguided on two counts. One is that for most people the primary purpose of whole life insurance is permanent protection against financial loss resulting from death—not the accumulation of savings. Secondly, even though people buy a continuous premium whole life policy, they need pay the premium only as long as they wish to keep the policy in force for its full face value. Policyholders may cease payment of premiums at any time after some nonforfeiture value has been accumulated. Rather than take this benefit in cash, they can convert the policy to one that is paid up for some amount less than the original face value of the policy. (This is discussed in subsequent sections.)

The preceding discussion is not intended to imply that limited pay policies are not desirable. Rather it is to stress the fact that, if lifelong death protection is the primary aim of the life insurance policy, it is best to purchase continuous premium whole life instead of a limited payment policy. Since more continuous premium whole life insurance can be purchased with the same number of dollars than limited payment whole life, persons having whole life insurance needs are probably best off using continuous premium life insurance when insurance needs are greatest. Once their insurance needs are reduced, they can convert their

Five ways to insure a life for $100,000

By varying the premium, death benefit, expiration date and cash surrender value, policies can be custom fitted to different needs. Diagrammed here are some typical policies issued to a 35-year-old man. For simplicity's sake they are nonparticipating policies, whose premiums are fixed by contract and are not affected by dividends.

5-year renewable term

Since this policy has no cash value, the $415 initial premium goes up every five years. The policy expires at age 70 unless converted to whole life by age 65.

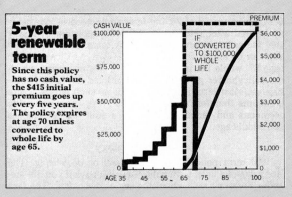

Whole life

To insure someone for life without ever raising the premium, reserves called cash values must be accumulated. Policy owners can take out the cash by giving up the insurance—or by living to 100.

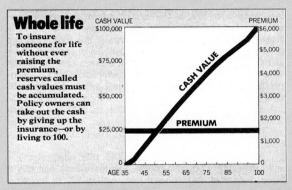

10-year non-renewable term

Another way of keeping premiums low is to make a policy nonrenewable. In this policy even the right of conversion to whole life expires after eight years.

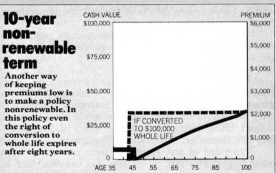

20-year decreasing term

Reducing death benefits monthly keeps premiums low—$299 here. For five years all the insurance in force can be converted to whole life with cash values; for the next ten years 80%; then none.

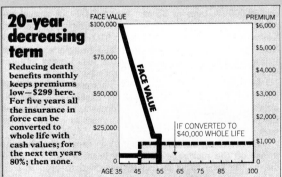

Term to age 65

This policy keeps the premium level. Overpayments in the early years make up for underpayments later, building up temporary cash value.

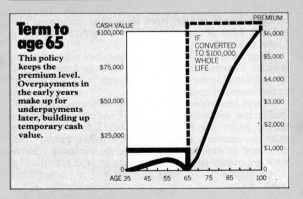

Source: "Six-Figure Life Insurance for Three-Figure Premiums," by Avery Comarow, excerpted from the March 1975 issue of MONEY Magazine by special permission; © 1975, Time Inc.

policy into a smaller amount of paid up life insurance. On the other hand, if people have sufficient life insurance already in force to protect against income loss, then they can effectively use limited payment policies as part of a savings or retirement plan.

Single Premium Continuous premium and limited payment whole life policies represent methods of acquiring life insurance on an installment basis. In contrast, a single premium whole life policy is one that is purchased on a "cash" basis. One premium payment at the inception of the contract buys life insurance coverage for the insured for the remainder of his or her life. The single premium policy has little use in the life insurance programs of most families. However, because of its investment attributes, the single premium life insurance contract does appeal to some as a medium for accumulating savings. In addition, in some instances the single premium policy can be an effective tool in planning for estate liquidity, which is discussed in Chapter 17.

Advantages and Disadvantages of Whole Life The most noteworthy positive feature of whole life insurance is that premium payments contribute toward building an estate, regardless of whether the insured lives or dies. This feature is due to the fact that the face value of the policy is paid upon death, or the cash value may be withdrawn when the need for insurance protection has expired. A corresponding benefit of whole life (except single premium) is that it permits individuals who need insurance for an entire lifetime to budget their premium payments over a relatively long period, thus eliminating the problems of unaffordability and uninsurability often encountered in later years with term insurance. The most frequently cited disadvantages of whole life insurance are that (1) more death protection can be purchased with term insurance, and (2) higher yields can be obtained on other investments. Like the negative aspects of term insurance, the shortcomings of whole life arise only when the policy is used in a manner inconsistent with its purpose. In other words, if maximum death protection is the predominant motive for the purchase of life insurance, clearly whole life should not be obtained. Similarly, if maximum return on investment is an objective, the funds available should not be put toward buying a whole life policy. However, if a person wishes to combine the acquisition of a given amount of death protection for the entire life of the insured (or until the policy is terminated) with a savings plan that provides a good return with high liquidity and minimum risk, then whole life insurance may be a wise investment.

Endowment Insurance

Endowment policies are those that offer life insurance protection for a stated period of time, such as twenty years or until age sixty-five. If the insured has not died by the end of the period, the policy may be redeemed for its face value. In other words, an endowment policy provides for the payment of the policy's face value upon the death of the insured or at the end of the policy period, whichever comes first. The endowment policy is similar to the whole life policy in that it combines savings with insurance protection. It differs, though, because the endowment contract does not provide coverage for the entire life of the insured, and it provides for savings accumulation at a faster rate than in a whole life policy. For example, a $10,000 twenty year endowment policy issued to a male age twenty-five would have a cash value of $10,000 when the insured became age forty-five. In contrast, the cash value of a $10,000 whole life policy does not equal its face amount until the insured reaches age 100. Of course, the annual premium per $1,000 of coverage under an endowment policy is usually substantially more than the rate per $1,000 of coverage under a comparable whole life policy.

Table 13-6 depicts a typical endowment insurance premium schedule. Because of its high cost, persons interested in life insurance for protection against premature death should never buy an endowment policy. Endowment policies are only beneficial to those who desire a systematic and semicompulsory form of savings. In Table 13-7, several types of whole life and endowment policies are compared on the bases of face value, accumulated cash values, and paid up amounts. The data in this table illustrate the trade-offs that exist among these policies in terms of the variables shown.

Other Types of Life Insurance

Credit life insurance, mortgage life insurance, industrial life insurance, special purpose policies, group life insurance, and variable life insurance are other types of life insurance that are readily available. However, with the exception of group life insurance, these types of contracts generally should be avoided.

Credit Life Insurance Banks, finance companies, and other lenders generally sell credit life insurance in conjunction with installment loans. Most often it is a term policy with a face value that decreases at the same rate as the balance on the loan. Although liquidating debts upon the

Table 13-6 Endowment Premium Schedule
(Premiums per $1,000 of Insurance; Minimum Policy Issued, $2,000—
Disability Waiver of Premium Included)

Age Nearest Birthday	Endowment at Age 65		10-Year Endowment		15-Year Endowment		20-Year Endowment		30-Year Endowment	
	Annual	Monthly	Annual	Monthly	Annual	Monthly	Annual	Monthly	Annual	Monthly
20	$17.04	$1.51	$95.01	$8.39	$60.48	$5.34	$43.46	$3.84	$26.93	$2.38
21	17.56	1.55	95.04	8.39	60.49	5.34	43.48	3.84	26.99	2.38
22	18.12	1.60	95.05	8.40	60.51	5.34	43.51	3.84	27.04	2.39
23	18.71	1.65	95.07	8.40	60.53	5.35	43.54	3.85	27.11	2.39
24	19.32	1.71	95.08	8.40	60.56	5.35	43.59	3.85	27.20	2.40
25	19.98	1.76	95.10	8.40	60.58	5.35	43.62	3.85	27.29	2.41
26	20.67	1.83	95.12	8.40	60.61	5.35	43.68	3.86	27.39	2.42
27	21.40	1.89	95.15	8.40	60.65	5.36	43.74	3.86	27.52	2.43
28	22.18	1.96	95.17	8.41	60.70	5.36	43.80	3.87	27.65	2.44
29	23.00	2.03	95.21	8.41	60.76	5.37	43.88	3.88	27.81	2.46
30	23.87	2.11	95.26	8.41	60.82	5.37	43.97	3.88	27.99	2.47
31	24.80	2.19	95.31	8.42	60.90	5.38	44.09	3.89	28.18	2.49
32	25.81	2.28	95.37	8.42	60.99	5.39	44.20	3.90	28.41	2.51
33	26.86	2.37	95.44	8.43	61.09	5.40	44.35	3.92	28.65	2.53
34	28.00	2.47	95.54	8.44	61.22	5.41	44.51	3.93	28.92	2.55
35	29.22	2.58	95.63	8.45	61.35	5.42	44.70	3.95	29.22	2.58
36	30.53	2.70	95.76	8.46	61.51	5.43	44.91	3.97	29.55	2.61
37	31.93	2.82	95.92	8.47	61.70	5.45	45.15	3.99	29.90	2.64
38	33.45	2.95	96.08	8.49	61.91	5.47	45.43	4.01	30.31	2.68
39	35.09	3.10	96.25	8.50	62.15	5.49	45.72	4.04	30.73	2.71
40	36.86	3.26	96.45	8.52	62.40	5.51	46.07	4.07	31.21	2.76
41	38.77	3.42	96.67	8.54	62.70	5.54	46.46	4.10	31.72	2.80
42	40.86	3.61	96.93	8.56	63.03	5.57	46.88	4.14	32.30	2.85
43	43.12	3.81	97.20	8.59	63.39	5.60	47.32	4.18	32.91	2.91
44	45.62	4.03	97.51	8.61	63.80	5.64	47.82	4.22	33.59	2.97
45	48.36	4.27	97.87	8.64	64.25	5.68	48.36	4.27	34.33	3.03
46	51.39	4.54	98.27	8.68	64.80	5.72	48.96	4.32	35.13	3.10
47	54.75	4.84	98.74	8.72	65.40	5.78	49.60	4.38	36.02	3.18
48	58.51	5.17	99.26	8.77	66.05	5.83	50.31	4.44	36.98	3.27
49	62.74	5.54	99.84	8.82	66.75	5.90	51.10	4.51	38.03	3.36
50	67.52	5.96	100.52	8.88	67.52	5.96	51.95	4.59	39.18	3.46
51	72.98	6.45	101.36	8.95	68.36	6.04	52.91	4.67	40.42	3.57
52	79.26	7.00	102.27	9.03	69.29	6.12	53.95	4.77	41.79	3.69
53	86.57	7.65	103.26	9.12	70.30	6.21	55.08	4.87	43.27	3.82
54	95.18	8.41	104.33	9.22	71.41	6.31	56.34	4.98	44.88	3.96
55	105.49	9.32	105.49	9.32	72.62	6.41	57.72	5.10	46.64	4.12
56	113.74	10.05	102.56	9.06	70.29	6.21	55.96	4.94	45.67	4.03
57	128.62	11.36	103.38	9.13	71.34	6.30	57.24	5.06	47.40	4.19
58	147.72	13.05	104.27	9.21	72.49	6.40	58.63	5.18	49.27	4.35
59	173.19	15.30	105.25	9.30	73.74	6.51	60.15	5.31	51.27	4.53
60	208.90	18.45	106.32	9.39	75.10	6.63	61.79	5.46	53.43	4.72

Note: All policies are participating.

death of a family breadwinner is often desirable, the funds for this need should be fulfilled through an individual's term or whole life insurance program. Buying credit life insurance per se is one of the most expensive

Table 13-7 **Comparison of Selected Life Insurance Contracts of Two Companies for a Male Age 25 at Date of Issue**
($1,000 Annual Premium for Each Contract)

Type of Policy	Company	Face Value	Cash Value at Age 35	Cash Value at Age 45	Cash Value at Age 65	Paid-Up Amount at Age 45	Paid-Up Amount at Age 65
Continuous Premium Whole Life	Co. 1	$71,377	$6,424	$16,987	$41,113	$37,687	$58,529
	Co. 2	59,490	6,961	18,502	37,717	31,273	48,153
Paid-Up Whole Life Age 65	Co. 1	63,870	7,026	18,650	45,092	38,332	63,870
	Co. 2	53,280	7,353	19,181	41,772	32,421	53,280
20-Pay Whole Life	Co. 1	44,117	8,816	20,823	31,147	44,117	44,117
	Co. 2	35,402	8,285	20,958	27,400	35,402	35,402
Endowment at Age 45	Co. 1	18,077	7,148	18,077	Matured at Face Value at Age 45		
	Co. 2	22,170	8,891	22,170			
Endowment at Age 65	Co. 1	53,500	7,661	19,771	53,500	28,195	Matured at Face Value
	Co. 2	45,872	5,148	16,452	45,872	26,000	

Note: All contracts shown are for participating policies.

ways to buy life insurance. Furthermore, contrary to popular belief, a lender *cannot* legally reject a loan because the potential borrower chooses not to secure life insurance.

Mortgage Life Insurance Mortgage life insurance is a form of credit life insurance designed to pay off the mortgage balance upon the death of the borrower. As in the case of credit life insurance, though, this need can usually be met less expensively by shopping the open market for a suitable decreasing term policy. The reason that credit life and mortgage life are relatively expensive is that lenders are often influenced by the amount of sales commission they receive in selecting the insurers with whom they place the coverage. And as might be expected, an insurer who pays high commissions is frequently one who charges a high premium.

Industrial Life Insurance Industrial life insurance is whole life or endowment life insurance that is issued in policies with small face amounts, often $1,000 or less. It is sold by persons who call on policyholders weekly or monthly to collect the premiums. The term *industrial* arose because, when these policies first became popular, the primary sales market was low-paid industrial wage earners. Because of its high marketing costs, industrial life insurance costs more per $1,000 of coverage than whole life and endowment policies that are issued with larger policy limits requiring annual or semiannual premium payments. Nevertheless, some insurance authorities believe that industrial life insurance offers the only practical way to deliver coverage to low-income families. Presently, industrial insurance represents only about 2 percent of the life insurance in force in this country, down from 11 percent just two decades ago.

Special Purpose Policies Certain types of policies frequently combine some form of term and whole life insurance for coverage on one or more members of a family. Although many of the special purpose policies are marketed under various company trade names, several general designations for these policies are: family income policies, family maintenance policies, multiple protection plans, and jumping juveniles. One appealing feature of certain family-type policies is that they may offer the guaranteed insurability of children. The policy may specify that when children reach a certain age (say, twenty-one or twenty-five) they may buy a specified type of life insurance at a predetermined price, regardless of their physical condition. While you may find that a certain special purpose policy will meet the needs of your family, more than likely these needs can be satisfied less expensively by separately purchased term and continuous premium whole life.

Group Life Insurance Under group life insurance, one master policy is issued and each eligible member of the group receives a certificate of insurance. Group insurance is nearly universally term insurance, and the premium is based on the characteristics of the group as a whole rather than related to any specific individual. Often group life insurance is obtained by employers as a fringe benefit for their employees. However, nearly any group can secure a group life insurance policy as long as the insurance is only incidental to the reason for the group. Many colleges and universities have both group life and group health insurance policies available to their students.

Comprising nearly 45 percent of all life insurance in force in the United States, group life insurance is one of the fastest growing areas of insurance. The amount of group protection in force has increased threefold just since 1965. Many group life policies now offer coverage not only for the group members but also for their dependents. In addition, nearly all group life policies provide that if individual members leave the group, they may continue the coverage by converting their protection into an individually issued whole life policy. Of course, after exercising the option to convert, these individuals assume all responsibility for the payment of premiums. The availability of group life insurance definitely should be considered when a family develops its life insurance program. However, because of its potentially temporary nature and relatively low face amount (often equal to one year's salary or more), it should fulfill only low priority insurance needs. Only in rare cases should a family rely on group life insurance to fulfill its primary income protection requirements.

Variable Life Insurance In variable life insurance policies the benefits payable to the insured are related to the value of the company's assets that support its payment obligation. The basic concept behind variable life insurance is that policyholders should be able to reap the benefits the insurer receives from investment returns in excess of the minimum return upon which premium computations are based. Furthermore, some persons believe that in periods of inflation a variable policy is essential for keeping an insurance coverage in line with the cost of living. However, while variable life may be a convenient way to guard against inflation, families can currently accomplish this just as well by simply buying additional policies as needed or purchasing contracts which give the policyholder the right to increase the face amount of the policy at stipulated intervals. Moreover, as recent experience has shown, a rising consumer price index is not necessarily accompanied by an increasing Dow-Jones Average. Consequently, variable life insurance cannot be relied on to replace fixed-dollar (nonvariable) life insurance to any significant extent, since there is no guarantee that the investment returns of the insuring company will increase with inflation.

Features of Life Insurance Policies

All life insurance contracts have various provisions which establish the rights and obligations of the policyholder and the insurance company. However, no standard or uniform life insurance policies exist. The wording of policy provisions and features varies among companies and according to the state in which the policy is sold. Nevertheless, even though the wording of the provisions may differ, a number of elements are common to nearly all life insurance contracts. These elements can be broken into two groups: (1) life insurance contract features, and (2) other policy features. Also important are certain financial advantages life insurance policies offer.

Life Insurance Contract Features

The key features found in most life insurance contracts are: (1) the beneficiary clause, (2) settlement options, (3) policy loans, (4) payment of premiums, (5) nonforfeiture options, (6) policy reinstatement, and (7) change of policy. Each of these important features is briefly described below.

Life Insurance That Changes When You Do

Those attractive young couples in the life insurance commercials always seem to be getting raises, moving into new houses, raising healthy children, sending them off to college and planning for a golden retirement. . . .

For people whose lives are running more normally—and less well—adjusting insurance coverage can present special problems. People who become ill or financially troubled often can't get or maintain enough life insurance coverage. A new type of insurance, however, offers greater flexibility than conventional policies for anyone whose insurance needs change through the years. It also provides new ways to avoid canceling policies in hard times.

"Adjustable life insurance," currently sold by two midwestern insurance companies, theoretically can provide for a lifetime of changing circumstances in one policy. Death benefits can be increased or decreased and premiums moved up or down to coincide with marriage, the birth of children and other major events in life. What's more, the policies now available offer this flexibility at a cost competitive with many conventional whole life insurance policies.

Adjustable life, sometimes known as "life cycle" insurance, combines the two basic types of life insurance, term and whole life. Term insurance provides coverage for a limited period of time, but normally builds up no cash value; whole life (or permanent) insurance combines coverage with a savings plan that builds up cash value. Adjustable life gets its flexibility by switching back and forth between these two types and by varying the periods covered by the term insurance. The term of coverage possible under an adjustable life policy is often longer than the typical term policy's one-, five- or 10-year maximum. If the amount of adjustable life term coverage remains the same over the years, so does the premium. With normal term insurance, by contrast, the premium increases with each renewal to reflect the increasing age of the insured person. Because the level premium means the client is overpaying in the early years, even the term coverage in an adjustable life policy builds up some case value.

Adjustable life was introduced by Minnesota Mutual Life Insurance Co., based in St. Paul; a similar policy now is sold by Bankers Life of Des Moines, Iowa. At least three other firms are considering the sale of adjustable life.

Not every life insurance buyer needs the special features of adjustable life. Mortgage insurance, for example, is cheaper in the form of term insurance that decreases along with the balance of the unpaid loan. . . .

Robert E. Hunstad, vice president of Minnesota Mutual, explains that adjustable life is designed to let the buyer focus on "the two essential questions of life insurance—how much coverage does the customer need and how much can he afford to pay in premiums?"

Adjustable life has a cost-of-living option, available on few other policies. Up to age 55, the policyholder is given a chance every three years to increase his coverage to correspond with changes in the consumer price index—up to a limit. . . . Although the increases typically would raise the premiums, the customer can keep payments the same by reducing the term of the coverage.

The policyholder must, however, accept each cost-of-living increase or he will no longer be offered the option. This is to keep someone from rejecting the increase in early years, then taking it later when he knows he is ill. But a policyholder who had always accepted these increases could keep boosting his coverage even while gravely ill.

Face value can be cut as well as increased. For instance, an adjustable life term plan expiring at age 70 might be switched to lifetime coverage paid up at 65 by reducing the death benefit.

A valuable feature of adjustable life is the ability to cut premiums without cutting death benefits by reducing the term of coverage or by switching from whole life to term. Ordinary policies may permit a change from term to more expensive whole life, but usually not the reverse. . . .

Money commissioned a cost study of adjustable life by Joseph M. Belth, professor of insurance at Indiana University and an expert on the cost of insurance to the consumer. . . .

As a first step, Belth measured the cost of adjustable policies when they are bought originally in a whole life form and not changed subsequently. He found the adjustable policies ranked about midway in cost among various whole life policies offered by Bankers Life and Minnesota Mutual. But when compared with policies from other companies, both adjustable policies were less costly than three-quarters of the 163 policies surveyed.

Belth then analyzed a situation where a policyholder decides he needs more coverage and can pay higher premiums. Once again, the adjustable policies proved higher in cost than some conventional policies from the same companies and lower than others. . . .

It's too early to tell just how well adjustable life is working for those who own it. But its flexibility could make initial insurance buying decisions less difficult. . . .

Beneficiary Clause All life insurance policies should have one or more named *beneficiaries*, the person or persons who receive the death benefits of the policy if the insured dies. Otherwise the proceeds are payable to the estate of the deceased and are often subject to prolonged legal and other procedures associated with estate settlement (see Chapter 17). In addition, if a beneficiary is not named, the distribution of the policy proceeds in the event of death may not end up as the insured would have desired. When naming the beneficiary, the policyholder should make certain the identification is clear. For example, a man could buy a policy and simply designate the beneficiary as "my wife." Later, if a divorce and marriage to another woman took place, a controversy could arise as to which "wife" was entitled to the benefits. Similarly, if children are the intended beneficiaries, problems can arise when other children become a part of the insured's family. For instance, if a man named "my children" as beneficiaries, would proceeds be payable only to his natural and legitimate children? Or would his adopted, illegitimate, or stepchildren also share in the proceeds? Since no definite answer to these questions exists, the need to precisely identify policy beneficiaries should be quite clear. As a precaution, a secondary beneficiary should also be named to reduce the possibility that the insurance proceeds would go to unintended persons via the estate. This could occur if the primary beneficiary were to die before or at the same time as the insured and a new primary beneficiary had not been designated.

Settlement Options Insurance companies generally offer several different ways in which death proceeds of a life insurance policy may be paid. The decision as to how the funds will be allocated may be permanently established prior to the death of the insured, or the beneficiary may be allowed to select the desired *settlement option* when the policy matures. The most common settlement options besides lump-sum cash payment are: (1) interest only, (2) payments for a stated period, (3) payments of a stated amount, and (4) income for life.

Interest Only Under the interest only settlement option, the policy proceeds are left on deposit with the insurance company for a period of time. In exchange, the insurer guarantees to make interest payments to the beneficiary during the time it holds the funds. In some cases the beneficiary is not permitted to withdraw the proceeds, and upon his or her death the funds are paid to a secondary beneficiary. In other cases, the beneficiary may have the right to fully withdraw policy proceeds at any time. The interest only option can be useful when there is no current need for the principal amount, or when the principal sum is large enough to provide a satisfactory annual income (in the form of interest) to the beneficiary.

Payments for a Stated Period With the payments for a stated period option, the face amount of the policy is systematically liquidated along with interest earned over a selected number of years. For example, a beneficiary at age fifty-five may not be eligible for social security benefits until age sixty-five but may be in need of a monthly income for that ten year period. Consequently, the option of receiving a monthly income for that duration may be more attractive than taking a lump sum. The amount of the periodic payment is determined by the face amount of the policy and the length of time over which the funds are to be distributed. For any given amount, the shorter the period, the larger the monthly benefit; and conversely, the longer the period of time over which the payments are made, the smaller the payment.

Payments of a Stated Amount The payments of a stated amount option is similar to the preceding alternative in that it provides for a systematic liquidation of the policy proceeds. It is different in that it provides for the selection of the amount of periodic benefit desired rather than the number of years over which income is to be received. The payment of a stated amount option offers more flexibility than the payments for a stated period, because beneficiaries usually retain the right to change the amount of income as their needs dictate. Under the stated period option, on the other hand, the term cannot be modified except that in some cases total withdrawal is permitted. In essence, the payment for a stated amount option can be used to accomplish the same objective as the stated period option. All beneficiaries need to do is estimate the period of time over which they will want to receive payments and determine the amount that will be payable. Then they can select the stated amount option to provide that amount of income. Should their needs change during the period, they can modify the terms of the settlement agreement.

Life Income Under the life income option, the insurer guarantees a certain payment amount to the beneficiary for the remainder of his or her life. In contrast to the preceding options, payments under the life income alternative are related to the age of the beneficiary at the inception of the periodic benefits. The amounts are essentially a function of the face value of the policy, interest rate assumptions, and the life expectancy of the beneficiary. (Technically, mortality rates rather than life expectancy are used in these computations. A *mortality rate* designates the number of deaths per 1,000 that will occur at specified ages each year, whereas *life expectancy* is the mean number of years of life remaining at a given age. Table 13-4, presented earlier, gives such data for a variety of ages.)

The life income option can be attractive to persons who want to be certain that they will not outlive the income from the policy proceeds and subsequently have to depend on others for support. Usually a company will agree under the life income option to guarantee payments for five or ten years to a secondary beneficiary should the original recipient die prior to the passage of that period of time. This arrangement is sometimes referred to as a *guaranteed payment life income option*. Of course, if the guaranteed payment life income option is selected, the monthly benefit is less than if the option providing income only for the life of the primary beneficiary is chosen. However, the younger the primary beneficiary when payments begin, the smaller the difference in the amount of monthly payments between the life income option and the guaranteed payment life income option.

Policy Loans An advance made by a life insurance company to a policyholder is a *policy loan*. These loans are secured by the cash value of the life insurance policy. A provision in nearly all whole life and endowment policies grants this right. Typically, the maximum amount that may be withdrawn is 95 percent of the policy's cash value. Although no specific repayment terms are necessary, any balance plus interest on the loan remaining at the death of the insured is subtracted from the proceeds of the policy. The rate of interest charged on policy loans is customarily 5 to 8 percent per annum and is stated in the policy at the time it is issued. Policy loans should not be obtained except in unusual circumstances because of the reduction of death proceeds that can result. One long-time advocate of whole life insurance has decried policy loans as "stealing from your widow." Although not all would agree with this emotional appeal, life insurance does provide basic financial protection for most families, and spending those proceeds prematurely is an unwise practice. On the other hand, because these loans are less expensive than borrowing from other financial institutions, they may appeal to certain persons who wish to keep their borrowing costs low and are not bothered by the accompanying loss of death proceeds.

Payment of Premiums All life insurance contracts have a provision that specifies when premiums are to be paid. With most insurers, the policyholder may elect the option of paying premiums on an annual, semiannual, or monthly basis. Some premium checks are mailed directly to the company, and in other instances the salesperson collects premiums from the policyholder. Another method of payment allows policyholders to pay premiums through an automatic deduction from their bank accounts. In the case of death of a policyholder who has paid premiums more than one month in advance, many companies refund these premiums along with the policy death proceeds.

Nonforfeiture Options As discussed earlier, a nonforfeiture option provides policyholders with some benefits in the event that a policy is terminated prior to its maturity. The laws of every state provide that all whole life and endowment policies (and term contracts which extend coverage over a long period) contain a nonforfeiture provision. In addition to a cash withdrawal, companies ordinarily offer the following options to the policyholder: (1) a paid-up policy for a reduced amount, or (2) a term policy for an extended period.

Paid-Up for Reduced Amount Under the reduced amount option, the policyholder receives a policy exactly like the one that was terminated except that it has a lower face value. In effect, the policyholder has purchased a new policy with his or her cash value at the single-premium rate. For example, assume that currently the cash value of a $10,000 continuous premium policy is $2,600 and that the insured is age fifty-two. The company would consult its rate book and find that a single premium of $2,600 for an individual at this age would buy $6,100 of paid-up whole life protection. Of course, under this option, the cash value would continue to grow because of the interest earnings, even though the policyholder is relieved of any further premium payments. This option is useful when a person's income and need for death protection decline while at the same time some coverage is still desired. Many people elect this option on whole life policies when the insured attains age sixty or sixty-five.

Extended Term The extended term option provides that upon the relinquishment of the cash value by the policyholder the company issues a term life insurance policy for the same face value as the policy that has lapsed. The period of coverage is determined by the amount of term protection a single premium payment equal to the total cash value would have purchased at the present age of the insured. The extended term option is usually the option that automatically goes into effect if the policyholder quits paying premiums and forwards no instructions to the company.

Policy Reinstatement While a policy is under the reduced paid-up option on the extended term option, the policyholder may reinstate the policy by paying all back premiums plus interest at a stated rate and providing evidence that he or she can pass a physical examination and meet any other insurability requirements of the company. *Reinstatement* means that the original contractual relationship between the company and the policyholder is revived. Most often the policyholder must reinstate the policy within a specified period (3 or 5 years) after the policy lapsed.

Change of Policy Many life insurance contracts contain a provision which permits the insured to switch from one policy form to another. For example, policyholders may decide that they would rather have a paid-up age sixty-five policy as opposed to their current continuous premium whole life policy. A change of policy provision would allow this change without penalty. In instances where policyholders are changing from a high premium policy to one with lower premiums (the opposite of the above example), the insured may need to prove insurability. This requirement reduces the possibility of adverse selection against the company.

Other Policy Features

In addition to the key contractual features described in the preceding section, a number of other life insurance policy features include: (1) a grace period, (2) a multiple indemnity clause, (3) the disability clause, (4) insurability options, (5) a suicide clause, (6) an incontestability clause, (7) a misstatement of age or sex clause, and (8) exclusions. A basic understanding of these features should provide you with a better feel for the coverages provided.

Grace Period The grace period permits the policyholder to retain protection for a short while (usually thirty-one days) after failing to remit a premium when due. If the insured dies during the grace period, the face amount of the policy less the scheduled premium is paid to the beneficiary.

Multiple Indemnity Multiple (most often double or triple) indemnity clauses double or triple the face amount of the policy if the insured dies as a result of an accident. This benefit is usually offered to the policyholder at a small additional cost. Many insurance authorities dismiss the use of a multiple indemnity benefit as irrational. This coverage should be ignored as a source of funds when programming insurance needs, since it provides no protection in the event of death due to illness.

Disability Clause A disability clause in a life insurance contract may contain either a waiver of premium benefit or a waiver of premium coupled with disability income. A *waiver of premium benefit* excuses the payment of premiums on the life insurance policy if the insured becomes totally and permanently disabled prior to age sixty (or sometimes age sixty-five). Under the *disability income portion*, the insured is entitled to a monthly income equal to five or ten dollars per $1,000 of policy face value. Some insurers will continue these payments for the life of the insured and others will terminate them at age sixty-five. Disability riders

"Herb, take out more life insurance."

Need, not intuition, should decide how much
life insurance is required.

Source: *Changing Times,* March 1977, p. 38. Reprinted with permission from *Changing Times*
Magazine, © Kiplinger Washington Editors, Inc., 1977.

providing waiver of premium and disability income protection are
relatively inexpensive and can be added to most whole life and endowment policies. Often, they are not available with term policies.

Insurability Options The policyholder who has an insurability option
may purchase additional coverage at stipulated intervals of time even if
the insured becomes uninsurable. This option is frequently offered with
the purchase of a whole life or endowment policy to buyers under age
forty. The increases in coverage usually can be purchased every three,
four, or five years in amounts equal to the amount of the original policy,
or $10,000, whichever is the lower. This option should be quite attractive
to individuals whose life insurance needs and ability to pay are expected
to increase over a five to fifteen year period.

Suicide Clause Nearly all life insurance policies have a clause which voids the contract if an insured commits suicide within two years (sometimes one) after its inception. In these cases the company simply returns the premiums that have been paid. If an insured takes his or her own life after this initial period has elapsed, the policy proceeds are paid without question.

Incontestability Clause All life insurance policies have an incontestability clause which gives the insurance company one to two years to investigate all information provided by the insured in the application. If during that period a material false statement is discovered, the company can seek a recision of the contract. After the elapsed period, though, the insurer is prohibited from challenging the validity of the policy regardless of whether the insured has died or is still living.

Misstatement of Age or Sex Notwithstanding the foregoing, the company can adjust the payment made under the policy at any time if the insured misstated his or her age or sex in the application. For example, assume that a male age thirty-five applied for a life policy by mail and stated that he was a female age thirty-five. The incentive for making this misstatement is that for a given amount of coverage, females of the same age as males are required to pay a lower premium because of lower mortality rates. If upon death ten years later the company discovered the error, it would award a sum equal to the amount of insurance that the premiums paid would have purchased had the insurer known the applicant was a male. Note that this is not technically a violation of the incontestability provision because the policy has not been voided but simply modified to conform to the facts. However, some observers say that the misstatement of age and sex clause is in conflict with the spirit of the incontestability rule and places an undesirable burden upon the beneficiaries.

Exclusions Although all private insurance policies have some types of losses that are excluded from coverage, life policies offer very broad protection. In addition to the suicide clause, only aviation and war exclusions are used more than infrequently. In aviation exclusions, the primary types of losses not covered are when the insured is a relatively inexperienced private pilot or is flying in military aircraft. No restrictions apply to fare-paying passengers of commercial airlines. In fact, most life insurers offer protection to the pilots and crews of scheduled airliners at standard rates. War exclusions often are inserted in policies in anticipation of or during periods of combat. Typically, they provide that should the insured die as a result of war, a return of premiums with interest will be made. War exclusions are intended to guard against adverse selection which could materially disrupt the mortality experience of the company and, correspondingly, its solvency. In certain other instances where the potential insured has a hazardous occupation or hobby, the company will either exclude coverage for that activity or charge an additional premium to cover the added risk exposure. However, seldom if ever would a company be able to modify the premium charged or coverage offered should the insured begin to live dangerously after the policy is issued.

Financial Advantages of Life Insurance Policies

In addition to the elements that make up the insurance contract and the other policy features, the following advantages of life insurance policies require discussion: (1) protection from creditors, (2) medium for savings, and (3) tax benefits of life insurance.

Protection from Creditors When an insured dies, all assets and liabilities are totaled and the heirs receive what is left after all legitimate claims against the estate are satisfied. However, the purchase of life insurance can be structured so that when death benefits are paid, the cash proceeds do not become a part of the estate. Even if the insured has more liabilities than assets, the proceeds would not be used to liquidate them. Similarly, creditors who are successful in securing judgments against persons with substantial accumulations of life insurance cash values most often cannot levy any claim on those cash values. State laws differ with respect to the rights of creditors to the death benefits or cash values of life insurance policies, but in nearly all cases, both can be better protected than assets such as stocks, bonds, mutual funds, and investment real estate.

Medium for Savings In addition to protection from creditors, life insurance can be an attractive medium for savings for the reasons of safety of principal, competitive return, liquidity, and forced savings. Many life insurance companies are more than 100 years old and have assets totaling into the billions of dollars. Even the banking industry encounters insolvencies more frequently than the life insurance industry. No major life insurance company has failed to meet its financial obligations in at least the last forty years. No other industry can match that record. Some wish to contrast adversely the financial return on the savings element in life insurance to investments in stocks, bonds, mutual funds, and real estate. However, such is an inaccurate comparison. These other media differ not only with respect to safety of principal but also in stability of earnings (risk), liquidity, and the contractual nature of deposits (premium payments). Unfortunately, the life insurance industry has spawned this erroneous exercise because of the overemphasis of "investment" in the sales presentation. More accurately, returns on life

A Life Insurance Quiz: How Much Do You Know?

The ten questions below provide some insight into the intriguing complexities of life insurance policies. See how many of these policy puzzles you can resolve.

1. A 27-year-old man in Utah designated a 37-year-old divorcee with eight children as the beneficiary of his life insurance. The man proposed marriage: she refused him. He told her that he could not live without her. Later she broke off with him, and on the same day he killed himself. The administrator of his estate went to court to keep the divorcee from collecting the life insurance, claiming she had "precipitated the suicidal act." A beneficiary is not entitled to collect if he murders the insured. Did the divorcee win? Yes ☐ No ☐

Yes. The Utah Supreme Court ruled that her conduct had not been so outrageous as to offend accepted standards of decency. A beneficiary who kills the insured in self-defense is also entitled to collect.

2. If you stop paying the premiums on a life insurance policy, the policy generally will lapse until you can prove that: A. You had amnesia or a similar physical or mental disability ☐ B. You are illiterate and couldn't read the premium notice ☐ C. You were kidnapped or otherwise forcibly detained ☐ D. None of these ☐

D. But an insurer cannot cancel a life insurance policy for one month after a premium was due. Many policies with cash values, such as whole life and endowment plans, require the insurer to convert them to "extended term" insurance for as long a period as the cash value will pay for.

3. A man names "Mary Smith, my wife" as the beneficiary of his life insurance. He divorces Mary Smith and marries Susan Jones. When he dies, who gets the proceeds? Mary Smith ☐ His wife ☐

Mary Smith. In most cases, the person named remains the beneficiary.

4. Many life insurance policies pay double the face value if the insured person dies of an accident. Which of the following causes of death would ordinarily trigger "double indemnity"? A. Sunstroke while golfing ☐ B. A gunshot fired by a guard while the insured is robbing a bank ☐ C. Russian roulette ☐ D. Going over Niagara Falls in a barrel ☐

A. If someone dies doing something that could obviously cost him his life, his death is generally not considered accidental.

5. In applying for life insurance, a man says he is 40 years old when he is 50. Three years later, he dies. His beneficiaries are entitled to the full amount of his life insurance policy because the two-year period of contestability is over. True ☐ False ☐

False. His beneficiaries would receive only the face value of a policy that a man of his true age would have obtained with the premiums he paid. For example, a $50,000 whole life policy would be reduced to about $34,000.

6. Whole life insurance gives you something that term insurance doesn't—a savings account. Approximately what is the average annual rate of return on the savings account after 20 years? A. 3% ☐ B. 4% ☐ C. 5% ☐ D. 6% ☐

B. Insurers don't disclose an interest rate on the savings account, or cash value, feature of whole life, but Professor Stuart Schwarzschild of Georgia State University recently figured it at 4.15% on average.

7. If you borrow against the cash value in a whole life policy, you must repay the money by a certain date. True ☐ False ☐

False. If you die or surrender the policy, though, the debt plus any unpaid interest is subtracted from the proceeds.

8. William A. White, an actuary for the New Jersey Insurance Department, is almost convinced that certain insurance policies should bear this notice in bold red letters: "The insurer general has determined that this policy is going to cost you a hell of a lot of money if you don't intend to keep it in force for more than a year or two." Which kind of insurance does he have in mind? A. Term life ☐ B. Whole life ☐ C. Disability ☐ D. Homeowners ☐

B. If you cancel a whole life policy during its first or second year, you will have accumulated little or no cash surrender value. You could just as well have purchased term insurance, which costs only about a third as much in premiums. The time to consider whether you really want whole life is before you buy it.

9. If you have adequate life insurance, which of the following can you easily do without? A. Double indemnity for accidental death ☐ B. Flight insurance ☐ C. Both ☐ D. Neither ☐

C. Your dependents will need the same amount to live on whether you die of sickness or from an accident.

10. On his life insurance policy, a man names his sister as beneficiary. In his will he leaves all his assets, including insurance, to his wife. Who receives the insurance proceeds at his death? His wife ☐ His sister ☐

His sister.

Source: "Twenty Twisty Questions about Insurance," by Warren Boroson, excerpted from the December 1976 issue of MONEY Magazine by special permission; © 1976, Time Inc.

insurance cash value should be compared to those of savings accounts and bonds of the United States government. In this area they compare favorably in providing *after-tax* returns ranging from 4 to 5 percent.

Tax Benefits Upon the death of the insured, the proceeds of a life insurance policy pass to the beneficiaries free of any state or federal income tax but may have certain death taxes levied against them (see Chapter 17). In contrast, after passage of the Tax Reform Act of 1976, other properties—such as stocks, bonds, and real estate—are subject not only to estate taxes but to income taxes on the capital gain at death (whether realized or unrealized). In fact, because these other assets (especially real estate) may not be liquid at the time the taxes become due, life insurance proceeds are often used to pay the resulting tax liabilities. Another tax advantage of life insurance is that when cash values are withdrawn from an insurer, income taxes are payable only on the amount by which the cash value exceeds the total premiums that have been paid. In practice, this excess seldom results because part of the premium that is paid is allocated to the death benefit cost incurred by the company during the time the policy is in force. Consequently it does not become a part of the cash value of the policy.

Companies, Costs, and Purchase Decisions

In order to proceed intelligently with the purchase of needed life insurance, it is essential to understand the alternative types of life insurance companies as well as the differences in life insurance costs. This part of the chapter not only looks at company types and how to measure policy costs, but it also examines the process of selecting the appropriate types of insurance, the agent through which to effect the insurance transaction, and the company from which to purchase needed insurance.

Types of Companies

More than 96 percent of the life insurance sold in the United States is issued by either a stock company or a mutual company. A *stock company* is owned by stockholders, while a *mutual company* is owned by its policyholders. Only one practical difference exists between these two types of insurers. Stock companies generally offer nonparticipating policies, whereas mutuals issue only participating policies. A policy is defined as *participating* when the policyholder is entitled to receive policy dividends which reflect the difference between the premiums that are charged and the amount of premium necessary to fund the actual experience of the company. However, when the base premium schedule for participating policies is established, a mutual company will estimate what it believes its mortality and investment experience will be and then add a more than adequate margin of safety to these figures. The premiums charged the policyholder are based on these somewhat exaggerated estimates. When realized company experience is more favorable than that estimated, a return of the overcharge is made to policyholders in the form of *policy dividends*. These policy dividends may be accepted by the policyholders as a cash payment, left with the company to earn interest, used to buy additional paid-up coverage, or applied toward the next premium payment. The dividend option selected is simply a matter of personal preference based upon the needs and wants of the individual policyholder. Note that it is advantageous to use the dividends to buy paid-up options in instances where more insurance coverage is desired since these additions are available at their "net" rates. This means that the rates contain no load for sales expenses and consequently provide an economical way to increase coverage.

Stock companies generally avoid this "overpayment" and "return of premium" by establishing premium schedules that provide for lower premiums than those required by comparable schedules used by mutual insurers. Policies that do not return overpayments in the form of policy dividends are referred to as *nonparticipating*. Stock companies may sell participating as well as nonparticipating policies. Still, the question that must be answered when choosing between mutual and stock insurance companies is which costs less over time—participating or nonparticipating life insurance. Unfortunately, neither is less costly in all cases. Some participating policies end up costing less than nonparticipating, and in other cases the opposite is true. In addition to mutual and stock companies, life insurance is also available through fraternal insurers; assessment companies; savings banks located in New York, Massachusetts, and Connecticut; and the federal government (excluding social security). However, the amount of life insurance in force by all of these nonmutual and nonstock insurers together is less than 4 percent of the total.

Life Insurance Costs

The traditional manner in which life insurance costs have been computed for purposes of comparison is known as the *net cost method*. Under this approach, the amount of premiums that is paid over a period of time (usually ten or twenty years) is totaled. From this sum the total dividends and cash value that are projected for the period are subtracted. Then the remainder is divided by the number of years in the period. To illustrate, assume that you are considering the purchase of a policy that would have an annual premium of $100 and that the guaranteed cash value along with the projected dividends during the first twenty years of the policy total $1,400. The net cost of the policy in this case would be $30 per year ([$2,000 − $1,400] ÷ 20). This amount can then be compared to similarly computed amounts for other competing policies. However, the net cost method has several flaws which detract from its usefulness. The first is that it does not consider the time value of money. A second problem is that the dividend amounts are only projections. Actual experience may be more or less favorable than indicated by these estimates. Third, the cost is computed only at a certain point in time. The rankings of the net cost of three policies at 10, 20, and 30 year periods could be different. And fourth, it considers only the cash involved in the contractual arrangement. Although the cash value of one policy may be larger, other dividend and nonforfeiture options as well as policy provisions may be more favorable in policies offered by competitors.

More recently, considerable attention has focused on the *interest adjusted method* of calculating the cost of life insurance. An advantage of this technique is that it recognizes the time value of money by applying a discount rate to the calculations. But all of the other problems still exist, and furthermore, the cost rankings of the policies being compared will change depending on the rate used in the discounting process. In addition, this method is much too difficult for general use by consumers. In order to use this approach, they would have to rely on the calculations of others. But the premium, dividend, and cash value structure at the time such calculations were made may have differed considerably from those prevailing at the time these consumers are shopping for their protection. Unfortunately, as can be seen from the preceding discussion, the development of meaningful cost comparisons among competing policies is almost impossible. The net cost and interest adjusted methods can provide you with some information, but you should be aware of their limitations.

Buying Life Insurance

The purchase of life insurance can be viewed as a two-step process. The first and most important step involves developing an estimate of your future financial needs and the types of policies that will best satisfy them. Next you should decide with which life insurance agents and companies you wish to talk. In practice, these steps are not usually independent of each other. In fact, in most cases the agent selects the potential policyholder rather than the other way around.

Preliminaries As was discussed earlier, life insurance is used to fill the gap in a person's financial program between the resources that will be available after death and those that will be needed. In addition, it can be effectively utilized as a savings medium. For most young families on limited budgets, though, the need for a large amount of death protection greatly exceeds the need for a savings plan. If you fall into this category, guaranteed renewable and convertible term insurance should account for the largest portion of your insurance protection. Most families also have the need for some amount of permanent insurance and savings, which a whole life policy can satisfy. Limited payment whole life and endowment policies should be purchased only when the primary need is savings instead of protection against financial loss resulting from death.

Selecting an Agent The selection of a life insurance agent is quite important since you will be relying on your agent for advice and guidance with respect to some very important financial decisions. It is best not to assume that just because agents are licensed by the state they are competent and will necessarily serve your best interests. What you need to look for when evaluating agents is their formal and professional levels of educational attainment. Does the agent have a college degree with a major in business or insurance? Does the agent have a C.L.U. (Chartered Life Underwriter) designation, which is awarded only to agents who meet certain experience requirements and pass college-level examinations in such fields as life and health insurance, estate and pension planning, economics, and federal income tax law? In addition, it is a good idea to observe how an agent reacts to your questions. Does the agent use fancy "buzz words" and stock answers? Or does he or she listen attentively and then after a period of thought logically answer your questions? These and other personal characteristics and mannerisms can provide you with information upon which to base your decisions. In most instances, it is wise to talk with several different agents before deciding from whom to buy. Also, do not make your decision while under the influence of a specific agent. Wait until you and your spouse (if you have one) have a chance to discuss the pros and cons of each agent. Then, when you have decided, call and ask that agent to come back for another visit.

Selecting a Company The process of selecting the company from which you will buy your coverages is a step that may precede to a certain degree the choosing of an agent. This approach is necessary since in the life insurance business most agents represent only one company. Consequently, before looking for an agent, you might want to develop useful criteria with which to screen out companies. Usually companies can be evaluated on the basis of their financial stability, reputation in the community and nation, liberality of policy provisions, and whether they offer participating policies (if this feature is important to you). In addition, some attention should be given to the relative costs of similar policies from the competing companies. For a view of how costs vary among twenty-five large life insurance companies, see Table 13-8. Note that the average annual cost (see column 6) of company number 25 is considerably greater than the cost for company 1. As a matter of fact, it

Table 13-8 Comparative Premium Costs for 25 Major Life Insurance Companies, 1957–1977: $10,000 Participating Whole Life Policy for a Male Age 35
(Figures on a per $1,000 Basis)

Rank[a]	Company	Premium Rate per $1,000 Age 35 (1957) (1)	Total Premiums 20 Years per $1,000 (1957–1977) (2)	Total Dividends 20 Years per $1,000 (1957–1977) (3)	Cash Value 20th Year per $1,000 (4)	Actual Net Cost per $1,000 (2)−[(3)+(4)] (5)	Actual Average Annual Cost per $1,000 End 20 Years (5) ÷ 20 (6)
1	Northwestern Mutual Life Insurance Co., Wisc.	$26.39	$527.80	$228.41	$380.72	$−81.33	$−4.07
2	National Life Insurance Co., Vt.	25.04	500.80	188.58	370.00	−57.78	−2.89
3	State Farm Life Insurance Co., Ill.	24.04	480.80	186.02	351.75	−56.97	−2.85
4	Mutual Life Insurance Co. of N.Y.	25.41	500.58	188.87	368.00	−56.29	−2.81
5	New England Mutual Life Ins. Co., Mass.	23.58	471.60	162.95	362.44	−53.79	−2.69
6	Equitable Life Assurance Society of N.Y.	23.41	468.20	153.62	367.00	−52.42	−2.62
7	John Hancock Mutual Life Ins. Co., Mass.	23.59	471.80	152.01	370.83	−51.04	−2.55
8	Connecticut Mutual Life Insurance Co., Conn.	25.61	512.20	199.12	362.44	−49.36	−2.47
9	Bankers Life, Iowa	23.44	468.80	150.34	367.00	−48.54	−2.43
10	New York Life Insurance Co., N.Y.	23.59	471.80	146.14	371.00	−45.34	−2.27
11	Massachusetts Mutual Life Ins. Co., Mass.	25.35	507.00	182.47	362.44	−37.91	−1.90
12	Phoenix Mutual Life Ins. Co., Conn.	26.39	517.24	188.04	367.00	−37.80	−1.89

13	State Mutual Life Assurance of America, Mass.	25.29	505.80	178.85	362.48	−35.53	−1.78
14	Mutual Benefit Life Ins. Co., N.J.	24.90	498.00	152.43	379.71	−34.14	−1.71
15	Penn Mutual Life Insurance Co., Penn.	23.87	477.40	141.55	366.96	−31.11	−1.56
16	Prudential Ins. Co. of America, N.J.	24.40	488.00	155.80	363.00	−30.80	−1.54
17	Franklin Life Insurance Co., Ill.	24.87	497.40	158.48	365.13	−26.21	−1.31
18	Pacific Mutual Life Ins. Co., Calif.	26.03	520.60	179.90	365.13	−24.43	−1.22
19	Metropolitan Life Ins. Co., N.Y.	25.00	500.00	155.12	367.00	−22.12	−1.11
20	Aetna Life Insurance Company, Conn.	27.96	559.20	205.81	372.00	−18.61	−0.93
21	Connecticut General Life Ins. Co., Conn.	27.67	553.40	197.05	372.00	−15.65	−0.78
22	Occidental Life Ins. Co. of California	23.38	467.60	112.84	372.00	−15.65	−0.78
23	Continental Assurance Co., Ill.	26.37	527.40	159.38	372.00	− 3.98	−0.20
24	Western & Southern Life Ins. Co., Ohio	24.16	483.20	112.85	363.00	7.35	0.37
25	Lincoln National Life Ins. Co., Ind.	27.84	556.80	167.01	362.44	27.35	1.37

aRank based on actual net cost shown in Column (5).

Source: Reprinted with permission from *1977 Life Insurance Facts* (St. Louis, Mo.: Standard Analytical Services, 1977).

can be seen that using the net cost method to rank the companies in Table 13-8, most policies have negative annual costs. It was pointed out earlier in the discussion of insurance costs that the net cost method (used in Table 13-8) suffers from a number of deficiencies; the preferred technique for measuring insurance costs is the *interest adjusted method,* which was also discussed earlier.

It is not uncommon to find that one company is preferable for your term protection while another company is more desirable for meeting your whole life needs. Age and size of company are useful indicators of the financial stability of life insurance companies. Unless good reason exists to do otherwise, you are probably best off limiting your choice of companies to those that have been in existence more than fifty years and have annual premium volume in excess of $50 million. Although these criteria screen out hundreds of smaller companies, they still leave more than fifty companies from which to choose. Information on financial stability can be obtained from *Best's Reports,* which are available in most university libraries.

Summary

This chapter has introduced you to the concept of risk and has explored various ways that risk can be handled by families. Among these methods are risk avoidance, risk assumption, loss prevention, and insurance. Risks that can be effectively handled by insurance must meet the following criteria: (1) a large group of people must experience them, (2) the loss involved must be fortuitous, and (3) the cost to the insurer of assuming financial responsibility must be relatively low—the losses covered must occur relatively infrequently but have a high potential severity. In order to determine the exposure to loss it can insure and the rates to charge, the insurance company performs the underwriting function.

The most widely accepted method for assessing the amount of life insurance a family should have is the needs approach. With this technique, the family estimates how much insurance it will need after a loss in order to pay for the following items: (1) debt liquidation expenses, (2) family income, (3) widow's income, and (4) the accumulation of special purpose funds. Once the amount of available resources is determined, it is compared to the total resources desired in order to find the amount of life insurance necessary to meet the financial needs of the family. Other approaches sometimes used to determine life insurance needs are the human life value approach and the multiple earnings approach.

The types of life insurance available to meet the needs of a family are term, whole life, and endowment. Term insurance is written for a stated number of years and terminates at the end of that period. Term insurance builds cash values only in rare instances where the period of coverage is relatively long (twenty years or more), and it offers a large amount of death protection at an economical rate for persons age forty or younger. Whole life insurance is coverage that is necessary to fulfill a need for death protection that will exist throughout the life of the insured. It also builds cash value and can provide a good way to accumulate savings. Endowment insurance is like term insurance in that it provides protection for a stated period of time. In contrast to term, though, endowment insurance matures to its face value, which is payable upon the death of the insured or at the end of the policy period, whichever comes first. Other types of life insurance include credit life, mortgage life, industrial life, special purpose policies, group life, and variable life.

A number of significant features of life insurance policies are: (1) the named beneficiary clause, (2) settlement options, (3) dividend options, (4) nonforfeiture options, (5) the incontestability clause, and (6) disability income and waiver of premium provisions. A variety of other policy features are often included in the life insurance contract. In addition, several favorable characteristics of life insurance external to the policy include the protection of cash values and death proceeds from creditors, its use as a competitive medium for savings, and the lower taxation of life insurance benefits. Mutual companies and stock companies are the two main types of life insurance companies. Comparison of life insurance costs can be made using either the net cost method or the interest adjusted method. Before purchasing life insurance, careful selection of both the agent and the company is important since differences exist in the quality as well as the cost of various types of life insurance.

Key Terms

adverse selection
beneficiary
Best's Reports
cash value
C.L.U. (Chartered Life Underwriter)
continuous premium (whole life)
convertible term
credit life insurance
decreasing term
disability clause
disability income portion
endowment insurance
exclusions
exposure to loss
fortuitous loss
group insurance
guaranteed renewable provision
human life value approach
incontestability clause
industrial life insurance
insurability options
insurance
interest adjusted method
life expectancy
limited payment (whole life)
loss prevention

mortality rate
mortgage life insurance
multiple earnings approach
multiple indemnity
mutual company
needs approach
net cost method
nonforfeiture right
ordinary insurance
participating policies
policy loan
reinstatement
renewable term

risk
risk assumption
risk avoidance
settlement options
single premium (whole life)
stock company
straight term
suicide clause
term life insurance
underwriting
variable life insurance
waiver of premium
whole life insurance

Review Questions

1. Define the terms (a) risk avoidance, (b) risk assumption, (c) loss prevention, (d) fortuitous loss, and (e) underwriting. Explain their interrelationships, if any.

2. Discuss the methods commonly cited for determining a person's life insurance requirements.

3. Name and explain the most common financial needs that must be satisfied after the death of a family breadwinner.

4. What is term insurance? What are the common types of term life insurance policies? Explain.

5. What are the advantages and disadvantages of term life insurance?

6. Explain how whole life insurance offers financial protection to an individual throughout his or her entire life.

7. Describe the variety of whole life policies that exist. What are the advantages and disadvantages of whole life insurance policies?

8. Define and discuss the endowment insurance policy.

9. There are some life insurance contracts which should be avoided. Explain why (a) credit life insurance, (b) mortgage life insurance, and (c) industrial life insurance fall into this category.

10. Explain the meaning of group insurance. How is it different from term insurance. How do employees stand to gain from group insurance? Explain.

11. What is a beneficiary? What is a second beneficiary? Is it essential to designate a beneficiary? Explain.

12. Explain the basic options that are available for payment of life insurance proceeds upon a person's death.

13. Explain the following clauses, which are often found in a life insurance policy: (a) multiple indemnity clause, (b) disability clause, (c) suicide clause, and (d) incontestability clause.

14. "Besides the regular policy features, there are in addition some important financial advantages of life insurance policies." What are these financial advantages? Explain each of them.

15. Distinguish between a stock life insurance company and a mutual life insurance company. As a purchaser of life insurance, which of these types of companies has most appeal to you? Explain.

16. "The purchase of life insurance can be viewed as a two-step process." Discuss the steps.

13-1 The Parkers' Insurance Decision: Whole Life, Endowment, or Term?

Case Problems

Charles and Judith Parker are a married couple in their late thirties. They have three children, ages twelve, ten, and four. Charles, who works as a product analyst for Ciba-Geigy, has money that he wants to use to purchase their first life insurance policy. Joseph Thornton, an insurance agent from Siegfried Insurance Co., has been trying to persuade Charles to buy a $15,000, twenty-five year limited payment whole life policy. However, Charles is contemplating buying an endowment policy. To further complicate matters, Judith feels that they should buy term insurance, since it would be more suitable to the needs of their young family. In order to resolve the issue, Charles has decided to consult Zachary Lawrence, a childhood friend who is now a professor of finance and insurance at the nearby state university.

Questions

1. Explain to Charles the differences between (a) a whole life policy, (b) an endowment policy, and (c) a term policy.

2. What are the advantages of a whole life policy over an endowment policy?

3. What are the basic types of term policies? Does term insurance have any advantages over whole life and endowment insurance?

4. Given the limited information above, which type of insurance would you recommend the Parkers buy? Explain your recommendation.

13-2 Comparing Insurance Coverages and Costs

William Street and George Butler, friends from Columbus, Ohio, want to adequately protect their families in the event of their early death. Each has been married for four years and is thirty years old. William is an aeronautical engineer with Continental Airlines, whereas George is a mechanical engineer with General Motors. Each enjoys good health and owns $50,000 worth of life insurance. William pays $709 in annual premiums, whereas George pays $421.

William's $709 premiums are payable until he reaches age ninety-six. After the first few years, a portion of his premium is viewed as cash value. At any one time, the cash value and death benefit will equal the face value of the policy. If he dies during the life of his policy, his wife and beneficiary, Trina will still receive the $50,000 face value. At sixty-five, the cash surrender value of William's policy will be $26,000. At this stage he will have an option to cash in his policy for the surrender value or to convert it into a $40,000 paid-up life policy.

George's policy is described as level term to age sixty-five. His $50,000 of life insurance will be in force and his premium payments will continue until he reaches the age of sixty-five, at which time he will no longer have any insurance. If, however, he were to die before reaching sixty-five, Sandra, his wife and beneficiary, would receive the $50,000 face value as the death benefit.

Over thirty-five years, William will pay a total of $10,080 more in life insurance premiums than will George. These excess premiums, if invested at 5 percent interest, would have amounted to approximately $26,000 over that time period.

Questions

1. If William and George both die before their policies terminate, is there any benefit for William's higher priced policy as compared to George's policy?

2. What will happen if they both live to age sixty-five? Which one is better off?

3. What advice would you give regarding selection of one of these policies?

Note: Interest on savings accounts is 5½ percent per annum. Government bonds pay approximately 7 percent per annum.

Selected References

"Back in the Dark about Life Insurance Costs." *Money*, July 1976, pp. 69–70.
Belth, Joseph M. *Life Insurance: A Consumer's Handbook.* Bloomington, Ind.: Indiana University Press, 1973.

"Bringing Sexual Equality to Insurance." *Business Week*, 23 May 1977, p. 116.

Degener, Jo. "How to Scale Down Insurance Costs." *Money*, April 1975, pp. 68–72.

Denenberg, Herbert S. *A Shopper's Guide to Life Insurance.* Harrisburg: Pennsylvania Insurance Department, April 1972.

Fogiel, Max. *How to Pay Lots Less for Life Insurance.* New York: Research and Education Association, 1971.

How to Select the Right Life Insurance Company. Des Moines, Iowa: Bankers Life Company, 1971.

"Know What Your Insurance Policies Really Say." *Changing Times*, January 1976, pp. 27–29.

"Life Insurance: How It Can Help You Build a Nest Egg." *Better Homes and Gardens*, March 1975, pp. 2 ff.

"A Life Insurance Policy That Costs Less." *Changing Times*, January 1975, pp. 23–24.

"Life Insurance: What You'd Better Know before You Buy." *Changing Times*, March 1977, pp. 37–40.

Mehr, Robert I. *Life Insurance: Theory and Practice.* Dallas: Business Publications, 1977.

Oehlbeck, J. Tracy. *Consumer's Guide to Life Insurance.* Elmhurst, N.Y.: Pyramid Press, 1975.

"Stretching Your Insurance Dollar." *Business Week*, 17 November 1975, pp. 125–132.

Tarrant, Marguerite. "Life Insurance for the Uninsurable." *Money*, March 1976, pp. 49–50.

"Variable Life Insurance—A New Kind of Policy." *Changing Times*, September 1976, pp. 39–40.

"What's Happening to Life-Insurance Dividends?" *Consumer Reports*, November 1976, pp. 659–662.

"What Your Life Insurance Can Do for You." *Consumer Research*, September 1975, pp. 11–14 ff.

"Who Will Collect on Your Life Insurance?" *Changing Times*, December 1975, pp. 37–39.

14
Health Care Plans and Insurance

A Preview of Chapter 14

In order to clarify the key aspects of health care plans and insurance, this chapter examines the following:

1. The need for adequate health insurance coverage.

2. The importance of health insurance and the impact of increasing health care costs on the health insurance needs of the individual.

3. The various types of health insurance, including disability income, hospital, surgical, medical expense, major medical, dental, and other special coverages.

4. The basic health care coverages available from government sources—in particular, federal social security programs and state worker's compensation plans.

5. The costs, benefits, and operating procedures of group insurance, Blue Cross/Blue Shield plans, individual health coverages, health maintenance organizations, and proposed national health insurance plans.

6. Ways of evaluating present coverages, of understanding policy provisions and features, of determining coverage requirements, and of selecting a health insurer.

Adequate life insurance is necessary to protect your family against losses that may result from death, but it is not enough. You are exposed to numerous other risks, including possible accidents or illness. Such misfortunes can burden you with sizable medical costs and/or disabilities.

504

They can also interfere with your ability to work, either temporarily or permanently. It is therefore imperative that you gain an understanding of how to assess your health care needs and select the type and source of health care coverage best suited to fulfilling them.

Since the middle 1960s, the health care delivery system in America has come under increased scrutiny. "Is the quality of our health care system adequate?" "Are sufficient resources available to meet the need?" "Should private organizations or government be the primary provider of health care services?" Although these are important questions with which society must deal, your time will be better spent learning about the key aspects of health care plans and insurance as they exist today. An understanding of the importance as well as the availability of health insurance is necessary in order to develop a health insurance plan that will provide you and your family with adequate protection against the sometimes devastating financial consequences of accidents and illness. Without adequate health care coverage you may find that the financial drain of medical expenses or lost income due to health problems, or both, will make it nearly impossible for you to achieve your stated financial goals. You therefore need to know the answers to questions such as: "Why worry about health insurance?" "How much health insurance is necessary?" "What types of health insurance coverages are available?" "What sources of health insurance exist?" "How should health insurance plans be prepared?"

The Need for Health Insurance

Health insurance pays for the expenses that are incurred when a person suffers an accident or illness. These costs include not only out-of-pocket items such as hospital and physician charges but also income which is lost due to disablement and other expenses which might arise. The need for insurance to provide for these expenses is dramatized by assessing the costs that could arise from a typical accident at home. For example, assume a man age thirty-five fell from a ladder while painting his house. An ambulance was summoned, and the insured man was taken to the hospital. There he was admitted, examined, x-rayed, and assigned to a semiprivate room. The results of the examination showed a broken leg and a sprained back. Treatment included setting the fracture, four days of traction for the back sprain, and four weeks of recuperation before returning to work. Total expenses and lost income for this disablement amount to $2,460, as shown in Table 14-1. Certainly charges of this magnitude could have a devastating effect on the family budget. Today most families recognize the large potential losses that can result from accident or illness and obtain health insurance to guard against them.

Unfortunately, the costs of treating the sick and injured have risen greatly during the last thirty years and are expected to go up just as much in the future. This fact further reinforces the need for an adequate health insurance program.

Table 14-1 **Disablement Costs of a Hypothetical Accident**

Ambulance	$ 35
Five Days of Hospitalization	750
X-Rays	85
Emergency Room Service	45
Physician	350
Traction Equipment Rental	85
Prescription Drugs	35
Anesthetist	75
Lost Wages (4 Weeks)	1,000
Total	$2,460

Increasing Health Care Costs

The costs of health care have been increasing at a rate which often substantially exceeds the rise in the overall consumer price index (CPI). In fact, as can be seen from Table 14-2, the costs of medical expenses have risen more than any other component of the CPI, with the exception of food. Of the various costs that comprise the medical care portion of the CPI, hospital charges lead the list in terms of price advances. Table 14-3 shows that hospital charges have more than doubled since 1967. Hospital room charges of $100 to $200 per day are not uncommon. Physicians' fees, nurses' salaries, and other products and services essential to health care also have increased in cost faster than the increases in price reflected by the overall consumer price index. Although the rate of increase in these fees and prices does not match the increase experienced in hospital rates, it is nonetheless significant. The cost of health care, though, is not uniform throughout the country. Wide variations do exist. For example, the average cost per hospital stay ranges from a low of $643 for 7.7 days in Wyoming to $1,875 for an average stay of 9.9 days in New York State. Table 14-4 depicts average hospital costs and lengths of hospital stays by state. The wide variation in costs should be obvious from examination of this table.

Several major factors account for the inflation that has occurred in the health care field. The chief cause most probably stems from the increased demand for health care services stimulated by the government's Medicaid and Medicare programs, as well as the rapid growth in the broad base of private health plans. More than ninety-five out of every hundred noninstitutionalized Americans are now eligible for at least some cost

Table 14-2 **Consumer Price Index (1967 = 100.0)**

Year	All Items	Food	Apparel	Housing	Transportation	Medical Care	Personal Care	Reading and Recreation	Other Goods and Services
1935	41.1	36.5	40.8	49.3	42.6	36.1	36.9	41.8	44.6
1940	42.0	35.2	42.8	52.4	42.7	36.8	40.2	46.1	48.3
1945	53.9	50.7	61.5	59.1	47.8	42.1	55.1	62.4	56.9
1950	72.1	74.5	79.0	72.8	68.2	53.7	68.3	74.4	60.9
1955	80.2	81.6	84.1	82.3	77.4	64.8	77.9	76.7	79.8
1960	88.7	88.0	89.6	90.2	89.6	79.1	90.1	87.3	87.8
1965	94.5	94.4	93.7	94.9	95.9	89.5	95.2	95.9	94.2
1966	97.2	99.1	96.1	97.2	97.2	93.4	97.1	97.5	97.2
1967	100.0	100.0	100.0	100.0	100.0	100.0	100.0	100.0	100.0
1968	104.2	103.6	105.4	104.2	103.2	106.1	104.2	104.7	104.6
1969	109.8	108.9	111.5	110.8	107.2	113.4	109.3	108.7	109.1
1970	116.3	114.9	116.1	118.9	112.7	120.6	113.2	113.4	116.0
1971	121.3	118.4	119.8	124.3	118.6	128.4	116.8	119.3	120.9
1972	125.3	123.5	122.3	129.2	119.9	132.5	119.8	122.8	125.5
1973	133.1	141.4	126.8	135.0	123.8	137.7	125.2	125.9	129.0
1974	147.7	161.7	136.2	150.6	137.7	150.5	137.3	133.8	137.2
1975	161.2	175.4	142.3	166.8	150.6	168.6	150.7	144.4	147.4

Source: Reprinted with permission from *Sourcebook of Health Insurance Data, 1976–1977* (New York: Health Insurance Institute, 1977).

Table 14-3 **Consumer Price Indices for Medical Care Items (1967 = 100.0)**

Year	All Medical Care Items	Physicians' Fees	Dentists' Fees	Optometric Examination and Eyeglasses	Semiprivate Hospital Room Rates	Prescriptions and Drugs
1947	48.1	51.4	56.9	67.7	23.1	81.8
1950	53.7	55.2	63.9	73.5	30.3	88.5
1955	64.8	65.4	73.0	77.0	42.3	94.7
1960	79.1	77.0	82.1	85.1	57.3	104.5
1965	89.5	88.3	92.2	92.8	75.9	100.2
1966	93.4	93.4	95.2	95.3	83.5	100.5
1967	100.0	100.0	100.0	100.0	100.0	100.0
1968	106.1	105.6	105.5	103.2	113.6	100.2
1969	113.4	112.9	112.9	107.6	128.8	101.3
1970	120.6	121.4	119.4	113.5	145.4	103.6
1971	128.4	129.8	127.0	120.3	163.1	105.4
1972	132.5	133.8	132.3	124.9	173.9	105.6
1973	137.7	138.2	136.4	129.5	182.1	105.9
1974	150.5	150.9	146.8	138.6	201.5	109.6
1975	168.6	169.4	161.9	149.6	236.1	118.8

Source: Reprinted with permission from *Sourcebook of Health Insurance Data, 1976–1977* (New York: Health Insurance Institute, 1977).

Table 14-4 **Community Hospital Statistics, 1975**

State	Average Cost to Hospital per Patient Day	Average Length of Hospital Stay (Days)	Average Cost to Hospital per Patient Stay
Alabama	$113.90	7.3	$ 831.50
Alaska	225.50	5.0	1,127.50
Arizona	175.20	7.4	1,296.50
Arkansas	102.20	6.5	664.30
California	217.40	6.6	1,434.80
Colorado	148.90	6.6	982.70
Connecticut	188.60	7.5	1,414.50
Delaware	162.70	8.3	1,350.40
D.C.	207.60	7.9	1,640.00
Florida	151.10	7.4	1,118.10
Georgia	138.90	6.4	889.00
Hawaii	152.10	6.9	1,049.50
Idaho	121.50	6.3	765.50
Illinois	160.10	8.0	1,280.80
Indiana	127.10	7.9	1,004.10
Iowa	109.80	7.8	856.40
Kansas	113.00	7.8	881.40
Kentucky	109.70	7.1	778.90
Louisiana	136.80	6.5	889.20
Maine	137.50	7.4	1,017.50
Maryland	181.00	8.3	1,502.30
Massachusetts	205.30	8.5	1,745.05
Michigan	166.10	8.2	1,362.00
Minnesota	121.90	8.8	1,072.70
Mississippi	102.20	6.9	705.20
Missouri	129.10	8.2	1,058.60
Montana	111.10	6.4	711.00
Nebraska	116.70	8.1	945.30
Nevada	182.50	6.5	1,186.30
New Hampshire	129.50	7.1	919.50
New Jersey	142.40	8.7	1,238.90
New Mexico	142.20	5.9	839.00
New York	189.40	9.9	1,875.10
North Carolina	114.80	7.6	872.50
North Dakota	98.50	8.3	817.60
Ohio	139.00	8.2	1,139.80
Oklahoma	128.60	6.7	861.60
Oregon	158.80	6.3	1,000.40
Pennsylvania	142.80	8.5	1,213.80
Rhode Island	188.20	8.0	1,505.60
South Carolina	113.80	7.3	830.70
South Dakota	98.50	7.0	689.50
Tennessee	113.80	7.5	853.50

Table 14-4 (continued)

State	Average Cost to Hospital per Patient Day	Average Length of Hospital Stay (Days)	Average Cost to Hospital per Patient Stay
Texas	$128.80	6.8	$ 875.80
Utah	148.20	5.6	829.90
Vermont	131.10	7.8	1,022.60
Virginia	122.40	8.0	979.20
Washington	171.60	5.6	961.00
West Virginia	109.50	7.6	832.20
Wisconsin	127.70	8.2	1,047.10
Wyoming	116.90	5.5	643.00
United States	151.20	7.7	1,164.20

Source: Reprinted with permission from Sourcebook of Health Insurance Data, 1976–1977 (New York: Health Insurance Institute, 1977).

reimbursement for losses resulting from accident or sickness. In addition, large acquisitions of expensive new health care equipment and facilities by hospitals and clinics have pushed costs upward. A poor distribution of demand for and the supply of health care facilities and services sometimes causes the inefficient allocation of health care resources. This poor distribution may also contribute to today's high costs of health care. Unfortunately, no immediate relief is foreseen. In light of these spiraling costs, the need for health financing plans is greater now than it has ever been and is expected to grow in the future. Few families can afford to assume the financial obligations that would arise if any member of the family required substantial medical attention.

Family Considerations

Of course, the need for health insurance is not consistent among all families. Certainly, the number of persons in the family and the current status of their health will affect the coverages that are required. Also, the income level of the family, the family members' personal habits, medical and family history, the total amount of present and future financial obligations, and whether or not the family depends on only one spouse for support will all influence its need for health insurance. The various types of health care coverages available as well as their application to solving health care financing problems are discussed in the following part of the chapter.

Types of Health Insurance Coverage

Around 1850, when health insurance policies were first sold, they were most commonly accident policies that paid a small amount if the insured were injured in a specific type of accident. As more health insurers began writing health coverages, the number of accident perils insured against increased. By the turn of the twentieth century, accident policies were being written against almost any conceivable risk exposure. At about this same time, health insurers were issuing "sickness insurance policies," which offered protection for a limited amount of income loss if the insured contracted any of several diseases named in the policy. Not until the 1930s was our modern concept of health care insurance born, when Blue Cross began selling policies that reimbursed individuals for the costs of hospital and surgical care. From the 1930s to the present, great strides have been made in health care plans in terms of coverages offered, amounts of reimbursement provided, and number of persons protected. However, no standardized policy has yet been adopted, and needed coverage is often obtained only through a collection of types of health insurance policies. Unfortunately, this approach may result in double coverage in certain areas, while other areas of need lack any coverage at all. Data depicting the number of persons with health insurance coverage and the types of coverage they have are shown in Table 14-5. Examination of this data reveals the fact that the biggest shortcoming in the health insurance programs of most families is the lack of disability income, particularly long-term disability income.

Table 14-5 **Number of Persons with Health Insurance Protection by Type of Coverage**
(in Thousands)

End of Year	Hospital Expense	Surgical Expense	Regular Medical Expense	Major Medical Expense	Disability Income		Dental Expense
					Short-term	Long-term	
1970	158,847	151,440	138,658	77,061	58,089	10,966	12,979
1971	161,849	153,093	139,399	80,252	59,280	12,284	16,347
1972	164,098	154,687	140,873	83,668	61,548	14,538	19,089
1973	168,455	162,644	151,680	87,839	64,168	17,011	22,476
1974:							
Under 65	161,604	156,846	149,291	89,278	65,282	17,799	N.A.[a]
65 and Over	11,536	9,588	8,879	1,766	—	—	N.A.
Total	173,140	166,434	158,170	91,044	65,282	17,799	33,297
1975:							
Under 65	165,357	158,518	152,157	90,125	62,971	18,396	N.A.
65 and Over	12,623	10,377	9,697	2,041	—	—	N.A.
Total	177,980	168,895	161,854	92,166	62,971	18,396	35,252

[a]Figures not available.

Source: Adapted with permission from *Sourcebook of Health Insurance Data, 1976–1977* (New York: Health Insurance Institute, 1977).

Even though many of today's health insurance policies provide much broader coverages than policies offered in the predepression era, the wide variety and quality of policies available today makes it imperative that one be cautious when shopping for health insurance. The individual can best guard against purchasing the wrong kinds of coverage by understanding the basic differences and uses of the various types of policies. Thus the following types of health insurance coverages are discussed below: (1) disability income, (2) hospital, (3) surgical expense, (4) regular medical expense, (5) major medical, (6) comprehensive major medical, (7) dental, and (8) other special coverages.

The Dollars and Cents of Getting Sick

Spiraling health-care costs are taking more and more billions of dollars out of the pockets of Americans every year.

Hospitals raised their charges 11.8 per cent on the average in the year ended last November [1976], and doctors boosted their fees 10.7 per cent, far outstripping a 4.5 per cent increase in the other costs of living.

Result is that hospital care in the U.S. now costs the average patient from $154 to $175 a day, compared with $48 in 1966 and less than $16 in 1950. That is a total increase of as much as 1,000 per cent in a generation—seven times the rate of inflation in the rest of the nation's economy.

Altogether, health care takes an annual bite that averages $650 per person, or $2,600 for a family of four. That is almost 11 per cent of the typical American's income.

Three fourths of the annual total is charged through taxes, insurance premiums and over-all inflation paid for by all wage earners.

With the rapid growth of Blue Cross, medicare and medicaid, for example, the public share of health-care costs now stands at 42 per cent. In the last four years, Government outlays for health have more than doubled to 39.5 billion dollars, almost one tenth of the federal budget.

Because such costs are mostly hidden, surveys show that Americans estimate their family medical expenses at an average of only $1,000 a year—less than half of the true figure.

Sharpest impact, however, is on the 17 per cent of Americans who have clearly inadequate protection under Government aid or insurance. Half of these people have no coverage at all, according to the Congressional Budget Office.

With the average hospital stay costing well over $1,000, an estimated 2.5 million persons under age 65 will have "catastrophic" expenses of more than $5,000 in the 12 months beginning October 1 [1977], these analysts figure. Even after insurance reimbursements, nearly 7 million families—1 out of every 11—will pay more than 15 per cent of their income to cover the soaring cost of getting sick.

Source: Reprinted from *U.S. News & World Report,* 28 March 1977, p. 37. Copyright 1977 U.S. News & World Report, Inc.

Disability Income Insurance

Disability income insurance is designed to provide families with weekly or monthly payments to replace income when an insured person is unable to work as a result of a covered illness, injury, or disease. Some companies also offer disability income protection for the unemployed spouse. It helps pay for the services that individual would normally provide. Disability income policies frequently include *waiting period* provisions which require that the insured wait a specified length of time after the inception of the disability before payment begins. A waiting period provision is similar to the deductibles that are found in property insurance contracts. The purpose of both is to omit coverage for the frequent small loss, which is very expensive to administer. A family can save a substantial amount in premiums by purchasing a contract that has a relatively long waiting period.

The maximum period for which disability payments are made normally ranges from thirteen weeks to age sixty-five. In some cases, a disability policy will state that payments will continue for a specified period if the disability occurred because of sickness (for example, five years) and another period if the disability resulted from accident (for example, age sixty-five). With most companies, the insured can trade off, say, an increase in the waiting period from seven days to ninety days for an increase in the duration of benefits from five years to age sixty-five. In fact, as can be seen in Table 14-6, the premium for a policy with a one year term and a seven day waiting period for the company shown is about the same as the premium charged for benefits payable to age sixty-five with a thirty day waiting period. Since the purpose of all insurance is to protect against a catastrophic loss rather than smaller losses that could be better handled through budgeting or savings, accepting this type of trade-off usually makes sense. Because the prolonged disability of the breadwinner of a family can have a severe adverse impact on its finances (often more than in the case of death), disability income insurance should be an integral part of the insurance program of most families.

Table 14-6 **Disability Income Insurance Premiums**
(Male Age 35, Class #1: Desk-Type Job)

Waiting Period	Term of Disability Benefits			
	1 Year	3 Years	5 Years	Age 65
7 Days	30.88	34.40	37.30	53.80
14 Days	24.40	29.10	32.00	47.90
30 Days	14.16	17.60	19.90	31.80
60 Days	9.70	12.75	15.00	26.20
90 Days	—	10.20	12.50	23.50
1 Year	—	—	10.90	19.50

Note: Premiums shown are annual charges per $100 per month of coverage.

Estimating Need The specific amount of disability income insurance to be purchased can be determined through the needs approach, which was developed in the discussion of life insurance in Chapter 13. The reader will recall that the first step involved calculating the monthly financial needs of the family. Because a prolonged disability often brings about additional expenses in the budget (i.e., uninsured health care costs), it is believed that even with some belt-tightening most families need at least 80 percent of their predisability take-home pay. With this amount, large reductions in savings or other assets in order to meet bill payments during the disability can be avoided. After the desired amount of income is computed, any existing income resources are totaled. Sources might include social security disability income payments, wage continuation payments, and income from other family members. The difference between the resources necessary and those available is the amount of disability income insurance required. Although most people need a competent life and health insurance agent to help make this determination, the example in the following section illustrates the appropriate procedures for estimating disability income insurance needs.

Disability Insurance Needs Example Assume that William Sweeney earns $1,400 per month and that after taxes and other deductions his monthly take-home pay is $1,050. William and his wife, Gertrude, believe that by trimming expenses they could manage to live on $900 cash per month in the event William suffered a long-term permanent disability. Resources available include social security payments of $400 per month and part-time employment for Gertrude, which could provide another $250 a month. Thus, with these income resources the Sweeneys would need to purchase a long-term disability income policy that would pay monthly benefits of $250 ($900 needed − $400 social security − $250 Gertrude's part-time job).

Tax Considerations In the past, there was a sick-pay exclusion that allowed a certain amount of *sick-pay* (that is, pay received for any illness), up to $100 per week, to be excluded from taxable income. The Tax Reform Act of 1976 replaced this exclusion with a $100 per week *disability pay* (that is, pay received only for a disability, not for just any illness) exemption. As a result of this change in the law, eligibility for tax relief in this situation, although still available, is now somewhat more restrictive. Because of the possible adjustment that would have to be made in programming for private disability insurance, you should determine how any benefits will be taxed at the time of purchase. Note that all social security benefits are tax-free. Also, remember that breadwinners whose annual earnings are relatively high—$25,000 and above—will need proportionately more disability income insurance because, as the level of income goes up, the percentage replaced by social security becomes smaller.

Hospital Insurance

Hospital insurance policies offer reimbursement plans covering the costs of hospital room and board and other expenses incidental to hospitalization. More persons in the United States are covered by some type of hospitalization insurance than any other kind of health insurance. Basically, hospital insurance pays for a portion of: (1) the per day hospital charges, which typically include floor nursing and other routine services, and (2) ancillary expenses, such as use of the operating room, laboratory tests, x-ray examinations, and medicine taken by the patient while hospitalized. Although a few hospital insurance policies will pay for an in-hospital private duty nurse, most do not. In some cases, the hospital plan will simply pay a flat daily amount for each day the insured remains in the hospital, regardless of the actual amount of charges levied. Numerous hospital plans now also offer reimbursement for some outpatient and out-of-hospital services, among which might be in-home rehabilitation or ambulatory center care, diagnostic and preventive treatment, and preadmission testing.

Surgical Expense Insurance

Surgical expense insurance provides coverage for the cost of surgery. Typically, a schedule of benefits will be available that prescribes the amount the insurer is obligated to pay for listed surgical procedures (for instance, $200 for an appendectomy, $100 for a tonsillectomy, or $400 for removal of a kidney). Sample surgical benefit payment schedules are shown in Table 14-7. The four schedules ($600, $1,000, $1,200, and $1,400) differ on the basis of the premiums charged for the policy. By paying a little more, the insured can receive benefits under a schedule providing higher maximum expense amounts. Usually surgical expense coverage is quite extensive and will pay for almost any type of surgery that is required to maintain the health of the insured. In the event a necessary surgical procedure is not named in the policy, the company will pay the amount listed for a comparable operation. The amounts shown in the schedule usually approximate the average fees charged in a specific geographic area. The cost of anesthetics and their administration is provided for in some surgical expense policies. However, more frequently these are paid under the additional benefit provision of a hospital insurance policy. Surgical expense policies may also allow payment for the treatment of tumors and other afflictions using x-rays or radium. Surgical expense coverage is typically sold in conjunction with a hospital insurance policy either as an integral part of that policy or as a rider. In

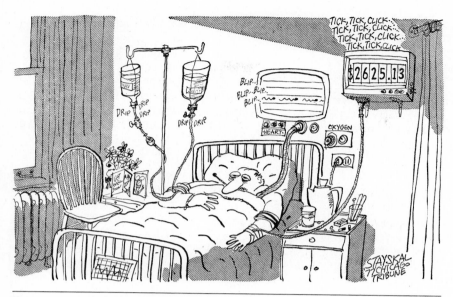

Rising Hospital Costs Make Hospital Insurance a Necessity
Source: Reprinted courtesy of the *Chicago Tribune.*

some cases, a surgical schedule is also available as a rider to certain accident policies.

Regular Medical Expense Insurance

Regular medical expense insurance can provide coverage for the cost of such services as physician fees for nonsurgical care in a hospital, at home, in a clinic, or in the doctor's office. Also covered are x-rays and laboratory tests performed outside of a hospital. These plans usually provide maximum amounts payable for services as listed in a schedule of allowances. Often the first few visits with the physician for any single cause will be excluded. This exclusion serves the same purpose as the deductible feature found in other types of insurance.

Major Medical Insurance

Major medical plans are those that provide benefits for nearly all types of medical expenses resulting from either accidents or sickness. As the name implies, the amounts that can be collected under this coverage are relatively large. Limits of $10,000 and $25,000 or higher are common, with some policies providing more than $250,000 of protection. The trend in recent years has been toward the higher benefit levels. For example,

Table 14-7 **Examples of Surgical Payments, Hospital-Surgical Policy**

Procedure	Maximum Payment			
	$600 Schedule	$1,000 Schedule	$1,200 Schedule	$1,400 Schedule
Appendectomy	$120.00	$ 200.00	$ 240.00	$ 280.00
Benign skin tumor not over ¼ inch in diameter, excision	12.00	20.00	24.00	28.00
Brain tumor, suboccipital craniectomy	450.00	750.00	900.00	1,050.00
Breast tumor, removal (one breast involved)	45.00	75.00	90.00	105.00
Cysts, incision and drainage of sebaceous cyst, not as hospital inpatient	6.00	10.00	12.00	14.00
Cystoscopy with ureteral catheterization, while hospital inpatient	45.00	75.00	90.00	105.00
Dilation and curettage of uterus (non-obstetrical)	45.00	75.00	90.00	105.00
Gall bladder, removal	180.00	300.00	360.00	420.00
Heart, replacement of aortic valve (open)	600.00	1,000.00	1,200.00	1,400.00
Hernia, repair of inguinal, femoral or epigastric	105.00	175.00	210.00	245.00
Hip or knee dislocation, closed reduction	60.00	100.00	120.00	140.00
Hysterectomy				
Subtotal or supracervical	165.00	275.00	330.00	385.00
Total (uterus and cervix)	180.00	300.00	360.00	420.00
Kidney, removal	240.00	400.00	480.00	560.00
Knee joint, excision of cartilage	150.00	250.00	300.00	350.00
Lung, removal	300.00	500.00	600.00	700.00
Proctosigmoidoscopy, initial, without biopsy (rectal examination by proctoscope)	9.00	15.00	18.00	21.00
Spinal fusion, with removal of disc	360.00	600.00	720.00	840.00
Suturing wound(s), not as a hospital inpatient, up to total of 2½ inches	6.00	10.00	12.00	14.00
Tonsils, or tonsils and adenoids, removal				
Under age 18	45.00	75.00	90.00	105.00
18 or over	60.00	100.00	120.00	140.00
Upper arm shaft, closed reduction of simple fracture	75.00	125.00	150.00	175.00
Varicose veins—injecting vein(s) of legs, not as hospital inpatient	3.00	5.00	6.00	7.00

Note: A more complete list of surgical operations and the related maximum payments is usually contained within the policy itself.
Source: Courtesy of Prudential Insurance Company of America, Prudential Plaza, Newark, N.J., 1977.

more than 25 percent of the persons presently covered under group major medical have benefits of $250,000 or more available. In contrast, in 1966 only 14 percent of these persons had policies with limits greater than $20,000. Major medical coverage was first offered in the early 1950s to supplement the basic coverages of hospital, surgical, and regular medical expenses discussed above. This basic concept still applies today since the other three medical and hospital expense coverages are available to meet the smaller health care costs while major medical is used to finance medical costs of a more catastrophic nature. More than three out of every four Americans are covered under some type of major medical health plan. The popularity of this insurance has grown more since its inception than that of any other kind of health insurance in history. Major medical plans are typically written with provisions for deductibles, participation or coinsurance, and internal limits.

Deductibles Because major medical plans are designed to supplement the basic hospital and medical expense policies, they frequently have a relatively large deductible of $500 or $1,000. In most plans, the deductible is on a per accident or per illness basis. This means that if an insured had a policy with a $1,000 deductible and suffered three separate accidents in the course of a year, each requiring $1,000 of medical expenses, the insured would not be eligible to collect any benefits from the major medical plan.

Participation or Coinsurance Another feature of major medical insurance is that most policies contain some type of participation, or coinsurance, clause. This provision stipulates that the company will pay some portion—say 80 or 90 percent—of the amount of the covered loss in excess of the deductible rather than the entire amount. The purpose of requiring insureds to participate as "coinsurers" is to reduce the possibility they will pretend to be ill and to discourage them from incurring unnecessary medical expenses.

Internal Limits Most major medical plans in recent years also have been written with internal limits. These internal limits place constraints on the amounts that will be paid for certain specified expenses, even if the overall policy limits are not exceeded by the claim. Charges which are commonly subject to internal limits are hospital room and board, surgical fees, and nursing services. The example in the following section illustrates how deductibles, coinsurance, and internal limits constrain the amount a company is obligated to pay under a major medical plan.

Major Medical Policy: An Example Assume that an insured person has coverage under major medical insurance that specifies a $1,000 deductible, an 80 percent coinsurance clause, internal limits of $75 per day on hospital room and board, and $500 as a maximum surgical fee. Assume further that the insured was hospitalized for fourteen days at $100 per day and required an operation which cost $600. Other covered medical expenses that were incurred with this illness totaled $1,200. Therefore, the total medical expenses incurred by the insured amount to $3,200, which includes $1,400 for hospital room and board plus $600 for the surgeon plus $1,200 for the other expenses. However, because of the coinsurance clause in the policy, the maximum the company has to pay is 80 percent of the covered loss in excess of the deductible. Before considering internal limits, the company would pay $1,760 (.80 × [$3,200 − $1,000]). The internal limit, though, further restricts the payment, since 80 percent of the $100 per diem hospital charge is $80 and the most the company has to pay is $75 per diem. (The internal limit on the surgery is not binding, since, after considering coinsurance, the insurer will have to pay $480 [.80 × $600], which is below the $500 internal limit.) Therefore, the insured becomes liable for another $70 ($5 per day × 14 days); the company's obligation is reduced to $1,690, while the insured must pay a total of $1,510.

Comprehensive Major Medical Insurance

A *comprehensive major medical insurance* plan combines the basic hospital, surgical, and medical expense coverages with major medical protection to form a single policy. In contrast to an ordinary major medical plan, the deductible under a comprehensive major medical plan is relatively small, often $100 or less. Some of these plans also have a more favorable participation feature than major medical policies since they may require no coinsurance on basic hospital and surgical expense claims. Most frequently, comprehensive major medical insurance is written under a group contract. However, some efforts have been made to make this type of coverage available on an individual basis.

Dental Insurance

Dental expense insurance covers necessary dental health care as well as dental injuries sustained through accidents. The coverage usually provides for oral examinations including x-rays, cleanings, fillings, extractions, inlays, bridgework, dentures, oral surgery, root canal therapy, and orthodontics. Of course, dental policies vary with respect to the number of these items included within the coverage. Some dental plans contain deductible and coinsurance provisions, and others have "first dollar protection"—they pay for all claims. Most present dental coverage is written through group insurance plans, although a number of companies do offer individual and family policies. However, since many types of dental insurance function more as budgeting techniques than as true insurance, the premiums are often relatively large in light of the dollar amount of coverage obtained.

Other Special Insurance Coverages

An examination of every type of health and accident insurance plan available would fill a book in itself. For the most part, however, policies other than the types discussed above fall into the classification of gimmicks, frills, or frauds. For example, numerous kinds of accident policies are available to cover persons as airline passengers on a given flight or for a specified period of time. They are just a form of gambling—not good insurance programming. Similarly, many hospital policies offered directly to the public through newspaper advertisements do not have a place in the insurance programs of most families. Now becoming popular is a version of the *dread disease health policies* that were commonplace earlier in this century. Today's renditions limit health care coverage to a specific type of disease or illness. Cancer policies appear to be the most common, with some organ transplant policies also being offered. The basic problem with buying policies that cover only a certain type of accident or loss is that major gaps in coverage will occur. However, the financial loss can be just as great regardless of whether the insured falls down a flight of stairs or contracts cancer, lung disease, or heart disease. Most limited peril policies should be used only to supplement a comprehensive insurance program if the coverage is not overlapping.

Five primary sources of financial aid for losses arising from accident or illness are available on a large scale. These are: (1) social security, (2) worker's compensation insurance, (3) group insurance, (4) Blue Cross/Blue Shield, and (5) individual health coverages. In certain parts of the country the need for health insurance coverage can be somewhat reduced by joining a health maintenance organization. Although not presently enacted, national health insurance legislation also is expected to provide protection within the near future.

Sources of Health Care Coverage

Social Security

Most people think of social security as a retirement system. It does, however, provide a considerable amount of coverage for losses arising from disability. In fact, the official name for what is commonly referred to as social security is Old-Age, Survivor's, Disability, and Health Insurance Program (OASDHI). Health benefits are provided under two separate programs: (1) disability income and (2) Medicare. Although the *Medicaid* program also provides medical benefits under social security, it is not discussed here since it is a public assistance program designed to provide benefit for those persons who are unable to pay for health care.

Disability Income The disability income benefits under social security can be quite important to families during child-rearing years as well as thereafter. Nearly all families in the United States are covered by social security. The only major exceptions are certain groups of state and local employees and most employees of the federal government, who have enrolled in a special system. In order to be eligible for disability income benefits, a covered employee needs twenty quarters (three-month periods) of coverage out of the forty quarters immediately preceding the date of disability and must have suffered a total disability that has been in effect for at least five months and is expected to prevent employment for a minimum of twelve months. After becoming eligible for disability benefits, the worker and his or her family can receive benefits for the duration of the disability, even if it lasts for life. The amount of the monthly family benefit paid on behalf of the disabled worker, say under age thirty-five, most often would range between 40 and 80 percent of his or her predisability monthly earnings. Table 14-8 provides a comparison of cash benefit payments for disabled workers given their status and predisability average yearly earnings.

Eligibility requirements for workers who become disabled before age thirty-one are more liberal. Benefits may be paid on behalf of young workers if they have coverage in one-half of the quarters elapsing in the

A Closemouthed Look at Bad Dentistry

The dental profession is getting tight-lipped about fees. The American Dental Association, which periodically surveys its members' fees, stopped publishing these findings in 1971, lest the public choose dentists by price alone.

Less constrained than their national organization, dentists in and around six U.S. cities recently provided *Money* with their prices for a dozen common dental procedures. Differences in the fees, which are averaged at the right, turned out to be related less to regions than to rents. City dentists tend to charge a bit more than those practicing in the suburbs and quite a bit more than those in rural towns.

The averages do conceal some huge spreads that aren't explained by high rents alone. A rural dentist in southern Alabama quoted $60 to $75 for root canal therapy—the removal of dead or infected nerve and blood cells from the canals and root chambers of a tooth. Dentists in high-rent sections of Los Angeles wanted $125 to $200 for the same work. Prices for a three-unit fixed bridge to replace one extracted tooth ranged from $300 in Scranton, Pa., to $1,000, again in Los Angeles. But price-wise patients in Los Angeles can find dentists charging under $500 for such a bridge.

Insurance companies that pay for dental work keep tabs on what fees are "usual, customary and reasonable," but this information is often kept secret lest it stimulate dentists at the low end of the range to raise their fees. The California insurance plans whose joint fee schedule is shown here demanded anonymity. The fees are lower than average partly because dentists accepting insurance payments don't have to pay collection agencies or write off unpaid bills.

Table 14-8 **Social Security Payments on Behalf of a Disabled Worker**
(Examples of Monthly Cash Disability Benefits, Effective June 1976)

Benefits Can Be Paid to a:	$923 or Less	Average Yearly Earnings after 1950[a]							
		$3,000	$5,000	$7,000	$8,000	$9,000	$10,000	$12,000	$13,000
Disabled Worker	$107.90	$223.20	$304.50	$385.60	$427.80	$452.20	$474.00	$516.10	$535.60
Disabled Worker and Wife at 62	148.40	306.90	418.80	530.20	588.30	621.80	651.80	709.70	736.50
Disabled Widow at 50	56.80	111.70	152.40	192.90	214.00	226.20	237.10	258.20	267.90
Disabled Worker, Wife under 65, and One Child (Maximum Family Payment)	161.90	341.20	561.90	687.20	748.70	791.60	829.50	903.10	937.20

[a]The maximum earnings creditable for social security are $3,600 for 1951–54; $4,200 for 1955–58; $4,800 for 1959–65; $6,600 for 1966–67; $7,800 for 1968–71; $9,000 for 1972; $10,800 for 1973; $13,200 for 1974; $14,100 for 1975; and $15,300 for 1976. The maximum family benefit for a young disabled worker and his or her family in 1976 is $959.40 a month, based on average earnings of $13,650.

Source: U.S. Department of Health, Education, and Welfare, Social Security Administration, *If You Become Disabled,* HEW publication no. (SSA) 76-10029, June 1976, pp. 14–15.

Extracting Some Dentists' Prices

Procedure	Average Fees Quoted by Dentists Surveyed in			Fees Paid by Several California Insurance Plans
	Cities	Suburbs	Small Towns	
Routine Cleaning	$ 16	$ 14	$ 11	$ 10
Examination with X-Ray Series	27	24	21	23
Silver Filling	13	10	11	9
White Filling	15	14	13	10
Extraction of One Tooth	17	15	13	9
Therapy on One Root Canal	125	126	104	75
Porcelain Jacket Crown	166	157	140	100
Full Gold Crown	150	164	126	90
One-Tooth Fixed Bridge	510	485	408	380
Complete Upper Denture	372	285	226	160
Fluoride Treatment	11	9	8	6
Periodontal Scaling[a]	173	104	103	48

[a]Cleaning the root area to relieve inflamed gums.

Source: "A Closemouthed Look at Bad Dentistry," by Barbara Quint, excerpted from the November 1974 issue of MONEY Magazine by special permission; © 1974, Time Inc. Illustration: Rudolph de Harak.

Our Multibillion-Dollar Medicaid Scandal

On New York City's Lower East Side, an undercover investigator for the U.S. Senate walked into a storefront medical center and complained of a head cold. Within a few minutes, he was given a general physical, an electrocardiogram, a tuberculosis test and medication—all charged to Medicaid.

• In Chicago, a handful of optometrists and optical stores enriched themselves by submitting thousands of fraudulent Medicaid claims. During one seven-month stretch, members of a single welfare family—none of whom had ever seen an eye doctor—turned up 55 times on phony claims. Taxpayers also paid for the "treatment" of patients whose addresses turned out to be vacant lots.

• On Long Island, N.Y., a nursing-home operator charged off to Medicaid a mink coat listed as "depreciation on movable equipment" and financed a trip to Hawaii as "dues and subscriptions."

Horror stories about Uncle Sam's once-hopeful Medicaid program are legion. The federal government, whose responsibility it is to oversee what is essentially a state-run program, estimates that of Medicaid's $19-billion annual cost, more than $3 billion is being lost to fraud, abuse and inefficiency—*twice as much as the entire budget for its first year of operation a decade ago.*

What was hailed as the greatest boon ever granted America's medically deprived has become the worst scandal in the history of federal social programs. But it could be only the beginning. Congress now appears headed toward eventual adoption of a national health-care program encompassing all Americans—costing taxpayers at least $60 billion in its first year alone. "If we cannot run relatively modest programs such as Medicare and Medicaid effectively and efficiently, then I do not see how we can venture forward with more extensive programs such as national health insurance," warns Sen. Charles H. Percy (R., Ill.), ranking minority member of the Senate subcommittee on long-term health care. . . .

Medicaid "Mills." Maria Gonzales (there are no real names in this composite illustration) awoke one sticky morning last June to the whimpering of her four-year-old son, Juan. She and her five children live on welfare in a three-room, airless tenement in New York City's Spanish Harlem. Worried that Juan might be seriously ill, Maria hurried him to a nearby storefront medical clinic—one of more than 350 that Medicaid has spawned in New York City alone. Unable to afford a babysitter, Maria took all the children with her.

Five hours later, she and each of the children had been needlessly examined by every one of the clinic's medical practitioners, ranging from an eye, ear, nose and throat specialist to a podiatrist. Her protests had been met with a "What do you care? You don't pay for it."

Juan, it turned out, merely had a nasty summer cold, and Maria was handed a prescription for a liquid antibiotic which, she was told, was in sufficient quantity for the other children to take as a "precaution." The cost of the visit and medication to the taxpayers: $200.

We are all victims, thus, in this con game that subjects thousands of big-city welfare patients to unnecessary, sometimes dangerous medical procedures. The personnel who staff such storefront clinics, usually foreign-trained doctors, are nominally independent operators who "rent" space by paying the owner a percentage—roughly 50 percent—of their billings to Medicaid. Thus, the doctors do as much business as possible to make it worth their while.

The operator of one New York methadone clinic also owned a Medicaid mill to which he sent his drug-addict patients periodically for extensive physical examinations, including a complete skull series. If a patient balked, his methadone dosage was heartlessly withheld until he submitted to treatment or examination. . . .

Reform Regimen. Late last year [1976], Congress appeared to have awakened to the scope of fraud and abuse in Medicaid. A series of sensational hearings generated a flurry of action in the Senate. A hastily drawn condensation of a much larger reform bill was shoved through the Senate by Sen. Herman Talmadge (D., Ga.), chairman of the Finance Committee's health-care subcommittee. But the House let the matter slide, despite warnings that if the situation in Medicaid wasn't alleviated the noble dreams of national health care would turn into a nightmare.

Now, Talmadge has reintroduced his anti-fraud and anti-abuse bill, and Chairman Russell B. Long (D., La.) of the Senate Finance Committee is committed to early action. To cure Medicaid's ills, the bill proposes:

1. A medical-care fraud unit should be established in every U.S. Attorney's office and each state agency administering Medicaid.

2. Conviction of Medicaid fraud should be made a felony instead of a misdemeanor, and the maximum jail sentence increased to at least two years. The maximum fine for conviction should be $25,000.

3. Specific performance criteria for states to follow in administering Medicaid—and periodic on-site evaluations of how they are conforming to these standards—should be established. States which do not correct deficiencies should lose part or all of their federal Medicaid matching funds for administrative expenses.

Beyond this handful of suggestions, we need the all-out determination of Congress, HEW and state authorities to end Medicaid fraud and abuse. The hour is late. But Congress has time to straighten out the massive Medicaid mess and restore it to its original purpose of aiding millions of poverty-level Americans.

Source: Excerpts from "Our Multibillion-Dollar Medicaid Scandal," by Don Thomasson and Carl West. *The Reader's Digest,* May 1977, pp. 87-91. Reprinted by permission.

period after they attained age twenty-one up to and including the quarter in which the disability occurred. A minimum of six quarters of coverage is required. A worker who is disabled prior to age twenty-one and whose disabled, retired, or deceased parent is covered under social security can draw benefits under that parent's account without ever having worked.

A very desirable feature of disability income as well as the other cash benefit programs of social security is that all payments are automatically adjusted periodically to reflect increases in the cost of living. No private insurance plan can make such a guarantee. Of course, the reason that social security can make this promise is that the financing mechanism is based on the assumption that taxes can always be raised, if needed, to fund the social security benefits. In addition to disabled workers themselves, certain children of disabled, retired, or deceased persons who had worked in social security covered employment are also eligible for disability cash benefit payments. Disability income can also be paid during periods of rehabilitation even though the recipient may have some type of gainful employment.

Medicare Medicare is a health care plan that has two primary components: (1) basic hospital insurance and (2) supplementary medical insurance. Although Medicare was primarily designed to help persons over age sixty-five meet their health care costs, it now also covers a number of persons under age sixty-five who are current recipients of monthly social security disability benefits.

Basic Hospital Insurance Under the basic hospital insurance coverage of Medicare, inpatient hospital services are included for ninety days per benefit period. A benefit period begins when an insured enters a hospital or skilled nursing facility and ends sixty days after the hospital or nursing home stay is terminated. In addition, a person has a lifetime "safety cushion" of sixty days of care which may be used at any time to extend coverage for a prolonged hospital stay beyond the standard ninety days per benefit period. Along with the coverage of hospital room and board, Medicare hospital insurance contributes toward the payment of all services normally provided to inpatients as well as covering stays for limited periods in post-hospital extended care facilities. Moreover, some post-hospital health services such as intermittent nursing care, therapy, rehabilitation, and home health aid are provided. Benefits offered under the basic hospital plan of Medicare are subject to certain stipulated deductibles, time limits, and coinsurance provisions. The funds to pay for Medicare benefits are derived from the social security taxes paid by covered workers and their employers.

Supplementary Medical Insurance (SMI) The supplementary medical insurance program under Medicare provides payment for the following items: (1) physicians' and surgeons' services that are provided either at home or in a health care facility; (2) home health service (visitations by a registered nurse); and (3) medical and health services such as x-rays, diagnostics, laboratory tests, rental of necessary durable medical equipment, prosthetic devices, and ambulance trips. Limited psychiatric care is also covered under this part of Medicare. In contrast to the basic hospital plan, this supplementary protection is a voluntary program. Financing is provided by charging premiums to those who elect to participate. These premiums are then matched by funds of the government from general revenues of the U.S. Treasury Department. No premium differential is assessed enrollees because of differences in their age, health status, or sex. The coverage under SMI is open to nearly any individual age sixty-five or over, as long as he or she is properly enrolled in the program and pays the required monthly premiums. SMI is similar to many other types of health insurance in that payments are subject to deductibles and the insured participates at the rate of 20 percent of costs incurred in excess of the deductible. It is important to recognize that SMI pays only 80 percent of the *allowable* amount of the bill—not 80 percent of whatever amount is charged by the physician for the service. Thus an insured may receive substantially less than 80 percent of his or her total bill.

Worker's Compensation Insurance

Worker's compensation statutes have been enacted in every state in the union. These laws generally provide for compensation to workers for job-related injuries or disease. Although the worker's compensation legislation differs in each state, in most cases compensation includes benefits in the form of disability income, medical expenses, rehabilitation, and scheduled lump sum amounts for certain injuries, such as dismemberment. There are wide variations among the individual states in benefit amounts and payment periods. A schedule of benefits and payment periods that is believed to be about average is shown in Table 14-9.

In most instances, covered employees become eligible for worker's compensation benefits when they show that an injury or illness has occurred in the course of their employment. Payments are made without questioning who was at fault—employee or employer—except in certain cases where the worker was intoxicated or acted outside the scope of his or her authority. The primary purpose of these laws is to lighten the burden of job-related injury or illness to the worker. The cost of worker's compensation plans in all states is borne directly by employers. However, the amount of premium charged is computed on a merit basis: those employers with the highest claims figures pay at the highest rates. Consequently, employers seek to reduce accidents and injuries to help

Table 14-9 **Scheduled Payments under Worker's Compensation Insurance—South Carolina**
(Specific Injuries, or Injuries for Which Compensation Is Payable for a Fixed Number of Weeks, Regardless of How Long Disability Lasts)

Injury	Number of Weeks Payments Continue
Thumb	65
First Finger	40
Second Finger	35
Third Finger	25
Fourth Finger	20
Great Toe	35
Another Toe	10
Hand	165
Arm	220
Foot	140
Leg	195
Eye	110
Hearing (1 Ear)	80
Hearing (Both)	165
Back[a]	300

[a]If an individual loses 50 percent or more of his back, he is considered 100 percent disabled.

Note: Where an employee received an injury which causes the loss of a member (eye, hand, finger, leg, etc.) or the permanent total loss of use of a member, compensation is payable at the rate of $66\frac{2}{3}$ percent of his average weekly wage not to exceed 100 percent of the state average weekly wage of the maximum for a fixed number of weeks.

Source: South Carolina Worker's Compensation Report to the Legislature.

keep premiums low. The employee is not required to make any premium payments for this coverage. Of course, self-employed persons who are covered under the law would have to make contributions for themselves and their employees. The four basic areas of coverage provided by worker's compensation insurance are disability income, medical and rehabilitation expenses, lump sum payments, and second injury funds.

Disability Income Disability income benefits are most often paid to covered workers suffering loss due to injury or disease. The amount paid represents a set percentage of their predisability earned wages up to some maximum amount. The duration of disability payments is as short as fifty weeks in some states and as long as a lifetime in others. The maximum weekly benefit payable is seldom more than one and one-half times the average weekly wage of workers within the state in which the worker is employed, and often much less.

Medical and Rehabilitation Expenses A basic objective of worker's compensation legislation is to help the recovery of employees and to assist them in reentering the work force as productive members of society. Thus the laws provide for the payment of hospital, surgical, and other related expenses, including such prosthetic devices as artificial limbs, which may be required to aid in the worker's recovery. In addition, a number of jurisdictions provide compensation for retraining seriously injured victims for new employment.

Lump Sum Payments Worker's compensation legislation also provides for the payment of lump sum amounts to employees who suffer dismemberment in a work-related accident or to their beneficiaries in the case of death. The lump sum amounts payable for any specific type of loss are usually listed in a schedule of benefits that applies to all covered workers. These scheduled amounts vary considerably from state to state. In fact, in some states, payment for the loss of an arm exceeds the payment allowed by other states in the instance of death.

Second Injury Funds Second injury funds are established by the states to operate in conjunction with worker's compensation statutes. Their purpose is to relieve employers of the additional worker's compensation premium burden they might incur if a worker already handicapped sustained further injury on the job. For example, an employer might be reluctant to hire a worker with one eye, because if that individual's other eye were lost, the injury would constitute total disablement under the law. And rather than being charged with an accident which resulted in the loss of one eye, the employer would be charged with a total disability. In light of the merit rating system used in worker's compensation, this would adversely affect the employer's claims experience and premiums. Established to relieve employers of this burden, second injury funds are financed in some jurisdictions from state tax revenues and in others from an assessment levied against worker's compensation insurers.

Group Health Insurance

Group health insurance consists of health care contracts that are written between a group (usually an employer, union, credit union, college or university, or other organization) and an insuring organization. The coverages of each specific plan are subject to negotiation between the group and the insurer. All of the health care coverages that have been discussed, except disability income, are widely available through group plans. Group insurance accounts for a large majority of all private health insurance premiums collected in the United States. As can be seen in Table 14-10, of the nearly $22 billion in health insurance premiums paid in 1975, more than $16 billion were for group insurance. In addition to private insurance companies, Blue Cross/Blue Shield plans—prepaid medical expense plans discussed in the following section—also provide

Table 14-10 **Health Insurance Premiums of Insurance Companies by Type of Policy and Type of Protection**
(in Millions of Dollars)

Year	Total Premiums	Group Policies			Individual and Family Policies		
		Total	Loss of Income	Hospital-Medical Expense	Total	Loss of Income	Hospital-Medical Expense
1970	$11,546	$ 8,149	$1,968	$ 6,181	$3,397	$1,104	$2,293
1971	12,777	9,170	2,189	6,981	3,607	1,154	2,453
1972	15,218	11,230	2,616	8,614	3,988	1,260	2,728
1973	16,587	12,109	2,716	9,393	4,478	1,485	2,993
1974	18,459	13,522	2,932	10,590	4,937	1,660	3,277
1975	21,833	16,687	3,031	13,656	5,146	2,076	3,070

Source: Adapted with permission from *Sourcebook of Health Insurance Data, 1976–1977* (New York: Health Insurance Institute, 1977).

health care coverage for groups. In fact, total premiums paid to Blue Cross/Blue Shield and a few other minor hospital-medical plans now also exceed $16 billion. Table 14-11 clearly indicates how the premium volume for both private health insurers and Blue Cross/Blue Shield has grown between 1970 and 1975 in relation to disposable personal income. In 1940 (not shown) only 0.42 percent of disposable personal income went for health care premiums, while by 1970 this figure had reached 2.91 percent. As of 1975, the figure had risen to 3.59 percent. The proportion of personal disposable income spent on health insurance is expected to continue to increase in the future.

Table 14-11 **Health Insurance Premiums and Ratio to Disposable Personal Income**
(in Millions of Dollars)

Year	Insurance Companies	Blue Cross/Blue Shield and Other Hospital-Medical Plans	Total Premiums (1)	Disposable Personal Income (2)	Ratio (Percent) (1)÷(2) (3)
1970	$11,546	$ 8,439	$19,985	$ 685,935	2.91
1971	12,777	10,058	22,835	742,811	3.07
1972	15,218	11,465	26,683	801,299	3.33
1973	16,587	12,908	29,495	901,663	3.27
1974	18,459	14,533	32,992	982,926	3.36
1975	21,833	16,943	38,776	1,080,857	3.59

Source: Adapted with permission from *Sourcebook of Health Insurance Data, 1976–1977* (New York: Health Insurance Institute, 1977).

The chances are that if you go to work for an organization of more than just a few employees, you will be covered by some type of group health care plan. In many group plans, the employer pays the total premium for basic coverage on employees and their dependents. In others, employees must pay the portion of their premium that provides protection for their family. Much of the rapid expansion of both benefits and persons covered under group plans has been a direct result of the collective bargaining process of unions and employers. In recent years many group plans have included, in addition to the coverages previously discussed, medical expenses for maternity (in or out of wedlock), abortion, alcoholism, mental and nervous disorders, and drug addiction.

Blue Cross/Blue Shield

In a strict sense, Blue Cross/Blue Shield plans do not represent insurance. Blue Cross contracts can be viewed as nonprofit prepaid hospital expense plans. They include hospitals that have joined together and, in exchange for a prepaid fee, agree to provide certain hospital services to members of groups protected by Blue Cross. Similarly, Blue Shield plans are nonprofit contracts providing for prepaid medical and surgical services. These plans serve as intermediaries between groups that desire these services and physicians who contractually agree to provide them. Although technically Blue Cross/Blue Shield organizations are nonprofit, they compete for business with private insurance companies (some of which are also nonprofit associations) and attempt to retain a portion of their income to finance future growth. However, if premium income is substantially larger than necessary to meet all expenses and surplus requirements, "dividends" are paid to subscribers in the form of either lower premiums or expanded coverage.

Currently, nearly 90 million persons are covered under Blue Cross plans, and 78 million are enrolled in Blue Shield groups. Blue Cross and Blue Shield organizations have been formed on a geographical basis and now number eighty-two and seventy-seven, respectively. Because they are producer cooperatives, benefit payments are seldom made to the enrollee. Instead, direct payments to the participating hospitals and physicians are the norm. When Blue Cross/Blue Shield first began, premiums were based upon a community-wide rating structure. No experience rating and rate adjustment were utilized. However, because of resulting adverse selection, the original rating system was dropped, and premiums are now calculated in much the same way as those for private policies. From the standpoint of the individual, little practical difference exists between the operations of Blue Cross/Blue Shield and group private insurers.

Individual Health Coverages

Individual health insurance policies provide protection directly to policy-holders and/or their families. Consequently, individuals can tailor the coverage to their needs. In contrast, an individual under a group plan is entitled only to the benefits that are available in the master group plan. All of the coverages discussed above (including disability income) can be purchased in the open market. It is also possible to convert existing group plan coverage to an individual plan when an individual leaves the group. Even though the protection afforded under many group plans is excellent, most families still need to supplement this coverage with an individual health plan. This situation is especially true with respect to disability income insurance for upper middle income wage earners. However, no generalizations can be made as to specific additions that are necessary because of the wide differences that exist among group health plans. In contrast to *group life insurance* (which was not recommended as a basis for a life insurance plan in Chapter 13), *group health insurance* can serve as the foundation upon which a family builds its individual health insurance program.

Health Maintenance Organizations

A health maintenance organization (HMO) consists of a group of hospitals, physicians, and other health care personnel who have joined together to provide necessary health maintenance and remedial services to its members. HMOs are also called group practice plans. Members are charged a monthly fee based upon the number of persons in the family. The fee entitles them to receive the various health care services on a preventive checkup basis as well as when needed. Health maintenance organizations may be started by the physicians and hospitals themselves, a community, a university, an employer, an insurance company, or another organization. They attempt to reduce the costs of health care to families and individuals through more efficient utilization of health care personnel and facilities. These plans are based upon the belief that by providing opportunities for preventive (as well as corrective) medicine, the long-run costs of health care can be minimized while at the same time the general health of society can be improved. The formation of HMOs has been encouraged by legislation of the federal government. Grants, contracts, and loan guarantees for the planning, development, and initial costs of HMOs are authorized under federal law. Still, even though many believe that HMOs are a way to meet the present and future health care needs of the country, not all of these plans have been successful; whether they will become as prevalent as Blue Cross/Blue Shield and private insurance is yet to be seen. It is interesting to note that Blue Cross/Blue Shield has already established HMOs in several states. This action may be an indicator of the future success of health maintenance organizations in general.

One well-known HMO that has been relatively successful is the Kaiser Foundation Program. This group practice plan was originally designed to provide health care for the employees of the Kaiser Corporation, who often lived in outlying areas. The Kaiser Health Care Plan is now open to the public as well as the employees of the company. Presently it has several million members, with hospitals and clinics in Oregon, California, and Hawaii. Generally, the cost of the health care services performed by Kaiser has been less than the average charges of other health care providers operating in the same geographic areas. However, the membership of the Kaiser plan to date has consisted of primarily middle-income wage earners. Current information tends to suggest that group practice plans that encourage more diverse groups, especially lower-income families, may not be able to duplicate the favorable experience of the Kaiser Health Care Plan.

Some Basic Facts about HMOs

For $50–$70 a month your family gets: Some or all of these services free—outpatient physician care, including annual checkups and emergency treatment as needed; unlimited inhospital days; short-term mental health treatment; x-ray and laboratory tests; physical therapy; radiation therapy; surgery; family planning and infertility services; injected medicine; obstetrical services; alcoholic and drug addiction treatment; preventive dental and vision care for children; home health care when needed; health education.

Some or all of these services at a reduced rate—complete dental care; complete vision care; facilities for intermediate and long-term care; long-term medical care and rehabilitation; prescription drugs.

You do not get—corrective appliances such as eyeglasses and artificial aids such as hearing aids; long-term mental health care; cosmetic surgery; long-term treatment for drug addiction and alcoholism; personal or comfort items and private rooms, unless medically necessary, during hospitalization.

Remember: As an HMO member you pay a monthly premium whether or not you employ any services, and you are expected to use HMO physicians and HMO facilities only. At the same time, studies have found that HMO members receive more preventive care, are subject to fewer premature deaths and perinatal mortality, experience a lower senior citizen death rate, and pay less money for health care, than fee-for-service patients holding conventional insurance policies.

Source: Reprinted by permission from "HMO Facts," Consumer's Digest, November–December 1975, p. 11.

National Health Insurance

In recent years a great deal of attention has been given to our health care delivery system by the news media, government officials, and others. As a result, a number of national health insurance plans have been proposed, although none has yet been enacted. The programs that have been suggested range in scope from a complete replacement of private health insurance with a government scheme that would cover the entire population to other plans that would preserve the private system while at the same time providing greater availability of health services to the poor and aged. Regardless of the approach that is taken, a national program must be more than simply a financing plan that increases the demand for health care. Such a plan must improve the efficiency and effectiveness of the manner in which health care is delivered to the public. Certainly, the mistakes that have been made with the Medicare and Medicaid programs should not be repeated in a national health insurance plan.

Health Insurance Planning

In planning your health insurance program, you should consider the following items: (1) present coverages, (2) important coverage provisions and features, (3) health insurance needs, (4) financial resources, and (5) criteria for selecting an insuring organization.

Evaluating Present Coverages

Your present health insurance coverages can be viewed in terms of two basic components: disability income and health care expense protection.

Disability Income The foundation of disability income protection for most families is provided by the social security program. No longer should social security be viewed as simply a retirement system that doles out a few dollars of subsistence on a monthly basis. Many young middle-income families are eligible for monthly cash social security benefits approaching $1,000 or more should the breadwinner become disabled. In addition to social security benefits, you should evaluate the kind of disability income or wage continuation plan that is offered by your employer. Nearly all corporate and government employers offer some disability income protection on a short-term basis. Many also allow sick leave days to accumulate over a period of time so that a healthy employee can build a valuable reserve of paid time off that can be used in the case of an accident or illness. As a final step, you should look at any individual policies that you currently have and determine both the amount of income and the time period over which it is to be provided. Most families do not have as much long-term disability income protection as is required to provide sufficient coverage.

Health Care Expense Protection In order to examine your present health care expense protection, you should first determine if you are covered under group health insurance plans. In many cases, workers may be covered under two or more group plans. For example, each member of a working couple may receive some coverage for the entire family from his or her employers. It is also worthwhile to examine the coverage offered by any individual hospital, surgical, medical expense, and major medical policy that you may have. The health insurance programs of many families are weak due to the fact that they have too much low dollar-loss protection and insufficient high dollar-loss protection. In other words, many families are overcovered on the more routine types of medical expense and undercovered on the less common, high-expense medical costs. Also, many have gaps in their health care packages as a result of placing too much emphasis on segmented or limited peril coverages.

Evaluating Policy Provisions and Features

Of all the types of insurance considered in this text, health insurance is probably by far the most difficult to discuss in a general sense. However, some of the most important features to be aware of include: (1) persons covered, (2) definition of accident, (3) effect of a change of occupation, (4) definition of disability, (5) house confinement requirements, (6) waiting periods and deductibles, (7) duration of benefits, (8) cancellation, (9) renewability, (10) policy limits, and (11) coordination of benefits. An understanding of these provisions and features is necessary in order to make sure that a policy provides for adequate coverage.

Persons Covered Some health insurance policies cover only the named insured, while others offer protection to all family members. Of those that offer family coverage, some terminate benefits payable on behalf of children at age eighteen and others continue them to age twenty-two as long as the child remains in school or is single. In the past, disability income policies were not ordinarily written to cover unemployed spouses because many insurance companies did not feel they had an adequate way of determining whether the person had actually become disabled or was simply claiming disablement in order to raise a little extra money for the household. More companies, however, are now beginning to offer this type of coverage, although the conditions under which the policies are issued are still rather restrictive.

Preview of Pending National Health Insurance: Legislation

In 1977 eighteen different bills concerned with national health insurance were submitted to Congress for its consideration. Six of them can be considered major. They offer a sampling of what the experts are thinking, what the health care industry is demanding, and what the public wants. Given on the next page are these six key health insurance plans listed in a sequence that runs from the relatively broad and generous to the relatively narrow and penny-pinching. In spite of these proposals, no one can predict for certain the future of health reform. What's your preference?

The Six Key Health-Insurance Plans

Bill	National Support	Estimated Cost by 1980	Administration	Financing	Benefits
Kennedy-Corman	A.F.L.-C.I.O., Committee for National Health Insurance.	$24.8 billion.	Special board within H.E.W.; regional and local offices will operate program.	Half to come from Federal general revenues, half from special taxes; 1 percent of payroll for employees, 2.5 percent for employers and self-employed.	Institutional services: hospital care, skilled nursing facilities up to 120 days. Diagnosis and treatment: physicians' services, lab and X-ray, home health services, prescription drugs (for chronic illnesses), medical supplies and appliances. Other services: physical checkups, well-child care, maternity, family planning, dental care (up to age 25), vision care and eyeglasses, hearing care and hearing aids. Patient cost-sharing: none.
CHIP	No formal support.	$11.3 billion.	Insurance through private carriers; states to supervise under Federal regulations.	Employer-employee premium payments, with employer paying 75 percent (65 percent first three years); special provisions for small employers and those with high increases in payroll costs.	Institutional services: hospital care, skilled nursing facilities up to 100 days. Diagnosis and treatment: physicians' services, lab and X-ray, home health services (up to 100 visits), prescription drugs, medical supplies and appliances. Other services: well-child care, maternity, family planning, dental care (under age 13), hearing care and hearing aids (under age 13). Patient cost-sharing: annual deductible* of $150 per person; 25 percent coinsurance,** with annual ceiling of $1,500 per family.
Ullman	American Hospital Association.	$25.1 billion.	Private insurance carriers under state supervision, according to Federal guidelines.	Employer-employee premium payments, with employer paying at least 75 percent; Federal subsidy for low-income workers and certain small employers; patients enrolling in a health-care corporation get 10 percent subsidy.	Institutional services: hospital care up to 90 days, skilled nursing facilities (30 days), health-related custodial nursing home care (90 days). Diagnosis and treatment: physicians' services up to 10 visits, lab and X-ray, home health services (100 days), prescription drugs limited to specified conditions, medical supplies and appliances. Other services: physical checkups, well-child care, maternity, dental care (under age 13), vision care and eyeglasses (under age 13). Patient cost-sharing: coinsurance (20 percent) or copayments*** (up to $5) on most items; special "catastrophic" provisions become effective when patient's out-of-pocket expenses reach a specified amount.
Fulton	American Medical Association.	$20.3 billion.	Private carriers provide insurance under state supervision; regulations issued by a new Federal board.	Employer-employee premium payments, with employer paying at least 65 percent; small employers get Federal help as do all employers with unusual payroll cost increases; self-employed pay own premiums but are assisted by income-tax credits computed on a sliding scale (the lower the income, the higher the credits).	Institutional services: hospital care, skilled nursing facilities up to 100 days. Diagnosis and treatment: physicians' services, lab and X-ray, home health services, medical supplies and equipment. Other services: physical checkups, well-child care, maternity, family planning, dental care (under age 18). Patient cost-sharing: 20 percent coinsurance, with an annual maximum of $1,500 per person and $2,000 per family.
Burleson-McIntyre	Health Insurance Association of America.	$11 billion.	Insurance administered by private carriers under state supervision; plan is voluntary.	Employer-employee premium payments, the ratios to be negotiated between them; low-income workers pay less; self-employed pay entire premium; all participants eligible for special tax deductions.	Institutional services: hospital care, skilled nursing facilities up to 180 days. Diagnosis and treatment: physicians' services, lab and X-ray (270 days), prescription drugs, medical supplies and appliances. Other services: well-child care, maternity, family planning, dental care (under age 13, one visit), vision care (under age 13, one visit). Patient cost-sharing: annual deductible of $100 per person; 20 percent coinsurance on all items, with annual family limit of $1,000.
Long-Ribicoff	No formal support.	$9.8 billion.	Employers and employees have two choices: to join Federal insurance program administered by H.E.W., or to buy private insurance from federally approved carriers, under H.E.W. supervision.	Employers pay 1 percent payroll tax and are allowed similar provisions for self-employed.	Institutional services: hospital care, skilled nursing facilities up to 100 days. Diagnosis and treatment: physicians' services, lab and X-ray, home health services, medical supplies and appliances. Other services: None. Patient cost-sharing: first 60 days of hospitalization not covered; first $2,000 in family medical expenses not covered.

*Deductible: patient's share of annual medical costs before insurance coverage begins.
**Coinsurance: the percentage of a given bill that is charged to the patient.
***Copayment: a flat rate charged to the insured patient on specific items (such as $2 per office visit).

Source: Richard Margolius, "National Health Insurance—The Dream Whose Time Has Come?" *New York Times Magazine,* 9 January 1977, pp. 12ff. © 1977 The New York Times Company. Reprinted by permission.

Definition of Accident Health policies that pay for losses caused by accident define an accident in one of two ways. Some have a liberal definition indicating that as long as the result of a given action is accidental, coverage will apply. This is called an *accidental injury clause.* Other health insurance policies contain an "accidental means" clause. Under this provision, both the act and the injury must have been accidental. Consider the following example: After cleaning leaves out of the gutters on his house, Steve Urse purposely jumped to the ground from the roof and accidentally broke his leg in the process. Payment would be made under the policy with an accidental injury clause, but no payment would be available if an accidental means provision applied, since the cause of the injury (jumping from the roof) was not accidental.

Change of Occupation In underwriting disability income policies, insurance companies consider the hazards related to the insured person's job. Consequently, people who work in dangerous occupations must pay a higher premium than those in less accident-prone positions. In order to protect the insurance company, most disability income contracts explicitly state that a lower level of benefits will be paid if an insured person switches to a more hazardous occupation during the policy period.

Definition of Disability In some disability income policies, people are defined as disabled if they no longer have the capacity to undertake gainful employment. In fact, this is the same definition used by the Social Security Administration to qualify a covered worker for disability payments. The practical enforcement of this provision, however, is often more liberal than might be expected from reading the policy. In contrast, more liberal policies classify insureds as disabled if they simply cannot pursue an occupation for which they have been trained. Under some coverages an insured person may be eligible for disability benefits if he or she loses both arms or both legs or, in some cases, one of each. In these instances no employment test would be applied in order to determine the benefit eligibility of the insured.

House Confinement Another requirement imposed by some disability income policies is that insureds must be confined to their home in order to become eligible for benefits. Obviously, this is a very undesirable provision.

Waiting Periods and Deductibles In order to reduce administrative costs and frequent small claims, nearly all types of health insurance policies include deductible and/or waiting period clauses. On individual and family policies, the policyholder usually has a broad range of deductibles and waiting periods from which to choose. Of course, with all

"Turns out your policy covers falling off the roof, all right, but not hitting the ground."

Understand Your Health Insurance Policy's Coverage!

Source: Changing Times, October 1972, p. 14. Reprinted with permission from *Changing Times* Magazine, © Kiplinger Washington Editors, Inc., 1972.

other things equal, the higher the deductible and the longer the waiting period, the lower the annual premium.

Duration of Benefits Another item that one should look for in health insurance policies concerns the duration of the period throughout which the company will pay benefits. For disability coverage, this time period typically ranges from six months to life. The benefit period under medical expense policies is quite often limited to three years after the first charge is incurred on a given claim.

Cancellation Many health insurance policies are written to permit cancellation at any time at the option of the insurer. Some policies explicitly state this; others do not. To protect yourself against premature cancellation, you should buy policies that contain a provision which specifically states that the insurer will not cancel coverage as long as premiums are paid.

Renewal Whereas cancellation pertains to termination of the contract during the policy period, renewal refers to the right of the insured to continue coverage upon expiration of the policy period. For maximum protection you should find health coverage contracts that are either guaranteed or noncancellable to at least age sixty-five.

Policy Limits All private health insurance contracts place limitations on the amount of benefits they will pay. Often specific dollar amounts are stipulated. In the absence of such specificity, the payments are limited to an amount considered "reasonable and necessary." *Reasonable* usually means the prevailing charges are in line with those given for similar services in the same geographic area. Remember that, in a fashion similar to major medical coverage, many health policies not only have maximum total amounts payable, but they also specify internal limits for certain types of expenses and services.

Coordination of Benefits In contrast to most property and liability insurance coverages, which are discussed in Chapter 15, health insurance policies are not contracts of *indemnity*. This means that insureds can collect multiple payments for the same accident or illness unless a "coordination of benefits provision" is included in their health insurance contracts. For example, many medical expense policies have a coordination of benefits provision with medical benefits paid under worker's compensation. In contrast, some companies widely advertise that their policies will pay claims regardless of how much other coverage the policyholder has. Of course, these latter types of insurance contracts are often more expensive per dollar of protection than those policies that provide for coordination of benefits.

Health Insurance Needs

As should be clear from earlier discussions concerning sources of coverage, most U.S. citizens receive substantial amounts of health insurance protection through the government programs of social security and worker's compensation and also under some form of group health insurance. Your individual health insurance program should be built around any of these coverages that apply to you and your family. The individual or family health policies you obtain should fill the gaps left by these types of programs. Because of the wide variety of group plans, generalizations about probable gaps in protection are difficult to make, with one exception: long-term disability income coverage. Of course, it is important to examine closely your major medical coverage.

Disability Income Most families are protected against disability income loss under social security. However, the size of social security benefits is based upon the career average monthly earnings on which social security taxes have been paid. Therefore, the longer you work and the more your income increases, the greater will be the dollar difference between your current earnings and your career average. Also, if you have a number of years of low earnings or no earnings covered under social security, your career average for social security computations will be reduced accordingly. Because of this possibility it is advisable for a family to have some long-term disability income protection in addition to that offered by social security. Since worker's compensation coverage is limited to disabilities that are job-related, it is best not to consider this coverage when developing your basic disability program.

Major Medical Another important area to check when planning health insurance coverage is the medical protection that is available for catastrophic losses. You should make sure that you are covered by a major medical policy with limits of at least $25,000 per person and if possible much more. It is a good idea to examine the possibility of increasing your deductible in order to use those funds for extending the limits of your protection. Remember, you should devote more attention to covering large losses than to protecting against losses of small amounts.

Considering Financial Resources

If the analysis of your current health insurance coverages received through government and group programs indicates that you need to purchase an individual or family health policy in order to fill in gaps, consideration must be given to the cost factor involved. Expenditures for needed coverage must be viewed not as luxuries but rather as essential to the adequate protection of your family's finances. If your financial resources do not appear adequate to purchase the needed coverage, you should reassess these needs and your budget priorities. Because adequate health coverage is so important, it should be given high priority in the budgeting process. The consequences of inadequate coverage can be rapid deterioration in your finances and possibly even personal bankruptcy. Such outcomes would probably prohibit you from ever achieving your personal financial goals. Thus it is best to make financial resources available to buy adequate health coverage. Of course, if the health care coverage you receive from government and/or group plans is adequate, concern with financial resources should not exist.

Selecting a Health Insurer

A broad spectrum of policy provisions and costs exists among health insurers. As a matter of fact, some companies offering policies with liberal provisions charge lower premiums than those with more rigidly defined features. The only way to buy health insurance intelligently is to shop around after determining your needs and compare policies on the basis of price and coverage offered. Unfortunately, since it is unsafe to assume that the highest priced policy is the best and the lowest priced the worst, this can be a difficult task. Until a more standardized comprehensive health insurance contract similar to the policies offered for automobiles and homes becomes available, most families must expect to spend considerable time and effort in order to develop a good health insurance program. As with other types of insurance, you should be concerned with the financial stability of the insurer and its claims settlement experience. Information on financial stability can be obtained from *Best's Reports*, which can be found in your library. Information about claims settlement and other important operating and sales practices of companies can often be secured through the consumer division of your state insurance department.

Summary

Because both the frequency and potential severity of economic loss resulting from sickness and accidents is high, health insurance is essential. The costs of delivering health care continue to soar, making some form of coverage all the more necessary. A variety of types of health coverage are available for meeting this need. Disability income insurance is primarily used to replace wages lost due to the disablement of a breadwinner. Because the largest gap in the health insurance program of most people is inadequate long-term disability income protection, this type of insurance merits close examination. Hospital insurance policies offer reimbursement for the costs of hospital room and board and other necessary expenses incidental to hospitalization. Surgical expense coverage pays for the cost of nearly all types of operations and surgical procedures. Regular medical expense insurance provides for the cost of such services as physician fees for nonsurgical care, x-rays, and laboratory tests. To protect against catastrophic medical expenses resulting from accident or sickness, major medical policies are available. Some health insurers offer a comprehensive major medical policy that combines basic hospital, surgical, and medical expense coverage with major medical to provide a package health care protection policy. Other less important coverages offered by some health insurers include dental expense policies, specified accident or sickness policies, common carrier (for example, airplane) accident policies, and supplemental hospital expense plans.

A number of important sources of health insurance exist. The often overlooked insurance portion of social security provides both long-term disability and medical and hospital insurance coverage. A source of financial recovery for job-related accidents or illnesses is worker's compensation, which often pays medical expenses, disability income, and a lump sum amount in the case of dismemberment or death. Within the nongovernment insurance market, group insurance is by far the most prevalent source of recovery. Group insurance consists of health care contracts that are written between a group (usually an employer) and an insurance company or Blue Cross/Blue Shield. Of course, a variety of individual health insurance policies are available from a large number of insurers. In recent years increasing attention has focused on health maintenance organizations (HMOs), which emphasize preventive medicine as opposed to remedial care as a means for delivering health care to the public. In the future, some form of national health insurance may replace many of the existing health insurance coverages.

In evaluating present health protection, individuals should first determine whether they are covered under social security and worker's compensation programs. They should also see what type (if any) of group plan their university or employer has available. People's needs for health insurance are influenced by the amount of resources they have external to health insurance, the size of their family, their present income level, and their tendency toward risk aversion. Health insurance policy provisions that individuals should be familiar with are those pertaining to persons covered, definitions of accident and disability, change of occupation, house confinement, waiting period and deductibles, duration and amount of benefits, cancellation, renewability, and coordination of benefits. It is also important for people to consider their available financial resources and determine the level of health insurance that they can afford. In selecting a health insurer, attention must be given to policy costs, the financial strength of the insurer, and whether the policy provisions are liberal or restrictive.

Key Terms

accident definition
benefit period
Blue Cross/Blue Shield
cancellation
coinsurance or participation clause
comprehensive major medical insurance
coordination of benefits provision
deductibles

dental expense insurance
disability income insurance
dread disease health policies
group health insurance
group practice plans
health maintenance organization (HMO)
hospital insurance
house confinement

indemnity
individual health insurance
Kaiser Health Care Plan
lump sum payments
major medical plans
Medicaid
Medicare
national health insurance
Old Age, Survivor's, Disability, and Health Insurance (OASDHI)

policy limits
regular medical expense insurance
renewal
second injury funds
sick leave
supplementary medical insurance (SMI)
surgical expense insurance
waiting periods
worker's compensation insurance

Review Questions

1. What factors have contributed to today's high costs of health care?

2. What is disability income insurance? Explain the waiting period provisions found in such policies.

3. Differentiate between hospital and surgical insurance.

4. What is major medical coverage? What are the common features of a major medical policy?

5. Describe (a) regular medical insurance, (b) comprehensive major medical insurance, and (c) dental insurance.

6. What is the other name used to refer to social security? Briefly describe the health benefits provided under social security.

7. What is Medicare? Explain the eligibility requirements and benefits provided by this plan.

8. What is the objective of worker's compensation legislation? Explain (a) lump sum payments and (b) second injury funds as they relate to worker's compensation.

9. What is group health insurance? Differentiate group health insurance from individual health insurance.

10. Discuss the basics of the Blue Cross/Blue Shield plans.

11. "Health maintenance organizations (HMOs) attempt to reduce the costs of health care to families and individuals through more efficient utilization of health care personnel and facilities." Explain basically how these organizations work.

12. Discuss the pros and cons of national health insurance. Are you for or against this type of program? Explain.

13. Describe the procedures used to evaluate an individual's current health insurance coverages.

14. List and discuss some of the important features that are likely to be included in a health insurance policy.

15. Briefly discuss the procedures for (a) evaluating present health insurance requirements, (b) considering financial resources, and (c) selecting a health insurer.

14-1 Evaluating Philip Mansfield's Health Insurance Coverage

Case Problems

Philip Mansfield was a self-employed window washer earning approximately $300 per week. One day while cleaning windows on the eighth floor of the First National Building, he tripped and fell from the scaffolding to the pavement below. He sustained severe multiple injuries but miraculously survived the accident. He was immediately rushed to the Mt. Sinai Hospital for surgery. There he remained for two months (sixty days) of treatment, after which he was allowed to go home for further recuperation. During his stay in the hospital, he incurred the following expenses: surgeon, $2,000; physician, $500; hospital bill, room and board, $60 per day; nursing services, $800; anesthetist, $100; wheelchair rental, $60; ambulance, $40; and drugs, $250. Philip has a major medical policy with LIC Corp. that has a $2,500 deductible clause, an 80 percent coinsurance clause, internal limits of $45 per day on hospital room and board, and $750 as a maximum surgical fee. The policy does not provide any disability benefits.

Questions

1. Explain the policy provisions as they relate to deductibles, coinsurance, and internal limits.

2. How much should Philip recover from the insurance company? How much must he pay out of his pocket?

3. Would any other policies have offered Philip additional protection? What about his inability to work while recovering from his injury?

4. Based upon the information presented, how would you assess Philip's insurance coverage? Explain.

14-2 Estimating the Disability Needs of Manuel and Teresa Fernandes

Manuel Fernandes and his wife, Teresa, have been married for two years and have a one year old son, Luis. They live in Detroit, where Manuel is employed as a welder on the assembly line at the Ford Motor Company. He earns $1,300 per month, of which he takes home $1,050. As an employee of Ford, he is entitled to receive the benefits provided by the company's group health insurance policy. In addition to major medical coverage, the policy provides a monthly disability benefit amounting to 20 percent of the employee's average monthly take-home pay for the most recent year prior to receiving the disability. In the instance of complete disability, Manuel would also be eligible for social security payments of $400 per month.

Teresa is also employed. She earns $300 per month after taxes working part-time at a nearby grocery store. The store does not provide her with any benefits. Social security benefits in the event she became disabled would provide monthly income of $200. Manuel and Teresa spend 90 percent of their combined take-home pay in order to meet their bills and provide for a variety of necessary items. The remaining 10 percent is used to fulfill their savings and entertainment goals.

Questions

1. How much, if any, additional disability insurance does Manuel require in order to provide adequate protection against his becoming completely disabled?

2. Does Teresa need any disability coverage? Explain.

3. What specific recommendations with respect to disability insurance requirements would you give Manuel and Teresa in order to provide adequate protection for themselves as well as their child?

Selected References

Boronson, Warren. "Diagnosing Your Health Insurance." *Money,* September 1974, pp. 39–52.

"Chances for Health Insurance—Bleak in '77." *U.S. News & World Report,* 14 February 1977, p. 35.

"Congress Catches Up with Medicaid Ripoff." *U.S. News & World Report,* 13 September 1976, p. 55.

Davis, Karen. *National Health Insurance: Benefits, Costs, and Consequences.* Washington, D.C.: Brookings Institution, 1975.

Gregg, John E. *Health Insurance Racket and How to Beat It.* Chicago, Ill.: Henry Regnery, 1973.

"Health Insurance for Older People." *Consumer Reports,* January 1976, pp. 27–34.

Hershman, Arlene. "The Race to Cut Medical Costs." *Dun's Review,* May 1977, pp. 48–53 ff.

"Insurance That Covers the Dentist Bills." *Changing Times,* May 1977, pp. 43–44.

Kennedy, Edward M. *In Critical Condition: The Crisis in American Health Care.* New York: Simon and Schuster, 1972.

Law, Sylvia A. *Blue Cross: What Went Wrong?* New Haven, Conn.: Yale University Press, 1974.

"Needed: A New Direction for Our Medical System." *U.S. News & World Report*, 28 March 1977, pp. 39–40 ff.

"One-Stop Health Care—Millions More Eligible." *U.S. News & World Report*, 12 January 1976, p. 64.

"Prevention or Cure? Behind the Shift in Health Care." *U.S. News & World Report*, 4 April 1977, p. 62.

"Unemployment Compensation: How It Will Help If You Need It." *Changing Times*, April 1975, pp. 7–10.

"Uproar Over Medical Bills." *U.S. News & World Report*, 28 March 1977, pp. 35–38.

"Your Health Insurance: Be Sure You Have What You Need." *Changing Times*, June 1977, pp. 45–47.

15
Property and Liability Insurance

A Preview of Chapter 15

In order to present the fundamental concepts of property and liability insurance and to outline methods of assessing the need for and adequacy of such policies, this chapter examines the following:

1. Types of exposure to loss, the criteria for an insurable exposure, the principle of indemnity, and coinsurance.

2. The key factors to consider when purchasing homeowner's, automobile, and other types of property and liability insurance.

3. The different forms of homeowner's insurance and variations in homeowner's policy coverage with respect to perils, property, losses, persons, locations, periods of coverage, and payment limitations.

4. Automobile insurance policy coverages, including liability provisions, uninsured motorists coverage, medical payments insurance, collision insurance, and comprehensive insurance.

5. The effects on automobile insurance of geographic location, type and use of automobile, driving record and personal characteristics of the insured, discounts or premiums, the claims settlement process, and the role of government in auto insurance.

6. Other types of property and liability insurance and the best way to select an insurance agent and a company from which to purchase needed insurance.

Because you own assets, you are exposed to a variety of causes of financial loss. Suppose a severe storm completely destroyed your house.

546

Could you afford such a loss? Most people could not. In order to protect yourself in the event of this and similar types of property loss, you need property insurance. Also associated with property ownership is the risk of negligence. For example, it is conceivable that you might one day be distraught over a personal problem, unintentionally run a red light, and kill a pedestrian. Because the consequences of this and other potentially negligent acts can cause financial ruin, appropriate liability insurance coverage is essential. Once you know how to assess your property and liability risk exposures, you will be able to select the coverages you need to assure the achievement of your personal financial goals.

American families and businesses are now spending more than $60 billion annually on premiums for property and liability insurance. Property insurance helps people guard against catastrophic losses to their real and personal property caused by such perils as fire, flood, wind storms, and many other calamities. Liability insurance offers protection against the financial ruin that could emanate from certain types of lawsuits. Although insurance outlays are quite large, only a small minority of families know what they are receiving for their dollars. Few people are aware of the gaps, overinsurance, and underinsurance that exist in their property and liability insurance programs. Since such inadequate insurance programs are completely at odds with the objectives of personal financial management, it is important to become familiar with the basics of property and liability insurance. This chapter discusses the property and liability risks that most families face and explains the coverages available to deal with them. However, before discussing property and liability insurance needs and available protection, attention is given to the fundamental concepts that underlie property and liability insurance.

The basic concepts related to property and liability insurance concern types of exposures, criteria for an insurable exposure, the principle of indemnity, and coinsurance. Each of these is discussed separately.

Some Fundamental Concepts

Types of Exposures

Most property owners face two basic types of exposures: physical loss of property and loss through liability.

Exposures to Property Loss Most property insurance contracts specify the property that is covered in the policy and name the perils (causes of loss) for which insurance proceeds will be available. However, some property contracts do offer protection on a comprehensive basis and limit coverage by excluding certain types of property and perils. The nature of these contracts imposes two obligations on the property owner: (1) developing a complete inventory of the property in need of insurance coverage and (2) identifying the perils against which protection is desired.

Property Inventory Most people neither fully appreciate the value of all the property they own nor attempt to itemize their property for insurance or other purposes. Nevertheless, an inventory of property should be prepared not only to aid in selection of coverages but also to assist in settling a claim if a loss occurs. All property insurance contracts require that an insured show proof of loss before reimbursement is made. Consequently, a prepared schedule of property with corresponding values can serve as evidence to satisfy the company. Ordinarily, families have a home, household furnishings, clothing and personal accessories, lawn and garden equipment, and motor vehicles intended for road use, all of which need to be insured. Fortunately, the majority of homeowner's and automobile package insurance policies provide coverage for these types of belongings. Many families also own items such as motorboats and trailers, motor vehicles intended for off-road use, business property and inventories, jewelry, stamp or coin collections, furs, cash, gold or silver bullion, manuscripts, important papers and documents, antiques, paintings, bonds and other securities, and items of special value such as expensive cameras, golf clubs, electronic recording and playing equipment, or citizen-band radios. Quite often coverage for these types of properties must be specially arranged with the insurer. In order to help policyholders prepare an inventory, many property insurance companies have easy-to-complete personal property inventory forms available. A sample of a portion of such a form is shown in Figure 15-1.

Identifying Perils As stated earlier, a *peril* is a cause of loss. Since certain perils cannot be reasonably insured against, very few property insurance contracts offer protection against every conceivable loss. Therefore, when obtaining property insurance protection, you should be certain to evaluate the various types of losses that are and are not covered by a policy. (Many persons feel a false sense of security after buying insurance because they believe that they are safeguarded for all contingencies.) For example, several perils which are uninsurable or demand special attention under many homeowner's or automobile insurance policies include flood, earthquake or earth movement such as mud slides, theft, mysterious disappearance, war or nuclear explosion, and wear and tear. In addition to limiting coverage resulting from certain perils, property insurance contracts also routinely limit coverage on the basis of location of the property, time of loss, persons involved, and the types of hazards to

Figure 15-1 **Personal Property Inventory Form**

Living Room				Dining and/or Family Room			
Items	*Model & Serial No.	Original Cost	Year Purchased	Items	*Model & Serial No.	Original Cost	Year Purchased
Books (see page 12)				Buffet			
Brick-a-brac (Total estimate)				Cabinets			
Cabinet, contents				China Closet			
Chairs				China (see page 11)			
Clocks				Chairs			
Curtains, Drapes				Curtain, Drapes			
Desk, Desk Sets				Glassware (see page 11)			
Fireplace Accessories				Lamps			
Lamps				Linens			
Mirrors				Mirrors			
Musical Instruments				Pictures, Paintings (see page 12)			
Pictures, Paintings (see page 12)				Rugs, Carpeting			
Stereo, Hi-Fi				Silver (see page 11)			
Phonograph				Tables			
Radio				Electrical Appliances			
Records							
Rugs, Carpeting							
Sofas				Other Articles			
Tables							
Television							
Other Articles							
Total:				Total:			

*Law enforcement officers will often not release recovered items unless the owner can identify them by a serial number.
Source: Insurance Record and Household Inventory, Courtesy of Farmers Insurance Group, Mission, Kansas, pp. 2–3.

which the insured is exposed. These limitations are explained further in subsequent sections of this chapter.

Liability Exposures Every day you face the risk that you might negligently cause property damage or bodily injury to someone else. For example, when golfing you might become impatient and tee off before the people in front of you are clearly out of range. If your drive struck one of these golfers and you were found legally liable for that injury, a judgment ranging into the thousands, or in some cases millions, of dollars could be levied against you. Of course, a debt of that magnitude could force many families into financial ruin and bankruptcy. Naturally, though, we all encounter many different liability exposures. Driving a car, entertaining guests in a home, and being careless during the performance of professional duties are some other common liability risks. However, even if we were never negligent and always prudent, we still would run the risk that someone might think that we were the cause of a loss and therefore initiate legal action. High legal fees required to defend against suits that may or may not have merit are another exposure most families encounter. Fortunately, various types of liability insurance are available for protecting families from losses resulting from each of these risks. Before discussing the methods available for insuring against liability exposures, the ways in which legal liability arises, as well as the defenses available for defeating claims, are briefly described.

Liability Based upon Negligence Legal definitions of negligence and liability have evolved over hundreds of years of court decisions and enactments of statutes, and these definitions are expected to continue to be modified as society's values change. In addition, specific rules of law not only vary over time, but their interpretations vary depending on judges, juries, and locations throughout the country. Consequently, only a general overview of these concepts can be presented here. A person is said to have been *negligent* when his or her behavior is inconsistent with the "reasonable man doctrine." This doctrine holds that if a person fails to act in a reasonable manner—as would one with normal intelligence, perceptions, and experiences common to the community—that person is said to be negligent. Evidence that an individual was negligent is only the first step in establishing liability. In addition, it must be proven that the defendant (the person accused of negligence) had a duty toward the plaintiff (the accuser) and that a breach of duty caused the plaintiff a compensable loss. If any of these elements is missing, the defendant is relieved from liability. The defendant can also escape payment if one of several defenses available against a charge of negligence can be successfully used.

Defenses to a Negligence Action The two most common defenses to a charge of negligence are assumption of risk and contributory negligence. Under the *assumption of risk defense*, the allegation is that some action of the plaintiff relieved the defendant of his or her duty to protect the plaintiff. For example, assume that Bill Putnam voiced his intent to try to cover a twelve mile stretch of highway in less than ten minutes on his motorcycle. If Janice Morris asked to go with him on this daredevil ride, she would forego any right to later collect from Bill should an accident develop because of his reckless behavior. With a *defense of contributory negligence*, the defendant maintains that the plaintiff contributed to his or her own loss by also acting in a negligent manner. This defense might be successful, for example, in a case where motorist A fails to yield the right-of-way (a negligent act) and is struck by motorist B, who has the right-of-way but is speeding. If it could be shown that the accident would not have occurred had motorist B been in reasonable control of his or her vehicle, motorist B's claim against motorist A might be defeated. However, because of the potential harshness of the doctrine of contributory negligence, some states have enacted *comparative negligence statutes*. Under this legislation an attempt is made to allocate the loss to each party in proportion to the degree each was negligent.

Note that the preceding discussion relates to the legal elements necessary for the successful defense against damages based upon a negligence action. In practice, though, juries often make awards which derive from their sympathy for the plaintiff rather than from the facts pertaining to the case. This is especially apparent in cases where the defendant is a large company.

Criteria for an Insurable Exposure

As was noted in Chapter 13, insurance can be an effective way to deal with risk only when the following conditions are met: (1) the loss covered is fortuitous, or accidental, (2) cost is relatively low—there is a low chance of a large dollar loss, and (3) there are a large number of similar exposure units. For certain types of property and liability exposures such as medical malpractice, products liability, and automobile collision and liability, insurance is becoming less and less able to provide the necessary protection. This undesirable situation is developing because losses in these areas are increasing in both frequency and severity, thereby pushing premiums beyond the levels that many insured persons are willing or able to pay. In fact, over the last several years property and liability insurers have lost billions of dollars through their underwriting activities. It is important to recognize that unless these losses are reduced to tolerable levels, fewer and fewer types of risks will meet the criteria of an insurable exposure. While some people believe that letting the state or federal government establish insurance operations for many types of property and liability coverages will solve the problem, such optimism is unjustified. Unless losses are reduced, premiums are going to increase regardless of whether private companies or the government offer these insurance coverages.

Principle of Indemnity

The *principle of indemnity* states that insureds may not be compensated by their insurance company in an amount exceeding the amount of economic loss. Most property and liability insurance contracts are based upon this principle. You might recall from Chapters 13 and 14 that in contrast, life and health insurance contracts are not contracts of indemnity. Four important concepts that are related to the principle of indemnity are implemented in property and liability insurance: (1) insurable interest, (2) actual cash value, (3) subrogation, and (4) other insurance.

Insurable Interest The concept of insurable interest is based on the notion that individuals who insure property must stand to lose something

Lloyd's of London—The Insurers Who Break the Rules

The concept of insurable risks and the Law of Large Numbers are rules to live by for most insurance companies. The typical insurance company requires that the likelihood of loss must be predictable, that the risk be spread over a wide geographic area, and that standards of acceptable risk be established. But Lloyd's of London is hardly a typical insurance company.

Lloyd's is actually not an insurance company at all, but an *association* of individual insurers who agree to insure risks that are not acceptable to more conventional insurance companies. The association has a colorful history that spans nearly three centuries since it began operations in a London coffeehouse in 1689.

Although the main business of Lloyd's is marine insurance, it is best known throughout the world for providing insurance against extremely unusual risk. Lloyd's has insured such body parts as Jimmy Durante's nose and Marlene Dietrich's legs. A Fat Lady in a circus once discovered she was losing weight and took out a policy to protect her career against such a disaster.

Most of the major bridges in the United States are insured by Lloyd's. Since the bridges are usually built by the issuance of bonds, the insurance covers not only damages to the bridges but also losses in revenue that the tolls would have provided.[a]

Lloyd's has paid off on numerous claims involving extremely large sums of money. When the *Titanic* sank in 1912, Lloyd's lost $3 million (a huge loss for that time). Hurricane Betsy resulted in a $100 million loss in 1965.[b]

[a]Denzil Stuart, "Report from London: Lloyd's Nonmarine Risks," *Best's Review*, November 1969, p. 48.
[b]"Lloyd's of London Wants $," *Forbes*, September 15, 1974, p. 77.

Source: Louis E. Boone and David L. Kurtz, *Contemporary Business* (Hinsdale, Ill.: The Dryden Press, 1976), p. 404. Reprinted by permission.

if that property is subject to loss, and they cannot receive more than the extent of their interest in the property in compensation for their loss. For example, assume that John and William own equal shares in an apartment house that has a market value of $100,000 (excluding the value of the land, which is uninsurable). If the building is completely destroyed, the maximum the insurer would pay to either partner is $50,000 since that is the extent of either's economic interest in the property. If these partners sell the property but forget to cancel their insurance policy and the property is destroyed by fire, the insurance company will pay them nothing because they lost nothing. However, ownership is not the only way someone can develop an insurable interest in a property. For instance, an owner of a dry cleaning operation has a legal obligation to return the clothing received in the course of business. If a fire damages the clothing, the owner may be liable to the customers for the value of the damaged clothing. Thus the proprietor—though not the owner of the clothing—does have a legal obligation to maintain it in good condition and may insure it in order to be protected in the event it is damaged.

Actual Cash Value The principle of indemnity also limits the amount an insured may collect to the actual cash value of the property. *Actual cash value* is defined most commonly as replacement cost less depreciation, although some insurers do guarantee replacement cost without taking depreciation into account. Since depreciation is usually deducted in order to obtain the actual cash value, only this case is considered here. If an insured property is damaged, the insurer is obligated to pay no more than what the property would cost new today (its replacement cost) less accrued depreciation. For example, assume that in a fire a homeowner lost two rooms of furniture which have a replacement cost of $5,000. The average age of the furnishings was six years, and they were estimated to have a useful life of ten years. Therefore, at the time of loss the items were subject to total depreciation of 60 percent (6 years ÷ 10 years)—in this case, $3,000. Since the actual cash value is estimated at $2,000 ($5,000 replacement cost minus $3,000 depreciation), the maximum the insurer would have to pay is $2,000.

Subrogation After the insurance company pays a claim, its right of subrogation allows it to request reimbursement from the person who caused the loss or that person's insurance company. For example, assume that you are in an automobile accident in which the other party is responsible for damage to your car. You may collect from your insurer or the at-fault insurer, but not from both (at least not for the same loss). If you receive payment from your insurance company, you must subrogate (transfer) to it your right to sue the other person. To collect the full amount from both parties would leave you better off after the loss than before it. Such an action would represent a violation of the principle of indemnity.

Other Insurance Nearly all property insurance contracts have an "other insurance" clause, which also supports the concept of indemnity. This provision prohibits insured persons from insuring their property with two or more insurance companies and then collecting full reimbursement for a loss from all companies. The "other insurance" clause normally states that if a person has more than one insurance policy on a property, each company is liable only for a pro rata amount of the loss based upon its proportion of the total insurance covering the property. For example, assume that John and William in the example above purchased two policies of $100,000 each on their $100,000 building. If a total loss occurred, each company would pay 50 percent, because the ratio of the coverage purchased from each company to the total coverage on the property is one-half ($100,000/$200,000). Similarly, if each of three companies had issued a $100,000 policy, their individual shares would be 33$^1/_3$ percent ($100,000/$300,000). Without an "other insurance" provision, insured persons could use duplicate insurance policies to profit from their losses.

Coinsurance

Coinsurance is a provision quite commonly found in property insurance contracts. It requires policyholders to buy insurance in an amount equal to a specified percentage of the value of the improvements to their property. If insureds comply with this requirement, they will be reimbursed for covered losses dollar for dollar up to the amount of the policy limits. Otherwise, payment is based upon a specified percentage of loss. For example, assume that John and William's fire policy on their apartment building, which had a value of $100,000 excluding the land value, contained an 80 percent coinsurance clause. This means that the policy limits must equal or exceed 80 percent of the value of their property less the value of the land, which is excluded because it is considered uninsurable. Further assume that they had run short of money and decided to save by buying a single $60,000 policy instead of a minimum of $80,000 (80% × $100,000) as required by the coinsurance clause. If a loss of any amount occurred, the company would be obligated to pay only 75 percent ($60,000 ÷ $80,000) of it up to the amount of the policy limit. Thus, on damages of $20,000, the insurer would pay only $15,000 (75% × $20,000). Clearly, it is important to closely evaluate the coinsurance clause of any property insurance policy you may buy in order to make sure that you will not have an unexpected additional burden in the event a loss does take place.

Although homeowner's insurance is often thought of as one type of insurance policy, four different forms (HO-1, HO-2, HO-3, and HO-5) are available to homeowners, and two forms (HO-4 and HO-6) are designed to meet the needs of renters and owners of condominiums (see Table 15-1). It is interesting to note that an HO-4 policy offers essentially the same protection as an HO-3 policy, except that coverage does not apply to the rented dwelling unit. In other words, a tenant who purchases an HO-4 insurance contract has the same protection as a homeowner who buys an HO-3 policy. The only exception is that the tenant does not need coverage on the real property because he or she does not own it and therefore has no insurable interest in it. All HO forms are alike in that each is divided into two sections. Section I applies to the home, its contents, and accompanying structures, and Section II is comprehensive coverage for personal liability and for medical payments and property damage incurred by persons other than the insureds. They differ, though, in that the scope of coverage under Section I is smallest with an HO-1 policy and greatest with an HO-5 policy. The coverage in Section II is the same for all forms. In the following paragraphs the important features of homeowner's forms HO-2 and HO-3 are emphasized because these are the policies that are sold most frequently. The coverage offered under these forms is basically the same; the differences lie only in the number of perils against which protection applies.

Homeowner's Insurance

Perils Covered

As mentioned previously, a peril is defined as a cause of loss. Some property and liability insurance agreements called comprehensive policies cover all perils except those that are specifically excluded in the policy, while others name the perils covered individually. The latter type is the more common variety and is called a *named peril policy.*

Section I Perils The perils against which the home and its contents are insured is shown in Table 15-1. The coverage on household belongings is the same for the HO-2 and HO-3 forms, but coverage on the house is comprehensive under HO-3 and named-peril in HO-2. Thus, an HO-3 offers the same coverage as an HO-2 for contents, but the same as an HO-5 for the house and other buildings. Whether homeowners should buy an HO-2 or an HO-3 form depends primarily on the amount they are willing to spend to secure additional protection. In some states, the premium differential is small and consequently an HO-3 policy is the better buy. In other states, though, the HO-2 form has a substantially lower premium. Also, the magnitude of the premium differential for the HO-2 and HO-3 policies can deviate materially among insurance compa-

Table 15-1 **Homeowner's Policies: Which Cover What?**

	House	Detached Garage or Workshop	House Contents and Unlisted Personal Property[b]
Basic Form HO-1	Damage by: fire; hail; lightning; windstorm; explosion; riots; aircraft; glass breakage; vandalism; smoke; vehicles (not your own); theft 100% of policy value	Same risks as at left 10% of policy value	Same risks as at left 50% of policy value
Broad Form HO-2	Same risks as HO-1 plus: collapse of building; weight of ice, snow and sleet; freezing; accidental damage to or from heating or plumbing systems; damage by electrical equipment; falling objects 100% of policy value	Same risks as at left 10% of policy value	Same risks as at left 50% of policy value
Special Form HO-3	All risks except: earthquake; landslide; mud flow; floods, tidal waters or waves; war; nuclear radiation; sewer backup and seepage 100% of policy value	Same risks as at left 10% of policy value	Same risks as list at left for HO-2 50% of policy value
Comprehensive Form HO-5	All risks except those specifically excluded under HO-3 100% of policy value	Same risks as at left	Same risks as list at left for HO-3 50% of policy value
Renters Policy HO-4	N.A.[a]	N.A.	Same risks as for HO-2 100% of policy value
Condominium Policy HO-6	N.A.	N.A.	Same risks as for HO-2 100% of policy value

[a]N.A.: not applicable.

[b]Not covered: animals, birds, or fish; cars, trucks, motorcycles, motor homes, and other licensed land vehicles; sound equipment permanently installed in a car, any recording equipment left in a car.

Note: Premiums vary, but homeowner's policies are fairly standard. These are Aetna Life & Casualty's for Paramus, N.J. HO-4 and 6 cover only personal belongings, since buildings are protected by the landlord's or condominium's policy. Fire department service charges are paid by people living outside fire department districts.

Source: "Shoring Up Your Homeowners Insurance," *Money*, May 1977, pp. 90–91. Reprinted courtesy of Aetna Life and Casualty Company.

Personal Property Off Premises	Temporary Living Expenses (in Percent of Policy Value)	Fire Department Service Charge	Personal Liability	Medical Payments per Person	Damage to Property of Others	Annual Premium on $50,000 House in Paramus, N.J. ($100 Deductible)
Same risks as at left 10% of policy value, but no less than $1,000	10%	$250 (no deductible)	$50,000	$500	$250	$144
Same risks as at left 10% of policy value, but no less than $1,000	20%	$250 (no deductible)	$50,000	$500	$250	$160
Same risks as list at left for HO-2 10% of policy value, but no less than $1,000	20%	$250 (no deductible)	$50,000	$500	$250	$169
Same risks as list at left 10% of policy value, but no less than $1,000	20%	$250 (no deductible)	$50,000	$500	$250	$258
Same risks as for HO-2 10% of policy value, but no less than $1,000	20%	N.A.	$50,000	$500	$250	Annual premium on $8,000 policy: $47
Same risks as for HO-2 10% of policy value, but no less than $1,000	40%	N.A.	$50,000	$500	$250	Annual premium on $8,000 policy: $47

nies. Because of its more limited coverage, the purchase of an HO-1 is recommended only for certain families; and, because an HO-5 usually costs more than most people are willing to pay, its popularity is also rather limited.

Section II Perils The peril insured against under Section II of the homeowner's contract is the negligence (alleged negligence) of an insured. As discussed earlier in this chapter, negligence is defined as failure to act in a reasonable manner. The coverage is called comprehensive personal liability coverage because it offers protection against nearly any source of liability (major exclusions are noted later) resulting from negligence. It does not insure against other perils for which one may become liable such as libel, slander, defamation of character, and contractual or intentional wrongdoings. For example, coverage would apply if you carelessly, but unintentionally, ran over someone with your car. However, if you purposely struck and injured another person, or attacked and harmed someone either orally or in writing, this liability coverage would not protect you from suits that might arise. As an additional feature of Section II, the insurer offers a limited amount of medical expense and property damage coverage to persons other than the homeowner's family in certain types of accidents involving insureds or their premises. The basic purpose of this coverage is to help homeowners meet their moral obligations and perhaps also to deter possible lawsuits.

Property Covered

The homeowner's policy offers property protection under Section I for the dwelling unit, accompanying structures, and the personal property of the homeowner and his or her family. In addition, coverage for certain types of losses also applies to the lawn, trees, plants, and shrubs. However, structures on the premises used for business purposes (except incidentally) are excluded from coverage, as are animals (pets or otherwise) and motorized vehicles not used in the maintenance of the premises. Of course, this means there is no coverage for motorcycles, autos, golf carts, or snowmobiles (an exception is small boats). Furthermore, business inventory (goods held by an insured who is a traveling salesperson or cosmetics and other goods held for sale) is not covered. Even though business inventory is excluded, business property (books, typewriters, working materials) is covered while it is on the insured premises.

As already noted, the homeowner's policy offers less protection than is desirable in many cases for such expensive items as jewelry, furs, cameras and photographic equipment, fine arts, antiques, and stamp or coin collections. To meet this need, insurers have developed *personal property floaters*, which provide additional coverage for the specific items named in them.

Types of Losses Covered

A person can suffer three different types of property-related losses when misfortune occurs: (1) the direct loss of property, (2) an indirect loss through the loss of use of damaged property, and (3) extra expenses that result from direct and indirect losses. The homeowner's insurance contract offers compensation for each of these types of losses.

Section I Coverage When a house is damaged by an insured peril, the company will pay a certain amount of living expenses that a family might incur while the home is being repaired. Also, in many instances, the insurer will pay for damages caused by perils other than those mentioned in the policy if a named peril is determined to have been the underlying cause of the loss. Assume, for instance, that lightning (a covered peril) strikes a house while a family is away and knocks out all the power, which causes the food in the freezer and refrigerator to spoil. The company will pay for the loss even though temperature change (the direct cause) is not covered directly in the policy.

Section II Coverage In addition to paying successfully pursued liability claims against an insured, the homeowner's policy includes coverage for: (1) the cost of defending the insured, (2) any reasonable expenses incurred by an insured in helping the company's defense, and (3) the payment of court costs. Since these three types of costs apply even in cases where the liability suit is without merit, coverage in these areas is an added benefit that can be of substantial value.

Persons Covered

The homeowner's policy covers the persons named in the policy and the members of their family who are residents of the household. A person can be a resident of the household even while temporarily living away from home. For example, college students who live at school part of the year and at home during vacations are normally regarded as residents. The homeowner's contract also extends limited coverage to guests of the insured for property losses that occur at the insured house, if the insured wants such coverage to apply. If the insured does not choose to file a claim for the guest's property loss, the guest will be reimbursed only if he or she can prove negligence on the part of the homeowner. If the home is financed, coverage for loss to the house will also apply to the mortgage lender, provided that the lender is named in the insurance policy.

Locations Covered

Although some insurance contracts (for example, automobile insurance contracts) have territorial exclusions, the homeowner's policy offers coverage worldwide. Consequently, an insured's personal property is covered regardless of whether it is loaned to the next door neighbor or is kept in a hotel room in Outer Mongolia. Coverage of property away from the insured premises is normally limited to 10 percent of the total amount of personal property coverage available. Coverage of property left at a second home such as a beach house or resort condominium is in effect only while the insured is actually residing there. Homeowners and their families have liability protection for their negligent acts wherever they occur. This liability protection does not include negligent acts involving motorized vehicles or arising in the course of employment or professional practice. It does, however, include golf carts when used for golfing purposes and recreational vehicles such as snowmobiles and minibikes when they are used on the insured premises.

Periods of Coverage

Most homeowner's policies are written for either a one year or a three year period. The advantage of the three year contract is that the annual premium is not increased during the policy period. All homeowner's contracts begin coverage at twelve o'clock noon, standard time, on the date of the policy and terminate at noon on the expiration date. In some states attempts are being made to change the inception of homeowner's policies to 12:01 A.M. of the date of issue.

Limitations on Payment

The insurable interest, actual cash value, subrogation, and "other insurance" features that restrict the amount paid under a property and liability insurance contract and thus enforce the indemnity principle have already been described. In addition to these items, replacement cost, policy limits, and deductibles can influence the amount an insurance company will pay for a loss.

Replacement Cost The amount necessary to repair, rebuild, or replace an asset at today's prices is the *replacement cost*. The homeowner's coverage on a house and the accompanying structures is based upon replacement cost coverage. This means that the insurer will repair or replace damaged items without taking any deduction for depreciation. The homeowner's contract is one of the few types of property insurance that makes available replacement cost coverage in lieu of actual cash value. In order for homeowners to be eligible for reimbursement on a replacement cost basis, they must keep their home insured for at least 80 percent of the amount it would cost to build it today exclusive of the value of the land. In periods of inflation, homeowners must either increase their coverage limits on the dwelling unit every few years or take a chance of falling below the 80 percent requirement. If the 80 percent condition is not met, the maximum compensation allowable for total or partial losses will be determined on an actual cash value basis. In some cases where the amount of insurance on the house is much less than the required 80 percent, the insuring company will pay even less than the actual cash value of the loss. This can happen because an insurer is not required to pay a higher percentage of the replacement cost amount than the total insurance on the building bears to 80 percent of its replacement cost. For example, if a person has only 50 percent of the replacement value insured, the insurer can limit the payment to $5/8$ (50% ÷ 80%) of the replacement cost even if the actual cash value of the loss is greater than this amount.

Neither actual cash value nor replacement cost has any necessary

Estimating the Replacement Cost of a Home

Using the multipliers provided in the table below, you can estimate how much it would cost to replace your house if it were destroyed by some disaster. For example, suppose your frame house, which cost $25,000 to build in 1955, is leveled by a tornado. To find its replacement cost, multiply $25,000 by 2.664, the 1955 multiplier for frame houses; it will cost you approximately $66,600 to have your home rebuilt. Note that these multipliers are calculated at the end of the year and take into account only the cost of building the house, not the land on which it is built.

Year Home Was Built	Type of Construction	
	Frame	Masonry
1976	1.000	1.000
1975	1.062	1.051
1974	1.139	1.127
1973	1.222	1.254
1972	1.331	1.361
1971	1.438	1.465
1970	1.584	1.600
1969	1.686	1.723
1968	1.793	1.844
1967	1.946	1.969
1966	2.039	2.053
1965	2.114	2.120
1960	2.376	2.385
1955	2.664	2.714
1950	3.073	3.166

Source: "What It Would Cost to Replace Your Home." Reprinted from *U.S. News & World Report*, 21 February 1977, p. 78. Copyright 1977 U.S. News & World Report, Inc.

relationship to the market value of a home. Because replacement cost and actual cash value relate only to the physical structure and do not consider the influence of location, as does market value, a home's market value can be in excess of its replacement cost or below its actual cash value. Also, even though a home is in an excellent state of repair, its market value may be lessened because of functional obsolescence within the structure.

Although coverage on the house is most often on a replacement cost basis, coverage on the contents is available from most insurers only on an actual cash value basis. Therefore, depreciation is taken into account in calculating the amount of any payments made for losses to furniture, clothing, and other belongings. The depreciation amount is subtracted from the current replacement cost of the items—not from what may have been paid for the property several years ago. And thus it is possible to collect more in insurance than the property's original price if the rate of inflation has exceeded the rate of depreciation.

Policy Limits In Section I of the homeowner's policy, the amount of coverage on the dwelling unit (coverage A) establishes the amounts applicable to the accompanying structures (coverage B), the unscheduled personal property (coverage C), and the additional living expenses (coverage D). Generally, the limits under coverages B, C, and D are 10, 50, and 20 percent, respectively, of the amount of coverage under A. For example, if the house were insured for $30,000, the respective limits for coverages B, C, and D would be $3,000, $15,000, and $6,000 (10% × $30,000; 50% × $30,000; and 20% × $30,000, respectively). Each of these limits can be increased if it is insufficient to cover the exposure. Also, for a small reduction in premium, some companies permit a homeowner to reduce coverage on unscheduled personal property to 40 percent of the amount on the dwelling unit.

In Section II, the standard liability limit (coverage E) is $50,000, and the medical payments portion (coverage F) normally has a limit of $500 per person and $25,000 per accident. These split limits under medical payments mean that no individual who suffers injury will be paid more than $500 but that as many as fifty people could be paid this maximum amount for the same accident. The basic amount of coverage for damage to the property of others (coverage G) is $250. Although these limits are the ones most commonly sold, most homeowners need additional protection, especially liability coverage. In these days of high damage awards by juries, no less than a $100,000 liability limit seems adequate, and a greater amount is advisable for persons with higher incomes and net worths. The liability limit with most companies can be increased for only a nominal extra cost.

Some Recent Innovations in Homeowner's Insurance

The record low temperatures during the 1976-1977 winter caused a good deal of damage from fires, burst water pipes, fallen trees, and other such perils. Thousands of families filed claims with their insurance companies, trying to recover whatever they could. But to their dismay, many of them didn't have enough insurance or the right kind of coverage. Given below is a checklist showing six innovations in homeowner's insurance that you should know about when purchasing such insurance.

Replacement-cost endorsement A typical home-owners policy insures household items for original cost less depreciation. If a 5-year-old TV set that cost $500 is damaged or stolen, the owner might recover about $250. Some insurers now offer, for an additional premium, personal-property coverage that pays full replacement value.

Debris removal If a storm causes a tree to fall on your house, a home-owners policy generally will pay for damage done to the dwelling and for getting rid of the tree. But if a tree falls without hitting the house, the policy will not cover the cost of removal. A debris-removal endorsement on the policy will pay this expense.

Mobile homes Special policies can protect these dwelling units and their contents from damage or theft and provide liability coverage in case someone is injured on the premises.

Condominiums Most companies offer policies that cover the personal property in a condominium unit. Agents recommend that condominium owners carry extra liability protection over and above what is included in the building's master policy.

Renters' policy Tenants usually have a substantial investment in personal property such as clothes, furnishings, bookshelves, room dividers. A special "tenants' form" policy insures such items against loss from fire, windstorm, theft, other perils.

Broadened coverage Many policies now include provisions such as these at no extra cost: reimbursement up to $500 for illegal use of credit cards; insurance against theft of personal items kept by children at school; coverage on tape decks and other sound equipment kept in a car but not permanently installed; increased indemnity for storm losses to trees, lawns and shrubs, from $250 to a new level of $500.

Source: "A Checklist for Buyers: Six Innovations in Home-Owners Insurance." Reprinted from *U.S. News & World Report,* 21 February 1977, p. 77. Copyright 1977 U.S. News & World Report, Inc.

Deductibles Each of the preceding limitations on recovery constrains the maximum amount payable under the policy. In contrast, deductibles place constraints on what a company must pay on small losses. Deductibles help reduce insurance premiums, because they do away with the frequent small loss claims that are proportionately more expensive to administer. The standard deductible in most states is $50 on the physical damage protection in Section I. However, deductible amounts of $100, $250, and $500 are available on an optional basis. The premium savings on policies with larger deductibles are often significant. For example, in some states an increase in the deductible from $50 to $250 results in an annual premium savings of $40 to $75 depending on the amount of coverage purchased. Homeowners should check with their insurance agents to see whether it is economically attractive to increase the deductible. Deductibles do not apply to the liability and medical payments coverage since insuring companies want to be notified of all claims, no matter how trivial. If companies did not adhere to this policy, it is possible that in some cases the insurer might be notified too late to properly investigate and prepare an adequate defense for a resulting lawsuit.

Automobile Insurance

Another asset that provides major exposure to loss for most families is the automobile. Both damage to this asset as well as negligence in its use can result in loss. As can be seen from Figure 15-2, motor vehicle accidents accounted for 46,000 deaths, 1,800,000 disabling injuries, and direct economic loss of more than $21 billion in 1975. In addition, indirect monetary losses to society result from police and legal costs, as well as from the lost productive capacity of capital and human resources. Fortunately, from the standpoint of the individual, the major portion of these costs can be insured against through life, health, and automobile insurance. Life and health insurance were discussed in Chapters 13 and 14, respectively, and the major features of automobile insurance will be discussed in the next several sections of this chapter. Because the frequency and severity of losses resulting from automobile accidents have been well publicized, all state governments have enacted legislation which relates to automobile insurance. Some of the basic types of statutes are discussed later in the chapter.

Coverages of the Family Auto Policy

The major coverages available under the family auto policy include liability, uninsured motorists, medical payments, collision, and comprehensive. Nearly all policies issued contain provisions for liability, unin-

Figure 15-2 **Motor Vehicle Accident Data, 1975**

Deaths 46,000
Disabling Injuries 1,800,000
Costs.. $21.2 billion
Motor-Vehicle Mileage .... 1,332 billion
Death Rate per 100,000,000 Vehicle Miles 3.45
Registered Vehicles in the U.S.............................. 139,200,000
Licensed Drivers in the U.S. 129,100,000

Accident Totals	Number of Accidents	Drivers (Vehicles) Involved
Fatal	39,900	56,100
Disabling Injury	1,200,000	2,000,000
Property Damage and Nondisabling Injury	15,300,000	25,500,000
Total (Rounded)	16,500,000	27,500,000

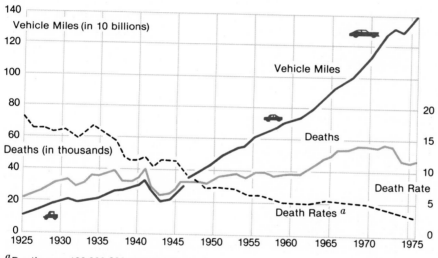

[a]Deaths per 100,000,000 vehicle miles.

——— Vehicle Miles

▬▬▬ Deaths

------ Death Rates

Source: Accident Facts, 1976 (Chicago: National Safety Council, 1976), p. 40. Reprinted courtesy of the National Safety Council.

sured motorists, and medical payments protection. However, many insureds choose not to purchase collision or comprehensive insurance.

Liability Policy Provisions Under the provisions of a typical automobile liability insurance policy, the insurer agrees: (1) to pay on the insured's behalf all sums for which the insured becomes legally obligated to pay because of accidental damages he or she has caused another, and (2) to defend the insured against another who is seeking compensation arising out of a covered occurrence. This provision for legal defense is quite important. It can mean a savings of thousands of dollars, for even a person who is not at fault in an automobile accident may be compelled to prove his or her innocence in court. Note, though, that liability insurance policies offer coverage for a defense only in civil cases. They do not provide for a defense against any criminal charges that may be brought against the insured as a result of an accident.

In addition to providing reimbursement for the damages of others and the costs of defense, the automobile liability insurance policy stipulates that certain supplemental payments may be made. Examples of supplemental payments include expenses incurred by the company in settling the claim, expenses incurred by an insured party at the time of the accident to render medical help to others, and all reasonable expenses other than loss of earnings incurred by the insured at the request of the insurance company (for instance, food and travel expenses).

Supplemental payments can also take the form of reimbursement for premiums up to $250 expended for appeal bond, bonds to release attachments of the insured's property, and bail bonds required of an insured as a result of an accident or traffic law violation involving an insured automobile. The amount of these supplemental payments is *not* restricted by the applicable policy limits. In other words, the insurance company does not reduce your policy limits by the amount it costs to protect you in these ways.

Policy Limits Typically, the automobile liability insurance policy provides for different policy limits depending on whether the damage is bodily injury or property damage. Policy limits to protect individuals against claims made for *bodily injury losses* are most frequently available in the following combinations: $5,000/$10,000; $10,000/$20,000; $25,000/$50,000; $30,000/$85,000; $50,000/$100,000; $100,000/$300,000; and $500,000/$1,000,000. (Note that some companies do not make available all of these various policy limits.) The first amount in each combination is a limit per individual, and the second amount is a limit per accident. For example, if you purchased the $50,000/$100,000 policy limits, the maximum amount any person negligently injured in an accident could receive from the insurance company would be $50,000. And the total amount that the insurer would pay to all injured victims in one accident normally would not exceed $100,000. Thus, if a jury awarded a claimant $80,000, the defendant whose insurance policy limits were $50,000/$100,000 could be required to pay $30,000 out of pocket ($80,000 award − $50,000 paid by insurance). For the defendant this could mean loss of home, cars, bank accounts, and other vital assets. In many states, if the value of these assets proves insufficient to satisfy a claim, the defendant's wages may be garnished (taken by the court and used to satisfy the outstanding debt).

The policy limits available to cover *property damage liability losses* are typically $5,000, $10,000, $25,000, and $50,000. In contrast to bodily injury liability insurance limits, property damage policy limits are stated as a per accident limit, without specifying any limits applicable on a per item or person basis. Often the combination bodily injury and property damage liability insurance policy limits are designated, for example, $10,000/$20,000/$5,000, where the first two amounts pertain to the available bodily injury coverage and the latter figure to the amount of property damage protection.

Single limit automobile liability insurance policies are available from some insurance companies. These policies specify a single maximum amount, say, for example, $300,000, per accident that can be paid to cover all losses incurred (bodily injury and property damage). The single limit liability insurance policy appears to make more sense than the so-called split limit coverages. Attempting to determine the total amount of damage one might cause appears to be a simpler task than determining internal per person limits, bodily injury limits, and property damage limits. However, single limit automobile liability insurance policies are not now widely available.

How to Cut the Cost of Insuring Your Car

From insurance authorities come these suggestions for holding down the expense of auto coverage—

• Put higher deductibles on your coverage for collision, fire and theft. A deductible of $200 instead of $100 will yield savings. If your car is old, you may want to drop collision or comprehensive coverage.

• Take advantage of safe-driver plans available in many States. They can save you up to 20 per cent on premiums.

• Check on other discounts for which you may qualify: good-student discounts, farmer discounts, reductions for owners of two or more cars, savings of 10 per cent on collision insurance for cars meeting federal bumper-impact standards.

• Shop around to see which companies serving your area offer the lowest premiums. You'll find it cheaper to pay premiums annually or semi-annually rather than monthly or quarterly.

Source: "How to Cut the Cost of Insuring Your Car." Reprinted from *U.S. News & World Report,* 23 February 1976, p. 47. Copyright 1976 U.S. News & World Report, Inc.

Persons Insured The automobile liability insurance policy extends protection to the named insured and residents of his or her household with respect to an owned automobile. In a majority of cases, an unmarried college student away from home would remain a resident of the household for automobile insurance purposes. Also protected are any other persons who use the automobile with the permission of the named insured as long as they abide by the scope of such permission. It is important to note here that the children of named insureds may not lend a parent's automobile or allow others to operate it unless the parent has authorized it. If such a loan were made without permission, liability insurance protection would not exist for the operator. Coverage also is afforded under automobile liability insurance to persons or organizations on whose behalf the automobile of the named insured is being driven. For example, if Marilyn Zorr were involved in an automobile accident while performing a service for the University of Wisconsin, her liability insurance would extend protection to the university.

In addition to offering liability protection to those operating the automobile of the named insured, automobile liability insurance extends coverage to the named insured while operating other nonowned automobiles and to his or her household relatives while they are operating any nonowned private passenger automobile or trailer. The important distinction here is between "any automobile" and a "private passenger automobile." The former has a much broader definition. Thus, for instance, a named insured is protected under his or her own policy while operating a rental truck, whereas other members of the household would not have similar coverage because the rental truck is not a private passenger automobile.

When a motorist who is involved in an automobile accident is covered under two or more liability insurance contracts, the coverage *on the automobile* is primary, and the other coverages are secondary. For example, if Bob Burnkrant, a named insured in his own right, is involved in an accident while driving George Clark's automobile (with permission), a claim settlement in excess of the limits of George's liability policy would be necessary before Bob's liability insurance would apply. If George's insurance had lapsed, Bob's policy would then offer primary protection.

Uninsured Motorists Coverage Uninsured motorists coverage is available to meet the needs of "innocent" accident victims injured by uninsured or underinsured motorists. Legislation requiring that uninsured motorists insurance be included in each liability insurance policy issued has been enacted in every state but one. However, the insured is allowed to reject this coverage in most of these states. An injured person can collect for losses under this coverage if an accident is caused by a negligent uninsured, underinsured, or hit-and-run driver. In many

"I'm sure glad for no-fault insurance. . . .
That makes it just as much the tree's
fault as mine!"

Understand Your Auto Insurance Coverage

Source: GRIN AND BEAR IT by Lichty and Wagner. © Field Enterprises, Inc., 1977. Courtesy of Field Newspaper Syndicate.

states, a person may also collect if the negligent motorist's insurance company is insolvent. Under the uninsured motorists insurance, an insured is legally entitled to collect an amount equal to the sum that could have been collected from the negligent motorist's liability insurance, if such coverage had been available.

Three points must be proven in order to receive payment through uninsured motorists insurance: (1) another motorist was at fault; (2) this motorist has no available insurance; and (3) a specified amount of damages was incurred. In all but seven states property damage is not included in this coverage, which means that under uninsured motorists coverage, you generally can collect only for losses arising from bodily injury. If the motorist and insurer cannot agree on the terms of the settlement of a claim under uninsured motorists coverage, the motorist can seek an attorney to negotiate the claim. If a mutually agreeable settlement still cannot be worked out, the insured has the right to have the case arbitrated by a neutral third party. In most cases, the accident victim and the company are then bound to abide by the decision of the arbitrator.

Policy Limits Uninsured motorists insurance is available at minimum cost (usually less than $6 per year). It often is sold with basic limits of $10,000/$20,000, with additional amounts available for a small increase in the premium. It is a good idea to buy uninsured motorists insurance with at least the minimum limits available. The cost of this coverage is small relative to the amount of protection it provides.

Persons Insured In contrast to liability insurance coverage, distinction is not made between the uninsured motorists coverage applicable to named insureds and that applicable to resident relatives. The unnamed members of the household are protected if injured in the named insured's automobile, as pedestrians, or as passengers in the automobile of someone else.

Automobile Medical Payments Insurance Automobile medical payments insurance provides for payment to eligible insureds of an amount no greater than the policy limits for all reasonable and necessary medical expenses incurred within one year after an automobile accident. It provides for reimbursement even if other sources of recovery, such as accident or health insurance, also make payment. In addition, in most states the insurer reimburses the insured for medical payments even if the insured proves that another was negligent in an accident and receives compensation from that party's liability insurer. As with liability and uninsured motorists insurance, a person does not have to be occupying an automobile when the accidental injury occurs in order to be eligible for benefits. For example, eligible insureds are covered for injuries sustained in traffic accidents, as pedestrians, or in motorcycle mishaps. This insurance also pays on an excess basis. For instance, assume that you are a passenger in an automobile of a friend and suffer $8,000 in medical expenses as a result of an accident. You can collect under your friend's medical payments insurance up to his or her policy limits. And you can then collect (up to the amount of your policy limits) from your insurer the amount in excess of what the other medical payments provide. Of course, you can also collect from the liability insurance of another person involved in the accident if that person can be shown to be at fault.

Policy Limits Medical payments insurance usually is available with per person limits of $500, $1,000, $2,000, $3,000, and $5,000. Thus an insurer conceivably could pay $30,000 or more in medical payments benefits for one accident involving a named insured and five passengers. Most families are advised to buy the $5,000 limit because even if they have other adequate health insurance coverages available, they cannot be certain that their passengers are equally well protected. Having automobile medical payments insurance also reduces the probability that a passenger in your auto will sue you (in those states that permit it) and attempt to collect under your liability insurance coverage.

Persons Insured Coverage under an automobile medical payments insurance policy applies to a named insured and relatives while occupying either an owned or an unowned automobile (with permission) or if struck by an automobile or trailer of any type. Protection also is generally made available to any other person occupying the owned automobile or an unowned private passenger automobile that is being operated by a named insured or a covered relative.

Automobile Collision Insurance Collision insurance is a first part property damage coverage that pays for collision damage to an insured automobile regardless of fault. It is written without outside limits, and the amount of insurance payable is the actual cash value of the loss in excess of a stated deductible. Remember that actual cash value is defined as replacement cost less depreciation. Therefore, if a car is totally demolished, an insured will be paid an amount equal to its depreciated value minus any deductible. In contrast to automobile insurance for bodily injuries, an insured cannot receive duplicate payments from automobile property damage insurance. Lenders often require the purchase of collision insurance on cars they finance. In some cases—especially when the auto dealer is handling the financing—the lender will attempt to sell this insurance. Generally, it is a good idea to avoid the purchase of automobile insurance from car dealers or finance companies. These firms have been known to sell policies covering only collision and excluding other coverages at premiums that are nearly large enough to insure the entire Hertz fleet. This is not to imply that all insurance purchases through automobile dealers or finance companies are bad. Still, a full-time insurance agent is better trained to properly assess and meet a motorist's insurance needs.

Individuals who purchase collision insurance may select from one of several *deductible* amounts available—$50, $100, or $250 in most cases, and for the most expensive automobiles, $500 or more. Significant premium savings often can be obtained by increasing the amount of the deductible. For example, one large automobile insurance company reports that a $50 deductible on a relatively new car can be purchased for an annual premium of $87, whereas the $100 deductible costs $60. Thus, a motorist who buys the $50 deductible is paying $27 for this additional $50 worth of protection. Note, however, that regardless of the amount of the collision deductible chosen, complete reimbursement is provided if an insured has an accident involving another motorist who has insurance with the same company.

Automobile Comprehensive Insurance Comprehensive coverage protects against loss to an insured automobile caused by any peril (with few exceptions) other than collision. As one might imagine, this coverage offers broad protection and includes but is not limited to damage caused by fire, theft, glass breakage, falling objects, malicious mischief, vandalism, riot, and earthquake. It is important to recognize that, contrary to popular belief, theft of personal property kept or left in the insured automobile is *not* covered under the automobile insurance policy. (It may be covered under the off-premises coverage of the homeowner's policy if the auto was locked at the time the theft occurred.) The maximum compensation provided under the comprehensive coverage is the actual cash value of the automobile. In recent years this coverage ordinarily has been written with a $50 or $100 deductible.

Why Auto Insurance Premiums Are Rising

These three figures clearly depict that through 1976 auto insurance premiums rose more slowly than the costs of auto repairs and health care—costs insurers must pay in claim settlements. It is a fairly safe prediction that auto insurance premiums will continue to rise to keep up with this inflation.

Automobile Insurance Premiums

The starting point for determining the automobile insurance premium is the rating territory. Since accidents are more likely to occur in some geographic areas than others, higher rates are applied where the probability of claims is largest. Even an insured who is the pillar of the community and has a sterling driving record will be charged the rates in effect for the territory in which he or she resides regardless of how high they might be. Usually the location where an automobile is principally garaged determines the applicable rating territory. Herbert Dennenburg, former insurance commissioner of Pennsylvania, stated that he had found a magic formula for reducing auto insurance premiums: "I moved from Philadelphia (a high-rate area) to Harrisburg (a low-rate area)." The effect of geographic location on the auto insurance premiums charged by one insurer is shown for several selected cities in Table 15-2.

In addition to the rating territory, other factors also influence the automobile insurance rates and premiums. Among these are: (1) the amount of use the automobile receives, (2) the personal characteristics of the drivers, (3) the type of automobile, (4) the driving record of the insured, and (5) applicable discounts.

Use of the Automobile If an insured has a nonbusiness automobile that is not customarily driven to work—or if an automobile is driven less than

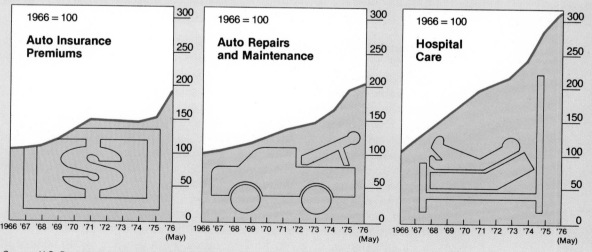

Source: U.S. Department of Labor. Reprinted from "Auto-Insurance Premiums Are Rising . . . But Not as Fast as Accident Costs," *U.S. News & World Report*, 19 July 1976, p. 69. Copyright 1976 U.S. News & World Report, Inc.

Table 15-2 **Annual Automobile Insurance Premiums
for Selected Cities**

Coverage	City and Effective Date				
	Columbia, South Carolina 6/9/76	Omaha, Nebraska 4/11/77	Boston, Massachusetts 1/1/77	Bismarck, North Dakota 6/28/76	Miami, Florida 10/1/76
Collision $100 Deductible	$ 92	$ 72	$ 620	$ 63	$ 87
Bodily Injury Liability (BI) $100,000/$300,000	126	106	117	46	425
Property Damage Liability (PD) $50,000	Included with BI	Included with BI	87	Included with BI	Included with BI
Comprehensive $100 Deductible	25	34	591	34	26
Total	$243	$212	$1,415	$143	$538

Note: All premium quotations are for a married male, age thirty-five, who has a clean driving record, drives to work less than ten miles one way in a six cylinder, automatic Ford Granada, and accumulates annual mileage of less than 7,500 miles. The same company in each city provided these rates.

Source: A major automobile insurance company.

three miles one way to work—it probably will be classified as a pleasure car. This is a favorable rating for the use classification. A motorist who drives more than three but less than ten miles to work will pay a slightly higher premium. And if an auto is driven more than ten miles each way to work, an even higher premium is charged. Generally, higher premiums are charged for automobiles driven for business purposes than for those that qualify for other classifications.

Personal Characteristics of Drivers Such items as age, sex, and the marital status of insureds affect the premium that is assessed for automobile insurance. As many young people and their parents realize, the rates applicable to youthful motorists can be relatively high. Figure 15-3 shows how the rate structure for certain young persons compares to the *base auto rate*. Generally, unmarried females age twenty-four or less and unmarried males age twenty-nine or less are placed in higher rate categories than individuals who are older. Married males under age twenty-five also fall into a relatively high rate category. Females above age twenty-four and married females of any age are exempt from the youthful operator classification and correspondingly need not pay the higher premiums. Insurance companies believe that such premium differentials based upon age are justified because of the great number of accidents that involve youthful operators. For example, as can be seen in Table 15-3, drivers under age thirty comprised only 33.9 percent of the motoring population but were involved in 51.1 percent of all auto

Figure 15-3 **Auto Insurance Rate Comparisons for Youthful Motorists**

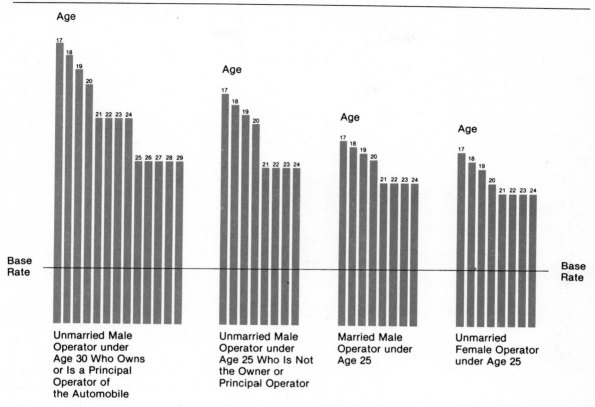

Note: The base rate includes no surcharges or discounts. It represents the auto insurance premium charged persons over thirty years old or married who drive a non–high-performance automobile for ordinary (nonbusiness) use and have clean driving records.

Source: Reprinted by permission from *A Family Guide to Property and Liability Insurance* (New York: Insurance Information Institute, 1976).

accidents and 50.0 percent of those accidents in which a fatality occurred.

Type of Automobile Automobiles may be classified as standard performance, intermediate performance, high performance, sports, and rear engine. As might be expected, if an automobile is not classified as standard performance, higher rates are usually charged. Autos that have high horsepower-to-weight ratios and more than three forward gears on the floor frequently are classified in higher rate categories.

Table 15-3 **Accidents by Age of Driver, 1976**

Age Group	Number of Drivers	Percent of Total	Drivers in All Accidents	Percent of Total	Drivers in Fatal Accidents	Percent of Total
Under 20	13,600,000	10.2	5,100,000	18.0	9,800	16.6
20–24	15,700,000	11.7	5,600,000	19.7	12,300	20.9
25–29	16,100,000	12.0	3,800,000	13.4	7,400	12.5
30–34	14,300,000	10.7	3,000,000	10.6	6,300	10.7
35–39	12,000,000	9.0	2,000,000	7.0	3,900	6.6
40–44	11,300,000	8.4	1,700,000	6.0	3,900	6.6
45–49	11,800,000	8.8	1,700,000	6.0	3,500	5.9
50–54	11,200,000	8.4	1,400,000	4.9	2,800	4.8
55–59	9,000,000	6.7	1,300,000	4.6	2,400	4.1
60–64	6,800,000	5.1	1,000,000	3.5	2,100	3.5
65–69	5,700,000	4.3	900,000	3.2	1,600	2.7
70–74	3,700,000	2.8	300,000	1.0	1,200	2.0
75 or Over	2,600,000	1.9	600,000	2.1	1,800	3.1
Total	133,800,000	100.0	28,400,000	100.0	59,000	100.0

Source: Reprinted by permission from *Insurance Facts, 1977* (New York: Insurance Information Institute, 1977).

Driving Record The driving records of insureds and those that live with them play an important part in the determination of premiums. Both traffic violation convictions and traffic accidents are normally considered in assessing driving records. The more severe types of traffic convictions are for driving under the influence of alcohol or drugs, leaving the scene of an accident without properly reporting it, homicide or assault arising out of the operation of a motor vehicle, and driving while having a revoked or suspended driver's license. In addition, but on a less severe basis, any conviction for a traffic violation that results in the accumulation of points under a state point system may result in higher insurance premiums. Included in this category are such violations as speeding, running a red light, failure to yield the right-of-way, and illegal passing. Typically, points under a state system are assigned only for moving traffic violations. Therefore, convictions for offenses such as parking violations, improper registration, lack of an operator's license, and lack of a valid safety sticker usually do not result in increased insurance premiums. In a number of states, a *premium surcharge* is made for traffic offenses. A surcharge schedule is shown in Table 15-4. Sometimes traffic violations do not directly enter into the premium computations but influence instead whether a motorist will be offered a regular policy or placed in an *assigned risk plan*. These plans have been organized in many states to provide automobile insurance to drivers who are refused coverage when they have sought it in a normal manner. Motorists who are placed in an assigned risk plan generally pay higher premiums.

Table 15-4 **Premium Surcharge Schedule for Traffic Offenses**

Offense	Surcharge
Driving under the influence where injury or property damage (over $200) results	$275
Hit and run	$275
Homicide or assault with auto	$275
Driving under the influence (no accident)	$170
Reckless driving where injury or property damage (over $200) results	$170
Racing on public highways	$170
Failure to stop for law enforcement officers when signaled	$170
Operating with suspended license or registration (including automatic suspension for lack of insurance)	$125
Operating motor vehicle without owner's permission	$125
Loaning driver's license to another	$125
False certification of insurance when applying for license or registration	$125
Reckless driving (no accident)	$ 60
Permitting unlicensed person to drive	$ 60
Each chargeable accident, over one (except as listed above)	$ 40
Each conviction over one for moving violations not listed	$ 40
One conviction, at any speed	No penalty
Two convictions, 10 mph under limit, or one conviction, 10 mph over limit, and one conviction, 10 mph under limit	Loss of safe driver discount only
Two convictions, 10 mph over limit	Loss of safe driver discount plus $40
Each conviction, less than 10 mph over limit, in addition to two convictions at any speed	Loss of safe driver discount plus $40
Each conviction, over two, 10 mph over limit	Loss of safe driver discount plus $60
Each conviction, any speed, when injury or property damage over $200 results	Loss of safe driver discount plus $60

Violations and accidents for the various drivers in a household will not be accumulated. If there are three drivers in a household, and each has only one minor traffic violation or chargeable accident, there is no surcharge.

But: if each of the three drivers has two chargeable violations or accidents, the surcharge is $120 ($40 + $40 + $40).

Source: Merit Plan, published by the South Carolina Insurance Department, Columbia, South Carolina.

Discounts Many automobile insurers give discounts, for one of a number of possible reasons, to individuals who purchase automobile insurance. Some give overall safe-driving discounts, and others give youthful operators lower rates if they have had driver's training. Youthful drivers may also receive discounts for maintaining at least a B grade average or by being on the dean's list at their school. These discounts apply to both high school students and college students. Nearly all insurance companies provide discounts to families with two or more automobiles if each of them is insured by the same company. Some also offer discounts to owners of compact automobiles. Several companies specialize in insuring certain portions of the general population. For example, a number of insurers accept only persons who are educators or executives, and others accept only government employees. While not offering discounts in a normal sense, these companies frequently do have lower premiums because, through more selective underwriting, they are able to reduce losses and operating expenses. It is also possible to secure lower premiums by purchasing automobile insurance from insurers that mass market through groups such as labor unions, credit unions, and employer plans.

Claim Settlement Process

When an automobile accident occurs, various steps should be taken to initiate the claim settlement process. After the claim is properly reported and filed, an insurance adjuster will attempt to settle the claim.

Initial Steps After an accident, the names and addresses of all witnesses, drivers, occupants, and injured parties, along with the license numbers of the automobiles involved, should be recorded. Law enforcement officers as well as your insurance agent or another authorized representative of your insurance company should be immediately notified of the accident. You should never admit liability at the scene of an accident or discuss it with anyone other than the police and the representative of your insurer. Remember, prior to determining who, if anyone, is legally liable for an accident, the requisites of liability must be established. Also, the duties of the police are to assess the probability of a law violation and maintain order at the scene of an accident—not to make judgments with respect to liability.

Adjustment Process Often, insurance agents will settle small local claims. In accidents of greater magnitude, the company will designate someone whose specific job is claims adjusting. This person may be an employee of the insurance company or an employee of an independent adjusting company. In either instance, the adjuster will be working on behalf of the insurance company, not for the insured. If an insured believes that the insurance company is not fulfilling its contractual obligation, he or she can hire an attorney or a public claims adjuster to negotiate the claim. As was indicated above, you can collect the actual cash value of your loss and your medical expenses under the collision, comprehensive, or medical payments coverage of your policy. Of course, the amounts paid are subject to the applicable deductibles and policy limits. However, if you are eligible to collect under the liability section of someone else's policy, you are entitled to receive reimbursement for all economic losses such as medical expenses, property damage, lost income, rental automobile charges, and any other reasonable expenses that were incurred because of the accident. In cases of bodily injury, benefit payments for general damages may also be required. *General damages* include compensation for such items as pain and suffering, inconvenience, and loss of a companion or partner.

The Government and Automobile Insurance

The annual losses from automobile accidents in the United States run into billions of dollars. Because of the increasing losses, most state governments have taken steps to encourage (and in many cases require) motorists to buy automobile liability insurance. These actions have primarily been in the form of financial responsibility laws and assigned risk plans. A summary of the liability insurance requirements in each of the fifty states is given in Table 15-5. Now, though, many states are forcing insurance companies to develop policies that conform with no-fault insurance statutes. And, indeed, federal legislation with respect to financial responsibility as well as no-fault insurance may soon be forthcoming.

Financial Responsibility Laws As their name implies, financial responsibility laws attempt to force motorists to be financially responsible for the damages they become legally obligated to pay as a result of automobile accidents. Two basic types of laws impelling motorists to assume financial responsibility have been enacted by the various states. The first variety is one in which all automobile owners in a given state are required to show evidence that they have liability insurance coverage prior to obtaining registration for their motor vehicles. Until 1971, only three states had these compulsory liability insurance requirements. However, approximately 50 percent of the states now require proof of insurance before registration.

In the second type of financial responsibility legislation, motorists do not have to show financial responsibility until after they are involved in an accident. If they then fail to demonstrate compliance with the law, their registration and/or driver's license is suspended. This latter type of law has been criticized on the basis that it allows negligent motorists to have one "free" accident. The problem with this arrangement is that even though the motorists who are not financially responsible lose their driving privileges, the losses to their victims may remain uncompensated.

Table 15-5 **U.S. Automobile Financial Responsibility Laws**

State	Liability Limits[a]	State	Liability Limits[a]
Alabama	10/20/5	Montana	25/50/5
Alaska	25/50/10	Nebraska	15/30/5
Arizona	15/30/10	Nevada	15/30/5
Arkansas	10/20/5	New Hampshire	20/40/10
California	15/30/5	New Jersey	15/30/5
Colorado	15/30/5	New Mexico	15/30/5
Connecticut	20/40/5	New York	10/20/5
Delaware	10/20/5	North Carolina	15/30/5
District of Columbia	10/20/5	North Dakota	10/20/5
Florida	10/20/5	Ohio	12.5/25/7.5
Georgia	10/20/5	Oklahoma	5/10/5
Hawaii	25/unlimited/10	Oregon	15/30/5
Idaho	10/20/5	Pennsylvania	15/30/5
Illinois	10/20/5	Rhode Island	25/50/10
Indiana	15/30/10	South Carolina	15/30/5
Iowa	10/20/5	South Dakota	15/30/5
Kansas	15/30/5	Tennessee	10/20/5
Kentucky	10/20/5	Texas	10/20/5
Louisiana	5/10/1	Utah	15/30/5[b]
Maine	20/40/10	Vermont	10/20/5
Maryland	20/40/5	Virginia	25/50/5
Massachusetts	5/10/5	Washington	15/30/5
Michigan	20/40/10	West Virginia	10/20/5
Minnesota	25/50/10	Wisconsin	15/30/5
Mississippi	10/20/5	Wyoming	10/20/5
Missouri	10/20/2		

[a]The first two figures refer to bodily injury liability limits and the third figure to property damage liability. For example, 10/20/5 means coverage up to $20,000 for all persons injured in an accident, subject to a limit of $10,000 for one individual; and $5,000 coverage for property damage.
[b]May be $25,000 single limit.

Source: Reprinted by permission of the American Insurance Association. Appeared in *Analysis of Automobile No-Fault Statutes* (New York: General Adjustment Bureau, February 1976).

No-Fault Statutes The concept of no-fault auto insurance is based upon the belief that the liability system should be discarded in favor of a system that reimburses without regard to negligence. No-fault insurance is designed to relieve the financial suffering of persons injured on the road. The principle is that "my insurance policy should pay the cost of my injuries, and your insurance policy should pay the cost of yours"— regardless of who is at fault in an accident.

Under no-fault statutes the driver, passengers, and injured pedestrians are reimbursed by the insurer of the car for any personal injury; the insurer thus does not have to provide coverage for claims made for losses caused others. Each insured party is compensated by his or her own company, regardless of which party is at fault. It is important to recognize that no-fault automobile insurance does not apply to property damage.

Since the middle 1960s, numerous advocates of reform have lobbied for no-fault auto insurance, alleging that liability insurance does a poor job of compensating victims of automobile accidents. These reformers believe that "too many of the injured receive too little compensation too slowly and too expensively." A typical criticism is as follows: The liability system that does not compensate you adequately and promptly when you find yourself compelled to make use of it is not reliable. Unfortunately, the critics of the present system have lost sight of the fact that liability insurance was never designed or intended to serve as the primary system for the compensation of the injured. Its sole purpose is to protect the assets of the insured, not to pay losses per se. This is the same concept behind all liability insurance.

The coverages of collision, comprehensive, and medical payments insurance, which were discussed earlier, are already on a "no-fault" basis. In addition, families can and should purchase widely available life, health, and disability income protection, which will protect them not only for losses resulting from auto accidents but also for nearly all other types of losses resulting from accident or sickness. In fact, numerous proclamations that we must have no-fault auto insurance so that people can be compensated for their losses have probably had a harmful effect, since they have detracted from any public understanding of the need for total insurance programming. Although there is no reason to be more concerned about the person who is injured in an automobile accident than for the homeowner who sustains injury while repairing his or her house, the widespread publicity given to the no-fault issue suggests that such concern may exist. On the other hand, because many valid arguments have been put forth by proponents of no-fault insurance, it appears that it will be a number of years before this controversy is resolved.

Overall, most of the no-fault laws that have been passed accomplish neither of their stated objectives—elimination of damage liability and provision for adequate compensation for all accident victims. The no-fault concept originally gained its largest public support because its advocates promised that it would contribute to lower auto insurance premiums. As might be expected, based upon the laws that are now on the books, it appears that these goals have not been attained. As a matter of fact, auto insurance premium increases have occurred in nearly all states with such reform legislation. Of course, as a result of economic conditions, insurance costs have also gone up in states that have not yet enacted no-fault legislation.

A Boost for No-Fault Auto Insurance

"No-fault automobile insurance works." This conclusion, contained in a Government study on experience in 16 States, is expected to improve the prospects for a federal no-fault automobile-insurance law.

The study was issued by the Department of Transportation on June 17 [1977].

No-fault insurance laws enable insured motorists to collect on personal-injury claims no matter who is at fault in a multicar accident. That's a sharp departure from the time-honored adversary system for determining who is at fault and who must pay the damages.

The DOT study concluded that:

• Benefits are more adequate and equitable in the States that have adopted the new approach.

• Payments are more prompt.

• The cost efficiency of administering auto-insurance benefits has improved.

• The burden on the courts and lawyers has been reduced as litigation has declined.

"No-fault does not necessarily mean higher insurance premiums," the report says, disputing opponents who argue that in some no-fault States, premiums have risen sharply instead of falling as predicted.

Inflation blamed. The principal reason for the premium increases in most of these States, says DOT, is inflation.

"No-fault plans of sharply varying objectives and character are widely seen as successes," the report says. "No problem has arisen in the implementation of no-fault for which there does not appear to be a readily available and feasible solution, given the political will to make the necessary change."

DOT's conclusions promise to add fuel to the already heated congressional debate over a federal no-fault law. The proposed measure would set minimum standards that States would have to meet within four years. In any State that did not, a plan mandated by the Federal Government would go into effect.

Supporting the law are labor unions and consumer groups. Opposing are the American Bar Association and the American Trial Lawyers Association. Insurance firms are split on the issue.

Hearings on the legislation are to begin in late June before a Senate committee. A House committee already has held seven days of hearings, and plans to hold more in July.

Source: "Fresh Boost for No-Fault Auto Insurance." Reprinted from *U.S. News & World Report*, 27 June 1977, p. 70. Copyright 1977 by U.S. News & World Report, Inc.

Laws in Effect During the last few years, a number of states have modified their automobile insurance laws. These modifications can be separated into three major categories, as given in Table 15-6. The most popular modification has been to prohibit liability lawsuits up to some dollar amount of medical bills ($500 or $1,000) except by persons suffering "serious" bodily injury. What constitutes a serious injury is defined in each state statute. However, because of the liberal definitions applied and the relatively low dollar thresholds, the right to sue for damages has not been thwarted materially by states enacting such legislation. In a few other states, first-party (i.e., no-fault) and liability insurance are compulsory under the law, but there are no restrictions on lawsuits at any level. In the remaining states that have enacted legislation, neither liability insurance nor first-party benefits are required of motorists. However, insurers are compelled to make these coverages available along certain prescribed lines. In only a few states has the impact of these laws requiring no-fault protection (i.e., first-party benefits) been great enough to aid the very seriously injured accident victim. Typically, the legislated limits on these benefits range from $2,000 to $5,000. However, under the Hawaii, Michigan, and New Jersey laws, payments can total more than $25,000. From the above, it is clear that the amount of auto insurance protection motorists are required to have varies from state to state. Many insurance companies provide for automatic adjustments in their policy-

Table 15-6 Recent Modifications in State Auto Insurance Statutes

Compulsory First-Party and Liability Insurance: Some Restrictions on Lawsuits[a]

Colorado, April 1, 1974	Kentucky, July 1, 1975	New York, February 1, 1974
Connecticut, January 1, 1973	Massachusetts, January 1, 1971	North Dakota, January 1, 1976
Florida, January 1, 1972	Michigan, October 1, 1973	Pennsylvania, July 19, 1975
Georgia, March 1, 1975	Minnesota, January 1, 1975	Utah, January 1, 1974
Hawaii, September 1, 1974	Nevada, February 1, 1974	Puerto Rico, 1970
Kansas, January 1, 1974	New Jersey, January 1, 1973	

Compulsory First-Party and Liability Insurance: No Restrictions on Lawsuits

Delaware, January 1, 1972	Maryland, January 1, 1973	South Carolina, October 1, 1974

Insurance Not Compulsory: First-Party Benefits Optional, No Restrictions on Lawsuits

Arkansas, July 1, 1974	South Dakota, January 1, 1972	Virginia, January 1, 1972
New Hampshire, October 1, 1971	Texas, August 27, 1973	Wisconsin, May 18, 1972
Oregon, January 1, 1972[b]		

[a]The term *first-party* here refers to no-fault insurance.
[b]First-party coverages must be provided in liability insurance policies covering private passenger vehicles.

Source: Reprinted by permission from *Analysis of No-Fault Statutes* (New York: General Adjustment Bureau, February 1976).

holders' coverage for out-of-state travel. It is a good idea to find out if your policy includes this needed benefit.

Other Property and Liability Coverages

While the homeowner's and automobile insurance policies represent the basic property and liability protection needed by most families, other insurance contracts of this type may be appropriate for some persons. Among those to be discussed here are the umbrella personal liability policy, mobile home insurance, boat insurance, recreational vehicle insurance, auto repair insurance, earthquake insurance, flood insurance, professional liability insurance, and group plans.

Umbrella Personal Liability

Persons with relatively high levels of income and assets may find the umbrella personal liability policy useful. It provides excess liability coverage for both the homeowner's and automobile insurance, as well as coverage in some areas not provided for in either of these policies. These policies are often sold with limits of $1,000,000 or more. In addition, some also include excess coverage for a family's major medical insurance. Limits of $25,000 are common for this latter protection.

Mobile Home Insurance

Mobile homes are now selling at the rate of 300,000 to 500,000 units per year. Because of this popularity, insurers have developed special package insurance policies for mobile home owners in the same manner as they have for owners of typical single family residences. Coverage on mobile homes may be written to offer protection on a comprehensive basis against the same perils that are protected on an HO-2 form. In addition, personal liability and personal property coverage is included. However, even though the coverage offered for mobile home owners is similar to that available for more permanent structures, rates per $100 of protection are typically higher for mobile homes since mobile homes present a greater loss hazard to insurers. Total losses are much more common on mobile homes than they are on single family residences.

Boat Insurance

Most people underinsure their boats. This situation is partly due to the fact that homeowner's policies do offer some limited protection for boat owners, which misleads many into a false sense of security. Insurance protection for boats should consist of liability, physical damage, theft, and medical payments. However, only boats less than twenty-three feet (or some other stipulated maximum) in length or those that have motors with under twenty-five horsepower are typically afforded liability coverage under a homeowner's policy. The physical damage coverage is limited to only a few perils, and in no case will reimbursement exceed $500. In addition, no medical payment is provided to persons injured in boat accidents off the insured premises. Consequently, for all but small fishing or sail boats, the coverage of the homeowner's policy is insufficient. Fortunately, though, this problem is easily remedied either through a boat and motor endorsement of the homeowner's policy or through a specially designed package boat owner's policy. These policies or endorsements typically contain liability, medical payments, and physical damage coverage. The liability and medical payments protection is similar to that offered in an automobile policy.

The physical damage and theft coverage under boat policies can be either very limited or comprehensive, excluding only a few perils such as nuclear explosion, warfare, and government action. Perils commonly insured against are fire and lightning, collision, overturning of a transporting land conveyance, windstorm, and theft. Other contingencies that can also be covered include damage resulting from submersion, vandalism, motor falling overboard, and burglary from a closed and locked garage or bathhouse. Because the physical damage and theft provisions of boat policies are not highly standardized, you should not assume that coverage exists for any given type of loss. Make certain your insurance agent explains what coverage applies and what losses are not covered.

Recreational Vehicle Insurance

During the last ten years, the use of personally owned recreational vehicles has risen substantially. Although no consistent definition of the term *recreational vehicle* exists among all insurance companies, the following vehicles generally fall within this classification: all-terrain vehicles, antique automobiles, dune buggies, go-carts, mini-bikes, trail and motor cross motorcycles, camping vehicles (both motorized and trailer type), snowmobiles, and customized vans. Generally, complete coverage is available for these vehicles, including bodily injury, property damage, liability, physical damage, theft, and medical payments. However, you may have to shop around for the policy that best fits your needs since, because of their specialized nature, not all insurance companies write coverage for recreational vehicles. In addition, the specific types of losses for which payment will be made is also likely to be more restrictive than for, say, a family automobile policy. Rates will also vary substantially, depending on the age of the driver, how the vehicle is used, and the geographical location of the policy owner. In insuring your recreational vehicle, as well as your boat, you need to discuss in detail with a property insurance agent how your recreational vehicle can best be insured in your state, giving particular attention to who, where, and what are covered.

Auto Repair Insurance

Some automobile dealers are offering plans whereby a person buying an auto can pay an additional fee to warrant the repairs resulting from specified malfunctions that may arise with use of the automobile. These plans, however, do not represent insurance but rather a simple arrangement whereby a fee is paid in exchange for contracted services.

Earthquake Insurance

Although most people think of California when earthquakes are mentioned, areas in every other state are also subject to this type of loss. At the present time, very few homeowners avail themselves of this coverage even though the premiums are relatively inexpensive in most parts of the country. Surprisingly, perhaps, the vast majority of Californians were without earthquake coverage when the major San Fernando Valley quake occurred in 1971.

Flood Insurance

Prior to the late 1960s, flood was regarded by most private insurers as an uninsurable peril because the risk could not be spread among enough people who were not located in floodprone areas. But in 1969, the federal government established a subsidized flood insurance program through the U.S. Department of Housing and Urban Development in cooperation with private insurance agents, who can now sell this coverage. In addition, the flood insurance program is encouraging communities to initiate land use controls in order to reduce future flood losses. Like earthquake insurance, few persons who are eligible for flood insurance have bought the protection, even though it is sold at low rates since it is subsidized by the government.

Professional Liability Insurance

Lawsuits against medical doctors for malpractice have increased substantially in recent years. And in fact, liability claims against nearly all types of

Medical Malpractice Insurance Is a Necessity for Doctors
Source: Copyright, 1976, Universal Press Syndicate.

professionals, including lawyers, architects, professors, and engineers, are also rising rapidly. Professional liability insurance is available to these individuals, but because of the increasing claims, rates are becoming much higher, and stricter underwriting standards are being imposed by insurers.

Group Plans

As a benefit to members of some groups (labor unions, credit unions, fraternal organizations, and various other organizations), group property and liability plans are being introduced. These plans, though, are not really true group plans as are life and health insurance agreements. Instead, they are arrangements for mass marketing automobile and homeowner's policies. The policies are still individually sold and issued. The primary benefit of group plans is that the lower marketing expense of the insurance company is passed along to the group members in the form of lower premiums. Some groups also have instituted *group legal insurance,* which is misnamed because technically it is not insurance. It is simply a fee-for-services agreement that the group enters into with a given law firm on behalf of its members. These plans typically cover only routine legal matters such as divorce, writing of wills, small claims settlement, and landlord-tenant problems. In some cases, though, the group member is entitled to certain lower charges on other needed legal services obtained from the same law firm.

Buying Property and Liability Insurance

When buying property and liability insurance, it is best to follow the same general guidelines that apply to the purchase of any other type of insurance. Begin by developing an inventory of exposures to loss and arrange these exposures from highest priority to lowest priority. Those losses that lend themselves best to insurance protection are the ones that occur infrequently but have a potential for high severity—for example, liability arising out of a negligence claim or damages to a home and its contents. Of less importance, but nevertheless desirable, is insurance to cover exposures to loss which could be disruptive to the financial plans of a family but would not result in devastating financial consequences. Such risks include physical damage to automobiles, boats, and other personal property of moderate value. Lowest priority should be given to insuring exposures that can easily be covered by savings or from current income. Low-dollar deductibles, for instance, usually serve only to increase premiums, and personal property of minor value, such as an auto that is just a few thousand miles from the scrap yard, normally does not merit coverage. In addition to inventorying exposures and deciding on appropriate coverages, it is important to exercise care in selecting both the property insurance agent and insurer.

Property and Liability Insurance Agents

Most property insurance agents can be classified as either captive or independent. A *captive agent* is one who represents only one insurance company and is more or less an employee of that company. Allstate, State Farm, and Nationwide are major insurance companies that market through captive agents. *Independent agents* typically represent between two and twenty different property insurance companies. These agents may place your coverage with any of the companies with which they have an agency relationship as long as you meet the underwriting standards of that company. Names of companies which may be familiar to you that operate through independent agents include Travelers, Fireman's Fund, and Aetna. It is difficult to generalize with respect to the superiority of agents. In some cases, you might find that an independent agent will provide the best combination of low-cost insurance and good service, while in other cases the captive agent might prove the better choice. The only generalization that can be made is that it does pay to shop around because there are wide differences in premiums charged and services rendered.

Property insurance agents should be willing to take the time to go over your total property and liability insurance exposures with you. There is much more to the purchase of property insurance than simply signing a homeowner's and an automobile insurance contract. Decisions must be made about limits, deductibles, floater policies, perils to be covered, types of property and uses, as well as other items that have been discussed throughout this chapter. Only an agent willing to talk with clients about these factors can adequately serve their needs. In property insurance, agents who meet various experience and education requirements and pass a series of written examinations may qualify for the C.P.C.U. designation. This abbreviation stands for Certified Property and Casualty Underwriter. On the whole, agents who have been awarded the C.P.C.U. have demonstrated an above average knowledge of this form of insurance.

Property and Liability Insurance Companies

Although the selection of the agent is probably the most important step in the purchase of insurance, some questions should also be asked about the company. Included among these are its financial soundness, claims settlement practices, and the geographical extent of its operations (this could be important if you are involved in an accident 1,000 miles from home). The agent should be a good source of information about the technical aspects of a company's operations, whereas friends and acquaintances often can provide insight into its claims settlement policy.

Summary

The basic coverages of property and liability contracts extend protection to insureds against the loss of their real and personal property from numerous types of perils and offer financial security from lawsuits based upon negligence. In order for an exposure to loss to be insurable, the loss concerned must be: (1) fortuitous, (2) improbable but severe, and (3) a risk that a large segment of the population faces. The principle of indemnity states that people should not be allowed to profit from their insurance—they should not be paid an amount in excess of their losses. This principle is supported by the concepts of (1) insurable interest, (2) actual cash value, (3) subrogation, and (4) "other insurance." Coinsurance is the provision found in many property insurance contracts that requires an insured to buy policy limits in an amount equal to a specified percentage of the value of the property.

Homeowner's insurance contracts for owners of residences are divided into two major sections. Section I covers the dwelling unit, accompanying structures, and personal property of the insureds, while Section II pertains to comprehensive coverage for personal liability and medical payments and property damage incurred by others while on the insured premises. The tenant owner's insurance form also contains these same two sections except that no coverage extends to the dwelling unit and accompanying structures. The major difference among the various forms of homeowner's insurance contracts is in the number of perils insured against. Because specific limitations apply to certain types of property covered under a homeowner's policy, special attention should be given to the following items of property: expensive cameras, jewelry, furs, and coin and stamp collections; business inventories; cash and bullion; important papers such as deeds and manuscripts; and some boats and recreational vehicles. Homeowner's insurance provides for the payment of all losses except the house and garage on an actual cash value basis subject to applicable deductibles and policy limits. Losses to the house and garage are reimbursed on a replacement cost basis if sufficient amounts of coverage have been purchased.

The family automobile policy commonly contains the following coverages: collision, comprehensive, medical payments, uninsured motorists, and liability. Collision coverage pays for physical damage losses resulting from collision accidents, whereas comprehensive covers nearly any other type of damage a person's car might suffer. Medical payments reimburse the insured for medical expenses incurred in an automobile accident, and uninsured motorists coverage pays for medical expenses and general damage. However, to collect under the uninsured motorists provision, the insured must show that someone else was at fault in the accident and that the person has no applicable liability insurance. Liability insurance is used by motorists to protect their assets if they should be found liable for damages in an auto accident. Other important topics related to automobile insurance include automobile insurance premiums, the claims settlement process, and government actions.

In addition to the major forms of automobile and homeowner's insurance, a variety of other types of property and liability coverages are available, including umbrella personal liability coverage, mobile home insurance, boat insurance, recreational vehicle insurance, auto repair insurance, earthquake insurance, flood insurance, professional liability insurance, and group plans. Before purchasing property and liability coverages, people should first evaluate their exposures to loss and determine the coverages needed. Both the insurance agent(s) and the insurance company should be carefully selected in order to assure that good coverage is obtained at a reasonable price.

Key Terms		
actual cash value		assigned risk plan
adjuster		assumption of risk (defense)

base auto rate
C.P.C.U. (Certified Property and Casualty Underwriter)
captive agent
coinsurance
collision insurance (automobile)
comparative negligence statutes
comprehensive insurance (automobile)
contributory negligence (defense)
deductibles
discounts (premium)
financial responsibility laws
general damages
group insurance plans
group legal insurance
HO-1, HO-2, HO-3, HO-4, HO-5, HO-6
independent agents
insurable interest
liability exposures
liability insurance

medical payments insurance (automobile)
named peril policy
negligent action
no-fault
other insurance clause
peril
personal property floaters
principle of indemnity
professional liability insurance
property damage liability losses
property exposures
property insurance
property inventory
reasonable man doctrine
replacement cost
right of subrogation
Sections I and II (homeowner's policy)
single limit automobile liability
surcharge (premium)
umbrella personal liability
uninsured motorists coverage

Review Questions

1. Briefly explain the fundamental concepts related to property and liability insurance.

2. Explain the principle of indemnity. Are there any limits imposed on the amount an insured may collect under this principle?

3. Edwina Livingston's luxurious home in the suburb of Broken Arrow was gutted in a fire. Her living and dining room were completely destroyed, and the property damaged had a replacement price of $25,000. The average age of the property was five years, and its useful life was estimated to be fifteen years. What is the maximum amount the insurance company would pay Edwina?

4. Explain the right of subrogation. How does this feature help lower insurance costs?

5. Describe how the coinsurance feature works. Assume that Clayton Barrow had a property insurance policy of $200,000 on his Beverly Hills

home. Would a 90 percent coinsurance clause be better than an 80 percent clause in such a policy? Give reasons to support your answer.

6. What are the perils against which most properties are insured under a homeowner's policy?

7. What types of property are covered under a homeowner's policy? Are the following included in the coverage: (a) an African parrot, (b) a Honda motorbike, (c) Avon cosmetics for sale, and (d) Tupperware for home use?

8. Describe (a) types of losses, (b) persons, (c) locations, and (d) periods that are covered under a homeowner's policy.

9. Describe replacement cost coverage and compare this coverage to actual cash value. Which is preferable?

10. What are deductibles? Do they apply to liability and medical payments coverage?

11. Briefly explain the major coverages available under the family automobile policy. Which persons are insured under: (a) uninsured motorists coverage and (b) automobile medical payments insurance?

12. Explain the nature of (a) automobile collision insurance and (b) automobile comprehensive insurance.

13. Describe the important factors that influence the availability and cost of auto insurance.

14. Describe the steps that should be taken to settle a claim when an automobile accident occurs.

15. Define *no-fault auto insurance*, and discuss its pros and cons.

16. Briefly describe the following property and liability insurance coverages: (a) umbrella personal liability, (b) mobile home insurance, (c) earthquake insurance, (d) flood insurance, and (e) boat insurance.

17. What guidelines should be used to distinguish between high priority and low priority risk exposures when buying property and liability insurance?

18. Differentiate between captive and independent insurance agents. What characteristics should one look for when choosing both an insurance agent and an insurance company from which to buy property and/or liability insurance?

Case Problems

15-1 The Sidwells' Homeowner's Insurance Decision

Phil and Anita Sidwell, ages thirty and twenty-eight, respectively, were recently married in Chicago. Phil is an electrical engineer with Geophysical Century, an oil exploration company. Anita, who recently graduated from Northwestern University with a master's degree in special education, is currently seeking a job. After living in an apartment for six months, the Sidwells have negotiated the purchase of a new home in a rapidly growing Chicago suburb. The Republic Savings and Loan Association has approved their loan request for $45,000, which represents 90 percent of the $50,000 purchase price. Prior to closing the loan, the Sidwells must obtain homeowner's insurance for the home. The Sidwells currently have an HO-4 renter's insurance policy, which they purchased from Phil's tennis partner, Kelly Duvall—an agent with Kramer's Insurance Company. In order to learn about the types of available homeowner's insurance, Phil discussed their situation with Kelly. Kelly offered a variety of homeowner's policies for Phil's and Anita's consideration. He recommended that the Sidwells purchase an HO-5 policy since it would provide them with the most comprehensive coverage.

Questions

1. What forms of homeowner's insurance are available? Which forms should the Sidwells consider?

2. What are the perils against which the home and its contents should be insured?

3. Discuss the types of loss protection provided by the homeowner's policies under consideration.

4. What advice would you give the Sidwells regarding Kelly's suggestion? What coverage should they buy?

15-2 Auto Insurance for the Turners

Marjorie and Rodney Turner, of Phoenix, Arizona, are a couple in their late twenties. Rodney is a loan officer at the Frontier National Bank of Arizona, and Marjorie works as a receptionist in Dr. Helen Bernard's Dental Clinic. At present, the Turners own one car. They have decided to use Rodney's Christmas bonus to buy a second car. One Saturday afternoon in late December, they visited Chuck Thomas's Auto Mall, where they purchased a fully equipped new Chrysler Cordoba for $6,200. In order to obtain insurance on the car, Rodney called his agent, Jack Cunningham, who represents Farmers Insurance Company. He explained to Jack his auto insurance needs, and Jack said he would investigate the various options for him. Three days later, Rodney and Jack got together to look over the various alternative coverages. Jack offered a number of proposals, including various combinations of the following coverages: (a) basic automobile liability insurance, (b) uninsured motorists coverage, (c) automobile medical payments insurance, (d) automobile collision insurance, and (e) automobile comprehensive insurance.

Questions

1. Describe the key features of the insurance coverages given above.

2. Are there any limitations on these coverages? Explain.

3. Indicate the persons who would be protected under each of the coverages given above.

4. What kind of insurance coverages would you recommend the Turners purchase? Explain your recommendation.

Selected References

Bickelhaupt, David L. *General Insurance.* Homewood, Ill.: Richard D. Irwin, 1974.

Boroson, Warren. "Those Picky Car and Health Insurers." *Money,* April 1977, pp. 93–99.

"Changes in Auto Insurance That May Affect You." *Changing Times,* April 1977, pp. 37–38.

Denenberg, Herbert S.; Eilers, Robert D.; Melone, Joseph J.; and Zelten, Robert A. *Risk and Insurance.* 2d ed. Englewood Cliffs, N.J.: Prentice-Hall, 1974.

"Doctors Still Hunt for Malpractice Insurance." *Business Week,* 12 January 1976, pp. 60–64.

A Family Guide to Property and Liability Insurance. New York: Insurance Information Institute, 1973.

Greene, Mark R. *Risk and Insurance.* Cincinnati, Ohio: South-Western Publishing, 1973.

Harris, Marlys. "Shoring Up Your Homeowner's Insurance." *Money,* May 1977, pp. 90–94.

"How to Cut Your Insurance Costs and Still Be Safe." *Better Homes and Gardens,* April 1977, pp. 86 ff.

"Insurance to Cover the Lawyer's Bill." *Business Week,* 18 April 1977, pp. 46–47.

"Making Your Auto Insurance Pay Off." *Changing Times,* August 1975, pp. 13–16.

Mehr, Robert I., and Cammack, Emerson. *Principles of Insurance.* Homewood, Ill.: Richard D. Irwin, 1976.

O'Connell, Jeffrey. *Ending Insult to Injury: No-Fault Insurance for Products and Services.* Urbana, Ill.: University of Illinois, 1975.

Seixas, Suzanne. "Meeting Car-Crash Costs Head On." *Money,* May 1976, pp. 120–121.

"Take a Fresh Look at Your Home Insurance." *U.S. News & World Report*, 15 March 1976, pp. 47–49.

"Where No-Fault Auto Insurance Stands Today." *Changing Times*, November 1976, pp. 13–15.

"Who Will Pay That Auto Insurance Claim?" *Changing Times*, August 1977, pp. 29–30.

"Your Valuables: Do You Have Enough Insurance?" *Better Homes and Gardens*, September 1975, pp. 6 ff.

Part 6

Retirement and Estate Planning

Personal Balance Sheet

Assets	Liabilities and Net Worth
Financial Assets	Liabilities
Nonfinancial Assets	**Net Worth**

This part of the text is devoted to two topics that should be given major consideration in the course of preparing and implementing personal financial plans: retirement planning and estate planning. Because both these subjects are not of immediate concern to most younger persons, many have a tendency to ignore them until it is too late to receive or optimize benefits. The individual who understands the importance and principles of both retirement and estate planning will work to build and preserve net worth that can provide a source of retirement income as well as benefits for heirs. Chapter 16 addresses its attention to retirement planning—particularly social security, annuity, and pension programs—and describes the potential benefits and costs associated with a variety of retirement goals. Chapter 17 considers the preparation of wills, establishment of trusts, and avoidance of estate taxes as these topics relate to the overall goal of estate planning.

16
Retirement Planning: Social Security, Annuities, and Pensions

In order to provide an understanding of the basic concepts and procedures involved in retirement planning, this chapter considers the following:

1. The primary sources of retirement income, which include social security, annuities, and pensions.

2. How to set retirement goals, estimate retirement needs, and evaluate sources of retirement income.

3. The role of social security in retirement planning—specifically, coverages, benefits, and provisions for the receipt of benefits.

4. The basic principle underlying annuities, commonly used annuity classification schemes, sources and costs of annuities, and factors to consider when purchasing annuities.

5. The major types, features, and classifications of pension plans.

6. Other kinds of retirement programs, such as Keogh plans, individual retirement savings plans, thrift plans, tax-sheltered annuities, profit-sharing plans, nonqualified deferred compensation plans, and professional corporation plans.

A Preview of Chapter 16

Although you may die before reaching retirement age, it is far more likely that at some time in the future you will either be forced to retire or will voluntarily choose to do so. You may be quite young, perhaps not even employed full-time, and retirement may be of little importance to you now. Such an attitude is typical, but unless you prepare retirement plans early, the chance that you will be able to retire when and in the fashion you desire will be reduced. You therefore need to find answers to questions such as: "How do I develop retirement plans?" "What benefits does social security provide?" "What is an annuity, and how can I use it?" "How does a prospective or existing employer's pension plan stack up?" The ability to answer such questions should enhance your chances of meeting your most distant—and possibly most important—personal financial goals.

Just as families must protect against loss of income resulting from death or disability during the working career of the breadwinner, so must they prepare for the reduction in earnings that will occur at retirement. People who do not plan properly often have to significantly reduce their standard of living and associated quality of life in order to make ends meet upon their retirement. Just at the point in life when they have the free time to travel, pursue hobbies, and indulge themselves in their interests, they find themselves unable to afford these activities. In order to avoid this kind of situation, it is wise to prepare and begin to implement plans that will provide for adequate retirement income. Even if you expect to accumulate a large amount of assets, you need to develop plans that will guide you in selecting those that can be liquidated in a manner that best provides income needed for retirement. This chapter focuses on the identification of the financial factors that should be considered in planning for retirement. Due to the uniqueness and changing nature of individual retirement needs, detailed guidelines for use in developing retirement plans cannot be presented. The discussion here begins with an overview of the retirement planning process and is followed by an examination of the basic sources of retirement income, which include social security, annuities, and pension plans.

Overview of Retirement Planning

Very few people in their twenties or younger have sufficient information to develop a complete plan for retirement. Uncertainty about inflation, social security, family size, the type of pension to which they might be entitled, and the amount of assets they will have accumulated by the time they are ready to retire make accurate forecasting virtually impossible. However, planning for retirement income does not require a crystal ball. It needs only to be founded on what appear to be reasonable assumptions at a given point in time. As personal and economic conditions change, necessary modifications can be incorporated into the retirement plan.

Unfortunately, too many of our senior citizens either did not or could not plan realistically for retirement income. Their economic situation contributes to the incidence of poverty in this country, which is higher among the aged than in nearly any other segment in the population. As indicated in Table 16-1, the median income of heads of households age sixty-five or over is less than that for heads of households in all other age groups. In Table 16-2, the sources of income for families whose heads of household are age sixty-five and older are reported for groups above and below the poverty level in 1975. The most apparent distinction between the below poverty and above poverty groups at the time these data were recorded was that, in addition to social security, the above poverty level families had a much greater incidence of income from earnings and

Table 16-1 **Median Family Income by Age (1970 and 1974)**

Age of Head	1970		1974	
	Number (in Thousands)	Median Income	Number (in Thousands)	Median Income
Under 35	12,481	$ 9,660	14,052	$12,730
14–24	3,190	7,631	3,344	9,604
25–34	9,291	10,359	10,708	13,914
35–44	9,342	12,085	8,873	16,513
45–54	9,396	12,941	9,418	17,575
55–64	7,313	10,723	7,373	14,210
65 and Over	5,797	4,990	6,600	7,170
Total Population	44,327	$10,454	46,315	$13,765

Source: Adapted from U.S. Bureau of the Census, Current Population Reports, series P-23, no. 39, and series P-60, no. 101 (Washington, D.C.: U.S. Government Printing Office, 1970 and 1974). Appeared in U.S. Bureau of the Census, Statistical Abstract of the United States, 1976 (Washington, D.C.: U.S. Government Printing Office, 1976), Table 662, p. 411.

Table 16-2 **Percent of Families with Head of Household Over 65 Years Old Receiving Various Types of Income, 1975**

Type of Income	All Income Levels (8,155,000 Families)	Below Poverty Level (721,000 Families)	Above Poverty Level (7,434,000 Families)
Earnings	49.6%	27.9%	51.7%
Public Assistance Income	2.7	11.8	1.8
Social Security Income	91.0	85.6	91.6
Supplemental Security Income	8.4	32.7	6.0
Other Transfer Income	12.3	4.2	13.1
Other Unearned Income	73.2	25.5	77.8

Notes: (1) Total percentages exceed 100 percent since some families have more than one type of income specified. (2) Based on 1975 statistics the poverty level was approximately $5,000 for a family of four.

Source: U.S. Bureau of the Census, Statistical Abstract of the United States, 1976 (Washington, D.C.: U.S. Government Printing Office, 1976), p. 420.

unearned income such as pensions, annuities, dividends, rental income, and interest than the below poverty group. This fact serves to reinforce the need to plan for retirement income in excess of that available from social security.

The first step in the retirement planning process involves the formulation of goals or objectives. Once these have been established, it is necessary to develop specific plans aimed at attaining them. These plans

Should Mandatory Retirement Be Extended beyond Age Sixty-five?

The problems caused by mandatory retirement have begun attracting the attention of Social Security actuaries and administrators, congressmen and corporations, pensioners and planners. They are finding that the practice is becoming impossibly expensive for business and government, each of which is paying out heftier pensions for longer periods. It has spawned dissension in labor and discontent among taxpayers who must pay the ever-increasing maximum Social Security tax each year. And it is creating stress for retired people themselves, many of whom bitterly resent being put out to pasture on the basis of a birthday. It's beginning to look as if compulsory retirement is a good idea whose time has passed. . . .

While many workers are finding it too costly to quit at 65, some employers are finding it increasingly expensive to allow them to. One reason is that people are living longer, which pushes up the aggregate of pension payments and can make comptrollers want to push up the retirement age as well. . . .

The government bears the chief financial brunt of compulsory retirement because of the Social Security benefits it must pay. And while the number of retired workers on Social Security is expected to grow—from 17.2 million in 1976 to 21.4 million by 1985—the agency's funds aren't keeping up. Social Security payments are already creating a deficit [see graph on next page] because the system is more generous than it can afford to be. Social Security retirement benefits are adjusted annually to keep pace with inflation. In addition, the taxable wage base is being adjusted upward annually. That means that although current retired persons' benefits only go up with the cost of living, workers still in the labor force will get not only the cost-of-living hikes once they retire, but also the advantages of the higher wage base they will be paying taxes on by that time. In some cases benefits will be more than the pensioner's salary was.

Furthermore, there will be fewer taxpaying workers to foot the bill for the retired generation. Since birth rates have fallen, the ratio of beneficiaries to workers is expected to rise from 31 per 100 this year to 52 per 100 by 2035. This could cause a ground swell against mandatory retirement among younger workers who otherwise would be more concerned with getting old bosses out of the way.

must consider both retirement income needs and the sources of retirement income available for meeting these needs.

Retirement Goals

Of course, people have many different types of goals for retirement. Playing more golf, fishing, traveling, and camping are examples of several of the more popular activities people anticipate. To have the income to

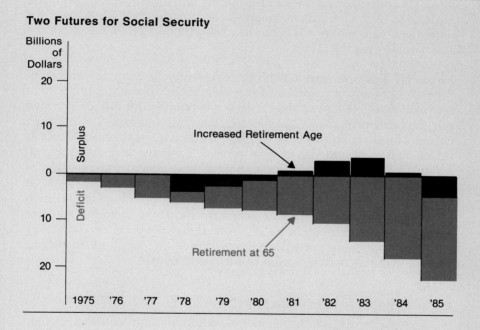

Two Futures for Social Security

Gradually raising the retirement age from 65 (brown) to 67½ (black) over a period of five years would eliminate the Social Security deficit temporarily and shrink it significantly over the long run. Other inflationary elements built into the system would keep the deficit from disappearing permanently, however.

Source: "Time to Rethink Compulsory Retirement," by Suzanne Seixas, excerpted from the April 1977 issue of MONEY Magazine, pp. 43–45, by special permission; © 1977, Time Inc. Figure sources are the Social Security Administration and the Treasury Department.

realize these goals, people should consider the age at which they will retire and what their financial position will be at retirement.

Age at Retirement Estimating when you are likely to retire is important because it affects the length of time that you have to earn and provide the necessary income. The 1960s saw the beginning of a trend toward early retirement. Many workers were electing to retire at age sixty, or even fifty-five. Over the last couple of years, a trend in the opposite direction, toward later retirement, has come into evidence; some people now remain in the work force until age seventy or longer. While these divergent actions may seem to be inconsistent, they really only indicate that fewer people are fitting their life patterns into society's preconceived mold. Of course, if you think that a shorter working career is for you, you must plan to place larger amounts of money aside each year for retirement than others who plan to work as long as they are physically and mentally capable.

Financial Position and Goals Your financial position at retirement depends not only on your plans for retirement but perhaps even more so on your choice of career and life-style. As pointed out in Part 1, which was devoted to financial statements, planning, and taxes, your career choice as well as your quality of life, or life-style, goals must be established realistically on the basis of projected income and expenditures. Although retirement was not mentioned, provision of some portion of income for use in fulfilling retirement goals should certainly be built into the financial planning process. Your projected financial position must be considered in light of relatively short-run financial needs as well as long-run retirement needs. You should not view merely putting aside temporarily unneeded or excess funds as retirement financing. Careful planning and allocation of funds is essential.

Estimating Retirement Income Needs

If all elements within the economy including your personal income remained static, estimating retirement income needs would be simple. But because both your personal budget and the general economy are subject to considerable change over time, forecasting retirement needs over a period of twenty to forty years can be quite difficult. Perhaps the best strategy is to plan for retirement in a series of short runs, rather than preparing a single long-run retirement plan. A good way of doing this is to consider your retirement income objectives as a percent of your present earnings. For example, if you would like to have a retirement income of 80 percent of your take-home pay, you, along with your life insurance agent or financial planner, could determine how much would have to be set aside each year in order to achieve this goal. Then, every three to five years you would reevaluate your planning in light of changes that may have occurred in both your personal situation and the economy. In fact, one of the most troublesome areas of retirement planning in today's economy is predicting accurately the long-term rate of inflation. An inflation rate of 6 percent over a period of thirty years can cause severe problems in a financial program that allows for only a 3 percent inflation factor. The actual computation of the amount to be set aside requires an understanding of social security, life insurance and annuities, and pensions and other investment devices, as well as the ability to use a variety of compound interest functions. Because the use of various interest-related financial factors is beyond the scope of this text, an example illustrating the retirement income estimation process is not included.

Sources of Retirement Income

The major sources of retirement income for wage earners are social security, annuities and life insurance cash values, employer pension and retirement plans, and individual retirement plans and savings. The remaining portion of the chapter describes the key characteristics of each of these. Of course, for individuals who have accumulated sizable estates by retirement age, income from stocks, bonds, real estate, and other business interests may also provide an important source of retirement income. Since these latter sources are discussed in the chapters devoted to personal assets, they are not given additional attention in this chapter:

Social Security

The Social Security Act makes available a variety of benefits in addition to the commonly known Old-Age, Survivors, Disability, and Health Insurance (OASDHI) provision. These include black lung benefits, supplementary security income (SSI), unemployment insurance, and public assistance and welfare services. In this part of the chapter, primary attention is given to the old age and survivor's portion of the act, since it has a direct bearing on retirement planning. The disability and health benefits of social security were discussed in Chapter 14, which is devoted to health care plans and insurance.

Basic Concepts

Generally, people have difficulty understanding the organization and operation of the social security system. An examination of four basic areas—financing, solvency, investment attributes, and historical perspective—can eliminate most of this confusion.

Financing The cash benefits paid under the social security program are derived from the payroll taxes (FICA), which are paid by covered employees and their employers. As pointed out in Chapter 4, the current tax rate is 11.70 percent, of which one-half, or 5.85 percent, is paid by the employee and the other half is paid by the employer. (See Table 4-1 in Chapter 4 for a schedule of past, present, and future rates.) Self-employed persons are also covered by social security. They must contribute 7.9 percent of their earnings up to the amount of the wage base. The maximum wage base on which taxes were computed in 1977 was $16,500. This amount is scheduled to increase each year at the same rate that the average annual wage increases.

Social security operates on a current funding basis. This means that the taxes collected today are soon thereafter paid out to social security beneficiaries. Although there is a social security trust fund, its purpose is only to act as a short-term financial cushion in periods when current revenues are insufficient to meet current obligations. This trust fund is not intended to be large enough to pay all benefits that have been earned under the program. Many covered workers incorrectly believe that their tax contributions are being held specifically for them by the Social Security Administration. Social security operates on the principle of an *intergenerational compact*. This means that today's working generation is paying for yesterday's workers, who are now retired, and tomorrow's workers will pay for today's workers when they retire.

Solvency People often remark that all of the social security benefit money will be gone by the time that they are ready to collect benefits. On the contrary, though, since revenues to pay benefits are derived from taxes, funds will be available as long as there is a work force to keep the system going. The basic financing problem to be overcome by the social security system stems from the fact that a larger percentage of our population will be "elderly" in future years than has been in the past. For example, as shown in Table 16-3, the percentage of persons age fifty-five or over has increased from 12.2 percent in 1930 to 19.8 percent in 1975.

Table 16-3 **Percent of Population Age Fifty-five and Over for Selected Years**

Age Group	Year					
	1930	1940	1950	1960	1970	1975
55 to 64	6.8%	8.0%	8.8%	8.7%	9.2%	9.3%
65 and Over	5.4	6.8	8.1	9.2	9.9	10.5
Total	12.2%	14.8%	16.9%	17.9%	19.1%	19.8%

Source: U.S. Bureau of the Census, *Statistical Abstract of the United States* (Washington, D.C.: U.S. Government Printing Office, various years).

This trend is expected to continue on into the twenty-first century. This means that proportionately fewer persons will be available in the work force to support the population of retired individuals (see Figure 16-1). Although current long-term projections of social security income and outgo do show deficits arising, these deficits will be countered by increases in the tax rates and by the correction of an unintentional error which was legislated in the method of computing benefits. Consequently, the probability that the social security system will "go broke" is no greater than the probability that the government will default on U.S. Savings Bonds.

Investment Attributes Many critics of social security condemn the program because they believe it does not produce as good a return on

Figure 16-1 **Proportion of Retired Persons to Work Force for Selected Years**

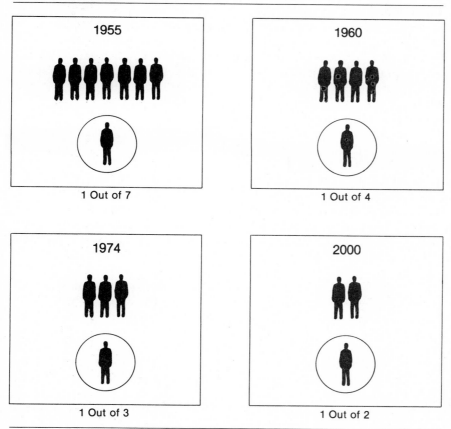

Source: Atlanta Journal and Constitution, June 5, 1977.

investment as would funds placed in a private retirement plan. These criticisms are faulty on several bases. First, this comparison is invalid because social security and an investment in, say, a mutual fund have very different benefits. If a covered worker dies at age thirty, his or her family could receive social security benefits ranging into the hundreds of thousands of dollars, even though that worker may have paid only several thousand dollars of taxes into the program. Had the same amount been placed in a mutual fund, the worker's family would merely receive the amount that had been paid in plus (or minus) any earnings (or losses) on the investment.

Second, social security is a compulsory social program which has an overriding social objective: the provision of a minimum level of benefit protection to all covered workers or their dependents. It cannot be appropriately evaluated on the basis of what it will return to any specific individual. Similarly, it is not possible to accurately assess the social value of the interstate highway system by measuring the returns to any one individual or group.

Third, nearly all of the calculations that attempt to compare social security to other "investments" have not acknowledged that social security is a dynamic program in which the benefit levels are constantly increasing. To assume (as most of these comparisons have) that the benefit levels in effect today will be the same ones in effect thirty or forty years from now is a gross error. In fact, as is shown in Table 16-4, monthly social security benefits for a person who retired in 1967 have risen faster than the cost of living. As a result of legislation enacted in 1972, social security benefits will increase automatically in the future as the cost of living goes up. Thus the social security program does provide favorable protection against the impact of inflation on benefits.

Historical Perspective When the Social Security Act was first passed in 1935, it covered only about one-half the work force and provided benefits only in the form of retirement payments to covered workers. Since that time, the program has been expanded greatly in terms of both coverage and benefits offered. Today more than 90 percent of those employed in the United States participate in this system, which now provides not only retirement benefits but also payments for survivors, disability income for workers and their dependents, and health care expenses for low-income and elderly families and individuals. Presently, more than thirty-three million persons are receiving cash benefits from social security totaling in excess of $80 billion annually.

Of course, the large growth of the social security program has placed increased tax burdens on covered workers and their employers. At the inception of the program, the social security tax rate was 1 percent levied against covered wages up to a maximum of $3,000. As late as 1950, the covered wage base was still just $3,000, although the tax rate had

Table 16-4 **Comparison of Monthly Social Security Retirement Benefits and the Consumer Price Index (CPI), 1967–1976**

Year	Benefits Payable in July[a]	Index of Payments	CPI in July
1967	$135.70	100	100.2
1968	153.34	113	104.5
1969	153.34	113	110.2
1970	176.34	130	116.7
1971	194.00	143	121.8
1972	194.00	143	125.5
1973	232.80	172	132.7
1974	232.80	172	148.0
1975	279.10	206	162.3
1976	297.10	219	(June) 170.1

[a]Assumptions—Payments to a male who:
1. receives no benefit for a spouse,
2. always earned more than social security wage base,
3. retired on 1 January 1967.

Source: Reprinted with permission from the *Journal* of the American Society of Chartered Life Underwriters, Vol. XXX, No. 4 (October 1976). Copyright 1976 by the American Society of Chartered Life Underwriters, 270 Bryn Mawr Avenue, Bryn Mawr, PA 19010.

increased to 1¹/₂ percent. However, since 1950, both the wage base and the tax rate have moved sharply upward. The 1977 tax rate and covered wage base were 5.85 percent and $16,500, respectively. Each of these is scheduled for periodic adjustments through the year 2011. Clearly, what started as a small social retirement system has evolved into a massive life, health, disability, and retirement system.

Whether social security has grown too fast and too much is a question frequently debated. Some maintain that it is nothing but a huge benefit scheme that is bound to fall apart. Others say that it needs to be expanded even more so that it becomes an all-encompassing cradle-to-grave security system for the entire population. While the former prediction is a bit too pessimistic, the latter is probably unrealistic in terms of the costs that the public is willing to bear. Nevertheless, nearly all agree that thus far the social security system has worked relatively well and has provided needed benefits to millions of people who might otherwise have had to turn to some type of pure welfare program in order to survive.

Who Is Covered?

Because of the broad coverage of social security, it is simpler to name who is not covered rather than list all of the types of employees to whom coverage extends. Basically, the following classifications are excluded from mandatory participation in social security: (1) employees of state and local governments, (2) employees of tax-exempt charitable or service institutions, (3) civilian employees of the federal government, (4) railroad workers who are covered under the Railroad Retirement Act, and (5) certain marginal employment positions such as newspaper delivery persons under age eighteen and full-time college students working in fraternity and sorority houses. By far the largest number of workers in these excluded classifications are employees of state and local governments and charitable organizations. These groups are not forced to participate because the federal government is not empowered to impose a tax on their employers. However, any of these groups may voluntarily participate in social security if a majority of the employees in it elect coverage. Unlike private employees, public and charitable employees who voluntarily enroll in the social security program also have the option of withdrawing after five years of participation. In fact, in recent years many of these groups have terminated their social security coverage agreement at the request of their members. Employees of the federal government do not participate in social security because they are covered by another retirement system that they believe is superior to social security and do not feel the need for additional coverage.

Benefits Important to Retirees

The basic social security disability and health care benefits were discussed in Chapter 14. Attention is given here only to the types of payments that can be important to retirees and their dependents throughout retirement: old-age and survivor's benefits.

Old-Age Benefits Workers who have become "fully insured" (the significance of this terminology is discussed later) during their employment careers are entitled to receive old-age benefits for life once they reach the age of sixty-five or elect to retire at age sixty-two. Of course, persons who elect to retire at age sixty-two receive annual amounts less than they would if they waited until age sixty-five before retiring. In addition, if the retired worker covered by social security has a spouse age sixty-five or older, the spouse is ordinarily entitled to a benefit equal to one-half of the amount being received by the retired worker. A spouse of a retired worker may also elect early receipt of benefits at age sixty-two, but the amount of the benefits is reduced by 25 percent of what it would have been had the receipt of benefits been put off until age sixty-five. Benefits paid to workers and their spouses who elect to receive these payments after age sixty-two but prior to age sixty-five are adjusted proportionately. In cases where the retired worker has a dependent child (or children), the spouse is entitled to a benefit, regardless of age, until the child (or children) reaches age eighteen. In addition, children of a retired, disabled, or deceased worker are entitled to monthly social security benefits if they remain full-time students in an approved educational institution. These benefits are payable until they leave school, marry, stop taking a full course load, or attain age twenty-two.

Survivor's Benefits If a covered worker dies, the spouse can receive survivor's benefits from social security. These benefits include a small lump sum payment of several hundred dollars followed by monthly benefit checks. The lump sum amount is paid automatically upon application. In order to be eligible for monthly payments, the widowed spouse generally must be at least age sixty or have a dependent and unmarried child of the deceased worker in his or her care. In cases where the children of the deceased worker reach age eighteen before the spouse attains age sixty, the monthly benefits cease and do not resume until the spouse does turn sixty. This period of time during which survivor's benefits are not paid to the spouse is called the "black-out period."

Benefit Amounts

The amount paid to the widowed spouse of a deceased worker is equal to 100 percent of the worker's Primary Insurance Amount (PIA). A retired worker and eligible spouse receive a payment of 150 percent of the PIA. The PIA is calculated from a scheduled benefit table based on the average annual covered wages of the worker. (Covered wages are wages up to the prevailing maximum on which social security taxes were calculated over the specified period of years.) Table 16-5 presents the PIAs associated with various wage levels. Note that payments made under the schedule do not remain constant but rather increase with the cost of living, as reflected in the Consumer Price Index (CPI). As can be seen from Table 16-5, the benefit payments on behalf of a worker with low covered earnings are proportionately greater than those paid on behalf of workers at higher wage levels. For example, with average annual covered earnings of $3,000, a widow or widower caring for one child could receive *yearly* payments of $4,017.60 ($334.80 per month × 12 months). In contrast, a widow or widower with average annual covered earnings of $10,000 would be eligible for annual payments of $8,532 ($711.00 per month × 12 months).

Thus, even though the employee with covered earnings of $10,000 earned three and one-third times as much as the worker with covered earnings of $3,000, benefits paid the former are only slightly more than two times those paid the latter. At present, only young workers with high earnings could have an average annual income for purposes of social security in excess of $10,000. This is true because it has only been recently that the social security wage base exceeded $10,000. Consequently, the career average for older workers, even those who earned the maximum, is likely to be under $10,000. Of course, in ten to fifteen years,

Table 16-5 **Examples of Monthly Social Security Payments or Primary Insurance Amounts—PIAs**
(Effective June 1976)

People to Whom Benefits Can Be Paid	Average Yearly Covered Earnings after 1950						
	$923 or Less	$3,000	$4,000	$5,000	$6,000	$8,000[a]	$10,000[a]
Retired Worker at 65	$107.90	$223.20	$262.60	$304.50	$344.10	$427.80	$474.00
Worker Under 65 and Disabled	107.90	223.20	262.60	304.50	344.10	427.80	474.00
Retired Worker at 62	86.40	178.60	210.10	243.60	275.30	342.30	379.20
Wife or Dependent Husband at 65	54.00	111.60	131.30	152.30	172.10	213.90	237.00
Wife or Dependent Husband at 62	40.50	83.70	98.50	114.30	129.10	160.50	177.80
Wife Under 65 and One Child in Her Care	54.00	118.00	186.20	257.40	287.20	321.00	355.60
Widow or Dependent Widower at 65 (if worker never received reduced benefits)	107.90	223.20	262.60	304.50	344.10	427.80	474.00
Widow or Dependent Widower at 60 (if sole survivor)	77.20	159.60	187.80	217.80	246.10	305.90	339.00
Widow or Dependent Widower at 50 and Disabled (if sole survivor)	56.80	111.70	131.40	152.40	172.20	214.00	237.10
Widow or Widower Caring for One Child	161.90	334.80	394.00	456.80	516.20	641.80	711.00
Maximum Family Payment	161.90	341.20	448.80	561.90	631.30	748.70	829.50

[a]Maximum earnings covered by social security were lower in past years and must be included in figuring your average earnings. This average determines your payment amount. Because of this, amounts shown in the last two columns generally will not be payable until future years. The maximum retirement benefit generally payable to a worker who is 65 in 1977 is $412.70.

Source: Social Security Administration, *Your Social Security*, HEW publication no. (SSA) 77-10035 (Washington, D.C.: U.S. Government Printing Office, January 1977), p. 17.

the average will increase substantially. Social security payments are not considered taxable income, regardless of the amount of other taxable income a recipient may have, and thus they have more value to the recipient than an equivalent amount of taxable income.

Retired social security beneficiaries, though, may have their benefit payments reduced if they have annual income from employment in excess of $3,000 per year. The applicable rule states that for each $2 earned in excess of $3,000, the beneficiary loses $1 in benefits. However, a person can receive unreduced monthly benefits in any month that earnings do not exceed $250, regardless of the amount of total annual wages. The amount a worker may earn without having benefits reduced is also scheduled to increase as the cost of living goes up.

The fact that there is a benefit reduction because of earned income is one of the most frequently criticized features of social security. Consequently, this so-called "earnings test" may be completely eliminated in the near future. Even though earned income presently can lead to benefit reductions, income from investments, savings, or rental properties does not reduce benefits. The principle that underlies the system in its present form is that social security benefits are intended to be wage replacement payments. Thus, if wages are still being earned (until age seventy-two), the offset described is imposed. And since the program is supposed to encourage thrift and retirement financial planning by covered workers, those who have accumulated savings and investments are not penalized.

Receiving Social Security Benefits

Social security payments are not simply automatically paid to eligible individuals (or their dependents) who have been assessed social security taxes. An application for benefits must be filed with the Social Security Administration, which then determines the applicant's eligibility for benefits based upon whether the covered worker had enough quarters (three-month periods) of participation in the social security system.

Retirement Benefit Eligibility In order to qualify for retirement benefits, nearly all workers today must be employed in social security covered employment for at least forty quarters prior to reaching retirement age. These quarters do not necessarily have to be consecutive. Once this forty quarter minimum requirement is met, the worker becomes *fully insured* and remains eligible for retirement payments even if he or she goes ten or twenty years without working in covered employment. Note, however, that in computing the average yearly earnings of covered wages, zeros are inserted for years in which no social security taxes were paid. This substantially reduces the size of monthly payments for which the retired is eligible.

Survivor's Benefit Eligibility A spouse and/or dependent children of a retired or deceased worker are eligible for monthly benefits if the worker was fully insured at the time of death or, in some special cases, if certain other requirements are met. The lump sum benefit mentioned earlier is payable if the worker was fully or currently insured. Workers are considered currently insured if they had six quarters of coverage during the full thirteen quarter period preceding the date of death.

Social Security and Retirement Planning

Obviously, no one can predict with any degree of certainty what amount of social security benefits will be paid to retirees thirty to forty years from now. For retirement planning purposes, however, it seems reasonable to

Some Inequities in the Social Security System

It is to be hoped that the inequities illustrated by the following examples will soon be eliminated by amendments to the Social Security Act.

1. Working Wives

Mr. A retired in January, 1976, at age 65. He had earned the maximum wage covered by Social Security, so is entitled to maximum benefits. His wife, 62, never worked in a job covered by Social Security.

Mr. A receives monthly	$387.30
Mrs. A receives monthly	$145.70
Total monthly Social Security benefits	**$533.00**

Mr. B and his wife are the same ages as Mr. and Mrs. A and retired at the same time. They earned the same total annual income as the A's, but Mr. B made two thirds of the total, and Mrs. B one third.

Mr. B receives monthly	$293.00
Mrs. B receives monthly	$154.50
Total monthly Social Security benefits	**$447.50**

2. Retirement Income

Mr. X is 66 years old and entitled to maximum Social Security benefits of $387.30 a month. He takes a full-time job paying $1,250 a month.

Earned income—$1,250 per month for 12 months	$15,000
Social Security benefits per year	None
Total annual income	**$15,000**

Mr. Y also is entitled to maximum Social Security benefits. He takes a job at $5,000 a month for three months only.

Earned income—$5,000 per month, January–March	$15,000
Social Security benefits, January–March	None
April–December total	$ 3,485.70
Total annual income	**$18,485.70**

Mr. Z, another retiree entitled to maximum Social Security benefits, does not take another job. But he has unearned income from investments of $1,250 a month year round.

Unearned income—$1,250 per month for 12 months $15,000
Social Security benefits, January–December . . . . $ 4,647.60
Total annual income **$19,647.60**

Note: Appropriate income taxes would have to be paid on earned and unearned income, but not on Social Security benefits. Earned income would be subject to Social Security payroll taxes.

3. Widows and Widowers

Mr. M, who has been working at a job covered by Social Security, dies at age 60. Mrs. M, also 60, has been receiving $8,000 a year in income not covered by Social Security. She becomes eligible for a widow's benefit of $271.60 a month.

Mrs. M's widow benefit—$271.60 a month for 12 months $3,259.20
Mrs. M's other income $8,000
Total income **$11,259.20**

Mrs. R also dies at age 60. She has had the same salary record in jobs covered by Social Security as Mr. M. Her husband, a 60-year-old retired federal worker, has income of $8,000 a year.

Mr. R's widower's benefit from Social Security . . . . None
Mr. R's other income $8,000
Total income **$8,000**

4. Payroll Taxes

Four wage earners pay Social Security payroll taxes [in 1976]. Here's how much:

Annual Wages	Social Security Taxes	Tax as Percent of Annual Wage
$ 6,000	$351.00	5.85%
14,000	819.00	5.85
20,000	895.05	4.48
30,000	895.05	2.98

Source: "Four Inequities: The Story in Dollars and Cents," reprinted from *U.S. News & World Report*, 26 July 1976, pp. 38–39. Copyright 1976 U.S. News & World Report, Inc.

expect social security to provide the retired average wage earner who is married with about 40 to 60 percent of the final salary or wage that he or she was earning immediately prior to retirement. This, of course, assumes that the retiree has had a full career working in covered employment. Social security should therefore be viewed only as a foundation upon which to build a retirement fund; in itself it is insufficient to allow a worker and spouse to maintain their preretirement standard of living. In the case of professionals who have annual salaries in substantial excess of the social security wage base, a much lower percentage of total preretirement wages will be replaced by social security. Consequently, both average and upper middle-income families must plan to supplement their social security retirement benefits with income from other sources. Two of these other sources that are widely available are annuities and pensions, the respective topics of the following two parts of the chapter.

Annuities

Since 1965, the number of individual annuity contracts in force with U.S. life insurance companies has increased from just over 1 million to more than 3 million. This growth has resulted primarily from the greater public awareness of annuities brought about by increased marketing efforts of life insurance companies. Furthermore, special legislation allows certain groups of taxpayers to use annuities in tax-sheltered retirement programs. This feature has also played a large role in the increase in purchases of annuities. In addition to the number of individual annuity contracts in force, another 8 million persons have annuity certificates under various group plans. In fact, about 75 percent of all annuity receipts collected by life insurers are remitted on behalf of group coverage agreements. The annuity principle, the classification of annuities, their sources and costs, and an evaluation of their place in retirement planning are discussed in the following sections.

The Annuity Principle

An annuity is actually the opposite of life insurance. As you will recall from Chapter 13, life insurance is the systematic accumulation of an estate for protection against financial loss resulting from premature death. In contrast, an annuity is the systematic liquidation of an estate to protect against the financial insolvency that could result from outliving personal financial resources. The period during which premiums are paid for the purchase of an annuity is called the *accumulation period*, and correspondingly, the period during which annuity payments are received is called the *distribution period*. Under a "pure" life annuity contract, for a given amount of consideration a life insurance company will guarantee regular monthly payments to an individual for as long as that person lives. These payments are composed of three parts: principal, interest, and survivorship benefits. The *principal*, of course, consists of the amounts paid in by the *annuitant* (person buying the annuity). *Interest* is the amount earned on these capital sums between the time they are paid in and when they are distributed. The portion of the capital sum that has not been returned to the annuitant prior to her or his death constitutes the *survivorship benefits*, which are, of course, paid to the survivors of the deceased annuitant.

By using mortality tables (see Table 13-4) and estimated investment returns, life insurance companies can calculate fairly accurately for a group of annuitants of a given age the amount of monthly payment that can be guaranteed to each individual without prematurely depleting the total amount of consideration that was paid in. Consequently, the financial risk of living too long is reduced from the individual's standpoint, while at the same time, by the law of large numbers, the insurer's risk is minimized.

Classification of Annuities

Annuities may be categorized by the following nonexclusive classifications: method of paying premiums, disposition of proceeds, inception date of benefits, number of lives covered, and method of calculating benefits. Figure 16-2 presents a flow chart depicting these schemes for classifying annuities.

Method of Paying Premiums The two methods used to purchase an annuity contract are the single premium and the installment method. As the name implies, a *single premium annuity contract* is one that is bought with a lump sum payment. Most single premium annuities are purchased just before retirement. However, if a given single premium amount is paid earlier, a larger monthly benefit will be received upon retirement. Quite frequently the cash values of death proceeds from a life insurance policy provide the funds used to acquire an annuity under the single premium method. Also, the vast majority of group annuities are funded with a single premium. As might be expected, however, many individuals who buy annuities do so by making a series of *installment payments* (most often annual) throughout their working career. During the period of accumulation, the contract serves as a medium for savings. If the annuitant dies before the distribution period begins, the premiums paid along with interest earned are given to the beneficiaries or the estate. In addition, the annuitant may either terminate the contract at any time and withdraw the cash value or simply stop paying the periodic installments and take a paid-up annuity for a reduced amount. One advantage of purchasing an installment-type annuity early in your career is that the monthly guaranteed receipt after retirement is based upon mortality

Figure 16-2 **Major Classifications of Annuities**

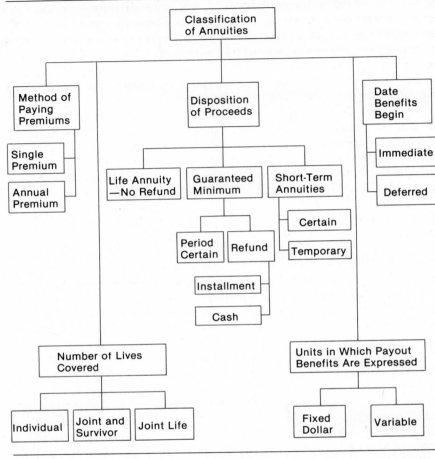

Source: Mehr, Robert I., *Life Insurance: Theory and Practice*, revised edition (Dallas, TX: Business Publications, Inc., 1977 ©). Reproduced with the permission of the publisher.

rates at the time the contract is negotiated. Even if the mortality rate improves, as is expected, you will not be required to pay the higher premium stipulated in contracts issued later on.

Disposition of Proceeds The four options that are most widely used in the distribution of annuity proceeds are the life annuity with no refund, the guaranteed minimum annuity, the annuity certain, and the temporary life annuity.

Life Annuity with No Refund (Straight Life) Under the life annuity with no refund option, the annuitant receives a specified amount of income for life, regardless of whether the period over which income is distributed turns out to be one year or fifty years. No refunds or payments are made to the estate or family when the annuitant dies. This disposition procedure entitles the annuitant to the largest monthly payments of any of the distribution methods. These larger payments result since, when the annuitant dies, the issuer (a life insurance company) does not have to distribute the principal, if any remains, to the annuitant's heirs. Only a minority of individuals select the life annuity with no refund. Most people who purchase annuities are opposed to "sacrificing" the large unused portion of their capital should they die relatively soon after retirement. However, this option often is used under group annuity contracts.

Guaranteed Minimum Annuities Guaranteed minimum annuities were developed to help overcome the emotional and economic objections to the straight life annuity. The two basic types of such annuities are: (1) the life annuity, period certain, and (2) the refund annuity. With each of these options, the annuitant designates a beneficiary who also may become eligible for benefits. Under the *life annuity, period certain,* the annuitant is guaranteed a stated amount of monthly income for life. In addition, the insurance company agrees to pay for at least a minimum number of years (five or ten, for example), regardless of whether the annuitant survives. A *refund annuity* provides that upon the death of the annuitant, monthly payments will be made to the designated beneficiary until the total purchase price of the annuity has been refunded. In place of the monthly payments, the refund may be taken in cash if so provided in the contract.

Annuity Certain A specified amount of monthly income for a specified period of years without consideration of any life contingency is provided by the annuity certain. For example, if an annuitant selected a ten year annuity certain, payments would continue for ten years after that individual retired, regardless of whether he or she lived two or twenty more years. The annuity certain can be used to fill a need for monthly income that will expire after a certain length of time. For example, a widow at fifty-two could choose a ten year annuity certain contract to fill the need for income until she reaches age sixty-two, when she plans to apply for social security benefits. Of course, survivorship benefits accrue under this method of distributing annuity proceeds.

Temporary Life Annuity Though similar to the annuity certain, the temporary life annuity differs from it in that benefits continue for the specified period only if the annuitant survives. If the widow above had chosen a ten year temporary life annuity but had died at age sixty, no further payments would be made under the contract. Since a survivorship benefit is not provided by the temporary life annuity, it provides a larger monthly income than the annuity certain. This is due to the fact that the insurer that sells the temporary life annuity may not have to pay the benefits over the stated period, while the insurer that sells the annuity certain must. Therefore, unless the above-mentioned widow had a beneficiary who needed extra income, she would be wise to select the temporary life annuity instead of the annuity certain. In actuality, annuitants purchase a temporary life annuity contract only infrequently for the same basic reason that they avoid straight life annuities—they do not want a major portion of the purchase price of their annuity to be "wasted" if they should die shortly after payments begin.

Inception Date of Benefits An annuitant often has the choice of receiving monthly benefits immediately upon buying an annuity or of deferring receipt for a number of years. Logically, the first type is called an immediate annuity and the latter a deferred annuity. An *immediate annuity* is always purchased with a single premium. It is most often used in conjunction with the cash value or death proceeds of a life insurance policy to create a stream of cash receipts needed for retirement or to support a widow and/or dependent children. A *deferred annuity* can be bought with either a lump sum payment or through an installment plan. This contract is quite flexible and can be issued with numerous options to the annuitant, in terms of both paying the consideration and receiving the proceeds. Most annuities purchased by individuals are installment-type deferred annuities, whereas those purchased under group contracts are generally immediate annuities.

Number of Lives Covered Most annuities are written on the life of one individual. However, in some cases it is desirable to include a spouse or other dependent of the annuitant. Such contracts are called joint annuities, and the most common of them is the joint and last survivorship annuity. Under the *joint and last survivorship annuity*, the monthly payments continue until the last survivor named in the contract dies. For example, assume that a husband and wife are covered under a joint and last survivorship annuity contract. If the husband dies first, payments will continue to be made to the wife for as long as she lives; while, if the wife dies before her husband, he still receives benefits for the remainder of his life.

These contracts can be written so that the same amount is paid monthly regardless of whether one or both parties are alive, or the benefits can be scheduled to decrease upon the death of the first mate. Most common, probably, is the annuity that initiates a one-third reduc-

"Until Harry got me this job, I didn't realize I was an important factor in his retirement plan."

Retirement Plans Should Be Made Jointly

Source: Changing Times, April 1969, p. 40. Reprinted with permission from *Changing Times* Magazine, © Kiplinger Washington Editors, Inc., 1969.

tion in benefits after the death of the spouse. The reasoning behind this plan is that, regardless of the popular expression, one *can* live "cheaper" than two.

Method of Calculating Benefits Most annuity contracts are written on a *fixed dollar* basis. This means that once a payment schedule is selected, the amount of monthly income provided does not change. In contrast, some annuity plans are available that adjust the monthly income provided according to the actual investment (and sometimes mortality) experience of the insurer. These latter contracts are called *variable annuities*. The advantage of a fixed dollar annuity is that the dollar amount of monthly income is guaranteed to the annuitant regardless of how poorly or how well the investments of the insurer perform. A major disadvantage, though, is that in periods of substantial inflation, the purchasing power of that dollar amount erodes rather quickly. For example, with a 6 percent annual inflation rate, one dollar is reduced in terms of purchasing power to approximately seventy-five cents in just five years.

In an attempt to overcome this disadvantage of the fixed dollar contract, the variable annuity was developed. With this plan, annuitants face a different risk. They cannot be certain how well the insurer's investments, which consist primarily of common stocks, will do. Annuitants take a chance that they will receive even a lower monthly income in absolute dollars than a fixed dollar contract would provide. Most people who participate in variable annuity plans do, of course, believe that they will at least be able to keep up with the cost of living. Unfortunately, though, common stock values and the CPI do not necessarily perform similarly. Figure 16-3 shows that even though the CPI rose approximately 90 percent between 1966 and the second quarter of 1977, Standard & Poor's Index of 500 common stocks increased by only about 22 percent during this same period. This recent experience has shown that a real risk of a reduction in benefits from variable annuities does exist. Indeed, as a result of the dip in common stock values, the payments made under many variable annuity plans during the early 1970s fell below the amounts paid by corresponding fixed dollar plans. Although most premiums paid into variable annuities are invested in common stocks, annuitants are sometimes given a choice as to whether they wish to have their monies placed in common stocks throughout the accumulation period as well as during the distribution period. In some cases annuitants may prefer premium build-up in a variable plan and then switch to a fixed dollar plan at retirement. In this manner they participate in the growth of the economy over the long working career period but guard against short-term recessions that may occur during retirement years.

Sources and Costs of Annuities

Life insurance companies constitute the leading source of annuities. Since the marketing and production for annuities and life insurance are similar, this development has been quite logical. The cost of annuities varies considerably with the age of the annuitant at issue, the age of the annuitant when payments begin, the method of proceeds distribution, the number of lives covered, and the sex of the annuitant. Table 16-6 presents the monthly benefits paid by several leading companies for selected types of immediate annuities. Note that substantial differences exist among the companies with respect to the amount of benefits payable. These differences confirm the need to shop around before making an annuity purchase. Note, too, that in every category the benefit

Figure 16-3 **Comparison of the Consumer Price Index (CPI) and Standard & Poor's (S&P's) Index of 500 Stocks**
(1966 to Second Quarter of 1977)

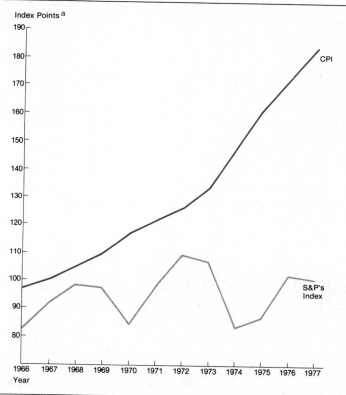

[a]The index values are yearly averages. The use of index yearly averages results in a much smoother curve than would the use of monthly or weekly values. For example, in 1970, the S&P Index was 90.31 in January, 75.59 in June, and 90.05 in December. The yearly average value was 83.22.

Source: Data are from the *Federal Reserve Bulletin* and *Standard & Poor's Statistics.* Reprinted by permission of Standard & Poor's. Figure (not including 1976 and 1977) from Mehr, Robert I., *Life Insurance: Theory and Practice,* revised edition (Dallas, TX: Business Publications, Inc., 1977 ©). Reproduced with permission of the publisher.

paid to females is less than the benefit paid to males. This is due to the lower mortality rates among women. The differences in mortality rates for males and females retiring at age sixty-five can be seen in Table 16-7.

An Evaluation of Annuities

The major value of annuities, for the most part, is that they are a source of income a person cannot outlive. While individuals might create a similar arrangement by simply living off the benefit of interest or

Table 16-6 **Benefits for Selected Types of Immediate Annuities by Sex and Age at Issue**

Company	Lifetime Only				Installment Refund				Life—10 Years Certain			
	Male		Female		Male		Female		Male		Female	
	65	75	65	75	65	75	65	75	65	75	65	75
Western National	$95.52	$131.94	$82.20	$111.06	$87.80	$111.72	$78.71	$98.92	$87.03	$101.64	$79.04	$95.09
United Benefit	78.87	111.26	69.62	96.84	72.00	93.75	65.81	85.80	73.52	90.48	67.15	85.25
John Hancock	85.55	116.02	75.93	102.03	79.50	100.64	72.75	92.00	79.80	95.38	73.35	89.82
Prudential	84.93	113.90	77.06	103.19	79.46	97.84	72.92	88.79	80.55	94.54	74.07	88.79
Equitable Life	89.39	119.85	78.27	104.73	82.34	103.77	75.07	94.47	82.81	98.14	75.86	92.57

Note: All annuities have a lump-sum cost of $10,000.

Source: Reprinted by permission from "Monthly Annuity Payments," *Best's Review, Life and Health Edition*, April 1977, p. 35.

Table 16-7 Survival Experience of 1,000 Males and 1,000 Females Retiring at Age Sixty-five

Age	Number of Males Surviving	Number of Females Surviving	Surviving Females as Percentage of Surviving Males
65	1,000	1,000	—
70	907	956	105%
75	775	882	114
80	596	762	128
85	383	584	152
90	179	357	199
95	49	144	294
100	6	29	483

Source: Reprinted by permission from "Men, Women, and Life Annuities," *Journal of Risk and Insurance*, December 1976, p. 558.

dividends from investments, they would find it difficult to engage in the systematic liquidation of their principal in a manner that would be timed to exactly coincide with their death. Often viewed as a disadvantage, however, are the returns on funds used to purchase a deferred annuity. They typically range from 4 to 6 percent, a relatively low rate that can often be matched or exceeded through alternative investment media. Because of this, some persons may prefer to accumulate retirement funds in another investment medium and then use these funds at retirement to purchase an immediate annuity. Note, however, that when a deferred annuity is purchased, the monthly benefit is guaranteed at the time of purchase, even though benefits may not be payable for thirty or forty years; thus, even if mortality rates for the elderly improve materially during the accumulation period, the annuity payments will not be reduced. On the other hand, if an immediate annuity is purchased, the monthly benefit payable is that which is in effect at the time of retirement. Thus the deferred annuity approach could very well produce a higher benefit even though the cash values during the accumulation period earn only a nominal rate of interest. This trade-off of low returns for the level of guaranteed future income should be considered when the use of annuities in fulfilling specified retirement income needs is being evaluated.

Pension and Retirement Plans

Accompanying the expansion of the social security program and the more recent increase in annuity sales has been the growth of employer-sponsored pension and retirement plans. Presently, approximately 60 percent of all wage and salaried workers in the United States are covered by such plans. In contrast, in 1940, when the social security program was in its infancy, less than 25 percent of the work force had the benefit of an employer-sponsored plan. This part of the chapter examines the reasons for the dramatic increase in both the number and scope of pension and retirement plans, the effects of this growth, the basic features of the various plans, the classification of plans, types of employer plans, other types of plans, and government influence on pension plans.

Reasons for Growth

Although there are many reasons for the widespread development of pension and retirement plans, three are probably most important. Basically, pension plans have been developed by employers (1) to attract and retain quality employees, (2) to meet the demands of collective bargaining, and (3) to provide low-cost benefits to owners and key managers of firms. Many employers have stressed and will continue to stress the advantages of their retirement plan in attracting and keeping valuable employees. In fact, numerous firms have more or less been forced to implement retirement plans simply as a defensive measure to counteract the effects of plans initiated by other employers who compete for the same workers. Of course, few representatives of these firms would go so far as to say that a good retirement plan encourages workers to put forth more effort. Nevertheless, evidence indicates that the lack of a good plan can serve as a job deterrent to prospective employees and may increase labor turnover, especially for employees age forty and older.

In 1948, the National Labor Relations Board (NLRB) ruled that pensions and other types of insurance are a legitimate subject for collective bargaining. Since that time, many employers have established new pension plans or liberalized the provisions of existing ones to meet or anticipate union demands.

Qualified pension plans, which are discussed later, allow firms to deduct for tax purposes their contributions to employee retirement programs. These contributions are not included in the taxable income of the employee. As a result, many firms, especially smaller ones, have established pension or retirement plans to help owners and key managers accrue funds for retirement that are not subject to federal income taxes. Of course, eventually, when the funds are paid out as benefits, income tax does have to be paid on them. As a result of the rules and regulations it established for protecting employees participating in private employer retirement plans, the Employee Retirement Income Security Act of 1974 (ERISA) may now contribute to a reduction in the number of new retirement plans started among smaller firms. This law is discussed in greater detail in a subsequent section of the chapter.

Effects of Growth in Plans

The growth of employer-sponsored retirement plans is important in two major areas. First, payments made under these plans represent a needed source of income to millions of retired workers and their dependents. More than 7½ million persons will receive in excess of $15 billion from private employer retirement plans this year. In addition, retirement programs sponsored by federal, state, and local government employers will provide another $18 billion to more than 4 million benefit recipients. As more employer plans mature, both the number of persons and dollar payments involved can be expected to increase substantially. The payments made to retired workers under employer-sponsored pension plans are in total still much less than those made by social security on behalf of retirees. But because a smaller number of persons are eligible for employer retirement benefits, payments to many individuals exceed the benefit amounts payable under social security.

The second major effect of growth in these pension funds is the related growth of their influence in the behavior of capital (security) markets in the United States. Assets of all pension and retirement programs (excluding social security) in the United States now total more than $300 billion. The largest portion of this amount is invested in corporate and government bonds as well as corporate stocks. In fact, pension and retirement funds as a group are now the largest institutional owners of the corporate stocks and bonds traded on the New York Stock Exchange. In addition, pension fund money is also becoming more widely available to finance mortgages on commercial and investment real estate.

Basic Features of Pension Plans

Apart from financing, which is discussed later, the basic features of pension plans that you should be familiar with pertain to eligibility requirements, the distinction between contributory and noncontributory plans, vesting, retirement age, and methods of computing benefits.

Eligibility Requirements In many pension plans employees must meet certain criteria before they become eligible for participation. Most common are requirements that relate to years of service, minimum age, level of earnings, and employment classification. Years of service and/or minimum age requirements are often incorporated into retirement plans in the belief that a much greater labor turnover rate applies to newly hired employees and younger employees. Therefore, to reduce the administrative costs of these plans, employees in these categories are excluded from participation. Pension plans which limit enrollment to employees who earn in excess of a given salary amount do so generally when the private plan is designed to integrate with social security. Social security is thought to provide adequate replacement of lost earnings for workers who receive relatively low pay, but employees who earn higher salaries need a supplemental plan in order to prevent a drastic reduction in income upon retirement.

Contributory versus Noncontributory Plans A retirement plan is considered *noncontributory* if the employer pays the total cost of the benefits. Under a plan with a *contributory* feature, the employee also bears a portion of this cost. Most pensions established by corporations are noncontributory. In contrast, nearly all plans for employees of federal, state, and local government require a contribution from the employee. In contributory plans, the employee's share of the costs is frequently between 3 and 8 percent of his or her annual wages and is typically paid through a payroll deduction. When employees who have participated in a contributory retirement plan terminate employment prior to retirement, they are legally entitled to some benefit based upon the amount of their contributions. Usually this benefit is a cash lump sum, but in some cases it can be taken as a monthly payment at retirement. Whether departing employees receive any benefit from the employer's contributions to the pension plan depends on the vesting feature of the plan.

Vesting The term *vesting* refers to the rights employees obtain to benefits in a retirement plan based upon their own and their employer's contributions. While employees' contributions vest immediately and can be withdrawn at any time, various conditions are often included in pension plans which limit the employees' interest in employer contributions. Frequently, vesting of employer contributions is based upon certain time requirements, amount limits, and form bases. Where there is a time requirement, the employee must work for the employer for a specified number of years prior to vesting. In some very liberal plans, no time restriction is applied and employer contributions vest immediately as earned. In others, vesting may not result for five, ten, or even twenty years. Recent trends have been toward reduction of the period that must elapse before vesting occurs, and five years is now most common.

When a limitation on the amount of vesting is included, the employer contributions become vested in stages. For example, a plan may stipulate that vesting of 25 percent occurs after five years of employment, 50 percent after ten years, and 100 percent at the fifteen year mark. Vesting can take different forms; in other words, the benefits employees receive when the employer contributions become vested vary in kind. In a growing minority of cases, the employee has the option of receiving a cash lump sum based upon these contributions. More frequently, though, the employee simply becomes eligible for a monthly check at retirement based upon contributions to date. Under a contributory plan, if an employee dies before retirement, generally his or her contributions are refunded without any death benefits being paid.

To illustrate the vesting process, assume that a medium-size firm offers a plan in which vesting of benefits becomes complete for eligible employees after ten years. The plan is contributory, with employees paying 3 percent of their salaries and the employer paying an amount equal to 6 percent of the employees' salaries. Under this plan, employees cannot withdraw as a cash payment the contributions made by their employer. The plan provides annual benefits in the amount of $11 per year of service for each $100 of an employee's final monthly salary—the amount earned during the final month in the employ of the firm. Therefore, an employee who worked a minimum of ten years for the firm would be eligible for a retirement benefit from that firm even if he or she transferred jobs at, say, age thirty-five. However, the value of the benefit for a worker who left the firm substantially before retirement age would be very small.

Two cases, one for a career employee and one for the minimum years of service employee, might help to clarify this concept. A career employee with forty years of service and final monthly earnings of $1,000 would be entitled to an annual pension of $4,400 (40 years × $11 × [$1,000 ÷ $100]). The employee with final monthly earnings of $1,000 who worked ten years and left the firm at age thirty-five would receive $1,100 annually at retirement (10 years × $11 × [$1,000 ÷ $100]). However, the inflation over the thirty year period elapsing before retirement would seriously diminish the purchasing power of the $1,100. Consequently, the employee might be better off simply withdrawing his or her own contributions (which always vest immediately) and terminating participation in the plan at the same time employment is terminated. Any worker who left the firm prior to accumulating ten years of service would be entitled only to a return of his or her own contributions (plus interest) to the plan.

Retirement Age Nearly all retirement plans specify a normal retirement age at which an eligible employee is entitled to start receiving benefits. In most plans, this age is sixty-five. Often pension plans also provide an early retirement age. In those cases, employees may begin receiving benefits prior to the normal retirement age, but the amount of the benefit payments is less than that they would have received if retirement had been deferred. Many retirement plans for public employees also give employees the option of retiring after a stated number of years of service (thirty or thirty-five) at full benefit, regardless of their age at that time. In the past, the trend in pension plans has been toward earlier permissible retirement ages. But since many have now begun to argue in favor of increasing the age for mandatory retirement, it is expected that fewer plans will further reduce the normal retirement age.

Benefit Computations The method used to compute benefits at retirement is spelled out in every retirement plan. Two general methods are most common: the defined contribution plan and the defined benefit plan. As the name implies, a *defined contribution plan* is one that specifies the amount of contribution that the employer and employee must make to the pension plan each year. At retirement, the worker is then awarded not a guaranteed amount but whatever level of monthly benefits those contributions will purchase. Factors most often considered to determine this level are age, sex, amount of contributions, and the amount of income that has been earned on the investment of the contributions.

Under a *defined benefit plan*, the formula for computing benefits is stipulated in the plan provisions. This plan allows employees to determine before retirement how much their monthly retirement income will be. Often the number of years of service and amount of earnings are

How Much Pension Is Enough?

It takes a long time to earn a good pension. John B. Moore, vice president of the Wyatt Co., a pension consulting firm, says, "In the typical private plan, you need to be at least 60 years old with 20 to 25 years' service before you get an adequate pension." Thus the penalties for retiring early, or for changing jobs too often in the middle years, can be severe. A good pension is the reward of the loyal and prudent—or, to look at it another way, the compensation of the timid and the unambitious.

To find out how much pension is enough, and how to get it, *Money* interviewed professionals in the pension field and some retired people, including three in Illinois who are living as happily today as they did when they were working. . . .

Rarely does a pensioner have as much income after retirement as before, but then he doesn't need as much because his expenses will drop. Reduced income taxes will be his biggest saving. A husband and wife each acquire an additional $750 personal exemption when they reach 65. Their Social Security income is tax free. Their reduced taxable income will probably be in a much lower bracket. Typically, a couple might go from a $20,000-a-year salary to a $15,600-a-year retirement income and find their federal income tax reduced from $3,000 to $1,360.

Retirement brings with it other spontaneous savings. If you are not going to and from work, you spend less on transportation. Without lunches downtown, food costs less. Without the need to impress customers and associates, you can spend less on clothes. Other savings can be achieved without much sacrifice. A two-car family can easily become a one-car family. Retired people have the time

prime factors in the formula. For example, a worker might be paid annually 1 percent of his or her final three-year average annual salary for each year of service. Thus, the benefit to an employee with twenty years of employment whose final three-year average annual salary was $10,000 would equal $2,000 per year (1% × 20 years × $10,000). Other types of defined benefit plans may simply pay benefits based upon: (1) a consideration of years of service but not earnings, (2) a consideration of earnings but not years of service, or (3) a flat amount with no consideration given to either years of service or earnings. Regardless of the method used to calculate benefit amounts, the employee's basic concern should be with the percent of take-home pay that the plan is likely to produce at retirement. A pension is usually thought to be good if when combined with social security it will result in a monthly income for the retiree of 70 to 80 percent of preretirement net earnings.

to look for bargains, to take advantage of off-peak rates or special rates for the elderly.

On the other hand, some expenses may go up. Retired people often find themselves spending more on travel than before. Eventually their medical expenses will almost certainly increase.

James H. Schulz, professor of welfare economics at Brandeis University, figures that to maintain a living standard in retirement similar to the living standard just before retirement, you need an income of 65% to 75% of your preretirement income, assuming no major changes in expenses. Other pension specialists put the range a little lower—at 60% to 70%. The calculations always include Social Security payments.

The Wyatt Co. discovered in a survey of the pension plans of 50 major companies that a typical corporate employee who retired in 1975 after 35 years' service got about 62% of his preretirement income—42% from his pension and 20% from Social Security. The spread at these 50 companies went from 54% at Boeing to 78.2% at Ford.

Schulz has observed that a highly paid employee needs proportionately less in retirement than a lower-paid one. Max Weil, a New York pension consultant, agrees. He contends, "A guy making $10,000 a year spends it all, and is going to need just as much when he retires. But a $50,000 executive is probably spending only $30,000. The rest goes into taxes, savings and investments. He won't need $50,000 when he retires." . . .

Source: "Building a 21st-Century Pension Right Now," by Jeremy Main, excerpted from the September 1976 issue of MONEY Magazine, pp. 38–39, by special permission; © 1976, Time Inc.

Classification of Plans

Pension plans are often classified according to whether they are "funded" and whether they are "qualified" under the requirements of the Internal Revenue Code.

Funding Pension plans must in some way provide for the financing of benefits that will be paid to retired workers. If the plan merely allows the employer to make payments to retirees from current income, the plan is said to be *unfunded*. One pension expert has called unfunded pensions "owe as you go" plans. This name is appropriate since employers accumulate liabilities throughout the working careers of their employees but do not necessarily put any assets aside to offset them. In the past, only a small minority of employees have been covered under unfunded pension plans. These unfunded plans have received a large amount of unfavorable publicity as being too risky for employees. And consequently, the Employee Retirement Income Security Act of 1974 (discussed in a subsequent section) sets forth minimum funding standards for pension plans.

Funded pension plans are those that formally establish charges against current income to allow for the pension liabilities as they accrue. The amount of liability that arises under the plan each year is determined by actuarial computations. (*Actuaries*, you will recall, are experts in calculating risks and premiums for insurance.) These computations take into account such factors as mortality rates among workers and retirees, potential and actual interest earnings, labor turnover, normal and early retirement ages, and salary levels. In order for a funded plan to be "actuarially sound," the assumptions concerning these foregoing factors must be realistic. In addition, the method of funding must be sound. Few persons advocate placing pension fund assets in speculative investments such as land development projects or commodity futures. On the other hand, many persons support the now more common practice of placing a large percentage of the fund assets in common stock investments.

Funding of pension plans represents an attempt to minimize the risk that benefits will not be available to an eligible employee upon retirement. Nonetheless, the unfunded plan of a large solvent governmental unit or a corporate employer sometimes can offer a better guarantee of payment than the funded plan of a financially weak firm. This may be particularly true where the primary objective of the actuarial assumptions of a funded system shifts from certainty of future payment to minimization of the employer's annual contributions to the plan. Requirements under the Employee Retirement Income Security Act attempt to control the lack of adequate funding in funded plans by requiring that "reasonable" actuarial estimates be used when calculating pension costs.

Qualified Pension Plans The Internal Revenue Code permits an employer making contributions to a retirement plan that is *qualified*—that meets a number of specified criteria—to deduct from taxable income its contributions to the plan. The employees on whose behalf the contributions are made do not include the employer's contributions in their taxable income until the benefits are actually received. Another tax advantage of these plans is that their investment income is allowed to accumulate untaxed. Qualification applies only to private employers. The retirement plans of governmental and charitable organizations do not have to meet qualification standards because they already have tax-exempt status.

Types of Employer Plans

Two basic types of qualified pension plans are popular: trust fund plans and insured plans. When an employer places its contributions with a trustee in a *trust fund plan* this trustee is then responsible for the investment of contributions and the payment of benefits. Under an *insured plan,* a life insurance company serves as the funding agency. In some cases, both a trust fund and an insurance contract are used. These plans are said to be *split funded*. Trust fund plans account for more than two-thirds of the employees covered under private pensions and nearly three-fourths of the assets held by private pension plans. Primarily smaller companies tend to use insured plans.

Other Types of Plans

In addition to the foregoing pension plans, numerous other mechanisms also exist for the organized accumulation of funds for retirement. Most frequently used are: Keogh plans, individual retirement savings plans, nonqualified deferred compensation plans, tax-sheltered annuities for special types of employees, profit-sharing plans, thrift plans, and professional corporations. When structured properly, each of these plans will also result in certain tax deferral advantages for the individual.

Keogh Plans The Self-employment Individual Tax Retirement Act of 1962—HR-10, frequently called the Keogh Act—gave self-employed persons the right to establish retirement plans for themselves and their employees that would permit them the same tax advantages available to corporate employees covered by qualified pension plans. The primary groups that have benefited from Keogh plans are professionals such as doctors, lawyers, and accountants, as well as owners of businesses that are not incorporated. Eligible persons can deduct from taxable income 15 percent of their earned income up to a maximum of $7,500 annually for placement in approved investments for retirement. Most often the investment media selected are bank savings plans, mutual funds, and life insurance annuity programs. Taxes are not levied against the investment earnings of these plans during the accumulation period. Funds may be removed from a Keogh plan prior to retirement, but a withdrawal penalty tax and income tax are assessed.

Individual Retirement Savings The enrollment in both qualified pension plans and Keogh plans grew steadily throughout the 1960s and early 1970s. Nevertheless, as of 1974, nearly 40 million persons in the work force were still without private pension coverage. (This, of course, does not include social security.) To ameliorate this situation, Congress wrote provisions into the Employee Retirement Income Security Act (ERISA) permitting these workers to establish their own individual tax-sheltered retirement plans. The basic difference between Keogh plans and individual retirement savings plans is that the former are designed primarily for self-employed persons whereas the latter benefit employees of companies and government who are not covered by an employer pension program. Employees who elect to participate in an individual retirement savings plan are allowed to make a tax-deductible contribution of up to 15 percent of their salary subject to a maximum of $1,500 per year. Although this deductible amount is relatively low, expectations are that it will be increased somewhat in the coming years. Three different funding arrangements may be used to accumulate savings under this program: an individual retirement account, an individual retirement annuity, and U.S. Retirement Bonds.

If an *individual retirement account* (IRA) is established, the employee's contributions are turned over to a trustee. Most often this trustee is either a bank or a savings and loan association. The trustee then invests the money as directed by the plan participant in such media as mutual fund shares, savings accounts, certificates of deposit, or other permissible investments. An *individual retirement annuity* may be purchased from life insurance companies. The annuity may be any one of the several varieties discussed earlier in this chapter, as long as it complies with specific regulations of the IRS. Nearly all major life insurers have now developed special annuity plans that are approved by the IRS, and they are marketing them widely. *U.S. Retirement Bonds* are a special series of bonds developed by the government to serve as a funding instrument for individual tax-sheltered savings plans. The bonds may be bought with face values of $50, $100, and $500. Interest is earned at the annual rate of 6 percent and is compounded semiannually. These bonds, just as the assets accumulated under the other types of savings plans, may not be used as collateral for a loan. Distributions of all the funds upon the retirement of the individual are treated as ordinary income to the recipient.

Keogh and Individual Retirement Account Investment Strategies

The counsel that investment advisers give to people with Keoghs or IRAs [individual retirement accounts] is generally the same: diversify. Split your funds between growth and conservative investments. Some could go into a mutual fund designed for growth, some into a bank's time-deposit account. Or a retirement planner could open a mutual fund Keogh or IRA one year, a bank time deposit the next. Many mutual funds open accounts for $1,000 or so and accept subsequent contributions as small as $25.

The earnings on municipal bonds lose their tax-exempt status when they're withdrawn from Keoghs and IRAs, so you should stay away from them. Capital gains likewise lose their special tax treatment when they're paid out as Keogh or IRA proceeds—except for capital gains that accumulated in a Keogh plan before 1974.

When you withdraw your IRA funds in a lump sum, it can pay you to use the normal five-year method of income averaging. Keogh investors who receive a lump sum get to use a special 10-year averaging method, however. If they receive $50,000, say, they must pay the tax in a single amount but they can calculate it as if they're paying taxes on 10 annual incomes of $5,000. What's more, they needn't include any other income in the annual averages; that's taxed separately.

The safest possible Keogh or IRA investment is government bonds—U.S. Individual Retirement Bonds for IRA investors, U.S. Retirement Plan Bonds for Keogh investors. They are sold in denominations of $50, $100 and $500 and pay 6% a year compounded twice a year. They can save you work, since you can buy them without having to choose a trustee. They're available directly from Federal Reserve banks and branches, or by mail from the Bureau of the Public Debt, Securities Transactions Branch, Washington, D.C. 20226.

Time-deposit accounts in a bank or savings association usually pay more than retirement bonds. But in choosing a time-deposit account for a Keogh or an IRA, keep in mind that some institutions charge nothing for administration; others charge up to $50 a year. Some banks let you withdraw from a time-deposit account before the designated withdrawal time without penalty if you have reached age 59½; others don't. One bank, Wells Fargo in California, promises that any IRA you open now will yield a minimum of 7½% a year until you reach 60. Its main office is at 464 California St., San Francisco 94144. The minimum deposit required to receive a yield of 7½% compounded daily is $200, and you must set up a six-year time-deposit account. As a bonus, you get a checking account with no monthly service charge.

Source: "IRA-Keogh Investment Strategies," by Warren Boroson, reprinted from the June 1977 issue of MONEY Magazine, p. 100, by special permission; © 1977, Time Inc.

Nonqualified Deferred Compensation Nonqualified deferred compensation plans are simply arrangements between employer and employee to defer payment for services rendered by the employee. Such agreements are most useful when an employee's future need for funds exceeds his or her present requirements. Often the potential exists for the employee to be in a lower tax bracket in the future when the funds are actually received. These plans are most common among highly paid athletes and upper echelon managers of large companies. Generally, no funding of the employer's liability under the deferred compensation agreement takes place. The employee is therefore nothing more than an unsecured creditor of the employer with respect to the owed wages. And the employee's eventual receipt of the deferred funds is contingent on the employer's continued existence as well as its financial capacity to pay. If all of the appropriate requirements are met, the earned compensation will not be taxable until the employee actually receives it. Nonqualified deferred compensation plans permit much greater flexibility as to who is covered, what the amount of compensation will be, and the conditions under which payment will be made than do qualified plans, which are subject to all of the cumbersome rules and regulations of ERISA.

Tax-Sheltered Annuities for Special Types of Employees Presently the Internal Revenue Code (IRC) allows employees of qualified charitable organizations and public school systems to exempt from current income annuities purchased on their behalf by their employers. This benefit can be supplemental to any other retirement plan that the employer sponsors for its employees. However, it is not without limit. The IRS requires the complicated computation of an *exclusion allowance* for each participating employee. This exclusion allowance is used to determine the maximum amount of annuity premium provided by the employer for the employee upon which taxes can be deferred. Generally, contributions up to approximately 20 percent of the employee's annual compensation are allowed. In the case where the employer is also making payments to an employer retirement plan for its employees, the amount available for the purchase of tax-deferred annuities is reduced accordingly. If an eligible employer does not contribute the maximum permissible amount in tax-sheltered plans for its employees, its employees may, on an individual basis, enter into a voluntary salary reduction agreement with the employer. The amount by which the salary is reduced (subject to the exclusion allowance) is then available for the purchase of the tax-deferred annuities. In essence, then, this IRC provision serves as an added benefit to eligible employees who wish to defer paying taxes on a relatively large percentage of their income. Of course, to take advantage of this feature, the employee must be earning more than his or her present budget requires.

Profit Sharing Profit-sharing plans are arrangements whereby the employees of a firm participate in the earnings of the firm. A profit-sharing plan may be qualified under the IRC and become eligible for essentially the same tax treatment as other types of pension plans. An argument in support of the use of profit-sharing plans is that they encourage employees to function at a higher level of productivity since the employees benefit directly when the firm prospers. Whether these types of plans actually accomplish this goal is still a subject of much discussion. One advantage of profit-sharing plans from the viewpoint of the firm is that they do not impose any specific levels of contribution or benefits upon the employer. In other words, when profits are low, the employer is liable for a proportionately smaller contribution to the plan. And when earnings are high, the firm pays proportionately more, and the employees benefit. In order to provide reasonable returns, many employers establish minimum and maximum amounts that will be paid as contributions to a profit-sharing plan, regardless of how low or high earnings actually are. The contributions from profit-sharing plans can be invested in life insurance annuity contracts, stocks and bonds of other organizations, or (in many cases) securities issued by the employing firm. Employees who opt to purchase the firm's securities may benefit twice. When profits are good, larger contributions are made to the profit-sharing plan, and the price of the shares already purchased is also likely to increase. For many years, Sears, Roebuck and Company has had one of the most widely known and best performing profit-sharing plans. Even many low-level Sears career employees who have taken advantage of it have reached retirement with stock ownership valued into the hundreds of thousands of dollars.

Thrift and Savings Plans Thrift and savings plans have been established by many employers to supplement pension and other insurance fringe benefits. Most plans provide that the employer will make contributions to the savings plan in an amount equal to a set proportion of the amount contributed by the employee. For example, in some programs employers will match employee contributions at fifty cents on the dollar up to, say, 6 percent of salary. An employee making $10,000 a year could pay $600 into the plan annually, and the employer would add another $300. These contributions are then deposited with a trustee who invests the money in various types of securities, including (or sometimes exclusively) stocks and bonds of the employing firm. With IRS qualified thrift and savings plans, the employer's contributions and earnings on the savings are not included in the employee's taxable income until he or she withdraws these sums. However, the employees' contributions are *not* tax deductible when they are paid into the plan and accordingly are not counted as income when returned to them.

"Hartwell, I have here the latest figures on our profit-sharing plan. You now owe the company three thousand five hundred and twenty-seven dollars."

Don't Forget: Profit-Sharing Benefits Depend on Profits!
Source: New Yorker, June 30, 1975. Drawing by Ross; © 1975 The New Yorker Magazine, Inc.

Usually thrift and savings plans have more liberal vesting and withdrawal privileges than pension and retirement programs. Often the employee's right to the contributions of the employer becomes nonforfeitable immediately upon payment, and the total savings in the plan can be withdrawn by giving proper notice. Those employees who terminate participation in such a plan, though, are frequently prohibited from rejoining it for a specified period such as one year. An employee who has the option to do so should seriously consider participation in a thrift or savings plan since the financial returns are generally quite favorable.

Professional Corporation Plans In recent years, the trend has been for groups of lawyers, medical doctors, architects, dentists, and other professionals to establish professional corporations. While the reasons for forming these corporations extend far beyond pension and retirement planning, often this is an integral part of the total program. As will be recalled, self-employed persons and members of partnerships can set up a tax-sheltered retirement program under a Keogh plan. But while it is attractive, a Keogh plan does not generally permit the development of nearly as attractive a tax-sheltered retirement fund as can be organized by a corporation. In addition, the tax rules related to providing other insurance fringe benefits are more favorable to corporations than those that apply to persons who are self-employed or members of a partnership. Consequently, if you choose to become a professional, it could be advantageous for you to explore with appropriate counsel the pros and cons of organizing a professional corporation.

Government Influence on Pensions

The two major areas of government influence on pension plans are the Internal Revenue Code requirements for plan qualification and the rules and regulations established by the Employee Retirement Income Security Act of 1974 (ERISA). The major stipulations of the IRC were discussed earlier in the chapter. At this point, therefore, attention is devoted to the most important features of ERISA. As the name of the act implies, the primary objective of ERISA is to increase the probability that employees who are covered by a retirement plan throughout their working career will in fact receive benefits upon retirement. ERISA covers nearly all

How the Stock Market Can Affect Retirement Income

The employees' shares of company profit-sharing funds are usually invested heavily in stocks that rise and fall with market prices. Therefore, the amount of income available from such funds can fluctuate greatly.

Example: Suppose that at the end of 1970, six employees had $100,000 each in a profit-sharing fund invested in stocks. As each retired at 65, his stake in the fund was cashed [in] and invested in a retirement annuity. Here is how the six would have fared, based on fluctuations in the value of the profit-sharing portfolio as measured by Standard & Poor's 500-stock index.

Date of Retirement, December 31	Employee's Stake in Fund	Monthly Retirement Annuity
1970	$100,000	$ 950
1971	110,787	1,052
1972	128,107	1,217
1973	105,861	1,006
1974	74,401	707
1975	97,874	930

Note: Figures exclude contributions or dividends after 1970.

Source: "Drive Is On to Cut Risks in Profit-Sharing Plans," reprinted from *U.S. News & World Report*, 2 February 1976, p. 71. Copyright 1976 U.S. News & World Report, Inc.

pension and retirement plans created by private employers engaged in interstate commerce. It does not cover plans sponsored by government, charitable organizations, or firms exclusively involved in intrastate commerce. The law only regulates plans that are in existence. It does not require firms to begin a retirement plan for their employees; nor does it prohibit them from discontinuing a present plan. Similarly, ERISA does not force companies to pay any minimum amounts to employees other than those specified in the plan.

Basically, ERISA prescribes minimum standards with which covered plans must comply. These standards pertain to provisions, funding, and administration of plans. Among the major items treated are vesting, eligibility for participation, definition of service, minimum funding requirements, disclosure to participants, and employer fiduciary responsibility. Another important provision of ERISA establishes the Pension Benefit Guarantee Corporation (PBGC). The purpose of this organization is to guarantee to eligible workers that certain benefits will be payable to them even if their employer's plan has insufficient assets to fulfill its commitments. The funding for the PBGC comes from charges that are levied against all employers regulated by ERISA. In essence, the PBGC is providing plan termination insurance to covered employees. Although the implementation of ERISA has not been problem-free, most observers agree that this law will go a long way in insuring that employees who have earned pensions will receive them.

Summary

The first step in the retirement planning process involves setting retirement goals which specify desired retirement age, financial position, and quality of life. Once these goals are established, the retirement income needs required to fulfill them must be estimated. Finally, it is necessary to evaluate and plan for sources of retirement income in order to achieve retirement goals. The basic foundation of a retirement program for most families is social security. The social security system is designed to accomplish social objectives more than to provide a "savings" plan for each individual who participates in it. Social security is financed on a current funding basis. Consequently, the fact that the system does not have a trust fund established that is sufficient to pay all accumulating liabilities does not mean that it is insolvent. While considerable publicity has focused on the insufficiency of individual social security benefits, such publicity has been somewhat misleading. Nearly all present beneficiaries of social security are receiving larger monthly checks than their tax payments could have purchased from private insurers. Important benefits paid by social security include those for disability, survivors, retirement, and health care.

Another major source of income useful in planning for retirement is the annuity contract. In recent years the sale of annuities has increased substantially. Basically, an annuity provides for the systematic liquidation of an estate. One of its primary advantages is that it can be arranged to provide payments for the entire remaining life of an individual, no matter how long that might be. The most important types of annuities are life annuities, guaranteed minimum annuities, annuities certain, and temporary life annuities. Annuities can be either fixed dollar or variable during both the accumulation and distribution periods. They can be written on the life of one individual or jointly on the lives of two or more persons. The latter variety is often used by a husband and wife. Private and government employer pension and retirement plans provide a third source of retirement income. These plans have experienced considerable growth throughout the last twenty-five years and now cover more than sixty million workers. Their basic features include eligibility requirements for participation, a specified amount of employee contribution (if any), a period required for vesting of the employer contributions, the stipulation of normal and early retirement ages, and a specified amount of benefits that will be provided upon retirement. It is important to understand the essentials of plan funding and qualification.

In addition to basic employer-sponsored pension programs, a number of other types of retirement plans are also available to certain employees and self-employed persons. Keogh plans permit the self-employed as well as members of partnerships to deduct for tax purposes a portion of their earned income to be used for retirement investment. Individual savings plans serve to accomplish objectives similar to Keogh plans except that the individual savings plan program applies only to employees of companies that have no established pension plan. Thrift plans are supplemental savings plans offered by some employers as a special benefit to encourage and stimulate employee savings. Under a special tax-sheltered annuity provision of the Internal Revenue Code, employees of charitable organizations and public school systems are permitted to have their employer purchase annuities for them on a favorable tax basis. Profit-sharing plans operate such that employer contributions are related to the annual earnings of the employing firm. Nonqualified deferred compensation plans are used to postpone earnings in an effort to defer and reduce the payment of income taxes. And, finally, professional corporations are a form of organization that provides a favorable tax climate for the establishment of retirement and other insurance fringe benefit programs. A significant piece of pension legislation, ERISA, was passed in 1974 in order to insure that workers who have become eligible for a pension through their employment actually receive the benefits that they have earned.

Key Terms

accumulation period
actuarial
annuity certain
annuity contract
contributory pension plan
deferred annuity
defined benefit plan
defined contribution plan
distribution period
earnings test
Employee Retirement
Income Security Act of 1974
(ERISA)
exclusion allowance
fixed dollar annuity
funded pension plan
guaranteed minimum annuity
immediate annuity
individual retirement account
(IRA)
individual retirement annuity
insured pension plan
interest (on an annuity)
intergenerational compact
(social security)
joint and last survivorship
annuity
Keogh plans
life annuity (straight life)
life annuity, period certain

nonqualified deferred
compensation
pensions
Pension Benefit Guarantee
Corporation (PBGC)
Primary Insurance Amount
(PIA)
principal (on an annuity)
professional corporations
profit sharing
qualified pension plan
refund annuity
retirement goals
Self-employment Individual
Tax Retirement Act (1962)
single premium annuity
contract
social security
special tax-sheltered annuity
split funded pension plan
survivorship benefits (annuity)
tax-sheltered annuity
temporary life annuity
thrift and savings plan
trust fund pension plan
unfunded pension plan
U.S. Retirement Bonds
variable annuity
vesting

Review Questions

1. Name and explain each of the steps in the retirement planning process.

2. What benefits are provided under the Social Security Act? Describe the basic operation of the social security system.

3. "Many critics of the social security program condemn it since they believe that it does not produce a good return on investment." Discuss why you agree or disagree with this statement.

4. Are all employed and self-employed persons covered under the social security program? Explain.

5. Discuss old-age benefits and survivor's benefits as applicable to retirees and their dependents under the social security program.

6. What is meant by the "Primary Insurance Amount"? Determine the yearly payment that Harold Holmes will receive. His average yearly covered earnings are $6,000, and he is fifty-two years old and disabled. Is Harold liable for any tax on this income? Use Table 16-5 to ascertain the Primary Insurance Amount.

7. Indicate the eligibility conditions necessary for a worker to be entitled to social security: (a) retirement benefits and (b) survivor's benefits.

8. Does social security coverage relieve you of the need for retirement planning? Explain.

9. What is an annuity? How does it differ from a life insurance policy?

10. Differentiate between a single premium annuity contract and an installment premium annuity contract.

11. Briefly explain the options that are most widely used in the distribution of annuity proceeds.

12. Describe and differentiate among: (a) an immediate annuity, (b) a deferred annuity, (c) a joint and last survivorship annuity, (d) a fixed dollar annuity, and (e) a variable annuity.

13. Why should you consider the trade-off between low returns and guaranteed future income when evaluating the use of annuities?

14. Discuss the main factors contributing to the widespread development of pension and retirement plans.

15. What basic features of pension plans should you be familiar with?

16. Indicate the distinguishing features of: (a) funded pension plans, (b) qualified pension plans, (c) trust fund plans, and (d) insured pension plans.

17. Describe and differentiate between Keogh plans and individual retirement savings plans.

18. Briefly explain the important features of: (a) nonqualified deferred compensation plans, (b) profit-sharing plans, (c) thrift and savings plans, and (d) professional corporation plans.

19. Describe ERISA and discuss its influence on pension plans.

16-1 Evaluating Percy Cooper's Retirement Benefits

Case Problems

Percy Cooper, age sixty, works as the general manager for a large chain of department stores with headquarters in Dallas, Texas. Although Percy has been with the company for thirty-five years and does not wish to retire in the near future, it is the company's policy that workers retire at sixty-five. The company has a defined benefit plan, which pays a retired employee 1½ percent of the final average salary per year for each year of service completed with the company. Besides the company pension, Percy will also be eligible for social security and Medicare. He has already paid off the mortgage on his $80,000 home and has no debts. His two children are married and do not depend on him for any financial assistance. Upon retirement he plans to go on a long vacation abroad, play golf, and fish. He does not anticipate any financial problems.

His wife, Charlene, currently fifty-one years old, believes that with his reduced income she will not be able to retain their maid, attend social gatherings, and make frequent visits to the country club. In short, she feels that, considering the benefits Percy is to receive, and taking into account the rising rate of inflation, they will not be able to maintain an acceptable standard of living once Percy retires.

Questions

1. If Percy's average salary in the last year of service with the company is $35,000, how much per year will the defined benefit plan pay him?

2. Do you believe that, given the quality of life the Coopers desire, the above amount will be sufficient? How would you view Charlene's opinion?

3. Assume Percy's average yearly covered earnings after 1950 were $8,000. Using Table 16-5, determine the annual social security payments he would be entitled to receive.

4. Express Percy's total annual retirement benefits received from the company and social security as a percentage of his annual preretirement salary of $35,000. Comment on this percentage and make appropriate recommendations to Percy.

5. Based on the information provided, evaluate the effectiveness of Percy's retirement planning.

16-2 Comparing Pension Plan Features: Which Plan Is Best?

Bill Carpenter and Gerald Shoemaker are neighbors, living in Kansas City. Bill works as a maintenance engineer for United Foods Corporation, Topeka Foods Division, while Gerald works as a foreman for U.S. Steel and Castings, Ltd. Both are married, have two children, and are well paid. Before Bill and Gerald joined their respective companies, there had been employee unrest and strikes. To counteract these problems, their firms developed job enrichment and employee motivation programs. Of particular interest are the portions of these programs that deal with pension and retirement.

Topeka Foods has a contributory plan, wherein 5 percent of the employees' annual wages is deducted to meet the cost of the benefit. An amount equal to the employee contribution is contributed by the company. The plan also includes a vesting feature, wherein 50 percent of the employer's contribution becomes vested after seven years of employment, and 100 percent after the fourteenth year. The retirement plan also establishes a normal retirement age of sixty for all employees and indicates that benefits upon retirement are computed according to a defined contribution plan.

Although U.S. Steel and Castings, Ltd., has a minimum retirement age of sixty, it provides for an extension period of five to six years before compulsory retirement. Employees (full-time, hourly, or salaried) also have to meet eligibility requirements. Further, in contrast to the Topeka plan, the U.S. Steel and Castings program has a noncontributory feature. Retirement benefits are computed according to the following formula: 1 percent of the employee's final annual salary for each year of service with the company is paid each year upon retirement. The plan vests immediately.

Questions

1. Discuss the basic features of the retirement plans offered by Topeka Foods and U.S. Steel and Castings.

2. Which plan do you think is most desirable, considering the basic features, retirement age, and benefit computations?

3. Explain how you would use each of these plans in developing your own retirement program.

4. What role, if any, could the purchase of annuities play in these retirement programs? Discuss the pros and cons of using annuities as part of retirement planning.

Boroson, Warren. "A Check on Your Social Security Savvy." *Money*, July 1977, pp. 75–80.
———. "Those Puzzle-It-Out-Yourself Retirement Plans." *Money*, June 1977, pp. 97–100.
Collins, Thomas. *The Complete Guide to Retirement.* Englewood Cliffs, N.J.: Prentice-Hall, 1972.
Corrick, Frank. *Planning Your Retirement Years: A Question and Answer Guide Showing How to Achieve Independence by Properly Planning for Retirement.* New York: Pilot Books, 1972.
"Forced Retirement: An Issue That's Riling Older Americans." *U.S. News & World Reports*, 4 July 1977, p. 75–76.
"How to Build a Pension Fund with an IRA." *Changing Times*, November 1976, pp. 39–42.
"In the Works: A Fairer but Costlier Social Security." *U.S. News & World Report*, 21 March 1977, pp. 55–86.

Selected
References

Jacoby, Susan. "All about Pensions and Other Retirement Plans." *Working Woman*, April 1977, pp. 14–18.

Melone, J. J. *Pension Planning: Pensions, Profit Sharing, and Other Deferred Compensation Plans.* Homewood, Ill.: Richard D. Irwin, 1972.

"Preserving Assets for a Secure Retirement." *Money*, November 1976, pp. 78–79.

"Rising Cost of Public Pensions—Can Taxpayers Afford Them?" *U.S. News & World Report*, 24 January 1977, pp. 84–86.

Rogers, Donald I. *Save It, Invest It, and Retire.* New Rochelle, N.Y.: Arlington House, 1973.

"Seven Points to Check in Your Pension Plan." *Changing Times*, March 1977, pp. 13–14.

Shore, Warren. *Social Security: The Fraud in Your Future.* New York: Macmillan, 1976.

"Social Security Needs More Than a Quick Fix." *Fortune*, June 1977, p. 97.

"Why Bigger Pensions Will Be Harder to Come By." *U.S. News & World Report*, 15 March 1976, pp. 77–79.

"Will Social Security Be There When You Need It?" *Changing Times*, February 1977, pp. 24–28.

"Your Pension: Will You Get a Fair Shake?" *U.S. News & World Report*, 25 July 1977, pp. 68–69.

17

Estate Planning: Wills, Trusts, and Taxes

In order to present the fundamental considerations related to estate planning, this chapter includes discussions of the following:

A Preview of Chapter 17

1. The importance of estate planning.

2. The basic steps involved in estate planning.

3. The important features of wills and procedures for preparing a valid will that can direct the estate in a fashion consistent with the deceased's desires.

4. The function of trust arrangements and the various types of trusts available.

5. The fundamental aspects of gift taxation and methods of bypassing or reducing gift taxes.

6. The federal and state estate tax laws and their impact on estate planning.

Someday you are going to die. Although this thought probably depresses you, its reality warrants attention. For if you do not give some consideration to the ultimate disposition of your accumulated wealth, chances are that little of your estate will be left for your heirs and beneficiaries to enjoy, such are the tax laws. Clearly, the importance of developing plans and taking action during your lifetime to assure that your wealth, or estate, is accumulated, preserved, and, upon your death, distributed in the desired fashion cannot be underestimated. This process, which is called estate planning, requires knowledge of wills, trusts, and taxes. An understanding of these components of estate planning and their interrelationships should make it possible for you to minimize the estate shrinkage that will occur after your death, while still achieving your lifetime personal financial goals.

The goal of estate planning is a continuous process of accumulating, conserving, and distributing an estate in the manner which most effectively accomplishes the estate owner's objectives. The emphasis of estate planning should be on personal objectives, the needs and desires of the individuals involved. In other words, estate planning should be "people planning." Not only wealthy people need to plan their estates; it also makes good sense for individuals of modest or moderate means. *Estate planning* can be defined as a goal satisfaction–oriented activity that uses tax minimization tools and techniques to provide the greatest financial security possible for an individual and his or her heirs or beneficiaries. The goals that generally motivate people to engage in estate planning most commonly include: providing for a comfortable retirement, taking care of self and family during a long-term disability, assuring financial security for family members in the event of the death of the head of household, and securing enough capital to meet college education costs and other special needs.

Planning occurs in every estate. Some planning is "controlled" by the estate owner and/or his or her professional counselors. Other, "uncontrolled," planning is done by the federal government and the government of the state in which the estate owner resides. Uncontrolled planning occurs when the estate owner forfeits the right to arrange for the disposition of assets and the minimization of tax and other estate settlement costs. This chapter discusses key factors in the estate planning process, particularly wills, trusts, and taxes. Special attention is given to types of planning and to the various means available for implementing estate plans.

Principles of Estate Planning

Individuals who wish to plan their estates must systematically uncover problems in a number of important areas and provide solutions for them. Table 17-1 itemizes the major types of problems along with their associated causes. These problems can be minimized or eliminated by maximizing the after-tax return on personal and business investments while minimizing the forces of estate impairment. Generally, the focus of estate planning is on reducing causes of estate impairment such as taxes and administrative costs. Techniques for accomplishing this objective are discussed in later sections of the chapter.

Table 17-1 **Potential Problems for the Estate Planner:
Their Major Causes or Indicators**

Problem	Major Cause or Indicator
Excessive Transfer Costs	Taxes and estate administrative expenses higher than necessary.
Lack of Liquidity	Insufficient cash. Not enough assets that are quickly and inexpensively convertible to cash within a short period of time to meet tax demands and other costs.
Improper Disposition of Assets	Beneficiaries receive the wrong asset or the proper asset in the wrong manner or at the wrong time.
Inadequate Income at Retirement	Capital insufficient or not readily convertible to income-producing status.
Inadequate Income, If Disabled	High medical costs, capital insufficient or not readily convertible to income-producing status, difficulty in reducing living standards.
Inadequate Income for Family at Estate Owner's Death	Any one of the above causes can trigger this problem.
Insufficient Capital	Excessive taxes, inflation, improper investment planning.
Special Problems	A family member with a serious illness or physical or emotional problem, children of a prior marriage, beneficiaries who have extraordinary medical or financial needs, business problems, and opportunities.

Who Needs Estate Planning?

Some form of estate planning is required by almost all adults who have dependents. A more technical breakdown of persons who should plan their estates can be made on the basis of either "people planning" or wealth.

People Planning Estate planning is important to those individuals with: (1) children who are minors, (2) children who are exceptionally artistic or intellectually gifted, (3) children or other dependents who are retarded, emotionally disturbed, or physically handicapped, (4) spouses who cannot or do not want to handle money, securities, or a business, (5) closely held business interests, and (6) property in more than one state.

Wealth From a standpoint of wealth alone, estate planning is essential for single, widowed, or divorced individuals with estates exceeding $120,000 and married individuals with assets exceeding $370,000.

Why Does an Estate Break Up?

Quite often, when people die, their estate "dies" with them. Sadly, the loss of the estate results not because they have done anything wrong but rather because they have not done anything. There are many forces which, if unchecked, tend to shrink an estate, reduce the usefulness of its assets, and frustrate the objectives of the person who built it. These include death-related costs, inflation, improper management, lack of liquidity, incorrect use of vehicles of transfer, and disabilities.

Death-Related Costs Last illness and funeral expenses are good examples of *first-level* death-related costs. Most people also die with some current bills unpaid and long-term obligations such as mortgages, business loans, and installment contracts outstanding. Unpaid income taxes as well as property taxes also constitute debts often payable by the deceased's estate. *Second-level* death-related costs consist of the fees of attorneys, appraisers, and accountants and probate expenses—so-called administrative costs—federal estate taxes, and state death taxes (some states have both an inheritance and an estate tax).

Inflation Death-related costs are only the tip of the estate impairment iceberg. Less obvious but often more damaging is the profound effect of inflation. Failure to continuously reappraise and rearrange an estate plan to provide a mechanism which will counter the effects of inflation can impair the ability of both financial and nonfinancial assets to provide steady and adequate levels of financial security.

Improper Management Business assets as well as some commercial real estate properties require continuous attention; often the estate beneficiaries are unable or unwilling to provide this needed care. The failure to note a change in consumer preferences or product or equipment obsolescence may result in a rapid decline in the value of a decedent's business or of various types of assets included within the estate.

Lack of Liquidity Insufficient cash to pay death costs and other estate obligations has always been a major factor impairing the value of estates. Forced sacrifice sales of assets with substantial income-producing power usually result in a disproportionately large loss of assets and family income. Furthermore, such sales—of the choicest parcel of farmland or a business which has been in the family for generations, for instance—often have undesirable psychological effects on the heirs. The outcome

Plan Your Estate: You Can't Take It with You!

Source: Saturday Evening Post, May–June 1977. Reprinted with permission from The Saturday Evening Post Company, © 1977.

can be a devastating emotional and financial blow. As a result of the Tax Reform Act of 1976, the sale of estate assets can generate still further problems because of what is known as the *carry-over basis tax trap*. For example, assume a deceased purchased property in 1977 for $50,000 and at the time of his death the value of the property had appreciated to $300,000. If the estate (or its beneficiary) sold the property for its $300,000 value, the $250,000 gain would be subject to an income tax. Generally, it would be treated as a long-term capital gain, which is taxed at a rate equal to one-half the normal tax rate and no greater than 35 percent. But, to add insult to tax injury, a second tax—the tax on "preference" items—can also be imposed on a portion of the gain. Together, these taxes can approach a rate as high as 50 percent.

Incorrect Use of Vehicles of Transfer It would be criminally negligent to put a high-powered car in the hands of a child. Yet assets are often put into the hands of beneficiaries who are unwilling or unable to handle them. Because of improper usage of vehicles of transfer, property often passes to unintended beneficiaries or to the proper beneficiaries in an improper manner or at an incorrect time. For example, spendthrift spouses or minors may be left large sums of money outright in the form of life insurance, through joint ownership of a savings account, or as the beneficiaries of an employee fringe benefit plan.

Disabilities A prolonged and expensive disability of a family wage earner is often called a "living death." Loss of income due to disability is frequently coupled with a massive financial drain caused by the illness itself. The financial situation is further complicated by a lack of attention given to the management of currently owned assets. This not only causes the growth of the family's financial security to cease but also diminishes the value of the estate with incredible rapidity.

The Estate—What Is It?

Your estate is your property, whatever you own. The *probate estate* consists of the real and personal property that a person owns in his or her own name that can be transferred according to the terms of a will at death. A distinction must be made between the probate estate and the gross estate, which may encompass a considerably larger amount of property. The *gross estate* includes all the property subject to federal estate tax at a person's death, both probate and nonprobate. Life insurance, jointly held property with rights of survivorship, and property passing under certain employee benefit plans are common examples of nonprobate assets that might be subject to federal (and perhaps state) estate taxes.

In addition, an individual may have property which is not probate property and will not be part of a decedent's gross estate for federal estate tax purposes, yet passes to his or her family and forms part of its financial security program. There are two types of such assets. One is the death benefit from qualified retirement plans such as pension, profit-sharing, and Keogh plans. Individual retirement account (IRA) death benefits might also fall into this category. Arranged properly, the proceeds from such plans pass outside the probate estate because of their contractual nature, are excludable from the decedent's gross estate for federal (as well as state, in many cases) estate tax purposes, and pass directly to the specified beneficiaries of the deceased. The other type of financial asset that falls into this category is social security. Payments to a surviving spouse and minor children are generally neither probate assets nor subject to federal estate (or state estate) taxes. Because of the freedom from administrative costs and taxes, this category of assets provides unique and substantial estate planning opportunities.

The Estate Planning Process

The estate planning process consists of a number of important steps. First, comprehensive and accurate data on all aspects of the family must be gathered. Table 17-2 summarizes the types of factual data required by professionals in order to prepare detailed estate plans. Second, the data gathered must be categorized into general problem areas, and estate transfer costs must be estimated. Third, with this information the estate plan is formulated and preparations are made for its implementation. The

Table 17-2 Classification and Types of Factual Data Required for Preparation of a Detailed Estate Plan

Personal Data
Names, addresses, phone numbers, family consultants
Family birthdates, occupations, health problems, support needs
Citizenship, marital status, marital agreements, wills, trusts, custodianships, trust beneficiary, gifts or inheritances, social security numbers, education, and military service

Property (except Life Insurance or Business)
Classification, title, indebtedness, basis, date and manner of acquisition, value of marketable securities, and location

Life Insurance

Health Insurance
Disability income
Medical expense insurance

Business Interest
Name, address, ownership
Valuation factors; desired survivorship control; name, address, and phone number of business attorney and accountant

Employee Census Data

Employee Benefits

Family Income
Income of client, spouse, dependent children, income tax information

Family Finances
Budget information, investment preferences
Ranking of economic objectives, capital needs, other objectives

Income and Capital Needs
Retirement: Age, requirement amount, potential sources
Disability: Required amount, sources
Death: Expected sources of income

Liabilities
Classification of liabilities, creditors, amounts, whether insured or secured

Factors Affecting Plan
Gift propensity, charitable inclinations, emotional maturity of children, basic desires for estate distribution

Authorization for Information
Life insurance

Receipt for Documents
Personal and business

Observations from Interview

Source: Copyright © 1977 by The American College. Reprinted from Confidential Personal and Financial Data form, *Advanced Estate Planning Casebook.*

objective of estate plans, of course, is to maximize the usefulness of people's assets during their lives and to achieve their personal objectives after their death. The final steps in the estate planning process involve testing and implementing the proposed plan.

Once the plan has been implemented, it is important to keep in mind that it is good only as long as it fits the needs, desires, and circumstances of the parties involved. As these elements change, the estate plan must also be modified. The birth of a child, a change of location, or substantial changes in income, health, and living standards are the types of events that indicate a need for a review. Even if none of these occur, a review of life insurance needs should automatically be scheduled at least once every two years, and a full estate audit should be made at least once every five to seven years. Because of the general complexity of the laws relating to estate transfer, the assistance of estate planners, life insurance professionals (C.L.U.'s), accountants, and attorneys is often necessary in the planning and evaluation process. Due to the complexity and individual nature of estate planning, more specific guidelines are not included in this chapter.

The Will

A *will* is a written legal expression or declaration of a person's wishes as to the disposition of his or her property to be performed or to take effect upon his or her death. The importance of a valid will can be illustrated in light of what happens when a person dies without one.

Absence of a Valid Will: Intestacy

Intestacy describes the state that exists when a person dies without a valid will. Some intestacy laws "draw the will the decedent failed to make" to determine the disposition of the probate property of persons who have died intestate. These statutes enumerate certain preferred classes of survivors. Generally, the decedent's spouse is favored, followed by the children and then other descendants. If the spouse and children or other descendants such as grandchildren or great-grandchildren survive, they will divide the estate, and other relatives will receive nothing. If no spouse, children, or other descendants survive, the deceased's parents, brothers, and sisters receive a share of the estate.

The disposition of a typical intestate estate can be illustrated by a simple example. Assume an individual dies with no valid will. That individual's separately owned property would be distributed as shown in Table 17-3 after deduction of debts, taxes, and state family exemptions. If the deceased leaves no wife or husband, child or descendant, parent,

Table 17-3 **Distribution of a Typical Intestate Estate**

Decedent Dies Leaving	Distribution	
Spouse and children or their descendants	Spouse receives one-third	Children receive two-thirds divided equally
Spouse and one child or its descendants	Spouse receives one-half	Child receives one-half
Spouse but no children or their descendants, and decedent's mother or father survives	Spouse receives $10,000 plus one-half of remainder	Father and mother or surviving parent (if one is already deceased) receive one-half of balance
Spouse but no children or their descendants, and no parent survives	Spouse receives $10,000 plus one-half of balance	Brothers and sisters receive other one-half of balance divided equally
Spouse but no children or their descendants, and no parent, brother, sister, niece, nephew, grandparent, uncle, or aunt survives	Spouse receives all	
Child or children but no spouse		Child or children receive all divided equally
No spouse and no children or their descendants, and decedent's mother or father survives		Mother and father receive all
No spouse and no children or their descendants, and no parent of the decedent survives		Brothers and sisters receive all divided equally

Source: Courtesy of Stephan R. Leimberg, Esq.

brother or sister or descendant, grandparent, or uncle or aunt or their children, the state normally takes all of the property. Had the deceased even in this situation had a will, the property could have been directed to some nonrelated individual or to a charity. Aside from having lost control of the disposition of property to individuals or charities, the person who dies intestate has also forfeited the privileges of naming a personal representative to guide the disposition of the estate, naming a guardian for persons and property, and specifying which beneficiaries are to bear certain tax burdens. In addition, with a valid will the amount of estate shrinkage can be minimized through the use of certain deductions and exclusions which may not result when a person dies intestate. The importance of a valid will—regardless of the size of an estate—must therefore not be overlooked in the personal financial planning process.

Preparation of the Will

A *will* can be defined as a written document that allows a person, called a *testator,* to determine the disposition of property at his or her death. A key characteristic of a will is that it can be changed or revoked at any time prior to the testator's (the will owner's) death. Upon the death of the testator, it becomes operative and applies to the situation which exists at that time. Will preparation, or drafting, varies with respect to difficulty and cost depending on individual circumstances. In some cases a two page will costing thirty-five dollars may be adequate, while in others it may be necessary to pay $500 to have a ten page will prepared. A will must not only effectively accomplish the specified objectives with respect to the distribution of assets, but it must also take into consideration the income, estate, and gift tax laws. Quite often, a knowledge of the corporate trust, real estate, and securities laws is required as well.

Information Requirements A properly prepared will should (1) provide a plan for distributing the testator's assets in accordance with his or her wishes, the beneficiaries' needs, and due regard to federal and state tax laws; (2) consider the changes in family circumstances which might occur after the execution of the will; and (3) be unambiguous and complete in describing the testator's desires. By following these general guidelines, the testator can generally develop a satisfactory will.

Use of an Attorney Will drafting, no matter how modest the size of the estate, should not be attempted by a lay person. The complexity and interrelationships of tax, property, domestic relations, and other laws make the "home-made" will a frivolous if not dangerous act.

Common Features of the Will

Although there is no absolute format that must be followed in will preparation, most wills contain eight distinct parts: (1) introductory clause, (2) direction of payments, (3) dispositive provisions, (4) appointment clause, (5) tax clause, (6) common disaster clause, (7) execution and attestation clause, and (8) witness clause. Each of these clauses is briefly described and illustrated below.

Introductory Clause An introductory clause, or preamble, would normally take the form shown:

I, _____, of the city of _____, state of _____, do hereby make my last will and revoke all wills made prior to this will.

The declaration of residence that is included here helps to determine the county which will have legal jurisdiction and be considered the testator's domicile for tax purposes. The portion of the clause related to revocation nullifies old and forgotten wills.

Direction of Payments The clause related to directing the estate with respect to certain payments of expenses is typically formulated along the lines of the example below:

I direct payment out of my estate of all just debts and the expenses of my last illness and funeral.

In many states, the rights of creditors are protected by law and such a clause is largely useless. However, the will of a married woman should contain a direction to pay debts. Otherwise, in a number of states the burden of funeral and medical expenses lies primarily on her husband.

Do's and Don'ts on Handling a Will

Legal authorities offer these suggestions for people who want to pass along property under a will:

1. Both husband and wife should have wills, and should update them periodically to take account of changing financial circumstances and family needs.

2. Tie your will to an over-all financial plan, including life insurance, jointly held property such as a home and bank accounts, and company-pension benefits with survivor provisions.

3. Have your will drawn by an attorney. While simple wills made without legal advice sometimes can be valid, State laws vary. An attorney can help avoid pitfalls.

4. Don't make bequests contingent on specific conditions or certain kinds of behavior by the beneficiaries.

5. If you have substantial property, don't ask a friend or neighbor to be the executor—the job is too time-consuming and complicated. Consider a bank, trust company or a specialist in financial management.

6. Keep your will where it can be found quickly. Leave a copy with your attorney or your bank. It is best to keep a will in a safe-deposit box.

7. If you want to change your will, don't write in a revision by hand. Consult your attorney. For legal reasons, even a minor change should be made formally.

8. Remember that property distributed under your will may be subject to estate taxes. Consider making some tax-free gifts during your lifetime to people you want to get your property.

Source: Reprinted from *U.S. News & World Report,* 21 June 1976, p. 73. Copyright 1976 U.S. News & World Report, Inc.

Dispositive Provisions Three examples of dispositive clauses are given below.

I give and bequeath to Allene Murphy all my jewelry, automobiles, books, and photography equipment, as well as all other articles of personal and household use.

I give to the Chicago Historical Society the sum of $100,000.

All the rest, residue, and remainder of my estate, real and personal, wherever located, I give in equal one-half shares to my children, Charlee and Lara, their heirs and assigns forever.

The first type of clause disposes of personal effects. A testator should make a detailed and specific list of intimate personal property and carefully identify each item. The second type of clause, called a *pecuniary legacy*, passes money to a specified party. The correct title of a charity should be ascertained by direct and discreet inquiry. Note that the popular name is seldom the correct or full legal name. The third clause describes the distribution of residual assets after specific gifts have been made. The share of a person who dies before the testator will normally pass to the other residual heirs unless provision is made to the contrary. Of course, this result varies from state to state.

Appointment Clause Examples of appointment clauses, which are typically included to appoint executors (the decedent's personal representatives), guardians, and trustees, as well as their successors, are given below.

I hereby nominate, constitute, and appoint as Executor of this last Will and Testament my beloved husband Elrod Wilmeyer and my brother, Charles S. Warren III. In the event any persons named herein predecease me, or for any cause shall cease or fail to act, then I nominate, constitute, and appoint as Executor of my said will in the place and stead of any or one of said persons named herein, the Farmers and Merchants Bank of Omaha, Nebraska.

I appoint my brother, Eugene Smith, guardian of the person and property of my son, Farnsworth, during his minority.

The first clause is used to appoint executors and alternates, whose responsibility it is to administer the estate of the deceased. The importance of naming an executor and alternate is highlighted in a subsequent section of this chapter concerned with the administration of an estate. The second clause shown is used to appoint a guardian. In many states, the surviving parent of an unmarried minor child can appoint a guardian of the person and property of the child. Often, the surviving parent is not allowed to become sole guardian of the property of a minor child.

Tax Clause An example of the tax clause is given below:

I direct that there shall be paid out of my residuary estate (from that portion which does not qualify for the marital deduction) all estate, inheritance, and similar taxes imposed by a government in respect to property includable in my estate for tax purposes, whether the property passes under this will or otherwise.

In the absence of a specified provision in the will, so-called *apportionment statutes* of the testator's state will allocate the burden of taxes among the beneficiaries. The result may be an inappropriate and unintended reduction of certain beneficiaries' shares or adverse income tax effects.

Common Disaster Clause A sample of the type of clause often included within the will to protect against a common disaster or simultaneous death follows:

If my wife, Ellarose, and I shall die under such circumstances that there is not sufficient evidence to determine the order of our deaths, then it shall be presumed that she survived me. My estate shall be administered and distributed in all respects in accordance with such assumption.

The assumption that the spouse survives is employed mainly to permit the marital deduction, which offers a tax advantage. Other types of clauses are similarly designed to avoid double probate of the same assets—duplication of administrative and probate costs. One such clause provides that the survivor must live for, say, thirty days in order to be a beneficiary under the will.

Execution and Attestation Clause An example of the execution and attestation clause is given below:

In witness whereof, I have affixed my signature to this, my last will and testament, which consists of (_____) pages, to each of which I have initialed, this _____ day of _____, One Thousand Nine Hundred and Seventy Seven (1977).

_____(Seal)

Every will should be in writing and signed by the testator at its end as a precaution against fraud; many attorneys suggest initialing each page after the last line and including a signature on the left hand margin of each page. Each page should, of course, be numbered.

Witness Clause The final clause, which helps to affirm that the will in question is really that of the deceased, is illustrated below:

Signed, sealed, and published by Terrell J. Michaels, the testator, as his last will, in the presence of us, who, at his request, and in the presence of each other, all being present at the same time, have written our names as witnesses.

It is wise to use at least three witnesses who sign in the presence of each other. Their addresses should be noted on the will. If the testator is unable to sign his or her name for any reason, most states allow the testator to make a mark and to have another person (properly witnessed) sign for him or her.

Requirements of a Valid Will

To be valid, a will must be the product of a person with a sound mind; there must have been no undue influence (influence that would remove the testator's freedom of choice); the will itself must have been properly executed; and its execution must be free from fraud.

Mental Capacity In order to be judged mentally competent, testators must have (1) a full and intelligent knowledge of the act they are involved in, (2) an understanding of the property they possess, (3) a knowledge of the dispositions they want to make of it, and (4) an appreciation of the objects they desire to be the recipients of their bounty. Generally such capacity is presumed; clear and convincing proof of mental incapacity is required to set aside a will, and the burden of proof is on the contestant.

Freedom of Choice A will is considered invalid if it can be shown that the testator was subject to the undue influence of another person at the time the will was made and executed. Threats, misrepresentations, inordinate flattery, or some physical or mental coercion employed to destroy the testator's freedom of choice are all types of *undue influence.*

Proper Execution To be considered properly executed, a will must meet the requirements of the state's Wills Act or its equivalent. It must also be demonstrable that it is in fact the will of the testator. Most states have statutes which spell out (1) who may make a will—generally any person of sound mind, age eighteen or older (age twenty-one in some states); (2) the form and execution a will must have—most states require a will to be in writing and signed by the testator at the logical end, preferably in black ink; and (3) requirements for witnesses. (No state requires more than three witnesses. It is recommended that this number sign as witnesses in the presence of the testator and each other. If at all possible, a beneficiary should not sign as a witness since in some states this would result in the disinheritance of that beneficiary.)

Changing or Revoking the Will: Codicils

A will is inoperative until the testator's death and therefore can be changed at any time until then. Wills should be revised for a number of reasons. Modification is generally in order if there is a significant change in the testator's (or the beneficiaries') health or financial circumstances; if births, deaths, marriages, or divorces have altered the operative circumstances; or if substantial changes in the tax law have occurred. An existing will can be either changed or revoked, although in certain states the "right of election," explained below, exists.

"His will reads as follows: 'Being of sound
mind and disposition, I blew it all.'"

Wills Vary in Complexity: Some Are Quite Simple
Source: New Yorker, February 5, 1972. Drawing by Modell; © 1972 The New Yorker Magazine, Inc.

Changing the Will In order to change an existing will, a *codicil*, which is
a legal means of modifying an existing will, is drawn up. It is used when
the will needs only minor modifications and is often a single page
document which reaffirms all the existing provisions in the will except the
one to be changed. The codicil should be executed in accordance with
the same formalities as a will and should be typed, signed, and witnessed
in the same manner. Where substantial changes are required, usually a
new will is preferable to a codicil. In addition, if a gift in the original will is
removed, even though substantial changes are not required, sometimes it
is best to draw a new will and destroy the old. This may avoid offending
the omitted beneficiary. Sometimes the prior will should not be destroyed, even after the new will is made and signed. This is especially true
where the testator is older or in poor health and the will may be
contested. One reason for retaining the prior will is that if the new will
fails for some reason (because of the testator's mental incapacity, for
example), the prior will may qualify. Another is that a prior will could

help to prove a "continuity of testamentary purpose"—in other words, the latest will (which may have provided a substantial gift to charity) was not an afterthought or the result of an unduly influenced mind.

Revoking the Will The revocation of a will may occur in two ways: a testator may revoke his or her will, or in some cases the law will revoke or modify it automatically. A testator can revoke a will by (1) making a later will which expressly revokes prior wills; (2) making a codicil which expressly revokes any wills; (3) making a later will which is inconsistent with a former will; and (4) physically mutilating, burning, tearing, or defacing the will with the intention of revoking it. The law automatically revokes or modifies a will under a number of circumstances, which vary from state to state. The more common ones are: (1) divorce, (2) marriage, (3) birth or adoption, and (4) slaying. If, after making a will, a testator is divorced, all provisions in the will relating to the spouse become ineffective. If a testator marries after making a will, the spouse receives that portion of the estate which would have been received had the testator died without a valid will—unless the will gives the spouse a larger share. If a testator did not provide for a child born or adopted after the will was made (unless it appears that such lack of provision was intentional), the child receives that share of the estate not passing to the testator's spouse that would have been given to the child had the deceased not had a will. And almost all states have "slayer's statutes" of some type forbidding a person who participates in a willful and unlawful killing from acquiring property as the result of the killing.

Right of Election Many states provide one further way a will can be changed: through the right of election. Some states give this right only to surviving spouses, while others extend a similar right to the testator's children. The survivor with a *right of election* has the right to "take against the will"—to take a specified portion of the probate estate regardless of what the will provides. One state, for example, allows a surviving spouse to take at least that share that would have been allowed had the deceased died without a valid will. This right is generally forfeited by a spouse who deserted the testator or participated in the testator's unlawful and willful killing.

Safeguarding the Will

In most cases, the original of the will should be kept in a safe deposit box together with deeds, contracts, and other valuable papers. Table 17-4 contains an executor's checklist of documents and information that should be kept in a safe deposit box. If each spouse has a separate safe deposit box, the couple may want to keep their wills in each other's boxes. Some states provide for "lodging" of the will, a mechanism for filing and

Table 17-4 An Executor's Checklist of Items That Should Be Kept in a Safe Deposit Box

__ (1) Birth Certificates		__ (7) Bonds, Stocks, and Securities
__ (2) Marriage Certificates (Including Any Prior Marriages)		__ (8) Real Estate Deeds
		__ (9) Business (Buy-Sell) Agreements
__ (3) Your Will (and Spouse's Will) and Trust Agreements		__ (10) Automobile Titles and Insurance Policies
__ (4) Life Insurance Policies or Certificates		__ (11) Property Insurance Policies
__ (5) Your Social Security Numbers		__ (12) Letter of Last Instructions
__ (6) Military Discharge Papers		__ (13) Additional Documents

List numbers of all checking and savings accounts including bank addresses and location of safe deposit boxes:

_____   _____   _____

_____   _____   _____

List name, address, and phone number of property and life insurance agent:

_____   _____   _____

_____   _____   _____

List name, address, and phone number of accountant:

_____   _____   _____

List name, address, and phone number of (current or past) employer. State date when you retired if applicable. Include employee benefits booklets:

_____   _____   _____

_____   _____   _____

List all debts owed to *and* owed by you:

_____   _____   _____

_____   _____   _____

List the names, addresses, telephone numbers, and birth dates of your children and other beneficiaries (including charitable beneficiaries):

_____   _____   _____

_____   _____   _____

_____   _____   _____

Source: Stephan R. Leimberg, *What to Do Until Your Legal Doctor Comes*, © 1977. Reprinted by permission of Stephan R. Leimberg, Esq.

safekeeping the will in the office of the probate court (also called orphan's or surrogate's court). In these states, this procedure satisfies the need to safeguard the will. Because it often takes a court order to open a testator's safe deposit box upon his or her death, some persons advise against keeping the will in one. Instead, it is recommended that the attorney who drew up the will and the testator's bank each retain a copy of it.

The Letter of Last Instructions

Frequently, people will have thoughts they want to convey and instructions they wish to have carried out that cannot properly be included in their wills. These suggestions or recommendations should be included in a *letter of last instructions* in the form of an informal memorandum separate from the will. Usually, it is best to make several copies of the letter and keep one at home and the others in the hands of an attorney or accountant to be mailed or delivered to beneficiaries at the appropriate time.

A letter of last instructions might provide directions with respect to: (1) location of the will and other documents; (2) funeral and burial instructions—often a will is not opened until after the funeral; (3) suggestions or recommendations as to the continuance, sale, or liquidation of a business (it is easier to freely suggest a course of action in such a letter than it is in a will); (4) personal matters that the testator might prefer not to be made public in the will, such as statements which might sound unkind or inconsiderate but which would prove of great value to the executor (for example, comments about a spendthrift spouse or a reckless son); (5) legal and accounting services (executors are free, however, to choose their own counsel—not even testators can bind them in that selection); and (6) an explanation of the actions taken in the will, which may help avoid litigation (for instance, "I left only $1,000 to my son, John, because . . ." or "I made no provisions for my oldest daughter, Melissa, because . . .").

Administration of an Estate

When people die, they usually own property and owe debts. Often, they will have claims (accounts receivable) against other persons. A process of liquidation similar to that which occurs when a corporation is dissolved must take place. In this process, money owed is collected, creditors (including the tax authorities) are satisfied, and what remains is distributed to the appropriate individuals or organizations. A local court generally supervises this *probate process* through a person designated as an *executor* in the decedent's will, or, if the decedent died intestate (without a valid will), through a court-appointed administrator.

An executor or administrator, who is sometimes also referred to as the decedent's personal representative, must collect the assets of the decedent, pay debts or provide for the payment of debts which are not currently due, and distribute any remaining assets to the persons entitled to them by will or by the intestate law of the appropriate state. Estate administration is important for many reasons. One of these reasons is that bank accounts and other contracts could not be collected without such a formal process because there would be no one who legally could bring suit or be entitled to give a release of liability. Another is that title to real estate could not be made marketable because there would be no assurance against the existence of a creditor with claims against the land. Due to the importance of the estate administration process, it is essential to select executors who are not only familiar with your affairs but who also exhibit good administrative skill.

Trusts

A *trust* is a relationship created when one party (called a grantor, settler, or creator) transfers property to a second party (the trustee) for the benefit of third parties (beneficiaries), which may or may not include the

---

A Four-Volume Will! A Videotaped Will! What Next?

The late Mrs. Frederica Cook, an early 20th-century American, made it into the *Guinness Book of Records* with a last will and testament in four volumes totaling some 95,940 words. For garrulous will makers today, technology has something new. It's now legal in Florida to videotape your directions to your heirs. A Jacksonville firm called Omni Video Optics will charge you $90 an hour for taping in black and white, $160 an hour in color; your heirs will have to pay $50 an hour for the playback. The firm has had seven takers so far—all still living.

Source: Excerpted from "Wills That Keep Your Heirs from Turning Gray," *Money,* December 1976, p. 96.

grantor. The property placed in the trust is called trust principal or *res* (pronounced race). The trustee holds the legal title to the property in the trust and must use the property and any income it produces solely for the benefit of trust beneficiaries. Generally, the trust is created by a written document. The grantor spells out the substantive provisions (such as how the property in the trust is to be allocated and how income is to be distributed) as well as certain administrative provisions. A trust may be *testamentary* (created in a will) or *intervivos* (created during the grantor's life). A trust may be revocable or irrevocable. Property placed into a revocable trust can be regained, and the terms of the trust can be altered or amended. Property placed into an irrevocable trust cannot be recovered by the grantor during the term of the trust. Although the establishment of trusts is generally for those with substantial means, the features of trusts as they relate to estate planning are briefly described in this part of the chapter.

Purposes of Trusts

Trusts are designed for any of a number of reasons. The most common motives are: (1) to attain income and estate tax savings and (2) to manage and conserve property.

Income and Estate Tax Savings It is possible to shift the burden of paying taxes on the income produced by securities, real estate, and other investments from a high bracket taxpayer to a trust itself or to its beneficiary, both of whom are typically subject to lower income tax rates than the grantor. The savings due to this rate differential coupled with the addition of the beneficiary's $750 personal exemption can be significant. Furthermore, dramatic estate tax savings are possible because the appreciation in property placed into such a trust can be entirely removed from the grantor's estate and can possibly benefit several generations of family members without adverse federal estate tax consequences.

Management and Conservation of Trust Property Minors, spendthrifts, and mental incompetents need asset management for obvious reasons. But busy executives and others who cannot or do not want to take the countless hours necessary to learn to handle large sums of money and other property often utilize trusts to relieve themselves of those burdens. The trustee assumes the responsibility for managing and conserving the property on behalf of the beneficiaries. The use of independent trustees has recently been employed by members of Congress and presidents to avoid potential conflicts of interest regarding investments. In some cases, the management ability of the trustee is held in reserve in case a healthy and vigorous individual is unexpectedly incapacitated and becomes unable or unwilling to manage his or her assets.

Selecting a Trustee

Four qualities are essential in a trustee. A trustee must possess sound business knowledge and judgment, have an intimate knowledge of the beneficiary's needs and financial situation, be skilled in investment and trust management, and be available to beneficiaries (specifically, this means the trustee should be young enough to survive through the trust term). A corporate trustee such as a trust company or bank that has been authorized to perform trust duties may seem best able to meet these requirements. A corporate trustee is likely to have investment experience and will not be incapacitated by death, disability, or absence. Unlike a family member, a corporate trustee can be relied on to be impartial and obedient to the directions of the trust instrument. Such objectivity has added value if there are several beneficiaries. On the other hand, a corporate trustee may be overly conservative in investments, impersonal, and lacking in the familiarity and understanding of family problems and needs that a family member would possess. Often a compromise is suggested: the appointment of an individual and a corporate trustee as cotrustees.

Common Types and Characteristics of Trusts

Although there are various types of trusts, the most common are the living trust, the testamentary trust, and the life insurance trust and pour-over will. Each of these is discussed separately below.

Living Trust A living (or intervivos) trust is one created during the grantor's lifetime. It can be either revocable or irrevocable. It can last for a limited period or can continue long after the grantor's death.

Revocable Living Trust The grantor reserves the right to revoke the trust and regain the trust property in a revocable living trust. For federal income tax purposes, grantors of these trusts are treated as owners of the property in the trust—in other words, just as if they held the property in their own name. Therefore, they are taxed on any income produced by the trust. Three basic advantages of revocable living trusts are often cited. The first is that management continuity and income flow are assured even after the death of the grantor. No probate is necessary since the trust continues to operate after the death of the grantor just as it did while he or she was alive. A second advantage is that the burdens of investment decisions and management responsibility are assumed by the trustee. A good example of this can be found in the case of individuals who want to control investment decisions and management policy as long as they are alive and healthy but who set up a trust to provide backup help in case they become unable or unwilling to continue managing the assets. This type of living trust is appropriately called a *step-up trust* because the trustee steps up to take the grantor's place in decision making and day-to-day management. A final advantage of the revocable living trust is that the terms of the trust and the amount of assets placed into it do not become public knowledge. Unlike the probate process, the public has no right to know the terms or conditions of a revocable living trust. Disadvantages of such trusts include the fees charged by the trustee for management of the property placed into the trust as well as the legal fees charged for drafting the trust instruments.

Irrevocable Living Trust Grantors who establish irrevocable living trusts relinquish title to the property they place in trust as well as the right to revoke or terminate it. Such trusts have all the advantages of revocable trusts as well as the potential for reducing taxes. Income produced by property held in an irrevocable living trust is taxed to either the trust or, if distributed, to its beneficiaries rather than to the grantor, who is usually in a higher tax bracket than either the trust or its beneficiaries. Disadvantages of such a trust relate to the fees charged by trustees for management of assets placed in the trust, the gift taxes on assets put into the trust, the grantor's complete loss of the trust property and any income it may produce, and the grantor's forfeiture of the right to change the terms of the trust as circumstances change.

Testamentary Trust When a trust is created by a deceased's will, it is called a testamentary trust. Such a trust comes into existence only after the will is probated. No tax savings are realized by the grantor with this type of trust since there is no divestiture of property until the grantor's death.

Life Insurance Trust and Pour-Over Will A will can be written so that it "pours over" certain assets into a previously established life insurance trust. This type of trust can be revocable or irrevocable and is created during the grantor's lifetime. The trust is named beneficiary of the grantor's insurance policies, and the trust may be "funded" (contain income-producing assets) or "unfunded." Generally the will contains a provision passing the estate—after debts, expenses, taxes, and specific bequests—to the specified trust. The trust contains provisions as to how those assets (together with insurance proceeds payable to the trust) will be administered and distributed. Such an arrangement provides for easily coordinated and well-administered management of estate assets.

Federal tax law provides for a tax on certain gifts made during one's lifetime (the gift tax) as well as on "death-time" gifts (the estate tax). Both lifetime gifts and death-time gifts are considered cumulatively and are subjected to the integrated progressive tax rate schedule given in Table 17–5. The tax on gifts is imposed on the right to transfer property and is measured by the value of the property transferred. The donor is primarily liable for the tax. The graduated table of rates presented in Table 17–5 is used for both gift and estate tax purposes and is known as the unified rate schedule. These rates are applied to all taxable gifts after a number of adjustments and computations are made. Due to the complex nature of the gift tax computation, an illustration is excluded from this discussion. This part of the chapter describes the fundamental aspects of gift taxes that should be considered in the estate planning process.

Gift Taxes

Transfers Subject to the Tax

Almost all property can be the subject of a transfer on which the gift tax must be paid. There is no tax on services one person performs for another; nor is the rent-free use of property a taxable transfer. A tax may be payable on cash gifts, gifts of personal or real property, and both direct and indirect gifts. For example, if a father makes the mortgage payments on his adult son's home, the payment is an indirect gift from father to son. In fact, almost any shifting of financial advantage in which the recipient does not provide consideration in money or money's worth may be considered a gift. Gifts are generally defined with reference to the *consideration* received. In other words, a transfer for less than adequate and full consideration in money or money's worth is viewed as a partial gift. Where some consideration is received by the transferor, the measure of the gift is found by subtracting the consideration received from the value of the property transferred. For example, suppose your father gave you a summer home having a market value of $40,000 in exchange for $5,000. The $35,000 excess of the value received over the consideration paid would be treated as a gift. Of course, if you gave no consideration for the property, its market value ($40,000) would represent the amount of the gift.

When Is a Gift Made?

The question of when a gift is made is important because it determines: (1) when the gift must be reported and the gift tax, if any, paid, and (2) the date at which the value of the gift is measured. Usually, a gift is made when the donor relinquishes dominion and control over the property or property interest transferred. For example, if a husband places cash in a

Table 17-5 **Unified Rate Schedule for Federal Gift and Estate Taxes**

Amount with Respect to Which the Tentative Tax Is to Be Computed	Tentative Tax
Not Over $10,000	18% of such amount
Over $10,000 but Not Over $20,000	$1,800 plus 20% of the excess of such amount over $10,000
Over $20,000 but Not Over $40,000	$3,800 plus 22% of the excess of such amount over $20,000
Over $40,000 but Not Over $60,000	$8,200 plus 24% of the excess of such amount over $40,000
Over $60,000 but Not Over $80,000	$13,000 plus 26% of the excess of such amount over $60,000
Over $80,000 but Not Over $100,000	$18,200 plus 28% of the excess of such amount over $80,000
Over $100,000 but Not Over $150,000	$23,800 plus 30% of the excess of such amount over $100,000
Over $150,000 but Not Over $250,000	$38,800 plus 32% of the excess of such amount over $150,000
Over $250,000 but Not Over $500,000	$70,800 plus 34% of the excess of such amount over $250,000
Over $500,000 but Not Over $750,000	$155,800 plus 37% of the excess of such amount over $500,000
Over $750,000 but Not Over $1,000,000	$248,300 plus 39% of the excess of such amount over $750,000
Over $1,000,000 but Not Over $1,250,000	$345,800 plus 41% of the excess of such amount over $1,000,000
Over $1,250,000 but Not Over $1,500,000	$448,300 plus 43% of the excess of such amount over $1,250,000
Over $1,500,000 but Not Over $2,000,000	$555,800 plus 45% of the excess of such amount over $1,500,000
Over $2,000,000 but Not Over $2,500,000	$780,800 plus 49% of the excess of such amount over $2,000,000
Over $2,500,000 but Not Over $3,000,000	$1,025,800 plus 53% of the excess of such amount over $2,500,000
Over $3,000,000 but Not Over $3,500,000	$1,290,800 plus 57% of the excess of such amount over $3,000,000
Over $3,500,000 but Not Over $4,000,000	$1,575,800 plus 61% of the excess of such amount over $3,500,000
Over $4,000,000 but Not Over $4,500,000	$1,880,800 plus 65% of the excess of such amount over $4,000,000
Over $4,500,000 but Not Over $5,000,000	$2,205,800 plus 69% of the excess of such amount over $4,500,000
Over $5,000,000	$2,550,800 plus 70% of the excess over $5,000,000

Source: Copyright © 1977 by The American College. Reprinted from *Advanced Estate Planning Casebook.*

bank account held jointly with his wife, no gift is made until the wife makes a withdrawal. Until that time the husband could completely recover the entire amount placed in the account. Similarly, when parents place property into a revocable trust for their children, no gift occurs since they have not relinquished control over the assets placed in the trust. But if they later make the trust irrevocable and thereby relinquish their right to revoke the gift, the transfer is considered a completed gift. For gift tax purposes, therefore, a transfer is not subject to gift taxes until the donor gives up: (1) the power to take or reclaim the property and (2) the right to alter the time or manner of enjoyment of the gift by the recipient.

Determining the Amount of a Taxable Gift

It is important to recognize that not all that is transferred by an individual is subject to a gift tax. Annual exclusions, gift splitting, charitable deductions, and marital deductions are all means of reducing the total amount for tax purposes. Each of these deductions is briefly discussed below.

Annual Exclusions Almost all gifts are subject to the gift tax, but for reasons of administrative convenience certain transfers, or "gift equivalents," are not counted. The gift tax law eliminates from the computation of taxable gifts transfers by a donor of amounts up to $3,000 to each of any number of donees. For example, a person could give gifts of $3,000 each to thirty donees for a total of $90,000 without paying any gift tax. Furthermore, the ability to give tax-free gifts of $3,000 per donee regenerates *annually*. This annual exclusion is available only for gifts of present interest in property—gifts which the donee has the right to use and enjoy immediately upon receipt. If the donee has to wait to use and enjoy a gift, it is then a gift of a future interest in property, and therefore the donor will not be allowed the $3,000 annual exclusion.

Gift Splitting Gift splitting is permitted in order to equate the tax treatment of married taxpayers domiciled in community property states with the tax treatment of married taxpayers domiciled in common law states. When a spouse earns a dollar in a community property state, half of that dollar is deemed to be owned by the other spouse immediately and automatically. If a gift is made of that dollar, each spouse is considered to have given fifty cents. Similarly, in common law states, a married donor, with the consent of his or her spouse, can elect to treat gifts as if they were made one-half by each spouse. Because of this gift-splitting option, if a wife transfers $6,000 to her son and the required consent is given by her husband, for tax computation purposes her gift is viewed as $3,000, and her husband is considered to have given the other $3,000. The total amount, because of the split, is entirely gift tax–free because a $3,000 annual exclusion is allowed to each spouse. The wife could give $6,000 to any number of donees and by splitting the gift with her husband avoid the tax on the entire gift. This tax reduction technique is available even if one spouse makes all the gifts and the other spouse gives nothing. Gift splitting is allowed, however, only for gifts to third parties.

Charitable Deductions There is no limit on the amount that can be given gift tax–free to a qualified charity—one to which deductible gifts can be made for income tax purposes. It is therefore possible for people to give their entire estate to charity and receive a gift tax deduction for the total amount. There would be no taxes, regardless of the type or amount of assets transferred.

Marital Deductions Again, in order to assure that federal transfer taxes have an impact on taxpayers domiciled in common law states similar to that on taxpayers domiciled in community property states, federal law permits a deduction for gift tax purposes on property given by one spouse

Gifts Are Taxed, Too

Many people are not aware of it, but the federal government taxes gifts that exceed certain amounts.

You are permitted to give any one person up to $3,000 each year tax-free, and you may make as many of those $3,000 presents as you like each year. A husband and wife can jointly give up to $6,000 to any one person each year.

Until last September [1976] you were also allowed a $30,000 lifetime exemption that could be used to offset gifts over the annual limits. Congress converted that exemption into a combined gift and estate tax credit. For 1977 the credit works out to a combined exemption from gift and estate taxes of about $120,000. (Under the previous law, you could pass on $90,000 of assets tax-free through gifts and your estate—$30,000 in gifts and $60,000 in bequests.) Congress also set up a single tax schedule for gifts and estates. Before, gift taxes were 25% lower than estate tax rates. State inheritance and gift tax laws don't necessarily parallel the federal provisions and should be checked before you make any sizable gifts.

Source: "Gifts Are Taxed, Too," *Changing Times,* December 1976, p. 38. Reprinted with permission from *Changing Times* Magazine, © Kiplinger Washington Editors, Inc., 1976.

Table 17–6 **Marital Deduction for Gift Tax Purposes**

Gift to Spouse	Marital Deduction
First $100,000	100%
Next $100,000	None
Over $200,000	50%

Source: Copyright © 1976 by The American College. Reprinted from *Advanced Estate Planning Tax Reform Act Supplement.*

to another. Table 17–6 itemizes the marital deductions permitted for various sizes of gifts to spouses. Assume, for example, that one spouse gives a gift of $200,000 to the other. The taxes on this gift would be determined as follows:

Gross Gift	$200,000
Less: Annual Exclusion	3,000
Includable Gift	$197,000
Less: Gift Tax Marital Deduction	100,000
Taxable Gift	$ 97,000

Only $97,000 of the $200,000 gift would be taxable as a gift.

Payment of the Gift Tax

A quarterly gift tax return must be filed when taxable gifts for the current calendar quarter plus taxable gifts previously made during the calendar year exceed $25,000. If annual gifts do not exceed $25,000 in one year, a gift tax return is not due until 15 February of the immediately following year.

Reasons for Making Lifetime Gifts

There are a number of tax-oriented reasons why estate planners recommend gift giving. The most important of these are discussed briefly below.

Gift Exclusion A single individual can give any number of donees up to $3,000 each year entirely gift tax–free. There are no tax costs to either the donee or the donor for making the transfer. If the donor is married and the donor's spouse consents, the gift tax–free limit is increased to $6,000, even if the entire gift was made from the donor's assets.

Estate Tax Savings A married individual with an estate of over $500,000 can save at least $500 in estate taxes by giving away $3,000. That is because estate taxes would consume at least that much if the property were retained in the estate. So the government is "funding" $500 or more of each $3,000 gift. For a single individual who is necessarily in an even higher estate tax bracket because the marital deduction is unavailable, the savings in estate taxes are even greater.

Gift Tax Exclusion Regardless of the size of the gift, if it is made more than three years before the donor's death, the gift will not be treated as part of the estate and subject to the estate tax. The estate tax savings from this exclusion can be significant.

Appreciation in Value One of the most important reasons for making a lifetime gift is that the appreciation on the gift from the time the gift is made will not be included in the donor's estate unless the gift is, for some reason, includable in the estate—as, for instance, it would be if the donor died within three years of making the gift. If Larry gives Steve stock worth $100,000, and it grows to $600,000 by the date of Larry's death five years later, only the $100,000 value of the stock at the time of the gift enters into the tax computation of Larry's estate.

Payment Limit After 1976, gift taxes do not have to be paid on gifts totaling $120,667 or less.

Impact of Marital Deduction Because of the gift tax marital deduction, the first $100,000 of a gift made to a spouse (in excess of the $3,000 annual exclusion) is entirely gift tax–free. It is possible, therefore, to combine the annual exclusion ($3,000), the gift tax marital deduction ($100,000), and the lifetime exemption or credit (worth $120,667) to give a spouse up to $223,667 without paying one cent in federal gift taxes.

Estate Taxes and Planning

The federal estate tax is levied on the transfer of property at death. The tax is measured by the value of the property which the deceased transfers (or is deemed to transfer) to others. The parenthetical phrase "deemed to transfer" is important because the estate tax reaches not only transfers that a deceased actually makes at death but also certain transfers made during the person's lifetime. In other words, to thwart tax avoidance schemes, the estate tax is imposed on certain lifetime gifts made to "beat the estate tax" or which are in essence the same as dispositions of property made at death. For example, if Max gives his son Eric $100,000 the day before Max's death, the tax law treats the gift as if it were actually made at Max's death. The $100,000 is therefore subject to the federal estate tax in addition to any applicable gift tax. This part of the chapter discusses key facts related to estate taxes and the estate planning process.

Computation of the Estate Tax

There are five stages involved in the process of computing estate taxes. The first involves determining the *gross estate,* the total of all property in which the decedent had an interest and which is required to be included in the estate. Secondly, the *adjusted gross estate* is determined. This is done by subtracting from the gross estate any allowable funeral and administrative expenses, debts, certain taxes, and losses incurred during administration. The calculation of the *taxable estate,* the third stage, is accomplished by subtracting any allowable marital deduction, charitable deduction, or orphan's deduction from the adjusted gross estate.

The computation of the *estate tax payable before credits* is the fourth stage. After determining the value of the taxable estate, any "adjusted taxable gifts"—which include certain taxable lifetime transfers not included in the deceased's gross estate—are added to the taxable estate. The unified rate schedule—the same one applicable to gift taxes, shown in Table 17–5—is then applied to determine a tentative estate tax. After this tentative tax is found, gift taxes the decedent paid on certain gifts are subtracted. The result is the estate tax payable before reduction by any available credits.

The final stage involves the determination of the *net federal estate tax.* Certain credits are allowed against the estate tax payable. These result in a dollar for dollar reduction of the tax. They are: (1) unified credit, (2) state death tax credit, (3) credit for foreign death tax, and (4) credit for taxes paid on prior transfers. After reducing the estate tax payable for any eligible credits, the net federal estate tax is payable by the decedent's executor, generally within nine months of the decedent's death. The form included in Table 17–7 depicts for a hypothetical situation the computations required to determine the net estate tax payable. The form is useful in following the flow of dollars from the gross estate to the net estate tax payable. Because of the technical nature involved in these computations, no further discussion of them is included.

State Death Taxes

More individuals are subject to state death taxes than are liable for federal estate taxes. This is because: (1) federal laws permit certain deductions such as the marital deduction that many state laws do not; (2) federal law exempts certain transfers that are not exempted under many state laws—for instance, death benefits under qualified noncontributory corporate retirement plans; and (3) the amount of property exempted from

Table 17–7 A Form for Computing the Net Estate Tax Payable

Line	Computation	Item	Amount	Total Amount
(1)		*Gross Estate*		$500,000
	Subtract Sum of:	(a) Funeral Expenses	$ 5,000	
		(b) Administrative Expenses	30,000	
		(c) Debts	20,000	
		(d) Taxes	5,000	
		(e) Losses	—	
(2)	Result:	*Adjusted Gross Estate*		$440,000
	Subtract Sum of:	(a) Marital Deduction	$250,000	
		(b) Charitable Deduction	—	
		(c) Orphan's Deduction	—	
(3)	Result:	*Taxable Estate*		$190,000
(4)	Add:	*Adjusted Taxable Gifts*		$100,000
(5)	Result:	*Tentative Tax Base*		$290,000
(6)	Compute:	*Tentative Tax*	$ 84,400[a]	
(7)	Subtract:	Gift Taxes Paid or Payable on Gifts Made within Last 3 Years	—	
(8)	Result:	*Tax Payable before Reduction for Credits*		$ 84,400
(9)	Subtract Sum of:	(a) Unified Credit	$ 30,000	
		(b) State Death Tax Credit	1,040	
		(c) Credit for Tax on Prior Transfers	—	
		(d) Credit for Foreign Death Taxes	—	
(10)	Result:	*Net Estate Tax Payable*		$ 53,360

[a]This value was calculated using the Unified Rate Schedule presented earlier in Table 17-5. The calculation was made as follows: $70,800 + .34($290,000 − $250,000) = $84,4000.

Source: Tools and Techniques of Estate Planning—After the 1976 Tax Reform Act, Stephan R. Leimberg, Herbert Levy, and Stephen N. Kendell, National Underwriter Company, by permission of the publisher.

tax under federal law is larger than that exempted by the laws of most states. There are three basic types of state death tax: a state inheritance tax, a state estate tax, and a credit estate tax. Each of these is briefly described below.

Inheritance Tax An inheritance tax, which is the most common type of state death tax, is a tax on the right to receive a decedent's property. The amount of the tax depends on the value of the property each beneficiary

"First the good news—you won't have
to pay any inheritance tax."

In Certain Instances Inheritance Taxes Aren't All Bad
Source: Lepper—Rothco Cartoons Inc.

receives and the relationship of the beneficiary to the deceased. In most
states beneficiaries are divided into categories. The lowest rates and
largest exemptions are allocated to lineal descendants or to those
beneficiaries most closely related to the deceased. For example, in
Pennsylvania, property left to a child of the deceased is taxed at 6 percent,
while the same property left to a cousin is subject to a 15 percent rate.
Real property held jointly with rights of survivorship by spouses is exempt
from state death taxes, while the same property held jointly by brothers is
subject to a 15 percent tax.

Estate Tax A state estate tax is imposed on the deceased's right to
transfer property and is measured by the value of the property transferred. It is therefore similar to the federal estate tax. Some states impose
both an inheritance and an estate tax.

Credit Estate Tax The credit, or "gap," estate tax is designed to bridge the gap between the state's inheritance and estate taxes and the maximum state death tax credit allowed against the federal estate tax. (See line 9b of the form for computing the net estate taxes payable presented in Table 17-7.) The credit tax is best illustrated by a simple example. If a deceased's taxable estate for federal estate tax purposes is $500,000, a credit of up to $10,000 against the federal tax is allowed for taxes paid to the state as death taxes. See Table 17-8, which gives federal estate tax credits for state death taxes, for determination of this credit. The amount of any state death taxes paid may be subtracted from the tax, provided, however, that the maximum to be subtracted not exceed the maximum shown in the table. If the state's inheritance tax amounts to only $8,000, an additional tax—a $2,000 credit estate tax—is imposed so that the total state death tax is increased to $10,000, the amount of credit given by the federal government for state death taxes.

Other Factors Affecting the Amount of State Death Tax Due Other factors that may affect the state estate taxes include: (1) state exemptions and deductions, (2) multiple state taxation, and (3) tax rates.

Exemptions and Deductions Not all property is subject to taxation. Generally, states exempt property transferred to the United States, to the state itself, and to certain charitable organizations. A few states exempt property passing to a surviving spouse. A number of states either totally or partially exempt life insurance proceeds unless payable to or for the benefit of the estate or its creditors. Most states allow deductions for administrative costs, debts, funeral and last illness expenses, and certain property taxes that are unpaid at the deceased's death.

Multiple Taxation Many individuals have summer and winter homes or land and other property in states other than where they live. Although most estates are taxed only by one state, in certain situations an estate or its beneficiaries may be liable for the taxes of more than one state. The right of a state to impose a death tax depends on the type of property involved. The general treatment of the major types of property is as follows.

Real estate, which includes land and permanent buildings, can be taxed only by the state in which the property is located.

Tangible personal property, which includes cars, boats, and household goods, can be taxed only in a state where it is situated. A boat, for example, is taxed where it is permanently docked. Its registry and location for insurance purposes are examined in order to determine its legal location.

Table 17–8 Federal Estate Tax Credit for State Death Taxes

Taxable Estate	Maximum Tax Credit
Not Over $150,000	8/10ths of 1% of the amount by which the taxable estate exceeds $100,000
Over $150,000 but Not Over $200,000	$400 plus 1.6% of the excess over $150,000
Over $200,000 but Not Over $300,000	$1,200 plus 2.4% of the excess over $200,000
Over $300,000 but Not Over $500,000	$3,600 plus 3.2% of the excess over $300,000
Over $500,000 but Not Over $700,000	$10,000 plus 4% of the excess over $500,000
Over $700,000 but Not Over $900,000	$18,000 plus 4.8% of the excess over $700,000
Over $900,000 but Not Over $1,100,000	$27,600 plus 5.6% of the excess over $900,000
Over $1,100,000 but Not Over $1,600,000	$38,800 plus 6.4% of the excess over $1,100,000
Over $1,600,000 but Not Over $2,100,000	$70,800 plus 7.2% of the excess over $1,600,000
Over $2,100,000 but Not Over $2,600,000	$106,800 plus 8% of the excess over $2,100,000
Over $2,600,000 but Not Over $3,100,000	$146,800 plus 8.8% of the excess over $2,600,000
Over $3,100,000 but Not Over $3,600,000	$190,800 plus 9.6% of the excess over $3,100,000
Over $3,600,000 but Not Over $4,100,000	$238,800 plus 10.4% of the excess over $3,600,000
Over $4,100,000 but Not Over $5,100,000	$290,800 plus 11.2% of the excess over $4,100,000
Over $5,100,000 but Not Over $6,100,000	$402,800 plus 12% of the excess over $5,100,000
Over $6,100,000 but not Over $7,100,000	$522,800 plus 12.8% of the excess over $6,100,000
Over $7,100,000 but Not Over $8,100,000	$650,800 plus 13.6% of the excess over $7,100,000
Over $8,100,000 but Not Over $9,100,000	$786,800 plus 14.4% of the excess over $8,100,000
Over $9,100,000 but Not Over $10,100,000	$930,800 plus 15.2% of the excess over $9,100,000
Over $10,100,000	$1,082,800 plus 16% of the excess over $10,100,000

Source: Copyright © 1977 by The American College. Reprinted from Advanced Estate Planning Casebook.

Intangible personal property—which includes securities such as stocks, bonds, notes, and mortgages—may, in the absence of interstate agreements, be taxed by several states. Generally, intangible personal property is taxed only by the state of the deceased's domicile. Unfortunately, if a deceased has residences in more than one state or does not clearly establish his or her state of domicile, two or more states can impose death taxes on the same intangible personal property.

Tax Rates The rates at which transfers or receipts of property are taxed vary widely from state to state. Some states have graduated rates similar to the federal tax, while others, such as Pennsylvania, have flat rates that do not grow progressively as the size of the estate increases. In fact, because the impact of state death taxes can be so significant, many individuals go "domicile shopping" at retirement to find a state with favorable rates, exemptions, and deductions.

Tools and Techniques of Estate Planning

The federal and state tax laws described in the preceding paragraphs provide both problems and opportunities to the estate planner. Estate shrinkage can be minimized and financial security maximized by judicious use of certain tax-oriented arrangements and maneuvers. Techniques of estate planning can be summarized by the four D's: Divide, Deduct, Defer, and Discount. These strategies are described briefly below.

Dividing the Estate Each time a new taxpaying entity can be created, income taxes are saved and estate accumulation is stimulated. Some of the more popular techniques are:

1. Giving income producing property to minor children, either outright or in trust. Since each child has an exemption and can receive up to $750 a year and pay no tax, a substantial income tax savings can be realized each year by persons in high tax brackets.

2. Creating multiple trusts for short-term periods. The income on the trust property is taxed to the beneficiary during the term of the trust, but the income-producing property is eventually returned to the grantor of the trust.

3. Establishing a corporation. Incorporation permits individuals in high tax brackets such as doctors or other professionals to save substantial sums by accumulating income in a manner subject to relatively lower income tax rates.

4. Fully qualifying for the federal estate tax marital deduction. This marital deduction allows an individual to pass—estate tax–free—up to

Planning Your Estate: Avoid the Common Mistakes!

A survey of bank trust officers conducted by the American Bankers Association reveals some very common errors people make when they plan to pass their assets to their families.

The Classic Blunder: No Will When people die without a will, the state in which they are domiciled writes one for them. The state follows a legal formula which the legislature believes best fits the average situation but may not best fit yours.

The Unprepared Spouse Each spouse should be aware of all the financial transactions taking place in the household in order to be prepared to take over financial management if a tragedy causes the death or incapacitation of the other spouse.

No Ready Cash Make sure your spouse has enough liquidity to pay for funeral costs, taxes, administration fees, debts, and daily living expenses until the estate is settled.

The Too-Rigid Will or Trust An ironclad will and trust agreement with severe restrictions may hamper the trustees' power to manage the estate as they see fit when family situations change and business takes unpredictable turns.

Paying Unnecessary Taxes Use the various options available to spare your beneficiaries the burden of unnecessary taxes on your estate.

Joint-Ownership: No Panacea It is a mistake to use joint ownership as a substitute for a will. Joint ownership has its disadvantages and should be avoided.

Selecting the Wrong Executor Selecting your best friend as executor to your estate may sometimes prove harmful, especially if he or she is not qualified or is in bad health. It is better to select your bank as executor and perhaps your spouse as coexecutor to assure that your estate will be managed with objectivity, expertise, and an understanding of its more personal aspects.

Ignoring Professional Help Writing your own will or making several changes in it without observing the legal formalities may cause your will to be declared invalid. Consult professional people rather than taking free advice from friends.

Failing to Update Your Will In an increasingly mobile society, with increasingly complex probate laws, it becomes more and more important to update your will and trust agreements whenever you have a change in family circumstances, move from state to state, or learn of changes in the law.

Source: Headings are from "Common Mistakes That Can Erode Your Estate," *Nation's Business,* March 1976, pp. 77–80.

$250,000 to a spouse (more if one-half the adjusted gross estate exceeds this amount). It also helps obtain the full advantage from the surviving spouse's unified credit.

Deducting Any dollar which is deductible from taxable income (or from a deceased's gross estate) is more useful to the taxpayer than a nondeductible dollar. The higher the income (or estate tax bracket), the more value that results from the privilege of deductibility. Some of the retirement plans discussed in Chapter 16 that enable an individual to obtain deductions for money set aside for retirement include: (1) qualified pension plans, (2) qualified profit-sharing plans, (3) Keogh plans, and (4) individual retirement plans.

Deferring Progressive tax rates (rates that increase as the income or size of the estate increases) penalize taxpayers whose maximum earnings (or estates) reach high peaks. This makes it extremely difficult to gain and retain financial security. Among the devices that help minimize the total tax burden by spreading income over more than one tax year or deferring the tax to a later period so that the taxpayer can invest the tax money for a longer period of time are:

1. Nonqualified deferred compensation plans for selected individuals in corporate businesses as well as private contractors.

2. The making of installment sales instead of cash sales so that the taxable gain can be spread over a number of years.

3. Private annuities, which are arrangements whereby one person transfers property to another, usually younger, family member. This recipient promises in return to pay an annuity to the original owner for as long as he or she lives. The income tax attributable to such an annuity can thereby be spread over a number of years.

4. Qualified pension and profit-sharing plans that allow tax deferral on the income and gains from investments.

5. Government Series E Bonds, since their earnings can be treated as taxable income at maturity rather than each year as earned.

6. Stocks that yield low dividends but provide high price appreciation because management is retaining earnings for company development.

7. Life insurance policies in which lifetime growth is not taxed and death values are income tax–free. If the insured survives, earnings inherent in policy values become taxable only as received, so the tax on any gain can be deferred over a lifetime.

8. Depreciable real estate that yields high write-offs in years when the estate owner is earning large amounts of taxable income.

9. Installment payment of federal estate taxes applicable to a business

interest. Payments can be spread over as many as fifteen years with only the interest being paid on the unpaid tax during the first five years.

Discounting After everything is done to accumulate an estate and reduce the income and estate tax burdens on it, there may still be a tax payable. There are two instruments which make it possible to, in effect, pay estate taxes at a discount: Flower Bonds and a special type of life insurance policy.

Flower Bonds are issued by the federal government and are now available through trust departments of banks, even to the terminally ill. They are sold at less than par but are redeemed by the government at par in payment of the federal estate tax. Savings are reduced, however, by inclusion of the bond at par in the gross estate of the deceased and by capital gains and preference taxes on the difference between the price paid by the decedent for the bonds and the amount at which they are redeemed.

Life insurance can be purchased by a person other than the insured or the insured's spouse, or by a trust, for an annual premium that is from 3 to 6 percent of the face (death) value of the policy. If proper arrangements are made, the proceeds of such insurance will pass to the decedent's beneficiaries free of income tax, estate tax, inheritance tax, and probate costs. Such proceeds may be used to pay death taxes and other probate costs.

Summary

The estate planning process involves accumulating, conserving, and distributing an estate in a manner that will most effectively achieve an estate owner's personal goals. The forces that often thwart the accomplishment of financial security for the estate owner and his or her family include death-related costs, inflation, improper asset management, insufficient cash to pay debts and expenses, improper or insufficient use of vehicles of asset transfer, and the prolonged disability of the estate owner. The estate planning process ideally consists of six elements or steps: (1) gathering of data, (2) identification of possible problems, (3) formulation of a plan and delegation of responsibilities for executing that arrangement, (4) testing of the plan, (5) plan implementation, and (6) periodic and regularly scheduled review of the plan.

Important privileges are forfeited when a person dies without a valid will. These include the right to decide how property will be transferred at death and who will receive it and the right to select someone to administer the estate, nominate a guardian, and decide who will bear the burden of taxes and administration expenses. The will should provide a clean and unambiguous expression of the testator's wishes, be flexible enough to encompass possible events or changes in family circumstances occurring after it is drawn, and give proper regard to minimization of federal and state taxes. A will is valid only if properly executed by a testator of sound mind. Wills can be changed by codicil or revoked by a later will. Estate administration can be described as a three-part process in which the decedent's personal representative, or executor, must: (1) collect the decedent's assets, (2) pay his or her debts and taxes, and (3) distribute any remaining assets to the appropriate beneficiaries.

The trust relationship arises when one party, the grantor, transfers property to a second party, the trustee, for the benefit of third parties, the beneficiaries. Trusts may be testamentary, intervivos, revocable, or irrevocable. The tax consequences of placing property in trust depend on which types of trusts are used. Trusts are designed primarily to accomplish one or more of three purposes: (1) to save income and estate taxes, (2) to provide asset management, and (3) to conserve trust property.

The gift tax law imposes a graduated tax on the right to transfer property during one's lifetime. The estate tax is essentially a levy on the right to make gifts at death. It is unified (coordinated with) the gift tax so that the rates and credits are the same for both. Once the estate tax is computed, certain credits are allowed and the resulting amount is generally payable within nine months of the decedent's death. State death taxes are also payable by a decedent's executor. The three types of state death taxes are: (1) an inheritance tax, (2) an estate tax, and (3) a credit estate, or "gap," tax. The four D's of estate planning—Divide, Deduct, Defer, and Discount—are used to define four categories in which every major tool or tax saving technique of the estate planner can be classified. Dividing involves the creation of new tax entities; deducting includes any type of retirement or employee benefit plan that provides financial security with before-tax dollars; deferring gives an individual the use of money that otherwise would have been paid in taxes; and discounting involves paying all expenses with "discounted" dollars.

Key Terms

annual exclusions	estate planning
apportionment statutes	estate tax
carry-over basis tax trap	executor
charitable deduction	first-level death related costs
codicil	Flower Bonds
credit estate "gap" tax	gift tax
death taxes	gift splitting
double probate	grantor

gross estate
inheritance tax
intervivos (living) trust
intestacy
irrevocable trust
letter of last instructions
life insurance trust and
pour-over will
living death
marital deduction
pecuniary legacy
probate
probate estate
res (trust principal)

revocable trust
right of election
second-level death related costs
step-up trust
taxable gifts
testamentary
testamentary trust
testator
trust
trustee
unified credit
unified rate schedule
will

Review Questions

1. Discuss the importance and goals of estate planning. Explain why estates often break up. Distinguish between the probate estate and the gross estate.

2. Briefly describe the steps involved in the estate planning process.

3. What is a will? For what major purposes is a will of importance? Describe the consequences of dying intestate.

4. Describe the basic clauses that are normally included as part of a will.

5. Indicate any requirements that exist with respect to who may make a valid will.

6. How can changes in the provisions of a will be made legally? In what two ways can a will be revoked?

7. Indicate what is meant by each of the following: (a) codicil, (b) right of election, (c) lodging of the will, (d) letter of last instructions, and (e) intestacy.

8. What is meant by the probate process? Who is an executor, and what role does the executor play in the estate settlement process?

9. Describe the basic trust arrangement and discuss purposes for which trusts are typically established. What essential qualities should a trustee possess?

10. Explain what is meant by each of the following: (a) trustee, (b) grantor, (c) beneficiary, (d) testamentary trust, and (e) life insurance trust and pour-over will.

11. What is a living trust? Distinguish between a revocable living trust and an irrevocable living trust.

12. Answer and/or describe the following as they relate to federal gift taxes:

(a) What is a gift?

(b) When is a gift made?

(c) Annual exclusion.

(d) Gift splitting.

(e) Charitable deduction.

(f) Marital deduction.

(g) Application of the tax rate.

(h) Payment of the gift tax.

13. Discuss the reasons estate planners recommend giving gifts. How and in what ways might gift giving help reduce estate shrinkage?

14. Explain the following as they relate to federal and/or state estate taxes:

(a) General nature of the estate tax.

(b) Computation of the estate tax.

(c) State inheritance tax.

(d) State estate tax.

(e) Credit estate tax.

(f) The amount of exemptions and deductions.

(g) Multiple estate taxation.

(h) Rates of state estate taxation.

15. "The tools and techniques of estate planning can be summarized by the four D's—Divide, Deduct, Defer, and Discount." Describe and discuss each of the four D's and their associated strategies.

Case Problems

17-1 A Long Overdue Will for Kris

Kris Pappadopolus, a Greek national, migrated to the United States during the late forties. A man of many talents and deep foresight, he has during his stay in the United States built a large fleet of ocean-going oil tankers. Now a wealthy man in his sixties, he resides in Palm Springs, Florida, with his wife, Veronica, age thirty-five. He has two sons, who are both high school seniors. For quite a while, Kris has considered preparing a will in order to assure that his estate will be aptly distributed if some unforeseen tragedy or natural cause takes his life. A survey of his estate reveals the following:

Ranch in Amarillo, Texas	$ 500,000
Condominium in San Francisco	200,000
House in Palm Springs	600,000
Franchise in Ice Cream Stores	2,500,000
Stock in Seven Seas International	5,000,000
Shares in Fourth National Bank	1,000,000
Corporate Bonds	3,000,000
Other Assets	200,000
Total Assets	$13,000,000

In addition to $1,000,000 for their education and welfare, he would like to leave his sons each 20 percent of his estate. He wishes to leave 40 percent of the estate for his wife. The rest of the estate is to be divided among relatives, friends, and charitable institutions. He has scheduled an appointment for drafting his will with his attorney and close friend, Leonard Wiseman. Kris would like to appoint Leonard and his cousin, Plato Jones, as coexecutors of his estate. In the instance one of them predeceases Kris, he would like his bank, Fourth National Bank, to act as coexecutor.

Questions

1. Does Kris really need a will? Explain why or why not. What would happen to his estate if he were to die without a will?

2. Explain to Kris the common features that need to be incorporated into a will.

3. What are the options available to Kris if he decides to change or revoke the will at a later date?

4. Give Kris appropriate advice for drawing up a will which will carry out his wishes.

5. What duties will Leonard Wiseman and Plato Jones have to perform as coexecutors of Kris's estate?

17-2 Estate Taxes on Phillip Colburn's Estate

Phillip Colburn, of Arlington Heights, Delaware, was sixty-five and in good health in 1976. He and his wife, Delores, had been married for thirty-five years. They had an adult son who had been made sole beneficiary of Phillip's and his wife's estate. When Phillip retired as chairman of the Vilanto Corporation in 1976, his net worth (estate) was valued at $1,000,000. The value had increased 6 percent by 1977. When Phillip died in 1977, he had no debts. Funeral costs amounted to $20,000 and the cost of administering the estate totaled $50,000. These two items are the only applicable deductions from his gross estate. Phillip left

$75,000 of his estate to his alma mater, Old State University. Four years prior to his death he had made adjusted taxable gifts of $160,000. No gift taxes were paid or payable on any of his post-1976 gifts. The unified credit available to Phillip's estate in the year of his death was $34,000. A state death tax credit of $3,800 was also available to the estate. Assume that the marital deduction of a maximum of either $250,000 or one-half of the adjusted gross estate could be taken. Using the format given in Table 17-7 as a guide to calculations, answer each of the following questions.

Questions

1. Compute the value of Phillip's gross estate at the time of his death.
2. Determine the value of his adjusted gross estate.
3. Calculate the value of the marital deduction available to his estate.
4. Determine the taxable estate at Phillip's death.
5. Calculate:
(a) the tentative tax base
(b) the tentative tax (using Table 17-5)
(c) the tax payable before credits
6. Determine the value of the net estate tax payable on Phillip's estate.
7. Comment on the estate shrinkage experienced on his estate. What might have been done to reduce this shrinkage? Explain.

| Selected References | Ashley, Paul Prichard, *You and Your Will: The Planning and Management of Your Estate.* New York: McGraw-Hill, 1975. |

Ashley, Paul Prichard, *You and Your Will: The Planning and Management of Your Estate.* New York: McGraw-Hill, 1975.

"Conserving Your Estate." *Business Week*, 26 July 1976, pp. 121–128.

Considine, Millie, and Pool, Ruth. *Wills: A Dead Giveaway.* New York: Doubleday, 1974.

"Could a Trust Fund Save You Money?" *Changing Times*, July 1975, pp. 37–40.

"Easing Estate and Gift Taxes: The New Plan, and Its Chances." *U.S. News & World Report*, 7 June 1976, pp. 68–70.

Freilincher, Morton. *Estate Planning Handbook—With Forms.* 2d ed. Englewood Cliffs, N.J.: Prentice-Hall, 1975.

Harris, Homer I. *Family Estate Planning Guide.* Mount Kisco, N.Y.: Baker, Voorhis, 1971.

"Latest on Planning an Estate." *U.S. News & World Report*, 30 May 1977, pp. 47–49.

"The Law and Your Will: A Lot of New Intricacies." *U.S. News & World Report*, 30 May 1977, pp. 49–50.

"Pitfalls to Watch For in Planning Your Estate." *U.S. News & World Report*, 18 December 1972, pp. 48–57.

"Should Heirs Pay a Capital Gains Tax?" *U.S. News & World Report*, 16 August 1976, pp. 45–47.

"Suppose You Die without a Will." *Changing Times*, January 1974, pp. 45–46.

"Tax Breaks That Help You Pass On More to Your Heirs." *Changing Times*, June 1977, pp. 7–11.

"Update Your Will Now or Your Loved Ones Lose." *Consumers Digest*, September/October 1975, pp. 18–20.

"Why Estate Planning Makes So Much Sense." *Better Homes and Gardens*, May 1976, pp. 36–40.

"Why You Should Make a Will and How to Go About It." *U.S. News & World Report*, 21 June 1976, pp. 73–74.

Ziegler, Richard S., and Flaherty, Patrick F. *Estate Planning for Everyone—The Whole Truth from Planning to Probate*. New York: Funk & Wagnalls, 1974.

Glossary

The chapter in which the term first is explained is given in parentheses.

Acceleration clause (12)   A clause that allows the lender to demand immediate repayment of the entire amount of the unpaid debt if the purchaser misses a payment.

Accrual basis (4)   A method used to determine income and expense under which items of income or expense are recognized when the obligation to receive or pay them is incurred.

Accumulation period (16)   The period during which premiums are paid for the purchase of an annuity. The amount paid in to the annuity is called the *principal*.

Actual cash value (15)   A value assigned to an insured property that is determined by subtracting depreciation from replacement cost. *See also* Replacement cost.

Add-on clause (12)   A clause that allows the lender to hold as security a number of items that are purchased over a period time; the lender does not release the security interest on these items until the entire loan has been paid off.

Add-on (interest) method (12)   A method by which the finance charge is added to the principal amount; the total is divided by the number of payments to be made to determine the amount of the monthly payment.

Adjusted balance method (11)   A common method of calculating interest on a charge account by which the interest charge is applied to the balance remaining at the end of the billing period (ignoring purchases or returns made during the billing period).

Adjusted gross income (4)   The amount of income remaining after subtracting allowable deductions from gross income in the process of determining the amount of taxable income.

Adverse selection (13)   The tendency for those who anticipate a loss in the near future to seek insurance more often than others in the general population.

Amended (tax) return (4)   A tax return filed to correct errors or to adjust for information received after the filing date of the taxpayer's original return.

American Stock Exchange (AMEX) (7)   The second largest organized security exchange, handling approximately 25 percent of all share volume on organized exchanges.

Amortized loan (12)   A loan in which the financing cost components for fixed interest rates are converted into equal monthly payments.

Annuity (16)   A contract that allows for the systematic liquidation of an estate to protect against the financial insolvency that could result from out-living personal financial resources. There are several different types of annuities, which may be classified by the following system: method of paying premiums (single premium, installment); disposition of proceeds (life annuity, guaranteed minimum, annuity certain, temporary); inception date of proceeds (immediate, deferred); number of lives covered (single life, joint and last survivorship); and method of calculating benefits (fixed dollar, variable).

Annual percentage rate (APR) (11)   The true rate of interest paid over the life of a loan.

Apportionment statutes (17)   State laws that allocate the burden of taxes among the beneficiaries in the absence of a specific provision for apportionment in a will.

Ask price (7)   The lowest price at which a security traded in the over-the-counter market will be sold.

Assessed value (9)   The value placed on a piece of property for purposes of establishing taxes due.

Assets (1,2)   Items that a person owns. They may be classified as financial (cash, savings, and investments) or nonfinancial (real estate, automobiles, etc.).

Assigned risk plan (15)   A plan that provides automobile insurance to drivers whose records would prohibit them from receiving insurance in a normal manner.

Assignment (wage)   *See* Garnishment.

Audit (4)   The procedure used by the IRS to validate the accuracy of tax returns.

Automatic reinvestment plan (8)   A plan which, if available, allows the mutual fund shareowner to elect to have dividends, interest, and capital gains realized on the fund's holdings reinvested in additional shares of the fund.

Average daily balance method (11)   A method of calculating interest on a charge account by which the interest is applied to the average daily balance of the account over the billing period. This method does not reflect purchases or returns made during the billing period.

Average tax rate (4)   The rate at which each dollar of a taxpayer's taxable income is on the average taxed. It is calculated by dividing tax liability by taxable income.

Balanced budget (3)   A budget in which the total income for the period equals or exceeds the total expenses of the period.

Balanced funds (8)   Portfolio of an investment company, consisting of the bonds, preferred stocks, and common stocks of a variety of industries or companies; such portfolios provide good but safe returns.

Balance sheet (1)   A key financial statement that presents assets, liabilities, and net worth, each measured at a specified point in time.

Balance sheet equation (2)   The accounting relationship among assets, liabilities, and net worth. The equation states that assets minus liabilities equals net worth.

Balloon clause (12)   A clause to an installment purchase agreement stating that the final payment will be considerably larger than all other payments.

Bankruptcy (technical) (2)   A state in which a person's or family's net worth is less than zero or in which a person or family is unable to pay bills as they come due.

Bear market (7)   A condition of the market in which stock prices generally fall. Bear markets are normally associated with investor pessimism, economic slowdowns, and government control. *See also* Bull market.

Beneficiary (13, 17)   A person who receives the death benefits of an insurance policy when the insured dies; also a person who receives proceeds from the estate of a deceased.

Bid price (7)   The highest price offered to purchase a security traded in the over-the-counter market.

Blue-chip stock (6)   A stock that is known to provide a safe and stable return. The company offering the stock generally provides uninterrupted streams of dividends and good long-term growth prospects.

Bond (6)   A certificate indicating that a corporation has borrowed a certain amount of money which it has agreed to repay in the future.

Bond discount (6)   The amount by which a bond sells below its face value. Bonds sell at a discount when similar risk bonds have higher interest rates.

Bond or preferred stock fund (8) The portfolio of an investment company that purchases diversified portfolios of either bonds or preferred stocks to provide safe, predictable returns to investors.

Bond premium (6)   The amount by which a bond's market price exceeds its face value.

Book value (6)   The accounting value of a firm which can be estimated by subtracting the liabilities and preferred stock value from the value of the firm's assets.

Broker-dealers (7)   Traders who make markets in certain securities by offering to either buy or sell them at stated prices.

Budget (3)   A tool for planning short-run income and expenditures in order to achieve long-run financial goals. The budget shows expenses and income within a given period of time.

Budget summary (3)   A statement that shows for each time period the estimated income, estimated expenses, amount of any surplus or deficit, and cumulative surplus or deficit.

Bull market (7)   A condition of the market in which stock prices generally rise. Bull markets are normally associated with investor optimism, economic recovery, and government stimulus. *See also* Bear market.

Bunching deductions (4)   A tax-reduction technique by which tax-deductible expenditures are used to lower actual expenditures in one year while raising them in the next.

Buyer's guides (10)   Publications such as *Consumer Reports, Changing Times*, and *Money* which provide information about and ratings and comparative statistics on furniture, appliances, and many other consumer goods.

Buy order (7)   An order to buy a specified number of shares of a security.

Call feature (6)   A feature often included as part of a preferred stock or bond issue that allows the issuer to retire the security during some specified period of time at a prespecified price. This feature is always included as part of a convertible security issue.

Call option (8)   An option to purchase a specified number of shares (typically one hundred shares) of a stock at or before some future date for a stated "striking" price. *See also* Put option.

Capital asset (4)   Property owned and used by the taxpayer for personal purposes, pleasure, or investment, such as a home, automobile, or stocks and bonds.

Capital gain (4)   A gain from the sale of a capital asset at a higher price than its original cost. Special tax treatment is given on long-term capital gains—those owned for more than one year—while short-term capital gains are taxed as ordinary income.

Capital loss (4)   A loss on the sale of an asset, which may be used as a tax deduction.

Capital market (7)   The marketplace in which long-term securities (those with lives or maturities greater than one year) are traded. All stocks and bonds are traded in the capital market.

Captive agent (15)   An insurance agent who represents only one company and who is employed by that company.

Carry-over basis tax trap (17)   A provision of the Tax Reform Act of 1976 that allows, essentially, double taxation on the sale of estate assets.

Cash basis (2)   The basis on which the personal income statement is normally prepared; only cash income and cash expenses are included on the income statement.

Cashier's check (5)   A check that a bank draws on itself in exchange for an appropriate amount of money.

Cash value (13)   An accumulation of cash in an insurance policy based on the way in which premiums are paid.

Certified check (5)   A check that has been certified to be good by the bank upon which it is drawn.

Charge account (11)   A form of credit extended to a consumer in advance of any transactions. The types of charge accounts are budget, credit, option, regular, revolving, and thirty-day.

Check (5)   A negotiable instrument which evidences a deposit withdrawable upon demand from a commercial bank.

Chicago Board Options Exchange (CBOE) (8)   The dominant exchange on which call and put options are traded. The options traded on the CBOE are standardized and are considered to be registered securities.

Closed-end investment company (8)   An investment company that issues only a fixed number of shares, which may in themselves be listed and traded on an organized security exchange.

Club account (5)   A savings account established at a financial institution for some special purpose, such as a Christmas fund.

Codicil (17)   A legal means of modifying, without revoking, an existing will. The codicil is attached to the will and becomes a part of it.

Coinsurance or participation clause (14)   A provision of most major medical insurance policies stipulating that the company will pay some portion, say 80 to 90 percent, of the amount of the covered loss in excess of the deductible.

Collateral (12)   An item or items readily marketable at a price sufficiently high to cover the principal amount of a loan. If collateral is named for a loan, the loan is *secured*; if none is given, it is *unsecured*. A *collateral note* is one that gives the lender the right to sell collateral in the instance of a default. A *chattel mortgage* gives the lender title to the property in the event of a default; and a *lien* is a legal claim that permits the lender to liquidate the items that serve as collateral in the event of a default.

Collateral trust bond (6)   A bond secured by the pledge of stocks and bonds owned by the firm issuing the bond.

Collision insurance (automobile) (15)   Automobile insurance that pays for collision damage to an insured automobile regardless of fault.

Commercial bank (5)   A bank that holds checking accounts and offers other types of savings accounts; a commercial bank also makes loans to qualified individuals and businesses.

Commodity futures   *See* Futures contract.

Common stock (6) The basic form of corporate ownership. It is a form of equity capital in that purchasers of common stock expect to receive dividends and/or capital gains in return for their investment.

Comparative negligence statutes (15) State laws that attempt to allocate loss to each party in proportion to the degree each was negligent.

Compounding (of interest) (5) Paying interest not only on the initial deposit but on any interest accumulated from previous periods.

Comprehensive automobile insurance (15) Coverage that provides for protection against loss to an insured automobile caused by any peril other than collision.

Comprehensive major medical insurance (14) A plan that combines the basic hospital, surgical, and medical expense coverages with major medical protection to form a single policy.

Confession of judgment (12) A clause in a sales contract that causes the purchaser to give up his or her right legally to disagree with respect to the debt should default occur.

Consumer Credit Protection Act (1969, 1975) (11) A wide-ranging law designed to protect credit purchasers, the most important provision of which is the requirement that both the dollar amount of finance charges and the annual percentage rate charged must be disclosed prior to extending credit. Also known as the Truth in Lending Law.

Consumer finance company (12) A company, sometimes called a small loan company, that makes secured and unsecured loans to qualified individuals. These companies do not accept deposits but rather obtain funds from their stockholders and through borrowing.

Consumer price index (CPI) (1) An index that reflects the relative cost of a "standard" bundle of goods and services measured in reference to a base year at which the index has a value of 100.

Contributory negligence (defense) (15) A defense against a negligence charge in which the defendant maintains that the plaintiff contributed to his or her own loss by also acting in a negligent manner.

Contributory pension plan (16) A retirement plan under which the employee bears a portion of the cost of the benefits. A retirement plan under which the employer pays the total cost is called *noncontributory*.

Conversion feature (6) A feature sometimes offered as part of preferred stock or bonds that allows the holder to convert the security into a specified number of shares of common stock over some specified period of time.

Corporation (6) A business firm that has been chartered by the state and given a type of legal status allowing it to become a legal entity. A corporation is said to be *closed* if its shares of stock are not publicly traded.

Coupon bond (6) A bond that provides interest coupons that are detached and redeemed by the holder at specified dates. These bonds are sometimes referred to as "bearer" bonds because they are owned by whoever holds them.

C.P.C.U. (Certified Property and Casualty Underwriter) (15) An insurance agent who has met various experience and educational requirements and passed a series of written examinations.

Credit bureau (11) An organization, typically established and owned by merchants and banks at the local level, which collects and stores credit information from its members and makes this information available for a specified fee to members who request it.

Credit card (bank and national) (11) A card issued by a commercial bank or private business that allows the cardholder to charge purchases at any store or business accepting it.

Credit life insurance (13) A type of life insurance sold in conjunction with installment loans that decreases at the same rate as the balance on the loan.

Credit limit (11) A specified amount beyond which a customer may not buy or borrow.

Credit scoring scheme (11) A method of analyzing a credit applicant's risk by assigning values to factors such as income, existing debts, and credit references.

Credit union (5) A mutual association owned by depositors. It draws together the deposits of its members and lends these funds out to other members.

Cumulative (preferred) stock (6) Stock requiring that all dividends not paid in previous periods accumulate. (Most preferred stock is cumulative.) These accumulated dividends must be satisfied prior to paying any dividends to the common stockholders.

Cyclical stock (6) Stock whose price movements tend to follow the business cycle.

Death taxes (17) The equivalent of federal *estate taxes*, these taxes include, at the state level, a state inheritance tax, a state estate tax, and a credit estate tax, which is designed to bridge the gap between the former two and the maximum state death tax credit allowed against the federal estate tax.

Debenture (6) An unsecured bond that is issued on the reputation of the firm.

Debt capital (6) Funds loaned to a business firm, such as corporate bonds.

Deductibles (14) Amounts not covered by an insurance policy, usually on a per accident or per illness basis.

The deductible is paid by the insured or by another insurance policy.

Deductions (from gross income) (4) Ordinary and necessary items of expense that can be deducted from gross income in order to determine the amount of adjusted gross income in the tax computation process.

Deed (12) A legal instrument used to transfer the title of real property from one party (the grantor) to another party (the grantee).

Default (6) The failure to pay interest (or principal) as required on a bond or any type of loan by a corporate, government, or individual borrower.

Defensive stocks (6) Often called countercyclical stocks, these tend to exhibit price movements that are contrary to the downward movements of the business cycle. Their prices are expected to remain stable during contractions in business activity.

Deficit (2) An excess of expenditure over income, resulting in insufficient funds that must be made up by either reducing savings or investments or borrowing.

Defined benefit plan (16) A plan in which the formula for computing benefits is stipulated in its provisions, thus allowing the employee to determine before retirement how much his or her monthly retirement income will be.

Delisting (7) The process of removing a security from trading on an organized security exchange.

Demand deposit (2) The term used in the banking and finance industry to refer to a checking account.

Demand-pull inflation (11) A kind of inflation that can result from "easy" credit. If consumers have too little difficulty in borrowing to purchase goods and services, the demand for these items may rapidly increase, thereby causing prices to rise.

Dental expense insurance (14) Insurance that covers necessary dental health care, such as oral examinations, cleanings, fillings, etc., as well as dental injuries sustained through accidents.

Depreciation costs (10) The amount by which the value of an item declines over a given period of ownership. It is the difference between the purchase price of an item and the price at which it can be sold at some future date.

Depression (1) The phase of the economic cycle during which the level of employment is low and the accompanying level of economic activity and growth is at a virtual standstill. This phase is generally accompanied by low prices for goods and services due to low levels of demand. *See also* Expansion, Inflation, Recession, and Recovery.

Disability income insurance (14) Insurance that is designed to provide families with weekly or monthly payments to replace income when an insured person is unable to work as a result of a covered illness, injury, or disease.

Discount (interest) method (12) A method by which the finance charges are calculated and then subtracted from the amount of the loan. The difference between the amount of the loan and the finance charges is then lent to the borrower.

Distribution period (16) The period during which annuity payments are made to the annuitant.

Diversification (7) The process of choosing securities having dissimilar risk-return characteristics in order to create a portfolio that provides an acceptable return.

Diversified common stock fund (8) An investment company that invests in diversified portfolios of common stock to provide a wide range of income-growth combinations.

Dividends (6) The distribution of earnings to the stockholders or owners of a corporation.

Dividend yield (7) The percentage return provided by the dividends paid on common stock. The dividend yield is most often calculated on an annual basis by dividing the cash dividends paid during the year by the current market price of the stock.

Dollar-cost averaging (7) A method of investing by purchasing a fixed dollar amount of a security at specified points in time. This approach forces the average cost of a security to remain at a reasonable level.

Down payment (9) A portion, usually 5 to 30 percent, of the full purchase price paid at the time of purchase; in the case of real estate, the mortgage covers the remaining cost.

Dread disease health policy (14) A policy designed to provide coverage for a specific type of disease or illness, such as cancer.

Dual funds (8) A special type of closed-end investment company that purchases securities having both income and growth attributes, in effect establishing two ownership groups.

Earnest money (9) A sum, usually 5 percent of the offering price, given to assure the seller of a home that a potential buyer's offer is in good faith.

Earnings per share (EPS) (6) The return earned on behalf of each share of common stock for a certain period of time. It is calculated by dividing all earnings remaining after paying preferred stockholders by the number of shares of common stock outstanding.

Earnings test (16) The amount a retired worker may earn without having social security retirement benefits reduced.

Effective rate of interest (5) The true rate of interest, or the rate actually paid over the period of time the funds are actually being used.

Electronic Funds Transfer System (EFTS) (5, 11)   A computerized information-gathering and processing system that eliminates the need for cash or checks, since all transactions can be made using a credit card.

Endowment insurance (13)   A policy that offers life insurance protection for a stated period of time, after which it may be redeemed for face value if the insured has not died.

EPA mileage rating (10)   The results of mileage tests conducted by the Environmental Protection Agency (EPA) to determine the number of miles per gallon various cars may be expected to get.

Equal Credit Opportunity Act (1975) (11)   A law making it illegal for a creditor to discriminate on the basis of sex or marital status when considering a credit application.

Equity (2)   The actual ownership interest in a specific asset or group of assets.

Equity capital (6)   Ownership funds invested in a business. A person buying corporate stock is contributing to the firm's equity capital.

Escrow payments (12)   Payments, such as those for insurance and taxes, which a homeowner makes in advance to the lender, who then uses them at the appropriate time to pay the necessary charges.

Estate tax (4, 17)   A tax levied by both the state and federal government on the value of an estate left at its owner's death.

Estimated taxes (4)   Taxes that must be paid on income not subject to withholding.

Excess itemized deductions   *See* Tax-table income.

Excise tax (4)   A tax levied by the federal government on the purchase of certain luxury items and services such as automobiles, gasoline, and tobacco products.

Exclusion allowance (16)   A computation devised by the IRS to determine the maximum amount of annuity premium upon which taxes can be deferred on annuities provided by qualified charitable organizations and public school systems to their employees.

Executor (17)   The administrator of an estate designated in the decedent's will.

Exemptions (4)   Deductions from adjusted gross income based on the number of persons being supported by the taxpayer's income.

Exercise price (6)   The price at which a right or warrant can be used to purchase a share of common stock. The exercise price is stated at the time of issue of either of these instruments.

Expansion (1)   The phase of the economic cycle during which the level of employment is high and the level of economic activity also remains high. This phase generally is accompanied by rising prices for goods and services. *See also* Depression, Inflation, Recession, and Recovery.

Fair Credit Billing Act (1975) (11)   A law designed to correct errors and abuses in credit billing and the poor handling of credit complaints; this law established time limits by which bills must be sent and complaints answered.

Fair Credit Reporting Act (1971) (11)   A law that regulates the use of credit information and allows consumers to have access to their own credit files.

Fair market value (2)   The price that an asset could reasonably be expected to be sold for at a stated date.

Federal Deposit Insurance Corporation (FDIC) (5)   An agency of the Federal Reserve System that insures almost all bank deposits held by U.S. banks.

Federal Insurance Contributions Act (FICA) (4)   The law establishing the tax levied on both the employer and employee. The tax is sometimes referred to as the social security tax.

Federal Reserve System (5) The agency of the federal government that governs the banking system.

Federal unemployment tax (4) A tax in addition to FICA that must be paid by the employer based on each employee's income. These tax proceeds are used by the federal government to pay unemployment benefits to qualified persons.

Financial assets *See* Assets.

Financial intermediation (11) The interaction between borrowers and savers at a financial institution. This mutually beneficial process channels interest paid on loans by borrowers into interest paid to depositors for the use of their funds.

Financial responsibility laws (15) Laws that attempt to force motorists to be financially responsible for the damages they become legally obligated to pay as a result of automobile accidents.

Fixed interest rate (12) A rate of interest that is fixed at the time a loan is negotiated.

Flower Bonds (17) Bonds issued by the federal government that allow the reduction of estate taxes by including the bonds at par in the gross estate.

Form 1040 (4) The form used by all individuals for filing their federal income tax return.

Formula timing (7) A plan for purchasing a security that attempts to force the investor to buy low and sell high by establishing certain indicators for buying or selling.

Fortuitous loss (13) A loss that happens by chance or accident—that is, its timing and/or occurrence are for the most part unintentional and unexpected.

Front-end load (8) An arrangement—typically under contractual savings accumulation plans—under which the purchaser of mutual fund shares must pay the total commissions on all planned purchases in the first few years of the plan.

Fundamental theory of stock value (6) Theory of stock value based upon the belief that the true value of a security such as common stock is dependent upon the expected stream of future earnings.

Funded pension plans (16) Those plans that formally establish charges against current income to allow for the pension liabilities as they accrue in order to minimize the risk that benefits will not be available to an eligible employee upon retirement. If a plan merely allows the employer to make payments to retirees from current income, the plan is *unfunded*.

Futures contract (8) A contract providing for the delivery of some commodity at some future date.

Garnishment (12) An arrangement by which a lender is allowed to collect a portion of the borrower's wages in the event of a default. The portion of an employee's wages that can be garnisheed is limited by the Federal Garnishment Law (1970).

Gift splitting (17) A way of reducing taxes in which a gift given by one spouse may be shared equally by the other spouse for tax purposes.

Gift tax (4, 17) A tax levied by federal and state governments on the giver of a gift. The amount of the tax depends upon the value of the gift given.

Graduated mortgage (12) A mortgage that has low interest rates in the first few years and higher rates thereafter.

Gross income (4) The total of all income (before any deductions) that is subject to federal taxes. Certain types of tax-exempt income are excluded from the gross income.

Group insurance (13, 14, 15) A master policy, usually of term insurance, that is issued for a group; each eligible member receives a certificate of insurance.

Group practice plan *See* Health maintenance organization.

Growth stock (6) A stock whose earnings and market price have increased at an above-average level over the recent past.

Head of household (4) A single individual who maintains as his or her home a household which is the principal residence of the dependent whom the taxpayer may take as an exemption.

Health maintenance organization (HMO) (14) An organization consisting of a group of hospitals, physicians, and other health care personnel who have joined together to provide necessary health maintenance and remedial services to its members.

Holder in due course (12) A third party to whom an installment loan has been sold.

Income averaging (4) A procedure available to taxpayers which allows them to spread their income evenly over a period of five years in order to reduce their tax liability in peak income years.

Income splitting (4) A technique used to avoid taxes involving the shifting of a portion of a taxpayer's income to related individuals in lower tax brackets.

Income statement (2) A key financial statement, it presents a person's or family's income, expenses, and contribution to savings or investment over a stated period of time.

Income stock (6) Stock having primary appeal for the dividend it pays out because it has a fairly stable stream of earnings, a large portion of which are distributed in the form of dividends.

Indenture (6) The legal contract that clearly states all obligations of the firm issuing a bond.

Individual Retirement Account (IRA) (16) A retirement plan for employees of companies who are not covered by an employer pension program. Under such a plan, the employees' contributions are turned over to a trustee, usually a bank or savings and loan association. The size and tax-exempt status of employee contributions are regulated by the federal government.

Inflation (1) A state of the economy in which the general level of prices is rising. It normally occurs during the recovery and expansion phases of the economic cycle. Its causes may be attributed to excessive demand or rapidly rising production costs. *See also* Depression, Expansion, Recession, and Recovery.

Installment loan (12) A loan that is repaid in a series of fixed, scheduled payments rather than in a lump sum.

Installment purchase agreement (12) A contract specifying the obligations of both the purchaser (or borrower) and the lender when a purchase transaction is being financed on an installment basis. Its four components are: a sales contract, a security agreement, a note, and an insurance agreement.

Insurability options (13) Options that allow the policyholder to purchase additional coverage at stipulated intervals of time even if the insured becomes uninsurable.

Interest adjusted method (13) A method of calculating the cost of life insurance that recognizes the time value of money by applying a discount rate to the calculation.

Interest penalty (11) A surcharge levied for late payment of a charge account or loan.

Interest rate risk (6) A risk affecting primarily fixed income securities such as bonds and preferred stocks. It results from changing market interest rates.

Intergenerational compact (16) The principle upon which social security works—that today's working generation is paying for yesterday's workers, who are now retired, and tomorrow's workers will pay for today's workers when they retire.

Internal Revenue Code (IRC) (4) The code that systematically outlines the federal income tax laws for corporations and all others. Originally established in 1939, it has been revised on numerous occasions; the most recent major revision was the Tax Reform Act of 1976. Implementation of the code is the responsibility of the Internal Revenue Service (IRS).

Intestacy (17) The state that exists when a person dies without a valid will.

Investment (6) The process of placing money in some medium in the expectation of receiving some future benefit.

Investment bank (2) A firm that specializes in selling new security issues, along with giving advice about pricing new security issues. *See also* Underwriting.

Investment club (7) A club formed to pool the money of interested persons for investment in certain securities.

Investment company (8) A company owning a diversified portfolio of securities that are professionally chosen on the basis of certain criteria. The most common type of investment company is the mutual fund.

Joint return (4) A method of filing a tax return available to married persons in which the gross income and deductions of husband and wife are totaled, and their taxes are calculated on a single tax return.

Kaiser Health Care Plan (14) A group practice plan originally designed to provide health care for the employees of the Kaiser Corporation but which is now open to the public. *See also* Health maintenance organization.

Keogh plan (16) A plan established by the Self-employment Individual Tax Retirement Act of 1962 (HR-10) under which self-employed persons have the right to establish retirement plans for themselves and their employees that permit them the same tax advantages available to corporate employees covered by qualified pension plans.

Lease agreement (9) A rental contract intended to protect the lessor (person who owns the property) from nonpayment or some adverse action of the lessee (person who leases the property).

Letter of last instruction (17) An informal memorandum containing suggestions or recommendations for carrying out the provisions of a will.

Leverage (9) The use of borrowing to magnify returns.

Liabilities (1, 2) A person's debts, which may result from department store charges, bank card charges, installment loans, or mortgages on real estate.

Liability insurance (15) A type of automobile insurance that pays for damages the insured has accidentally caused another and for the insured's defense against another who is seeking compensation arising out of a covered occurrence.

Lien *See* Collateral.

Life insurance trust and pour-over will (17) A provision in a will that allows certain assets to be "poured over" into a previously established trust.

Limited liability (6) The concept under which an investor in a business cannot lose more than the amount of his or her investment.

Limited partnership (9) A type of partnership in which the limited partner is legally liable only for the amount of his or her initial investment.

Limit order (7) An order to either buy a security at a specified price or lower or sell a security at or above a specified price.

Line of credit (11) The total amount of credit customers are allowed to charge.

Liquid balance (5) Money held in a form that can be readily converted into cash without a great deal of expense or administrative effort.

Liquidity (2) The ability of assets—financial or nonfinancial—to be readily converted into cash.

Listed securities (7) Securities that have met the necessary prerequisites of an organized security exchange and are therefore traded on the exchange.

Load fund (8) A mutual fund on which a transaction cost associated with either purchase or sale is levied.

Loan origination fee (12) A fee paid to the lender for making a loan.

Lump-sum payment (14) A payment under worker's compensation of a specific amount for specific types of losses.

Magnetic Ink Character Recognition (MICR) (5) A magnetic coding imprinted on checks and deposit slips to speed up the check- and deposit-clearing process.

Major medical plan (14) An insurance plan designed to supplement the basic coverages of hospital, surgical, and regular medical expenses; the latter are designed to cover smaller health care costs, while major medical is used to finance medical costs of a more catastrophic or long-term nature.

Maintenance margin (7) The minimum percentage equity an investor must maintain in a stock purchased using borrowed funds.

Marginal propensity to consume (1) The percentage of each dollar of income that a person spends for consumption, usually higher for lower-income persons than for higher-income persons.

Margin purchases (7) The buying of securities using some borrowed funds; the percentage of borrowed funds is limited by both law and brokerage firms.

Marital deduction (17) A deduction allowed to married persons for gift tax purposes by which one spouse may make a tax-deductible gift to another.

Market makers (7) Persons who specialize in creating markets for certain securities by offering to buy or sell a given security at specified bid and ask prices.

Market order (7) An order to buy or sell stock at the best price available at the time the order is placed.

Market rate of interest (6) The rate of interest paid on similar risk types of instruments in the marketplace.

Market risk (6) Factors such as changes in political, economic, and social conditions, as well as changes in investor tastes and preferences, which may cause the market price of a security to change.

Medical payments insurance (automobile) (15) Insurance that provides for payment to eligible insureds of an amount no greater than the policy limit for all reasonable and necessary medical expenses incurred within one year after an automobile accident.

Medicaid (14) A public assistance program under social security that is designed to provide medical benefits for poor persons who are unable to pay their health care costs.

Medicare (14) A health care plan administered by the federal government designed to help persons over age sixty-five and others who receive monthly social security disability benefits.

Money market (7) The marketplace in which short-term securities are traded.

Money market fund (8) An investment company portfolio containing short-term debt instruments such as certificates of deposit and treasury bills.

Monthly Investment Plan (MIP)
(7) An arrangement that allows investors to invest $40 to $1,000 in New York Stock Exchange securities every month or three months.

Mortgage, chattel *See* Collateral.

Mortgage bonds (6) The most common type of secured bonds that have real property such as land, buildings, or equipment pledged against them as collateral.

Mortgage insurance (12) An insurance policy on the life of the borrower that names the lender as the beneficiary, so that if the borrower dies, the mortgage is automatically paid off.

Mortgage loan (12) A loan in which the lender, for self-protection, takes the legal right to the property for which the loan is made in case the borrower defaults.

Multiple indemnity (13) A clause that doubles or triples the face amount of the policy if the insured dies as a result of an accident.

Municipal bond fund (8) An investment company portfolio consisting of municipal (tax-exempt) bonds.

Municipal bonds (6) Bonds issued by state or local governments for financing certain projects. The interest earned on these bonds is tax-exempt.

Mutual company (5, 13) A company that is owned by its depositors or policyholders.

Mutual fund (8) An open-end investment company that invests in a diversified portfolio of securities. It issues and repurchases shares as demanded and therefore does not have a fixed amount to invest, as in the case of a closed-end investment company.

Mutual fund fund (8) A mutual fund that owns a diversified portfolio of shares of other mutual funds. It spreads risk over a large group of securities.

Mutual savings bank (5) A special type of savings institution, much like a savings and loan association, found mostly in the New England area. The depositors are owners of this type of institution.

National Association of Securities Dealers (NASD) (7) A self-regulatory agency made up of all brokers and dealers in over-the-counter securities. It regulates the OTC securities markets.

National health insurance (14) A much-discussed form of insurance coverage under which the government would assume all or part of the costs of health care services.

Negligent action (15) An action inconsistent with the "reasonable man doctrine"—the doctrine that if a person fails to act as would one with normal intelligence, perceptions, and experiences common to the community, he is negligent.

Net asset value (NAV) per share (8) The price at which a mutual fund will sell or buy back its own shares based upon the current value of the securities which it owns.

Net cost method (13) A method by which the amount of life insurance premiums that are paid over a period of time is totaled, and from this sum the total dividends and cash value that are projected for the period are subtracted.

Net earnings (4) The amount of earnings an employee takes home after the employer has made all required as well as requested deductions. Also called "take-home pay."

Net worth (1, 2) Often considered the amount of personal or family wealth, it is determined by subtracting all liabilities from all assets.

New York Stock Exchange (NYSE) (7) The largest and most prestigious organized security exchange; it handles a majority of the dollar volume of securities transactions and accounts for approximately 65 percent of the total annual share volume on organized exchanges.

No fault (15)   A concept of automobile insurance that favors reimbursement without regard to negligence.

No-load fund (8)   A mutual fund on which no transaction costs are charged.

Nominal rate of interest (5)   The stated rate of interest on a loan or savings deposit; this rate does not necessarily represent the true rate of interest being paid on the funds.

Nonfinancial assets   *See* Assets.

Nonforfeiture right (13)   An option that gives the policyholder the portion of those assets that had been set aside to provide payment for the death claim that was not made. The amount is given to the policyholder when the policy (whole life or endowment) is canceled.

Nonqualified deferred compensation (16)   An arrangement between an employer and employee to defer payment for services rendered by the employee. Such an agreement is most useful when an employee's future need for funds exceeds his or her present requirements.

NOW account (5)   The negotiable order of withdrawal (NOW) is similar in appearance and behavior to a checking account except that it often requires advance notice of withdrawal. It can be viewed as an interest-earning checking account or as a savings account against which checks can be issued.

Odd lot (7)   A quantity of less than one hundred shares of a security.

Open-end investment company   *See* Mutual fund.

Option (8)   A contract that permits one to either purchase or sell a specified security at a predetermined price within a certain period of time. *See also* Call option and Put option.

Overdraft (5)   A check written against an account for more money than is in the account.

Over-the-counter market (OTC) (7)   The market on which the securities of smaller, less well-known firms are generally traded.

Partnership (6)   A business owned by more than one person and operated in the interest of all owners. Its income is normally taxed as personal income of the owners, and their liability is not limited to their investment in the business.

Par value (6)   The stated value sometimes placed on stock certificates and assigned to the stock. It reflects the minimum price at which the stock could sell without causing the shareholder to assume any liability for the firm's actions.

Passbook account (5)   A regular savings account at a financial institution.

Pension Benefit Guarantee Corporation (PBGC) (16)   Established by a provision of the Employee Retirement Income Security Act of 1974 (ERISA), this organization guarantees to eligible workers that certain benefits will be payable to them even if their employer's pension plan has insufficient assets to fulfill its commitments.

Performance fund (8)   An investment company portfolio that emphasizes performance as measured by the total return earned on the shareholders' investments; the investment strategies are speculative.

Personal property floaters (15)   Special clauses of property insurance policies that provide additional coverage for specific items named in them, such as jewelry, furs, and antiques.

Point (12)   A fee, equal to 1 percent of the mortgage amount, charged to raise the annual percentage rate of the loan or to pay the lender for making the loan.

Policy loan (13)   An advance made by a life insurance company to a policyholder secured by the cash value of the life insurance policy.

Portfolio (7)   A combination of stocks and bonds owned by an investor.

Pour-over will   *See* Life insurance trust and pour-over will.

Preemptive right (6)   The right given to existing stockholders to be given an opportunity to maintain their proportional ownership when a new issue of common stock is made.

Preferred stock (6)   A special type of ownership or equity capital that provides for a stated dividend payment that must be made prior to paying any common stock dividends. A preferred stock may be cumulative or noncumulative and participating or nonparticipating, depending on the way dividends are paid.

Prepaid interest (4)   Interest expense that is paid in advance of its actually being owed.

Prepayment clause (12)   A clause that allows for payment of a loan prior to its maturity date. This clause often contains a penalty charge for prepayment to prevent the borrower from refinancing with another lender.

Preventive maintenance (10)   Maintenance, usually on automobiles, which is designed to reduce the need for future repairs.

Previous balance method (11)   A method of computing interest charges by which interest is calculated on the outstanding balance at the beginning of the billing period; this is the most expensive method for the consumer.

Price-earnings ratio (P/E) (6)   A ratio calculated by dividing the prevailing market price per share by the earnings per share. This ratio is viewed as an indicator of investor confidence in a given security.

Primary insurance amount (PIA) (16)   An amount calculated from a scheduled benefit table based upon the average annual covered wages of the worker for social security benefits.

Primary market (7)   The market in which new securities are sold to the public. Only new issues are traded in this market.

Principal (6)   The face value of a debt instrument that would be received by its holder at maturity.

Principle of indemnity (15)   An insurance principle that states that an insured may not be compensated by his or her insurance company in an amount exceeding the amount of economic loss.

Probate (17)   A process of liquidation that occurs when a person dies. The deceased's debts are collected or paid, and the remaining assets are distributed to the appropriate individuals or organizations.

Probate estate (17)   The real and personal property a person owns in his or her own name that can be transferred according to the terms of the will. The probate estate differs from the *gross estate* in that the latter refers to all property subject to federal estate taxes at a person's death, both probate and nonprobate.

Professional liability insurance (15)   Policies designed to protect such professionals as doctors, lawyers, architects, professors, and engineers in the event that they are sued for malpractice.

Profit sharing (16)   An arrangement whereby the employees of a firm participate in the earnings of the firm. Such an arrangement may qualify as a pension plan.

Progressive tax (4)   A tax schedule in which the larger the amount of taxable income, the higher the rate at which the income is taxed.

Property insurance (15)   Insurance that provides coverage for loss to such items as one's home, furnishings, boat, etc.

Property tax (4)   A tax levied on the value of various items of property owned by the taxpayer, such as real estate, automobiles, and boats.

Prospectus (7)   A document made available to prospective security purchasers by the issuer describing the new security being issued.

Proxy (6)   A written statement used to assign a stockholder's voting rights to another person.

Purchase contract (9)   A formal agreement to purchase a house, which states the offering price and all conditions—including repairs, inspections, closing date, and so on—required by buyer and seller. It is a contractually binding agreement.

Purchasing power risk (6)   A risk resulting from possible changes in price levels in the economy that can have a significant effect on the prices of securities.

Put option (8)   An option to sell a specified number of shares (typically one hundred shares) of a stock at or before a specified future date for a stated "striking" price. *See also* Call option.

Qualified pension plan (16)   A retirement plan that meets specified criteria established by the Internal Revenue Code.

Quitclaim deed (12)   A deed that gives the grantee whatever claim the grantor had on the property and completely relieves the grantor of further risk.

Random walk theory of value (16) The theory that stock price movements are strictly random events.

Real estate investment company (9) A corporation that sells its shares and uses the proceeds to make real estate investments.

Real Estate Investment Trust (REIT) (9)   An unincorporated business that accumulates money for investment in real estate ventures by selling shares to small investors.

Recession (1)   The phase of the economic cycle during which the level of employment is declining and the overall level of economic activity is slowing down. This phase is often accompanied by steady or declining prices for goods and services due to declining demand for these items. *See also* Depression, Expansion, Inflation, and Recovery.

Recovery (1)   The phase of the economic cycle during which the level of employment is improving and the economy is experiencing increasing activity and growth. *See also* Depression, Expansion, Inflation, and Recession.

Regional stock exchanges (7)   Stock exchanges other than the so-called major stock exchanges (NYSE and AMEX) that deal primarily in securities having a local or regional appeal.

Registered bond (6)   A bond on which interest checks are automatically mailed to the bondholder—that is, the bond is registered in the name of the owner.

Regulated investment company (8) An investment company that has met certain conditions, the most important of which is the distribution of almost all earnings to shareholders.

Regulation Z (11)   A statement issued by the Federal Reserve Board outlining the directives for complying with the Consumer Credit Protection Act.

Reinstatement (13)   A revival of the original contractual relationship between the life insurance company and the policyholder upon payment of all back premiums and satisfaction of the insurability clauses of the policy.

Remedial loan society (12)   A nonprofit organization that operates in a manner similar to a pawnshop in that it lends against physical assets, which are held as collateral. Such an organization is designed basically to provide loans to the poor.

Replacement cost (15)   The amount necessary to repair, rebuild, or replace an asset at today's prices.

Reverse stock split (6)   A stock split in which each old share of stock is exchanged for less than one new share of stock.

Right of election (17)   The right of a surviving spouse to take a specified portion of the probate estate regardless of what the will provides.

Rights offering (6)   An offering of new shares of corporate stock to existing shareholders on a proportional basis relative to their existing ownership. *See also* Preemptive right.

Round lot (7)   One hundred shares of a security or some multiple thereof.

Rule of 78 (Sum of the Digits) (12)   A rule used to determine the portion of the total finance charges the lender receives when a loan is paid off prior to its maturity.

Sales finance company (12)   A company that purchases notes drawn up by sellers of certain types of merchandise—typically more expensive items such as automobiles, furniture, and appliances.

Savings accumulation plan (8)   An arrangement under which an investor makes scheduled purchases of a given dollar amount of shares in a mutual fund.

Second injury funds (14)   Funds established to relieve employers of the additional worker's compensation premium burden they might incur if a worker already handicapped sustained further injury on the job.

Secured (and unsecured) loans   *See* Collateral.

Securities (1, 6)   Obligations of issuers that provide purchasers with an expected or stated return on the amount invested. The two basic types of securities are stocks and bonds.

Securities and Exchange Commission (SEC) (7)   The agency of the federal government that has the responsibility of enforcing the Securities Exchange Acts of 1933 and 1934. This agency regulates the disclosure of information about securities as well as the operation of the securities exchanges and markets in general.

Securities Investor Protection Corporation (SIPC) (7)   An agency of the federal government that insures each brokerage customer's account for up to $50,000 of securities and $20,000 of cash balances held by the firm.

Security exchanges (7)   Forums—either organized or over-the-counter—in which buyers and sellers of securities can be brought together to make transactions.

Self-employment tax (4)   A tax that must be paid to the federal government by self-employed persons. The proceeds of this tax are used to provide self-employed persons with the same benefits regularly employed persons receive through the FICA tax.

Sell order (7)   An order to sell a specified number of shares of a given security.

Senior debts (6)   Debts or bonds to which debentures are subordinated; these debts have a senior claim on both income and assets.

Settlement options (13)   The various ways in which the death proceeds of a life insurance policy may be paid, such as interest only, payments for a stated period, payments of a stated amount, or income for life.

Short sale (7)   A transaction made in anticipation of a decline in the price of a security. It involves selling borrowed securities with the expectation that they can be replaced at a lower price at some future date.

Simple interest method (12)   The method by which interest is charged only on the actual loan balance outstanding.

Single payment loan (12)   A loan made for a specified period of time at the end of which full payment is due.

Small Business Administration (SBA) (10)   An agency of the federal government whose purpose is to provide advice, loans, and other services to owners of small businesses and to those who are about to begin a small business.

Sole proprietorship (6)   A business owned by one person and operated on his or her own behalf; its income is taxed as personal income, and the owner's liability is unlimited.

Special savings account (5)   A savings account that offers slightly higher interest rates than a passbook account but in exchange requires the saver to maintain a specified minimum balance and/or to maintain that balance for a specified period of time. Certificates of deposit are one example of this type of account.

Specialty fund (8)   A common stock fund that invests in the shares of firms within a specific industry.

Stock averages (7)   An index or average of a group of stocks that is believed to reflect a given industry or the entire securities market. These averages are used to gauge the behavior of the securities market.

Stockbroker (7)   Sometimes called an "account executive," the stockbroker purchases and sells securities on behalf of clients, to whom he or she provides advice and information.

Stock company (13)   A company that is owned by stockholders.

Stockholders' report (7)   Sometimes called an *annual report,* it includes a variety of financial and descriptive information about a firm's operation during the year.

Stock split (6)   A trade of old shares for new shares typically initiated by management in order to either increase or reduce the price of stock.

Stop-loss order (7)   An order to sell a stock when the market price reaches or drops below a specified level.

Stop payment (5)   An order to the bank not to make payment on a check that has been written.

Striking price (8)   The price at which an option (call or put) can be exercised, normally a price set close to the market price of the stock at the time the option is issued.

Subordinated debenture (6)   Unsecured bond that is given a secondary claim (with respect to both income and assets) to that of other bondholders or lenders.

Supplementary medical insurance (SMI) (14)   A voluntary program under Medicare that provides payments for such extra services as at-home care and laboratory and x-ray costs. This program requires the payment of premiums by those who participate.

Surplus (2)   An excess of income over expenses, resulting in a positive contribution to savings or investment or a reduction in outstanding debt.

Survivorship benefit (annuities) (16)   That portion of the capital sum that has not been returned to the annuitant prior to his or her death and that is paid to the survivor.

Syndication (real estate) (9)   A limited partnership that invests in various types of real estate and is professionally managed. There are various types of real estate syndicates—such as single property and blind pool—involved in specific kinds of real estate acquisitions.

Systematic withdrawal plan (8)   A plan that allows the mutual fund shareholder to be paid specified amounts each period.

Tangible property (1)   Tangible items of real and personal property that generally have a long life, such as real estate, automobiles, jewelry, and other physical assets.

Tax credits (4)   Certain deductions from their tax liability that taxpayers may be eligible to receive.

Tax-exempt income (4) Certain types of income, such as disability payments and child support payments, that do not have to be claimed as part of the taxpayer's income for tax purposes.

Tax-exempt securities (4) Bonds paying interest that is not taxed as income. These securities are issued by various state and local governments and are often called "municipals."

Tax-sheltered annuity (16) An annuity that is exempted from current income.

Tax shelters (4) Certain types of investments that provide tax "write-offs" (deductions). These tax shelters typically involve real estate and oil-related investments.

Tax-table income (4) Adjusted gross income less excess itemized deductions (deductions in excess of the zero bracket amount).

Term life insurance (13) Insurance that covers the insured only for a specified period, most often five years, and does not provide for the accumulation of any cash values. The most common types of term insurance are straight term, renewable term, convertible term, and decreasing term.

Title insurance (12) Insurance taken as a form of protection against the possibility that the title to a property for which a loan is made will be found faulty.

Total return (on a security) (7) The return received on a security investment over a specified period of time. It is made up of two basic components—the dividend (or interest) yield and capital gains.

Treasury bill (6) A short-term (91- to 360-day) debt instrument issued by the federal government that is considered to be a safe investment.

Trust (17) A relationship created when one party (the *grantor*) transfers property to a second party (the *trustee*) for the benefit of a third party (the *beneficiary*). The property placed in the trust is called *trust principal* or *res*. A trust may be *testamentary* (created in a will) or *intervivos* (created during the grantor's life). It is either *revocable* (capable of being regained, and the terms of the trust altered or amended) or *irrevocable* (not recoverable by the grantor during the term of the trust).

Trust fund pension plan (16) A pension plan in which the employer places its contributions with a trustee, who is then responsible for the investment of contributions and the payment of benefits. If an insurance company serves as the funding agency, the plan is called *insured*, and when both a trust fund and an insurance contract are used, the plan is called *split funded*.

Truth in Lending Law *See* Consumer Credit Protection Act.

Umbrella personal liability (15) A policy that provides excess liability coverage for both homeowner's and automobile insurance, as well as coverage in some areas not provided for in either of these policies.

Underwriting (7) The process of selling a new security issue, a task normally carried out by an investment banking firm. If a group of investment banks carries out the process of underwriting, the group is referred to as an *underwriting syndicate*.

Underwriting syndicate (7) A group of underwriting firms (i.e., investment banks) who accept the responsibility for selling a new security issue.

Unified rate schedule (17) The graduated table of rates used for both federal gift and estate tax purposes; these rates are applied to all taxable gifts.

Unlimited liability (6)   Liability that can extend beyond the amount of money an investor has put into a business (e.g., the liability of a sole proprietorship or partnership).

U.S. Retirement Bond (16)   A special series of bonds developed by the government to serve as a funding instrument for individual tax-sheltered savings plans.

U.S. Savings Bonds (5)   Bonds issued in various denominations and maturities by the U.S. Treasury to assist in financing federal government operations.

Variable life insurance (13)   Insurance in which the benefits payable to the insured are related to the value of the company's assets that support its payment obligation.

Variable rate mortgage (12)   A mortgage that allows the mortgage rate to change over the life of the loan in response to economic conditions.

Vesting (16)   The rights employees obtain to benefits in a retirement plan based upon their own and their employer's contributions.

Waiting period (14)   A provision of some disability income policies that requires that the insured wait a specified length of time after the disability before payment begins.

Waiver of premium (13)   A clause that provides for automatic payment of premiums should the policyholder be unable through disability to make the payments himself or herself.

Warrant (6)   An instrument that gives the holder an opportunity to purchase a specified number of shares of common stock at a specified price over a designated period of time.

Warranty (10)   A guarantee, usually written and generally transferable, of the general reliability and quality of a product.

Warranty deed (12)   A deed in which the grantor warrants that the title to the property has no flaws.

Whole life insurance (13)   Insurance designed to offer financial protection for the entire life of the individual. Cash values are accumulated under this type of insurance.

Will (17)   A written document that allows a person, called a *testator*, to determine the disposition of property at his or her death.

Worker's compensation insurance (14)   A type of insurance paid for by the employer and designed to compensate the worker for job-related injuries or disease.

Yield-to-maturity (6)   The annual rate of return that a bondholder purchasing a bond today and holding it to maturity would receive on his or her investment.

Zero bracket amount (4)   A specified amount of a taxpayer's income to which a zero tax rate applies. A taxpayer can use this blanket deduction instead of itemizing personal (non-business) deductions.

Index

F